Anna

Southern Voices from the Past: Women's Letters, Diaries, and Writings

This series makes available to scholars, students, and general readers collections of letters, diaries, and other writings by women in the southern United States from the colonial era into the twentieth century. Documenting the experiences of women from across the region's economic, cultural, and ethnic spectrums, the writings enrich our understanding of such aspects of daily life as courtship and marriage, domestic life and motherhood, social events and travels, and religion and education.

Anna

The Letters of
a St. Simons Island
Plantation Mistress,
1817–1859

Anna Matilda Page King

Edited by Melanie Pavich-Lindsay

The University of Georgia Press
Athens & London

© 2002 by the University of Georgia Press
Athens, Georgia 30602
All rights reserved
Designed by Louise OFarrell
Set in Janson by G&S Typesetters
Printed and bound by Maple-Vail
The paper in this book meets the guidelines for
permanence and durability of the Committee on
Production Guidelines for Book Longevity of the
Council on Library Resources.

Printed in the United States of America
06 05 04 03 02   c   5 4 3 2 1

Library of Congress Cataloging-in-Publication Data
King, Anna Matilda, 1798–1859.
[Correspondence. Selections]
Anna : the letters of a St. Simons Island Plantation
Mistress, 1817–1859 / Anna Matilda Page King ;
edited by Melanie Pavich-Lindsay.
p. cm.
Includes bibliographical references (p.) and index.
ISBN 0-8203-2332-2 (hardcover : alk. paper)
1. King, Anna Matilda, 1798–1859—
Correspondence.   2. Plantation owners'
spouses—Georgia—Saint Simons Island (Island)—
Correspondence.   3. Saint Simons Island (Ga. :
Island)—Biography.   4. Plantation life—
Georgia—Saint Simons Island (Island)—History—
19th century.   5. Saint Simons Island (Ga. :
Island)—Social life and customs—19th century.
6. Agriculture—Georgia—Saint Simons Island
(Island)—History—19th century.   I. Pavich-
Lindsay, Melanie, 1951– II. Title.
F292.G58 K56 2002
975.8'742—dc21
2002000718

British Library Cataloging-in-Publication Data available

Contents

Preface

Written in the heyday of King Cotton, the letters of Anna Matilda Page King of St. Simons Island, Georgia, contain much of what makes a good novel. Money, politics, love, pain, power, death, honor, and longing are ongoing themes in more than one thousand letters Anna wrote to her parents, husband, and children between 1817 and 1859. As in any good story, the supporting characters —husband, children, grandchildren, and servants—play important roles in the development of the plot, but it is the life of this elite woman in the antebellum South that is presented at center stage.

The Georgia Sea Islands provide a dramatic setting for Anna King. Tree-lined roads, sea breezes, and the fragrance of roses fill the pages of these letters, as do mosquitoes, perilous heat, and persistent fevers. Anna's world was inhabited not only by her family and neighbors, but by the enslaved people of her plantation and others on the island as well. On an almost daily basis, ill-nesses, births, and deaths within the slave quarters and beyond occupied her thoughts and, therefore, her letters. Messages were regularly passed between black and white members of the King household, if no more than a brief "the servants all beg to be remembered." In a few cases, Anna's pen kept members of enslaved families in touch with each other. However, while they enter and cross the stage, the bondpeople of Retreat remain, in Anna's writing, periph-eral to her story.

The Old South, with its myths and realities, has fascinated natives and non-natives alike for more than one hundred years. Through fiction and nonfic-tion, films and plays, southern antebellum life, as it was or as it is imagined, has gained a worldwide audience. Moreover, the stereotype of the southern belle has captured the imagination of women and men alike. Through the writings of women of the Old South we can more fully explore these powerful stereo-types. Certainly they need exploration. Henry Louis Gates Jr. writes in the fore-word to Catherine Clinton's *Tara Revisited: Women, War, and the Plantation Leg-end,* "Of the various communities of agents that created nineteenth-century American life, it is the inner lives of women, along with those of people of color, which remain largely *terra incognita* even to late twentieth-century readers. And of the various communities of nineteenth-century women, none is more complex or enigmatic than that of women in the South."[1]

As one of these "women in the South," Anna King used letters to family and friends as both a means of communication and a sorely needed opportunity to pour out some of her innermost thoughts. Part letter, part diary, her letters speak of the ebb and flow of everyday southern life and her struggles to cope with the ongoing responsibility of putting food on the table, nursing her "family black and white," and keeping faith with a disappointing husband. She shared with diarist Ella Gertrude Clanton Thomas the early promise of a life of ease, if not comfort, and the consequences of marriage to an unsuccessful and remote man. Like Thomas's diary, Anna King's letters give us new insights into the transition of southern belles into southern wives and mothers.

Other writers have offered their own perspectives on the lives of the white and black inhabitants of St. Simons. Fannie Kemble's controversial account, written between 1838 and 1839, of life at Hampton Point on the north end of the island and at Butler's Island on the Altamaha River tells of the beauty of the region, but also of the appalling cost to those in bondage and servitude. Today, the novels of Eugenia Price find wide readership for their stories of the people and events of the island's plantation past, particularly the lives of its women. Life in the antebellum South captures our attention, stirs our imagination, and begs to be understood.

Anna King emerges from her letters as both ordinary and extraordinary. She stands out as a more than competent manager of her children, grandchildren, and plantation at a time when an elite woman's sphere did not extend much farther than her front door. Men, as husbands and fathers, occupied the role of provider and protector from the dangerous and potentially corrupting outside world. Women, as wives and mothers, presided over hearth and home, maintaining order, comfort, and safe haven within those circumscribed walls. Women in the antebellum South generally married at a younger age and had more children than their northern counterparts. And unlike women in the world to the north, most elite southern women were isolated on large tracts of land, deprived of the community life available to women in towns and cities. Plantation mistresses were responsible for producing most of the goods and services required by the members of their household, including, in many cases, the education of their children. They relied on visits from family and friends for emotional support and a sense of community. While slavery provided an ever-ready labor force, it also produced a potentially dangerous mix of cruelty, exploitation, affection, devotion, jealousy, and violence. Moreover, slave-owning families lived in an atmosphere of constant sexual tension between owner and owned, the big house and the back quarters.

As the daughter of a rich planter and the wife of a prominent public figure, Anna could be expected to subscribe to a typical, if not stereotypical, model of elite female life within the South's rigidly defined society. However, while she was trained for and accepted her roles as wife, mother, and plantation mistress, she stretched and at times redefined the boundaries of those roles. Moreover, her letters point to the need for an expanded model of the lives of elite women in the antebellum South. Stephen Berry explains that a "systematic analysis has never been made of how much time planter professionals spent at home in the first place, nor has much been said about the impact of such absences on the families left behind."[2] The absence of her husband for nearly half of their thirty-four-year marriage is one of the most interesting aspects of Anna King's life.

Anna's circumstances and choices set her apart from other women of her class. She was an only child and did not marry until she was twenty-six years old. The training she received from her father in plantation management and his provisions for her in his will were also unusual for the time. While William Page could not change his daughter's legal status as a woman, he successfully circumvented her husband's control over at least a part of her fortune.[3] We will never know whether Page acted out of concern for the "rights of women," because he lacked a male heir, or because he recognized the unique talents of his daughter. His decision to place his St. Simons property, including a portion of those enslaved there, beyond the reach of Anna's husband may have been based solely on his distrust of Thomas Butler King's talents or motives. By training and parental intent, then, Anna participated in the traditional male sphere of business and agriculture. She cultivated seed, supervised planting and the construction of buildings, managed a large labor force, and brought her crop to market. It may well have been this ability to manage Retreat inside and out, as well as her fortune, that moved Mr. King to propose marriage.

Anna also embraced her traditional role as an elite woman in the antebellum South. She had been trained by her mother to assume that role and often relished her domestic responsibilities. She nurtured, protected, and guided her children from infancy to adulthood. With an attention that bordered on the obsessive, she fed, nursed, dosed, and advised them. She planned for their education and future, and she never missed an opportunity to remind them of her sacrifices and their responsibility to fulfill all their fond parents' hopes. She was mistress to more than one hundred enslaved men, women, and children, and with similar dedication and fervor provided for their care. In fact, her sense of self in relation to Retreat's bondpeople forms a fascinating part of her letters. Though she never questioned her innate superiority to them, she wrestled with and wrote about the extent to which intimacy and affection blurred the racial divide.

Anna King excelled both at creating a warm and loving environment for her husband and children and at offering generous hospitality to extended family and friends who were frequent visitors at Retreat. And, for much of her married life, she did all this without the presence of the requisite "organizing principle" of her world—a husband, father, and master.[4] Anna's letters to her husband from 1842 onward form an almost constant chorus pleading for his return. She complained regularly, and at times bitterly, of his long absences. Without him she had no one with whom to share the responsibilities of raising children and running Retreat. But St. Simons Island was too small an arena to contain T. B. King's lofty ambitions, and her pleas fell on deaf ears. Even within a busy household, Anna was lonely. She struggled for more than thirty years to love and be loved by a man who became more illusion than flesh and blood. Anna's struggle to bring her husband home and his striving for wealth and success on a grand scale formed the opposite poles of their marriage. What Anna King experienced the least in her daily life, and longed for the most, was the love and support of a husband at home.

Nevertheless, she worked hard to create the image of a loving, self-sacrificing, even attentive father, when in reality T. B. King saw less and less of his children. Yet, their children grew older and their needs more expensive and pressing. The ability of the land to yield the crops necessary to support the household grew ever more precarious, and the needs of the enslaved people and the tensions of slaveholding never ceased. But Anna worked tirelessly until her oldest son, Butler, came home to fill some of the spaces left vacant by his father. He preferred, as he often said, the life of a planter, and as Steven Stowe points out, he was unusually sensitive to Anna's needs. In choosing his mother's world over his father's he became the emotional center of his mother's life at Retreat.[5] The responsibility she so longed to share with her husband would fall to her son to shoulder.

Businesswoman, doctor, nurse, teacher, accountant, and horticulturist are only some of the roles she performed—and performed well. She was a practical and often forthright woman, and most of her writing lacks deep insight into her own or anyone else's actions and behavior. She often appears more acted upon than agent in her world. She does not come across as a confident woman who relished her place as head of her household. Nor did she have a rich intellectual life. Anna King was a gossip as likely to be scathing in her judgments as generous. In her letters we encounter both a blatant racist and anti-Semite and a loving, even doting, mother and grandmother. In the end, she may even seem very familiar.

Yet it is also possible to look beyond one woman's story, no matter how absorbing or poignant, to the greater significance of this voice from the past. Catherine Clinton writes, "Southern women may never emerge from the trappings of myth and nostalgia, but by systematically exploring the lives behind those images, the thorns as well as the blossoms, our historical understanding will broaden, deepen, and eventually reshape our perceptions of the plantation era."[6] Anna King's letters are just such a rich source of knowledge about her time and place. Woven into the pattern of her daily life was the ritual of sitting at desk or table to "hold communion" with those she loved most. To the very end of her life she bound her family together with paper and pen. Through her words the curtain shielding the past is drawn back and we enter Anna King's parlor, dining room, and even her bedroom. We hear her conversations and private thoughts, experience a world both familiar and foreign. Her letters present an individual life at a crucial point in the complex history of American race, class, and gender relationships. In them we witness one woman's navigation within the world of patriarchy and slavery. The addition of her letters to the growing list of published diaries and letters from the pens of nineteenth-century southern women may very well reshape our "perceptions of the plantation era"—and, perhaps, our understanding of the present.

Notes

1. Clinton, *Tara Revisited*, 11.
2. Berry, "More Alluring at a Distance," 864.
3. For a more complete discussion of women's property issues in the nineteenth century, see "Loopholes: Separate Estates" in *The Free Women of Petersburg*, by Suzanne Lebsock.
4. Drew Gilpin Faust writes that "the plantation embodied the hierarchical structures of southern paternalism. It functioned as the most important instrument of race control, and it similarly worked to institutionalize the subordination of white women, for the master was the designated head of what he frequently characterized as his 'family white and black.' Within this social order men and women, boys and girls, slave and free learned the roles appropriate to their age, gender, and race. . . . Male prerogative and male responsibility thus served as the organizing principle of southern households and southern society; white men stood at the apex of a domestic pyramid of power and obligation that represented a microcosm of the southern social order" (*Mothers of Invention*, 32).
5. Stowe, *Intimacy and Power in the Old South*, 242, 249.
6. Clinton, *Tara Revisited*, 213.

Acknowledgments

Almost ten years ago I walked onto the property that was once Retreat Plantation and into the cemetery for the enslaved people and their descendants. There among marked and unmarked graves I first encountered Neptune Small. I had little idea then that he and many of the people he knew would come to be an integral part of my life. My initial intent was to learn about the lives of the enslaved people at Retreat, but Anna Matilda Page King proved irresistible. While reading her letters I have often felt as though I had stumbled into an empty house and begun pulling open drawers and looking under beds. I have come to know the Kings, and some of the people who lived and worked at Retreat, well enough to feel in a sense like part of the family.

That first trip to Retreat and my encounter with Neptune Small led to hours spent reading the King family's letters on microfilm at the library of Agnes Scott College in Decatur, Georgia. That work was turned into a senior thesis under the guidance of Michele Gillespie, my teacher, mentor, and friend. I am a historian largely because of her passion and skill as a teacher. Catherine Clinton has remained interested in and supportive of my work for nearly ten years. It meant a great deal when I first met Catherine to be taken seriously as a researcher and writer. I hope to pass that welcoming into the fold on to my own students. When I was a graduate student at Clemson University it was William Steirer who pushed me to think clearly and argue convincingly. It was often a trial by fire, but he spurred me on to edit Anna King's letters into a thesis.

I am now a doctoral student in the Social Foundations of Education program at the University of Georgia. It has been my great fortune to meet and work with Ron Butchart, who has from the very beginning called me colleague and friend. Moreover, he has read parts of this manuscript and painstakingly commented on them. I have had few teachers of his quality and dedication, and his criticisms and suggestions have made this a much better book than it would otherwise have been. Daniel Bascelli at Spelman College has rescued this manuscript more than once. His computer skills and generosity are greatly appreciated. I thank Malcolm Call for his belief in the value of Anna King's letters and for his patience while I completed the manuscript. Jennifer Comeau Reichlin and Jon Davies played important parts in bringing this book to completion. The staffs of the Southern Historical Collection at the University of North Carolina, Chapel Hill, and the Georgia Historical Society in Savannah have been continually helpful to a novice and then insistent researcher. This work would not have been possible without their generous assistance. Edwin R. MacKethan III has not only shared his time, family photographs, and other documents but has read and made corrections to portions of this book. Melinda Conner painstakingly copyedited the manuscript and graciously waited while I responded to her suggestions—most of which appear in these pages. She, too, has done much to improve my work and I am grateful. Any errors that remain are mine alone.

Families come in different ways. We are born into one, marry into another, and choose to become members of others along the way. In all kinds I have been mightily blessed.

One of my families has grown out of deep friendship and love. It began when my husband, Arturo Lindsay, met Jim Winchester, a fellow faculty member at Spelman College, at graduation. Through Jim we were introduced to a circle of friends who are sisters and brothers all. We have spent many hours eating good food, drinking good wine, and talking trash. Barbara Marston, Larry Slutsker, and their daughters, Emma and Sarah; Jim, Eve Lackritz, and their children, Sophia (my goddaughter) and Adrien; Mary Potter and Tim Craker; and Louis Ruprecht—scholar, writer, teacher, gardener, and baker—have all added more than they can know to my life and work.

My friend and sister, Lisa Tuttle, artist and collaborator, has been vital to my development as a historian and to this project. We began a conversation seven years ago about my research on Anna King and her work as an artist, and we are still talking. Through my research and her visual art we created an installation work titled "Retreat: Palimpsest of a Georgia Sea Island Plantation." Initially, we hoped to create a space where people could find themselves and "the other" and begin to make connections. We hoped it would also be a place where conversations could begin about what divides and connects us. It has been a wonderful journey. We recently asked Lynn Marshall-Linnemeier, who has created work based on the lives of four of the enslaved women at Retreat, to walk with us. Lisa has listened patiently to my complaints and fears. She has transcribed and proofread letters and slave lists. She has believed when I couldn't —seen the book finished when I felt most overwhelmed. Through our work together and the pieces she created for the people of the story—Anna and Rhina, Annie and Georgia, my encounter with the past at Retreat has grown deeper and more meaningful.

Mtamanika Youngblood and George Howell are also close and cherished friends who have supported and congratulated me at every turn. I rely on their sense of history and love of art. Sandra Eleta opened her house in Portobelo,

Panama, and her heart. Our conversations and time spent in the hammocks on her porch have brought insight and inspiration.

There is the family I married into. My in-laws, Louise and Arthur Lindsay, have lived across the street from us for the past ten years. Long before they left New York to come to Georgia they welcomed me into the family with open arms and loving hearts. Mamá, like my mother, comes from a family of strong women, and they too have made me one of their own. My mother-in-law has been a second mother and has nourished both my body and my spirit. I can always count on a delicious meal and her prayers. Pop has also been a loving parent. He is a man who stops in the middle of the street to listen to the birds, and like Kris Kringle, he leaves his cane in the corner of our kitchen to let us know he has been there. Our dogs Minka, Zuzu, and Machito benefit from his kind attentions too. He comes when we are late to let them out and turns on the lights.

My family has also come to include my brother-in-law Richard and his family Mokwong, Ricky, and Margot; my brother-in-law Jorge; and my stepson Urraca Lindsay, his wife, Racquel, and their children, Troy and Isaiah.

My family of origin is large and loving. My four grandparents were, in a sense, my first history teachers. Rosella Barron Blitva and Nichola Blitva, Ukrainian and Serbian, and Anna Schuty Pavich and Michael Pavich, Czech and Serbian, linked me both to my cultural inheritance and to the twentieth century. Their experiences spanned much of that century. Nichola in particular, who died just a few years ago at the age of 103, made me aware of the time and events one lifetime can span. My mother's family, the four daughters of Nick and Rose, have been an integral part of my life since childhood. In Pennsylvania and in Maryland, in church and around the kitchen table, I grew up with them and their children. Their love, laughter, and music sustained me then as it does now. To my aunts and uncles: Bette Ellsworth and John Ellsworth, Patte Sweeney and Jack Sweeney, Nicholas Blitva and Carole Kovacevich Blitva, Romayne Laichak and Henry Laichak, and to my cousin-sister Bernadette Leah Sweeney I give thanks.

Though we live in different cities I remain closely linked to my brother, Milan Pavich. His daughter and son, Kassia and Paul, I have thought of as my own. They have brought me much happiness. My sister-in-law, Ricki Schnayer, and my niece, Rennie Ament, have added much to our family. It is a great gift when families grow wider and deeper roots.

My mother and father, Mildred Blitva Pavich and Milan Pavich, always provided a vital foundation of love and support. From endless dancing lessons to seemingly endless stints at school, they have stood behind and beside me. My father's experiences growing up just beyond the blast furnace of a steel mill and as a soldier in World War II are with me still. History and good writing were important to him. I hope he would be proud of the work I have done here. My mother, the strongest and most efficient woman I know, continues to amaze and inspire me. As a nurse during World War II she did what I wish I could have done. As a wife, mother, homemaker, and school nurse she has worked tirelessly. She is an accomplished painter and recent graduate of Florida Southern University. I treasure her friendship and regret that the busyness of our lives intrudes on the amount of time we spend together. She has been one of my most significant supporters in the completion of this project. There is never a moment when I do not feel her love for me, and for that I am more grateful than I can say.

It is to my husband, Arturo, however, that this book is dedicated and without whom it would never have been possible. It was through him that I met Anna Belle Lee Washington, an artist on the island who first took me to visit the ruins of Retreat plantation. Since then Arturo has suffered along with me for seven years to see this book completed. While I struggled he kept reminding me that it would do no good to produce a near perfect manuscript if no one ever read it. When we met, I was an ex-dancer and dance teacher. It was Arturo who first suggested that I go back to school and who knew I could do whatever I dreamed. His belief in me has never wavered. It is through his example, however, that I have learned the most. He is an artist and scholar, a friend and teacher. I have seen his ability and willingness to engage with students at a deep level—to listen carefully and advise wisely. He can talk to anyone, anywhere. He makes friends wherever he goes, and there are few places in the world where we could travel without being invited into someone's home. I have been inspired by his energy and dedication to making the world a more humane and just place to live. Despite his hectic teaching, lecturing, traveling, and painting schedule he never fails to cook delicious meals. Ethiopian, Indian, Italian, Chinese, Thai are only a few of the cuisines I can come home to on any given night. His love and support have been my mainstay. My love for him and my gratitude are unending.

Finally, I thank Neptune Small for opening the door and inviting me to step through.

Editorial Policies

While I have tried to preserve Anna King's voice and the idiosyncrasies of her style, I have throughout this volume imposed certain changes in order to make her thoughts more accessible and her words flow more easily for the reader.

I have inserted breaks in the form of paragraphs where it seemed clear to me that she was moving from one subject or thought to another, and I have capitalized words where helpful. Anna, like many of her contemporaries, frequently used dashes in place of commas and periods. I have replaced dashes with commas and periods where necessary and have in all cases abbreviated long dashes within and at the end of paragraphs. I have not, however, changed her ampersands to "and" or "&c" to "etc."

My other corrections and additions appear in brackets. I have added the full spelling of some abbreviated words and names to prevent confusion. I have also added letters when I felt they were intended but omitted. If Anna wrote "you" when clearly she meant "your," it appears in the text as "you[r]." Question marks in brackets indicate words that were indecipherable. I have indicated damage to a letter resulting in missing words or sentences by inserting "[torn]." In the few cases in which an entire page was missing from a letter I have added "[page missing]." I have let stand Anna's dating of letters though I have included place-names when her location would otherwise be unclear.

Anna never included apostrophes to indicate possession or added a period after the titles Mr., Mrs., or Dr. I have not changed this punctuation, believing that, in the case of the possessive form, it is understandable within the context of the sentence. In instances where Anna opened but did not close quotation marks or parentheses, I have added or omitted them depending on the content.

Much more problematic was ordering Anna's spelling. She often used such British forms as *rumour, labour, shewn, endeavoured,* and *favour* and abbreviated words ending in "ed" with "t" as in *blest, helpt,* and *crampt*—but not always. She also randomly, though consistently, divided words, as in *can not, some thing, any thing, no thing,* etc. They remain as written, as do the misspellings that occurred in the course of a lifetime of letter writing amidst the pressures of a busy life. Anna often asked that the reader of her letter excuse all errors. I ask you to do the same.

Introduction

The Golden Isles of Georgia form a barrier against the sea along the state's nearly 150-mile coastline and include the islands of Ossabaw, St. Catherine's, Sapelo, St. Simons, Jekyll, and Cumberland.[1] Beginning in the sixteenth century, Creek Indians migrating from the mainland to the coast following seasonal patterns of hunting, gathering, and planting experienced invasions by first the Spanish, then the French, and finally the English. General James Oglethorpe, arriving in 1733, established settlements along the coast and founded the city of Savannah. The territory between the Savannah and Altamaha Rivers was designated the Colony of Georgia, to be governed for twenty-one years by a board of trustees made up of twenty-one prominent Englishmen, including Oglethorpe. Spanish settlers, missionaries, and soldiers soon abandoned their efforts to colonize the Sea Islands, and the territory between the Altamaha River and the Florida border became known as the *Debatable Land*.[2] St. Simons Island, whose name originated from the mission San Simon, established by Spanish missionaries in the sixteenth century, was chosen as the best strategic site for a fort to defend the colony from the Spaniards, who still owned Florida.

On a high point just at the center of the western side of the island, Oglethorpe built Fort Frederica, named in honor of Frederick Prince of Wales, to protect the town within its walls as well as the newly established colony. Frederica's inhabitants included artisans and farmers who established a thriving town of tree-lined streets and two-story dwellings of brick and tabby.[3] Lands within the town walls and larger tracts within its vicinity were successfully developed and cultivated. The island's notable citizens included a doctor, a schoolteacher, and a midwife. Charles Wesley along with his brother John, who founded the Wesleyan Methodist faith, preached to the townspeople. A smaller outpost, Fort St. Simons, was established at the southern end of the island and a road was built connecting the two fortifications.

When war was declared between England and Spain in 1739, Oglethorpe was ordered to invade Florida. His attempts to defeat the Spanish at St. Augustine proved fruitless, and he returned to St. Simons assured of Spanish retaliation. The 1742 Battle of Bloody Marsh, in which Oglethorpe's army of 650 men routed 3,000 Spanish invaders, ultimately secured the island and the colony for England. By 1743 Oglethorpe had returned to England; his soldiers withdrew, and the English settlers moved inland.

Much of Frederica, however, was destroyed during the Revolutionary War. In addition, islanders loyal to the Crown moved to the West Indies to wait out the conflict, but returned to rebuild after it was over. At war's end, British troops evacuated Savannah, and Georgia became an independent state. Although John McIntosh Mohr, leader of a group of Scots, had petitioned the trustees of the colony in 1739 to ban the introduction of slavery, it had come, as had long staple cotton and the great plantations on which it was grown.[4] An influx of planters from South Carolina looking for rich new land, combined with the invention of the cotton gin, enabled coastal Georgia to find its place in the agricultural empire of the Old South. Among the many families who became rich from land and the enslavement of Africans and their descendants were the Pages of South Carolina.

Major William Page had been a friend and neighbor of Pierce Butler in the Beaufort District of South Carolina before moving to St. Simons to manage Butler's plantations there.[5] He was paid one thousand dollars annually and instructed to build a wharf and a manager's house.[6] It was Page's plan, however, to buy his own land, and in 1804 he purchased property at the southwestern tip of the island from Thomas Spalding. Page named his property Retreat and became wealthy growing Sea Island cotton.[7] Before long he had established himself as one of the leading citizens of the island and the state. This was an era of great development when newly cultivated soil produced superior crops and captured Africans were delivered straight to the island's shores.

Major Page's plantation grew around a house rebuilt by Thomas Spalding after the original residence constructed by his father, James, was destroyed in a coastal storm. It was a replica of Orange Hall, James Oglethorpe's house in Frederica, and was patterned after houses constructed in the West Indies. It was a "raised cottage" of one and a half stories, with shuttered porches and a full basement.[8] The main house faced the beach and, across the sound, Jekyll Island. There was a detached kitchen, and over the course of approximately twenty years a schoolhouse, guesthouse, cotton barn, corn barn, and greenhouse were added.[9] Two hundred yards behind the plantation house sat the overseer's house, a slave hospital, and, within sixty yards of the hospital, a slave cemetery.[10] A short distance to the east was a row of slave houses that faced the beach.

The two-story hospital, made of tabby, had an attic with two rooms where the enslaved women who served as nurses could sleep. Downstairs, a nine-foot-wide central corridor divided two rooms that measured fifteen by twenty feet each. In a 1942 article, Dr. Joseph Smith Jr. described the building: "A great chimney ran up in each partition between two rooms; this gave a fireplace in each room. Every room had two windows."[11] The two floors were just alike; the lower one was used for women, the upper one for men. The walls were sixteen inches thick, and the whole building measured forty-eight by twenty-seven feet. Slave houses on Retreat were also made of tabby and were built to accommodate two families. Each side of the house contained two rooms on the first floor, a dormered second floor, a set of stairs, and a fireplace (which opened on both sides of the house from a central chimney).[12]

Among the most celebrated aspects of Retreat were the gardens. More than one hundred varieties of roses grew within the horseshoe-shaped "formal" garden, which was bordered by a hedge of crepe myrtle and an outer edge of oleanders. The walks in and around the rose garden included a shell walk bordered by oak trees, a cedar walk bordered by cedar trees, and a rose walk between two rows of rose bushes. There was a fruit orchard containing orange, olive, and date trees.[13] Family members and friends sent new and unusual varieties of plants from all over the world. Thomas Wentworth Higginson wrote in 1863 that Retreat's garden "was the loveliest spot I have seen in the South, filled with hyacinthe odors."[14] Although plans had been made to build a larger, more elaborate dwelling on the property, Retreat remained a relatively modest-looking estate.

Anna Matilda Page, born in 1798, was the only child of Major Page and Hannah Timmons Page to survive childhood.[15] She grew up in a world of gentlemen farmers and their ladies surrounded by the natural beauty of St. Simons: forests of live oaks draped with Spanish moss, longleaf pine, magnolia, palmetto, cypress, cedar, sea myrtle, and red-berried cassina along with marshes and wide stretches of beach.[16] She was attended to and supported by the labor of more than 150 "servants." Every comfort her parents could afford was provided. Anna was tutored at home and by William Browne at neighboring Cannon's Point[17] and was given French lessons by Mrs. Henri Du Bignon of Jekyll Island.[18] Yet Major Page also insisted that his daughter's education include a thorough knowledge of the day-to-day management of the plantation—even, in at least one instance, to supervising the construction of "plantation buildings" during one of his many absences.[19] Anna made her debut at a ball given in her honor at the home of William Scarbrough on West Broad Street in Savannah. Called "sweet Anna" by her father, she was said to be much sought after by the young men of the island and mainland.[20] Anna fell in love with an Englishman, Charles Molyneux, and agreed to marry him, but her father and his uncle could not reach an agreement on dowry. The relationship was severed, and she was left broken hearted.[21] She afterward extended her time as a belle, and it was not until 1824 that she consented to marry Thomas Butler King of Massachusetts. The *Darien Gazette* reported the marriage:

> We Bachelors
> Whom love abhors
>   And whom each fair despises
> May envy those
> More lucky beaus
> Who woo and win those prizes
> That we in vain
> Have strove to gain
> Through endless days of sorrow
> Yet we may pray
> If not today
> Our times may come tomorrow

> Married: At Retreat, St. Simons Island, on the 1st. inst.
> by the Rev. Edmund Matthews, Thomas B. King to
> Anna Matilda, only daughter of Major William Page.[22]

Thomas Butler King, son of Daniel and Hannah Lord King, was born in Palmer, Massachusetts, on August 27, 1800. He attended Westfield Academy and studied law with his brother Henry and Judge Garrick Mallery. Of his eight brothers, John David, Stephen Clay, and Andrew also immigrated to Georgia. T. B. King, it was said, could serve as the stereotype of the aristocratic southern planter. He was handsome with a pale complexion, cleanly modeled face, piercing gray eyes, firm chin, and lips that met in a stern line.[23] Upon his marriage to Anna, King acquired not only a wealthy and accomplished wife but access to the most elite circles in Georgia and the South as well. He also gained a capable manager who would provide him with the opportunity to pursue public life on a national as well as international scale.[24] Thomas Butler King had married well.

Initially, married life was good. Anna and Thomas traveled in the North and started a family. Their early happiness was marred only by the death of Anna's parents in 1826 and 1827.[25] The estate left by William Page was valued at $125,000 and included land; enslaved laborers; and stock in the Bank of the United States, the Planter's Bank of Savannah, and the Bank of Darien, Georgia. By trust, the cotton plantation on St. Simons and fifty of those enslaved and their issue, or "increase," were left to Anna and her children; the balance of the estate went to Page's other legal heirs, who included T. B. King.

The King children came at regular intervals, beginning with Hannah Matilda Page, born in 1825 and named after both her grandmothers. The next child, William Page, was born in 1826 and died in 1833 at the age of six. In 1829 Anna had a second son, Thomas Butler King Jr., and in 1831 a third, Henry Lord Page King. A daughter, Georgia Page, was born in 1833; followed by Florence Barclay in 1834; a son, Mallery Page, in 1836; Virginia Lord in 1837; John Floyd in 1839; and, finally, Richard Cuyler in 1840.

While Anna was giving birth to ten children, her husband bought land and bondpeople and invested in the development of both the island and the mainland. Within five years of his father-in-law's death King bought an additional 150 acres in Waynesville, a summer resort near Brunswick, Georgia, situated near mineral springs, and built an "elaborate cottage" that they named Monticello. Planters from Glynn, Wayne, and Camden Counties built a community of summer residences there along with a clubhouse and meeting grounds. In 1830 T. B. King purchased an additional 4,700 acres on the Satilla River where he grew rice and began construction of a third residence, Waverly. He was elected to the state legislature, beginning the career in politics that would last his entire life. As King was expanding his planting interests he realized the advantages associated with developing the port of Brunswick. "Situated on a deep tidal creek called Turtle River that extended some twenty miles inland," notes King's biographer, Edward M. Steel, the port of Brunswick "afforded deepwater anchorage for vessels. To the east and north [the] Turtle River opened into Saint Simons Sound, a protected body of water with inland links north to Charleston, South Carolina and south to the Saint Mary's River in Florida. Direct access to the Atlantic from the sound was provided by the mile wide channel between Saint Simons Island on the north and Jekyll Island on the south." If a canal were built to connect the Altamaha River (twelve miles north through swampy lowlands) with the Turtle River, Brunswick might develop into a port rivaling Savannah. As a state senator T. B. King had the opportunity to "guide" laws favorable to the development of that canal and a railroad.[26]

"By his thirty-fifth birthday," writes Steel, T. B. King "was the father of a large and growing family, the master of 355 slaves, and a planter with extensive holdings."[27] Yet, King's success was not to last. Within twelve years of his marriage to Anna, all but Retreat and the fifty enslaved people left directly to her by her father (and their "increase") were seized against T. B. King's debts — debts amassed through the failure of crops, economic downturns, and the elaborate financial schemes he constructed to support the expansion of his plantations and business ventures. The financial constraints thus placed on a once-pampered belle were not as great, however, as the burden of what would become an almost constant separation from her husband, who expanded his political and business careers in an effort to regain his lost fortune.

After beginning his political career as a states' rights advocate and member of the Georgia Legislature, T. B. King was elected to the U.S. House of Representatives in 1838. He joined the alliance that became the Whig party, advocating, among other things, a national bank and a protective tariff. He lost his seat in 1842 but was reelected to Congress in 1844, 1846, and 1848. He played a key role in the development and expansion of the U.S. Navy and supported federal subsidies for mail steamship lines and the development of rivers and harbors. In 1849, after failing to gain a cabinet position as secretary of the navy, he was sent by President Zachary Taylor as a special agent to the newly acquired territory of California. A year later he resigned from Congress when President Millard Fillmore appointed him collector of the Port of San Francisco at a salary of $10,000 per annum. King invested heavily in California land and large-scale mining during this time. After an unsuccessful bid to become California's senator in 1852, King resigned his post as collector. Though he had been gone from St. Simons for more than two years, he did not return home after his defeat. Rather, he launched plans to build a transcontinental railroad from Texas to the Pacific coast along the thirty-second parallel. During the next few years he traveled to England on mining business and throughout Texas promoting the Southern Pacific Railroad Company.[28]

A talented visionary and promoter, King was unfortunately an unsuccessful financier. In his dealings in the 1830s with the Brunswick and Altamaha Canal & Railroad Company and the Brunswick & Florida Railroad, and in the 1850s with the Southern Pacific Railroad, he built financial structures based on inflated values and high-sounding promises. In both cases, what began with great promise and "boom" ended, in part as a result of the Panic of 1837 and the Panic of 1857, in "bust."[29] While his political career brought him national recognition, his failures as a businessman drove him to the brink of economic ruin. Hounded by creditors for almost twenty years, King was protected from financial ruin by Retreat and his father-in-law's trust.

Meanwhile, the children, the Retreat household, and the business of managing a large-scale planting operation consumed Anna King's time, energy, and emotions. As her children grew, they continued to receive her almost constant attention, and as young adults, her confidences as well. Hannah Page, nicknamed Tootee, married William Audley Couper in 1845 and provided Anna with grandchildren and adult female companionship. Living at nearby Hamilton, where William served as the plantation manager,[30] she frequently visited her mother and, when that was not possible, wrote letters and notes. Tootee and Anna supported one another emotionally as well as physically. They exchanged food, servants, and remedies and shared child care and nursing chores. Both women married relatively unsuccessful and disappointing men, but each succeeded nevertheless in raising a large family of sons and daughters. (See appendix 1 for the Page-King family tree.)

Georgia, the next eldest daughter, supplied her mother and the household with a beautiful singing voice and a quiet, pious demeanor. She was an able, and at times disciplined, student who was particularly attached to her older brother Lord. It was Georgia who entertained guests and tutored the younger children. She worked hard to be the pride of both parents.

Florence was a joker and trickster who frequently tried her mother's patience. Less confident in her gifts as both a student and vocalist, she tended toward shyness and, occasionally, laziness—especially in her schoolwork. Called Flora, Flo, and sometimes Poya by her family, Florence was attuned to family life, parties, and the most recent gossip.

Virginia, known as Appy, was quiet, at times studious, and somewhat sickly. She suffered as the youngest daughter in a large family with diminishing means, an absent father, and an increasingly distracted mother. Less inclined toward "domestic" pursuits than her sisters, Appy emerges from Anna's letters as nervous and withdrawn, oppressed by the insulated and at times stagnant world of Retreat.

By contrast, the King sons hunted, fished, and trod on their mother's flowers. The boys lived in "Grasshopper Hall," a two-story addition attached to the main house by a breezeway. Thomas Butler King Jr., always called Butler or Buttie, preferred the life of a planter to that of a scholar. Though he attended college, Butler returned to the island to serve as a surrogate husband, father, and master. He also traveled for extended periods with T. B. King in California and elsewhere and assisted him in his public and private work. While he spent more time with his father and knew him better than his siblings did, Butler preferred home life to the world of politics and big business.

Henry Lord Page, known as Lord or Lordy, was considered the most talented of the King sons and was the child his parents and siblings expected to attain greatness. Lord was a wavering scholar and intermittent worker, but an ever-ready traveler, escort, and dancing partner. While Butler longed for a quiet life among the places and people of coastal Georgia, Lord looked on the world as his arena. Although he believed himself another "Washington or a Napoleon, a Bishop or a Tom Paine,"[31] he never lived up to his own or his parents' expectations.

The middle son, Mallery, served both plantation and brothers—he was Butler's companion at Retreat and Floyd's counselor when they were away at school together. Most often called Mall or Malley, he, like his sister Virginia, sometimes got lost in the shuffle. By the time he was finished with school and ready to find a job as an engineer, he was needed at home. Lord was away at school, and Butler had to remain at the ready to travel on business for the plantation or for his father. Mallery waited for an opportunity to strike out on his own, but like a good son and brother stayed on to aid Butler in the fields as Retreat's worn-out lands yielded less and less cotton.

John Floyd, called Floyd or Fuddy, and Richard Cuyler, known as Cuyler and Tip, were the youngest of the King children. They spent less time at school than their older brothers and more time in the woods and on the waters surrounding St. Simons. Anna worried about their "roughness" and despaired of ever finding good yet affordable schools for them. Both boys, but especially Floyd, remained close to their mother as well as their nieces and nephews at nearby Hamilton.

Anna's sons went to preparatory schools and colleges—to Athens, Georgia; Cambridge, Massachusetts; New Haven, Connecticut; and Charlottesville, Virginia—and traveled often between New York and Florida. Lord went to Europe while Butler accompanied his father to Texas, California, Mexico, and Panama. Lord and Mallery also traveled with their father in Texas, Louisiana, Georgia, and Virginia. The King daughters paid visits to friends on St. Simons and in Brunswick, Darien, and Savannah. Three King daughters traveled north to school and to visit resorts and medicinal springs in Virginia and New York. All the King children, with the exception of Tootee, spent time with their father in New York City and with friends and family in Philadelphia and Allentown.

Though often separated, the members of the King family relied on and loved one another deeply. On returning with his father from California in 1853, Butler wrote to Anna of their reunion with brother Lord: "Of course you know better than I can tell you the sweet joy we felt at meeting him. I don't know how he and father conducted themselves when the event took place but he[,] Lord and I made perfect *girls* of ourselves. I have not kissed a *man* for so long a time that it tasted real funny."[32] The three youngest King daughters, strongly attached to parents, brothers, and each other, remained unmarried until the onset of the Civil War. Georgia wrote to Lord in 1857: "I think Mother is a little anxious fearing I will be an old maid. But the truth is, we have been exalted so much in our opinion of ourselves and each other that we are hard to please. Mother and you boys I don't think would be pleased to see us select any one and yet you would be sorry for us never to marry and we have been brought up so to respect your opinions that we are perhaps not sufficiently independent."[33]

And ever present in all their lives, but obscured by the invisible wall that circumscribed and defined their existence, were the enslaved people who planted, hoed, picked, cooked, nursed, ironed, sewed, and served them. Though Rhina, Clementine, Lady, Pussy, Toney, Quamina, Annie, Neptune, Jane, Christiann, and Sukey are some of those regularly named in Anna's correspondence, they are never truly known. Appendix 2 lists the bondspeople of Retreat, from Anna's original "inheritance" through the roster of 1853. To Anna they were "servants" both depended on and dependent. She could live with them, work with them, nurse them, love them, even despise them, but she could never see them as deserving her fullest attention or sympathies. Rarely in her letters does she talk about their lives independent of her own. Her racism, like that of many people of her time, was inherited, constant, and unquestioned. She never wavered in her belief that it was her right to own other human beings or in her understanding of the duties of that ownership. Anna never saw her enslaved workers as fully human. Indeed, even though slavery was a hotly debated issue within nineteenth-century American life and many called for its abolition, few people anywhere in the country supported the idea of social equality between the races.

There were many visitors to Retreat, both family members and friends. Anna's cousin Amanda Fitzallen Scott Woolley and her husband, the Reverend Vardy Woolley, were regular guests.[34] Amanda was, in essence, the sister Anna never had, and the two women maintained a lifelong bond of love, friendship, and support. The childless Woolleys loved, and were loved by, the King children. Mrs. Gale came to Retreat to be the children's nurse and remained there until her own death, cared for by Anna and her former charges.[35] The Coupers, Wyllys, Armstrongs, Johnstons, Browns, Bourkes, Hazzards, Grants, Frasers, Du Bignons, Caters, and Jaudons were among the families who inhabited the world of Retreat and St. Simons Island, and their names fill the pages of Anna's letters.

John Couper of Cannon's Point was among the early settlers of the island to grow rich on cotton and the enslaved. The square three-story house had a wide veranda and large porticos on each end. It was built on a foundation of tabby, the upper floors were of clapboard, and the entire structure was painted white with green shutters. John Couper married the former Rebecca Maxwell of Sunbury, Georgia, who was sixteen years his junior. They had five children: James Hamilton, Anne, John Jr., Isabella, and William Audley. Anne Couper and Anna were close friends, and in 1845 William Audley Couper married Anna's oldest daughter, Hannah Page.

James Hamilton Couper and his father were known as naturalists, horticulturalists, and agricultural experimenters. They produced long staple Sea Island cotton, sugarcane, dates, olives, oranges, lemons, vegetables, and exotic flowers. J. H. Couper graduated from Yale in 1814 and managed and later owned Hopeton plantation in the Altamaha River delta. He married Caroline Georgia Wylly in 1827 and the couple had five sons and two daughters.[36]

The Goulds arrived on the island during its post–Revolutionary War period of expansion. James Gould, a native of Massachusetts, built the first lighthouse on St. Simons in 1810 and was appointed the first light keeper (a position he kept until 1837). Gould and his family lived in the adjacent keeper's house until they purchased land on the island after the War of 1812. St. Clair plantation, approximately 900 acres, ran across the center of the island from Black Banks River to Dunbar Creek. The two-story house was built of tabby with wings on each side. When James Gould's wife died in 1820, his oldest daughter, Mary, took over as mistress. Mary, like Anna King, had a great love of roses and planted them "so successfully and in such abundance that the place took the name of 'Rosemount.'" She was said to be a capable plantation manager, and she continued to manage St. Clair after her father's death and until the onset of the Civil War.[37]

The Wyllys, loyalists during the Revolution, returned from self-imposed exile in the Bahamas afterward. Captain Alexander Wylly, who married Margaret Armstrong, added a tract known as the German Village to his father's original purchase and named his plantation The Village. Their children included daughters Susan, Matilda, Caroline, Frances, and Heriot; and sons Alexander and John. The youngest of the seven Wylly children, Caroline, married James Hamilton Couper in 1827. The youngest son, John Armstrong, was killed in 1838 by Dr. Thomas Hazzard over a long-standing argument concerning the property line that separated their two plantations. Dr. Hazzard was arrested and charged with manslaughter, but he was never convicted.[38]

The Caters, a Huguenot family originally from South Carolina, owned Kelvin Grove plantation on the island. Thomas Cater bought his first tract of land on St. Simons in 1790. His only son, Benjamin Franklin Cater, married Anne Armstrong, niece of Captain and Mrs. Alexander Wylly of The Village. Their daughter Ann married James P. Postell of South Carolina. One of the largest plantations on the island, Kelvin Grove came to include several large tracts of land, including the one on which the Battle of Bloody Marsh was fought.[39]

The Demeres were an old and respected St. Simons family. Captain Raymond Demere, who came to Georgia with Oglethorpe, built Harrington Hall, which sat one and a half miles east of Fort Frederica. His son, Raymond Demere Jr., was a Revolutionary War hero who developed an island plantation, Mulberry Grove, during the early years of the nineteenth century.[40]

Work by the enslaved people at Retreat and many of the other Sea Island plantations was done by task, with each person assigned a particular job based on age, gender, ability, and physical condition. When their jobs were completed for the day, Retreat's bondpeople were free to attend to personal business—to

direct their own time and labor.[41] They cultivated their own fruits and vegetables, and hunted and fished to supplement the rations of meat and cornmeal
handed out by their mistress. They raised their own chickens, turkeys, and
hogs, and, when needed, sold them to Anna for her table. In addition to their
rations they were given shoes, clothing, utensils, and sometimes, for favorite
servants, shawls, fans, straw hats, handkerchiefs, and even jewelry. Great skill
was needed navigating the waters in and around the island, and among Retreat's laborers were expert oarsmen and mariners.[42] While Anna's inclination
and sense of duty as a slave owner resulted in a modicum of stability, failing
crops, falling cotton prices, illness, accidents, and death constantly threatened
to change their lives. All knew they could be sold at any time, separated from
their families and all that was familiar and loved.

Of primary concern to Anna as a wife, mother, and plantation mistress was the
health of those under her care at Retreat. She wrote constantly of the state of
health of her husband, children, guests, and bondpeople. She asked constantly
for reports of the health of absent family members and offered advice and
sometimes preventatives and cures for the health risks associated with traveling to towns and cities north and south.

However, plantation inhabitants, white and black, were particularly subject
to a number of diseases. K. David Patterson writes in "Disease Environments
of the Antebellum South" that "the health of antebellum southerners reflected
the region's harsh disease environment." Climate, economics, and human activities created "favorable conditions for mosquitoes, which transmitted diseases, for worm eggs and larvae, and for a host of waterborne protozoa, bacteria, and viruses, [that] existed for much of the year." Infectious diseases were
a major cause of death for adults and children alike, though the rate of death
among infants and children was especially high. Todd L. Savitt explains in
"Black Health on the Plantation: Masters, Slaves, and Physicians" that "the
state of slave health depended not only on disease immunities and susceptibili-
ties, but also on living and working conditions." During the warmer months,
"intestinal diseases caused by poor outdoor sanitation and close contact with
the earth became common." Insects also spread disease. Mosquitoes carried
the parasites responsible for yellow fever and malaria, and "flies transported
bacteria such as *Vibrio* (cholera), *Salmonella* (food poisoning and typhoid), and
Shigella (bacillary dysentery); the virus that causes infectious hepatitis; and the
protozoan *Entameba histolytica* (amoebic dysentery) from feces to food." Im-
properly cooked pork carried the parasites responsible for trichinosis, and the
primitive sanitation conditions under which enslaved people lived promoted
infection by other parasitic worms as well.[43]

Scarlet fever, a contagious disease that causes a high fever and scarlet rash, was especially feared. Also called scarlatina, it became quite virulent for a time in the nineteenth century (it existed in a milder form during the colonial period, as it does now). Scarlet fever sufferers required constant nursing, and the disease was often deadly for children. Slave children were even more vulnerable given the conditions under which most lived—poorer nutrition and sanitation, and crowded living quarters.[44]

Also abetted in its spread by poor sanitation and crowding was tuberculosis. Consumption, as it was called for most of the nineteenth century, was difficult to diagnose in its early stages and unpredictable in its course. Sheila Rothman explains that "physicians divided consumption into three separate stages . . . the first stage [was] marked by a dry persistent cough, an irritation in the throat, pains in the chest and shoulders, a slightly accelerated pulse, and some difficulty in breathing, particularly during exercise. . . . The second stage brought more intense and debilitating symptoms. The cough . . . produced mucous materials and pus. . . . A 'hectic fever' periodically broke out, spiking twice daily and marked by a rapidly accelerating pulse (to a rate of 120 a minute)." The ruddy complexion caused by the fever gave consumptives "a deceptive appearance of good health. . . . During this second stage ulcers appeared in the throat, causing a continual hoarseness and making it painful to eat or speak above a whisper." Only with the third and terminal stage did the diagnosis become certain. Emaciated and hollow-cheeked, the consumptive literally wasted away. "The lungs now sounded hollow (either to the ear or through the stethoscope), and the cough, known as the 'graveyard cough' or 'death rattle,' was distinctive and unmistakable, enabling physicians to say that the disease had spread to the lungs." The "ghostly and cadaverous appearance" was a clear sign that "the person had 'gone into a consumption.'"[45]

The 1860 federal census reported that cholera infantum, one of the most common and frightening causes of infant illness and death, occurred five and half times more often in the South than in the North. Also known as "summer diarrhea," doctors knew little of its cause or cure. The symptoms included severe diarrhea, vomiting, headaches, dehydration, and debilitation. Endemic and virulent, cholera struck children between the ages of six months and two years beginning in late spring and lasting through the early autumn. Susceptibility to cholera infantum coincided with early weaning. Physicians at that time recommended that mothers wean their children early, between the ages of six months and one year, unaware that breast milk contains antibodies that protect children from disease. Weaning from breast milk to other liquids often brought illness and sometimes death.[46]

Notes

1. In *Georgia's Land of the Golden Isles*, Burnette Vanstory writes, "The coastal islands may have been termed 'golden' by early explorers in search of treasure, but they came to be known throughout the world as the Golden Islands in 1717 when Sir Robert Montgomery planned his 'Margravate of Azilia,' the margravate to include Ossabaw, St. Catherine's, Sapelo, and St. Simons. With an idealistic dream of establishing a settlement that would be an earthly paradise, the Scottish nobleman formed a syndicate of wealthy Londoners and wrote a *Discourse Concerning the Design'd Establishment of a New Colony*, extolling the beauties and opportunities of the region, to which he gave the well deserved Denomination of the Golden Islands" (Vanstory, *Land of the Golden Isles*, 1, 4–5).

2. Ibid., 5.

3. Tabby (sometimes referred to as "tappy") is a building material of the Georgia coast made of lime (from burnt oyster shells), sand, oyster shells, and water mixed together, poured into a form, and tamped down to produce a dense, firm material resembling concrete. See Cate, *Our Todays and Yesterdays*, 56.

4. Bell, *Major Butler's Legacy*, 537; Cate, *Our Todays and Yesterdays*, 70; Green, *St. Simons Island*, 23–30; Vanstory, *Land of the Golden Isles*, 1–81, 106–112.

5. He managed both Hampton (or Butler's Point), a cotton plantation, and Butler's Island, a rice plantation southwest of the island on the Altamaha River.

6. Bell, *Major Butler's Legacy*, 155, 538–539.

7. Spalding experimented with long staple cotton sent to him from the Bahamas (but developed on the island of Anguilla in the West Indies). It was successfully cultivated on St. Simons and became known as Sea Island cotton, highly prized in the markets of England for its color and long fibers, which were woven into the finest cotton in the world. See Green, *St. Simons Island*, 41.

8. Marye, *Story of the Page-King Family*, 12; Vanstory, *Land of the Golden Isles*, 175, 176.

9. The corn barn, two stories with a loft, was made of tabby and used for storing corn and fodder. The first floor also housed the plantation's best horses. One of only two structures that remain standing today, it is owned by the Sea Island Company and is used as a clubhouse for a golf course built on former Retreat land. The cotton barn was made of wood and had four floors and eight windows. The first floor held the cotton gins; the second, the equipment used to grade and bale the cotton. This building could be seen for many miles at sea and was used by sailors as a guide after Confederate soldiers destroyed the lighthouse on the island. In fact, it appeared on U.S. government and geodetic maps as *King's Cotton House*. See Cate, *Our Todays and Yesterdays*, 123, 125–126; Margaret Davis Cate Collection, Georgia Department of Archives and History [hereinafter GDAH], microfilm roll 3175; Vanstory, *Land of the Golden Isles*, 134; Wheeler, *Eugenia Price's South*, 36.

10. The Retreat slave cemetery is now bordered by a golf course. Descendants of the plantation's slaves are still buried there among marked and unmarked graves.

11. Smith, "A Slave Hospital of the Old Deep South," 7.

12. One of the two plantation buildings still standing on former Retreat property is a slave house bordering an area (former cotton fields) that was once called New Field

and is now part of the island's airport. Originally six houses stood in a row, and a seventh sat across a road that ran from the "main house" to the fields. It is owned by the Sea Island Company and is used as a gift shop called the Tabby House. See Green, *St. Simon's Island*, 58.

13. Cate, *Our Todays and Yesterdays*, 125; Huie and Lewis, *Patriarchal Plantations of St. Simons Island*, 30.

14. Thomas Wentworth Higginson, born in 1823, was a Unitarian minister, author, and soldier during the Civil War. He served as colonel of the first Negro regiment during the war and with the Freedman's Bureau afterward. His books include *Army Life in a Black Regiment*. See Cate, *Our Todays and Yesterdays*, 123.

15. A note found in the William Audley Couper Collection of the Southern Historical Collection, University of North Carolina, Chapel Hill [hereinafter WAC, SHC], lists ten children born to the Pages. Florence Marye states that "by the time Anna Matilda was born in 1798, six of the eight earlier children had died, often soon after birth. The other two, and a child born in 1802, died in 1801–1804, leaving Anna Matilda as the only one to survive childhood" (Marye, *Story of the Page-King Family*, note 5, 111–112).

16. Vanstory, *Land of the Golden Isles*, 2.

17. In 1803, John Couper hired an Englishman, William Browne, to run a school for his children. Young Anna Page rode on horseback between Retreat and Cannon's Point to receive daily lessons. See Wheeler, *Eugenia Price's South*, 32–33.

18. Jekyll Island was named by Oglethorpe after Sir Joseph Jekyll, Master of the Rolls, who contributed 600 pounds to the establishment of Georgia as an English colony. In 1791 the island was purchased by a group of Frenchmen, one of whom bought out his partners a few years later. Le Sieur Christophe Poulain de la Houssaye du Bignon (who shortened his name to Poulain du Bignon) repaired the old tabby buildings on the island, planted Sea Island cotton, and became rich. He and his wife, Margaret, had two sons, Henri and Joseph. In 1807, Henri married Ann Amelia Nicolau; they lived at Jekyll with their children—Charles, Eliza, Henry, Sarah, Katharine, John Couper, Joseph, and Eugenia. It was with Ann Du Bignon that Anna took French lessons. See Cate, *Our Todays and Yesterdays*, 45–46.

19. William Page wrote to his daughter from Newport, Rhode Island, in August 1823, "In my reply I was not as particular in some plantation concerns as I may have been. I will repeat part and add to it. If you have not *positively* engaged *Up Country* Lumber, do not as so—let the Scaffold Etc. alone and do the best with what is on hand. The Lime and moving bricks for the 8 chimnies percevere in—the worst is the loss of the Cotton Crop. . . . *Give orders* to *open the drains not haul up* nor *hoe* but to take off all the sprouts *with knives* and *continue to as so until the first Nov[ember]* in doing which there will be a chance to take in what may be made and to produce a late crop" (William Page to Anna Matilda Page, August 28, 1823, Thomas Butler King Papers [hereinafter TBK], SHC). See Huie and Lewis, *Patriarchal Plantations*, 29.

20. Huie and Lewis, *Patriarchal Plantations*, 29; Vanstory, *Land of the Golden Isles*, 133; Wheeler, *Eugenia Price's South*, 32–33.

21. Marye, *Story of the Page-King Family*, 25.

22. Vanstory, *Land of the Golden Isles*, 176.

23. Steel, *T. Butler King of Georgia*, 1.

24. Ibid., 2–3.

25. The following notice of the death of Anna's mother appeared in the *Darien Ga-zette* and the *Georgia Republican* and *Savannah Republican* on October 14, 1826: "Page, Mrs Hannah, Consort of Major William Page died September 28, 1826, 68 years, at Retreat Plantation, St. Simon's Island, Georgia." See Warren and White, *Marriages and Deaths, 1829–1830*, 97.

26. Steel, *T. Butler King*, 8–9, 166.

27. Ibid., 5–7.

28. Ibid., 28, 35, 42, 47, 51, 62, 65–97, 105–115.

29. Ibid., 166–167.

30. Tootee married William Audley Couper on January 15, 1845. Her marriage to the youngest son of John Couper joined two prominent St. Simons families. Hamilton, adjacent to Retreat, became the property of Isabella Hamilton Corbin under the trusteeship of James Hamilton Couper on the death of James Hamilton.

31. Henry Lord Page King to Thomas Butler King, April 7, 1848, TBK, SHC.

32. Thomas Butler King Jr. to Anna Matilda Page King, March 16, 1853, TBK, SHC.

33. Georgia Page King to Henry Lord Page King, December 15, 1857, TBK, SHC.

34. Amanda Eliza Fitzallen Scott was an heir of William Page. She was married on February 22, 1832, to Rev. Vardy Woolley by Simeon L. Stevens, M.G. Anna always referred to her cousin's husband as "Mr. Woolley." See Cate, *Our Todays and Yesterdays*, 246, 269.

35. Florence Marye states that "there was a Scottish head nurse affectionately called Mammy Gale to help in this task [child care]. Her husband, captain of a sailing vessel chartered by Mr. King, died while in port in Savannah. His wife, a former child nurse, was glad to turn back to her old calling. A son was placed at Bethesda, the famous orphan school near Savannah. He became a successful man, but his mother chose to remain in service with the Kings until the end of her life" (*Story of the Page-King Family*, 45).

36. Bell, *Major Butler's Legacy*, 515–516; Vanstory, *Land of the Golden Isles*, 111–118; Wheeler, *Eugenia Price's South*, 29–30.

37. Vanstory, *Land of the Golden Isles*, 194–195.

38. See Huie and Lewis, *Patriarchal Plantations*, 20–21; Wheeler, *Eugenia Price's South*, 37–39.

39. Huie and Lewis, *Patriarchal Plantations*, 36; Vanstory, *Land of the Golden Isles*, 141.

40. For more on the Demeres, see Cate, *Our Todays and Yesterdays*, 72–73, 181–182; Vanstory, *Land of the Golden Isles*, 199.

41. Though the origins of the task system are not known, it was brought to coastal Georgia by South Carolinian settlers. It had been in use in the South Carolina low country since the early eighteenth century. Betty Wood writes in *Women's Work, Men's Work* that agreements reached between owners and bondpeople about appropriate workloads were vigorously protected. For a more detailed discussion, see pp. 14–21.

42. Wood explains,

On most lowcountry plantations bondpeople had ready access to two of the main prerequisites for fishing and hunting: boats or canoes, often of their own manufac-ture, and firearms. From the mid 1750s they were not denied the right to be in pos-session of guns with which "to hunt and kill game, Cattle, Mischievous Birds, or Beasts of Prey." In theory, guns could be carried only in the presence of a white per-son and had to be returned to the owner or overseer after their use, which could not

be on the weekend. In practice, not all owners strictly enforced these require-
ments. . . . Hunting expeditions involving the use of firearms were usually made in
the company, and thereby under the direct supervision, of the bondperson's owner
or a male member of the owner's family. However, particularly trusted bondpeople
might be allowed to hunt alone. (45)

43. See Selected Pages from the Record Book of Retreat Plantation; Savitt, "Black
Health on the Plantation," 152–153; Patterson, "Disease Environments of the Antebellum South," 338, 340.
44. McMillen, *Motherhood in the Old South*, 149–150.
45. Rothman, *Living in the Shadow of Death*, 16–17, 132–133.
46. See McMillen, *Motherhood in the Old South*, 115–121, 123.

August 29, 1817, to February 9, 1847

How grateful I am to you for writing so punctually—the time passes so much more rapidly and pleasantly when I can get two letters each week.

In these letters, Anna moves from her days as a belle into her life as a mature married woman. During this period she and the nine children she bore lived on the various properties T. B. King had purchased and developed, and she began to learn to cope with his frequent and prolonged absences.

Retreat, August 29th 1817

To Major William Page

Tho I have not yet received an answer to my letter written some weeks since, I trust that tomorrow's post will favor me with as lengthy an epistle, as your first; be assured that I am not a little proud, to think, that your letter to me, is more lengthy than that has been yet, received from you. It again becomes my turn, to dedicate a few hours in communication to my dear father, intelligence of your affectionate family at Retreat. I am happy to state that we all continue to enjoy our usual health, the poor negro's have been extremely sickly within the last three weeks. As many as 26 have been taken with the fever, but many thanks to the Almighty disposer of all events, the most of them are now in a state of convalesency. The Island begins now to put on a very unhealthy appearance, Mr Armstrong and two of his daughters are very sick; as is also Mr & Mrs Mathews, and one of their little children, Mr Abbott, and all of his children, and Mr Goulds children. It is very sickly on the Main particularly the inhabitants of Brunswick, Carpenter Cole, lost in the course of one week, his wife and *two* children.

Mr Boyd came over last Sunday—he mentioned that he had written to you the day previous to his coming over; when he returned my aunt accompanied him leaving, Cousin's Mary and Thomas with us the latter of whom I am happy to state is almost entirely recovered, from his late disposition.

Last week some sailers called here, and sayd that they were in search of two deserters from some vessel at Fernandina, and offered a reward to Richard and Toney if they would detain them, should they stop here, they observed that they did not care for the men, who *should* be hung; but they wished very much to recover the boat which was [a] fine, large, sail boat.[1] The negro's accordingly were on the look out, the following day a boat was discovered at our landing place which answered the description which was given by the pursuers of the runaways but as there was [?] no one here to take possession of the boat, and crew, they remained unmolested, frequently changing their position along the beach, but never left the boat. The next morning Mother sent over to request Mr Baillie and Mr Dyer to come to Retreat. They arrived just as Mr Boyd did; The poor creatures so soon as they saw Mr Boyd coming down in your large boat, with a number of Negro's, doubted not their being inpursuit of them, they left their boat and endeavored to conceal themselves in the Marsh. Mr Baillie and Mr Boyd had them brought up, and strictly interrogated, the unfortunate creatures appeared so much alarmed and told so pitious a story that they were treated with much levity. Mr Baillie recognised the white to be one who formerly worked at Mr. Coupers, in the capacity of a carpenter; and knowing that James Couper wanted one, he gave him a note to James.[2] the other a yellow man declared himself free, but as he had no ticket to proove him so, Mr B–l–e advised him to leave the Southern States as soon as possible; or else he would be sold.[3] The boat Mr Baillie has detained and has written to the owners informing them where she is &c. Mr B requested Mother to call on him when ever she is at a loss, declaring that he would with pleasure render her any service in his power.

I know that you will participate in your friend General Floyds fatherly feelings when I inform, you that my dear Mary Hamilton has made him a grand father; the aff[licted] [o]ld gentleman I am informed grows worse day [?] piece of news for you; Mr Bruce Wright was last evening married to his Cousin Miss Burnet; I have been informed that he purposes giving a ball, soon as he arrives at his place on this Island; delectable weather you will no doubt think, for tripping it on the light fantastic toe. My Mother and Cousins unite in love to you and accept in imagination a kiss from your affectionate child
Anna Matilda

1. Richard appears on the 1853 list as number 48. He was born on August 19, 1810, which would have made him ten days short of his seventh birthday on the day this letter was written. Toney is number 21 on the list from William Page's will. On the 1853 list Toney is recorded as number 7, born May 22, 1808, making him nine years old in August 1817. It seems unlikely that a seven-year-old and a nine-year-old would be placed in a position to subdue two runaway men. See appendix 2.

2. James Hamilton Couper was named after his father's close friend, James Hamilton, a planter, shipper, and London merchant. His property, Hamilton, on the south-

ern end of the island was adjacent to Retreat, and his wharf (known as Gascoigne Bluff during the time of Oglethorpe) was the island's main shipping point.

3. Free blacks were required to carry proof of their status such as "a copy of an emancipation deed or county court decree." John Hope Franklin and Loren Schweninger write in *Runaway Slaves* that "free blacks were arrested and jailed as runaways on numerous occasions. . . . [T]he general assumption was that blacks were slaves until they could prove otherwise" (184).

Savannah 26th February 1823

My beloved Mother

Your very welcome letter of the 22nd I had the happiness of receiving this afternoon. Words are inadequate to express how truly rejoiced I am to hear that beloved friends at Retreat are well and I know that it will convey equal pleasure to you to hear that I am in good health. The severity of the weather has not made me feel otherwise—than a little more stupid[1] than ordinary and has to be sure confined me much to the house. Our friends are all well with the exception of Mrs Marshall who has been some what indisposed from a cold. You were doubtless much shocked when I informed of the death of Miss Harris. I have been frequently to see the afflicted family who appear to be somewhat more resigned to their loss. I regret very much to hear of the extreme illness of Mr Bowers—and I fear you[r] next letter will apprise us of his death—if so his family will meet with a dreadful dispensation and will be much to be pitied.

I went with Mr McNish the other day to look at some fresh crackers which I think will suit you—I did not send any thing by Capt Porquet who remained here but a few days, but hope by the next opportunity to send on most of the articles. The trunk I will be obliged to have opened as there was no key to it nor could the Capt give any account of it.

It will probably amuse you to hear how I have past the last week. On Friday Col and Mrs Marshall gave a dinner party the company amounted to twenty-five ladys and 15 gents—Miss Wylly[2] and myself among the former. Every thing was in style—we were however obliged to leave immediately after as we had to prepare for the Ball in the evening which was at the exchange. We went about 8 oclock and remained until 3 A.M. I danced a great deal and was much pleased of course as is always the case when I can dance as often as I feel inclined. Mrs Camochan was there—who made many kind inquiries after you and papa. The room [was] as large as it was crowded with ladys at least 3 to 1 of the other sex. The next day I went to hear an oration which was delivered in the theatre by Mr Hall McCalister. The House was much crowded—as all the Companies in town were present the Hussars occupied the pit and the Blues and Guards the second row of Box's. The lower was given up to the ladys and privates. Mr McC acquit himself very well. In the evening we went to hear a lecture from the *Catholic Bishop of England*—he certainly is the most eloquent man I ever heard. The church is crowded every night and his eloquence his precepts and the example he holds out are to the admiration of all who are capable of understanding him. On Sunday we went to Church—Mr Snodgrass was also eloquent. In the afternoon a Methodist minister preached and in the evening I had an opportunity of hearing Mr Capers with whom I was highly pleased. There were 81 ministers of that denomination in this City. Last night I went to the theatre—Hilsons first night for this season. The play was fortunes fool or what to pay—the afterpiece Nissakin [?] or Sprig of Laurel neither of which I was much pleased with.

I received a letter the other day from Eliza Grant.[3] I have since written to her stating that I would wait for her and hoped she would not remain longer in Charleston than the time before mentioned. I likewise wrote to Isabella requesting that she with one of her sisters would return here with Eliza to visit St Simons once more. I feel for Cousin Mary as I know she does not like writing but tell her I think it will be doing her a piece of service to remain away as long as I can and that on my return I shall expect to find her quite an expert *pen woman* and that she cannot learn younger. Maria is now here she has been in Town almost the whole of the time I have.[4] I expect to go out next week to remain untill Eliza returns. Tell my dear papa that I shall behave so prettily on my return that he will forget that I was ever absent.

Mrs Paine is now in Town—I saw her today. Last Sunday nine gentlemen called to see *me* among whom was Mr *Tom Young*. Mr Joe Jones and Mr King Senr[5] dined here on Saturday—the former made many kind inquiries after yourself and papa. I had a letter last week from Amanda[6] she mentioned that she intended to return home the first of March and could not come here which I regret very much and I know she would be much pleased at having an opportunity to visit Savannah. The McNishes appear anxious that she should do so.

Good night my beloved mother. May God bless and preserve yourself—my dear father Cousin Mary and all with you is the fervent prayer of your affectionate Daughter.

A M Page

1. Anna means "stupid" as "in a state of stupor; dazed; stunned; stupefied."

2. "Miss Wylly" refers to one of the daughters of Alexander and Margaret Armstrong Wylly of The Village on St. Simons. In 1848, Mrs. Wylly and her unmarried daughters were living at The Village. See Hull, *St Simons, Enchanted Island*, 45; Vanstory, *Land of the Golden Isles*, 189–190.

3. The daughter of Dr. Robert Grant, owner of Grantly, Evelyn, Elizafield (along the

Altamaha River), and Oatlands plantations (on St. Simons). Grantly and Evelyn were large tracts of rice, cane, and cotton fields with settlements for slaves and overseers. Elizafield was the family's home (named after Dr. Grant's mother), and Oatlands their summer home (where they escaped the malarial seasons associated with rice planting). Wheeler, *Eugenia Price's South*, 36–37.

4. Isabella Timmons was Anna's cousin. Cousin Mary may also be a Timmons relation. I am unable to identify Maria.

5. Mr. King Senr may refer to Roswell King Senior, former overseer of Pierce Butler's Hampton Point (on St. Simons) and Butler Island plantations. He was recommended to Butler by Anna's father, William Page, and his son, Roswell King Junior, succeeded him as overseer. I do not believe Anna is referring to her future husband, Thomas Butler King.

6. Amanda Fitzallen Woolley, Anna King's first cousin.

Savannah 10th March 1823

My dear Mother

You have I trust received my last letter likewise the one written the week before by which you will learn that I am—with Mr and Mrs McNish and Mr Speakman and all other friends—are in good health—and I fervently pray that my beloved parents and Cousin are enjoying the same blessing. I write you today as I shall not have an opportunity of replying to your next by the return Mail as I shall not be in Town on Wednesday.

I received a letter yesterday from Isabella Timmons—the family were then all well. She mentioned having received the potatoes and oranges which they were very thankful for. They have not yet determined if any of them will return with Miss Grant. I have been disappointed in not hearing from Eliza Grant since I wrote you last but from what Isabella says I think I may calculate on her returning at the appointed time. I presume by this Amanda has returned. I am pleased to hear that her visit was an agreeable one. My only regret is that she was disappointed in her visit here and I am sure she would have spent a very pleasant time of it.

Last Saturday Mr Swarbuck and Mr Speakman and myself with Mr and Mrs McNish and Mr Wm McNish (who has been spending a few days with his brother) spent the day with Miss Jane in Country.[1] The day was pleasant and I think that I never enjoyed myself more. In front of the house is a very beautiful Lawn on which 70 sheep with a number of cows—geese and in fact poultry of every description were grazing. On this Lawn are a number of beautiful Cedar trees—and near the foot of one a pond. To be romantic I endeavoured to personate a Shepherdess—took a *book and lute* with me and seated myself at said Cedar. The rest of the company were strolling about—or seated on the bank of [the] Pond. We all enjoyed it much and returned home to tea.

Yesterday I went to the Episcopal Church and in the evening to the Presbyterian. This evening Mrs Marshall, Mrs Isaac, Mr Swarbuck, Miss Scarborough[2] & myself and several others intend going to the Theatre. The Play is the one taken from Ivanhoe—Mr Hilson will be Isaac the Jew.

I have seen Mr Bunch frequently—they are well and beg to be kindly remembered to you all. I have just heard from Mr Brown. Poor man his sufferings have been great indeed he has been perfectly delirious for the last five days—his poor wife is but little better. He was in a sleep when the servant was there and the Physicians think if he awakes more composed there may be yet some hope—but it is feared he will never awake more. Poor Mrs Brown how dreadful will be her situation. Susan Wylly has been staying there for several days.

Mr McNish tells me that he expects [Captain] Porquet in daily. With this expectation I shall have the trunk packed. Your Bonnet I have not yet procured—I could only find 2 pair of scissors chains in Savannah. I do not like them—yet as I know you to be anxious for them I have purchased them. I beg that those articles which I shall send belonging to the negros may not be given out until my return.

Cousin Marys linen is with yours and my fathers—the quality will show which is hers. I must now beg that my dear Mother will use her influence with my indulgent father to permit me to remain as long as he first promised me. You know that when I return I shall be with you as much as you can desire—and really my dear Mamma you know I am *getting old and* cannot much longer enjoy the pleasures of the world. So do pray my dear Mamma get him to indulge me. There is no danger of my losing my heart this time.—[3]

Should anything occur between this and the morning worth relating I will add it—at present—I have nothing further to say. Give my best love to my dear papa and Cousin Mary. Mr Mc[Nish] and Maria desire their love and best regards to you all. Good morning. May God bless and preserve you—and on my return may it be my happiness to find you all well and happy.

Your affectionate Daughter

A M Page

1. Miss Jane Elizabeth Johnston of St. Simons and Savannah and her sister Ann Mary would remain Anna's friends for many years. The Johnstons were the orphaned daughters of Thomas and Mary Dews Johnston of Savannah. Thomas Johnston was a distant relative of John Couper (of Cannon's Point, St. Simons), with whom the girls lived after their parents died. In 1819 Ann Mary Johnston married John McNish, a Scot who had worked as John Couper's clerk and bookkeeper but later became a prosperous cotton broker in Savannah. For further details, see Vanstory, *Land of the Golden Isles*, 184–185; Wheeler, *Eugenia Price's South*, 26.

2. This is most likely Julia Henrietta Scarbrough, youngest daughter of William

and Julia Scarbrough, at whose mansion on West Broad Street in Savannah Anna was formally introduced at a ball given in her honor. Wheeler, *Eugenia Price's South*, 33.

3. Anna may be referring to her broken engagement to Charles Molyneaux.

Retreat 27th January 1827

My Dear Miss Jane

I was but just recovering from a tedious fit of sickness—when informed of the second loss sustained by your dear Sister.[1] Most sincerely did I mourn for the loss of one who has ever shewed me kindest attention—and deeply did I commiserate the misfortune which had befallen my dear friends altho aware that my condolence would afford no relief. Yes—I should have written to you ere this—but for my *unexpected confinement* which took place two days after receiving the distressing intelligence. Alas whilst lamenting the second calamity which in so short a time of each other had befallen your family—little did I think that we too were to lose another beloved member of our already bereaved family.

My poor Fathers death was indeed a dreadful shock to me. It is true that for months past his life was a burden to him but yet his presence was dear to me— and when it pleased God! to take unto himself my Angel Mother—it was sweet to think that I had yet one dear Parent left. Before you came to the Island last spring he had (what we feared was) a fit of apoplexy.[2] But he has appeared so much better since then when you saw him—that we did not apprehend a recurrence of it. On the 11th [January] he had a slight attack but soon appeared perfectly himself came out to dinner and tea both of which he partook very heartily of. And when Mr King left him at 10 oclock that night he had every prospect of passing a comfortable night. But alas the fit returned about six the next morning—and at 12 he breathed his last. He appeared to suffer no pain only when they attempted to raise him up was quite insensible and never even so much as moved a finger during that time. My poor dear Father alas you are gone—and Oh! may you be reunited to my beloved Mother in that world where the wicked cease from troubling and the weary are at rest. How Melancholy—how changed is our once happy family.

It is wonderful how I have been sustained through my various afflictions— it is surely through the Mercy of God! but why should I question it. I who could never lose a favorite cat without grieving—would weep for days at the death of a friend—I who never suffered the bare idea of losing my Mother or Father to enter my thoughts without suffering the most acute agony. Yes I who have suffered so much—have through the Mercy of my God! been supported through their death—an alarming and tedious illness and during my perilous

illness on Christmas morning—with no other aid save that of my faithful old
Sarah now 78 years old.[3] My dear Amanda had to dress the child[.] Mr. King
sent for Dr Grant and Mrs Eustice—also for Dr Fraser[4] but as I was only sick
three hours all was safe ere any one of them arrived. My dear little William
Page continues to do well—altho premature by several weeks. My Hannah
Page is perfectly healthy and is one of the most lively talkative little creatures
in the world.[5] My dear Husband ever kind and attentive to me is well. Have I
not many instances of his divine goodness? Have I not still more blessings than
I deserve? Yes my dear Miss Jane I feel that I am still greatly blest and that I
must endeavour to be happy—and will do so too. I will try and imitate my
Mother in every respect—which will lead to contentment if not to happiness.

I have understood that yourself and your dear Sister have gone for a while to
the Country. I would that she could be persuaded to come and stay with me a
while—your presence would be highly prized by me. I shall I fear be often
alone with Amanda and the children—as Mr King will be obliged to leave
home often. He is now in Darien[6]—and I assure you I feel his absence very severely. Do dear Miss Jane try and induce her to come.

Mr Fraser[7] left the Island on Wednesday on his way to Savannah to sail for
England. There was a most unpleasant occurrence took place at Dr Grants on
the day of Elizas *intended* nuptials—poor girl I feel for her most sincerely. As
Anne Armstrong was there and intends to give Mrs S Armstrong the particulars in vindication of Dr Grant I refer you to her.[8] Should you chance to see
that lady I should not have named the affair—but I think all who feel an interest in the Grants should know the truth of the matter.[9] I received Hannah
Pages cloak, hat and shoes—all of which I much admire and return you thanks
for the same. It is now late and I must conclude. Pray make acceptable my best
love to your dear Sister and Kiss dear Mary Jane.[10] Amanda unites in love with
me to you both. God Bless you dear Miss Jane.

Yours sincerely and gratefully
A M King

1. Ann Mary Johnston McNish lost her young son in October 1826 and her husband in December. Vanstory, *Land of the Golden Isles*, 185.

2. A stroke.

3. Old Sarah is number 1 on the 1839 list and recorded as eighty-six years old, but
no birth date is given. See appendix 2.

4. Dr. Robert Grant was a summer resident of the island, and Dr. William Fraser
(of Savannah) the brother of Lt. John Fraser. John Fraser married Anne Couper
(daughter of John and Rebecca Couper), and William Fraser, Frances Anne Wylly.
Wheeler, *Eugenia Price's South*, 33.

5. Anna, married to Thomas Butler King in December 1824, had by January 27, 1827, given birth to two children, Hannah Page and William Page (named for Anna's father). William Page, the only child Anna was to lose in childhood, died at age six of an unspecified "fever."

6. Darien, established as a Scottish settlement in 1736, sits on the mainland near Sapelo Island on a branch of the Altamaha River (named the Darien River). Its history is closely tied with that of the coastal islands, and it was an important port, lumber town, and commercial center. Vanstory, *Land of the Golden Isles*, 75–76.

7. Lt. John Fraser, husband of Anne Couper Fraser.

8. Anne Armstrong was a niece of Margaret Armstrong Wylly who later married Benjamin Franklin Cater of Kelvin Grove, St. Simons. Mary Wheeler writes that Benjamin Cater's father, Thomas, was killed by his overseer, who was having an affair with Benjamin's mother, Elizabeth Cater. She says, "the night Thomas Cater was killed, a faithful slave carried young Ben to Retreat Plantation the home of Maj. William Page. As guardian, William Page made sure that Ben was educated at Yale before he assumed charge of the Cater estate at Kelvin Grove Plantation." Anne Armstrong died in 1835 giving birth to twins, one of whom died with her. Her sister Margaret (named after their aunt Margaret Armstrong Wylly) married Benjamin Cater after coming to Kelvin Grove to care for the surviving baby. Wheeler, *Eugenia Price's South*, 20–21. I am unable to identify Mrs. S. Armstrong.

9. The nature of the "unpleasant occurrence" is unknown.

10. Mary Jane was the daughter of Ann Mary Johnston McNish.

Retreat 10th May 1828

My Dear Miss Jane

Your kind letter with all of the articles which you procured for me have been safely received. I really fear you have thought it ungrateful my not acknowledging them sooner. I have been extremely busy whilst at home—have been again to visit Mrs Scott—at the same time I think I may have answered your affectionate letter but you know dear Miss Jane I am a very poor correspondent. I was happy to learn by your letter that yourself—your dear Sister and Mary Jane were well which blessing I sincerely hope you may still be in the enjoyment of. Also that little Amanda Anderson was well and not a little gratified to learn that those dear little girls the (Speakmans) were enjoying your kind care and attention. I have no doubt but what my little girl would have been highly delighted to have made one of the happy group. She is well—dear William is very thin. He is getting out six teeth which I presume is the cause. He is still very lively. Amanda, Mr King and myself are as usual.

Mrs Couper I fear has given over the idea of visiting you this spring—I have lately been favored by a visit from her. She continues to be troubled with bad colds. I saw a part of the family on Sunday last a[t] Church—all were well they said at home. Mr Fraser left the Island on the 8th on his way to Charleston to Embark for England. I feel very much for poor Ann as it is uncertain I believe when he will return.[1]

Mrs Roswell *Junr* and Mrs Ralph King have been down at Hampton for several weeks—the balance of the family are expected down shortly. The above mentioned ladies spent the day with us on Wednesday last.[2] I presume you have heard that Mrs Hogan has had a Son (Robert Grant Junr)[3] the Doctor is gone to the Havanna. She is to go in the fall. Dr and Mrs Grant were here last week—they appear to be quite reconciled to her leaving the US. Mr and Mrs Cater have both somewhat recovered their health they were here this afternoon. The Wyllys are all well at present—Mrs James Hamilton Couper is now on a visit to them. Mr and Mrs [Eustice?] are well in fact I hear of no complaints among the neighbours.

We poor birds of passage, are just on the wing for our Northern *home*.[4] What would I not give were it possible for us to remain here the year round. The idea of again mixing with strangers is to me almost insupportable. We contemplate leaving home on the 25th for Savannah as our passage is to be taken in the good Ship *Macon* to sail on the 1st June. I hope I may have the happiness of seeing you in Savannah—if but for an hour. What are your movements to be this Summer? North? or South? If the latter—I would press the use of our house etc on your service—but that fear of its being sickly prevents me. That I would however leave to your better judgement. We will talk it over when we meet. I must however say that I am selfish enough to hope that you will also go North.

I have not seen Mrs Bowers except at Church since you left—some how or other I can never get there. I hope my dear Miss Jane to hear from you ere I leave home—but I will not tax your goodness too far should you find you have no time to spare. Give my love to your dear, dear, Sister and a kiss to sweet Mary Jane. Mr King and Amanda unite in love and regards to you both. Tell little Amanda that her parents and little Sisters and Brother are well—that Mary is now going to School and if she does not mind will learn faster than what she does (which I however doubt much as I am sure Amanda is the most fortunate child in having you as a friend and instructor). I hope you may not be disappointed in her but may reap your reward both here and hereafter for the kindness shewn her. The children are both long since gone to bed—but I may venture to say that both send a kiss to *little* Mary Jane. Excuse this scrawl dear Miss Jane and all its errors

And believe me as ever

Your [torn page]

1. Anne Sarah Couper Fraser and Anna were childhood friends on the island. Anna attended school at Cannon's Point with the Couper children. Anne Couper is the main character of Eugenia Price's popular trilogy of novels based on eighteenth- and nineteenth-century St. Simons Island.

2. Mrs Roswell King Junior was the former Julia Maxwell of Midway, Georgia. Roswell King Junior was the overseer of Maj. Pierce Butler's plantations on St. Simons and Butler Islands, and he and his wife lived at Hampton Point on St. Simons. Both he and his father were known for their harsh treatment of Butler's slaves. Malcolm Bell writes that "the elder King's untiring efforts and capability as a planter did much to make Major Butler a rich man, a goal Roswell King pursued with relentless determination that warped his sense of decency in his relations with the hundreds of black slaves he controlled." In addition, his son too "punished with vengeance and by the time he wed Julia Maxwell had sired several mulatto children by plantation women." After coming to Hampton, Julia Maxwell King ordered the punishment of Judy and Scylla "for bringing her husband's children into [the] world" (Bell, *Major Butler's Legacy*, 531–532).

3. Mrs. Hogan's son, named after her father, Dr. Robert Grant.

4. Florence Marye writes that when William Page died, T. B. King wanted to invest in the development of Brooklyn, New York, but Anna disagreed. "They therefore agreed on the purchase of a house in Newport, Rhode Island, where a summer colony of their friends from Charleston, South Carolina was in full bloom" (Marye, *Story of the Page-King Family*, 42).

Monticello 4th November 1839

Many thanks my dear Miss Jane for your affectionate and very acceptable letter. It was quite an unexpected pleasure I assure you; therefore was the more highly prized. I have now very few correspondents, no regular one indeed. Consequently have lost the little talent I once may have possessed for letter writing. Yes dear Miss Jane it was so pleasant to get a letter from you. I felt disposed to acknowledge my sense of your kindness as soon as the mail would allow. I was however so low in spirits I concluded I would wait the return of my dear husband. Thank God! he returned home quite safe on Thursday last. He is well save a cold taken on the way home. Our children to are well. With so many blessings I ought to be content yet the idea of so soon losing his society will obtrude to dampen all present enjoyment. Such is poor human nature.

I was much grieved to hear today that dear Ann Fraser has again been afflicted that she has lost one of her dear little children.[1] Mrs Gale was so informed by one of Mrs Jas Coupers servants. How truly do I feel for her. I will write to her on the morrow. It is some comfort to know that we have the sympathy of our friends. I know by sad experience that it availeth little yet that little shall be offered to her who I have always loved. I will not expect her to an-

swer my letter but do you dear Miss Jane do me the favor to say how herself
and other children are. I have heard that the scarlet fever prevails and that the
dear little Sophia was its victim. I have a great dread of that disease.[2] When
Quamina[3] returned from the Island he informed me that it was at Hampton
and Cannon's Point[4] but as you said nothing about it in your letter I had a hope
that his account was exaggerated. This is to me a year of gloom. How much
more so to poor dear Ann Fraser. May God! in his mercy support her under
her severe afflictions.

I have seen the most of your acquaintances on the Sand Hills also Mrs Delaroche since your departure. They all expressed much regret at your short stay
among us. Their sincerity I hope you do not doubt. I am sure you cannot mine
and I hope dear Miss Jane if we are still *occupiers of Monticello* you will not wait
for a letter and be chilled by a "shall be happy to see her." But will come prepared to make us a long visit. God! only knows how matters may be with us ere
then but I will not trouble you with my painful anticipations of evil.

Our children are all at home and I, as inefficient as I really am, have undertaken to instruct the three elder ones until we can do better. It is a long story
and an unpleasant one so I will not undertake to pain your kind and generous nature by relating the ingratitude, *selfishness* and unkindness of their *uncle*.[5] Georgia and Florence still go to Miss Burton—who tho' a very excellent teacher of
young children is not calculated to instruct girls and boys of the age of our
elder children. Georgia is most anxious to undertake her promised letter to
you. I can hardly convince her she cannot write well enough. Our dear little
Mallery is about as well—at all events he uses his arm as well as before he received the last injury. His restlessness caused him to get several switchings as
painful as it was for me to punish the poor little sufferer—but it had a very
salutary effect in sobering him. Little Virginia is getting quite fat again and [?]
also Floyd. I cannot be too grateful that the[y] are all in such good health as
they at present enjoy.

I hope you have heard good accounts of your dear sister and Mary Janes
health. Pray when you write give to both of them our love and regards. I am so
sorry that in the hurry of your departure I forgot to give you the dried peaches
which I was so pressing you should receive. I have *a bushel* at your disposal if I
could only get them to you. Remember dear Miss Jane you are to come hereafter without first thinking it necessary to apprise me of the pleasure you intend us and come prepared to *rest* after the fatigue of your journey by land and
water and not runaway before your friends can realize the happiness of having
you with them.

Give my love to all who still hold me in their remembrance. Mr King desires
his best regards to you. H[annah] P[age], Butler, Lord, Georgia, Florence,

Mallery, Virginia and Floyd all send their love and kisses to you. Mrs Gale is quite recovered and thanks you [?] the kind message you left with me for her.

> Very truly and affectionately
> Your friend
> Anna M King

1. Lt. John Fraser had died July 18, 1839, at Hamilton, leaving his wife and ten children, ranging in age from twenty-two years to seven months, with little money and numerous debts. The epitaph on his tomb as recorded by Margaret Davis Cate, however, gives his death date as January 18, 1839. Sophia Julia Fraser died November 1, 1839. Ferguson, *The Couper Family at Cannon's Point*, 121–130; Cate, *Our Todays and Yesterdays*, 274.

2. See McMillen, *Motherhood in the Old South*, for more on scarlet fever.

3. Quamina, number 20 on the 1853 list, was born January 22, 1794, and died in March 1860 (see appendix 2). Someone added to a page in Anna's daybook of "Deaths of negros from June 1854 (Deaths)": "Quamina—most honest & true—a faithful servant & good man after a short illness of 24 hours departed this life [illegible] March 1860."

4. Hampton was the home of Major Pierce Butler on the northern end of St. Simons. Butler also owned Butlers Island, a rice plantation northwest of St. Simons on the Altamaha River. After growing rich on both Sea Island cotton and rice, he moved in the early 1800s to Philadelphia, leaving the day-to-day management of his holdings to Roswell King. His grandson's wife, Fannie Anne Kemble, made both Hampton and Butler's Island famous when her *Journal of a Residence on a Georgia Plantation in 1838–1839* was published in 1864. John Couper and his plantation at Cannon's Point gained a reputation for unrivaled hospitality and culinary excellence. Couper's chef, Sans Foix, was said to be able to debone a whole turkey and maintain the roasted bird's shape. Wheeler, *Eugenia Price's South*, 23–28.

5. Anna is referring to one of her husband's brothers.

Monticello 2nd December 1839

My dear Miss Jane

I received your very acceptable letter whilst I was on a short visit with my dear husband and children to Waverly. I desired dear Miss Jane to have acknowledged your kindness sooner than this but since Mr Kings departure my time is very much taken up with endeavouring to instruct our three elder children all the morning and the rest of the day to our younger ones; and house hold, as well as out door matters. I have more to do than I can attend to—but perhaps it is well that it is so as I am thereby prevented from brooding over the absence of my dear husband and other ills I have to contend with.

I have yet to acknowledge my dear Anne Frasers letter. I was most grateful for her early reply to mine. I did not even expect it. How pleasant to me to find that she yet loves me. You know dear Miss Jane how sincerely I have regretted that much to be lamented break in our former intercourse. How gratified I would be if I could but see her if but for a few hours. How rejoiced am I to find that she so humbly submits to the will of an all wise providence. May he increase her faith. But may he in his mercy stay his chastening hand. And may the dear children he has spared to her be her comfort and stay through life. Oh it is dreadful to see a beloved object consigned to the grave. It is dreadful to a believer but Oh! how much worse for those who have no faith in our precious saviour who feel not the mercy of our God!

I was truly shocked to hear of the cruel murder of poor Peter Mitchel and was at the same time informed that his poor wife died last summer and that Mrs Albirty (Mary Sadler of St Marys) from nursing Mrs Mitchel imbibed her complaint and she too died after great suffering. And again your excellent friend Mr P Houston of Savannah. The death of the last named can only be regretted on account of his children and friends. I have been told he was a truly devout Christian. Do you recollect the apprehensions for his safety you expressed to George Houston? Susan Johnston told me that he looked the picture of health when she left Savannah but a short time since. So it is my dear Miss Jane the old and the young the worldling and Christian all[—]all are passing off of the busy scene. Their places are filled by others and they are soon forgotten by the world.

I have indeed great cause to rejoice and be grateful for the health of our beloved children. How long I am to be this blessed God! alone know[s]. Let me be thankful for the present blessing. I have had four letters from their kind and beloved father since he left us—the last was on the 26th just as he was leaving Savannah for Charleston. He was then well. I hope he is now safe in Washington City. He will be obliged to be out in January to attend a R[ail] Road meeting. I hope then to see him if but for a day. Should you conclude on visiting Philadelphia do oblige him by placing yourself under his care.

Gentlemen who passed here in the stage for Tallahasse on *Thursday* left *New York* only the *Sunday before*. The stages have commenced running tho they have not yet got fairly under weigh. It is enlivening to see them passing shut up as I am in these dreary pine woods in winter. I have not seen any of my neighbors except Capt Abrahams since my dear husband left me. But I believe they are all well.

I sent by *Lady*[1] the peaches and Tootee sent her pigeon peas for your doves. I wished to have asked Mr A L King to have taken them to Brunswick as it was probable J[ohn] Fraser or W[illiam] Couper may be at court.[2] But his vehicle was so crowded that I disliked to trouble him with even a little more weight. Mr King has given Dunham[3] on the Island such strict orders not to have any communication with any other place on the Island for fear of scarlet fever that I do not know how you will get them. I told Lady to give them in charge of Mr Dunham and desire him to contrive some way to get them to you without running any risk.

I now my dear Miss Jane avail myself of your kind offer by requesting you to purchase for Hannah Page [stained] myself a *bonnet.* You see by the sum enclosed [stained] that I wish for very plain ones. Our circumstances are so much reduced by the loss of crops that I feel no desire to dress more that [*sic*] just to avoid looking shabby. I should like mine trimmed plain with dark ribbon for winter. Hannah Pages according to her age—or rather I should say *size.* If it will not give you too much trouble I would be glad to receive them in all this month by requesting the Messrs Kings to send them to Brunswick to the care of A L King. He would take charge of them for me. I know you too well to hesitate asking this favor of you.

The children all send love and kisses little Floyd is a noble looking boy just now. He has 6 teeth and can raise himself up to a chair—he is very strong and healthy. Little Virginia speaks very plain. Mallery is very fat and rosy and uses his arm with much ease. Georgia and Florence get on very well with their lessons at Miss Burtons. The former is very anxious to improve in her writing that she may write to her father and dear Miss Jane. Hannah Page, Butler, and Master Lord get on well as I can expect under the *teacher* they have. At all events it prevents their losing all they had previously learnt. I have I fear tired you with my very long letter. Pray pardon its prolixity. Mrs Gale has been again quite ill. Poor woman I fear her constitution is much broken by her frequent attacks of her old complaint. My love to dear Anne Fraser and say I will gladly answer her affectionate letter as soon as I can do so. It is now very late and I have yet a long letter to write. My love to Mr and Mrs Couper and the Wyllys and Mrs. Bartow.[4]

Yours truly
A M King

1. Lady is number 6 on the 1853 list, born on November 11, 1786. See appendix 2.

2. A. L. King is Andrew L. King, brother of T. B. King. For a short time before moving to Cuba to manage, and then own, a sugar plantation, he was involved with his brother in the development of the port of Brunswick and the Brunswick & Florida Railroad. He and his wife, Louisa, were in and out of Anna's good graces several times during the course of her life. Vanstory, *Land of the Golden Isles,* 202–205.

3. John Dunham was the overseer at Retreat for many years. He often wrote directly to Thomas Butler King on the condition of the crop, animals, and slaves. On June 14, 1848, he reported, "There is, and has been, some sickness among the Negroes. The oxen at Newfield are in beautiful order and the pasture is very fine. The horses are

not fat, but in pretty good plight. I shall be through the fifth hoeing on Friday. Some of the corn I have been compelled to hoe over three time to keep down the young crab grass" (Lane, *Neither More Nor Less Than Men*, 113).

4. Isabella Couper Bartow was the sister of Anne Couper Fraser, James Hamilton Couper, and William Audley Couper. Her husband, Rev. Theodore Bartow, was ordained in South Carolina and became rector of Christ Church in 1830. Wheeler, *Eugenia Price's South*, 11.

Monticello 31st December 1839

I wrote to you my dear Miss Jane about the first week in December and as you spoke of not leaving the Island before the 15th of the month directed my letter to the care of Mr Couper. I have been expecting to hear from you week after week but as each one brings disappointment, I begin to fear my letter has never reached you. I am the more anxious as my necessities had induced me to avail myself of your kind offer to procure me what I may require in Savannah. I therein enclosed thirty dollars begging the favour of you to get Hannah Page and myself a bonnet. After the letter was gone I heard that bills of the Bank of Darien and its branches were ten percent below par all the money I then had was of that description I could send no other—but thought I would wait to hear from you what amount I should again forward to make up the deficientcy.

I presume you are now in Savannah or at your favorite Hermitage. I therefore shall direct this letter to the care of Mr Ralph King in Savannah. Do dear Miss Jane let me hear from you as soon as you receive this. Your unfortunate peaches I gave in charge of Lady who was to go from W[averly] to St S[imons] in a vessel hourly expected at the former place when she left here the first week in Dec. Instead of which she was kept waiting there until two days before Christmas when she was sent down in a boat. I hope she will have the wit to send them to Cannon's Point and let your friends have the good of them if you are not to get them.

I hear very regularly from my dear husband his health was good on the 21st. I am in constant dread of his suffering from the excessive cold of this hard winter. I am grateful that I am able to say that our children are all well.

You will I hope excuse this short letter as I am now in much haste to give the children their breakfasts. Tomorrow I trust will be the beginning of a new year of happiness to you. May we both my dear Miss Jane arise with hearts better fitted to serve our Maker than we have ever done. With feelings of deep gratitude to my God! that I and mine have been permitted to see the close of this year. And with a hope that all is well with you—I am dear Miss Jane

Your affectionate and faithful friend
A M King

Waverly, 3rd March 1842
Jas Hamilton Couper Esq

My dear Sir

It cannot be unknown to you that the unfavorable seasons for some years past, and the almost annual ravages of the caterpillar have cut short the crop of Sea Island cotton on the coast of Georgia, and in some locations almost destroyed it.[1] My husband has probably been one of the greatest sufferers from these successive disasters. At a time when negros were selling from five to six hundred dollars round in gangs—he unfortunately purchased largely; relying on the proceeds of his cotton crops to enable him to make payment, but the almost total failure in some years, short crops and low prices in others, have prevented him from realizing the means to meet his engagements.[2] The result is that his creditors have seized and taken from him all his property which in the condition of the country and at present Prices will probably not pay his debts.[3] This may render it necessary for me to call on your friendly aid as one of my Trustees, to protect the property bequeathed in my Fathers will for the benefit of myself and children.[4]

I do not impute any blame, or mismanagement to my husband, nor has his misfortunes, in the slightest degree impaired my confidence in his integrity, or his ability to manage property. Nor is it my desire to give you unnecessary trouble. I simply ask that you will stand the friend of my fathers child in case my husbands creditors shall after taking all his property attempt to seize that upon which I can alone rely for the support of a family of nine children most of them small—and at that peculiar age when instruction and parental support are essential and necessary. I do not know that my husbands creditors will disturb me but in case they attempt it I desire permission to call on you and Mr Joseph Jones—my other trustee—to protect my property, as my husband cannot act and I can rely alone upon my Trustees.[5]

It is my desire that my husband be left as your, or my agent, in the management of my plantations and business generally.

If my memory serves me a copy of my Fathers will was sent to you soon after his decease. If you cannot lay your hand upon it I will send you another immediately.

I send you enclosed, a list of the 50 negros left to me in the will, with their increase.

Pray let me hear from you as soon as convenient—Direct your letter to Waynesville.

My kind regards to Mrs Couper

Very respectfully
Your obedient servant
Anna Matilda King

1. Frederick Wilkinson places the "Cotton Caterpillar" and the "Cotton Boll-Caterpillar" among the most devastating cotton pests. The former lays hundreds of difficult-to-detect eggs on the underside of the upper leaves of the plant. Several generations may be produced during a growing season, thus preventing the plant from putting out leaves and buds. The latter is similar in its life history to the first but attacks the newly formed boll. See Wilkinson, *The Story of the Cotton Plant*, 35–36.

2. Of the years between King's marriage and his financial losses Steel writes: "Besides enlarging and improving his wife's property, he extended his operations to the rice-growing area of the mainland in 1830 when he bought for $12,000 part of the Middleton Barony, comprising some 4,700 acres on the Satilla River. Six years later he offered to purchase the rest of the Middleton Barony for $7,000. His planting ventures were so successful that he planned to finance this purchase and a similar one of 800 adjoining acres out of two years' profits." Unfortunately, Steel continues, in the mid-1830s "cotton prices on the world market began a downward trend that was to last for ten years. The Panic of 1837 had struck hard at the cotton grower, although the total effect was not immediately apparent." King's "optimism had led him to pile one undercapitalized company upon another and in their management he had misinterpreted the trends of the economy." His "financial affairs, precariously balanced for so long, came tumbling about his ears in January 1842. On the 17th of the month he drafted a letter to his creditors confessing his inability to pay his debts, even with the forced sale of property. He had received no adequate offer for the one hundred slaves that he had put on the market. So gloomy was the prospect that he left Washington . . . with the intention of resigning his seat and settling his affairs. From February until May he remained at home arranging for the disposal of his property—Waverly Plantation, the summer cottage at Waynesville, and the slaves" (Steel, *T. Butler King*, 6, 16–17, 40).

3. Steel writes that "the *Savannah Republican* of March 5, 1842, contains the notices of the U.S. Marshal's sale of 246 slaves and nearly 20,000 acres in three counties to satisfy judgements against King. Later references in the King Papers make it clear that the sacrifice of this property still left King in debt" (*T. Butler King*, 177).

4. William Page's will read, "I give and bequeath unto Joseph Jones, Esq. of Liberty County and unto Mr James Hamilton Couper of Glynn County, as Trustees, and in trust for the Sole use, benefit and behoof of my affectionate daughter Ann Matilda, at present the wife of Mr Thomas Butler King. To her and to her heirs, not subject to the debts or to be under the control of her present, or any future husband, or husbands she may have the following property a part of my Estate real and personal. Viz. All my lands or landed property situated on St Simons Island with the improvements there on. Also my household furniture, bedding and bed linens, table linens & plate. Also all my cattle and stock of every kind on said Island. Also the following named fifty negro slaves with their increase" (Page Will, GDAH).

5. Before legislation was passed to protect married women's property, it could be confiscated by her husband or creditors. Trusts such as the one created by Page were women's only means of protection. See Hellerstein et al., *Victorian Women*, 305.

2nd June 1842
[Retreat]

My dearly beloved Husband

I had intended commencing this letter at a leisure moment when I would be able to write to you a long letter but that moment is only to be had at night & now my *eyes* will not bear that so in great haste I have retired in H[annah] Pages room (the office) on a *rickety* table—bad pen & mind full of trouble. I write to say your wife and children are well but the negros are very sickly. A most distressing *disentary* has attacked.[1] Polly, Jane, Anthony Sukey & Clementines youngest child, the two first & the last are exceedingly reduced. I can get nothing to check it. Peggy also sick, *Hannah* has been also quite sick & seems falling into bad health. Smart was taken with fever on Sunday night & by Tuesday swelled all over.[2] So you see I have my hands full and in the midst of this a *house full.*

The day before yesterday Mr Harrington & family came down to take passage in a Brig to go out over this bar. The weather was very boisterous. The motion of the vessel laying in the sound was very sickening. So that I could not do otherwise than ask them up. The wind sticks obstinately to the NE and now my family numbers *20.* You will say where do you put them all. I have put all the little ones up stairs, taken birth with Tootee myself, & given them my room & their white servant the Sopha in our parlour. Sturtevant now sleeps in the cotton house but eats in the same place. He will go to McIntoshs when I leave.

Wilson is now laying the foundation of the house. I believe including Mr S[turtevant] there are five carpenters at work. I am nearly *eaten out.* The corn and bacon and nails came last week. I have given Mr Harrington your room door key if your land lady charges you with a *new lock* bring *the old one home.*[3]

We had a very good rain the day my last letter was put into the office & since then another which I hope will save our corn crop. Toney begged me tell you that he saw two cotton blossoms on the 28th May.[4] That the last rains brought up all the seed—some that has lain in the ground since the *first planting.* The cotton crop is improving. We have had less than any where else. I am told up at the Sand Hills & Buffalo they have had a great deal & I believe some hail. Dunham I believe writes to you by this mail & will probably give you a better account of the crops than I can.

This is now the 2nd of June. I will endeavour to leave by the 15th but the sickness of these negros have put me sadly back. I have been obliged to take Ruthy out of the field to help Rhina wash.[5] Clementine has to cook breakfast & supper. Elizabeth Cuyler has been spending some days up the Island—having Davy[6] & the buggy. Oh I wish I could only be once more alone with my own dear husband & children. It has cost me more to keep house one month on this Island than all the time I staid at Waverly.

Mr Harrington desires me to say that Mr Cuyler sent him the paper that it just got to Brunswick in time for him to have it executed & forwarded.

I received your short letter by the vessel which brought the corn. I do hope & pray I may hear from you by this Mail. Mr Harrington says you got on safe to Wilmington. I feel very anxious about you. For mercy sake be careful of yourself & if my life is of any value to you or your children write me often. I have too much to trouble me without having this to contend with too.

I think Butler & Lord still feel the influence of your late *visit* at home. They do not give me quite so much trouble. I enclose a letter from Henry.[7] I have not read it. Neither do I ever care to read another letter from his pen. I hope and trust you still keep your calmness & firmness and that your health may be spared. I feel truly anxious about you. I fear you will be for making up for lost time and over taxing your strength & thereby injuring your health. It is of no use my preaching to you but if you have any value for [torn] life or reason *let self for once be your* [torn] *care.* The children are all in school [torn]. They desire a great deal of love & kisses [torn].

May God! be more merciful to you my beloved than your fellow mortals have been. May *he* in mercy bless & restore you to your devoted wife

A M King

1. For more on diseases, see Patterson, "Disease Environments of the Antebellum South," 152–153; and Savitt, "Black Health on the Plantation," 338, 340.

2. Polly, born August 20, 1801, is number 33 in Major Page's will and number 70 on the 1839 list. Jane is number 2 in "50 Negros with Their Increase," but is listed as "purchased" on the 1853 list. Anthony is listed as one of Ruthy's children on the list of "50 Negros with Their Increase" but does not appear on any of the other lists. There are two Sukeys. One appears on the list from Major Page's will as number 35. Sukey 2d is listed on "50 Negros with Their Increase" as Alic and Maryann's child. Sukey Jr., born April 14, 1830, appears on the 1839 list as number 86. Clementine or Clementina is listed in Major Page's will, on the list of "50 Negros with Their Increase" as number 18, and as number 90 on the 1853 list. Hannah Junr. (born December 20, 1842) appears as number 15, making Hannah three months pregnant in June 1842. Smart, born March 30, 1812, is number 11 on the list from Major Page's will, number 91 on the 1839 list, and number 68 on the 1853 list. See Page Will, GDAH; appendix 2.

3. I believe she means that if T. B. King can procure a lock from his landlady in Washington, Anna won't have to buy one if she wants to replace the lock after Harrington leaves.

4. Edward Steel writes that T. B. King "relied especially on the driver, Tony, who

in the later years when an overseer was employed made separate oral reports on production figures" (*T. Butler King*, 32).

5. Rhina appears on the list "50 Negros with Their Increase" as Myrtilla's daughter. She is number 76 on the 1839 list, her birthday given as May 21, 1825; and number 104 on the 1853 list. Ruthy Junr., born May 12, 1808, is number 4 on the list from
Major Page's will, number 51 on the 1839 list, and number 31 on the 1853 list but does
not appear on the 1859 list. Ruthy 2d, born May 24, 1828, is number 87 on the 1839
list and number 61 on the 1853 list. See appendix 2.

6. Four Davys appear on the 1839 list. Davy Piles, number 185, was born in 1805;
Davy number 224 is recorded as a body servant born in 1813; Davy number 237 was
born in 1824; and Davy number 332 is noted as being ten years old. See appendix 2.

7. Anna is referring to Henry King, Thomas Butler King's brother, who lived and
practiced law in Allentown, Pennsylvania.

5th August 1842
[Monticello]

My dearly Beloved husband

Your welcome letter of the 25th came to hand by the last Mail. How grateful I am to you for writing so punctually—the time passes so much more rapidly and pleasantly when I can get two letters each week. I rejoice to hear that
your health is better and that you were about leaving for a healthier place. I pray
God! you may obtain what you seek—health and strength—and I will hope a
little flesh too. Hannah Page says she is sleeping better at nights for several
days past retaining her food. Butler has one of the afflictions of *Job* just now
having a very "sore boil." This is the only ailment now in this family.

By the last mail I had a letter from Andrew & one from Louisa[1] also one to
you which I forward. Mumford sent me another letter yesterday which I returned as I did Tisons last unread. Those people really persecute me and doubtless tell a great many lies. Well we have had to submit to a great deal and a little
more trouble will not kill us—so it is only the work of man.[2]

I had hoped to have heard from the Island before I wrote today but Davy has
not yet returned. I sent him down on Tuesday to get the boys ponies. The
weather was very stormy after he left—it rained all Tuesday and the wind at
the NE. Cleared off on Wednesday so cool as to make fires *necessary* to our comfort. For the last three days we have had fires in every room the atmosphere
clear and delightful. Just our pleasant October weather—Thermometer vary-
ing from 60 to 70 degrees. I fear there has been a storm some where to cause
so great a change—though this has been a remarkably cool summer and as yet
very healthy but there is so much water on the flat lands it will no doubt be

sickly should the rains now cease. I think it very strange that I have not yet received the order from Mr Cuyler to get the gins from Waverly.

I hope you will be able to write to me longer letters. I want you to write all about your dear self. I shall not make this a long letter being rather hurried. As you will not probably receive it until you return to W[ashington] it is not so important, as I shall I hope be able to write to you a longer letter by the Tuesday mail. H[annah] Page says she will write to you again very shortly—but begs you in the mean time to answer her last letter. Georgia is half crazy to be allowed to add a post script to this. I hardly think she will have time. The children talk daily of your return and long to see you.

I take great delight in our garden. It is very pleasant to spend my afternoons down there with our dear children—each one employed in some way or other. Butler is of the greatest assistance to me he superintends the out door matters and I think will be of great assistance to you should you continue to be a planter. He is not afraid of hard work.

I implore of you my beloved to be careful of your health. If my life is of importance—how much more is yours. The children send a great deal of love

Your devoted wife

A M King

My dear father

I wish you would come home for I wish to see you very much it seems that I never wished to see you more than now I declare it seems there is something missing every day when the stage passes i wish It would stop in You must write to me for I think after I miss you so much I think after I miss you so much I think you may write to me.

Your affectionate daughter

G P King

Poor Georgia has not done herself justice in writing in so much haste. I will let it go as it is. In looking over my papers I find I have but one copy of my fathers will. I do not like to part with this one. I think you have one of the copies with you—which you can let Henry have.

God Bless you my beloved

A M King

1. Louisa, Andrew King's wife, is reported in the family narrative of Florence Marye to have been a "Miss Louisa Murdoch, Boston governess to the King children. She was entrusted by Charles Amory of Boston to carry to Mr. King the gift of the famous Warwick vase carved from the live oak timber from Retreat Plantation used in the original construction of the now remodeled frigate Constitution" (*Story of the Page-*

King Family, 54). There is no evidence in Anna's letters, however, to indicate that Louisa Murdoch King ever served as a governess to the King children.

2. Referring to the financial difficulties caused when King's expanded planting operations and his plans to build railroads and canals failed, precipitating him deep into debt. See Steel, *T. Butler King*, 8–9, 166.

9th August 1842

My dearly beloved husband

Since the acknowledgement of your having been sick I would be still more distressed at not hearing from you by the last mail had you not mentioned your intention to leave Washington City for a short time. I flatter myself my disappointment is owing to your change of situation. I look forward to the coming mail with much anxiety fervently praying I may hear good tidings of your health. Hannah Page is better our other dear children are all well. The cool weather is gone and we again have heat though I think this has been a most delightful summer.

I heard from the Island through Davy I also had a few lines from Dunham. The cotton had suffered from the drought which caused it to shed badly. And the wind last week did considerable damage. So to end the whole I suppose little or nothing will be made. Every one speaks gloomily of cotton crops. The rice crop I believe is very fine this season. I am trying to get all I can to grow in our garden here—but the *ground seems almost tired.* I have *Ned*[1] here his *legs* are both in a dreadful state. I will try and get some advice for him. Davy says he heard no *complaints* on the Island.

Every afternoon the dear children and myself go down to the garden. We walk and work until dark. This garden is indeed a very pleasant resort to us. We had very poor fruit this season and now but few vegetables but the corn & potatoes look well also the arrow root & cane.[2] Quamina certainly deserves much credit for having so much done. I have permitted him to go to the Island. Davy says the cotton had began to open—but none yet gathered.

By the way I received a long letter by the last mail from my cousin W. P. Molett.[3] He is very much disposed to be our friend but he is very much put out by your not answering his letter—he attributes it to *pride* on your part. Do my husband write him one of *your own letters.* Do *not lose* so *important a friend to your poor wife & children by want of a little civility on your part.* Write to him. He requests I will show you his last letter—which I would enclose but for fear of its never reaching you. Do my husband oblige me by writing—tell him all your present intentions as his advice even if you do not mean to follow it—*he has made a for tune* & knows how to turn one penny to make it grow into a pound.

At all events he is a friend worth securing to your family when a little civility is all he requires.

Mr Couper went to the Island on Saturday and returned last evening. I have not heard what he thought of our little crop there. I fear the winds of last week has done it great injury. I really apprehended a regular storm. Davy came up on Saturday & brought the boys ponies. You never saw a happier little pair of boys—they now leave home at day light for school—take their breakfast at the Lodge but return to dinner. Mr Cuyler sent me an order on Alex [?] Atkinson for the gins—but nothing more. I asked for an order to remove the *timber wheels* and every other moveable article from the place. I rather think he forgot my wants in the pressure of his business. His health was better. He says he will send me Mr Barriens opinion this week.

I hope you will gain what you seek in leaving Washington—health—you scarcely imagine how anxious I am about you. Now your anxiety is divided into 11 parts your 9 children your wife and our *little all*. Mine is centered in you alone.

Lovat Fraser is back again. I never saw any one gain flesh faster than he has done. He leaves again in two weeks. Poor Park Gigneliat is still very low and John his brother—is in a very bad way—one of the brothers *Scott* is a dreadful object as helpless as a babe. He cannot even walk but is carried about like a child. I really think poor Mrs Gigneliat is to be pitied. I am told it is delightful to see the devotion of the *well members* to the afflicted ones of that family. Henry who is quite a youth takes Scott in his arms with so much tenderness and walks him about as a fond mother would a sick babe. How thankful we aught to be that we have so healthy a family.[4]

I am anxious about H[annah] Page she is decidedly dispeptic poor girl.[5] She is obliged to restrain the little appetite she has & then sit still for at least an hour after or else Up it comes. Mr Edward Houston said he was afflicted in that way for years.

Georgia says she was never so anxious in all her life to see you as she now is & she is sure when you hear this you will not let it be long before you do come home. They are all very anxious to see you & talk a great deal of the happiness they anticip[ate] enjoying on your return to us. The servants behave rem[arka]bly well. They seem to wish to do all in their power to relieve me of trouble. I must now conclude my beloved one may God! in Mercy bless guide & comfort you. The children send a great deal of love & a bushel of kisses.

Your devoted wife

A M King

1. Ned is listed as number 41 on the list from William Page's will. There are two Neds on the 1839 list: Ned number 84 was born on August 12, 1821; Ned number 329

is listed as ten years old. On the 1853 list Ned, born in 1821, is listed as number 57. See appendix 2.

2. Arrow root (which derived its name from its use as an antidote for poison arrows) is a tropical American plant of the genus *Maranta* with large leaves, white flowers, and starchy roots.

3. Mr. Molett was a Timmons cousin who was a successful planter in Alabama. Anna had written to him asking for a loan. While he was unable to comply with her request, he wrote to Thomas Butler King advising him on planting as well as economizing.

4. Anna's description makes it seem likely that the family was suffering from tuberculosis, or consumption. See Rothman, *Living in the Shadow of Death*, for more on the disease.

5. Dyspepsia is a general term for indigestion.

11th & 12th August 1842

My dearly beloved husband

Your kind letters of the 28th & 30th Ult[1] reached me yesterday. A thousand thanks for your affectionate remembrances of us. I rejoice to hear you were able to *run* up that *memorable* hill it is one proof of health tho' you do not say as much on *that important subject* as I could wish. I know you never like to dwell much on your own state of health—you are always for putting *the best foot* foremost. When you get this letter I beg you will just sit down & write me an exact account of your health—how you look, how you feel, if any *fatter*, your appetite and every thing about your dear self. You know how anxious I am about you—pray be particular & tell me *more of yourself*.

I should not I suppose recognize Staten Island could I visit it now. How beautiful it must now look with those improvements—yet Melancholy when we reflect on the changes which have taken place since you took me there six months after we were married. Then we had kind parents & enough of the worlds goods to make the future a pleasing anticipation. Alas! how changed!!! But thanks to the Mercy of God! we are not left entirely penniless. We are far better off than many others are. Far better off than we deserve to be. I feel more and more my base ingratitude to my God! & to you too my dear husband. When blessed with plenty I suffered trifles to make me unhappy. I find I can bear up much better than I thought it possible under real troubles than I once could under *imaginable ones*. This I attribute solely to the Mercy of that All Wise Being whose will it is we should be brought low. I am still blessed with a beloved husband who is both willing & able to exert himself for his family. We have yet nine of the ten children He has given us and not entirely destitute of the means to support & educate them. They too are in health. And if my table is not so sumptuously supplied as formerly, if my attendants are fewer I have yet enough for real wants & have not been driven yet to the necessity of cooking or any such drudgery. I find by carrying my own keys I see exactly how fast things go. By attending to my pantry it is kept far cleaner than Almarene[2] did. I have to scold far less. In fact I am happier now than I have been the last three years. *If*, *you could only be at home & free from all your enemies.*

It grieves me to hear you say "if I could remain here a few days longer my health would be much benefitted." I fear my beloved it is for want *of the means* that your stay is shortened. Oh! that I but possessed once more a fortune for your dear sake. You know husband I never valued money for *my own* gratification. Your wants & those of the dear children have always been my first consideration—even the necessities of the negros I have considered before my own. But enough of this.—

H[annah] Page is better—looks better but occasionally still spits up her food. The other dear children are quite well as is also dear Sarah Houston. The servants are better. On Tuesday Mr Plant, Doctor Follin, Francis Scarlett, Mr Feller & Burril Brown called & were all here at the same time. This afternoon Mr Plant, Miss Elizabeth Hazlehurst & Mr Robert so you see we meet with some *politeness.*

I consulted Dr Follin about *Ned.* He says his whole system is deranged & that he has dropsy of the *chest.* He thinks as he is young he may be relieved and said if I would send him to Bethel—where he resides—he could attend to him with far less expense to me & more justice to Ned. His legs are so bad he aught not to do any work so I have sent him.[3] Poor fellow he seems very anxious to get well & I now regret more than ever not bringing him up when I came.[4] Hannah is better but still not well. Burril Brown says his father has a remarkably fine crop. He counted *20 open boles on one stock of cotton* some days ago &c &c. There was a terrible *hail storm* at Waverly the other day but it did not extend to Mr Browns.

By the way the Mr Campbell who with his little boys were at Retreat in April is married to an old maid of 49 in Savannah 15 years his junior, old Miss Bell Robertson a cousin to the Johnstons. I believe I wrote to you that his second son had had his left hand shot off. And your old favorite Miss Margaret Telfair[5] is married too to some great man in England. She is about the same age. I think this has been a fortunate year for *Old Maids.* I would not be surprised to hear that Miss Jane Johnston was married but "as Mrs McNish has not yet seen the man that Mary Jane should marry" I suppose Aunt Jane has not either as regards herself.[6]

There will be church here on Sunday—Mr Stephens will preach. I wish I could conquer my repugnance to *seeing a certain family.* I would go. Mrs McCay & Miss Scarlett will be at church. Mr Stephens is considered a very good preacher. I suppose you saw Mr McKean[7] whilst in N.Y. He very kindly sent me a number of Brother Johnathan & some little Books for Malley & Virginia.

Florence charged me when going to bed to tell you she hopes soon to write well enough to send you a letter. Malley said I must still write for him "that he wants to see you very much & hopes you will soon come & bring his *half dollar knife.*" Appy now wishes she had taken the physic then you would have brought her something. Floyd too speaks confidently of getting a knife. Little Tip looks very knowing but can say nothing further than *kiri* too. He is a very sweet little fellow and is in fine health. Our removal to this place has certainly benefited him.

I had a letter from Elizabeth Cuyler by the last mail—her father had been again sick but was better. Margaret was then in bed *with fever.* This is what I feared. She was in very high health when she left us. Elizabeth too is not well. She regrets very much having returned to Savannah. Mr Cuyler was confirmed and took the sacrament last Sunday.

I had written thus far last night my candle burnt out & my eyes became dim so that I fear I have made many mistakes. To wait til the mail morning I write in too much haste. I have too many interruptions to write during the day & at night my eyes will not let me do much in way of reading or writing so you will have to put up with this scrawl. We are all well this morning. Since the *blow* and rains we have had one week of dry weather at first cool & delightful but now warm enough through the day, and yesterday a pleasant shower. We have not experienced a single hot night this summer. From what you say I rather think *our summer has been cooler than yours.*

You know why I am so anxious for those castings—the necessity of our being in funds early in November. I hope they may now soon arrive. The cotton house [is] finished & a little cotton got out so that we may be enabled to bring in our odds and ends. I sent you by last Fridays mail a letter from Andrew. And in my letter of Tuesday begged you to write to Mr Molett.[8] He seems hurt at your never having replied to his letter to you. Address to "Portland Dallas County Alabama." Lovat Fraser is still on the Sand Hills—he however leaves for N.Y. in a week. Poor young man he seems pleased with the sea & prepared to work his way through life as a sailor. I am surprised at the determination of Henry Barclay. There seems no necessity for him to become a carpenter but he aught to know his own business better than I can. I feel every day more anxious for our own dear boys. Soon we shall have to turn them off to shift for themselves—and ill calculated are they to bear with the trouble of this world. I hope the time is now near at hand when you will stay at home & give them by your example & precepts better instruction than I have been able to impart. Believe me husband your constant absences for the last 10 years have been of incalculable injury to your family.

I find Mrs Houston a most desirable companion for our daughter as well as a very pleasant one to myself. No one can be m[ore] amiable or correct in their deportment than Sarah Houston. Oh! [torn] can her father treat her so cruelly? Mr Houston comes up every [Satur]day night & leaves again on Monday morning. They give me no trou[ble] and he sends me each week sufficient to prevent their being any expense in venison, beef, and chickens. He also provides for his horse & they do their own washing. I must now conclude as it is breakfast time & the children are getting impatient. They all send a *thousand* kisses to there dear father and hope ere long to see him at home. May God! bless you my beloved & may we meet again in health peace & happiness.—

Your devoted wife
A M King

[Enclosed with Anna's letter of August 11 and 12]

Monticello, August 15th 1842

My dear Father

I hope you will excuse my not having written to you long ere this, it has been my intention to do so ever since you left, I have begun more than one letter to you but always thought that they were either to badly written, or, had not enough in them, to send; but I have determined what ever may happen to this one, I will send it, as my dear mother says I must and should write to you. And to tell you the truth I am half jealous of Tootee, who has written to you twice.

Butler and Lord both send their love and say that they will ask Mr Dutton to let them write to you in school hours as they canot write good by themselves, they say that they like him very much indeed he is very kind to them. do My dear father write to me soon as I am most anxious to hear from you. I wish congress would make hast and adjourn as I feel your long absence more and more every day please as soon as you can come home for we all [?] require you here very much indeed.—

If you do not come home soon you will not know little Tip Mamma has put short frocks on him and he looks very sweet I wish you could just see him he is very proud of his pantalets. He tries very much to talk and can say a few words some times.

Dear father My hand is very tired so I hope you will excuse this bad writing as Tootee says I can write to you very soon.

All the children send their love love and a kiss to you

Believe me your affectionate daughter
G P King

1. This is an abbreviation for "ultimo," meaning "the previous month."

2. Almarene appears on the 1839 list as number 307 and twenty-eight years old. She does not appear on the 1853 list, but under "Deaths of negros from June 1854" Anna wrote "Almarene July 1855." See appendix 2.

3. Dropsy is an accumulation of fluid in the body, or congestive heart failure. Ned's heart disease was so advanced as to produce fluid in his chest (which the physician could hear) and in his legs (causing them to swell). Information from Barbara Marston, M.D., Emory University School of Medicine, Atlanta, Georgia; and Larry Slutsker, M.D., Centers for Disease Control and Prevention, Atlanta, Georgia.

4. A copy (in what appears to be Anna's handwriting) of an undated letter concerning the King's summer residence reads:

> Mrs King is now prepared to offer her summer residence near Waynesville to you at the price proposed last spring, with a *reasonable* allowance in addition, for the services of the boy who has been kept there to take care of the place. The price will therefore stand this.

> | Price in April 1842 — | $500.00 |
> | Interest 2²/₃ years to this date | 97.00 |
> | Title papers & recording | 11.00 |
> | | $608.00 |

> The services of Ned to be added.—If you will pay the whole amount on the first January, or one half *then* and the balance the 1st April Neds services will be thrown in or not charged.

> Mrs King could obtain more for the establishment, but as it has been offered to you she and myself deem due to you [?] the offer.

> The privilege of removing such shrubs, flour [*sic*] and fruit trees from the garden as she may desire, and a few loose white pine boards from the carriage house is reserved. Also all the moveable valuables & furniture &c. You can have possession some time this month.

> Please let me hear from you as soon as possible on the subject.
> With much respect & esteem
> I am very truly yours
> Signed (Thos Butler King)

> Col Joseph Wiggins
> Near Waynesville

> I confirm the above
> Anna Matilda King
> I also reserve the large iron pot set in brick in the wash kitchen. (TBK, SHC)

5. Margaret Telfair was the daughter of Alexander Telfair, "the Princeton-educated son of an early Georgia governor, a trustee of the Independent Presbyterian Church, and chairman of the Savannah Theater" (Lane, *Architecture of the Old South Georgia*, 127).

6. After the death of her son and husband, Ann Johnston McNish built a house near Cannon's Point on four acres of land she leased from John Couper for one dollar per year and which she named Long View. Vanstory writes that "here Ann and her young daugh-

ter could be near the Coupers, and Mary Jane could know the pleasant island life that
Ann had enjoyed as a girl. . . . In 1843 Mary Jane McNish was married to Leighton Wilson Hazelhurst, the son of Robert and Elizabeth Wilson Hazelhurst, whose families
were among the earliest settlers of Glynn County" (*Land of the Golden Isles*, 185–186).

7. Thomas Swasey McKean, an 1828 graduate of Harvard, was the tutor of the
King children.

27th December 1844
[Retreat]

My dearly beloved Husband

I am sadly reduced in the *paper line* but cannot let that be an excuse not to
write to you. My last dated the 23rd I gave to Davy to have Mailed at Brunswick. Malley was the same day taken with violent fever, pain in his head & side.
I was very much alarmed and watched him with painful anxiety—but thanks
to the Mercy of God! his fever lasted but 24 hours and the pain wore off with
the perspiration and he is again well. And our H[annah] Page, Cuyler & Floyd
all seem to have got over the worst of their attacks. Ann Gale has been quite
sick too but is better. We have three cases now in the hospital. *Smart* is the
worse off in fact quite ill. He was doing very well 'til last night when he re-
newed his cold and has had a relapse. Pussy[1] seems to think him a little better
than he was a few hours ago. Butler & Lord have got over their colds. I have
no doubt we shall have cases enough after the holy days. That man Chevalair
has not yet landed our goods. This is truly provoking.

Mr Williams from St Marys came here on Friday and remained until this
morning with Mr Kahn—*they* left together this morning for Genl Clinches
plantation. James King[2] came on Saturday spent the day and night and when
he was going away yesterday asked me to let Butler & Lord accompany him
home. As they had no amusement here I thought it would be as well to let them
go. They will be back tomorrow none the worse I hope for their visit.

I could not spare Almarene to send to the office yesterday so that I have not
received your letter which I hope to do tomorrow. My cold distresses me very
much. I do not know what can make me so unwell but it does seem as tho' I
cannot get over my head aches—but I cannot spare the time to lay down in the
day.[3] And I am thankful I am able to be up.

I do not know when Mr Kahn intends to leave us. I suppose he is waiting
your return. I am fully persuaded that he is a first rate teacher to smart apt children but I am equally certain that he *scolds too much*. He seems ever finding fault
with one or the other. He actually is *quarrelling* the whole time with one or the
other of the children. But I am afraid Mr MacKean will be too high in his price.
We must do as Mr Couper does. He does not give more than half of what you

give Mr K. He writes to the president of Yale College for a young man of such & such qualifications who will be willing to come out for one year at such a price. The President looks around—there are a great many who for a few hundred dollars will come out for a year or two years. Do see if you cannot write to Mr Dwight. I know Butler & Lord can now lose no time Butler especially is so backward. It really makes me melancholy to think how little they have gained in the last year. I talk to them in every way I can. I never let an opportunity pass to urge them on.

I wrote to Mr Anderson[4] to day for some house hold supplies and shall write to Mrs Matthais a[nd] beg her to get a few things for myself and the children. I have delaid until I can do so no longer hoping the price of cotton would *rise*, but there seems no demand for it. I am sure you have enough to drive you crazy —and surely I cannot be sufficiently thankful [to] God! for giving you strength to bear it as you do. May this be continued to you my own dearly beloved Husband. If the sale of these 70 negros would pay *all* demands I would feel perfectly happy, but it is only the *beginning*.[5] But far be it [last line on the page is missing] *hope* in your noble breast. Hope on—but do not let it deceive as it has before done & induced you to incur *fresh debts*. I wish we could get rid of *all* at *there value* and leave this wretched country. I am more and more convinced it is no place to rear a family of children. But this is not to be done at present and we must bear as we best can all the ills of our situation. To bring up boys on a plantation makes them *teranical* as well as lazy, and girls too.

I suppose you will soon be coming out. Oh! how I dread your journey!!! May the God! of Mercy protect you from all harm. Oh my husband my heart is sick from trouble. It seems to me I have no comfort. If you do get home safe it will be but to leave me again. I know it cant *now be helpt*. I also know there is no use to repine—so I will stop.—

The children send you a great deal [of] love a[nd] ma[ny] kisses. They will I hope soon be all well again.

I heard yesterday that poor suffering Mrs Abraham was even lower than when I saw her. *It* has become now so *offensive* it is really terrible to stay in the room with her. It made *me very sick* even after I got home.[6] She told me that she knew it was so & that for that reason she preferred being alone. I do not think she can hold out much longer. As soon as she dies the Capt will go to *Thomas County*. He seems attentive to her.

Do excuse my miserable scrawls. My head aches my pen & paper are both so miserable.

God! bless you my own dear love, guard you from all harm, and guide you in all you do.

Your devoted wife
A M King

I have just received your dear welcome letter of the 19th. I thank you my beloved husband for your punctuality. I am afraid after reading this scrawl you will pay me no compliment on *my firmness*. But we all have our weak moments. I think you are taking a great deal of trouble if you are going to N.Y. solely on account of Mr M[c] K[ean]. It would have been as well to have let him come to you unless you had to pay his expenses. I am for saving every dollar for a little *leak* will after a while drain off a great swamp. Dupree writes me he will not levy until he hears from you. His letter has relieved me of some anxiety. God! bless you again & again my own dear love

Your devoted wife

1. Pussy is number 17 on the list from William Page's will; number 104, birthdate February 20, 1794, on the 1839 list; and number 89 on the 1853 list. She worked for many years as a nurse in the hospital and seems to have had a measure of autonomy in dealing with her patients. Anna generally praised her work. See appendix 2.

2. James King was the son of Stephen King, Thomas Butler King's brother.

3. Though Anna was remarkably healthy throughout her life, she suffered from chronic (possibly migraine) headaches that increased in intensity as she grew older.

4. G. W. Anderson Brothers was the Kings' factor, or agent, in Savannah. Factors sold the cotton and rice crops of local planters (for an average commission of 2.5 percent) and supplied plantations with goods available only in the city. In addition, they extended credit and/or paid bills—charged against the current or future sale of crops. Commerce or Factors Row stood on a bluff overlooking the Savannah River and included offices and, on the riverbank below, warehouses. William Cullen Bryant wrote of seeing "long trains of cars heaped with bales, steamer after steamer loaded high with bales coming down the rivers, acres of bales on the wharves, acres of bales at the railway stations" in Savannah (Lane, *Savannah Revisited*, 133). Also see Vanstory, *Land of the Golden Isles*, 98.

5. Evidently, seventy more slaves had to be sold to cover T. B. King's debts. Steel, *T. Butler King*, 40–41.

6. The intensity of the odor that Anna describes could be caused by certain types of cancer or bacterial infections including those associated with bedsores. Information from Drs. Marston and Slutsker.

9th Feb—1847

My dearly beloved husband

I was again disappointed yesterday no letter from you—not even a news paper no intelligence *from* you later than the 19th Jan. This to say the least of it is *discouraging* for I am not certain that my letters to you meet with any better treatment. Writing is to me by no means an agreeable employment as the use of glass's are painful to me. But still I write regularly once a week to you & believe you do the same to me.—

Well! we cant help ourselves—& have to put up with these Democrats from the President down to the Post Master of Frederica P[ost] O[ffice].[1] *I can hear nothing of those highly prized plants*—I fear *we may consider them a total loss.*

If the family were not well I should have told you so at the beginning of my letter. H[annah] Page is *still up*, little Anna had quite an *attack* the last Thursday from her teeth & for 2 days was quite sick—but thank God! she is quite well again—tho' with the loss of some flesh.[2] Our own dear children are in their usual health. My dear Amanda still remains with me which is a great comfort to me. My last letter to you was delay'd—the boat did not pass until *Friday* evening.

Mr James [Hamilton] Couper says he has not yet received yours & Mr Cuylers *consent* to sell *Oatlands*[3] so he can do nothing to effect the sale *until he gets it.—Pray attend to this.* Mr Petrigrue writes me that the papers came safe to hand & are all satisfactory.

The papers speak confidently of an extra Session. I hope & trust it will not be—I can scarce believe the present congress is so near its close. What happiness to be allowed to hope in a few short weeks we may have you once more at home. Oh! dearest you cant desire it as much as we do—there are so many of us to be made happy by your presence. I pray Gods! mercy you may be permitted to return as soon [as] steam can bring you after the 4th of March. Do my dear husband be careful of your health. I hope you will be able to procure Mr Woolleys Boat for he seems to have set his heart on getting one through you. I am sorry I sent for Amanda when I did—but I had every reason to think poor Tootees time was come. I know she has so much to do at home but she says she will not leave me until it is over.[4]

On Saturday last the Gaston landed a very nice cheese directed to Mrs A M King—care of G. W. Anderson & Brother Savannah & again on Sunday the boat landed *another cheese* directed in exactly the same way. I would really laugh if the Gaston lands another on Saturday. I hardly think you sent them as it is the last thing you would send us—as you do not think cheese *wholesome.* I rather think we are indebted to the Jaudons for these fine cheeses. I told Mr Wright I thought his Mother must have sent them—but he looked as though he *doubted it.*

Mr & Mrs J H C[ouper] have been spending a few days at the point. Mr Brown[5] spent this evening with us. Mrs Cater speaks of going North the coming summer. John Demere is her manager & has promised her 25 bags of cotton this year.

The children all unite in love & kisses to you—be sure to write to Mr Cuyler if you have not yet done so. I hope & trust I may hear from you by the next mail. I shall be miserable if I do not hear from you. I had quite a long letter from Mr McKean the other day—he is now living near Boston.—

I do not think my letter will be found very interesting—but some how I am

kept very nervous by H[annah] Pages situation & my eyes pain me to night.
Amanda sends her best regards. God! bless & preserve you dearest Husband

Your devoted wife

A M King

1. James K. Polk, a Democrat from Tennessee, and his supporters took his election
in 1844 as a mandate for U.S. expansion. As a result of the Oregon Compromise and
the Mexican War, the United States made huge territorial gains (from the Pacific coast
to the Continental Divide) and was faced with the unresolved and volatile question of
the expansion of slavery. T. B. King, a Whig and an opponent of Polk and the Mexican War, was also the spokesman in Congress for his party. King wrote to his daughter in 1846, "The Oregon debate is still going on in the Senate—I think enough has
transpired to show that we shall not have war—Tho' the prospect was very gloomy at
the commencement of the session—I do not now entertain a doubt that the western
men designed to throw the Country into a war and that *with* or without a *knowledge* of
this design they had at the beginning induced Polk to adopt their policy—He seems now
to have become alarmed and they are ready to take off his scalp" (Steel, *T. Butler King*,
57). Given the political climate and King's views and allegiances, it seems little wonder
that Anna expresses such a negative view of Democrats—from the White House to her
local post office.

2. Hannah Page King (Tootee) married William Audley Couper on January 15,
1845. "Little Anna" is Tootee's first child. T. B. King wrote to his daughter from
Washington in March 1846, "I have your dear kind letter of the 10th Inst. ["Inst." is
an abbreviation for "instant," meaning "of the present month."] Thank you with all my
heart for it—It is quite impossible for me to say why I have not written to you—I have
felt [?] anxiety than could be expressed in a volume. . . . Your dear bright infant has also
shared [?] painfully my sleepless anxiety for its dear mother. . . . I cannot express how
thankful I am that you are so well and long to see my grand daughter; your mother says
she resembles her father" (T. B. King to Hannah Page King Couper, March 21, 1846,
TBK, SHC).

3. Oatlands was owned by the Robert Grants, who had purchased it soon after
the turn of the nineteenth century. It was used as a summer home until 1834 when
Dr. Grant and his wife, Sarah Foxworth Grant, retired to St. Simons Island and Oatlands, giving their Altamaha River plantation, Elizafield, to their son Hugh Fraser
Grant (who married Mary Fraser). When Dr. Grant died, his wife returned to
Elizafield to live with her son and his family. Afterward the property was owned by the
Coupers. T. B. King and Mr. Cuyler evidently purchased all or part of Oatlands at
some point and were now ready to sell. However in 1853–1854, Butler King was plant-
ing about one hundred acres at Oatlands, so the sale evidently never took place. Huie
and Lewis, *King's Retreat Plantation*, 14–16; Vanstory, *Land of the Golden Isles*, 186–187;
Wheeler, *Eugenia Price's South*, 36–37.

4. Evidently Tootee was again pregnant and soon to deliver.

5. Rev. Mr. Brown of Christ Church.

May 23, 1848, to April 11, 1850

I have no *human aid* to look to if sickness visits my family or plantation—all eyes are turned to me for all the wants in sickness or in health.

Although her husband and older sons moved away from her protective care during these years, life at Retreat continued to consume Anna's time and energy. Her grandchildren, too, became a constant focus of her attentions, and letter writing an essential component of her most intimate relationships.

Retreat 23d May 1848

My dearly beloved husband

On Sunday I had the happiness to receive your most welcome letter of the 14th Inst—wanting just one day of *being a month* after the last letter I had received from you, as that was the 15th of April. I[t] does seem passing strange what does become of your letters. If those curious Post Masters would but send them to me after satisfying their curiosity I would be thankful. I was very miserable about you but this letter has quieted me somewhat. As the convention is to be held in Philadelphia on the 7th June & you think Congress will adjourn on the 20th I hope you will have nothing to detain you and that I may hope to see you by the 25th of June—but I dare say (as has always been the case) you will not return as soon as I shall expect you. I hope you have received my long letter of 8 pages fools cup.[1] As I could not well write at Mr Woolleys I made up for the loss of one week by the length of that letter.

Last week my letter was short. I was low spirited and half sick. I feel very little better now—but will try and tell you all I can. Butler still looks very badly but says he is well. Lord is very thin & pale—but does not give up. Malleys knee is quite well—Georgia has had a bad cold. The rest of the family including Tootee & her babies are as usual. On Saturday we had a fine shower. On Sunday noon a good sprinkle & at night a *very* fine shower. It has been raining heavily on the maine yesterday but none here. We have been very much more fortunate than the folks at the North end. Mr J H Couper called to see us yesterday—& said his crop was suffering very much it being *six* weeks since they had had enough rain to lay the dust. We have had *six* good showers here since he had had one. His health is now quite restored. He desired *very particularly* to be remembered to you. "Madam" intended coming down with him but was prevented by company.

Mr J H C[ouper] *congratulated* me on your renomination.[2] God knows it gives me no pleasure. I dare say I would have been *mortified* had your *name been rejected* but you promised me you would not consent to be again put up for *a target to be shot at.* And I believed you! Oh! my husband you cannot feel our constant separation as much as I do—or you would not think of going again. How will you manage to go on the canvass—we have neither horses or the means to obtain them. Now do not think I "scold" but you seem to forget how miserably [?] I am at home to get the most common comforts of life. You speak to Butler of his going to College. How can either of them go *without Andrew's fulfilling his promise*.[3] Have you heard from him further on the subject? You say my beloved that you "are working hard for myself & the children"? You have certainly built up a *proud name for yourself*—but I fear that will be all. You see my own dear husband I have much time *to think* & all I can think—I can see no way open to escape from difficulties. If you would but stay with us, how much better it would be—how much happier I would be. I have said all this before— I would not repeat—but think you must have forgotten.

In my last I mentioned the visit of Miss Cuyler & Miss Fannin the latter after staying two nights went to the Wyllys but is to return here. Mr & Mrs P[aul] Demere & Miss Martha[4] came down on Thursday last. Her object in coming was to get the services of Dr Sylvester who had promised to be on the Isld by the 15th. After remaining two days with us Mr Demere & his sister returned home leaving his wife and children with us. She is still here. I find her a most lovely character, ladylike, prudent, amiable—so kindly disposed to all. Her children give me no trouble—she has them under good management. Dr Sylvester & his assistant came here this morning so you may suppose I have a pretty full house. I long to be once more alone with the family—for you may be sure it takes no little contriving & cunning catering to get enough to put on the table. *Mr Couper* says "at this season of the year every body should go out visiting it is so hard to find a table."[5] And it does seem so for Mrs Postell[6] & children are on the Isld & some other strangers expected. I believe I would willingly run too if I knew where to go to. I wish you would try and get time enough to write me all your plans & intentions. I have been calculating on the pleasant time we would have when you returned in June but now I suppose you will scarcely be home at all with us. I have heard nothing from Louisa for a long while.

On Saturday evening the young people went to Mrs Wyllys by invitation and on their return tell me I may expect the most of that family with Miss Gould

& Miss Armstrong here to tea this evening—such being the case I have not waited for night to write to you but will add how the evening comes off. The flower garden looks very well these rains have saved me much labour in watering. The fushias continue blooming. The Fizanthus has entirely overgrown its frame & I do not know how to dispose of it. Mrs Paul [Demere] is in perfect raptures with the whole. I enjoy the beauties of it as much as ever. I will now conclude until tonight.—

The young people kept it up until half past twelve—they danced you may be sure but it was warm—music bad &c. I was tired but tried to be agreeable. The fact is I think it was a dull affair. I have nothing new to add. I hurry off the mail boy—hoping I may be blest with another letter from you. The day is hot & sultry. I hope it will bring us a shower. All the chicks send love & kisses to you. God! bless you my beloved & restore you to us in health peace & happiness.—

Your devoted wife

A M King

1. Neither the eight-page letter to which Anna refers nor a reply from T. B. King is extant.

2. King was facing, in Steel's words, "the recurrent problem of the politician, re-election." Although Anna clearly believed that he would not stand for reelection, "his political friends encouraged him to run again, and he began making plans with his closest supporters on the choice of delegates to the nominating convention and on publicity for the race" (Steel, *T. Butler King*, 60).

3. Andrew had agreed to pay both Butler's and Lord's expenses at college.

4. Paul and Martha Demere were Raymond Demere Jr.'s grandchildren. At Raymond Demere Jr.'s death in 1829, his grandsons, Joseph, Lewis, John, and Paul inherited the Harrington property. John Fraser Demere, son of Paul and Annie Fraser Demere and the fifth generation of the family, was born at Harrington Hall in 1841. Anne Fraser Demere was the daughter of John Fraser and Anne Sarah Couper Fraser. She is buried in Christ Curch cemetery and her epitaph reads in part: "Sacred to the memory of Anne R., wife of Paul Demere, who departed this life on St. Simons Island, Geo., Sept. 15, 1841, in the 24th year of her age." By 1848 Paul Demere must have remarried. See Cate, *Our Todays and Yesterdays*, 274; Vanstory, *Land of the Golden Isles*, 199.

5. Southerners were renowned for their hospitality. "Visiting" provided one of the few opportunities women had to travel, though it was always under the protection of a male family member or friend. Catherine Clinton recounts one southerner's "tale of extraordinary hospitality: 'I have often been told of the gentleman and his wife, who, being asked to dine at a residence on St. Simons, found that during the meal a boat had been sent to Darien, fifteen miles distant for their luggage, and that so much pleased were host, hostess and guests with one another, that the stay was prolonged until two children had been born to the visiting couple'" (*The Plantation Mistress*, 176–177). The "gentleman and his wife" referred to here were John and Rebecca Couper of Cannon's Point. While Anna's guests never extended their visits quite so long, she entertained regularly particularly during spring and summer. Also see Hull, *St. Simons, Enchanted Island*, 60.

6. Benjamin and Anne Cater's daughter, Ann, married James P. Postell of South

Carolina. James Postell kept a valuable library of literary as well as scientific works, and was a conchologist, ornithologist, and lepidopterist. His collection of more than six thousand classified and labeled shells was given to Roanoke College in 1876. See Cate, *Our Todays and Yesterdays*, 151; Huie and Lewis, *King's Retreat Plantation*, 36; Vanstory, *Land of the Golden Isles*, 199–201.

[Written on the envelope:] I write a long letter by this days mail which I hope you will get at the same time but that you may open this first.—

12th July

Butler says he feels that he is getting better—Tip had no fever yesterday & is at his books today.

Your own
Anna King

Retreat 11th July 1848

My dearly beloved husband!

Your hasty letter of the 3d Inst reached me on Sunday the 9th. I should have been delighted to get a letter which had travelled so smartly had it contained one word of how you were & when this everlasting Congress would adjourn. As it did neither I must acknowledge it was *unsatisfactory*. I have (you see) taken *half the sheet you* wrote on to tell you how we are getting on.

I have given Butler no medicine I have not tried catapasm [*sic*] [1]—because the pain *was not such* for which you once applied them to him. The pain no longer troubles him. He now only complains of that sick *indescribable* feeling— *irritability*—quick *pulse*—& *beating of the heart*. For these Dr Blakewood recommended "perfect quiet—& Colletons Bitters as a tonic & Quinine in small doses." The latter gives head ache so he stopt it. I sent him to Hamilton where he staid one week driving his sister over every evening in her buggy. Mr Couper has built a remarkably convenient & nice bathing house. The quiet, bathing, & tonic benefitted him very much. And but for a bad cold he took on Saturday would be much better. I gave him freely of lightwood tea yesterday & he says the soreness of his chest is much relieved & that he has not been troubled with his old feelings for several days & *assures me he is much* better. So much for him. Lord says he is getting on—as he takes it coolly. That is he lives up stairs from breakfast until sundown & does not let *multiplicity of garments* distress him. He is very cheerful & full of hope that he will make a respectable entrance into College. I will now conclude in order to save the mail—with love & kisses from the children

Your devoted wife
A M King

1. Anna misspelled "cataplasm," a poultice made of flour, mustard, meal, bran, flax-seed, or similar substances commonly applied to sores, inflammations, etc.

Answer this minutely & as quickly as possible. AMK

Retreat, 11th July 1848

My dearly beloved husband

I have just folded & directed a short letter to you written on the *blank side* of the letter I got from you on the 9th. I had hoped to have got a long letter or at all events you would have told me *how you were* & what hope you had of *adjournment* but not one word on *either subject*. I do hope that dear Butler is better. I wished him to remain another week at Hamilton but he was unwilling to lose so much time. His cold was very troublesome yesterday but that too is evidently better today. The rest of the family are in their usual health—tho' Cuyler did have some fever yesterday. He is quite cheerful this morning & I hope will have no return of it. The weather has been so *hot* the last ten days we have had several cases of fevers among the field people—but not of an obstinate character. Tho' I have two cases I do not know what to do with. *Anthony* and *Maryann*—the former seems to have some inward complaint—which Pussys skill cannot reach the latter has symptoms of derangement (you know her mother old Liddy was deranged).[1] I have been blistering her very freely which is all I can do for her.[2]

From Monday the 3d until Saturday 8th it was very warm—a strong dry westerly wind—which dried & parched up every thing. On Saturday we went to Hamilton for the day—from 11 to 6 we had two very fine showers. The next day it rained powerfully here & again yesterday. These rains were very timely as both corn & cotton were suffering from the dry hot winds. If we do not get too much now we will be thankful. In Florida, Camden, Wayne & McIntosh they have had already too much.[3] God! has thus far bless'd us with good seasons & a promising crop.

I have been hoping against all people & the newspapers could tell me that you would be home before your sons left for College—I fear after all it cannot be. No time is now to be lost. I wrote to you a long letter (giving you extracts from Louisa's letter) on the 4th Inst. I do hope you received it in due time. I wrote to *her* & sent on my letter by Margaret Cuyler who left us on the 5th. I requested Mssrs G W A[nderson] & B[4] to forward my letter by the *very first opportunity*. Louisa requested to be "informed as quickly as possible the sum necessary for the out fit &c of the boys." Now it seems to me we have both *slumbered* over this matter. I have no means of raising the money myself.

From a Catalogue Butler received of Franklin College[5]—the terms seem
to be—

Board for 9½ months	from $76 to $114 dollars
Tuition, servants [?] library fees &c	50.50
Washing	9.11
Fuel	5.10
	$140 to 185 dollars for nine & a half months.

This of course does not include out fit or travelling expenses. $50—in ad-
vance—that is if he enters on the 15th January he pays 30—& on the 1 August
$20. I dare say you can get the terms of Cambridge from some of the members
from Massachusetts.[6]

Mr J H Couper goes to Athens the first week in August. *I am very anxious
Butler should* accompany him. *He* being one of the Trustees—would be a great
advantage to our son, & I hope you will be able to make the *arrangement for
him* to do so & that you will write to Mr J. H. C[ouper] requesting him to take
upon himself his *introduction*. We cannot expect to hear from Louisa in time for
Butler & unless her next letter & mine too travel quicker than her last did I fear
too late for Lord. It would be a sad thing for Lord enough to discourage him.
He has worked so hard to fit himself to enter. It is of the utmost importance
you give these matters your earliest & best attention.

In writing all this I am trembling with fear that you may be sick & unable to
move in this matter. If so in Mercy get some one to write for you do not keep
me in suspense. You know dearly beloved husband I would not add (if I could
help it) the weight of a feather to your other cares. I would not, (if I could help
it) give you one uneasy thought but *I am powerless*. If otherwise what pleasure
it would be to me to just do what you bade me do (for you)—to say the word
& it was done.

I had every hope when you left me that this session would terminate in June
or the first of the month. The *Intelligencer* even now speaks of September!! Do
my love give me your opinion. When will you come to us? I would not have
you do an act that would reflect the slightest discredit on your name. I would
not (if I thought I could influence you) ask it—as much as I desire to see you.
I am only afraid *they* may get you to go elsewhere after the adjournment. Tell
me when it is probable I may be blest with your presence. Tell me all about
your dear self. I think I have said all I could say on this subject—of our sons
going to College and perhaps I ought now to close my letter—but it is against
my conscience to send you *blank paper*.

I must go on to say we once more have a quiet house. M C[uyler] got off
safely on Wednesday last & we heard on Sunday of her safe arrival &c. Geor-

gia now has her time to herself and is studying very hard. She has had much to make up but will try and get time to write you by this mail. Butler says he will write next week. Mr Brown[7] called here a few evenings ago. I told him I would be glad to see Mrs Brown here—he said "Susan would be most happy to come but ([?]) she feels a little delicacy as neither you or your daughters have call'd—cant you let them just call—they speak to Mrs Cater pray adopt the *French fashion*." What the french fashion is I know not so I just told him I could not call on Mrs Brown as long as she lives at Mrs Caters & so ended the matter.[8] Mr & Mrs W [Armstrong] & Miss Susan are now at JD['s] late residence. We are invited there this evening to tea but the horses are in the plow. Mrs Charles Grant has at last had a *daughter* no doubt there is great rejoicing. Our dear daughter H[annah] Page is as usual. Little Anna is as sweet as ever. Willie still has his pull backs from his teeth poor little boy he gives me much trouble during the day—but sleeps well at night which is a great comfort to both himself & me.[9]

I had a letter from Mr McKean on Sunday. He seems much attached to the whole family—he says his *home* is Cambridge—where his sisters reside. His only brother is still suffering from paralysis in his lower limbs. I hope this kind feeling towards us will be of service to our son Lord. I shall reply to this letter of his by tomorrows Mail. I now write my letters on Tuesday & send the letters to the office as soon as it is light in the morning to save horse & boy from the heat of the day. I hear that Mr J H Coupers negros are suffering much from Measles.[10] I hope & trust it may not get here.

The children seem so anxious for your return. The servants too are constantly enquiring when you will get back. Mr B[rown] requested me to thank you for the valuable documents you have sent him. William Couper received some on Sunday with which he seemed much pleased. And Butler has read the pamphlet you sent him. He has loaned it out or I would try & find time to do the same. God! bless & preserve you my dearly beloved. Oh! how much I do want to see you! The children send love & kisses—& all sorts of endearments. The servants beg to be remembered—Your devoted wife

A M King

1. Maryann is number 39 on the list from William Page's will; number 80 on the 1839 list, her age given as thirty years; number 47 on the 1853 list, where she is noted as having been purchased. Her birth year is shown as 1802. Liddy appears on the list from Major Page's will and on the list "50 Negros with Their Increase" as number 37; there is a cross next to her name on the latter. A note says that "of the original 50—4 have died marked by a cross." This list was most likely compiled in 1842 when Anna wrote to her trustee James Hamilton Couper. See appendix 2.

2. Charles Rosenberg writes that "the popularity of 'counterirritation' in the form of skin lesions induced . . . through chemical or mechanical means, was based on the

assumption that the excoriation of one area and consequent suppuration could 'attract' the 'morbid excitement' from another site to the newly excoriated one, while the exudate was significant in possibly allowing the body an opportunity to rid itself of morbid matter, and of righting the disease-producing internal imbalance" (Rosenberg, "The Therapeutic Revolution," 51, n. 8).

3. Camden, Wayne, and McIntosh are neighboring counties.

4. Unable to identify.

5. Franklin College, founded in 1785, would become the University of Georgia. In the winter of 1848, Butler wrote a long letter to his father explaining why it was "impossible" for him to enter Cambridge "or any other Northern University." "For though I have studied *very hard* for the last three years, I find that my mode of studying latin & greek has been entirely *wrong*—that is I have never studied the construction—as I ought to have done—But have tried to get my lessons by merely finding the meaning of the words. Consequently I know very little more about latin & Greek—than I did two years ago." Butler explained his plans for the future based on an honest assessment of his interests and talents. Knowing full well what his parents expected of him, he argued that Lord, not he, possessed their father's "brilliant talent & desire to distinguish himself in the world." More than anything else, Butler said, he wanted to live on the island and be a planter ("I flatter myself that I *may* make a good farmer"). Thomas Butler King Jr. to Thomas Butler King, February 25, 1848, TBK, SHC.

6. Lord was studying to take the entrance exams at Harvard College.

7. Rev. E. P. Brown became rector of Christ Church in 1844 but also served St. David's Church in Glynn County. "He served both churches alternately on the Sabbath—a most exhausting duty but faithfully performed until interrupted by the war." He is listed in the 1850 Glynn County Census as forty years old, married to Susan W. Brown, and having a three-month-old daughter, Mary. See Holmes, *"Dr. Bullie's" Notes*, 193–194; *1850 Census of Georgia (Glynn County)*, comp. Rhea Cumming Otto, 1973, GDAH.

8. I am unable to determine why Anna could not call on Mrs. Cater.

9. Willie, Tootee's second child, was named after her brother, William Page King, who died at age six. Willie was evidently staying with his grandmother at the time.

10. Measles posed a major threat not only to Anna's slaves but to her children and grandchildren as well. See Patterson, "Disease Environments of the Antebellum South," 158.

Retreat 5th September 1848

My beloved Lordy

You have ere this passed the much dreaded ordeal have been examined & *I trust been admitted.* I see by the papers upwards of 70 had been admitted in the Freshman class. If you have been so fortunate as to stand the test I hope & trust your whole mind will be bent on study. So that in the end (if God! in mercy spare your health & life) you may come off with honor to yourself and Oh! my son with deep heartfelt gratification to your parents & friends. I believe my dear son you have ambition enough to try for this but I fear you love pleasure too. Yet I trust you will not forget that the world is now before you & that it depends on yourself whether *you will rise among the greatest or sink with the lowest.* God! keep you my beloved boy from all harm. May he be your guide—your protector—your friend! I hope to hear from you tomorrow. I hope also to hear from or see your father from whom I have received no intelligence since the letter I received with yours of the 18th August from N.Y. Butler has written to me every week since he left until the last—but I hope all is well with him.

We have not omitted writing to you regularly & shall unless sickness prevents continue to do so. What has become of Mr. Savage?[1] I think he may have written to me. I may enclose in this a few lines to him as I do not know his address. I had a long letter from Mr McKean. He expressed himself anxious to serve you in any way he can. And should he see cause to offer you advice I trust my dear son you will take it as it will be intended all in kindness.

Your sister & her little ones left us yesterday. They were well—we feel more lonely than ever—now they are gone. And the weather is so intensely hot—& *ruinously* dry—the cotton *crop is seriously injured by it*—the grass all dried up. You would be surprised to see how parched up everything is. I fear those living on the main will suffer much from fever—as there must have been much water on the land when this drought set in.

Mrs. W[illia]m Armstrong has been very sick since the day of Mrs. Abbotts funeral—poor old lady she has little strength to stand a fever. I heard also that John Fraser[2] was sick but hope he will not be as ill as he was two years ago. I believe I mentioned that *Sam*[3] had brought measles on the place. I had hoped until this morning that I would be as fortunate as Mrs Wylly was but one of his sisters children broke out with it this morning & I now fear it will spread. In burning off the margin they found poor little Weasels bones—and not ten feet from them was burnt in his coil an immense rattle snake & in the immediate neighborhood Dunham killed three other large rattlesnakes. I hope poor little Weasels *murderer* was among them.

I hope to hear from you tomorrow or on Sunday. I know you will have enough to do to attend to your studies—but I yet hope you will find time to write to us once in every two weeks—we can scarcely expect more from you. Georgia will add a few lines to this. They all join in love to you my dear boy. I hope to write you a more cheerful letter when I again address you. Be careful of your health & do all in your power [to] gratify the love—ambition & pride of your devoted Mother.

A M King

1. John Savage, the former tutor at Rereat, remained friendly with the family and later proposed to Georgia (she refused him). Lord became his law partner in New York City in 1860.

2. John Fraser was the son of Lt. John Fraser and Ann Sarah Couper Fraser (thus also the nephew of William Audley Couper).

3. Sam appears on the list "50 Negros with Their Increase" as Ruthy's son. He is number 56 on the 1839 list, birth date December 1, 1829; and number 36 on the 1853 list. See appendix 2.

Wednesday 28th September 1848

My dearly beloved Lord

I have just received your most welcome letter of the 16th I have read it aloud *twice* & expect to read it again & again—for every child & servant will want to hear all you have said, & then I shall send it to Tootee & let her enjoy it. For Oh! my beloved boy I have been so anxious about you. I opened the Mail bag with "fear & trembling" fearing there would be no letter from my own dear boy! Thank God! you are able to say you are well. I write you by this days Mail. But I am so anxious to acknowledge your highly prized letter I cant wait until Saturday!

I am rejoiced to hear that you are well—that you are so comfortably situated & that you have so fully made up your mind *to study*. If you continue to study my own beloved Lord I *know* you will succeed. Do not let the disappointment at Cambridge *dishearten you*.[1] Forget *that* in your endeavours, to let *those gentlemen* see you are capable of coming up with the *best of them*. You have the *capacity* & I know my own beloved boy—you will put "your shoulder to the wheel" & not give up. I admire your forbearance in not going to see those sights. After your relaxation from Study & all the excitement of your life in N.Y. &c &c has subsided you will feel it more easy to bend your whole mind to study. I think after all dear Lordy (if we can forget the mortification of the thing) it is best you should be where you are.[2] We have had such poor teachers for you (except Mr Savage) it was not *your* fault you were not prepared. And then you will gradually get into the ways of the Yankees. It is pleasant to think it is for the best. You must keep up your spirits my son do not give way to any thing that is discouraging—try to overcome every obstacle in the way of your obtaining knowledge, & if God! in mercy spares you life & health—come out the *pride* & joy of your devoted Parents. Lord! you little know how much I love—I doat on you. May God! of his infinite mercy & goodness bless & preserve you—raise your young heart to *him* my son & you will feel you have a friend above all earthly help to lean on. I will write a few lines to the kind Dr & Mrs Perry—thanking them for their present kindness to you which I trust my beloved boy you will continue to deserve. I know you will not neglect to write to us whenever you can do so with out interfering with your Studies. You must be careful of your health *& clothe warm* for you will soon begin to feel the severity of a Northern winter. God! grant you health!!

We heard again from Butler today—he is well. *Steve*[3] tells me *Henry* has had a *regular fight* with a young man *& Flog'ed* him soundly.[4] *Poor Steve* he is kind hearted fellow but what a misfortune my dear Lord. I do not know when to believe him! I am thankful this is a fault neither you or Butler are guilty of.

Georgia will *cry* again I suppose when she reads your long letter. That Georgia is a dear good girl! & I know you love her. Florence looks very well now. They with Malley accompanied Steve to Hamilton to see the latter off in the Steam boat last Night & Tootee sent & requested me to let them stay the night. Steve got off very early—I am expecting the girls back momently and Miss Rebecca with them.

I have not seen Tootee for more than a week. She looks prettier & is *more happy* now than since her marriage. Her husband *is devoted* to her & the children. He seems to watch her every movement & has *co[n]fessed his* sins & implored her pardon for all the *causes* he has given her for unhappiness. This is her reward my son her patient forbearance, her perfect conduct as a wife—has wrought this happy change. It would make your heart glad to see how perfectly happy your dear Sister is. W[illia]m has no idea that *I* ever had *suspicions* of him —but acknowledged that *he thought Butler* & *you* had. But *mum is the word*— let by gones be by gones. I only hope all may now go well.[5] Dear little Anna talks a great deal about *you* & *Butty*. Willie is getting on very well. But as Tootee intends writing to you very soon I will leave to her all she has to tell about her babies.

I believe I mentioned the hurt Malley got—but his foot is now well. Tip had a touch of fever on Monday but is up & about again. The Measles go on slowly. Clementines Bell[6] fell & broke her arm fortunately it was below the elbow & easily managed. Toneys Jane has been in an awful state for several weeks after having had convulsions for days—she had a baby—then the convulsions returned & for all the last 5 days she is quite *crazy*.[7] She has not slept a *wink* since Saturday last—this cannot last much longer. The child still lives.

You would be gratified to see the joy your letter has diffused over *all* of us. I got up this morning feeling like an *Old Woman*. I now feel as blithe as either of those *young Southern girls* you danced with at the *Astor house*. Poor Mrs Gale seemed as glad as any one & prays God! to bless you. The servants *grin* at me where ever I meet them—so glad are we all to hear that you are well. I am writing in great haste for the Mail—As I am anxious you should know how happy your dear letter has made us. You may expect a letter every week—tho we shall have but little news to give you. The Isld is very dull & no prospect of its being otherwise. Unless indeed *Miss Hazzards*[8] *return* may produce a change. I have not been at the NE[9] this year & do not know that I shall go there at all. The old gentleman promises us a visit when your father gets back.[10]

Next Monday will be the Election—& the first Monday in November will determine whether we are to continue under Locofoco rule & see once more the Sun of prosperity rise on our now benighted country.[11]

I will give your message to Malley—he has killed some birds with your gun but says he finds it rather heavy. All who are at home sends *lots* of love to you—the servants all beg to be remembered. And now my beloved I will close this scrawl as you are doubtless tired. May God! bless you my Son—May He bless you with his choicest blessing is the constant fervent prayer of your fond

Mother
A M King

I would write to Mr Savage if I knew his address. Butler had a letter from him.

My own dear Brother

You, I suppose ere this have received my three former hurried letters, and are surprised you have not got the one I promised to write after my return from visiting our dear Fan.[12] But dear Brother I have—not yet gone, "and *that* is not the worst of it." As we expect dear Father every boat of course we cannot go *now*, and so I dont expect to go for sometime after he arrives. I should like to go *after* father comes, on account of the *Album*[13]—but except for that, I should before, as I do not like, as he has so short a time to remain at home, to leave him.

In my other letters dear Lord, I have asked all the questions, concerning your *entering* &c. So I will not weary you by repeating them, and hope in a few mails to have them satisfactorily answered.

We were all so *very* much disappointed last Sunday on receiving no letter from either of our absent ones but hope next mail to be more fortunate. I got a letter from Butler last Wednesday—and he amused me very much by telling me how many times the *bell rang* every day. I wonder if *your* college has such a *quantity* of *Bell ringing* in it!

Last night—Mother, F[lorence], V[irginia] and I were looking at your picture. Oh! Lord—how much it is like you! We all kissed it for good night and *I* could scarcely help my ready tears from falling upon it. *Dear* Lord will you not send me one of your pictures? Do please! Now I suppose you will say "Why ain't *one* enough?" But I say no! Mother and Tootee having one you know will make *me* none the richer. Oh! Dear Lord if you but knew *half* how much I would value it, you would not hesitate *one* second!! I intend to try to prevail upon dear Butler also.

Florence wrote you by the last mail and begs you to write her soon. Now dear Brother I do not wish—you to tax your pleasure hours—*one instant*, to write *to me*, but I can only beg you to write whenever you *can* possibly do so conveniently—for you *cannot* think how much pleasure even *a few* lines gives me. Clementine told me the other day this message for you—and *Tootee* says *you* must tell it to Mr Savage—she says—"Tell Mass Lord the *servants* & particularly *Clementine*, are very much *mortified*—at his not having sayed a word about Mr Savage"!!! She told me *particularly* to put it in, so you see I have done so.[14]

Oh! Lord I am so anxious to hear what you have been doing. I want to talk about it all the time.[15] As I have hardly any thing to say on "*our subject*" as I have not yet gone up to see Fannie—But wait in patience and you will hear all!! Good bye now—my dearest Lord, write soon to your devoted sister

Geo

1. Four days earlier Anna had written, "You can scarcely *feel it* more than we do. But my own dear boy *on you alone* depend your *future* successes. Mr McKean in his letter to me expresses much sympathy for you & says 'only *15* were admitted *clear* out of *75*— Others were admitted on condition of passing satisfactory examinations in certain branches at the close of the first term.' I am glad my dear child you were not the '*only black sheep.*' Your Sister Georgia *blubbered* right out when she heard you were not admitted. But let it pass my son. Yet let me hope you will not forget what you *then* felt— so as to induce you to study hard & be ready to pass '*Clear*' next spring" (Anna Matilda Page King to Henry Lord Page King, September 24, 1848, TBK, SHC).

2. Lord was attending Exeter Academy to prepare to retake the Harvard entrance exam.

3. Steve (Stephen), Stephen Clay King's son.

4. He may have been referring to Henry King.

5. It is difficult to know what "all the causes he has given her" were. As was typical for women of Anna's time and class, she does not reveal her son-in-law's confessed sins, which may have been anything from excessive drinking to liaisons with other women, including enslaved ones. However, five months later she wrote to Lord, "Your Sister looks *younger* and *prettier* than she has done since her marriage. But tho' there is now a change for the better *all confidence* is lost & without confidence no married *woman can be happy*" (Anna Matilda Page King to Henry Lord Page King, February 11, 1849, TBK, SHC).

6. Clementine's Bell is most likely Isabella, born April 12, 1846, and listed as Isabel on the 1859 list. See appendix 2.

7. Jane may have been suffering from preeclampsia or eclampsia, a complication of pregnancy that causes hypertension in the mother, although these symptoms could also have been caused by gestational diabetes or a high fever from an infection. Information from Eve Lackritz, M.D., Centers for Disease Control, Atlanta, Georgia.

8. The Hazzards—Colonel William Wigg and Dr. Thomas Fuller—owned adjoining plantations on the island, West Point and Pikes Bluff. Both brothers were members of the state legislature and were known for their expertise at boat racing and hunting. Colonel Hazzard wrote a history of Glynn County, and his brother wrote articles on both medicine and agriculture. A bitter dispute over the property line separating Hazzard property from Wylly property resulted in the murder of John Armstrong Wylly in 1838 by Thomas Hazzard. The Miss Hazzard mentioned here may

have been William's daughter Mary, then eleven years old. 1850 Census, Glynn County, GDAH; Vanstory, *Land of the Golden Isles*, 191–192.

9. The northern end of the island.

10. John Couper.

11. "Locofoco" refers to the radical wing of the Democratic party. A locofoco was a type of friction match. Anna wrote on the 24th, "I wrote to you a few lines in Florences letter by last Wednesdays mail—I therein told you that after staying but *two* days at home your dear father had left us for the Canvass. I hope he will be able to stand the fatigue & may soon return home—for I do require his presence—I feel so much depressed" (Anna Matilda Page King to Henry Lord Page King, September 24, 1848, TBK, SHC). Thomas Butler King Jr. and Lord King enthusiastically supported their father's bid for reelection to Congress and believed Zachary Taylor would win the presidency. Both King and Taylor were elected.

12. Fannie E. Grant. In the 1850 census she is listed as seventeen years old. Georgia, born in 1833, was therefore the same age.

13. Unclear.

14. Judging from Clementine's message, the house servants at Retreat seem to have been fond of Mr. Savage.

15. Certainly the King children were devoted to each other, but it must have been difficult for Georgia and her sisters to watch their older brothers move beyond the confines of the island to an education and world they could not know.

1st December 1848
The anniversary of my marriage night—

My own dear Lord!

I have not written to you for a long time more than a post script here & there. But you know how visiting puts me out of regular habits. I did think I would write you all about our visit to Mr Woolley and to *Satilla* but I suppose Butler has told you all about it. But he could not have *told* you what I felt when I found *I had to do it*. Neither will I attempt it. So let it pass my dear boy. Your dear father wrote you a few hasty lines on leaving home & Georgia wrote you a hasty letter on Wednesday to which I added a few more. I have just finished a letter of 12 pages to your Aunt Louisa & have yet to write to your father for tomorrows mail so I will just go on to say we are all in our usual health who are at home. That is G[eorgia, F[lorence] V[irginia], F[loyd], T[ip] myself & Mrs Gale. Butler will be back on Sunday & will be able to give you an account of his visit on the maine. I have not seen your sister since Wednesday but believe they are well. You have been informed of your Father & Malleys departure.[1] Poor dear Malley! how I grieve to part with him but I hope it will be for his good! I send you a Newspaper of the 25th wherein you will notice your fathers arrival &c. He wrote me but a few hasty lines as he had much to occupy his time—he left there on Tuesday the 28th & I hope is now safe in Washington City. I fear poor Malley was very sea sick he was in such high health. Your father stopped at the Pulaski but M[alley] staid at Mr Cuylers.

Margaret & Mrs Matthais have written a most pressing invitation to Georgia to spend the winter with them & say your father has given his consent. I nevertheless have *withheld* my consent. Poor Georgia would be delighted to go for a few weeks—but not the whole winter—but when she goes into a City I would desire a more prudent Chaperon than I guess M[argaret] C[uyler] would be. I have a great mind to write to your father *that I have consented to her going.* He had no business to give *me* the annoyance of refusing when he had consented. He has forgotten my letting you & Butler go to Savannah because he had promised Bourke[2] that you should do so.

I am glad you intend spending your holy day with your father. How glad dear Malley will be to see you. I can scarce yet realize that the dear boy has left us. Poor child he went off in less than a weeks warning—but your father said he would fit him out in Washington. Now that Malley is gone Floyd will have no one to beat him so poor Tip will have to receive all Floyd has to inflict—& have no one *to pass it to.* I regret very much that your Sisters are losing so much time. I mentioned to your Aunt Lou that if Mrs Lara did not come out at once we would have to get some one else.[3]

I suppose Butler mentioned to you the death of poor Sturtevant. We all regret his death exceedingly. *L L W Harris*—landed at Hamilton when the Steamer stopt for your father & Malley. He was "as drunk as drunk could be." He had been at Waynesville to try and get a school there—but I suppose failed as he could not say enough against the people or the place. Mr & Mrs Brown are now on the Parish they speak of going to house keeping but seem in no hurry to begin. They were anxious to stop here but it was "no go." They have put up at Hazzards on condition that she instructs Miss Sarah in Music drawing &c and he, Masters Miles & Thomas Hazzard. I do not like either of them & wish they had left. Mr J H Couper & *lady* leave Hopeton tomorrow on their way North. How I envy her her happiness—willingly would I go with them for the happiness of seeing you my dear boy. I hope Sunday will bring us a letter from you. Do try and write home at least *once* in *two* weeks. And tell us if you still like your boarding house. I hope so. As I have taken it into my head it is a good one. I know you will try & behave like a gentleman where ever you are. Write me all about the family.

So Savage is engaged. I am glad to hear it & hope the young lady is worthy of him. G[eorgia] says she will take particular pleasure in telling Mrs Hazzard of it. When is his father to be married? I owe Mr S[avage] a letter but do not know when I shall be able to write to him. I must also write to Mr McKean. H[annah] Page and myself are both anxious to send you oranges but do not know how to get them to you—perhaps Dr Perry could put you in the way. If so let us know & they shall be sent forthwith. Dear Malley filled up the *vacancy* of his trunk with oranges said he intended to save some of them for you. But as they were freshly gathered I fear they will not keep.

Stars youngest colt got *snag'd* the other day. But wonderful to relate it has got over it—so there has been two wonders on the place. The woman Jane has an infant two months old[4] & a snag'd colt has recovered. Mengas Fraser has returned wonderfully improved in manners & appearance so say the folks. Now his Mother will bore us more than ever with her Ming![5]

I suppose Butler has informed you that the new road to N[ew] G[round] was being made. Your father has devoted the labour of all the field men for 2 weeks on it and had he been at home himself it would have been completed in that time but you know what Dunham is at *jobs*. They did more last week over worse ground than they will do this week. A direct line from Sukeys house to N[ew] Field—it cuts off more than a ¼ of a mile 30 feet wide with a ditch on each side. From New Ground gate you can see Sukeys house.[6] Your father got permission to use his road hands for the purpose—the labour is great for there were several low places to be filled up & one continued mass of Palmata roots to cut through. Your father has ordered trees set out all along the road—& it will take 500 trees to go the distance. I doubt Dunhams accomplishing it.

I must now bid you good night my beloved Lord. May God! in mercy watch over & guard you from all danger. Oh! my Son! May he in mercy draw your young heart to love him as you aught to do & may we meet again in health peace & happiness. Your Sisters & little brothers send you much love. Mrs Gale sends her love & best wishes for your health & happiness. The servants all beg to be remembered.

Your devoted Mother

A M King

My dearly beloved brother

I am sorry that I have *no* time to write to you by this *mail*, but as Georgia and I are going to see Sarah Hazzard to day I will not have time—It is time for me to go and dress. I will write you a *very* long letter by the next mail.

Your devoted Sister

Florence

---

1. Mallery was being sent to a northern preparatory school.
2. Captain Tom Bourke was married to Sarah Du Bignon.
3. Aunt Lou is Louisa King, and Mrs. Lara a young woman she and her husband, Andrew, had taken in. Mrs. Lara's husband was either killed or had simply disappeared,

and she worked as a governess/teacher to support herself. She reappears at the center of a major family squabble in later letters.

4. Jane Jun. was born September 10, 1848. See appendix 2.

5. Mengas was Menzies Fraser, son of Dr. William Fraser and Frances Wylly Fraser. Dr. Fraser died in 1837 en route to Saratoga Springs in New York of heart failure (he was, with his brother John, attempting to reach the springs to regain his health). In 1838 Frances and son Menzies were persuaded to take a trip on the steamer *Pulaski* accompanied by James Hamilton Couper and a Mrs. Nightengale and her infant daughter of Cumberland Island. While at sea the ship's boilers exploded and 77 of the 131 passengers died. J. H. Couper, however, saved both women and their children. See Wheeler, *Eugenia Price's South*, 39–40.

6. There were eight houses at "New Field." One, the Tabby House, still stands near the McKinnon Airport. This may have been Sukey's house. See Cate, *Early Days of Coastal Georgia*, 79.

6th March 1849

My dearly beloved Lord!

I have not received a line *from* you since your letter of the 14th January. And your father wrote me *he* had not since the one he enclosed to me. I see Wm Couper has received *two* letters from you since you entered Yale.[1] That of the 18th Feb I had the pleasure of perusing—& grateful am I to hear you were then in health. May God! in mercy grant to you a continuance of that great blessing. Malley has been very sick with the mumps & fever. It was fortunate for him that he was under the care of your dear father—poor little fellow. As soon as he was convalescent he wrote to G[eorgia], F[lorence], V[irginia], & myself & again the next week to G[eorgia], V[irginia], & myself which made 7 letters we received in one week. Mr Woolley wrote to Cousin Amanda *from Washington* on the 25th—which is the latest accounts I have received of your father and Malley. On Sunday last I had a letter from our dear Butler. Poor fellow he was suffering from a violent cold. I am very uneasy about him—for you know how little care he takes of his health & how hard it is for him to shake off a cold. Oh! my beloved Lord—you children can have but little idea—how much anxiety I feel for your health & welfare. I implore of you my son to be careful of your health!—

I wrote to you on the 14th & 17th Feb & Georgia wrote on the 24th. I believe those are the dates. All of which I hope you have received. I do hope tomorrow will bring me a letter from you & I fervently pray you may be able to say you are in health. Since the 16th Feb we have had a continuation of most unpleasant weather. Cold & boisterous—I really thought the house I sleep in would be blown over & during the day there was no moving out on account of the clouds of dust & sand.[2] It has done sad havoc with the orange trees & my beautiful flower garden—the cold on the 19th killed a great many of my choice plants. I almost determined to give up the garden—but I dare say I will after the first good rain be working in it as hard as ever.[3] I had the pleasure of having your Sister & the children here on Saturday. She told me she had just finished a long letter to you and doubtless has told you all about Anna, Willie and Isabella.[4] They really are three very fine children. Your Sister *looks* better than she had done since her marriage. Poor dear child she had gone through a terrible ordeal. God! grant she may *not again be tried*. If so her life may be spared—but not her mind.—

I hope to see your dear father & Malley next week. Oh! Lordy what would I not give could you & dear Butler be here too! I do hope you will be able to come out in August—but that will be a most unfavourable season to come South but I will not now fret about the probable consequences "sufficient for the day is the evil there of." G[eorgia] F[lorence] V[irginia] F[loyd] & Tip have just been having their teeth attended to by Dr Stilwell.[5] Do you know the little fellow has actually brought out *his wife*. Wm says she is rather pretty & is as fat as he is lean. Your Sisters & brothers are well. Cousin Amanda returned from Savannah quite sick but I am glad to say she is now in her usual health. Mrs Gale too is well all unite in love & regards to you. The servants all beg to be remembered.

I wrote to Mr Savage long ago—but he has not had the *manners* to answer it—or as Malley has it "scribble me back." I saw H[orace] Gould the other day—he enquired kindly after you boys. I have been no where since the ploughing season began & really have nothing new or interesting to tell you. We have been expecting Stephen Kings family here ever since the measles disappeared but now I hope they will not come until your father returns home. It is possible Mrs Hugh Grant may make me a visit for a change of air—poor woman she is in wretched health. I have not seen Mr or Mrs J H Couper since their return—but frequently hear of them & that they are well. The Misses Corbin had not made their appearance on Sunday last. Miss Susan Johnston intends visiting the Isld ere long. On the 22 Feb the Glynn rangers (Minus the Capt *Coronet* & one or two others) united with the Camden troop to celebrate the day at Jefferson. A fine saddle was cut for & won *by young Myers*. After the parade they had a dinner—in the evening a *ball*, *Supper* &c &c. A year ago you would have thought it fine—but now I suppose you would turn up your nose at such rustic affairs. Little Malley writes that he expected to go to the Inauguration ball!![6] If I could but have heard the music & partaken of the *supper* I would be satisfied. Not so Georgia—what would she not give to be at it? Not to eat, but to dance.

I hope my beloved Lord you are getting on with your studies & will continue to do well. Be careful of your health my dear boy! Give my love to Hamilton.[7] The children desire to be remembered to him also. Florence has been writing to you but she has been so taken up with having her teeth attended to that I fear she has not done herself justice. I wish I could have written you a more amusing letter my boy—I am thankful I have no misfortune to recount. May God! in mercy bless—guide & guard you. And Oh! my child may we meet in health & happiness is the constant prayer of your devoted Mother

A M King

F[lorence] was so *nervous* on account of getting her teeth fix'd—she could not finish her letter to go today. We have had quite a scene with Rhina—I wanted to have her bad teeth extracted. Maria[8] was more courageous tho she said "it fair play made the water pop out of my eye." We are all as usual today. God! bless you my boy—

Your Mother
A M King

Tootee & the babies have just come in she sends her love & the babies send kisses.—

Your devoted Mother
A M King

1. It is unclear why Lord decided to take the entrance exam for Yale rather than Harvard.

2. Anna wrote to Lord on February 29, "On Friday 16th we had (after a night of sleet) a *real snow* storm. I never in all *my life* saw so much snow—it lasted from 7 A.M. to 2 P.M. & some remained on the back shed even until Sunday. Which was a most disagreeably cold windy day. it continued to grow colder until when we got up this morning the water in the bucket was frozen tho' a fire was burning in my room until late in the night" (Anna Matilda Page King to Henry Lord Page King, February 29, 1849, TBK, SHS).

3. On February 11 Anna had described the garden to Lord saying, "I have made a still further addition to my garden. The slip between it & the path to the gate is now all in geraniums &c &c I have a number of perfect *white double Japonicas* this winter as many as 11 open at one time on one plant. They are really beautiful. I have added a number of new roses to my collection—Mr Bourke kindly sent me several. Major Bowen 3—& from others I have several varieties—You[r] favorite 'hearts ease' are in full bloom & the largest flowers I ever saw. Thousands of violets—&c &c—so that tho it is but Feb. I could afford '*nose gays*' to dozens of belles" (Anna Matilda Page King to Henry Lord Page King, February 11, 1849, TBK, SHC 3).

4. Isabella Hamilton Couper, the third child of Tootee and William Audley Couper, was born August 1, 1848.

5. Dentistry, though considered nominally a part of medical care (physician-dentists

established the Baltimore College of Dental Surgery, the first dental school in the country, in 1840), was not given the same respect during the nineteenth century as medicine. Most doctors considered the filling and pulling of teeth akin to carpentry rather than the art/science of diagnosing and healing the body. One was a trade, the other a profession. See Numbers, "The Fall and Rise of the American Medical Profession," 101, 190–191.

6. He was to attend the inauguration of Zachary Taylor.

7. Hamilton Couper was a fourth-year student at Yale and Lord's roommate.

8. Maria is number 47 on the list from William Page's will. There are three Marias on the 1839 list: number 73, born December 1, 1917; number 209, born in 1814; and number 250, born in 1829. On the 1853 list Maria, born December 1, 1817, is recorded as number 98. Maria Junr, number 29 on the 1853 list, born May 11, 1845, may have been her daughter. No Maria is listed in 1859. See appendix 2.

[Written on the envelope:] The Mail arrangements are altered the Mail going North *closes* on *Tuesdays* and *Fridays*—but the letters from the North are received as usual on Wednesdays and Sundays. Your letter only reached me on this, 4th—I have acted on it as quickly as I could.

5th April 49

My own dear Lord

I received your note inclosed in your letter to Georgia yesterday. I rejoice my beloved son to hear of your being in health and hope that blessing will be continued to you. How little is this blessing valued by those who possess it— it is only those who feel its want who can appreciate its value! I cannot but be anxious for you boys. To be sick at home is distressing enough—how much more so to be laid on a bed of suffering far away from friends! I am sure your dear father can tell you the difference. And poor Mr Woolley how much he felt the want of the attentions of his good wife—to whose care he returned when barely able to crawl about. He with dear cousin left me on Monday for Col-[one]ls Isld. He is better—but scarcely able to bear the excitement of the disagreeable business which hurried him off. The man to whom he sold his plantation and every thing he possessed except his bed—bedding & wearing apparel and who mortgaged him 10 negros as well as the place to ensure payment turns out one of the biggest villains you can well imagine—& does not own in his own right one dollar—the negros & mules being his wifes. So poor Mr Woolley will have to take back his place & lose all they have made way with—or lose the whole. This is hard to be borne. I only mention this (as one instance) that there are others who have trials as well as we have.

I wish you had mentioned the sum necessary for your wants the coming term & beg you will let me know as near as you possibly can—the sum necessary *for the year*. I must insist on your keeping as true account of your expenditures—it is due to us to know how it goes and it will give you a better value of it. Mr Andrew King has never *sent* but the $500 you have already had between you. If we could be correctly informed the sum absolutely necessary—we could try & be always ready to meet your demands. I think you told me that Mr J H Couper told you that Hamilton cost him between 4 & 500 including all his expenses per annum. And I should think you could not possibly require more than he does—you know my beloved son—there is no sacrifice we are not willing to make for the education of our children. I know your ambitious disposition will avail itself of every chance to obtain an education & rest assured we will do all in our power to give you a fair chance but economy in every shape must needs be practiced in order to get on. [A mark appears here that resembles the drawing of an animal's paw.] *I shall ask this day Mr Anderson to forward you at once one hundred and fifty dollars and hope that will* answer. So dear boy let us drop the subject for the present.

I hope by this time your dear father is with you—tho' when Malley wrote on the 29th March he was still in Washington. I have not heard from him since the 21st. You must not be annoyed at his not answering your letters. You must have seen when with him—how much he had to occupy his time & every thought. And I believe he has been just as busy since as he was before the adjournment. I will pass over the injustice he has met with. He ever has been & ever will be an object of jealousy—to judge Berrien & the Up Country members.[1] If I was clear of my embarrassments & cotton would but bring a good price I would far rather he would come home and let us plod on on the down Hill of life on what we have than ever to look for his reward from a country for which he has spent so much time—labour—& Money. I wish your father had sent Malley home with Mr Woolley as it seems he had left Mr Abbotts school —poor little fellow he is very home sick. I hope my love you have got over yours as no one can study with a discontented mind.

In my note inclosed in Georgia's letter of last week I mentioned Butlers anxiety to return for good in November. I am most reluctant he should do so and still more so to have him at *his age* settle down as a negro driver on this Isld unless Tom Bond & L[ovat] Fraser were in California. The latter I do not fear as much as the former because Butlers eyes are wide open to his faults but facts have come to my knowledge about Master Tom which has entirely changed my opinion of him & I desire no further association between him & my own dear good Butler. Young men should be careful who they select as *friends*. Do you my darling Lord be careful. Above all avoid those who fear not their God! who trust not to the merits of the Saviour. All other vices will follow in the tracks of these. I have tried my beloved child to instill in your young minds the im-

portance of religion & live in hopes that ere I die I may see my prayers answered for one & all of you dear children who God! has given to my keeping.

I have not seen your dear Sister since Tuesday. She & her little ones were
then well. You know I have no carriage horses & I never like to stop a plough.
Star took it into her head to die the other day—so the others have to work the
harder. Old Hicky came down & tuned the piano this week—so that G[eor-
gia] can play with more satisfaction to herself & others. Old Mr Gould was
here not long since—he paid *you* so many compliments—I really had to change
the subject. I felt myself beginning to blush—but God! be praised—it was
not with shame. I see by the papers that Mr J H C[ouper] accompanied Mr
Corbin as far as Savannah. The last account from Hopeton gave us the pleasure of hearing all were well there. I had a long letter from Mr Savage not long
since which I have answered. All join in love to you my beloved Lord. God! in
mercy be your friend—your guide—And may we meet again in health—peace
& happiness.

My best regards to Hamilton.

> Your own Mother
> A M King

I wish my beloved Lord you could now see my pet garden—tho I have lost
some—and others are cut down by the severe cold—still it is beautiful. I wish
I could see you now culling my prettiest—I do not think I could find it in my
heart to scold even that you did jump over my beds. We are also eating strawberrys—G[eorgia] will write you next week—All send love—God! bless you
my boy.

> Your Mother
> A M King

1. When Zachary Taylor was elected president in 1848, Thomas Butler King, who
campaigned for him and was a strong advocate for the navy (as a member of the House
Committee on Naval Affairs), hoped to be appointed secretary of the navy. Though
there was support for his appointment to the cabinet in the North, Georgia Whigs did
not favor him. Alexander Stephens, an adviser to Taylor on cabinet appointments and
a fellow Georgian, wrote, "I did not at first have any serious thought about Mr. King
of our State being put at the head of the Navy. But recent rumours awaken my apprehension. Now my dear Sir this will not do. You know Mr. King, but I know the people
of Georgia. And if you will allow me I will suggest to you that Mr. Crawford at the head
of the War Department or Mr. Toombs Atty General will suit us much better." On
March 5 it was announced that George W. Crawford of Georgia would be secretary of
war and William Ballard Preston of Virginia, secretary of the navy. Although partisan

politics destroyed King's bid for party favor and national recognition, Taylor awarded him with a mission to California and later appointed him collector of the Port of San Francisco. Steel, *T. Butler King*, 69–71.

15th May 1849

My own beloved Lord

I do not like a single week to pass without some one of us writing to you.— I have to thank you for your long letter from Springfield but have not time to do so as I would wish. I have much to take up my attention & find it harder to collect my thoughts every time I have to put them down on paper. On Friday dear little Willie was very ill—I staid both that day and the next with your Sister—but he is about again—I fear as the warm weather approaches his attacks will be more serious—but Gods! will be done!!!—The other little ones were unwell too but they all dined here on Sunday. We have had a visit from Miss Clayton & Tom Bond—they only staid three days. We feel under deep obligations to this young lady & her Mother for many kindnesses shown your dear brother in Athens. She is a month younger than Georgia & is a very amiable young girl. She seemed to enjoy her short visit to us exceedingly—& would not rest until I had let her take one of your de———pes[1] up with her. The one without the hat I look on as a prefect treasure & can never refrain from kissing it whenever I look at it. I dare say you would rather I had loaned it to Miss Fanny whose low country manners would not allow her to beg as hard as Miss Augusta did for it.

Miss Margaret Cuyler—came with Miss Picot[2]—came for 2 weeks but has already prolonged it to *three*. She is on the whole more bearable—than on her former visits. She showed us the likeness of her *intended* Mr Daniel Elliot. She makes no secret of her engagement. But they are not to marry immediately. She goes north this summer. On Sunday we had a letter from Andrew addressed to your father on the 18th April urging your fathers making him a visit. I do hope your fathers letter reached him in time for them to meet in Havanna. I begin now to hope that I shall soon hear from your beloved father. Oh! my son—you know not what your poor mother suffers from anxieties of every sort. May God! in mercy protect the beloved ones who are absent from me as well as these dear ones who are left with me. I can scarce yet realize that your beloved father is so far away—that so long a time must elapse before we can meet again. Oh! That we may indeed meet again!!![3]—

We are much pleased with Miss Picot—I hope she may be able to give satisfaction. The children all seem anxious to please her—but they are all so deficient it will be a hard task for her I fear. She is very much the lady in her manners—highly accomplished & apparently very amiable. Mr Bartow dined here yesterday—Mr James H Coupers family are all down except himself—he was appointed Executor to old Dr Troup—& I believe is seeing into his business. Mrs Smith (E Bond) & *Mrs Brown* have each a daughter. Mr Brown has already been trying *Homapathic* on *"our little daughter."* Georgia will write to you in all this week—she has very little leisure now as you may suppose. I hope you will enjoy your visits—& that you have secured a friend in your Cousin John. Mr Savage owes me a letter—I am glad he had not answered it as I would rather hear from him after he has seen you. I hope you will not remain a week in N.Y. it will be too expensive. I also wish you would write to you Uncle Andrew. Direct to the care of "Samuel M Noyes Esquire. Matanzas." You must tell him how much is required to Support you at College as it is what I cant find out from either you or Butler.[4]

If you wish to write to your father—Direct to the Honble T Butler King. MC Sanfrancisco—Upper California—*"the postage is free."* I did not intend to send you such a scratch but *I am nervous* & unhappy—but Thank God it is no worse with me. All send love to you you cant think how pleased poor Mrs Gale is that you never forget her in your letters. The servants all beg to be remembered—God bless you my son

Your devoted Mother

AMK

Give our best regards to Hamilton—Miss Annie Cater has returned home for vacation looking fat & course.

1. Daguerreotype.
2. Adele Picot, the King children's new teacher, was from Philadelphia, where her father operated a school. In 1851, Georgia, Florence, and Virginia attended the Picots' school at 15 Washington Square.
3. Steel writes:

> Although King failed to receive from Taylor the appointment which he coveted, the President called on him to help solve the most important and delicate question which faced the new administration, the political future of California. . . . King's letter of instructions from Secretary of State John M. Clayton enjoined him to carry out several duties. In addition to carrying dispatches to the naval and military commanders in California, he was to assure the people of California of the President's concern for their welfare and his efforts in their behalf . . . [and advise them] on the adoption of measures best calculated to promote the President's wishes. Another duty was to acquire information about the country. Finally, King was to report immediately any attempt to establish an independent government or to alienate any territory gained by the treaty of Guadalupe Hidalgo. (*T. Butler King,* 71, 73)

4. Written in between the lines is "you will pay the postage to Havanna."

4   Wednesday 20th June 49

My own dearly beloved Husband!

How grateful I am for your affectionate and most welcome letter of the 15th & 17th May—dated at Panama What a load of anxiety it removed from my mind for your safe arrival at that place—as I am under the impression that the greatest difficulty would be between Chagres & Panama. Now that I have heard that you had got so far—I am in great apprehension you would be made sick by all the *fatigue, exposure & discomfort* you had undergone. What a terrible journey to you my dearly beloved husband! Oh m[a]y God! in mercy grant *fever* may not be the consequence of so much exposure. What a pity you were so long detained in Panama! You complain of the fatigue (That is not to be wondered at—) but I tremble lest that feeling of *lacitude* may not be the fore-runer of fever. I will try & hope for the best!

I had just sent off my third letter to you—via New York to go in the Crescent City on the 30th Inst & hope you will get it in due time. I have not received the *one* you sent me from *Chagres*. I first read your dear letter to the children. Then I read it to Mrs Gale. Then to Lady & Polly. Then to Hannah & Old Jane. How much oftener I shall be asked to read it I know not. When I was *telling* Pussy & Clementine *"all about you"* Boney[1]—said "Tank God! Misses I feel much better since you hear from Mossa." *He* is sick poor fellow. I shall send it to Tootee to read and then it leaves not my bosom by day, or its place under my head at night, until I have the happiness to get another from you to take its place.

That must be a beautiful country! *If* you could have had *dry weather* and *better accommodations* & *several* other *ifs* it would have been delightful. If you escape fever you will be considered a *tough* subject. You have been always blessed in your journeys with exemption from sickness or serious accidents. I pray God! you may be as fortunate in your present journey and that after all the *toil, exposure—risk & sacrifice*—you may be *rewarded accordingly*. It is indeed a terrible sacrifice this of being so far sepparated—to be so little together as we are! I know you are doing for the best—and I try to bear with patience your frequent long absences. This *looking forward* near six months yet for the time I may *hope* to see you is terrible. Oh! m[a]y God! in mercy grant we may meet again in *health—peace* and *happiness*. You bid me unite with you in setting a proper example to our dear children! My nonattendance at Church is *I hope the worst* example I have shown them. This I plead guilty of—& will try to amend it.

When I concluded my letter to you yesterday—I told you it was then raining. It continued to increase until it *poured down* water—the yard—garden— every where covered—but it blew almost equally hard. We have not had such a rain or blow since last October when you were on the canvass. It had been blowing since Sunday night. This morning it has been raining *elsewhere*, but has with us been hot & sultry. I was amazed to find that I *could find dry dirt* in the garden after such a deluge. But the earth was so parched the water ran off as oil would. Dunham tells me the corn is not as much broken as would have been expected—& is more benefited by the rain, than injured by the wind. Neither is the cotton injured. The wind is still E[ast]. I hope it will not come on the blow again.

What must be the feelings of that *wretched woman*! but she must have been destitute of all proper feeling to have acted as she did. The daughter who committed suicide is most to be pitied both soul & body lost! If the husband feels that he has never been *unfaithful* to his miserable wife He is indeed to be pitied—*tho! that would not make her crime the more excusable*. It is a *horrid business view it as you will*. It seems to me these *crimes* are becoming more common. Think you not that your sex is to blame? There are too many faithless husbands —*Tho* (I repeat) *that* is no *excuse for the wife*—two wrongs (as you always say)— do not make a right.

Monday morning 25th June

Yesterday I had the pleasure to receive a letter from our dear Butler his health is much better—Wm Couper had also a letter from our Lord—who was well. We are all in our usual health at this place. Thank God! For so much blessing. Yesterday too I obeyed your desire—I gathered our six children (now at home) into the two buggys & went to church.[2] The ride was an uncomfortable one but I felt *happier for having gone*. Our neighbors congratulated me on having heard from you. For in truth I believe the most envious must *pity* me. I do indeed feel that mine is a most responsible situation. Responsible to my God! to my husband! to my children!!! "The spirit truly is willing, but the flesh is weak." I cannot do all that is required of me—I pray to God! for aid. I find myself constantly looking *for aid* from you my beloved! What a misfortune to all of us your being so little at home! When Oh! when will you again remain at home? This subject I will drop as it is useless. I will do all I can to rear your children.—

I received a letter from Mary Henry yesterday.[3] She writes very affectionately—expresses much gratification from Lords visit to them—pays him a great many compliments and ends by saying Lord had carried off a *half bushel* of *dutch hearts* when he left Allentown. She complains much of *your neglect* of *her husband—your never visiting him—never answering his letters—*That *you have not a brother who loves you better or one more deserving of your love & confidence* than her husband is &c. I will make as many good excuses for you as I can. And wish if you can you would write to Henry. I should think he would doubly appreciate your letter if it came *all the* way from *California*.

What an awful distance it is in truth! I did not believe it was so distant until I examined the Map! What difficulties you encountered in getting to Panama! How do I now contrast the comforts of our *homely home* with those miserable negro huts—your supper of hard biscuits & coffee—the least palatable refreshments could be offered you, my love. Then to sit crampt up in a boat day after day—deluged with rain—but even that was preferable to that hazardous & m[o]st uncomfortable ride from Gorgona to Panama. I hope & trust you felt no ill effects from that *pitch into the ditch*. I bless *the Engineer* for giving you a better horse. Your new white hat must look bad enough by this. I hope & trust when you return you may fare better. Willingly would we take some of those heavy showers here. We have had none since the 20th. Since then until today the weather has been dry, clear, & cool—this morning it was exceedingly warm until 12—when the sea breeze came in.

On Saturday Wm Couper gallanted his wife, Fanny & Susan Fraser, Miss Cunningham, Georgia & Florence to spend the day with the Dubignons on Jekyl. I had charge of the three dear little ones who with our four younger chicks, Miss Picot & mammy Gale dined on broiled chickens &c. Miss P[icot] was invited to accompany them but preferred staying at home. She does not like visiting.[4] We continue to be highly pleased with her. I think her plan of instruction admirable—the children are attentive & respectful & I hope will make a good return to you for the expense & trouble you are at, to obtain a good teacher for them. The Party from Jekyl did not return until near dark—they had a rough time in returning with a strong sea breeze & flood tide. I ran away into the garden keeping a servant to watch & tell me how they got on (you know what a miserable coward I am) & right glad was I when the boat touched the shore, when G[eorgia] & F[lorence] got out, & Anna & Isabel were put on board to proceed on to Hamilton. I have not seen Tootee since (Wm drove the young ladies to Church yesterday) tho I hope to have that pleasure this evening or tomorrow.

Miss Isa Cunningham goes back to Savannah tomorrow night. I will get her to take charge of this letter to be mailed for the *Falcon*—And add more to the childrens letter to leave this [island] on the 29th. Our neighbors are all well except poor old Mr Armstrong he is going rapidly now. His daughter Susans devotion to him is *beautiful*. Whether she has been *scandalized* or not—her devoted attention to her feeble minded mother & unfortunate father renders her an object of praise & admiration.

When you speak of those beautiful flowers on the banks of the river Chagres how much I wish some of them were in my garden—be sure & bring me *some seeds*. But husband! in mercy do not think of *returning by land.* The papers are full of the sufferings of those who have gone to California by land—they say "more human bones will be left on *the plains* than were left on the battle fields in Mexico."[5] They begin too to talk of the Mexicans intention to resume their possession of California. All this tends much to increase my anxiety for your safety. I dare not suffer myself *to think*. What an undertaking is yours my beloved husband! I wonder what would tempt—J H C[ouper] or S[tephen] C K[ing] to make such a journey by land or water. To undergo what you undergo? May God! of his infinite goodness and mercy *guide, guard,* prosper & restore you to us in health & happiness. I am in a constant state of painful anxiety for your health & safety. I imagine ten thousand ills that may befall you. And it seems to me if I only had you back—I would be willing to live in even one of those *"miserable palm* leaf huts" if I could only keep you with me.

The last papers bring us the news of *J. K. Polks death.*[6] May his soul be at peace!

We are getting alarmed about the Cholera. I pray God! it may not reach San Francisco. *Sulphur* taken in small doces is said to be a sure cure. I do not dread it for myself—but Oh! how much do I dread it for our beloved Butler—Lord— & these dear children—as well as for the negros.

Tuesday 26th

Our dear Tootee did come over yesterday evening with the Misses Fraser— Isa Cunningham—her two children & husband. Poor Isa C is in very bad spirits just having heard of the death of her sisters youngest child. We are all to go over there this evening. Little Willie is still with me. He is learning to talk very plain. He got hold of a *case knife* yesterday & commenced trying with it, to mend a *pen to write* "to poor Tom and tell him to come home from "Talliforny."[7] His health is improving.

The weather is very dry and very hot. I had hoped after the storm of last week that the drought was broken. I do hope when it does again rain we shall not have as terrible a blow. I think it strange Louisa has not written to me since you saw Andrew. Oh! my beloved husband how much do I pine for your return. You say you hope to conclude your business by the first of November! That seems a long time to look forward to—and yet how many will be laid low ere that time comes round! No words can express what I feel for you. Oh! my beloved husband what a sacrifice you are now making for your children! May God! in mercy grant these efforts may be crowned with success—& that we may have the unspeakable happiness of seeing you once more safely restored to us! I can scarce yet realize you are so far away! Hard—hard have you laboured for a *reputation* to leave your children but that will not give *them bread*. Surely some more substantial reward is in store for you—That the time will come—when you my beloved may rest from your labours & enjoy some return for all you have done for *others—and for your country at large.* It seems to me *you are* always to labour for an *uncertain reward,* if Genl Taylor does not come up to his promises.

I would I could go where we could put our children to school—without having them taught at home. There is no emulation—nothing to rouse them up. All the same ding dong every day business—then the expense is so great—but this can never be done unless you had an Office—a sure income & where you could be more with us. Think you that time will ever arrive?

You only mention Capt Ringgold & Major Garnet—what has become of Capt or Col Allen? I trust the Cholera has not stopt Mr Calhoun.

Alex Wyllys son went on by land to join Col Fremonts[8]—his friends are very unhappy at not having heard from him since he left the State. He is of *Lords age*—his grand father Spalding gave him his out fit & is to give him $500 a year.

The papers are loud against the Democratic Party—who are combining in all parts to mar, all in their power, the efforts of Genl Taylors administration for the good of the country. What a set of villains they are!!!

I trust my beloved you will avoid running into any danger—remember my beloved you are our only earthly stay!! They tell me I must not expect another letter for at least 50 days from the Date of your leaving Chagres—perhaps I may not expect one so soon—but I trust I may hear from you next Month. And Oh! May God! grant I may hear from you, that you are in health—safety and likely to prosper in this extra ordinary Mission. Genl Taylor ought *not* to have required so great a sacrifice from one who has *done so much* to exalt him. Hang such confidence!—it is like paying a brave soldier the *complement* for his bravery—to make him lead *a Forlorn hope*!!! I hope you will be able to write me long letters—let me hear particularly how your health is—how the climate agrees with you.

I hope these letters may reach you—As I am sure you must be anxious to hear from us. The children will also write by this opportunity. Praying Gods! choicest blessing on you I am your devoted wife.

AMK

1. Cupid, born July 21, 1777, is number 25 on list from William Page's will, number 21 on the 1839 list, and number 1 on the 1853 list. See appendix 2.

2. Christ Church, Frederica, was organized in 1807, making it the second oldest Episcopal church in Georgia. The first wardens included Robert Grant and William Page; the vestrymen were George Abbott, John Couper, Raymond Demere Jr., James Hamilton, and Joseph Turner. The first church building, erected in 1820, was destroyed by Union soldiers during the Civil War. Vanstory, *Land of the Golden Isles,* 144–145.

3. Mary King was the wife of T. B. King's brother, Henry King, of Allentown, Pennsylvania.

4. It is clear that Adele Picot endeared herself to the Kings and became a companion to her charges, accompanying them on visits to friends and family on the island and mainland. Yet she remained somewhat aloof, often declining invitations to stay home to read or sew instead. Elizabeth Pryor suggests that many northern teachers, though treated like family members, "preferred to spend their free hours by themselves, reading or walking in the countryside, rather than participate in the family's social life" (Pryor, "An Anomalous Person," 370, 377).

5. Though the earliest trail west dated from 1776, traveling overland to California or Oregon was still arduous and dangerous. It took five months to travel by covered wagon from the western border of Missouri to Oregon.

6. James K. Polk died June 15, 1849, in Nashville, Tennessee.

7. Thomas Butler King's grandchildren called him Uncle Tom.

8. John C. Frémont was an explorer, lieutenant in the corps of topographical engineers, and U.S. senator from California in 1850–1851. In 1848 he organized an expedition to explore the mountains of California, reaching Sacramento in 1849.

22nd June 49

My beloved Lord

I wrote you a few hurried lines on Tuesday last but having had the happiness to hear from your dear father I again write you a hurried letter. His letter was dated 17th May from Panama—which town he reached on the *6th*. The Steamer *Panama* arrived *there* on the same day and your father had the prospect of leaving that miserable place on the 17th. He does not assign any reason why the Steamer stopt so long at Panama. He had in her a *birth* in the *best state room*—which would be a great luxury after all he went through after leaving the Steamer *Orus* [and] Capt Tucker on the *river Chagres*. This gallant *officer* did not leave your dear father until he saw him safe in Panama. Soon they had to leave the *Orus* and take to a boat—the river being too low for the Steamer they went in this way three days—poling or rowing as the water would allow, stopping at night at negro villages—sleeping in Palm leaf huts. The first night they had to drive out pigs & cattle to get a place to hang up their hammocks in. The third night they got to Gorgona—where he was more comfortably lodged by the *Engineers*. The next day they mounted miserable little ponies—their baggage put on to mules—from the rains—it rained on them every day—their progress was very slow—the ponies bogging up to their knees in clay—at length your fathers Poney—went head over heels, & threw him about ten feet into a deep ditch—fortunately he was not hurt and soon mounted again—soon after one of the Engineers over took the party & gave your dear father his Poney—when he got on better—they took the whole day to travel 28 miles—the distance from Gorgona to Panama—where they at last arrived wet to the skin—& completely fagged out. Panama is a real negro town—nothing but the most squalid negro population. The climate hot & damp. Your dear father says he felt much as he does here in August & September—but hoped when he should arrive in San Francisco—he would feel well again. He speaks of the great beauty of the Country so far—of the agreeableness of his companions Col Garnett & Lieutenant Ringgold and nothing so feelingly as of the sacrifice he is making for his beloved children. God! knows my beloved boy whether this beloved husband and father will ever return to us!—he has under taken a *hard mission* and all for the benefit of his children. Strive my son to reward him for so doing—by your application to your studies & by your correct conduct. It will be delightful to gratify him. I wish I could send you his letter.

We had quite a storm of rain & wind on Monday until Wednesday morning. It did not do as much harm to the corn as we apprehended it would—the rain did more good than the wind did harm—that is on this place—the cotton was not injured. I have not heard how others have fared. Your sister accompanied by Fanny & Susan Fraser & Miss Isa returned last evening from Cannon's Point all were well there. Poor old Mr Armstrong is very ill—poor old gentleman—I fear he is near his last. His face is getting rapidly worse—that his friends can[t] desire to see his days lengthened—as there is no cure for his cancer. Miss Susan is still unwell—poor thing she has much to contend with.

I am very unhappy about dear Butler—am most anxious to hear from him again. I wrote in my last begging you to write more frequently—All send love to you my beloved Lord.

> Your own Mother
> A M King

24th July 1849

My beloved Son Lord

I wrote you a few lines by the last Mail & enclosed to you Mr J. H. Coupers kind letter to me on the subject of your return home.[1] That evening we had a call from Hamilton—Who gave me the pleasing assurance "that you were well & doing well" when he left you. For this comfort I am first thankful to God! for keeping you in health & next thankful to you my boy that you are making good use of your time. By this time I suppose you are thinking seriously of your visit to us. I hope & trust you will *strictly* follow Mr Coupers kind advice. *Advice given me at my own earnest solicitation & intended for your own good—your safety & there in my happiness.*

I would particularly request *you will come direct to Savannah* in the *Tennessee* or *Cherokee* which ever may offer at the time you may be ready to start. That you will leave New Haven so as to be as short a time as possible in N.Y. that whilst in N.Y. you will strictly avoid the infected Parts—be careful in your diet —Clothe warm—*avoid especially* night air—sleep with your windows down. I hope and trust you may meet the *Florida* boat in the river & thereby avoid going at all to Savannah. On your way out—Your going first to see Butler *is not advisable*. We are most anxious for your safety my beloved boy—even more so than to see you—as much as we ardently wish that pleasure. And be sure to have "cholera drops" always at hand. I look forward to your return with a trembling heart. Oh my own dear boy—if a weak mothers desire to see her son after being one year absent should cause evil to befall him—what will not that poor Mother suffer!! I have put my trust in God! & I trust his Mercy may protect you from all harm.

I am sure you will be sorry to hear *that Hamilton is now sick his fever* his mother is fearful is caused by passing through Charleston. Others think it is occasioned by a cold. Mr J H Couper is also in bed from an attack of *Cholera Morbus*, not *ill*, but sick enough to keep his bed. Jimmy & Margaret have also fever—and among the negros at Cannon's Point there has been three cases of *Cholera Morbus*. At present we are all in our usual health. For this mercy we cannot be sufficiently grateful. How long we are to be blessed God! alone knows. I hear no fears expressed for the safety of Mr Couper or his children & earnestly hope their health will soon be restored. We have had a great deal of unpleasant weather—damp, & cool enough with some to render extra clothing necessary. But the two last days have been fine—& Dunham is hauling in fodder enough I hope to support Rocket[2] whilst you stay with us.

It will cost you $50 to go & return from Athens—but I value not the money. It is your safety I think of. Before the time arrives for you to return to New Haven we will I trust be able to see our way more clearly—& I pray God! the country may be more healthy so that you may make your brother a visit. You may imagine my dear boy that I have a great deal to be anxious about. I have no *human aid* to look to if sickness visits my family or plantation—all eyes are turned to me for all the wants in sickness or in health. It would therefore be cruel in either children or servants to run unnecessary risks. I have a strong hope *if you will follow* Mr J H Coupers kind advice that your coming home will be attended by no evil consequences. And Oh how I do long to see you my beloved Lord. I would that Butler could be at home at the same time—but his vacation is but for one week. His ill health has occasioned him much loss of time—which he regrets very much—as well he may—for every moment is now precious to both, aye to all of you.

I am getting painfully anxious to have another letter from your dear father it is now over three months since he left us—and 2 months & 8 days since his last letter was written—(that is the last I have received). May God in Mercy preserve him in health & prosper him in his Mission. He has undertaken a work that will cause hard labour both of mind & body. God Grant him success—but above all—may he be restored to us in health, peace & happiness. Poor Old Mr Armstrong still lives—his daughter Susan is nearly worn out— he has now been five weeks in bed. I was there last evening.

Your Sister was here yesterday—she will be over again this evening & will take Willie home. I am sorry to part with the little fellow—he is now looking very well & getting to be quite "*a boy.*" Isabel weaned very easily & was much improved by her stay of 10 days with me. Poor Mrs Gale devoted herself to the care of her during the day—I took the charge at night—& the dear little one between us was well taken care of. Anna has been very little with me of late— she is indeed a sweet intelligent little creature.

Georgia says she will write to you next week—do dear Lordy write me as often as you can. I am very anxious about your health & safety. I have had another kind letter from your uncle—he mentions having received Butlers letter—I hope you have written to him. It is a respectful attention due from both you & Butler to the only uncle who has shown the least interest in you. Andrew asks to be informed of the amount necessary for your yearly schooling & support at College—As he wishes to arrange as far as he is able the payments. Of this you can inform me as I wish to write to him early next month.—

We expect Mr & Mrs Brown this evening to stay until *tomorrow evening*— do you not envy me! Mr Bourke must have a dull time of it on Jeky[ll]. He is expected to pay Wm A Couper a visit ere long. I hope he will bring his wife over with him. She is indeed a dear sweet woman.

The children send you a thousand loves—Mrs Gale begs to be kindly remember'd. The servants always beg to send you huddy. Lady still talks of her Old Mas Hamilton[3] with great pride—she says she "know's you will turn out well." God bless you my beloved Son—write me often or I will think you are sick. May God bless you my son & may we soon meet in health, peace and happiness is the fervent prayer of your

Devoted Mother
A M King

My eyes still very troublesome writing quite a task to me.—

1. James Hamilton Couper advised in a letter written July 15, 1849, from Cannon's Point:

In the present state of things I think he runs no risk of cholera by returning home, if he will make arrangements so as to avoid remaining any length of time . . . where the cholera exists, and be careful in his diet and in avoiding all exposure. I would suggest to him if [he] decides to come on to adopt the following course. To be gov-

erned in his election of Charleston or Savannah by the latest accounts of the health
of these cities, which he can ascertain in New Haven by enquiring at the office of
the newspapers. To leave New Haven in time only to reach New York to meet the
departure of the Steamer. If he is compelled to pass the night in New York, to take
his lodgings high up in the city, and to keep out of the night air and the infected dis-
tricts—On his arrival in Charleston to leave it as soon as possible. My impression
is that the train leaves immediately on the arrival of the steamer. If compelled to remain an [*sic*] night to house himself before sunset, and sleep with his windows
down. . . . If he goes up the Country from Savannah, and is detained in that city, to
avoid the night air and to confine himself to the hotel. . . . Lord should provide himself with a small vial of Cholera drops consisting of Laudanum, camphorated spirits, and cayenne pepper, which all the apothecaries will compound for him. On the
first symptoms of diarrhea he should take it. He should go warmly clad, and it will
be well for him to wear flannel. Let him avoid the night air, and cold winds. He
should be very particular in his diet, eating moderately of poultry, beef, mutton and
lamb bread and rice; and avoiding all fruits and vegetable, fish, lobsters, crabs, [?]
[?]. If he will follow these directions he will incur but little danger, even in passing
through a cholera district. (James Hamilton Couper to Anna Matilda Page King,
July 15, 1849, TBK, SHC)

2. Lord's horse.
3. I don't know why Lady would have called Lord "Mas Hamilton."

21st August 1849

My own dearly beloved Husband!

Georgia & I wrote you a hasty letter on Friday last—since then we notice
that the *Falcon* is expected to stop at Savannah on her way to Chagres. I have
therefore another opportunity to thank you again for your dear letter of the
28th—and to acknowledge the rec[eip]t of your *expected* letter written on your
arrival at San Francisco. Oh! My beloved how much have I to be grateful for.
What a fearful passage you had in the Panama. How unconscious we were of
all the dangers which threatened you—for all the discomfort & even sickness
you experienced. Oh! My God! I thank thee, that all ended so well. What a new
world you have entered into. How strange every thing must appear to you.
How relieved you must have been *at the reception given you* surely dear husband
greater honours could not have been expected. I treasure them in my heart—
& hope your Political enemys may yet have cause to regret *they would not let you
be in the cabinet.* My heart is too full I feel that I cannot express my feelings in
words. I am much relieved to hear the climate has restored your health. I cannot appreciate all you have undergone since you left me. I can only pray God!
in his mercy to guide, guard, prosper & restore you to us in health & happiness. Oh! My beloved—how fearful the risks you run—how endless the fatigue—what labours of both body & mind. Oh! That you may be able to stand

it—you certainly are a wonderful man! Who would have believed it if told ten years ago—what you would accomplish in that time.

Old Mr Couper is in *ecstacy* at your success so far—dear old gentleman he seems as proud of you as if you were his own son. I have sent the "bill of fare" to Butler. It does indeed seem strange that in so far off a country—you should receive so many honors. I have indeed been blest the last few days—first came your letter of the 28th. This was joyful—that day a fine rain which was much needed. On Sunday morning we had the happiness to welcome home our dear Lord! who arrived safe & well—a few hours later came your letter from San Francisco—& a letter from dear Butler—telling us he had returned to Athens in improved health—And then dear husband we were all in our usual health— even dear little Isabel who had been so sick began to improve & is getting better daily. Have I not cause to be thankful?

Dear Uncle Tom do come home to your little Anna. Willie wants to see you too dear Uncle Tom.

You see I was interrupted by the arrival of H[annah] Page & her babies—as soon as Anna & Willie heard I was writing to you they insisted on writing to you too. Anna thought she could hold the pen herself—but Willie let me have the guidance of his hand—the *words are their own.* I have to write whenever I can steal a moment from poor little Isabel. She is quiet with no one but with me—poor baby it is pitiable to see how fever—heat—teething & weaning have reduced her. I have had a great deal of trouble with her—but am glad to have relieved her poor mother of the fatigue—for tho I am the *grandmamma* I can stand more fatigue than H Page can. The weather is very hot & debilitating. This is Wednesday the 22nd. Lord received by this days mail your *franked* new paper. He will write you by this opportunity—I see by the paper that the *Ohio* is expected to touch at Savannah—I am now sorry I sent my letter by the way of N.Y. It may get lost—& I do not care to repeat in this what those letters contained. Mr Dunham wrote to you the state of the crop. Toney tells me the cotton still promises well.

I am quite put out by the *piano failure.* It is much a draw back to the girls to be without an instrument. On Monday Mr & Mrs Bourke, Lord—baby & I— spent the day at Hamilton. The dear old gentleman could talk of nothing else but *you.* I told you of the death of poor old Mr Armstrong. Of Mr J H Couper's panic about the Cholera. We begin to feel quite secure from it tho' we may yet suffer from it. I cannot imagine the reason—but all my young turkeys are dying since yesterday I have lost all but *3* they just jump up & then fall down dead. This is a sad disappointment to me—but I am glad it is no worse—for the negros thus far are unusually healthy. Mr & Mrs Brown leave the Isld this day *for*

Boston. He never thought it worth while to ask the permission of the Islanders to do so—I only hope he will not return. Tho' I suppose he is as good as any other we may get. There has been a great revival at Waynesville. First the Baptists had a meeting which lasted 5 days & then the Methodists for 4 days. We certainly have been unfortunate on this Island in our ministers. But we need only our own consciences to lead us to Him who died for us!! Oh my husband when I think how you have escaped when others were cut off! how can I be sufficiently grateful! Oh! My God! tho' [*sic*] alone can know my gratitude—Oh! How fervently I pray for the Holy spirit to descend on me & mine! May my prayers be granted!—

I fear you will find this letter a disjointed affair—but I can only write whilst the baby sleeps—for she will be quiet with no one else but me. This is now the 24th. The weather *hot* & *dry*—I do not think we have had so hot & dry a summer since 45—that is at this place—the folks on the Maine continue to receive their copious rains. Mr and Mrs Bourke left here yesterday. They both requested to be remembered to you. I am sorry Mr Bourke is out of employ. He seems to feel it very much. The papers are full of "what could carry you to California." All sorts of guessing going on. This is very amusing to old Mr Couper—who sincerely "hopes the results may confound your enemies." Lord will write to you by this opportunity. And I think dear husband this will be my last letter as I see the papers say this mail is intended to meet the Pacific mail of October. And you hope to leave California in November. I[t] does seem so strange that so long a time is required to get a letter to you. What will you not have undergone before we meet again. Does it not seem like a dream to you? It does to me. In fact my mind seems in a constant confusion. I cannot yet realize that you are so far away. Oh! May God in mercy grant we may meet again in health—peace & happiness.

We are all in our usual health all complaining of the terrible heat—Miss Picot looks a great deal better than when she first came—but complains much of the heat. The children say they cannot study for the heat—tho dear Georgia sticks to her books all day—she is so mortified that she cannot go on with her music—but how can I get a piano? The Indians have again been at work in Florida—a Steamer past here this morning with troops & I hope they will now put a final stop to their murders. Lord is very anxious to see Butler before he returns to Yale. I think it well he should do so—for it may be long ere he has an other opportunity. His health is very good—he seems to think he can undergo as much *as you can.* This I doubt!! I will now conclude and let some of the children fill up this Page—May God! bless and prosper you my beloved husband—above all may He restore you to us in health & happiness—Oh! Be careful of your precious health—remember the wife & children dependent on you for happiness. The negros are delighted to hear that you are (or were) well—they cannot comprehend the distance you are from us—Mrs Gale sends her best regards. H[annah] Page says she wants to write to you—but may not be able. I have received congratulations from all my neighbors on my hearing from you. Praying Gods! choicest blessings on you I am your devoted wife

A M King

My dearly beloved Father!

I have but a few moments during recess to say how rejoiced I am to hear you were well when you wrote on the 28th June. Though 2 months has past since then we yet hope you continue to enjoy health. May God!! bless & restore you to us is the prayer of your affectionate daughter

Florence

My dear beloved Father

As Florence says "I have but a few minutes to write to you." Oh father how strange it does seem you should be so far away. How much we want to see you. I hope we may all meet you in health and happiness. your affectionate daughter

Virginia

My dear Father

Now that Lord has come home it seems as if I miss you more than ever. Dear Father how much I wish I could have accompanied you. I think I could have been of some assistance to you; tho' I do not think I should have enjoyed the passage on board the Panama. I am thankful you were well when you last wrote. Do be careful of your health for the sake of your affect[tionate] son

M P King

[Written on the envelope:] If Mr King has returned to New York City the Post Master will oblige by forwarding this immediately to him addressed to the Astor House N.Y.

21st February 1850

My dearly beloved husband!!!

On Sunday last I saw your arrival announced in the *New York Enquirer*. On last Wednesday (yesterday) Georgia received a long letter from Lord giving her a most glowing description of the few happy days he had spent with you in New York. By the *Intelligencer* of the 12th I saw your arrival in Washington City announced. This surely must be all a dream? It cannot be possible that you would so long neglect to write me! I do not intend to reproach you! Lord says "Father will probably remain two or three weeks in Washington then return here before [he] proceeds home." As there is a probability of your remaining [?] long[er] I have ventured to write this to offer you my heartfelt congratulations on your safe return.[1] No words can express my gratitude to our God! for His mercy in permitting you to return & in health. I wrote to you when we thought you would leave California in Dec & sent my letter under cover to the Capt of the [?]—thinking you would return in that ship. When your last letter dated the 1st Dec reached me I again wrote & enclosed my letter [to] Andrew—who in his letter to me said "he would be in Havana [to] meet you." As I find the Steamer you came in did not touch [in] Havana—you could not have received that letter either. But I suppose Lord told you all we have written to him—therefore I need not repeat.

In your last letter you said "I intend to purchase the best piano I can find on my arrival in N.Y. if you are not supplied." Finding the children were losing so much time I got Mr Picot to purchase me one at 90 days credit for $453—some odd cents—including the insurance. This is or will be due on the 8th March. If you have the means I would be very glad if you can pay this note of mine. We have sent very little cotton on & I will be difficulted to raise the amount at so early a day. I hope when you pass through Philadelphia on your return to New York you will be able to see Mr Picot. His daughter continues to give every satisfaction.—

Lord says you have been most generous in your presents to him. I do not say he is not worthy—I would only remind you there are eight others at home equally entitled to you[r] remembrance. For myself all I ask is for my lawful share in your affections. Bring me back your heart unchanged & I ask no more. But if you have any curiosities—do not bestow them on others. Your children will prize them more than any one else will.—

The Mails are very irregular—but I hope this may not be delayed. Praying the choicest blessing of God! on you—& that we may soon have the happiness to welcome you home I am as ever your devoted

Wife
A M King

My dearly beloved Father!

I cannot express to you what great joy we all felt Sunday on hearing of your arrival in the Atlantic shore [?] once more. Oh dear Father when shall we see you again? When we first saw that you had returned we fondly hoped to see you again some time this week, but as Lord tells us you will be obliged to remain in Washington for some weeks I am afraid we shall not be able to see you for two weeks or ten days at least. I thought when I commenced this my beloved parent I should be able in at least a measure to tell you how happy I am at the mear idea of seeing you again. Oh! dear Father I—we all, have suffered so much on your account, hearing that you were ill—very ill & then not being able to reach you[2]—I hope you will never again go so far away from us. I dont think dear Mother could stand it, She looks very badly now, nothing will improve her but your return, So you must not leave us again dear Father. Lord wrote me a long letter yesterday & told me how much he had been enjoying the few days in New York. Lord speaks much of your kindness and is proud of his Father, which of us is not? I am sure I am very proud of you my dear Father. I am certain that since Washington there has never been so great and good a man! Don't consider this flattery. I never flattered in my life and I am sure I may be allowed to tell my parent how much I love him. Do you know Father that I am afraid I love you too much! This may be nonsense but it is no less the truth. Do my beloved parent hasten home to dear Mother and all of us. Dear Mother has a great deal to worry and distress her, I don't know how she bears it as well as she does. These little annoyances are much more trying than great troubles. Don't you think so? But I must not commence on these subjects for they are too much in the abstract. I have learned the "Marsailles Hymn" to play for you when you come. And if I am not such a little fool as to make a mistake, it will do very well do you think? I actually am more timid now than when I first took lessons on the Piano—I suppose the reason is that I think persons expect more of me & this makes me nervous or rather fidgety for I can't bear to be thought nervous. Don't you dislike nervous women? I think you do—I wanted to write this very nicely so as to show you how much dear Miss Picot has improved my writing but the paper is not good & I have to use it as Mother commenced her letter. Now dear Father when you come home, I hope you will tell us all about California! I hope you will not be as silent as you generally are, for we are as curious as the good people of N.Y. every bit—I am only afraid you will have talked out all you had to say. I hope not however. And indeed, so that I could but see your dear face again, I believe I would even give up the great pleasure of hearing you talk—May I not enjoy both?—My dearest Father I could fill pages in writing you. But the bell has rung & I must go to practice the "Marsaelles Hymn." I will imagine your picture to be yourself—I have often done it before. Every one sends love & kisses &c. Boney declares he will be so glad to see you that he will never work again! Good bye dear Father.

Your ever devoted daughter
Georgia

Feb 22d 1850

I am quite wild with joy at the idea of so soon seeing you at home dear Father, how distressed we have been about you. But now that you have been spared to us—I hope you will never again leave

Your affectionate daughter

Appy

My dear father

I am most happy to hear of your safe return to N.Y. And equally so to hear that your health is so good. We fully expected to see you here on Saturday next but from what Lordy says we fear you will be detained some time longer—I know you will come as soon as you can

Your affectionate Son

M P King

My dear Father

I am very glad to hear you have quite recovered your health & that we may soon see you once more at home. I have learned to shoot & have killed a great many birds, some hawks & rabbits. Do not be uneasy, I am very careful with my old long single barrel gun; it shoots first rate. Do come as soon as you can.

Your affectionate son

Floyd

22d February 1850

My dearest Father

It is useless to try to describe to you our happiness Sunday last when Mallery (who had just returned from Savannah) told us that you had arrived in N.Y.— Oh! dear Father how anxiously we all look forward to your return home, I suppose Mother & Georgia have told you every little piece of news that is of any interest, Georgia received a long letter from Lord on Wednesday, & it was mostly about you & ofcourse that made it all the more interesting to us—Dearest Father I hope before many weeks are over, you will have returned home, It is quite late & I can think of nothing that has not already been told you, so I really hope you will excuse this short & very badly written P.S.—I hope my dear Father that you will not take this as a specimen of my penmanship, for my pen is very bad, the paper not good—I am sure you will be very pleased with our dear Miss Picot, she is so kind & amiable, that we all are very much attached to her, & I do not know how any one could know her without loving her, Good night my dearest Father, hoping soon to see you here in good health, I am with much love your

devoted daughter
Florence

My dear "Father"

In the hope that you will excuse the liberty I take in thus addressing you, I beg leave to offer my congratulations, and wish you a speedy return among the dear ones who are so fondly and anxiously expecting you.

Respectfully your "daughter"
Adele [Picot]

Hon. T. Butler King

My dear Father

I am very glad to hear you will so soon be at home Mother will not let me shoot—but I hope you will—all I can doo well is to cut wood I am getting very strong Your affectionate little boy

Cuyler

P.S. I hope you are quite well dear Pa

Dearest Father

I cannot allow this piece of blank paper to remain [?] unfilled when I am so anxious to converse with you tho it only be on paper—I must certainly tell you of my new accomplishment. I am sure you would never guess— Shooting Yes indeed dear Father I have killed ten robins. I hope when you return you will allow me to go out shooting hawks with you. Will you? I shall be very good & pull the trigger at the right time. We all got playing last night & Miss Picot wrote you a few lines too. She is a very sweet lady & I know you will like her—Do you intend telegraphing Butler that he may meet you in Savannah? We received a letter from him on Sunday & he was quite well. Breakfast is waiting so I must go—Good bye dear Father

Your affectionate
Georgia

Do bring your desk & other trap[ping]s from Washington you will feel the want of them here—Do not be alarmed at what Georgia says about my health —I am quite well—only I have grown old in looks very rapidly—owing to the constant anxiety I have suffered.—

1. Anna's sarcasm is understandable. Her husband had returned to the East from California without having written or telegraphed his plans to her.

2. See the letters below.

From R. M. Price to Anna King

[August 30, 1849][1]

Dear Madam,

You will doubtless perceive by the papers that Mr King has been ill with the prevailing disease of this place, the dysentery, he is at my house and had the best medical and other attention. I am most happy to inform you that he is now convalescent and is only prevented from writing you, by the prohibition of his medical advisor who is unwilling he should undergo the excitement of writing. I beg leave to advise you that Mr King shall receive every attention and care while here and that he is now entirely out of danger.

I am dear Madam Very Respectfully,
Your Obt Servt Rodman M Price

My dearly beloved Anna,

The Dr has forbid my attempting [to] write, but I am permitted to add by way of P.S. that I am rapidly recovering. The steamer goes out one day sooner than I expected or I may have given you something better than this scratch. Pray do not feel the least alarm on my account. I hope to be up and out in a day or two, Kiss the dear children a thousand times for their affectionate father and your ever devoted,

T. Butler King

P.S. I hope this attempt to write will not alarm you more by its appearance than my having written it would have done. My room is dark of course and I am suffering from weakness.

I am most happy madam to be able to confirm the many favourable reports that will reach you of your husband's condition. I subjoin this postscript at his request, lest some exaggerated accounts that have been published here, may reach you, and occasion unnecessary distress and alarm.

I have the honor to be Madam yours Most
Respectfully,
A. J. Bowie, Surgeon, U.S. N[avy].

1. The location of the originals of this letter and the next is unknown. Transcribed copies received October 29, 1948, from Alexander Heard from "the papers of Marie Nisbet wrapped together and marked John Nisbet Marye," TBK, SHC.

From C. Ringgold to Anna King

[September 1, 1849]

My dear Madam,

My friend Mr. King wishes me to address you a few lines by the Steamer which sets our today for Panama. Your husband has had an attack of dysentery for the last two weeks, and he is now much better, he would have written to you himself, but the Doctor deems it prudent he should not exert himself, and expose his eyes to the light. Mr King has lately returned from a visit to the interior of the country, and the weather being very warm, perhaps caused the attack which he had been seized with. Dr. Bowie of the Navy, has been his attending physician, and his skill has easily overcome anything serious. In a few days we both hope to proceed to Monterey, to attend the sitting of the Convention, which meets today. Mr King wishes me to say in great kindness and affection he will write by the next steamer, of 1st Oct and give you the particulars of his sickness under his own hand. I have been constantly with him, and he has had every convenience the town can afford. I hope tomorrow, he will leave his bed, and in a day or two, be enable[d] to take exercise.

> With great Respect I am my dear Madam
> Your Obt Servant
> Cadwalader [Ringgold], United States Navy.

28th March 1850

My own dearly beloved husband

Your most welcome letter of the 20th reached me yesterday. I am most grateful to our most merciful God! that you are better. May he in mercy restore you to us in health! How little we value the great blessing until deprived of it. Now that you have finished your report I hope it may not be long ere we are blessed with your presence at home. I think the business which further detains you must be important else you would not longer delay. I am heart sick with hope deferred. But I will try & be patient I know you will not stay away longer than you are compelled to. I feel that my letters have been shorter than they ever heretofore have been. But I always write under the impression that your mind is so occupied you have little leisure to read further than what strictly regards the health of your family. To keep your mind easy on that head [?]—I have written twice every week since your being in Washington—And after the first two weeks I felt confident you would have left ere my letter reached that place—as you will observe on the back of at least two of them. I did not know how you were circumstanced & felt annoyed at being obliged to ask you to pay for the piano. I hope by this that matter is settled—for by the last Mail I had a letter from Mr Picot reminding me that my note was due on the 8th March. I think Miss Picot will remain another year if her Mother will consent. I feel that her continuence will be of vast importance especially to our dear Georgia—who is doing all in her power to improve in every respect. Miss P[icot] endeared herself to us all by her exemplary conduct. I am sure you will admire & esteem her. The amount of Salary is large & beyond the means of the plantation. I am thankful you are able to assist. God! knows you have worked hard enough & suffered more than enough for what you may gain.—

I am much relieved to hear you do not intend to come on by the land route. It would be very imprudent your doing so. If you value my happiness be careful of your precious health. I am glad my short letters have alarmed you. Tho I know you say what you do not think. No. I have loved you too long—to begin now to change. I feel that tho' long absent—still I am blessed with a beloved husband whose life & happiness is of more value to me than all the world besides—even California with all its gold!—

Our dear old friend Mr Couper was buried yesterday. On Monday night I received an urgent request from Mr Brown to come to his wife—who was ill & had no one with her but negro women. I was not very well—& little Isabel had fever. I did not go until the morning—when I got there her infant was born—but she was in a very dangerous state. I remained until after dinner—her danger was then over. When I received a note from Georgia begging me to come home as Tootee had arrived from Hopeton & was in so nervous a state as to require my presence. The dear old gentleman expired on Monday night—After the most intense suffering of 4 days. He previous to that, had complained of no pain—May God! be praised for all his mercies—We hope his precious soul is at rest. Like the thief on the cross we hope his prayers were heard. Yes, the dear old man prayed to God! Prayed to his Saviour for Mercy. Oh my husband—how relived I was to hear this. It took away most of my sorrow for his departure. Dr Sullivan said if he survived this illness he would probably never know a days health. We met the body yesterday at Frederica. Our dear Butler had arrived the night before—So that we had 8 children & one grandchild to show this last respect to one who has ever been our friend. His interest in you continued to the last. His last effort to read was to read your "card" which he could not—but it was read to him. The last absent person he spoke of was you. He wondered what could detain you & hoped Genl Taylor would do some thing for you. This more than he had said for days before & more than he ever spoke at one time after. Mr J H Couper was very ill with Pleurisy—when his father died but was a little better yesterday when William left. Hannah Page grieves much. Her children are still with me—but will go home this evening.

Our dear Butler heard that you were expected to arrive in Charleston last Saturday. He hastened down to meet you there. When he got to Charleston & found you had not come—he said he found it difficult to resist the temptation to go on to Washington. "Nothing prevented his so doing—but the apprehension that you may not like it." He things [*sic*] he would have been sick if he had not come away when he did—Several young men were sick & he felt very unwell. He is a dear noble fellow this same Butler. Georgia had a letter from Lord yesterday. He was anxiously expecting you to arrive in N.Y.

Since writing the first part of this letter—I have had some conversation with Miss Picot. She says so far as she is concerned she would be willing to remain some time longer with us. But she fears it will [be] difficult to persuade her Mother to part with her longer. Before you receive this you will doubtless have seen her parents & I hope they may consent to her remaining. I am so anxious on G[eorgia] & F[lorence's] account—she should remain. Butler will remain until you come. I do hope and trust you will now soon be here. Do not let it be a whole year—it is now going fast on to it since you left us after your short visit of six days. I have had our flower garden weeded twice since your arrival in N.Y. it is looking now very pretty. That man Douglas has not sent my roses— bad luck to him! The cotton is all up but it is so cold I fear it will be killed— So we will not be as well off as those who have been behind hand in planting. There seems so much uncertainty of this letter reaching you. I discouraged Georgia & Butler from writing as they desired to do by this Mail. I hope in Gods! Mercy you will not again be detained by sickness—I would rather even that pleasure should keep you—as cross as that would make me—than that you should again in the slightest way be indisposed. True love is always jealous. I never before so much regretted my plain Exterior—I know no one can have a more constant heart—but I would wish again to be young. I desire beauty & accomplishments that my husband may be as proud of me as I am of him. I know you do not like to read a crossed letter.[1] I will therefore conclude. Miss P[icot] sends her best regards. Mrs Gale her kind remembrances. The children send a thousand loves and kisses—And hopes for your speedy return. The servants say they are worn out waiting to see you. And now my own dearly beloved husband—I must say adieu. God! of his infinite mercy and goodness keep you from all harm. And may he permit you to return once more to us in health peace & happiness—is the fervent prayer of your devoted wife—

A M King

1. "Crossing," or crosshatching, involved filling a page of paper from top to bottom, then turning it horizontally or diagonally and writing across what had already been written. While it saved both paper and postage, such writing was not always easy to read. Anna had, in fact, crossed half of the last page of this letter.

11th April 1850

My own dearly beloved Husband

I cannot imagine what detains you in Washington or why you do not write to us! I am most painfully anxious about you. God! in mercy grant you are not again confined to a bed of suffering! Dearest husband when shall we meet again? I believe your detention is caused by necessity. I know you are doing all for the benefit of your children. Yet it is hard to have you stay away *so* long. If you would only write *once a week* there would be some relief to my suffering. But this continuel silence (to think only three letters since your return from California). This dread that you are ill. The soul harrowing fear that harm may befall you—drives me almost crazy. I can settle down to no employment. Do in mercy write to me oftener—if you can't come.

I see a vile slander on your "report" in the *Intelligencer* of the 3d.[1] Jones is the mans name bad luck to him I say. I know you possess great coolness. Oh! exert it all. I am so thankful you have done with Politicks. I cannot endure the slander which all public men are subject to. And you above all others who I know have done so much for the public good and at so great a sacrifice. And have been so ill requited.

I wrote some two weeks ago & addressed my letter to the Astor House New York. Georgia wrote by the Tuesday mail & addressed it there also. I do not think this will reach Washington in time to meet you there & hope it may not be in time to find you in N.Y. that you may be now on your way home. But I cannot resist writing. I judge you by myself. If you are still detained I know you will be glad to hear from us, & if not, I will have past a half hour in communing with my greatest earthly blessing. You will perhaps say "we are too old to talk love to each other." If that be your opinion I differ from you. I feel that years have but increased my love for you. I feel as much pleasure in writing to you now as the most love sick damsel of 17 would to her lover. More a great deal— no woman can love—lover or husband—more ardently, tenderly than I do you. If you in truth love me equally you will be glad to get this letter & will not fail to answer it. If unfortunately you are still detained.

We are in our usual health. Our dear Butler is getting in despair he fears he will be compelled to return to Athens without seeing you. I now wish he had gone on to Washington (as he was much tempted to do when he got to Charleston & found you had not come on) but he feared you would not approve of his doing so. We have much cause to be proud of our dear Butler. He is a fine high souled fellow. I had a most affectionate letter from Lord yesterday. He was anxiously expecting to hear of your being in N.Y. I hope when he returns to N[ew] H[aven] he will be able to resist company & accomplish what he was sent there for, a good education. Miss Picot seems disposed to remain longer with us if her mother will consent. The price is great—but the advantage to the children—especially Georgia & Florence is of no small importance. She is a lovely character.

Our dear H[annah] Page & her little ones are pretty well. She is still nervous & complains of pain in her chest. William is fat & hearty—working hard for but little pay. G[eorgia], F[lorence], M[allery], V[irginia], F[loyd], & T[ip] are able at all time to eat their full allowance. Poor G[eorgia] has not grown taller but she is all my fond heart can desire her to be in character. She seems to have the good will & admiration of all who know her. She is a dear sweet child. Florence is improving in every respect. Malley is as fat as ever. He is very affectionate & obedient to me. Virginia is a little vixen—but smart & has her good points. Floyd is still old rough & ready. Ready at all time for hard work or hard knocks. Our youngest boy, dear little Tip, is pretty much the same. You will find your grandchildren much grown—Willie much improved—he dearly loves me. I believe he is my pet—tho' I cannot throw Anna aside & little Bell will claim her share of notice. Mrs Gale is often sick poor dear old Mammy—she is always trying to console me & find excuses or reasons for your silence or delay. The servants all say "they have dreamed about you so long all for nothing."

The Bishop has been on the Island he preached on the 3d & 4th & gave us most excellent sermons. I had attended Church the Sunday before he came so you see I was at Church three times in one week. Mr Brown is more prosy every time I hear him. He did manage to read the service a little louder when the Bishop was present. The Bishop called to see us on the evening of the 3d. I was enabled to give him some fine strawberrys & then he went over our flower garden—& made many pretty compliments on its beauty &c. He says if he can find some one to take charge of them he will (in the Autumn) send me a great many cuttings. This will be so much clear gain. I wish you were here to see how very pretty the garden now is. We had quite a storm of rain & hail one night last week. When it began to hail my first thought was the flower garden—but very soon that was forgotten in consideration of the cotton & corn. It did not last long, & to my astonishment the next morning I found it had not done the slightest injury either here or at Newfield.

We had some frost last week which killed some of the cotton. I believe all is going on pretty well on the plantation. I fear I have committed a great error in not having the cotton sooner in market. I was advised not to ship early as the prices in April would be higher than sooner. Only 27 of white and 3 of stained were sent early—that sold at 30 & 11 c[ents]. I sent on 55 bags the first of this month & now the price is fallen. God! help me! I am always trying to do for the best & am ever doing wrong.—

Have you yet written to Andrew? I shall write to Louisa by the *Isabel* on the

15th. As it is so uncertain this reaching you I will conclude—as I have yet to write to Lord & Louisa by this Mail. All send love & regards to you. The servants beg to be remembered. Praying Gods! choicest blessing on you my dearly beloved husband I am devotedly your

A M King

The paper is so thin & I have no envelopes. I am so wasteful as to send two sheets.

1. When King had left Washington for California ten months earlier, Whig party members from both the North and the South agreed that California should be admitted to the Union. Since then, the question of whether California was to be admitted as a slave state or a free state had divided southerners and northerners in Congress. President Taylor wanted the people of California to decide, as set forth in the constitution they would soon submit. However, both Whigs and Democrats charged that Taylor had attempted to influence that decision by sending Thomas Butler King to California. On his return, King was immediately embroiled in the controversy, although he denied having received instructions from the president or his cabinet and insisted that he had made no attempt to influence the people of California concerning their decision. See Steel, *T. Butler King,* 76–81.

June 23, 1851, to May 16, 1852

You did not go North to visit—see sights—or eat dainties—you were sent there to finish your education.

T. B. King traveled once again to California, and this time he took Butler as his assistant. The family was further separated when Mallery was sent to school near New Haven, and Georgia, Florence, and Virginia attended Mr. Picot's school in Philadelphia. Anna worried constantly about the safety, health, and well-being of her far-flung family. As always, she wrote regularly to all her "dear absent ones" of all that concerned those left at home and those away.

Retreat 23d June 1851

My dearly beloved Mallery

I thank you my good son for your affectionate letter of the 13th. But for your consideration I should not have heard from any of you beloved ones at the North. I had a very kind letter of the 14th from Mrs Jaudon—which (but for your letter) was calculated to make me uneasy about your sisters—as she expressed much uneasiness at their not arriving by the morning train from New Haven to New York.[1] I required letters to cheer me yesterday—the papers are full of a terrible fire which has destroyed Millions of dollars of property in San Francisco—among the other buildings the Custom house. I see many hotels have been burnt & I very much fear your beloved Father & brother were among the many who were without shelter that night.[2] I dread the next account we shall get. I know on such an occasion as that—that neither your Father or Brother would shrink from giving every aid in their power. Oh! God! grant they may be safe & well.

It gives me pleasure to find that you my dear boy have some idea of the sacrifice I have made of my own comfort & happiness for your good. Keep this in remembrance my beloved. Remember that this sacrifice is made *entirely* for your own good—And tho' to see my children ornaments to the family will give me happiness still the good will result to your own self. Remember all I have tried to instill in your Mind. I need not repeat—& God! will bless all your endeavours to do right.

83

I am sorry that your sisters staid so short a time in New Haven as Mr Picot's holydays is so near it was scarce worth while their hurrying on to Philadelphia. I[t] was kind of Adele to go to New York to meet them. I wish I could have been in a corner to peep at you & dear Appy spending your quiet evening together. Dear Appy I feel very much for her—for there are many rough corners in her disposition which will have to be smoothed off by her intercourse with strangers. And dear Florence—how did she seem to like New Haven. As to dear little Georgia she never loses her self possession. I am sure dear Lord had reason to be proud of such sisters. Your Sister has had but one letter from William— writing the day he arrived in New York. We shall be expecting him home by the last of this month. I hope he will be pleased with his trip. It was a great relief to me his going with your Sisters—& your dear Sister being with me at this time is a great comfort.

We are all in our usual health except Mrs Gale. Poor old woman she suffers very much with her leg—& it will be a long while before she can walk again.[3] She has indeed been singularly unfortunate. Poor Hannah is much better & is able to help in the pantry again but she will never be well again. The weather for the last week has been really stormy—the rain was very acceptable—but the wind did some harm to the corn. My poor pigs feared [sic] badly. I have lost no less than 21. You see they were pretty poor—& the cold rain & wind just put them out of their suffering. I hope now the grass will grow & thus keep the others as well as the poor cattle & horses from starving to death. A vessel put in here after the wind subsided—with the loss of one mast—her bow [?]—yawl— &c. She was loaded with cotton from Savannah bound to New York. I think as she had not cotton on deck they must have thrown over the deck load. She could only carry one sail—& is gone the inland route to Savannah. Last week a rattle snake struck the finest ox we had & killed him in a few minutes.

On Sunday—(yesterday) I attempted to go to Church. Anna, Willie, Tip & myself in the carriage Floyd on Rocket—when we got near there we met Mrs Caters & Miss Armstrongs carriages. The ladies told me Mr Brown was sick & there would be no Church. So we turned back & pearing that Miss Mary Gould had arrived we call'd in to see her. She is by no means as fat as when she left us 25 months ago. She asked very kindly after all of you dear absent ones. Mr Bourke went on a pleasure trip to Florida last Wednesday in the *Welaka*— they had terrible weather for it. He took Middleton[4] on with him & about an hour ago the boat past here on its return to Savannah. They had a band of music on board (Middletons fiddle makes a part of it). The boat came near in & with the glass I could see Middleton playing—the tune they play d was "Oh! Susannah." It only served to make me feel more melancholy. It reminded me of each & every one of you absent ones.

I am very much obliged to Mr Russell for that new rule of his. If you could only compare the two letters—the one he saw & the one he did not see—you would be surprised at the difference in the spelling. Do dear Malley try & correct your spelling. It will be a little hard at first—but soon you will find it come[s] quite easy. I shall write to Lordy by this same Mail—therefore will not charge you with any message to him. I am glad his spirits are so good—you must give my compliments to Mr Russell.

I have a pair of canary birds—& Floyd and Tip are trying to raise three doves—we are going to try and raise a number of birds—for *my* amusement. Miss Anne Cater from one pair of canaries had raised 12 young ones this year—when the other night a cat got into the cage & killed the old Mother & father & 7 young ones. It must have been very trying to Miss Annie—they have still 7 canaries left. I fear I shall not be so successful with mine.

I sent yours and Lords hats to Mr Bourke who got Mr John Cunningham to take charge of them—I hope you have got them safe & that you like them. Mr Henry Floyd send them to you as *presents*. I would rather have paid for them.

I hope you will be able to read this scrawl. I have not had time to write as carefully as I usually do to you. Floyd would have gladly written to you could I have spared the time to help him. I have written twice to members of Stephen Kings family & have received no answer. I do not wish to write again—but if I can find out where D[aniel] Lord is staying I will inform you. Your Sister—Floyd, Tip, Anna, Willie, Isabel, King,[5] Mrs Gale all send much love & kisses to you. The servants all beg to be remembered to you. Praying the choicest blessings of God! on you my own beloved Malley—I am as ever

Your devoted Mother
A M King

1. Earlier in the month Florence, Georgia, and Virginia had traveled with their brother-in-law, William Couper, to New Haven, New York, and then to Philadelphia to attend Mr. Picot's school. Evidently, Adele Picot's mother did not want her to remain any longer with the Kings and Anna was determined to continue her daughters' education. Butler wrote his mother in July, "You cannot realize the joy I felt to see how well you bore the departure of the *girls*— . . . As to Father's opinion of G[eorgia] F[lorence] & V[irginia]'s going to Philadelphia—give yourself no uneasyness—the uneasyness it would *cause you* was the only objection in the minds of eather of us—the very great advantage it will be to them *all*—especially Georgia and Florence is *incalculable*—and as I wrote Sister it is the best step that had ever been taken in the education *of any of us*" (Thomas Butler King Jr. to Anna Matilda Page King, July 1851, TBK, SHC).

2. On May 11, 1851, Butler, who was working for his father in San Francisco, wrote to Anna of the fire:

The papers . . . will be full of it—but no one who was not here at the time can have the most remote ideas. The flames broke out about half past ten—or eleven oclock on the night of the third of this month—and by daylight of the next morning—as much property was destroyed as was in the great fire of four or five days in *New York* all most the whol City was in ashes in six hours—oh! what a cite it was—Father very unfortunately had just left that afternoon to go up into the country for a day or two—the first time he has been away for an hour in months—I saved all the important papers of the Custom House—and I had the money down in the vault—but whilst I was attending to the papers at the Custom H—the fire spread all over town and burned the Hotel at which we were stopping—and if it had not been for one of the porters of the *C.H.* who happened to see the house must burn we would have lossed every rag of clothing we had as it was I lossed a bout half I had—But one good thing is there are thousands and thousands worse off—there were hundreds burned to death—the fire came upon them so quickly—that though they knew it was coming they had not time to escape—I came very near being in the same fix—for the steps (that is stair case) were all on fire when I came out of the Custom-House—I got a little burned but I had put some buckets of water by me and after doing all I could I threw the water over my self put my hat over my face and made a rush—after all that when Father came he *found a great deel of fault* because I did not do more—when every one here knows how I acted—well he was not here—so he knows nothing of what a fire in this climate is—when every thing is as dry as tinder at this season of the year—and the wind blows a gale every evening—why even the strong brick blocks that every one thought would stand fire—went like so much trash—the wood on the inside was so dry it would burn from the heat of the wall—But I will leave this subject as I can give you no idea of what has taken place—I only know it has made me ten years older in the ways and things of this world of sin and trouble—I am afraid you will see an account of the fire in the papers before you get this letter—and be uneasy for fear F[ather] D[avy]—or I have been injured so I will write to N.Y. to have you telegraphed to announce our safety. *Oh! My own Dearest* Mother how I did wish for you the morning after the fire when I had been working all night nerely burnt to death—had no place to go to—(for every respectable hotel is gon) and feeling sick and worn out I thought if I only could have you or one of the girls to rub my head—though I did have a very pretty young Lady to do the same thing—but I dont love her—. (Thomas Butler King Jr. to Anna Matilda Page King, May 11, 1851, TBK, SHC)

3. Anna wrote to Lord on June 13 that Mrs. Gale had fallen that morning and broken the small bone of her left leg but asked that Anna not tell Georgia about it. Anna Matilda Page King to Henry Lord Page King, June 13, 1851, TBK, SHC.

4. Middleton, born December 2, 1827, was Clementine's son and is listed as number 106 on the 1839 list, number 92 in 1853, and number 31 in 1859 (see appendix 2). It is unclear why he would have been traveling with Mr. Bourke.

5. Butler King Couper, born in 1851, was the fourth child of Tootee and William Audley Couper. He was also called King, Kooney, and Cooney.

No 14 in all   Retreat 14th July 1851

My beloved my own Florence

I have just finished writing a long letter for Mrs Gale—addressed to you three dear girls & adding a postscript to it from myself to dear Georgia—I wrote her a long letter beginning on Friday & ending on Saturday the 12th. Yesterday was sacrament Sunday—I desired to partake of that solemn & most holy ordinance. So when I met Charles[1] on our way to church & saw how rich I was in letters—I would *not suffer myself to read those from Philadelphia*—fearing they would be as distressing to me as the ones I had received last Wednesday from G[eorgia] & V[irginia]. I wished to be in Charity with all. I read dear Lord & Malleys letters up to the 7th July found that they were well had Mr Bourkes long & kind letter—one from Mrs Houston—one from Mary Floyd. I did not let go from my grasp your dear letters for more than a few minutes at a time all the while I was in church—but did not break a seal until I got back home & in Mrs Gales room when I first read for her your affectionate letter—and then one after another until I got through all of them. I am thankful to God! my own precious child to find that you are rather improving in health—I am also thankful to perceive you are trying to think better of matters & things at No 15. I can only hope as time wears on you will not only improve in health but be more reconciled to the great difference between that spot & your own dear home. You cannot more ardently desire to the return to us than we do to have you with us again. Could you take a peep at us you would scarce realize it to be the same family.

We are very *still* here. Miss E[u]phemia [Cunningham]—the little boys & myself look very unlike the large happy family who so lately surrounded the family board—But my child I could bear this painful as it is could *I think the end for which we are separated would be accomplished*—I wish you would tell me exactly how you employ your long & lonely days. I fear my beloved ones—there are too many precious hours wasted in "crying over spilt milk." I was grieved beyond expression by your letters up to the 29th June. I even mentioned in my letters to your Father and brother how unlike what I had expected was your treatment at No 15—I am now sorry that I did but really *your Sisters* seemed so very unhappy I could not keep silence on the subject with your Father & dear Butler. Your last letters are much more moderate and I cannot *but hope* you will go on improving in your likes until in a short time you will find it *bearable*. When I think how Adele was treated by *us all* I cannot but contrast our treatment of her with that of her family of you my precious ones. It is hard my poor Flora to increase your appetite by bitters then give you "2 little dry crackers" to satisfy your hunger. You should eat more at meals—I hope they do not stint you there too. As to the *sheets.* That is quite a Yankee notion of economy of labour & money. Tho' I never knew this cunning of *changing sheets*—I believe in boarding houses—*not Hotels* one pair of sheets is allowed every week when two persons sleep in one bed, for a *single bed*—the sheets must remain on 2 weeks. Adeles sheets were changed regularly *every* week—neither did I count the pieces she sent into the wash. I pay for your washings—hers was done gratis. But let us drop the subject. So long as your health improves—so long as they improve your education—I will try & bear our separation.—

I have written to you in my letter of the 4th of July about money matters. I can only hope the amount I had in Mr Jaudons hands may not have been swallowed up in his failure. If that is safe you will have the means to go to your Uncles with dear Malley—And whilst he is with you you will I trust be a little happier. We are the *creatures of circumstances*. Therefore on circumstances our separation depends. I can only hope & pray that when we do meet again it will be in *health & happiness*. You must try my beloved child to give satisfaction—not only in your lessons—but in your general deportment—And be as prudent in your correspondence with the *Grants* as you have been with *me*—you talk a little plainer to Mrs Gale—I have been surprised to see how much more *guarded* you have been than *Georgia* & Appy. I would be *pained* if I thought you were not perfectly open & candid with *me*. It is your duty to tell me all that concerns yourselves but you cannot be too guarded in your conversation or correspondence with others—which ever of you wrote to the Grants—they have *published it to every one who go near them*—They will keep no *secret for you*. Do my own dear Florence be careful of what you say.—

On Sunday when we got near the fork of the road it came on to rain powerfully—Floyd had to get into the carriage—it saved him very little. We had to ride up to the church door & got our feet & skirts quite wet even then. It soon ceased raining after we got into Church—but when we were returning we rode through a number of puddles of water—the rain did not reach the Village or extend to Mr Goulds. It seemed so strange to ride through water over a solid road & then so soon get into dust & deep dry sand we really require the rain— I was therefore sorry that we got none. I had a long letter from dear Malley & a longer one from dear Lordy—he had just had a letter from your beloved Father up to the 30th May. He and dear Butler were at that time quite well. It will be terrible if the $2,000 he sends Lord has been lost by *Mr Jaudons failure*. The second $1,000—was sent in case the first had not reached Lord—Only one intended to be used by Lord. Dear Lordy is so elated by his prospect of visiting Europe—It will be a great dissapointment if he can't now go—but let me hope for the best.

Mary Floyd has been quite unwell Rosalie has I suppose answered your letter. I am sorry G[eorgia] has not written to Mary—M really I believe sincerely loves Georgia—her love is entirely *disinterested*. Mr Bourke says he has forwarded Georgias letter to Sarah[2] who with Kate & Eugenia Dubignon are in the Up Country—Mr Bourke says "I met Dr. Delaroche this morning who told me his daughter had barely life in her. She has a baby of a day or two old"—Mrs Delaroche is also with her poor suffering daughter. I deeply feel for her. Rhina was at Mrs Armstrongs yesterday & says the 2 *Miss Northups are going to leave Mrs Cater on Friday next for good.* How hard it is to have a child educated in this part of the world. Well has Mrs Houstons sister called to see you yet? Sarah H—says she expected her sister to call & see you—How kind of you my own Florence to be satisfied to remain without your sister—that she may enjoy a day & night at Dr Mitchels—I think you should have first been taken there—as your health requires it most. I rather think both you & dear Appy drew back when it came to the point—you must try to get over that feeling of yours—you lose much innocent enjoyment by it. I am deeply indebted to Dr Mitchel for his kindness to all of you. Your dear Father will in some way reward him for it.—

Poor Black is now Brown—I will try & get you a piece of his rusty locks. The horses all look miserably. They miss poor *Alic.* I shall not enjoy a fig this season—they are now very fine everyone says—The melons have not been good—the grapes promise well. If I can get any thing to preserve I will send you some *if* you think it will not give *offence.* I am glad to see from Miss Picots letter that you have received you[r] box. I hope her baggage has reached Philadelphia by this—I have written twice to Mr Anderson about it. Lord speaks of seeing you in three weeks from the date of his letter which was dated the 7th Inst. I hope it will be a *drop* of sweet in your tasteless cup—But my children you should not have *leisure* to be lonley. *It is only at night when I cannot see to read or write that I feel my* loneliness. Do as I do—occupy your mind & read—write —practice any good employment that is improving to you. You did not go North to visit—see *sights—or eat dainties*—you went there to *finish your education.* When Miss Picot gets back tell her plainly your 2 *crackers are not enough*— They would not have satisfied her here as lunch. If she is with you—tell her I thank her for her letter & will answer as soon as I can—You must be careful that no one gets hold of my letters but yourselves. By the way Ann Cater— begs you for your Daguerreotype—you can get it taken for her if we have the means. Tootee has the three single ones taken of you—Georgia & Appy in Savannah—I will give Amanda the group taken in Savannah—if I can get one taken in Philadelphia of *you Mal & Appy.* That of Lord & Georgia is fine—I still have two of my beloved Butler.—

I am sorry that I did send you on so early—but you know I could not do otherwise I could not let you be exposed to the danger of getting fever—neither could William have gone with you in August. The servants send you all a thousand blessings—Miss E[uphemia] C[unningham] sends her love. Your little brothers send kisses—Floyd says he will soon write to dear Appy. You must each one kiss the other for me. I have not seen Tootee since they all dined here on Saturday last. I must now stop my own precious Florence—May God! bless you my *own* darling child. Cling close together you three dear lambs of one fold & I trust God will mercifully restore you to your devoted mother

A M King

P[?] According to your request I send the letters you ask for—Tho they are not with the postage.

1. William Page's will lists a Charles as number 19. On the list of "50 Negros with Their Increase" Rose's children are recorded as Charles, William, Caesar, and Norton 2d. Charles is number 108 on the 1839 list, birthday October 6, 1818; and number 91 on the 1853 list, birthday May 1818. See appendix 2.

2. Sarah Bourke, the daughter of Henri and Anne Du Bignon, was married to Captain Thomas Bourke.

Retreat, 21st July 1851

[To Mallery]

Thank you my dear affectionate & attentive son for your letter of the 11th Inst. I wish you could have mention'd Lord, he is the only one of you 5 dear ones that I did not hear from yesterday. I have not yet received the letters which I know your dear Father & Brother wrote to me by the Mail of the 1st of June—And I have heard through their letters to Lord—yourself & to Mr Bourke that they were well at that time—and though this relieves me of anxiety—Still I wish I could get my letters. I can never tire in reading their affectionate expressions of love for me. I would their letters could come more regularly & more direct.

I suppose by this time it will have been *decided* whether Lord goes to Europe or not. It seems like a troubled dream to me his ever having thought of going. I know that I am very weak in many ways—I am particularly so when any of my beloved ones is exposed to the danger of the seas. I feel most miserable when I know you are on the water. Though I know that the kind providence which watches over you when under the same roof with me—has equal care & mercy over you whether you travel by land or water—still I feel different. I pray constantly for you beloved ones—m[a]y my prayers be granted. Lord has never told me of his arrangements *particularly*. If he goes—*I hope he will see that you will want for nothing that he can have you provided in.* And you my darling boy will have no one *to look to for guidance but your God!* Pray to Him my own dear Malley—Pray to God! to be your guide to bless all your endeavours to do right —for strength to resist all temptation to do wrong. If you pray (*really desiring His Heavenly guidance*)—rest assured you will receive the assistance you need

& pray for. Remember my beloved son—that tho your dear Father & Mother cannot *see your acts—do not hear your words—do not know your thoughts*—That our great God! *sees—hears—knows! sees all you do—hears all you say & from him no secret thought can be hid.* This is wonderful but not less wonderful than *true*.[1]

Tuesday 22nd

I had just got to this length when I saw dear Tootee—& all the children with Wm driving up in their carriage. They were all well—before they left us Miss Mary Gould came. She staid until 10 oclock so I had no time to continue my letter last night. Cousin Amanda would not let me write last night & played me an ugly trick this morning—I slept soundly & she would not wake me until breakfast was ready—now between company last night & sleeping late this morning I am crampt for time & cannot write either to you or to the dear girls as long letters as I would wish. I accompanied your cousin to visit Mr Hazzard & Miss Gould last Thursday—I also stopt to see Mrs Tom Armstrong who was quite sick.

Cousin Amanda leaves us in two days & has promised to return here on the 2nd week in August—Mr Woolley only remained one day with us. He has to go to Savannah on the 15th August to receive the *Planter* the new accommodation boat. We are all looking for the arrival of this boat with impatience. We find the present boats so unaccommodating they will land nothing but passengers nearer than Old Town.[2] Our ice comes to us all melted. I shall miss my dear Cousin very much.

I saw by the last papers that poor Mr Frost has been killed in a duel & have heard that Capt Henry Clark last week killed a man in St Marys & has run off. I hope my son you will learn to control your angry passions. It would be an awful thing for you to be killed whilst in a passion or for you to kill a man from passion. Try my boy *to govern yourself.*

Mrs Gale is getting on Slowly. Your dear little brothers are quite well— They are trying to raise birds—they work hard for them but the poor things will die. Mr Dunham went to see his mother last week—I was fearful the negros would injure his monkey & had it brought to the house—Master Jack is a very *dirty fellow.* I would not have him to take care [torn] his tricks amuse for a short time—but it soon become[s] [tire]some. Jack has taken a great liking to me & to Maria [torn] cann[ot] [torn] Amanda or Rhina—neither can they [torn] him [torn] [to]uch them.

We have been suffering for want [torn] rain but yesterday we had a very fine one. The figs now in full season—they brought in a *bushel basket full* of perfectly ripe ones this morning. Oh! how I wished I could have set the basket before you, Lord, G[eorgia], & Appy—dear Florence does not like figs. The grapes are fast ripening. I am now shingling the Old House—It makes no little noise & dirt.

I have yet to write to your sisters & must close this hasty scrawl. I wrote to Lord yesterday. Cousin Amanda & Mrs Gale join your little brothers in much love to you. The servants all beg to be remembered. May God! bless you my beloved son is the constant prayer of your devoted Mother

A M King

1. Anna had double-underlined beginning with "God! *sees* . . . " to the end of the paragraph.
2. I am unable to identify Old Town.

Retreat Thursday evening
7th August 1851

My dearly beloved Flora

I would follow your advice my own dear child & write to you but once a week had I received your promised letter yesterday—I try to think "all is well" with you beloved ones—but still my anxious fears will prevail—I had looked forward to the Mail yesterday for some thing to cheer me but I got nothing but bad news paper news. I see there has been another great fire in that devoted City San Francisco. The telegraphic account is very short—& no particulars mentioned—I am dreadfully anxious about your beloved Father & brother.—

I have not yet heard whether my beloved Lord went to Europe or is yet in N.Y. I feel anxious about each & every one of you beloved absent ones. The weather has been excessively hot the past week & I fear you dear girls feel the heat of that city. I can only hope that the mail on Sunday may do away my apprehensions—I had more than all this distress on me yesterday—Pussy came early in the morning to tell me Liddys[1] little baby was very sick—but was better than it had been all night. As several of the other babies had had the same complaint & got over it I did not feel very uneasy—I did all I could do for it—but it *died* before dark! I am thankful it was not a grown person or a larger child—tho the little thing had grown finely & was very promising. *Nanny* lost that little boy *Henry* on Tuesday last. William is indeed unfortunate with little negros—The death of that poor little boy is not *so* much to be regretted.[2] I have not seen your sister since Monday—I have not heard from her since yesterday. I could not go over yesterday evening on account of that sick baby & Miss Gould was here too—I would have gone this evening but have been expecting Mrs Fraser & her daughters all day. Mrs Hazzard—Miles—Sarah & "Carney" were here on Tuesday evening—they took tea with the little boys & myself—Sarah told me that your little parcel to Eugenia Grant was safely received by her. I suppose you will hear from Jenny on the subject. It seems Col Hazzard sends over to Cartwrights every Saturday—by one of the servants sent—Sarah entrusted your parcel. I wrote a long letter to Adele by the Tuesday Mail—I also wrote a long letter to dear Geo & sent a draft on Mr Jaudon for $100—to enable you dear children to go out of the City if a *proper* opportunity offered. I mentioned your wish to Adele—I hope you will try & over come that shyness of yours. You possess as good talents as your Sister Georgia—It only requires to be drawn out. You must have more confidence in your abilities—Do not give way to low spirits—or despondency. Help your poor Mother to *hope* for the *best*. What would we be without hope—Hope which concerns this world—& hope which concerns the world to which we are all hastening! I think my own precious Child you seem more home sick than either Geo or Appy—Do my love try & be reconciled to remaining to finish your education. You must feel convinced that you cannot suffer as much as I do.—

Mrs Gale is still able to come down stairs—she sits at table too & is busy making a dress for herself. I gave her a fine peach this evening—she said she wished you dear girls & poor Malley only had the beautiful peaches I gathered this evening—They are nearly over. I have preserved a goodly quantity & shall send you a share—much better than those which went with the melon. Those were not ripe enough & were common peaches from Jekyl. I think our trees have borne more than 2 bushels this season of as fine peaches as I could desire. The grapes are remarkably sweet—they too are nearly over & are also the figs. The melons are still plentiful. I have given away most of the grapes. Mary Gould says she never ate finer—Old Mr Gould & Old Mrs Armstrong relish them exceedingly. I hope they will be as fine the next summer that you are home. I intend to try & get more peach trees from the North this Autumn.

One week from tomorrow & I hope my dear Cousin Amanda will be here. I know she will be delighted with her beautiful cup—Mr Woolley will not stop here on his way to Savannah. Misses Cunningham had more favourable accounts of their Fathers health poor old man I hope for his daughters sake he may be permitted to return to Savannah. He seems to be the last link which keeps that family together. I suppose you correspond with Jinny Grant & know more about them than I do—I have heard nothing *from* them since the week after you left home. I have my flower garden now in nice order—tho it has suffered much this summer from the drought. The little rankins are nearly all dead—I got old Peter to make me some frames for the roses—great awkward things they are. I have sent to New York for wire to shut in the office door & windows. My little canaries are quite well & as I have had the non pareals now 11 days & they are quite well I hope they will live. If the little negros would let the nests alone I could catch more as I did these. These which I have are the real non pariel not such as you have seen me try to raise—They are

smaller and more beautiful.[3] Mrs Wilson has raised 20 mocking birds this season & I do not know how many non pariels & other birds. Floyd & Tip have
been very unfortunate with their mourning doves & mockingbirds—They
have now 6 mocking birds & 2 Turtle doves which promise pretty well. The
fact is they are entrusted to the tender mercies of Christiann & she is a faithless little huzzy.—

It seems hard that my two last letters to you should be written when I was
under depression of spirits—I hope my beloved child I may have less cause to
be anxious when I next write. I wish you would tell me exactly how you pass
your time—do you *speak* French—practice your music? I tried one evening to
play on the piano—but my fingers were stiff & my mind was on some thing
else. When you write again tell me all about your dear brothers & about your
dear selves—you never mention Judge Mallery—has he paid you no attention? Has Harriet Hazelhurst ever called to see you? I owe Mrs Houstown a
letter—but do not know when I shall answer it. Mrs Hazzard & Sarah desire
their love to each of you. In fact whenever I see any of the neighbors they always beg me to send there love or regards to you. You seem to be affectionately
remembered by all on the Island. Poor Mrs Gale is ever speaking of "the
girls"—poor old woman I know she feels very lonely since you went away. The
servants all beg to be remembered to you dear girls and to dear Malley. I feel
anxious to hear from Louisa—it appears stirring times in Cuba—God! grant
no harm may befal them—Gonzales came South in the same boat the Cunninghams did when they came in June. They said he went by some other name
& looked very worn. I have no objection to the Cubans succeeding but I do not
want any American to have a finger in the pie.—

Kiss your dear Sisters & my precious Malley for me for your little brothers
& for Mrs Gale. Tell Appy that Floyd now rides the little sorrel horse—he
seems gentle—I wish they were as earnest in learning their books as they are
in many other things—riding—bird raising &c. I must now conclude my
beloved child—I am sorry I cannot give you a more cheerful letter—I am so
anxious for all of you beloved ones. May God! bless—protect—& guide each
& every one of you my precious my beloved absent ones is the constant prayer
of your devoted Mother

AMK

My love—regards & compliments to Adele Mrs P[icot] her daughters &
Mr Picot.

8th

We are as usual this morning—I have just heard from Tootee—Miss Euphemia
& Joe Bond had fever yesterday—Miss Isa not well—our dear ones in their

usual health. I trust the next mail may dissipate the anxious fears of your poor Mother

AMK

1. Liddy, born April 15, 1823, is number 41 on the 1839 and 1853 lists. See appendix 2.

2. It is unclear why Anna would have this attitude about the death of Henry. However, it may have something to do with her son-in-law's earlier confessed sins.

3. A nonpareil is a painted bunting (*Passerina ciris*).

2nd September 1851

My own dearly beloved Flora

This being the Mail by which I must write to California I would have let this one Mail pass without bearing a letter to you—but as Tootee has not written I know you will be uneasy unless you hear how those dear little ones are getting on—And I would not have you made uneasy when a few lines (even if written in a hurry) can relieve your anxiety. I am grateful to be able to say the dear children are much better. Anna looks & is as usual—Willie has had no return of fever—& tho he looks thin & pale—still I hope he has entirely got over his attack. Isa looks badly yet—but I hope too she will now do well. King is quite well & getting to show temper *when contradicted*. Floyds arm is doing well—otherwise he is in his usual health. Tip is quite well—Mrs Gale was sick yesterday from eating too heartily of roasted duck—but is better today. Miss Isa is quite well—Miss Euphemia still with fever & very weak. My health is as usual. The negros healthy. Now is not that a pretty fair board of health? God! grant it may be no worse. There is a great deal of Catarrh fever going about. Fanny Fraser has had this fever even longer than Euphemia has—but is not so weak poor—Euphemia has not been in good health for some time. She is very low spirited too which is much against her recovery. Mrs Gales health & the sickness of Euphemia have given me much additional care "but what cannot be helped must be endured." I am very grateful that these cases are not *in my own family*. Mr & Mrs J H Couper have been sick but are better. Miss Caroline Harris & Miss Gould are sick—but not seriously so—Dr. Wilson was here last evening to see Euphemia—I hope the medicine he has ordered me [torn] do her good—I would be so glad to see her up again.—

The Mail on Sunday brought me letters from your dear Father & Butty. Also dear Georgias letter to me—& those sweet affectionate notes to Floyd from yourself—Geo & Adele—the dear little fellow was very much gratified. Tootee, William & the chicks were here on Saturday evening—were here when the Mail came & was here again last evening. When we get letters they are con-

sidered as common property between her & me—tho' I will have her give me
all of mine to keep as so many treasures.

Georgia mentioned that she had received a letter from dear Butler up to the
15th July—the same date as theirs to me—consequently I can give you nothing that will be new from them. We cannot sufficiently feel the great Mercy our
God! has shown us by having kept them that far in health & safety—From
what Butler writes me there are too many bad people in that Country. God!
protect our precious ones from harm! Yesterday my thoughts seldom wavered
from you beloved girls—It was the day for you to commence your regular
school. I some how feel most for you my Flora—you have so little *confidence in
yourself.* You must endeavour to over come this feeling my precious child—
Keep in mind how proud & happy it will make *us all* if you reap the advantages
now offered you. A few more months my beloved child & you will have left
school—and my own darling—if you live to look back on your school days you
will say & feel they were your happiest days. Rouse up now all your energy—
believe—or determine to conquer all difficulties & you will accomplish all that
is required of you. I am afraid to look forward—still I some times find my self
doing so—When I may hope to see my sons & daughters our pride—When I
shall see my three darling girls admired for their accomplishments—& es-
teemed & loved for their virtues. If life is spared us—it depends on yourselves
whether I am to be so much blessed or not. I have had you constantly in my
thoughts—& fervently have I prayed God! to open your minds to instruction—& to guide you all in the right way. You cannot my love wish to be at
home more ardently that [*sic*] I desire to have you here. If you only could know
the pain it costs me to send you away—& deprive myself of your loved presence for *your own* good you would try & gratify my fond desire for your improvement—you would try & cause me to realize my expectations. I feel now
very much for dear Malley poor boy! He is now to leave you & go among those
who care not for him. My own beloved precious boy! May God protect &
guide him. I wanted to write to him by this Mail but I doubt if a letter will now
find him in Philadelphia.

So you really saw Mrs Henry King. I am perfectly certain I wrote to inform
her when you would be able to visit her. I am nevertheless glad that you have
an opportunity of making the acquaintance of your Uncle Henry. He is a noble
minded man but is under the dominance of a Yankee wife—whose worst fault
may only be *selfishness.* I hope you will each give me your own account of the
visit. I am so sorry to hear of the failure of John King—I love him for his
kind[n]ess to dear Lord & Malley—And he would be kind to you too I think if
he could meet you. I am getting very anxious to hear from dear Lordy—I wish
he had not gone to Europe. His doing so has added much to my anxiety on ac-

count of you beloved absent ones—I try to feel & be satisfied—that he is under the same kind providence which has heretofore protected him. I can only pray this protection may be continued to him. And that the time may come when all of you beloved ones may be permitted to return to your home. Let me Oh! God! once more see all of these & beloved ones return. Let them unite with these precious ones now near me—injoining their thank giving with me to the throne of Mercy—& Oh! what words could express my gratitude my joy!!!—

Dear Georgia still begs me to get the double gowns made up at home. I have already decided it would be *better* to have them made up in Philadelphia. In the first place—I may not get the material best suited for them. Then I *will not* be able to get them cut as she wishes them—& lastly it is so difficult to get any thing sent on. *Request Mrs Picot have them made at once for you*—It would cost more than $10—for me to get the Material & send them to you & then after all they may not suit you. I shall have to send a parcel to Mally—I can send Appys dress & your bonnet then. Do provide yourselves with whatever is necessary for your comfort—I would not have you suffer for want of any thing necessary. I only beg you will be prudent & waste not. I wish you would tell Georgia—I am sorry she lost her account book but would feel easy if I could think that [this was] the only loss you girls have met with. It is difficult to get rid of careless habits you did not try to conquer whilst at home. You have felt this I am sure.

Miss Armstrong was here yesterday—she made a call of some three hours—which played the mischief with my letter writing. Floyd says I must tell you—He & Tip & the dogs killed 2 opossums yesterday—That he has now but 2 birds & Tip has none. But as Miss Harriet Wyllys birds are all dead and Miss Susan has lost her Mocking bird—you must not attribute the loss of his to mismanagement. My birds are yet well—As mine cost money & have a whole room to themselves—it would be hard to lose any of mine. The owl will not die—He gives no trouble—but is getting in the way. Kiss your dear Sisters and dear Mall (if he is with you) for me. Floyd & Tip send you kisses—Misses C[un-ningham] send their love. Mrs Gale sends much love & thanks you over & over again for the S[l]ippers & cup. She says tell Appy the slippers are as real comfort to her & to tell the rest of you that her tea tastes as good again when drank from the cup you sent her. The servants all beg to be remembered—They say they are most dead to see you all—Poor Hannah has been laid up lately—tho poor thing she can never be well again. Give my love to dear Adele—I hope for your sake she intends taking a part in the school. I will answer her affectionate letter as soon as I can. My love to Mrs P[icot]—& her daughters & best regards to Mr P[icot]. God! bless you my own dear Flora.—

Your devoted Mother

AMK

ᴘs—You will find this letter full of errors but I cannot help it—I have not even time to read it over. The medicine Dr Wilson gave poor Euphemia has made her very weak. I would give much could I see her *better*. Isa had a letter from her Sister on Sunday telling her that Miss Newel was very *ill* in Savannah—I am sorry to hear this—she had improved so much by her stay on the Island. I am too glad she was not taken sick *here*. She would have given us all more trouble than poor Euphemia has who gives less than any other sick person I ever knew. I hope my beloved ones you may escape fever I feel very anxious about you all. God! protect you my darlings—Mrs Gale is down stairs this morning

Your own devoted Mother

ᴀᴍᴋ

Retreat 29th September 1851

My own dearly beloved Georgia

You see I have taken an extra size sheet of paper to write on—because I intend to *say a great* deal to yourself—Florence & Appy. I cannot call this a leisure day—but I am alone. I have heard Floyd & Tip spell their lessons & read one—& have permitted them to go over to Hamilton for the day. Their first visit there since Floyds accident. Yesterday Isa Cunningham, Floyd & Tip & myself set out for Church. The weather cool—bracing & beautiful. When we reached the negro houses at New Field we met Charles with the Mail. The Mail always excites us—not as it used to excite you children—but the excitement to me is most painful. And poor Isa dreaded to hear of her poor Old Father. I thank my God! I had letters or intelligence from each of you beloved ones at the North & a letter from your dear Father & Butler—My joy was *almost* full. But poor Isa received the most distressing account of her poor old Father.

The letter which they ought to have received on Wednesday got to town after the mail had left. These letters were to inform E[uphemia] & Isa that their only parent barely breathed—there was not hope of his again rallying & to hasten their going to see the last of their poor old Father. We of course turned back home. It would have grieved your tender heart to witness the distress of these poor girls. Their Father has long ceased to be a support to them. Particularly since their Mothers death—he has called for all their tender cares & attentions to smooth his downward path. This duty tho' trying to health & patience they have beautifully discharged—His death will sever the last remaining link which has so long bound that family together will be severed. These three girls will have to seek other homes—will *have to support themselves.* Just contrast their condition with yours my beloved daughters. You have never had a *real* want that was not supplied. It *has been my study from the day you were born to the present moment*—To cherish you, support you—educate you. Think how many really necessary comforts I have denied myself—Think how your devoted Father has toiled night & day to raise you to be among the first of the land—Think of the sacrifices he has made & continues to make to enable him to give you a finished education. Think of the lonely state I have reduced myself to that you my beloved ones should have every advantage of education that money can purchase. Think all this over—then ask yourselves—if you are trying to repay us in any way—for all this sacrifice of feeling & of money. This part of my letter I address more especially to you my beloved Florence & to you my dear little Appy.

In Mr Picot['s] letter of the 22nd Inst he writes this "Miss Georgia, I have every day more reason to think, is a very intelligent young lady, and I must add *of the highest promise*. She has done a great deal so far—but she might have done more not that she is not diligent enough or lacks attention and application, but simply because she is too impulsive and attends too much to things which a young lady in her position ought *in my opinion* to disregard, or neglect. Her correspondences & that of her Sisters have occupied *too much time*. They write & receive more letters than any pupils I have ever had. They have with their companions too much *frivolous* chit chat in a word there is too much waste of time. They are all, I am happy to state again, in perfect health and I begin to think that I shall now be able to require more effort, more study, from Miss Florence, who has again assured me *this very afternoon* that she is extremely well. Florence & Virginia have done very little—the former, indeed, almost nothing. The latter has, at times convinced me that she is quite intelligent, & could give great satisfaction. I am sorry to say F[lorence] & V[irginia] do not show that docility which *I know* Madam you so earnestly and frequently recommended—but my duty compels me to inform you of every thing it is important you should know, concerning your children—to enable you to co operate with me to the obtention of *our* object. PS. Please recommend to your daughters not to form any plan of pleasure or *other*, without first consulting us. I warn'd them enough against school friendships—The young ladies we have with us, are all very good, but they are all young, inexperienced & too impulsive."

This now is what your beloved Father writes to me in his letter of the 15th August. "Butler has received letters by the last Steamer from Lord & Malley—but none from Georgia, Florence, or Virginia—Pray say in your letters to them that they must write to me by every mail. There is no idea that gives me more horror in *my exile* from my family as that my *children*, for *whom I am labouring*, may forget me—I am sure, while they remained with you they would be constantly reminded of me. I hope they are all quietly at school—Our daughters must study French & Spanish! I hope Florence & Virginia will become more reconciled to their *music*, especially vocal music—I hope and *desire* that you will communicate your views & *commands* to them *constantly*. I suppose for a while they will be in a *whirl* of excitement—This will I hope soon wear off & then I trust they will be earnestly engaged in the *business* of education. Now is the time for them to improve and I hope if it pleases Heaven I am permitted to return I may find them all my fond heart can desire."

It almost sickens me to repeat over & over the same lesson to you dear children. If it would do you any good I would write my eyes out in giving advice— But I am almost discouraged. You my Georgia seem to be making an effort to improve in your book learning—will you not try to improve *in every* other respect? Do so my precious one—& you will have a sweet reward, *that of an approving conscience*. In what words my own sweet Florence am I to urge you on in the path of duty! I have exhaus[t]ed every effort to convince you that we are seeking for you that—which will result to your own individual good—by sending you to school. There is nothing worth having to be gained *without labour*. You are now 17 years old. You have a mind capable of improvement if you will only exert its powers. You have now every opportunity to do so. If you will but try I am certain you will succeed. Do not abuse the gifts of God! by giving way to your indolent habits. If you will exert yourself for the sake of your fond parents—sisters & brothers—surely you will for your own sake. Look at Miss Eliza Dubignon—the Fraser girls—& others that I could name. They had not as many advantages as we have given you—still had they improved those they had how different—how much happier and more attractive they would be. If you can do nothing else you can be *docile*.

Now my little Appy why cannot you at all times give satisfaction to your teachers? Why disappoint my fond hopes—why make my poor heart bleed. You are now old enough to know right from wrong—did you ever feel *happier* for being *idle*—*disobedient* or *saucy*? I am sure you never have. Why then do you ever commit either of these faults?[1] Now my beloved children in giving you advice in giving you opportunities to obtain an education—Whose good do I seek yours or my own? It is true my fond heart would be gladdened could I see my beloved children all it desires them to be—still the real benefit will be yours alone. Do not blame Mr Picot for writing me that letter—he was only doing *his duty*. I am satisfied he is only seeking to make you—what he knows we desire you to be. I have entreated of you to be cautious in forming school *intimates*. In rearing you dear girls I have endeavour'd to make you *virtuous*, *pure minded*, *pious* girls. I believe you to be the first—The second can too soon be contaminated by an impure associate. To sum up the whole be diligent to improve—be respectful and obedient to your teachers. Keep ever in mind the

object for which I have sent you to No 15. I did not send you there for pleasure—but for profit—a wealth once obtained—none but God! can deprive
you of. Do not my beloved give me occasion again to remind you of all this—
I have already in my former letters—desired you would never attempt accepting an invitation or going any where without first consulting the opinion &
consent of Mr & Mrs Picot. They are as responsible for you whilst at No 15—
as I am when you are under my guidance. I feel satisfied Mr Picot is *deeply interested in your* welfare—neither will he (at fitting times) debar you of innocent
enjoyment.

Now as to your too many correspondents. I have thought you spent too
much of your present valuable time in writing letters—I wish you to abridge
the number. As great happiness as it is to hear from *each of you once a week*—I
will consent to receive but 1 *from one of you (a week)* then every two weeks you
can write one of you to Tootee—twice a month you *must all write to your dear
Father & one or the other of you to dear Butler.* One write to Lord the other to Malley once every *two weeks.* I *decidedly recommend* you dropping for the present *all*
other corespondents—your reasons cannot give offence to your friends—even
if it did—better offend them *than disappoint the fond hopes of your noble Father* &
devoted Mother! Could you see the anguish these dear Cunninghams are suffering at parting with their only parent—you who have so devoted a Father so
devoted a Mother would try to give them all the happiness you can whilst we
are doing so much for you. If you do not—bitter will be your regret *when we
leave you*!!

Your Sister invited me to dine with her today—but independent of its being
writing day—Mrs Gale is very unwell & I have two very sick negros—I felt it
my duty to remain at home. It is a long time since I have been at Hamilton &
the day was so inviting. The weather is cold enough for blankets on our beds
& fires morning & evening—real beautiful Southern Autumnal weather. Such
weather as this when my mind is distressed—but adds to my misery—all nature seems to be smiling on the nothingness of man. Yesterday at this time I as
little expected a death on the place as it was possible for poor human nature to
be sure of life. After this hour Pussy told me *Allen*[2] was sick & she wanted flax
seed to make him tea. After Tootee went away I thought I would just walk up
& see him. I found him exceedingly ill—I did all I could for him, poor little
fellow, but of no avail, he is gone. I trust to a happier home. It seems we are not
to be rich in negros. But it is Gods! will & I try to be resigned!!! We have been
so bless'd with health among the negros. I had hoped death was far away! but
it too frequently happens it is at our door when least we expect it. I am thankful to God! it is not worse—A little negro died at Hamilton last night. I think
Allen's sickness was caused by green groundnuts. They have been making such

havoc in my patch I would not wonder if more suffer by them. Hamilton Couper returned home on Saturday night last his eyes are yet in a bad way. It was Isa['s] & my intention to go to the North end this week—I shall do so in a few days if I possibly can leave home. I believe they are all doing very well all getting well—The Wyllys are still at the Point—Miss Gould was here on Friday evening last. She told me she had been dreaming of you three girls. I hope Wednesday may *bring me* another letter from our dear Lordy. Tootee & the children are to spend tomorrow with me. I would I could have made this a cheerful letter my dear child but I feel it my duty to offer you the best advice in my power. Try & persuade your dear Sisters to do better. Kiss them both for me. Your brothers send ¹/₂ bushel of kisses—Mrs Gale a goodly number. The servants all beg to be remembered. God! bless & guide you in all things is the prayer of your devoted Mother

AMK

Poor *Fly* was killed by a snake on Friday night last.

[Enclosed]

30th September 1851

My own dear Poya

    I have again searched for a Heliotrope flower without success. I send you a sprig of the plant & a lemon leaf. I wish I could press in a cluster of the flowers & some of the beautiful ripe limes now on the tree. See how ready I am at all times to gratify your slightest wish my own dear Florence—Why will you not gratify your Mother by exerting yourself to learn. You & Virginia must read attentively the long letter I send today to dear Georgia—it is intended more for you & Appy than for her. I will write to you by the Friday Mail. We are as usual today. The sick negros are reported rather better—Kiss your Sisters for me. My regards to Mr Picot & love to Mrs P[icot] & her daughters. All here send love kisses & Huddys to you beloved ones

Your devoted Mother
AMK

1. Appy's daughter, Florence Marye, recalled that

Georgia was an earnest student and law-abiding; Florence, no student at all and sadly homesick. My mother, little thirteen-year old Virginia, so intellectually precocious she kept her teachers on the jump, was so naughty she nearly drove them crazy. Once, given as punishment the copying of an appalling number of moral precepts, she instead wrote in flawless French a witty and slightly scurrilous romance involving the old gentleman next door, Mademoiselle, and that good stout lady's father confessor. No one dared lay a hand on her in punishment, as at the first move she would begin screaming "I'm going to have a fit; I'm going to have a fit!"; and if not heeded, she threw such convincingly faked convulsions that the uninitiated sent hurriedly for a doctor and even the most hardened were left undecided what to do. Such a tomboy that she was nick-named "Tommy," neither the long-suffering Picots, ruffled hoops, nor ruffled pantalets kept her out of the sacred tree tops of the City of Brotherly Love. (*Story of the Page-King Family*, 56)

2. Allen does not appear on any of the lists in appendix 2.

Monday 14th October 1851

My dearly beloved Florence

I fear I shall not be able to write as long a letter this time as I desire or as you are entitled to—but when I tell you all I have to do & to think about I am sure you will think I have done well even to write so much. In the first place let me through you thank thank [*sic*] dear Adele for her affectionate letter—dear Geo for her short hurried one & Appy for hers to Mrs Gale & the boys. Yesterday I received one of your dear Fathers hasty letters—but I was glad even for that—he said Butler was writing me a long letter by the same mail (up to the 1st September) but that letter has not yet come to hand. Your dear father said nothing about health—but as he did not speak of sickness I am allowed to hope they are well.

In reply to dear Georgias *very* earnest request that I should immediately write to Mr Picot & request his indulgence during the stay the Grants may make in Philadelphia—I expressed my opinion very candidly in my letter to her by the last Friday mail. The Grants past Hamilton on *Friday*—having taken the boat a[t] Brunswick & on Sunday after I received a letter from Jinny—saying she had just received a letter from Florence "in which she begs me to write to you immediately & be[g] you to let them stay with us *if* we go to Philadelphia. I mean by we Fanny, Dr Troup & myself—Fanny is to leave L'Pool on the 20th of this month. If Fanny *possibly* has time she will certainly go to see the girls." It would not be the entire loss of two days (as Jinny says "we will not remain longer than 2 days in Philadelphia") that I value as much as the *impression those two days will leave on your minds.* I would of course wish the desire you feel to see Fanny & Jinny gratified—but your staying two days with the Grants at a Hotel seems not what your Father would approve of. If *Mr & Mrs Grant* were of the party it would *alter* matters. Oh! my beloved girls if you could only appreciate the deep all absorbing desire I have for your *entire* welfare you would not ask me to do that *which may not be right* or force on me the pain of refusing your request. Georgia [asks] only to be allowed to stay with the Grants those hours not devoted to study. This seems more reasonable. I will leave it to *your discretion* and to Mr Picots prudence. If he thinks you can afford to lose the time to be all day with the Grants—I will not object. If you will make up your minds to let this indulgence have no bad influence on your minds so as to distract your thoughts from your studies—I will not object. Before you go further read this part of my letter to Mr & Mrs Picot & consult them on the matter. I very much fear you are letting the possibility of meeting the Grants occupy now too *much of your thoughts.* I am sorry *they* have gone in your way. I have had *some experience* of this influence Fanny exercises over Georgia & Jinny over you. But I will hope better things of you both. I will hope, you will not grieve your poor self sacrificing Mother by *giving Mr Picot cause to complain of* either one of you my precious children—*it goes like daggers* to my heart whenever I hear that any one of you are deserving of censure. I would have been very glad to have known when Mr Grant was going—but I heard nothing of it but through your letters until I heard that they had actually gone—for they must have left Savannah before Jinnys letter reached me. I wish you could have thought of answering my question concerning your brother Lord—I have never under stood when he expected to be back. I wish you would let me know if you can.

I am grieved to say dear little King has had fever ever since Friday—it is caused by *teething*—on Friday morning Tootee found he had two teeth & soon after she found he had fever caused by the upper teeth—the gums are much swollen. I could not go to her on Saturday because Mrs Fraser & her daughters were here—I had expected dear Tootee to spend Saturday also with me, but Kings being sick prevented her coming. And on that day I had 22 sick negros—which increased to 32 before Sunday night. Thank God the most of these have gone out to day—but some half dozen fresh hands have come in—as Pussy was of the number when so many were down I would have "gone by the head" had not Amanda been with me. Pussy is still sick—I have Sukey & Mily[1] *as nurses.* The fevers are caused by the dry weather & NE winds—all the negros seem to have colds. I am thankful it is no worse & as the wind changed today & it looks like rain I am in hopes this state of things will soon change for the better. This fever or worse type has been all over the country—we have been so free of sickness here that I really flattered myself we would escape—it is well for us it did not take place at a more busy season. Your dear Cousin went to Hamilton for this day—but returned to me this evening. Amanda the boys & myself went to Hamilton yesterday evening—We will go again tomorrow that is if I can leave the place. Mrs Gale is again about, your Cousin—your brothers & myself are in our usual health.

Mrs Fraser & her daughters leave for Goshen on Wednesday. Mrs John Demere *requires* her Mothers presence. Fanny F[raser] still looks thin. Mrs Fraser tells me that Susan has entirely recovered her health—herself & Rebecca were at Marietta when they last wrote. They now speak of going to live at Marietta—Rebecca is at this time negotiating for a house for them to live in—but you know they are always at such plans. Mrs Dr Fraser is determined to go & live in Savannah so goes the world. I would I could just run away from this place for a few months. I must say I am tired of my tread mill life. We are speaking of going to Lands end—but you know I would not leave any of the negros sick. I would not have told you so much about the sickness here—but that I have long made up my mind it was best never to hold back any thing from the knowledge of my husband or children—you must not let it make you uneasy on account of the white family—we—that is your brothers & myself *are perfectly* well and these fevers do not seem fatal. Of course I cannot no one will die of it [*sic*]—but my experience so far shows that it is not of a fatal nature. Flora² & her infant both had this cold but enough of this—I hope my next letter will give you better accounts.

I hope you have had letters from Butler dear good boy he is very attentive in writing to us. Your dear Father expresses great solicitude for your welfare this letter was written in reply to the one I told you I had written to him in *July*. The anxiety that letter gave him is I hope been removed by those I *afterwards* wrote. So if Butler wrote to you dear girls you had better be careful *that no one sees it.* He is apt to say what he thinks. I have just finished three very long letters one to your Father—1 to Butler & 1 to your Uncle Andrew. I have yet to write to Malley. Poor fellow he will have to put up with a short letter this time—I would have devoted Saturday to writing but that Mrs Fraser was here & the attention I was obliged to pay the darkies. Mrs F[raser] & Fanny begged I would give their love to you girls when I next wrote. Also Miss Armstrong requested the same—she spent the whole morning here—Cousin A[manda] did not meet her. Alic Couper expects to go to New Haven in about 3 weeks—I did not understand whether Hamilton goes on or not—you dear girls ask for cane—I would be ashamed to send you what we have this year. The joints are very short & it is as hard as ribbon cane owing to the drought. I have lost more than half the oranges—by splitting but there are still a good many on the trees. If I could have heard when Jinny was going—I would have requested her to take charge of the dress of Appys you asked me to send on & I would have sent you some preserves. As it is I must wait until the *Planter* comes on & trust to Mr Andersons sending them to you. Cousin A[manda] your little brothers & Mrs Gale send you much love & many kisses. I am particularly anxious you & Appy would make up your minds to taking singing—as well as—dancing lessons—it is your dear *Fathers* express wishes that you cultivate your voices. I will write to Mr Picot before long to know if you can spare the time from your other more necessary lessons—to attend to singing. I shall not have time to read this over—you must make allowance for all mistakes. Kiss each other for your devoted Mother

AMK

The servants all beg to be *remember'd*.—

1. Mily or Miley, appears on the 1839 list as number 196, born in 1836. See appendix 2.
2. Flora is number 283 on the 1839 list and number 78 on the 1853 list, birthday April 26, 1818. See appendix 2.

Retreat 23d October 1851

My dear Sister Florence

To convince you, *that I am better* Mother will write whilst I dictate an answer to your affectionate letters. My fever lasted 58 hours but Cousin A[manda] & Mother have allowed me to get up today. I have put on my warm clothes & as it is quite cool we have a fire in the room—my amusement all morning has been keeping this fire up with the aid of our *man Henry*.[1] Now Poya! I know that I got this fever because I disobeyed Mother but you see I thought I could bear the hot sun & have been made to suffer for my disobedience—have had to keep my bed two days—covered up in blankets drink gruel & warm teas— which I dislike almost as much as I did the castor oil—& what is worse still— I cannot run about out doors & will get no ten cents tomorrow. Now do you not think I am well punished? You seem very anxious about *Black*. I have the pleasure to inform you *he is really fat* & glossy. Mr Dunham has been indulging him a long while—how Mr Black will look when the working season is over I can't say. At any rate I hope he will not be gull'd again—Mother has purchased working collars which will I hope prevent this injury to the horses. I guess Poya when you see my Miss Kate—who is Sister to your precious Black—you will wish me to exchange with you. Kate is larger than black—better form'd & al- together better looking. I do not think you need envy us the *cane*. When I tell you that neither Floyd or *myself care for it* you may be sure it is not *worth* eat- ing. Floyd & myself are [?] trying our luck at fowls. I have 3 hens & Floyd has 6. We built a new fatning coop for Mother & have got back our old hen coop. We have no dogs but D[aniel] Lords sick *Noony*. This is bad. We miss Lion & poor Fly—not a little. Floyd will get Mother to answer dear Appys letter. If I write more he will have nothing new to say. Kiss dear Georgia & Appy & Miss Picot for me. Maria is just toasting some bread for me—I wish you were here to help me eat it. Dear Sister I want much to see you all again & hope that happy day may yet arrive to your affectionate brother

R. Cuyler King

Retreat 23d October 1851

My dear Sister Virginia

You doubtless think it is high time I should be inscribing a letter to you with my own clumsy fist but the fact is I find it a difficult matter now even to write my copies—my hand is still stiff—but it will wear off.[2] As you are looking forward to riding as one of your delights when you return home— I take pleasure in telling you that your horse is now quite gentle—paces pleasantly & with a nice new saddle & bridle you will look quite *like a young lady on him especially if you have your rough* brother Fuddy as an escort. I have been riding him since my arm got well. Tip still sticks to old Cherry. My horse is no great beauty—I can't get her fat even with my ½ pint of corn night & morning—with any one else she refuses to go ahead but as soon as I mount her she is very manageable she knows my voice so well. I call her *Rosetta*. Tip has told Poya that we are again trying to raise chickens. Your hen has turned off two broods since you left one of 5 & now 7 fine chickens—so Mother owes you for 12. If you wish I will take charge of your hens—tho' they may do best left to themselves. If you & Miss Rosalie ride out together (if you ride your horse) you have less jolting & less laughing. This evening will decide the fate of the *owl*. He will live—& it is not pleasant to kill a pet thing even if that pet is an owl. Since the corn is in a rat proof barn we do not need an owl. If Mr Brown wants it—we will give him the owl if he will send for it. Mr Brown is to be here this evening. I can find no birds to kill the feathers of which are suitable for fans. I wish I could get you & dear G[eorgia] & F[lorence] some pretty fans—to give to the ladies who have been kind to you. I have just got through my lessons for the day & feel like stretching my feet. I therefore bring my letter to a close. Mother will write you all about the sick—& how Mrs Gale is getting on. Kiss dear Georgia & Florence for me. I love you all very much. Oh! dear Appy how glad I will be if it pleases God! to permit dear Father—Butty, Lordy Malley & you dear Sisters to return safe & well once more to old Retreat the loudest noise now heard in this old house is that which the canaries make—they are singing now with all their might—kiss dear Miss Picot for me too—tell her I love her as much as ever I did.

Your affectionate brother
J Floyd King

My dearly beloved Flora!

Your brothers have filled up two pages to yourself & Appy. I must have my say now to you. I have the pleasure to acknowledge your dear letter received by yesterdays Mail. How rejoiced & grateful I am my own sweet Flora to hear that you were well & *that you are determined* to avail yourself of your present *very great* opportunities to obtain a good education. Mr Picot—I presume may be *very particular*. All I ask of you my precious child is to try your best to improve your mind & that you will try to abide with *his rules* & be *respectful in your demeanor not only to him but to his wife & daughters or any other teacher you may have.* I feel satisfied that Mr Picot *is anxious* for your welfare. How pleasant it will be to you dear girls to feel when you leave No 15, *that you deserve to be mentioned with respect & esteem by all who knew you at that house.*[3] It is quite in your power to attain this my darling children. I have been perhaps too indulgent a Mother to my children—My desire has ever been that you obey me *from love.* You must learn to obey your teachers from knowing it *to be your duty.* I do hope I may hear *no more complaints.* I am delighted to see your number is one higher—try my love to mount yet higher—I ask this for your own sakes more than for mine—because the *advantage will be to yourselves more than to me.* As proud & gratified as good reports would make me.

Our dear little Tip has himself told you that "he is up today" and I hope with care he will have no more fever. Our dear Tootee was here yesterday evening looking remarkably well & so cheerful—She promised to spend this day with us but this morning William sent to request Amanda to go over as your dear Sister was very unwell. Amanda went—I could not leave Tip for a whole day—but will go over this evening & hope before I close this letter to give you better accounts of your dear Sisters health. From what William says in his note I presume her attack is similar to those she had before you left us—& which I had hoped she was done with.

I have but one negro sick today & that one is Rhina—she has been ailing some time but would not lie up until yesterday she was oblig'd to do so. I can but hope she will soon be better. Mrs Gale is getting along better. She thinks her back is stronger—her bodily health is better than it has been a long while but [for] lameness she would be well. Poor old woman she misses you girls very much. You know I did think of giving her Floyd & Tips room—but she preferred remaining in her own & then F[loyd] & T[ip] are too large to sleep in my room & too young to be sent far away from me. In this way Mrs Gale has many solitary hours—Tho I give her all the time I can spare from my other more important duties. She said she had a long message for you—one she made up last night—but it was forgotten when I asked her, "what I should say to you, for her." One thing she does remember "that when I send you 'pelican' you will be careful never to be seen with it on your head—for fear it may bring you in trouble."[4] I hope in a week or ten days to send you the dress you want & some preserved peaches. The oranges will not be ripe for 6 weeks yet. And I fear the cane will never be any better than it now is.

I see there are dates up to the 15th September from California. Nothing being said of your dear Father encourages me to hope for good tidings when I receive his & dear Butlers letters. I hope no one will make love to Buttys letter to me this time as was the case with his letter up to the 1st Sep. I am convinced that he did write to me. I begin to give up all hope of your dear Fathers being made Senator, as by the papers I see the Democrats have carried the State of California. I try to believe "that all that is—is right." All is in the hands of a Wise Providence & I will try to submit with patience to His divine will.

Lord promised to write to all of us from Paris. I cannot feel easy about that dear son until I know he is safe back at his books. God! grant him a safe return to me once more. If his life has been spared I doubt not he has derived much benefit by his hasty tour. My dear Malley never misses a week in writing to me. You are all very attentive & I do thank you all for your frequent letters. I wish you would tell me *more of yourselves.* How do you all look? Any of you grown taller?—have you & Appy grown *straighter.* Do my Florence keep back your shoulders & tell Appy to do the same. Has my sweet Geo much colour? Tell her *beware of bad colds*—the same to you & Appy. My darlings, Malley & you dear girls did not comply with my requests about the daguerreotypes. I am not to be cheated out of them. At the same time you can have one taken for Annie Cater.

1. Henry, born February 11, 1846, is number 101 on the 1853 list and also appears on the 1859 list. See appendix 2.

2. Anna wrote to Mallery for Floyd on Tuesday, October 7, "Yesterday was the first day I have attempted to write since my arm was broken so I cannot write to you but by Mothers hand—" (Anna Matilda Page King to Mallery King, October 6 and 7, 1851, TBK, SHC).

3. Written in between these lines was "I have never treated him or his [wife] with any disrespect."

4. Unclear.

Monday 3d November 1851

My own dear Florence

I fear my own dear Flora this letter will be as hurried as the one I wrote to Georgia by the Friday Mails. But I cannot very well help myself. I had intended making up for my short letter to my precious Geo—by giving you & her an unusually long letter by this Mail—but I have yet to write to your dear Father—Butler, Lord, Malley & Mr Woolley—besides some letters of business—& have only a part of two days to do it in. I should have been made uneasy about you dear girls today—having received *no* letter from either of you—had I not received a few hurried lines from dear Adele—she not only assures me that my dear girls are well but that you had the pleasure of a few hours visit from dear Lordy. Oh! how grateful I am to hear that he has really reached the U.S. in health & safety. Praise God! for this mercy! I had also a few lines from our dear Malley. I cannot think why I did not get your letters?—for Adele says your letters had been sent to the Office before she wrote her hurried letter. Thank her for those few lines.

I gave dear Geo a hasty sketch of my visit to Cannon's Point on Thursday last. After I had sent off my letters on Friday I had then to attend to the little boys. In the evening your Sister—Wm & *all* the little ones came over. She insisted so much that we should spend Saturday with her—that we did so—going soon after breakfast your brothers preferred riding on the ponies—Neptune[1] was busy so Charles drove us over. I concluded it best to send him back—as soon as we got to Hamilton. We found dear Tootee complaining of sore throat—but the 4 little dear ones quite well. I never saw Anna, Willie & Bob looking better than they now do—& as to King—he is really a very lovable boy—so *perfectly* good—so lively he is even showing his two little white teeth. His efforts to talk are amusing he says Ma Ma & pa pa—& when any one tells him to say these words—he watches earnestly our mouth & fix[es] his lips—before he will bring out the sound. William had gone to Oatlands so we had the house to ourselves. Floyd & Tip amused the 3 children & themselves—by mending broken toys & building houses for them—Our Cousin, Tootee & myself past the day pleasantly in sewing & talking—you beloved absent ones were our especial subjects to converse about. Just when I was beginning to feel very hungry William came. We had a very nice dinner indeed—after which Wm the boys & children went out—Amanda—Tootee & myself sat down again to our needles until near sun down—When I requested the horses may be put to the carriage & in spite of all Tootee could say to the contrary I mounted the front seat—took reins & whip in hand—(Amanda occupying the back seat) & set out for home. I have not had so pleasant a drive since you left me. Cousin A[manda] told me old stories & opened the gates—I listened to her & thought of by gone days—when I was young & free from cares—when Amanda & myself used to ride alone just where ever our fancy directed. The little boys got safe home just as I was beginning to be uneasy about them—we first went up to see Mrs Gale & tell her how we had spent the day—then we had tea after which Amanda the boys & myself walked on the beach near to the light house & back home before eight o clock.

We intended going to Church today—but it was very warm & looked like rain. I had scarce got through reading to your brothers when Charles came in with the mail—I am grateful it brought me no bad news. From a letter I received from De Witt & Morgan—I learn that the *Planter* would *positively* leave Baltimore on the 1st October—which was *yesterday* you know—So I cannot expect to keep my dear Cousin longer than one week more with me. I have promised to make my visit on the *Planter*[']s second trip South which will be about the 17th Inst. This may give me a chance of hearing from your dear Father & Butler up to the 1st October. If nothing prevents—Amanda the boys & myself will go up to Hampton Point on the coming Wednesday—I am anxious to see Dr Wilsons birds—Amanda & the boys wish to see the place. In the event of our carrying through this plan we will dine at the Wyllys—or Hazzards which ever Amanda may prefer.

Before you receive this you will have met with & *parted* from the Grants & I very much fear this meeting will only have made you more home sick—you my precious Florence. I can only hope my beloved child that you now *feel the importance of an education*—that you will have the good sense to turn your whole mind to improvement. Your present *advantages are very great.* Do *not let your time be wasted.* Think dear Flo—how much pain it costs your dear Mother to be so long separated from you. Think dear girl at what a sacrifice & by what labour your dear Father makes the means to educate you dear children. I am sure when you *reflect* on all this you will *exert yourself to the utmost to improve*— You must try & learn to *speak French & Spanish with ease.* If you will only throw aside that false modesty which is so much against your success you will find you will get on much faster—never mind if you do some times make mistakes—*no one can expect you to be perfect at once*—practice is every thing. Try my own dear Flora to fulfill my fond expectations—that you will do all in your power to gain information & accomplishments. Do not let it be said when you get back "I cant see what good sending her to Philadelphia has done." Your Father particularly desires you & Appy shall learn to sing—dance—speak french & Spanish. Do not disappoint that beloved—that best of Fathers! I feel *no* fear of Georgia not doing her best to improve—my apprehension is for *you & Appy.* Do my darling child try & do your best. And rest assured my beloved child you will be all the happier if you do. I would make it my rule (if I were in your place) to speak nothing but french under Mr Picot['s] roof (unless persons called to see you who cannot speak french). I would try & obey to *the letter every rule* of the house. I would *prove* that it is not for *want of trying* that you do not give *perfect Satisfaction* to all your teachers. Try this plan for one week—at the end of that time I am convinced you will be better satisfied to try another week and so on as long as you remain at No 15. If you will do this I will *thank you my Flora.* for it will remove a great weight from my heart. Do you & dear Appy try hard to improve—Oh! do my loves.—

When I got no letters from you I was in hopes you had written to your Sister—but I fear from my hearing nothing from her this evening—that she has been no more fortunate than I have been. Had it not been for Adeles letter I would have been miserable about you dear girls. I will wait with all the patience I can muster until the Wednesday Mail. From what Butler says in his last letter to me I fear there is a very little prospect of your dear Father being made Senator—if he is not God! knows when he will return. I can only hope the happy day may arrive when *we shall all meet* again—I some times wonder how *I do bear* to be so separated from you beloved ones. I try hard to be patient—hoping all will result to the benefit of you beloved ones. It will be hard for me to suffer so much & you obtain no good! I will hope for a full reward!—

Mrs Gale is once more able to come to table. She has set her heart on going home with Amanda & I hope the change will do her good. I will just stop now & fill up this page on Tuesday morning. Hoping I may be able to say then as I now do—we are all well.

Monday morning

Whilst at supper table last night—who should walk in but our friend Mr Woolley. Mrs Gale had been talking all day about his coming—we could not drive it out of her head—that there was no probability of his so doing—but so she would have it—& so it did happen. He received notice to day that the *Planter* would leave Baltimore on the first—& would rather be in Savannah a day before she gets there than after her arrival. He will go on in the *Walaka* today—he is well & in good spirits. He says Old Steve came on in the Sunday boat young Steve & his Mother are having their portraits taken. Steves is to be full length—price $150. At the great Fare held at Macon last week a great many persons had their pockets picked among the number Mr Plant—Old Scarlett, Dr Riley—Henry Gigniliat—& Mason Tison. So these 4 last come home feeling small. This evening Wm, Tootee—the chicks & Cousin Amanda came over—they give a most laughable account of the manner in which Mr Woolley got on board the *Welaka*. The *Magnolia* came just after the *W[elaka]*—Woolley would have preferred the *M[agnolia]* but in his hurry he did not see her. In the hurry of the Capt of the *W[elaka]* to secure a passenger he run his boat on the marsh—& stuck for some minutes—but I cannot tell it as Tootee & Amanda do—so I will not attempt it. Tootee says it is now 5 weeks since she has heard from any of you. What can have become of the letters I should have received yesterday from you—but for dear Adeles hasty letter I would be very unhappy about you dear girls. I must now conclude this scrawl. Kiss your dear Sisters for your Cousin, brothers, Mrs Gale & myself. Give my love to A[dele] & her Mother & Sisters & regards to Mr Picot. The servants all beg to be remembered affectionately to you my darling girls Praying the choicest blessings on you three.—

I am your devoted Mother

A M King

1. Neptune, Neptune and Sukey's son, is number 43 on the 1839 list, birthday September 15, 1831, and number 45 on the 1853 list. See appendix 2.

Thursday afternoon 13th Nov

I have just dismissed my little school & with much pleasure sit down to have a wee bit communion with you my darling beloved Florence. I know it will rejoice your affectionate heart to hear that we are all in our usual health—all jogging on in our usual hum drum way. Little Willie was as well the next day after his attack as tho' he had had no fever at all poor little fellow it seems a difficult matter for him to keep well—he & his old ailments seem hard to be separated for good. I hope yet to get to see him as healthy as Floyd & Tip are. Our dear Cousin is still with me. She received letters from friend Woolley yesterday who says "the *Planter* got to Savannah on the 10th she fully comes up to his expectations—is a fine boat &c. The *builder* was expected to arrive in the *Planter*—but for some reasons not mentioned he did not neither had he arrived on the 11th. Mr Woolley was compelled to remain in Savannah to await the coming of this said builder (Mr Brown)—thought it possible he may arrive & all matters arranged so that the boat could leave S[avannah] on Thursday & be here tomorrow. So you see we are still in doubt. Amanda has been ready for a start ever since Tuesday morning—Mrs Gale put on her new dress & best cap—& for two days sat the picture of impatience—all for nix. So now they look forward to move off some time tomorrow. Mr Woolley also mentioned that—the part owners who were in Savannah (Old McDonald—Mumford & Mr Woolley) intended giving a pleasure trip to who ever chose to accept the compliment on Wednesday evening—but the weather was any thing but pleasant—but more of this at some future time.

Last evening as unpleasant as it was—we rode over to see our dear ones at Hamilton. William met us at the gate & requested us to go into the Hospital to see two very ill negros. We found them very ill. My good Cousin discovered at once that old Amey had been deceiving William—she had not followed his orders—& we three set to work to try & mend matters—soon dear Tootee was added to our number. I wonder what those vile abolishanists would have said could they have looked in on us. William with his own hands helping to put on blisters—dear Tootee making arrow root. Cousin A[manda] feeding the poor girls &c &c. We were pressed very much to stay all night as it rained a little—Amanda & the boys were willing to do so—but I did not like to leave Mrs Gale all night—or the house either without having made arrangements for doing so before leaving home. We took tea & returned—I was met at the front door by I[s]hmael[1] with 3 chickens to sell—Ned—who wanted thread— & Rhina who was anxious to be first to tell us that Big Sarah[2] had a baby & that some things were wanted which neither Maria or herself could find—so you see it is very well we did come home.

The weather is fine today & I expect your dear Sister will ride over after dinner. Yesterday Tootee received a little box containing a *broach*—from Tom Bond—he wrote her a very affectionate letter begging her acceptance of the broach as from a brother. William teased her very much about receiving presents from young men—who were really *no brother* of hers. The children were delighted with the broach—King made a grab at it. I have heard nothing of Joe Bond later than what Ann Bond wrote to Isa Cunningham "that he was at West Point." When Joe was on the Island—he picked off a leaf of my wax plant— nam'd it & planted it in one of my box's—it has looked fresh and well—yesterday I had to remove the earth in the box & found that the leaf had put out roots most beautifully. Joe did not tell me whether he named it for Georgia— Florence or Virginia or little Anna—I rather guess it was after little Anna for I believe *she* loves Joe better than either of her Aunts do.

I received by yesterdays mail my beloved Butlers letter up the 1st October— also one again from dear Lordy & again one from Euphemia Cunningham. I like very well to hear from friends—but it adds much to my letter writing. I wanted to write to dear Adele by this Mail—but I have several letters to write which must go tomorrow. Give my love & a kiss to dear Adele—tell her I love her more & more for her kindness to you my darling girls. I hope my own dear Florence your next report will show a higher number. Now my child you are old enough to feel the advantages of a good education—of correct deportment—I feel satisfied you *will* endeavour to improve rapidly now—for your school days are drawing to a close my beloved girl—now is the time for you to exert yourself. If you *will do so*—I am sure you *will never* regret it—if you *do not* rest assured *you will* look back with pain & regret on every idle or misspent hour you have wasted. If Mr Picot scolds you—do not think that he does so because he does not like you. I am satisfied in my own mind he is *really anxious* for your welfare. I am certain if you will seriously reflect on every scold you have received—you will acknowledge you had not fully done your duty. I have said all I can on the subject of your taking singing lessons. It is your dear Fathers expressed wishes that you & Appy should cultivate your voices. Appy yet has time to do this at a future day—but you have not. But *if you cannot now spare the time from your other lessons*—why then you *cannot please your father*. You have *naturally* a very sweet voice—but you would never sing. I hope you are speaking French now with more ease—the more you try the easier it will be until in a short time it will be no task. How comes on your Spanish—remember I have a paper here which I wish much to have translated. I hope to hear again ere long from your Aunt Lou and that she may be able to tell me all is again quiet in Cuba. It would be a great misfortune if they are obliged to leave that country just now. If I were in Andrews place—I would sell out at once & come to this country. Tho' from what I can perceive this country will not I fear much longer remain the United Republic it now is. I hope you dear girls write regularly to your dear Father & Butler. Two mails had arrived in California without carrying letters from *me*. This of course makes them both very uneasy. I hope my letters may not be lost—Tho' I know they both know me too well to attribute their not getting letters to neglect on my part. I could spend my whole time in writing to you beloved ones—it forms my greatest happiness to write to you all & to read your dear letters. I will try & not injure my eyes—so that this pleasure may last as long as I live—for I cannot expect to keep all my loved ones with me. No the time is near when you will all be scattered—not as you now are only for a few months—but for life. This is a melancholy fact!—

By the return of the *Planter* to Savannah—I will send you sweet meats—oranges—&c &c—I will take care to inform you (in time) what I send—& can only hope they will go safe—& that it will give you half the pleasure in eating them that it does us in sending them. Cane & oranges are both unusually inferior this season—from the long drought. It really seems as tho we shall never have rain again sufficient to wet the earth. But I am grateful that I have no greater misfortune to complain of. I had expected your dear Sister until this moment when I have received a note begging us to go again to see those poor negro girls—we will go—but with little hope of doing them any good. Cousin A[manda], your brothers & Mrs Gale unite in much love & many kisses to you beloved daughters. The servants all beg to be remembered. May God bless you all my own sweet children—my love to Mrs Picot & her daughters & my best regards to Mr Picot.

Your devoted Mother

A M King

1. "50 Negros with Their Increase" lists Ishmael as one of Binah's children. On the 1839 list Byna is number 4 followed by Ishmael, who is noted as a driver, birth date August 14, 1807. Ishmael 2d, born March 9, 1828, Clementine, and Frank are listed as Byna's children. On the 1853 list Ishmael (2d) is listed as number 110. See appendix 2.

2. Sarah, born March 31, 1824, is number 99 on the 1839 list and number 83 on the 1853 list. See appendix 2.

Saturday 22 November

My dearly beloved Florence

This is but Saturday & Tuesday must come before this letter can leave your old home but I have made up my mind (if nothing happens to prevent) to leave home on Monday evening for Hamilton & on Tuesday your Sister, her children, your brothers & my self hope to start for our long promised visit to Lands End. Tomorrow I hope will bring me pleasant intelligence from all of you loved ones at the North & perhaps from those beloved ones far off in California *if* so—*if* I can hear you were all well—I would leave home with a lighten'd heart Hoping & trusting "all is well."

It is very annoying to be writing when the mind is taken up with expecting some certain thing or event—such is my present case. I am expecting the *Planter* to take the long promised boxes &c to you dear ones. Yesterday forenoon we were all so busy Tootee spent the morning here. Herself, Anna, Willie, Bell, Floy[d], Tip & myself—Then Quam, Neptune, Clementine, Maria, Rhina, Mily, Christian, Old Peter too—all all had a finger in the pie—such giving of orders—such doing & undoing was never seen before. It was cold too—& you may depend on it there were frequent truants to be seen running off to warm our fingers. This morning Mr Dunham kindly marked with his *own ink* the boxes & barrels. The box marked "to be kept dry—this side up with care" you will find but two box's—some ground nuts, & the remains of the fine Pomegranates I have been keeping for you. There are 4 packages of arrow root 1 for Lord, 1 for Mrs Picot, 1 for yourselves & 1 I wish given to Mrs Dr Mitchel with my grateful acknowledgements.

In the other box are two night gowns one for you & one for dear Geo. I recollected you may be in want of winter night dresses & made up these two to help you through the cold weather. I send the skirt of Appys dress—& your old friend "Pelican." You will I hope be pleased with the swiss Muslin dresses *Clementine has braided for you* I think she does deserve some credit for doing them so nicely & so neatly. I saw Miss Newel braiding a childs dress—& took it into my head to make Clementine try her hand on one for each of you. I could not get the braid in S[avanna]h & by the time I got it from New York the warm weather was near over. I hope you will be able to wear them next spring. I send muslin for bodies & sleeves—I thought the muslin not fine enough—sent for more—before it came I despaired of getting any finer & one was nearly finished before the other Muslin came. Now I have this other muslin still—And if you dear girls will tell me how you would like the *skirts tucked* I will set Clementine to work at them as soon as the warm weather approaches. I love to see you all in *white*—the most becoming dress in my opinion for young girls—*Typical of purity*. I regret I had but the one pattern for braiding—Rhina put in

6 of her pin cushions—one for each of you dear daughters—one for Adele—
one for Caro & one for Soph.[1] She also sends you those sweet potatoes you will
find in the next size box. In it you will find 4 gars peaches—1 water melon—1
(an attempt) grape. The two small gars of black berrys is all I had. I sent that
more as medicine than preserve. I am told it is excellent for *hoarseness* or a
cough & you know how apt dear Geo is to have both. Just take a tea spoon full
whenever the cough is troublesome or hoarseness distressing. You will fine [*sic*]
the preserved peaches good I think. In this box are also a few lemons (the tree
is now more covered with young fruit & blossoms than it was in the Spring).
You have one box with the best cane William had & a barrel of oranges. I send
Mr Picot's little boys one barrel of oranges. William intends to send you a jug
of Syrup. I hope all these will reach you safe & in as good order as they leave
me. My potatoes (as usual) are inferior or I would have sent you some. Rhina
got those few from her friend Celia.[2] It was very pleasant to see how each one
white & black tried to pack these things that they should go safe to you dear
children. I must request that you will ask the favour of Mrs Picot to have *these
box's* put away for you—they will answer to pack away your things when you
are leaving No 15. I am particularly anxious my jars should be preserved with
care. I had great trouble to get these & but for friend Bourke should not have
succeeded. Mrs Picot has one—you had two this summer & now here are
8 more. The boys I hope will take care of the 4 I have sent to them today. I have
very fine brandy peaches. I think them really delicious—but I *feared* to send them
to you. Neither have I sent any to your brothers—But I know how to make
them now & I hope my darlings I may see all of you enjoy what I may make
next summer. I look forward with trembling to the future—Thus far we have
been singularly blessed—God! has indeed been merciful! Let us praise His
Holy name!!!—

Anna was a little unwell last Thursday but is better now. We are all looking
forward with pleasure to our visit to Cousin Amanda—God! grant I may
spend a happier time than I did the last. I have just finished a hurried letter to
dear Adele—I am sure my precious Flora that you are mortified that so poor a
report should be sent me. I will not scold or find fault with you my beloved girl.
I will only just say you know what will make me *happy* & what will make me
miserable—I am sure your affectionate heart will *induce* you to try & make me
the *former.* I would not wound the feelings of any of you especially when we are
separated—I may have done so in my last letter to my beloved Georgia—But
I cannot endure that one so faultless as Georgia really is—should so weakly
cling to one who really cares so little for her. Now Flora—if Fanny really loved
Georgia as much as G[eorgia] loves F[anny] would she have allowed near *six*
months to elapse *without writing*? Do not *believe* that Fanny wrote any other

letter than that of the 22nd October. And she would not have written that *one* had she not met Lord. Why should her letters come without *failing* to her parents? How did I get every one Lord wrote to me? It was *easier* for Georgia to get letters from Europe than either Mr Grant or myself. But enough! I am only sorry that a girl of Georgias superior mind can be so gulled.

Just now Pussy sent to tell me Sarah's baby would not nurse—& she thi[n]ks it has lockjaw.[3] This is almost as severe a blow to me as it is to poor Sarah who has lost so many children with this distressing complaint. It is now 10 days old & I never lost one before so old with lock jaw. But I will not complain! it is by the hand of Him who knows best. One thing seems certain we are never to grow *rich* by the increase of our negros.

I have been all day trying to write letters all this beautiful cold day—but I make out badly—will be thinking of the *Planter* (by the way the old *Ivanhoe* just now passed here going south).

Monday 2 o clock P.M.

I will now finish this scrawl my own dear Flora. I was much disappointed yesterday by receiving not even a line from either of you beloved girls at No 15. In my letter to Georgia by the Friday Mail I acknowledged yours & dear Appys by the last Wednesday Mail. I think Georgia may have written to me! I do not expect letters from you by *every* mail. I know you have but little time to write letters. Latterly Georgia has not written as often to me or Tootee as you & Appy have. I will not complain if her leisure moments have been *profitably* spent. Yesterdays Mail brought me a letter from dear Mal—one to Tootee from Lord & one to me from *dear Butler*—but it was dated 4th October. The dear boy expected me to receive this letter before I should get the one of the 1st as he sent it by express. I hope he will not try that new route again. I would be sorry if all their letters were as long coming as this one has been. Not hearing from you yesterday made the day seem a long one to me. Just about dark we saw the *Planter* going up the river. Here have we been looking out for her ever since Saturday morning. The poor negros have had to watch & take care of the things in the flat day & night—expecting every minute to see the boat. Well she did get here this morning & took off the freight. When you will receive your share I will not pretend to say. I can only say I hope you will receive them safe & enjoy all that is eatable. I did want so much to send you cake but there was not an egg to be had for love or money. I have not seen Tootee since Friday morning. She was prevented coming here yesterday evening by Mr & Mrs Walker being at Hamilton. William is gone over to Court—he is very sorry he could *not* send you the Syrup it all turned *to sugar*. I am glad to be able to say Sarah's baby may get over this *tightness* of *jaw*. Pussy was certain it would die.

But the 9th day being past—I did not give it up—& as it can nurse very well I hope it will live. Little Alonzo[4] has also been very sick but he too is better & no one else is sick.—

I see by the papers that Hamilton Couper arrived in the last Steamer from N.Y. I hardly think he went [to] Philadelphia. I guess we will not get to Fancy bluff *tomorrow*. I am not sorry to wait a day or two longer. The Wednesday mail *may* bring me letters from California & from one or the other of you beloved girls at No 15. I wish I could just send you the white Japonicas now open 7 beautiful flowers on one plant. Putting them in jars have been a great improvement to the looks of the plants. I keep my eye on the Hileatrope—you shall have the first flower it produces. I must now just add that the cards I enclose were received yesterday unfortunately I lost the seal. Kiss my beloved Georgia & Appy & tell them each to give you a kiss for me. God! bless you all my precious children—God! grant I may be rewarded for all I now suffer from this painful separation by the benefits hoped for—& the safe & happy return of each & every one of you beloved ones to your devoted Mother

A M King

Your dear little brothers send many kisses & lots of love to you three. *The servants all* beg to be remembered.—

25th

In consequence of some injury to the *Isabel*—I fear my letters to your dear Father & Butler will again be detained. I desire particularly that one or the other of you dear girls will write to them by the very next Mail from *New York for California* & let them know how we all are by the last accounts you shall receive. Tell my dear Appy that it is probable I will not write to her by the Friday Mail—If we do get off in the *Planter* I dare say I shall have enough to do. We are all pretty much as we were yesterday. It rained all night—& the weather still unsettled. Kiss each other over & over for your devoted Mother

AMK

1. Caro and Soph are Adele Picot's sisters Caroline and Sophia.

2. Anna kept a detailed record of the goods she purchased from her bondpeople and how much she paid. She bought chickens, eggs, fish, turtles, fruit, to name but a few items, and paid from a few cents to $5–10 depending on the item, the quantity, and the time of year. It is clear from her letters that she relied on this "informal economy" to feed her family and many guests as well as to obtain such necessary items as baskets and fishing nets. Selected Pages from the Record Book of Retreat Plantation, GDAH.

3. Lockjaw is a symptom of tetanus. It was common in slave infants, who died when they could not nurse. The tetanus bacteria were most likely introduced through the um-

bilical cord, either via dirty hands or instruments used to cut it, or possibly when slave women used dirt (mixed with water) to seal the wound. This is still done in areas of Africa today and could represent an African practice retained by enslaved women. Information from Drs. Marston and Slutsker; Savitt, "Black Health on the Plantation," 317.

4. Alonzo does not appear on any of the lists in appendix 2.

Retreat 14th December 1851

My own dearly beloved Florence

I know you will be delighted to receive again a letter dated from your loved home. If dear Geo has received the letter I sent from Lands end by the last *Friday Mail* you will have heard it was our intention to return home on that day. Mr Woolley started for the Bluff by the time it was light to see if the Boat was in sight. Rhina woke us all up before sunrise & we all were in a bustle to be off as soon as we could get some breakfast—Mr W[oolley] came back—no boat— nevertheless he hurried us all off by eight oclock—some rode in Mrs Scarletts carriage some in Mr W[oolley's] buggy—some walked & some rode in the ox cart. We were sorry to leave poor Mrs Gale by herself—But when we left the house we had no doubt but that this boat would take us off before twelve oclock. Cousin A[manda] put up for our lunch all that was left from breakfast —cold mutton, cold turkey, ham biscuits, cheese—& added cake & jumbles. When we got to Fancy Bluff—still no boat! For an hour or so, we were *very impatient*. But finding this did *no good*, we set too to amuse ourselves. Mr Owens gave us up his house—desiring we should call on his servant for what ever the house afforded, that we required. So King was served some milk.

We then visited the distillery saw the process of making spirits of turpentine & Rosin?—got ourselves bogged in the "*raw material*"—& took some time & trouble to clean off. We loitered about watching for the *Planter* until 2 oclock, when we concluded to eat our dinner. Thinking our being at the house, would prevent Mr Broad & Mr Owens from getting their dinner comfortably, we went down to the Warm House & Steam Boat landing. Mr Woolley had given Willie a pair of goats—they were tied by the legs & were like ourselves *rather impatient*. Then there were coops of poultry to go in the Steamer & Millions of Sand flies to help our annoyances—I verily believe the dinner quieted all of us—we all seemed better satisfied with ourselves—each other & even the Sand flies after we had eaten. After this we became quite cheerful—night came on & with it rain but light wood was plentiful—& with the crude rosin large fires were *kindled out doors. The children enjoyed this very much*. We could not return to Mr Woolleys as the boat may arrive at any moment. Eventually about ten oclock Rhina descried the Steamers light coming up the creek. William had been joking Willie about his goats—one of the gentlemen was leading Willie by the hand to the landing—I heard him say to Dr Austin—"I expect now the Capt of that Steamboat will be apt to take my goats from me, but I mean to tell him he cannot do no such thing." Our dear cousin went on board with us.—

When I went into the ladies cabin—I was requested by a lady "not to bring in a light or make a noise because the lady in the opposite birth was very ill— had taken laudanum &c"—I said I was sorry to have disturbed them & as we expected very soon to leave the boat, I would leave the cabin to them. The Mother of the sick one begged me "to come near to her & she would tell me all about her daughters sickness"—she had got but a few words further when the daughter called out pettishly "*hush ma'* I *want to be quiet*"—So I came out. We stopped at Col[onel]s Island for Sarah & Miles Hazzard & Campbell Mc-Donald—then at Blythe Island for freight. I felt sorry for the Mother of this sick woman & asked Dr Austin if he would go in & see her—he humanely consented to do so—& I once more entered the cabin. They readily consented to see the Doctor—The daughter asked "if he was an old man"—the Mother begged me "to come in & remain during the Doctors call." I satisfied them both—the Dr was young but was a married man & I would come in with him— as soon as we were seated both Mother & daughter began to tell the symptoms &c. The Mother was making a very long story of it—Where they came from— how they had been recommended to come South—How *luxuriously* they had lived in Virginia—how starved they had been in Florida—The Daughter calling out "now stop Ma' let me tell the Doct.["] The Mother would cease for a moment & then strike in again—When the daughter would again beg her to stop—eventually she said "Stop Ma' I feel *cross*—I must talk myself to the Dr["]—I left them at this. When he came out he said he had succeeded *he hoped* in persuading both Mother & Daughter to "stop" talking for the night. I could not but be sorry for them both—as there was sickness in the case—& they were two lone women & among strangers in a Strange land.—

We find the *Planter* a very pleasant boat—& will I hope do well. It was some time before either Anna or Willie could be persuaded to lie down—Bob soon for got all the cares of life in a sound sleep. Poor Willie sat bolt upright—every time his goats would bleat out—his eyes would look bigger—I was glad when he could no longer keep awake. As it was so late I concluded it would be best for me to land at Hamilton—Eventually at near one oclock we got our feet once more on old St Simons—Mom Jane had no idea of spending the balance of the night within reach of home so she footed it home. I sent orders for the carriage & cart to be over by the time it was light. I shipped my baggage home & as soon as breakfast was disposed of, I hurried over in quest of letters from you beloved ones. I found one from your beloved Father up to the 1st No-

vember, 2 from Mal—Yours, Georgias & Appys up to the 29th November—
one from Lordy & a long one & two short ones from Adele & her Brothers—
And these my darlings are the last I have received from you dear girls. This
days Mail brought me a letter from our beloved Butler up to the 1st November
& one from each of those dear boys in New Haven. Dear dear Florence I
am so unhappy about you my own dear child—Why is it you are so *desponding*.
In what way am I to induce you to throw aside you[r] *timidity* or *apathy* (I do
not know which predominates) to hinder your reaping the advantages of your
present opportunities. Say my own dear child do you wish *me to bring you home
alone* & leave your sisters. *If you say so—as much as it may grieve & mortify your
Father your Sisters & brothers & myself—I will do so rather than you should be so utterly wretched as I imagine you to be from your last letter.* God! Know[s] my beloved child our only inducement for sending you to No 15—is for your own
good. If I *can afford* it my desire is to keep you & Georgia only one year at
Mr Picot's school when that is finished (if God!! in Mercy spares your lives) you
two will have done school. You would all return home & we then would have
to think where Appy will next go. I feel the *responsibilities of both Father &
Mother*—as your poor Father is too far off to decide what had best be done for
you dear children. Our desire is to give *each of you an* equal chance of obtaining
a good education—& we have already done more than most parents would
have thought (with the means we have), they could afford. But we have strained
every means in our power—If the idea of singing lessons distresses you—give
it up—But in mercy to yourself (if not to us) try & get on in your other
branches. Let the hope of pleasing & gratifying that dear far distant Father—
those loving Sisters & brothers & your devoted Mother—Stimulate you to exertion—throw off your timidity you have talents, *use them*. Think nothing impossible for you to learn which others have learnt. Do my Flora try.—

Mrs Gale prefers remaining longer with Cousin Amanda—I would not object to this but that her being there may confine our good Cousin at home. (I
was called off & made the above digression before finishing with my letters.) I
am grieved to hear you have been so sick—And tho' both Geo & Adele tells
me you have got over your attack—my getting no letter later than the 29th Nov
this being the 14th Dec makes me *truly miserable*. You know my darling Flora
you cannot bear *damp feet*. How many have forfeited their lives by imprudence
in this particular. Flora my darling what would become of your poor Mother
if _____.[1] God! protect you my precious ones. Oh! may He in Mercy grant
that we may all meet again in this world. I had also today a long letter from Euphemia C[unningham]. She writes to me so affectionately & seems so grateful
for the attentions I bestowed on her last summer. She sent me 16 roses of various kinds from Mrs Stodards garden. I will cultivate my garden with greater

care than I ever did—thinking all the while how pleased you will *all* be to find
it improved when you get back. I watch the Heliatrope every time I am going
to write to you hoping to find a flower to send you. As yet there are none. You
have doubtless heard from Butler if not from your dear Father up to the 1st Nov.
Neither of them speak of returning—Oh! that I could once more see you all
around my table—I think I would then be content to die—rather than again
endure all the pain & anxious fears from your absence which I now endure.
Mrs Gale charged me with a great many messages of love to each of you. She
seems never tired of talking about you dear girls—I really believe she loves you
dearly. Our dear Cousin A[manda] & Mr Woolley speak of you with affection
& pride—They drink from the cups you sent them & never fail to tell strangers or visitors from whom they came. I think they must feel very lonely now.
Amanda said she really dreaded to go back on Friday night—H[annah] Page,
Wm, 4 children & servt, Floyd, Tip myself & 3 servants—& two gentlemen
(who came from S[avannah] to see Mr Woolley in the *Planter* on Tuesday & left
with us on Friday)—15 persons taken out of the small home left quite a gap.

I found all pretty well when I got home yesterday morning all were delighted
to get us back again—I really thought the women servants would have kissed
me & the *he ones* wring off my hands. The birds sang louder and the flowers
looked more beautiful. The Japonicas—are far handsomer than they have ever
been before since I owned them. I brought Anna home with me—dear little
creature she has been so very happy but her Parents came over directly after
dinner & William said he has been *so long* separated from his family he wanted
to have them all around him once more for a few days. Tootee tells me that she
really expects to go to Savannah directly after Christmas. I hope nothing may
occur to prevent her so doing—she needs some re creation. If she does go—
she will leave Willie & Bob with me taking only Anna & King with her. King
is the best baby I ever knew—he is really a sweet little fellow. I have got to the
end of my 4th Page & how beautifully straight & neatly it is written but you
will I trust be able to read every word I have written.[2]

15th Dec.

I hope & trust you are all as well this disagreeable chilly rainy morning as your
little Brothers & myself are. I think after this we shall have some stinging cold
weather. How do you bear the cold—I hope you dear girls clothe warmly. You
must spare no expense for your real & necessary comforts. Christmas is drawing near. I am particularly delighted to find from his letter that your dear
Brother Lord intends to join Malley & yourselves in visiting your Uncle &
Aunt. But you must be careful my darlings to avoid *taking cold.* I have heard
nothing from or of any of our neighbors since my return. I am so sorry that

Mrs Bourke should have returned to Savannah without my having the pleasure of seeing her here. I fear she may think I aught to have remained at home to receive her. Had I done so Tootee would have done the same & would probably have given up going altogether. I have not heard one word of Fannie [Grant] Troup since her return home. Had she been sick I would have heard of it. I am sorry I hurt my beloved Geo's feelings by my manner of writing about Fannie. My *change* of feeling for Fannie is from her change of conduct to Geo. This commenced from the time Fan & Jinny went to Carolina & it has been increasing ever since. Tell Geo not to fret herself from fearing Fanny's silence is caused by her being ill. I do hope & trust the Wednesday Mail may bring me letters from you beloved ones & that these letters will tell me of no more colds—head or heart aches. Give my love to dear Adele I will answer her letter ere long. Tell the little boys I will do the same *if* I can find time. Thank Eddy for the prints. Floyd & Tip send you lots of love & kisses the servants all beg to be remembered. Kiss each other for me. I may not have time to write to dear Appy by the Friday mail—I say this fearing you may be uneasy if you do not hear from me. My health is good—few are more blest in this respect than I am. God! bless you my darling Florence—May His infinite Mercy restore in health & happiness all you beloved ones to your devoted Mother

A M King

1. Anna left out the word and drew a line here.
2. In fact, the writing on this page is uneven.

                                                          18th January 1852
My own children

I thank you my beloved children for your most welcome letters up to the 8th Inst. It took a perfect load of care off of my mind to hear you were once more safe at No 15—& were able to tell me up to that time you had not suffered from that terrible ride to Allentown. I have not time now to write & thank your uncle & Aunt for their kindness to you all—I received your letters on Saturday (yesterday). The Wednesday Mail did not come until Friday night—there was no Mail from the Island on Friday—& today there is no Mail. I received yesterday also a letter from dear Mallery who informed me of the disaster to Mr Russells establishment. It seems a true saying "trouble never comes alone." I thank God! that dear Mall was absent at that time—it not only prevented his suffering at the time but also saved some of his clothes—for he writes me that his books were all burnt & his *clothes stolen*. I am very sorry that Lord went to West Point—I have not received a line from him since the 15th Dec. It would have been such a comfort to me could I have received a letter also from him yesterday.

On Monday I sent you a hurried account of that awful catastrophe. I went over to Hamilton & saw the passengers get on board the *Welaka*—I found dear Isabel Cunningham at Hamilton. When the account of the disaster reached Savannah on Sunday the 11th—it was reported that *all* were lost. Isa determined to come to my support. When she heard my precious ones were spared still she determined to come. She left Savannah in the [?] which boat was sent out by the owners of the ill fated *Magnolia*.[1] Contrast this conduct with that of Miss Gould & her sister [unreadable] word since the disaster—never mind it does us no harm.

On Tuesday morning in the *midst of the most severe snow storm* I have ever witnessed Christiann ran in *to tell me* "*Herbert*[2] *was all* burnt up" depend on it—I was there *in an instant & found* him badly burnt—you know how much spoilt he is. Clementine had left him & Bell in her room & came in to wait on Breakfast. It was snowing so much I did not like to go to the negro houses or have Pussy come to me—so I sent Clementine to see how the sick were. In this time Mr Herbert had got playing with fire—his clothes took fire—Poor little Bell tried to extinguish the fire by brushing him with the broom no one who heard him cry—thought any thing of it—knowing he always made that fuss when his Mother left him. After a while little Tilla[3] went in—She had the presence of mind to dash a bucket of water over him—his face—neck—under one arm stomach & knees were severely but not *dangerously* burnt. I was (as you may suppose) terribly frightened—Thank God! he is now doing very well. Alic Boyd[4] was very badly off—from a violent cold—the inflammation ran high—I was very much alarmed about him. I put on a large blister—& now thank God! I am able to say he is doing well. Jimmys[5] face is healing fast—Richard is very much better—Mr Dunham is able once more to be about. Oh! my children help me to praise God! for all His mercies. The more I reflect—the greater seems the mercy extended to me The amount of property lost is not ruinous—20 bags Mr Dunham says is uninjured—I consider my loss in cotton 5 bags—which would have brought me $500—but when I look on the mercy which spared me my beloved children my good overseer & my dear negros—I dare not murmur at the loss of a few hundred dollars. You my darlings must make up this to me by *taking in knowledge to the full*. I have to write several other letters tonight & must not give you a lecture now.—

Our dear Cousin was at Waynesville in church—when Mr Woolley came to the Church door & said "The *Magnolia* is blown up & every soul lost." This he had just heard from the Mail carrier—Amanda rushed out—& it took them but 2 *hours* to reach home. Soon they learnt that my children were saved—but it was reported that I had lost all my cotton & had 2 negros killed. They had no way of getting down before the following Thursday night. They landed at Hamilton (ei) Amanda & Mrs Gale—& came to me after breakfast. Our dear Cousin is very unwell. Mrs Gale—had got fat & could get about with much more ease—but she took a bad cold & is consequently very unwell. I hope she will be better in a day or two. Our Cousin leaves us on Tuesday—but has promised to return to me in a short time. Tootee—Isa & the three oldest children were here yesterday & today. They will spend tomorrow with us—& if nothing new occurs to keep me at home I will go over with Amanda on Tuesday. Mr Woolley will stop for her in the *Planter* at Hamilton.

My 2 box's of sweetmeats have been fished up out of the wreck—but are of course spoilt—I am so sorry for those I was sending to Mrs Jaudon & Mrs Mitchell. As I sent Mrs Picot last year—and as Adele wrote to me her Fathers request that I should send no more to No 15—I regret the loss of hers less. I made them with loaf sugar & they were very nice & beautiful. The Hamilton negros fell in with a whole barrel of my oranges—which they appropriated to themselves. I had sent away my last oranges. I must not forget to mention that this piece [blank] was a Pitcher presented by 3 of the passengers to William & Tootee—with W[illiam] & H[annah] P[age]'s names engraved on it.

I cannot write any more for my candles warn me I shall not have light enough for my other letters—Do not be uneasy about my health my beloved children—I am as well in body as ever I was. Your little brothers, dear Cousin & Mrs Gale send thousands of loves & kisses—God bless you my own precious children

Your devoted Mother
A M King

All the servants beg to be remembered—Rhina remained until this evening with Tootee.

19th

The family are as usual the negros no worse this morning. Kiss each other for your devoted

Mother
A M King

I would re commend your sealing with wafers—Appys last letters came open'd to us—

1. In her entry on Hamilton plantation Margaret Davis Cate describes the "awful catastrophe" mentioned above:

A terrible tragedy occurred here in 1850. The *Magnolia*, one of the early side-wheel steamboats that plied the inland waters from Savannah to Florida, carrying both passengers and freight, had loaded cotton at the wharf at Hamilton and was preparing to leave when the boiler exploded. Passengers and freight were hurled in every direction. Most of the passengers had been on the side of the boat near land watching a tame fawn grazing nearby when the explosion took place, and, as it happened, were as far removed from the boiler as it was possible to be. Had it not been for this, more of them would have been killed. As it was, many lives were lost and dozens terribly burned and wounded. William Audley Couper who was living at Hamilton at the time, improvised a temporary hospital on the second floor of his barn—a large tabby building still standing at Hamilton. Bales of cotton were cut open to make beds, and doctors were brought from Brunswick and from Darien, some of whom remained for weeks ministering to the sick. The survivors of the *Magnolia* sent Mr. and Mrs. Couper a silver pitcher, suitably inscribed, as a token of their appreciation of the kindnesses shown them. (Cate, *Our Todays and Yesterdays*, 134)

While Cate dates the accident to 1850, Anna's letter is dated January 18, 1852.

2. Herbert (number 95) was born July 7, 1849. See appendix 2.

3. "Negros with Their Increase" records Myrtilda, or Tilla, as Maria's child. She is number 99 on the 1853 list, born December 6, 1840, and number 77 on the 1859 list. Her daughter Anne, number 78, is recorded as three months old, as is Tilla's youngest brother, Herbert, making Tilla and her mother, Maria, pregnant at the same time. See appendix 2.

4. Alic Boyd is number 33 on the 1839 list, no birth date recorded; number 12 on the 1853 list; and number 1 on the 1859 list. See appendix 2.

5. A Jimmy is number 1 on the list from William Page's will. A second Jimmy, born April 28, 1838, is number 50 on the 1839 list, number 25 on the 1853 list, and number 70 on the 1859 list. The latter list records another Jimmy, number 45, thirty-six years old. This could be the Jimmy from William Page's will recorded in 1827. See appendix 2.

11th February 1852

My own dearly beloved Florence

I have just received your affectionate letter of the 4th. I had began to feel *neglected* by you my own dear Flora but getting 2 letters in 5 days does away that impression. I know you will feel anxious & uneasy until you hear of the safe return of your dear Sister & her little ones—I will therefore at once tell you that they landed safe at Hamilton yesterday morning. I felt very miserable about them. The fog was so dense I dreaded the *Welaka* & *Planter* running against each other. I walked alone down to the creek dreading every moment to meet a dead body. I had scarcely got to the extent of the beach when I saw through the mist the *Planter*—I of course soon got back to the house & sent over an express to enquire after our dear ones & soon had the relief of knowing they were safely landed. Our dear Tootee & Anna came over just when we were sitting down to dinner. They were both in high spirits & as well as I could expect them to be. This morning Tootee sent for the Frasers. So I am once more alone. I really pity poor Tootee—but they are her husbands relations & the trouble & expense must be borne. I received dear Adeles letter with yours—I rejoice to hear that her excellent Father is better. God! grant he may soon be well again. It is now just two o clock—will you believe that I see from my window Miss Mary Gould riding up. I have cooked no dinner today for your Sister kept Floyd & Tip to dine at Hamilton—I must go & play the agreeable.—

Well Miss Gould came at 2 oclock & remained until sun down. The object of her visit was to get Plants from the flower garden—grapes & fig cuttings—well of course this took Rhina the whole afternoon. It also prevented my going to Hamilton—But still her being here was a kind of relief. On Monday just after I had sent off my letters to the Office—they came in & told me Capt Mc-Neltys body had been found between this & the light house. Jimpa[1] was going along with his hogs—saw a body floating by—waded in & drew it to the shore then came & told Mr Dunham of it. He was of course in a terrible state of de composition—& would not have been recognised but from the papers in his pocket book & the gold chain attached to his watch which Mr Dunham at once recognised. I will not harrow your feelings—but barely add that the watch & pocketbook I put into a tin box & directed it to Mr McNelty. The body I had placed into a box made for the purpose. These Mr Dunham took charge of & as the *Welaka* was passing (the same day) they were put on board at the creek. This you know was on Monday—on that day Dembos[2] body & the body of another negro were found at Hamilton. This morning before breakfast Peter found the body of another white man just opposite the last negro house. It was in a far worse state than the others were—I have had real trouble to get it buried. In the first place I have *given boards* for the five who died at Hamilton & could scarcely find enough to make a box for poor McNelty's body. Then this one was in such a state it was difficult to manage—& even more so find boards. Then Dunham was sick & *I had actually to attend to it myself.* The body was in such a state I would not let the negros put their hands into the pockets—consequently we do not know who it is. The face was gone & the little hair left was *red* which shows that it was not McGuire for the lady passengers said Mr Mc-Guire had black hair. I do earnestly pray no more bodies may come on this shore—if they do I have not a board left to make them coffins—neither will I allow my people to handle them. The Owners of the *Magnolia* have sent men with a Schooner to get up the wreck. I think it the place of those people to see to the bodies—I cannot do any more than I have already done. It seems as tho' I am never to be done with *losses* from that explosion. But let us drop the painful subject.—

Your dear Sister left with Mr Bourke her daguerreotype to be sent to you dear girls—I presume that she wrote to you. Her stay here last evening was not long—and then their was so much talking I did not ask her if she had written to you whilst in Savannah. I have not seen dear little King—he is not what any one can call *beautiful*—but he is a very *bright intelligent* looking little fellow & withall—he is the *best* baby I ever knew. Isabel is decidedly the best looking of the children & as sweet as she is pretty. But Willie *loves me so much I am obliged* to love him more than either of the others, tho' I do love them all very dearly. I missed them very much last night & today—but I will soon be reconciled to the loss of their sweet prattle. How strange it is that we *can* be reconciled to great misfortunes. It is wisely & humanely ordered that such should be our nature. Do not suppose that I have yet become reconciled to this painful separation from a beloved husband & Six of my darling children. Could you my children only know the *loneliness* the pain I suffer—you would *each one strive* to repay me by *your doing all in your power to improve*. I shall send you Adele's letter to read. It pains me *exceedingly* to perceive there *yet* so much dissatisfaction given by you three dear girls. I have written you *pages* of the *best advice I am capable* of giving. You are all old enough & have a good share of common sense. You all must be conscious when you are *neglecting your present great advantages* or breaking the rules. Oh! my children if you love your poor Mother—if you regard the approbation of your noble minded Father. Throw aside your idle habits your *impatient* tempers—& for the remainder of your stay at No 15 endeavour not only to improve every moment of your time—but also to give entire satisfaction to your teachers. God! alone can know all I suffer from your absence from me *& you must know & feel that I suffer*—& what is this for? *that you may be properly educated.*

I am *surprised* my own dear Flora at your asking me to have *your singing lessons discontinued*—I had got *worn out myself in asking you to sing*. But *when your own beloved Father wrote to me from that far distant country—to which he went soley to make his family more comfortable—particularly "desiring that you & Appy should be made to sing."* Could I do otherwise *than desire you should take lessons?* Can I now desire you to relinquish them? I am sure had you *reflected* one moment you would not have made the request. Nature has bestowed on you & Appy just as sweet a voice as it did on my own little Georgia. You know how much pleasure it affords us all to hear her sing—to hear you & Appy join your voices with hers will delight us. Then again Adele complains of your being careless of your health—& will *keep pins* in your mouth. Oh! Flora have some pity on your poor Mother! Could you my child see the number of persons afflicted with consumption who flock south every Winter—you would be careful to avoid taking cold at the North. If you regard not your own life I cannot expect you my child to regard me [*sic*] happiness—But for your own sake I *implore* of you to be more *prudent*. We are expressly forbidden "not to tempt the Lord our God!" God has blest you all with sound constitutions—but the very strongest may fail. Many who are now *dying from the effects of colds* in Savannah may have been even stronger at your *age than you are now*. Do not my child disregard the admonitions of dear Adele or of those who wish you well. The *pill story I am ashamed of*—Willie would not have been guilty of such *childishness*. Now my darling read with attention all the advice I have given you in this letter. You can little know the pain it always (but especially when you are far away) gives me to find fault with you or any one of you beloved children—But I would be wanting in my duty to you should I with hold giving advice when I know you need it.—

It is my desire to go over to see your Sister tomorrow—poor thing she has her hands full. They brought home Middleton—he (I hope) will save her some trouble. Old Duncan became unbearable—so Nancy now cooks. I hope Rebecca & Lizzie will not remain much longer on the Island those two Demeres give so much trouble. It is either *Physic* or *food* the whole time. Susan speaks of remaining some time with Tootee. Mrs Clinch sent each of them 2 dress's by Tootee & John Fraser sent them each one dress—So that makes 4 dresses each one has received since they came to the Island—& almost every family on the Island are helping them sew. I believe Mrs Dr Fraser also sent them dress's—H[annah] Page said they had a large box of goods sent them.[3] Dear Tootee brought me a pair of Sugar tongs as a present. I gave her money to get herself a silver Soup ladle. She sent you a lock of Kings hair in a little trinket—poor little fellow it was hard to find a pinch of hair long enough for the purpose. Poor Tootee had very little money of her own—I think Middletons wages should have been given to her.[4] She bought a very nice gold pencil for herself & had her Daguerreotype taken for Cousin Amanda—some one (she thinks it was Mrs Cunninghams white nurse) spoilt the likeness & stole the gold pencil—It was done the very morning they left. Amanda tells me—that when William went with Mr Woolley alongside of the *St Matthew* on Tuesday last—they (or William) saw Henry Gigneliat on board—poor fellow he is going once more in pursuit of health. Dr Nichol (so says some gossip) will not consent to his daughter marrying Henry until his health is restored—of that there seems but little hope.[5] The Hazzards told us on Saturday last that they had heard—that the other sister & Postell are to be married right away.[6]

Miss Mary Gould was here last evening—she looked very badly. In fact Mary G[ould] looks ten years older than when she left St Simons 2 years ago. I fear she is doing herself much injury by this cold water system. She strongly recommended my "*packin*" Tip—but I could not be persuaded to do so. I had a letter (a very kind one) from Mr Savage by the last Mail—I also had a very affectionate one from dear Euphemia Cunningham—her health improves slowly. She requested me to send her & Isa's love to you whenever I write. Mrs I Cunningham is in a rapid decline the Doctors give no hope of her recovery. E[uphemia] & Isa sent me two pair of excellent strong gloves "to save my hands from rose thorns." Mrs G[ale] a pair of nice warm mits—F[loyd] & T[ip] each a nice knife. To Wm they sent a cup & saucer—very pretty—but of *equal size with* the one dear Butler gave me. To Tootee they sent neck ribbons & a pretty collar—to the children candies—& to Pussy—(what she most wanted)—tobacco. I wrote to Euphemia & your Aunt Henry Mary—as well as to dear Geo & Malley—by the Tuesday Mail. My dear Amanda is not well—I really believe that she not only loves you all most fondly—but that *she is proud of the love & attention you all show her.* Mr Woolley speaks of you all with affection *& no little pride.* It did seem to do him double good to take his tea—milk or coffee from his beautiful cup. As soon as he left us Amanda would no longer drink out of hers—for fear it may get injured. It is very gratifying to me to see my children affectionate & respectful & attentive to one who I so dearly love as I do my Cousin Amanda—She is worthy of all the love & respect *we are capable of feeling.* I shall go over to Hamilton after dinner to see your dear Sister. Poor John Davis is dead—he died last night after an illness of only a few days. From what I can understand his case was a severe one & he had no attention. How much better off are our slaves than the poor in *any country* whether they be white or black.

Friday morning 24th

I found your sister much better last evening. It was so *cold* I've concluded it would be better for *dear* Amanda to remain at Hamilton the night than to return with me through the cold night air. I could not remain from my little boys. I found Mr. Brown here—come to preach for the negros & stay the night. Your dear Sister sends much love to you dear girls—She said it was her intention to write to you dear Flora by this very mail. And that she fears you think she has been neglectful latterly the sickness of dear little King—her greatness of needlework—& now her own sickness have prevented her writing to you. She hopes to do so very shortly. William is looking remarkably well. The dear children are all now well—tho' poor little King has not yet regained his flesh or healthy colour. You know how sweet the three elder children are—but you can only imagine the sweetness of Master Butler King. I have requested cousin Amanda to send me word early to day—how dear Tootee is—if much better I will not go over until after dinner—if otherwise I will go as soon as I dispatch the letters for the mail. This attack of Tootee's is just like those she had before you left us—*but not so severe as those were.* I have every reason to hope she will be quite well again in a day or two. Rhina is better—I have not yet asked her about the letter in French. The servants are very much gratified by your particular mention. Our good old mom Jane continues to cook my dinners. Lady & Polly to wash & iron the clothes. Pussy is often sick but when up attends the sick. Maria has been sick but was soon up again—for a wonder Clementine has not laid up since you left us—may be the trip to Savannah has made a change in her cons[t]itution. Poor Hannah has been better all summer—I require nothing more from her than what she feels able to perform— Poor Hannah! At present I have no one on the sick list but Rhina—She is my right hand & I miss her very much—but I hope in a few days she will be well again. Christiann grows more stupid & lazy. I have little Annie[7] now to brush the flies she is smart little thing. Daddy Quamina is taking particular pains to cultivate some quote "Scops" for you dear little girls. How comes on your Spanish? Be sure to learn to speak it fluently or you can not see your uncle and aunt in Cuba. Cousin A[manda] told me last evening to be sure & send love & kisses to you dear girls. Mrs. Gale sends much love—your dear little brothers have themselves written. The servants one & all beg to be remembered. I kissed the *babies* for you when at Hamilton. Give dear Adele a kiss & thank her for her kindness to my daughters. Kiss your dear Sisters for me—My love to Mrs. P[icot] & best regards to Mr. P[icot]. Excuse this hasty scrawl—I have yet more letters to write. May God! bless you my own dear Flora—bless you & your dear Sisters—

> your devoted Mother
> A M King

I may add a few lines to this before Friday. After all I have gone through today I could not sleep tonight—it is the best thing I could do—to write. Kiss the belov'd girls for your devoted Mother

AMK

Mrs. Gale would blow me up if she thought I had written 4 Pages without telling you she is better & sending her love. Your little brothers are quite well & send kiss's. Alic B[oyd] is getting on—Herbert too is mending a little—no one else sick. Once more God bless you my darling child

> Your Mother

AMK

10 o clock

I have been hoping to hear from Hamilton before it was time to send off my letters—Even whilst writing this far I received a note saying our dear Tootee had a good night—is free of fever this morning & I hope when her medicine operates will be quite well again. It has been so cold—we were glad to have fires to warm by. Mrs. Gale will go with our dear Cousin & I hope soon to make the long talked of visit to Lands end. The Miss's Parland have a great many beaux—& but little instruction to improve their minds or manners. I see that Mrs. Hopkins & daughters have returned to Savannah.

Rhina is very much better this morning & I have no one else sick among the darkies. Mr. Brown says his little son give[s] no trouble whatever & that *Susan* is better this [torn] than [torn] of her other confinements—I have given [torn] owl to Mr. Brown as a *pet*. My birds are quite well—I am in great haste my darling Flora—as I have yet Floyd's lessons to attend to & to see after out door business. Kiss again & again your beloved Sisters for me—Kiss dear Adele & tell her how much I feel her kindness to you all. Cheer up my sweet Flora—try & get on with your studies—rest assured you will never regret the hours you devoted to that purpose. God! bless you my darling child.—

> Your Mother,
> A M King

1. Pussy's son James is number 109 on the 1839 list, birth date January 25, 1829; and number 96 on the 1853 list, where he is noted as James or Jimpa. See appendix 2.

2. Dembo does not appear on any of the lists in appendix 2.

3. Anna had written: "From what the girls tell me—Selena saved all of her own & her Mothers wardrobe—Susan saved her own & part of Rebeccas—The most of Mrs Demeres & her husbands & childrens clothing were saved—I rather think if the truth was told—the house—some bedding & some furniture is all—but this to poor John Demere is a most serious loss. From my heart I pity him & his wife" (Anna Matilda Page King to Florence Barclay King, January 28, 1852, KWC, GHS). Also see Anna's letter to Tootee dated September 28, 1852.

4. Slave owners commonly hired out their slaves—to other planters and to mines, mills, foundries, or to work on railroads and canals, depending on their skills. Some owners allowed the bondmen to keep part of their earnings or to pay money toward the purchase of their freedom. For more on this, see Franklin and Schweninger, *Runaway Slaves*, 36.

5. The following entry for 1852 appears in "Glynn County's Oldest Marriage Records": "Dec. 7—Henry G. Gignilliat and Miss L. M. Nicholes" (Cate, *Our Todays and Yesterdays*, 249–250). Either Henry Gignilliat regained his health, Dr. Nicholes relented, or the gossip was untrue.

6. In the same record: "Dec. 2—Dr. C. G. Postell and Miss M. W. Nicholes, by Rev. J. S. Screven" (ibid.).

7. Annie, number 105 on the 1853 list, was born February 9, 1842, and was Rhina's only child. See appendix 2.

Retreat 29th Feb 1852

My own beloved Florence

The Capt of the Mail Steamer has again carried our Mail South—& we will not get it before Wednesday. This is truly provoking—I hope it may contain letters from you beloved children. Tho' I know you cannot write to me every Mail—still as your last letters were dated the 16th I think I may expect letters on the 29th. In my last letter to dear Geo I acknowledged having received all three of your letters. And the one from Adele. This I sent to Geo—I wrote to her my entreaties *to try & prevail* on you my own dear Flora to *give up all those practices of which Adele complains.* You are doing yourself *great injury*—you are *cruelly distressing your poor Mother*—and what would your *Father say & feel if he knew this?* My beloved child have you *no regard for our sufferings?* If you continue to keep pins in your Mouth in a few years you will have no teeth. If you continue to *swallow them*—in a *short time you will die a most dreadful death!* If you will expose yourself to colds by leaving off your Flannel & drawers or any other imprudence you *will die of consumption* or Pleurisy. You have sense enough to know all this yourself and *you have been warned.* How can I persuade you to *take advice.* Oh! my Florence you can have no idea how much it distresses me to write this to a beloved child—who is so far from me—who *I may never see again!* Adeles letter grieved me—still I thank her for informing of your practices—*she simply did her duty.* It is not only silly in you—but wicked—you are committing *deliberate suicide.* Will you now give over causing such distress to your poor Mother? If you have the least *compassion* you surely will. You can have no idea of the constant state of painful anxiety I am kept in. Every day brings its trials—It does seem hard—*that my children should willfully add to my troubles.* If I remember right—Miss Picot did not complain of your lessons. If you are doing better at them—I do sincerely *thank* you my child. I have no doubt you all have trials—which you think great—but if you could change places with *me*—*your* trials when compared with mine you would find mere trifles. I do most fervently hope & pray I may hear no more complaints of yourself or Sisters.

I gave dear Geo all the wishes of your beloved Father—I wrote to Miss Picot my desire that you & Appy should devote the most of your time to French—Spanish & music. I know you are by no means a finish'd English scholar. Still this will be your best opportunity to acquire the above branches. Mr Picots ill health I fear will be a disadvantage to the school. Tell Geo—to write me exactly how matters are. I do hope you beloved Girls will keep in mind the necessity of exertion. Let nothing deter you from trying to improve. Time is flying & vast sums expending. Make up your minds to gain all you possibly can before the 1st of July.

Yesterday afternoon I called to see Mrs Armstrong & Susan went with me to see Mrs Cater. Many kind enquiries were made about you dear girls. Mrs Cater is even more lonely than I am. I really feel sorry for her—her carriage driver & man of all work Jacob had been kicked by a horse & badly (tho' I trust not fatally) hurt. She told me that Annie has been very sick from sore throat—was getting quite home sick &c. If you desire to write to her direct to Miss Annie Cater—care of Madam Du Pre[1] Charleston S.C. Mrs Cater also told me that she heard from the Wyllys that Old Mrs Grant was exceedingly ill. I have heard nothing of Mr H Grants family. I fear you will scarce make out that name I will try it again Du Pre—Ah that is it.—

Yesterday the Miss's Wylly—Rebecca Fraser—little Rebecca Demere & their little maid Becky went to Hopeton—RF has taken her final leave of the Island—she requested me to give her love to each of you. Elizabeth intends spending a few days with Mrs Horace Gould—so dear Tootee will have only Susan with her & has promised to spend Tuesday with me—wind & weather & Kings health permitting. The dear little fellow will be a whole year old on Tuesday. Your brothers & myself went over to Hamilton this evening. All pretty well—tho' EF fancied Matty to be sick. I saw only Susan—Elizabeth & Matty were shut up in the upper castle room. I received a long letter today from dear Mrs Paul Demere—she as usual makes more affectionate enquiries after you dear absent ones. She says the infant is very large & quite pretty—he was born on the 13th January. Susan Fraser told me this evening that John Demere had determined to hire out his negros & trying to get an overseers birth on the Brunswick Canal. Mr J H C[ouper] (in the event of his getting a birth on the Canal) offered him possession of Mr Barretts summer residence at Cartwrights for his family to reside in. I do hope for his wife & childrens sake that John Demere may be able to do this.

Tootee says she has written to you dear girls. I am now employed on letters to those beloved ones in California. I have 4 pages written to each of them. I will not quite finish them until tomorrow or Tuesday. I am determined this time to send my letters in full time. Last Mail was delayed some 23 hours. In fact since the loss of the *Magnolia* the Mails have been so irregular—there is no dependence to be placed in them. The remains of that ill fated boat remains bottom up where it has been since the 9th January. It is a perfect eye sore to me. Even more so since being informed that I need not expect to be paid for my loss's. The owners deserve no commiseration for their loss. They seam no way disposed to even help themselves—had the wreck been raised soon after the disaster—not only would the passengers (who did not find their baggage)—have recovered their trunks but they (the owners) would have saved much belonging to the boat.

Alic Boyd has got through his 7th week—I hope in another week he may use crutches.[2] Little Herbert is now getting on smartly tho' his sores are not yet well. We have been blessed with a fine rain—I actually rode through puddles of water (even on our road) this evening & it rained several hours after dark. This will enable us to put in the crop with some certainty of getting it up. My flowers too will be benefited. I hope on Wednesday to hear when the *Planter* will be repaired—we feel already the inconvenience of her loss. I have freight waiting in Savannah—with no prospect of getting it before the *Planter* is repaired. I hope by her very first trip dear Cousin Amanda will make us a visit. Mrs Gale would be pretty well but for a sore on her leg. And she is *so contrary* I fear it will not get well directly. Poor Mrs Gale she has suffered a great deal & must remain a cripple to the end of her days. I received by the return of the boat which carried up the ladies yesterday the book Georgia gave to the care of Mrs Huger. I have loaned it to Mrs Gale—as I have no time for reading at present. I must now conclude my own dear Florence. I doubt not you will detect many errors in this letter—But I cannot help it. I may not read it over. Your little brothers send a great deal of love to each of you. Mrs Gale would fill a whole sheet if I had time to write all she wishes to say to you. The servants all beg to be affectionately remembered. Kiss each other for me. My love to Adele & kind regards to her Parents and Sisters. With fervent prayers for your welfare & happiness—I am your devoted & most affectionate Mother

A M King

March 1st

William has just come over with the brother of the poor fellow who we picked up & buried here. This Mr McGiven is from New Jersey & says he cannot rest until he places his poor Brother along side of his Parents in New Jersey. I could not refuse giving assistance & yet it is hard to run such risks for my negros to have twice to handle this putred corpse & for which I may not even *get thanks*. William says he left all well at Hamilton—I hope nothing may occur to prevent dear Tootee from spending tomorrow with me. We are all as usual this morning. Spring begins to show itself—even tho' the beautiful green of the oranges is not seen. God bless you my beloved Florence—May His mercy & goodness restore you all to your devoted Mother

AMK

---

1. Anna has written over the name and then written it above.

2. On January 28 Anna wrote "Alic Boyd is doing as well as a broken thigh will let him" (Anna Matilda Page King to Florence Barclay King, January 28, 1852, KWC, GHS). He may have been injured in the explosion of the *Magnolia*.

Retreat 15th April 1852

My dearly beloved Florence

By the Tuesday Mail I wrote to dear Georgia. I also addressed a few hurried lines to dear Adele. This is now your turn dear Flora to hear from me & I thank God! I have no particularly bad news to give you. Latterly every letter I have written has told of severe illness or death. We—that is your Sisters family your brothers and myself are as usual. Mrs Gale has again been sick—but is better poor old woman her state of health is very bad. I had the pleasure yesterday of having dear Tootee & the children with me. William went fishing for drum & she came to cheer me with her loved presence. After I dismissed your brothers Floyd came & asked my permission to go with Mr Dunham across the sound to fish. I said *no*—he bore the refusal so well I was half tempted to call him back & tell him he may go. How much did I afterwards congratulate myself at not having done so. Mr Dunham & March[1] were oarsmen—*Charles* at the helm—soon the wind began to blow—the sound very rough—William was in his life boat & was better man'd—he came a cross the sound like a bird—whilst Dunham & March in the old "Conastoga" laboured over. I was uneasy enough about them—how much more I would have suffered had Floyd & Tip been with him. You may suppose how squally matters looked when William was uneasy for their safety. He landed at the creek & walked up along the beach watching Dunhams progress. The best of it is, Dunham did not catch a single fish. I hope it will deter him from going again.

The weather promised rain—so Tootee left me directly after dinner. It is well she went then as it rained until near bed time. As glad as I would have been to have her remain the night—she thought it her duty to return home & I would not press her to remain. I heard from her this morning they were all well. Floyd & Tip caught a nice mess of crabs yesterday & have just returned from a like expedition—so I shall have crabs for dinner. I was distressed by what I heard *from Tootee that Mr Hugh Grant said to William*. I perceive from this *that you have not followed my advice*. Those Grants are the *Telegraphs* of the County. *Whatever you write to them is made as public as the returns of an electionaire. From what Mr Grant told William openly in Brunswick—you have been far more communicative to Jinny Grant than you have ever been to your sister or myself.* I can only *hope* no *evil* may result from this *imprudence*. I can say no more than I have already said to you & your sisters on this subject. Were I to forbid your writing to those Grants—I do not *think you would obey me*. Time will convince you that *I am right* & *you wrong*. William also saw his brother who very kindly said if I intended bringing you home this summer he would take charge of you—I have nearly made up my mind to accept his kind offer for the reasons I gave Georgia & Lord in my last letters.

My *only* letter by the last Mail was from Mr Bourke. I did hope to have heard from one or the other of you dear girls. It does seem to me, as there are *three* of you—I may hear oftener from you. To receive letters from you loved ones is so great a pleasure to me. Tootee had a letter from Isa C[unningham] yesterday. Mrs John C[unningham] continues much the same. I sincerely hope as the spring advances Mr Picots health will improve. It is enough to make his wife & children miserable to see him suffer so much. Does Adele still give you music lessons? I hope to find a great improvement in all of you & I do long to hear the piano again. Our only music is the song of the birds. By the way "Tootee" is hatching out some young ones. I do hope the lice will not take those from me. Mrs "Bourke" is sitting—if she does no better this time I shall sicken of her.

The late rain's has vastly improved my gardens. The flower garden is now really beautiful—never so much so as now. Did Appy get those 3 shrubs safe. I wish I could send you each a bouquet this evening & some green pease for your dinner tomorrow. The birds have made love to my strawberrys—I am much annoyed you may be sure at this but I have submitted to this as well as to many other *disappointed hopes*. Mrs Richardson & Miss Mary Gould were here this afternoon—we walked round & round the garden plucking those beautiful roses until they formed a monster "nosegay." Mrs R leaves for Baltimore on Tuesday next—she tells me the Miss's Parland go on at the same time on their way to New York to some school there. Mr Long told William that he was to be married very soon to a young lady *in Savannah* & Mr Grant among other things told William that he intended sending Jinny & Sally back to Bishops school—but I suppose you know more of their plans than I do. I have heard nothing of Stephen Kings family since my last letter to your sister Georgia. I wrote to Mrs S C K[ing] as soon as I heard of her affliction—but do not expect her to answer my letter. There was a most destructive fire in Savannah last Sunday night & a less one the next night. The loss by the first estimated at $300,000—$50,000 of which falls on Mr Lamar & on which there was no insurance. As the month of May approaches I begin to dread another great fire in San Francisco—God! grant that (should there be one) your dear Father & brother may not be among the sufferers. Oh! my Florence what a blessing it will be if we are all permitted to meet again in life—in health & in happiness—this last can be *increased* or *lessened* by the exertions you are making *to reward your parents for all they are doing for your welfare*. Do not let it be said that you have wasted your time—much can be gained even in the short time you have left. I very much fear that Mr Picots sickness has been *unfortunate for you*. Your dear Father seems anxious you should continue at school another year! This *is to be considered*. Had you exerted yourself the past year it might not *have been deemed necessary*. Mrs Cater is now in Augusta. I do not think it was worth while sending Annie to Charleston for *less* than 3 months. I have not heard if it is Mrs Caters intention either to send her daughter back to Charleston or to give her further home instruction. Miss Emma Postell is to accompany them back to the Island & (as I understand) to spend the summer with Annie. I have heard nothing further of Frank Scarletts marriage.

Your sister pressed me much to spend the day with her tomorrow but I will not go unless Mrs Gale is able to get down stairs—I give her *all the time I can spare* from my other duties. Still she has many solitary hours poor old woman. I verily believe I am the greatest slave in Georgia—there is not a moment I can call my own. The boys occupy 4 hours of the morning & then I have so much else to do. Nothing goes on exactly as I wish it—but I cannot help it. Quamina has come to the conclusion it will be best to cut down the orange trees. We have been waiting to see how they would put out—it is done slowly & badly. This will take from the place its greatest beauty but it can't be helped. The sour oranges are as much injured as the sweet. Tell Appy that two of her hens will have the honor of hatching out my Shanghai—Malay & Java chickens—but I will pay her for them the same I would pay had the eggs been for her. I never knew fowls & Turkeys more backward than they are this year. As to ducks I have not an egg yet. But as others are more fortunate you need not fear starvation. Mrs Gale sends much love to each of you your dear little brothers send lots of kiss's. The servants all beg to be remembered to you. Give my beloved Geo & Appy each one of your sweetest kiss's for me & tell them each to give you one in return. My Florence I do long to see you all again—May God! in mercy permit us *all* once more to meet in this world. It is a world of trial & sorrow but there is another & a better world to which each day brings us nearer. May we each find a place "in that house not made with hands Eternal in the heavens." Do you my beloved children try for an entrance into that house. Praying the choicest blessings on Father, sons & daughters—I am as ever your devoted Mother

A M King

16th

We are all pretty much the same this lovely morning. Tip just brought in a whole hand full of sweet roses. I wish you had them. Give our love to dear Adele & that affectionate Soph. Also to Mrs Picot & Caro. Give a morning kiss to my precious Geo & Appy. God! bless you my own dear Flora.

Your own affectionate Mother

A M K

---

1. March, born August 14, 1806, is number 3 on the list from William Page's will and number 46 on the 1839 list, which notes him as a driver. See appendix 2.

Retreat Sunday night
16th May 1852

My own dear Florence

I had the happiness to receive your most welcome letter of the [blank] on Wednesday last & today received one from dear Appy of the *5th*—from Malley (at Rockville) of the *7th* & from Lord of the 10th Inst. It does seem strange that it should require 5 days longer for your letters to reach us than Lords. It is no fault this time of yours dear Flora for your letter & Appys to Tootee were post marked 6th of May—Appys the same to me. I am indeed gratified to a Merciful God! who permits you all to be able to say you *are in health*. What a blessing this is to me & to us all. Depend on it my own Flora, *health is a great blessing*. Your dear Sister—with Wm and the children came over as usual this Sunday evening—she brought me the letters she had received from you & Appy.

Yesterday the dear ones at Hamilton your little brothers & myself accepted an invitation from Mr & Mrs J H Couper to dine at Cannon's Point. I would scarcely have gone so *hot* a day but I wished to beg the favor of him to take you a little money & Mrs J H C[ouper] to take charge of a parcel for you girls which contains 2 thin coloured dress patterns for each of you & white swiss Muslin sufficient to make 3 dress's, 3 collars & 3 pair one for each of you under sleeves & neck ribbons—these coloured dresses I selected as the prettiest of the samples sent me—you will see I have pin'd on the names—on each article *except* the *under* sleeves & ribbon. Well these dresses I wish you will have made up as quickly as you can. You may have preferred selecting that number of dresses according to your own fancies—but I fancied these. I hope you will like them. Mr & Mrs Couper were exceedingly kind yesterday. They offer to take charge of you home. Dearly beloved children as anxious as I am to see you again, I have my fears that you may be made sick by returning home at that season. But what am I to do? I have not the means to let you 5 go travelling or boarding. Now if Mrs Henry King would give you all a most pressing invitation to stay with her until Nov. I verily believe I would consent rather than that you should run the slightest risk of being made sick by returning in July & August. What misfortune it is to be poor! And alas my children I have to tell you of another death among our people. Emoline died this morning after 8 days— & what is very distressing to me I have a number of others sick—with the exception Linda[1] & Frederic[2] every one of Suckeys family are sick. Mily is *very* sick—When I returned home last night I found Emoline so low & Mily just about to be ill. I made her come to the sick house—fearing the effect E-s death would have on her. This morning when I went into the sick house to see Mily[.] Rose's twins[3] were bawling & little "Mary Wylly"[4] squalling. When I mentioned this in the presence of Mrs Gale—she insisted that Mily should be given up to her to nurse in her own room as Mily had kindly nursed her through many sickness's. So Mrs Gale & myself have been Milys nurse to day poor girl she had scorching fever & God! alone knows how it is to terminate. I am as you may suppose in great distress of mind—I have my hands & head as well as heart full of trouble. The season is so hot & dry after such terrible winds the cotton crop is miserable. Oh! you can have no idea of what I am undergoing—But God! be praised for so great a mercy—I hear that you are all well. My dear Tootee & her children are well your dear little brothers are well—& have yet health & strength to enable me to see to the sick. What a comfort it would be if I could get the advice of a good Physician. I have sent for Dr Wilson—tho I have but little confidence in his skill. If Cousin Amanda could only have come last week—what a relief it would have been to me. Rhina is very much out of health—I sent her to Darien to Dr. Sulivan but he did not seem to think much was the matter with her. After she came back she expressed so great a desire to go to Amanda that I sent her off to Fancy Bluff last Tuesday. I have since heard from Amanda who with Mr Woolley intend coming down this coming Thursday. They will find me I fear not only in trouble but in dirt—for Neptune being sick I have no one to scrub. I earnestly pray for a resigned spirit—to bear with resignation & patience the afflictions sent me. I cannot be sufficiently grateful that this sickness is not among my children. I have not time dear Flora to write you the news of the Island. You will so soon see Mr & Mrs J H Couper & Margaret I refer you to them for all news of the Grants. With the exception of the note I got from Jinny *after* she started for the North & Mr Grants message about cotton seed I have heard nothing *from* the Grants. Mr Bourke wrote me a very long letter by this days mail. Rebecca Fraser is still with Mrs Bourke. Mr Bourke & Sarah invite you girls to stop with them on your way home—but I am in hopes you will not be compelled to stop in S[avanna]h. Mr B says Mrs Cater & Annie are still in Augusta. Mr & Mrs J H C[ouper] saw Stephen Kings family when on their way to Savannah. Mrs S C K[ing] expressed her self as perfectly resigned to Martha's death & both Mr & Mrs Couper told me that Stephen C. King was looking remarkably well—& *in fine spirits* full of the anticipated pleasures of their North Western excursion. Mr Bourke informs me that Mrs John Cunningham cannot last many days longer. Oh! this death— how terrible it is!!

Mr J H C[ouper] is certainly very kind to me. I am sorry I used such harsh expressions as those contained in my last letter to Geo—I must however entreat you to *be guarded in all you say* to her or Margaret. Hamilton does not accompany his parents he seems to feel this very much. It must however be a relief to Mr & Mrs Couper that he remains with his brothers. Their first plan was to meet the *Welaka* at the cut but they have now determined to take boat at

Hamilton. I fear I shall not be able to accept Tootees invitation to see them de-part. This is the Mail by which I am to write to those beloved ones in Califor-nia—how it grieves me that I cannot tell them better news of the health of the negros & the crop. But thank God! I trust I may be able to say the dear ones at Hamilton & under this roof are well. Kiss your sweet sisters for me—for your brother & Mrs Gale. Give my love to dear Adele—my best regards to Mr Pi-cot—Madame & the young ladies Caro & Soph. I will add just a line on Tues-day God! in mercy grant it may not be to impart further misfortunes. I must now bid you good night my own dear Flora. Praying the choicest blessings of God! on you my sweet child & on all you beloved absent ones & (tho' death has removed several who would have rejoiced to see you return) let us all unite in earnest prayer that the family may all meet again in health & happiness.—

Your devotedly affectionate Mother

A M King

1. "50 Negros with Their Increase" lists Linda as one of Neptune and Suckey's chil-dren. She is number 35 on the 1839 list, birth date April 29, 1838; and number 46 on the 1853 list. On the 1859 list she is number 48 and appears with her husband, Jimper (number 47). See appendix 2.

2. Frederic, born February 3, 1843, is number 42 on the 1853 list. On the 1859 list his name is spelled Frederick. See appendix 2.

3. Rose is number 12 on the list from William Page's will; number 92 on the 1839 list, her birth date January 2, 1814; number 69 on the 1853 list; and number 124 on the 1859 list. See appendix 2.

4. Mary Wylly is number 76 on the 1853 list, birth date June 5, 1850; and number 129 on the 1859 list. See appendix 2.

June 7, 1852, to November 15, 1852

Tootee dear as long as I live & have a husband—I will never again leave home without him.

After a painful separation from her husband and six of her children and a period of sickness and death among Retreat's bondpeople, Anna was compelled, by nervous exhaustion, to go North to recuperate. Reunited with Georgia, Florence, Virginia, Lord, and Mallery, she spent the summer and fall writing to Tootee, who remained on St. Simons, as well as to T. B. King and Butler in California.

7th June 1852

My dearly beloved Lordy

From dear punctual Malleys letter of the 29th Ult. which I received yesterday I rejoice to hear you were both well at that time. Tootee had a long letter from Georgia & we both had letters from dear Butler, & I one from your dear Father those from the two latter were up to the 3d May. How grateful I am to God! that you were all able to say you were well. Oh! my son in the midst of all these my trials at home, I feel that God! has been yet Merciful. So far as I know, my husband my children are spared to me. With them I may yet enjoy the balance of my days on earth—without them—what would be to me all the riches of this world? but as dross!—

Your dear Father *decidedly disapproves* of my bringing you 5 dear children home before Autumn. Did I go contrary to his advice—& either of you should be made sick—what would be my feelings? To leave your sisters without proper protection would not do. I may be difficulted to raise the means to support us all even in the most economical way—but it is perhaps the wisest plan for me to join you all. The fact is Lordy I do believe if I stay here I must sink under my nervous state. For years has this been growing gradually worse. The sickness & death this time seems to have been too much for me. I can only hope the meeting with you all the change of scene will restore my mind to its former state & enable me better to bear the trials we are all subject to in this world of trouble.[1]

This nervousness has been growing gradually on me for years—But for this fatal sickness on the plantation I could have borne on & have thought myself well off—even when compelled to bear a longer separation from you loved ones. But the death of these negros & the sickness which still prevails on the place has broken me down. I feel that I must go away from the place or sink under my troubles. I shall leave home with deep regret carrying with me many cares on my mind. The leaving of your sister & her children not the least of these cares. But she would not leave her husband even if we had the means of her going with me. I can do nothing for these sick people myself. I have had two skillful physicians to them. The one left us on Saturday night, the other goes this evening. Even if I had the means to bribe them to longer stay—they could not neglect their other patients. They tell me these now sick are doing well—but others may occur. Well I have done all I could I can do no more. I can only trust in the Mercy of God! that no more will be taken from me. Toney is able to go out, & Dunham says he is better but neither of them are capable of doing full duty. The negros are disposed to give all the trouble they well can—as is always the case when they see a chance to impose. I have never suffered so severely by being a slave holder & I am so heartily sick of being one that I would even sell at a sacrifice if I could sell out altogether. But I must have patience & trust in Gods! Mercy that health may be restored to the place. I cannot but think the location of our negro houses has been the cause of all the sickness—the negros come home heated from their days work—sit down in front of their houses in the sea breeze get a violent check of perspiration then follows fever—but 3 of the new ground negros have been sick & those of a less violent type—there are fevers at Hamilton but not of a serious character. In fact we have been more unfortunate this year than any one else on the Island. *Rhina* is in decided bad health. I shall take her with me. I hope it will be the saving of her life. But it is no use my telling you any more of my troubles. God! grant I may meet you all in health. And I do hope you will all try by your good conduct to be a comfort to me.

My dear cousin Amanda & her good husband have been perfectly devoted to me. They have just lost a boy about your age from drowning. Capt Stevens lost a man he had just given $600 for by drowning—& James Gould lost a boy last week—(they suppose drowned at Blackbanks). Well these are terrible shocks—but to lose them in this way one [at a time]—is not like seeing so many ill & do what you will so many die in one family.[2] But the Will of God! be done. I cannot be sufficiently grateful that this sickness & death has been confined to my negros! But we will trust in Gods! mercy that the worst is now over. That this cloud will pass over & that sunshine & *joy* may once more be ours—this affliction I trust will work its own good by convincing us of the uncertainty of all worldly riches—& induce us more earnestly to seek that which man cannot take from us & which God! will bless & increase a thousand fold.

I think Tootee wrote to you by the Fridays mail. As it is necessary I should practice the most rigid economy I would like to locate in some retired pleasant village where I could put Floyd & Tip to school—& where perhaps your sisters could continue to receive instruction. We must not expect a gay—but we can hope for a happy meeting. Mr. & Mrs. Woolley are going North—To have dear Amanda with me at least a part of the time will be a great comfort—& happiness to me. Your dear Sister is a perfect little heroine—she has been staying with me since Amanda & Mr. Woolley left on Saturday. It is determined that we are to leave the coming Thursday. I hope I may not give it up at the last moment. I have no inducement but the pleasure of see[ing] you all a few months sooner. As to my health I could bear even what I am now suffering if I thought yourself & sisters & Mall would do as well without as with me. Your dear Sister—brothers & the babies send much love to you. Be careful of your eyes dear Lordy. May God! grant we may all meet again in life—in health & happiness is the earnest prayer of your devoted Mother

A M King

1. Tootee wrote to her father on June 5,

I have but a few moments but hasten to write a few lines to tell you of my dear Mother—She wrote you yesterday and told you all that has passed within the last two months at Retreat—Her health has suffered severely and Dr Curtis says there is no remedy for the present state of nervous derangement except entire change of sene and climate. . . . First she thought of going alone with Mrs & Mr Woolley. . . . But my dear father I think you would prefer that my husband your son in law—should be her escort—so as he thinks the same and my dear Mother only refuses as she fears my being left alone—I insist that he shall go—And dear Father you may be sure that he will take all care of her. Pray dear Father write mother *approving* of this move for she has taken it in to her nervous head that you Father dear may not like it—I know my Father that if your voice could be heard from that far off land it would be loud in your wish for her to go—as indeed I and Dr C—& all of us think that if she remains here there is no telling how long we may have her with us— It will benefit her so much. (Hannah Page King Couper to Thomas Butler King, June 5, 1852, WAC, SHC)

On July 14 Thomas Butler King replied,

In my distress about your dear mother your letter of the 5th Ult gave me much consolation—I feel quite sure that under the protection of your good husband she will be as well taken care of as circumstances will permit and that she will be comfortably lodged in some quiet place where she may enjoy the society of your brothers and sisters and be cheered by pleasant scenes and the company of agreeable people—You cannot imagine my dear Tootee, what a shock the intelligence of your dear mothers indisposition has given me—I am in a constant *whirl* of business which gives little time for reflection and requires all my energies to manage—This is a *sad* relief to me—yet *it is* a relief—Else I know not what I should or could do—I am struck almost dum by the idea that your dear Mother, who has ever enjoyed such strong health has at last been prostrated by a derangement of her nervous system— It will now avail nothing to imagine *how* it has been done—Her exposure has been, I am sure, mostly unnecessary, but I should not now say so to her. She has taken the best means to recover and may God! in His mercy bless and restore her to health— I shall await the arrival of the next mail in fear and trembling—If she can but escape fever until her arrival in the healthful atmosphere of New Jersey, all will be well— What I dread is fever at sea—but the voyage is now so quickly performed by Steam that there is much less danger than formerly in a sea voyage—I hope for the best . . . I am greatly indebted to your good husband for taking charge of your dear mother—Pray tender my best thanks to him— . . . Pray write to me frequently— The intelligence of your dear mothers indisposition has made me almost as nervous as she is presented to be— . . . I cannot say how soon I shall return—If God in his mercy grants our prayers for the recover[y] of your dear mother I may remain here until November or perhaps longer—In fact I could not get away sooner, were I to resign tomorrow such is the extent and nature of the business of which I have charge—This seperation is painful and distressing in the last degree—My motives in coming here were good—May Providence bring good out of it. (Thomas Butler King to Hannah Page King Couper, July 14, 1852, WAC, SHC)

2. Anna wrote to Florence on June 1, "Poor Sukey died this morning. Liddy & Linda are yet in a very precarious state. I have great dread lest the death of their Mother will have a serious effect on them. We attribute poor Sukeys death to her grief for Mily. She seemed to bear Emolines death as well as we could expect, but when Mily died she seemed plunged into a state of apathy from which nothing could rouse her. On Saturday her fever returned & we could do nothing to save her" (Anna Matilda Page King to Florence King, June 1, 1852, TBK, SHC).

Sunday night 13th June
[Savannah, Georgia]

My own beloved child

It is very probable I may not have time to write to you tomorrow so I will just give you a few lines before I go to bed. Oh! my Tootee it does seem strange that I have you to write to in addition to my other dear absent ones—my sweet child I do feel this separation from you very much. I never see a little child in the street but I fancy I can see some resemblance to our dear little ones but not one of them is as pretty as yours. I wrote you by the mail yesterday before the Southern mail came in. I then had to go out shopping—a most disagreeable occupation to me. I was out all the morning *trudge trudge*. Mr Woolley, Amanda

& myself went to that famous London House store. I did run up a bill of $15.55 cts—but think I could have got just as good & as cheap at De Witts & Morgans. Mr Woolley & Amanda did pretty much all their shopping there. I then came back to this truly friendly roof & after dinner off again I went.[1] In our preambulations we encountered dear William—he was in McClesky & Nortons, he joined us—took us into an ice cream shop where he & Mr Woolley ate twice as much ice cream as we could. We then went to a new confectionary establishment kept by *Monsieur* N Lefort, Proprietor of the "Paris house" there we met Mrs McDonald & Sue Johnson eating ice cream. My object in going into this establishment was to purchace you some cake, as you forbid my getting candy for the chicks—it did seem hard that you all should be deprived of candy because dear Bob would have it & it would give her tooth ache. But as neither William or myself could bear that she should have an ache we passed by the beautiful candies.

I must before I go further thank you for your comforting letter—thank you & Mr Dunham too for the comforting news you both give. I pray God's Mercy on those poor negros that they may indeed all be better, & may live to welcome me back. It requires no little resolution on my part to keep from getting into the *Planter* tomorrow and going back to you. But for those dear ones who I have not seen for more than a year I certainly would do it. It worries me that I should be the cause of keeping William so long from you. I know his presence is so necessary to your comfort & happiness. It is very selfish in me my permitting him to accompany me. God! in mercy protect you all & grant to your good husband a happy & safe return to you my love.

Last evening Mr Cuyler & Margaret called—they staid here a long time. Margaret is the same old seven and sixpence—Mr Cuyler is no longer a handsome man, he was very kind however. Mrs Matthau had called when I was out. Lizzie I believe I mentioned had called—I met her & Dick in the streets yesterday. In the presence of Mr Cuyler Margaret gave me an invitation to dine with them tomorrow & ask[ed] William to accompany me. All that Mr Cuyler said was to ask where William was staying—I did not say I would dine with them or that I would mention the matter to William. Mrs Johnston made a long call on me in the evening—& was the same as when we were on the Sand Hills. I had invitations from the Cuylers—Mrs Johnston & the Cunninghams to go to church today. But some how I preferred to go with Cousin A[manda] & Mr Woolley to their church, so they called for me & the boys. We had a most excellent sermon this morning from the Presiding Elder. On our way to church this evening we had the *pleasure* of meeting Mrs Charles Grant. She was in one of her nervous excited humors—saying what an attack of nervousness she had had the last few days—Dr Sullivan in attendance &c. This evening she sent to ask me to go to church with her after tea but I was too tired—for after church Amanda, Mr W[oolley], the boys & myself had been overhauling the new part of the city. Every body must have known that we were country folks. The City is really rapidly building up. If I could sell my lands on the Island & purchase a house here, the hire of the negros would *maintain us beautifully*. William should come too—he would soon find something to do. Is it not a delightful plan? Let us think of it!—I feel such a kind of horror of St Simons.

When we got back I found dear William & John Cunningham here, the former regretted very much he had not gone to walk with us—I felt even more sorry I think than he was & had I thought of the walk before leaving for Church I would have sent Middleton for him.[2] Mr C[unningham] says his wife is not so well today—will you believe it that woman has had the *conscience to miscarry*. The Doctors say if she *does again* she will die right away, & if she could have kept it—she would have recovered. This is what Sarah told me this evening. This was the reason *she* was so ill some time ago.

Dear Sarah Bourke is just as kind to me as tho' she was my own child, so gentle—so thoughtful. Poor child she has much to worry her at this time & yet any one to see her would not suspect anything. Poor B[ourke] has been in a frolic & will carry it on. I have not set eyes on him since I came, he stays out all day, at night he staggers home & is assisted up to his room, he is off again as soon as he gets up in the morning. I am *grieved* for Sarah. I would leave the house & go either to the Cunninghams (who have press'd me to divide my time with them)—or to stay at the house Amanda stops at—but I fear it will not only be talked of—but that [Sarah] will be hurt if I do. I consulted William & he thinks I had best remain where I am. Poor, poor Bourke—what a ship wreck he is making of his own & his sweet wifes happiness. It is impossible that any one can be more amiable or patient than Sarah is. I am trying to persuade her either to go with us North or go South this summer. If she goes South I know you & William will do all in your power to induce her to visit you. Remember my child that all that I have left behind in the way of comforts is at your service.

The 1 dozen doyles only cost 56¼ cts. I send them to you. The 4 pair of gloves I hope will fit you. The bread I hope you will enjoy, as I send $1 worth—which is more than you can use—I want you to send Dunham a loaf—& give a *little* of it to the sick negros. *Two pieces* of the ginger cake give to Ishmael if he is able to eat it.[3] The two straw hats are for Neptune the black for dresses & 2 black silk handkerchiefs are for Liddy & Linda.[4] The two tin coffee pots are for Cupid & Toney. The Iron pot is for Quamina. Tell my precious babies— that I will bring their toys when I return—& that they must think of me when they eat the cakes. I went through the market on Saturday evening—how I wished you could have had some of the good things I there saw, such splendid beef, Mutton, Pork, & the finest vegetables I ever saw—*tomatto* in abundance, & even water Melons, *for which* they asked one dollar a piece. I thought if I could just have *transferred* all that meat & all those vegetables to Retreat the negros would not have the conscience to be sick any more. I have written you a long letter with very little in it. But I feel like a cat in a strange garret, & some what bewildered. I do hope we may not leave before the Mail gets in on Wednesday. And Oh! how I pray you may be able to give me good news of all I left behind—first of your own dear self & children, then my poor negros—Mr Dunham & the place & of Mrs Gale. Tell her I have not seen her grand child—but Mrs Branch told me yesterday that she had seen him very lately & that he was perfectly well. I must say good night—Amanda will wish me to add a few lines for her in the morning. Praying the choicest blessings on you my precious child I am your devoted Mother

AMK

I was awoke this morning by a cry of "fire." You may depend on it I was up & awoke the boys quick enough—Rhina soon came up & said "it was close by." The poor boys were hurrying on their own clothes & urging me to do the same. Soon after Mr Woolley came & begged me not to be alarmed as there was no danger to us. The fire is still burning—it commenced in a carpenters shop & communicated to a large brick building belonging to a Mr Cohen which is yet burning & even now there is another fire down at Yamacraw.[5] It is very fortunate that these did not occur in the night—or even yesterday when the wind was high. This is a lovely morning, calm bright & beautiful God! grant it has dawned on *all* I hold dear in as good bodily health as it does on your little brothers & myself. The boys tell me Amanda was at the fire & that 2 brick houses & the carpenters shop are consumed. This must have been designedly done.

The basket in which the bread goes belongs to Sarah do take care of it & restore it safe to Sarah. Rhina seems better. I hope all may be for the best that I take her with me. The expense is the least consideration with me. You must tell my good Pussy that I think constantly of her. Should any thing befall her, I would indeed meet with a serious loss. I pray God! no more will be taken from me yet a while. I saw 4 funeral processions yesterday—3 white & 1 negro, there may have been others—but there are a great many people in this place. Tell Lady to be sure & try & raise & keep the poultry well. And Maria must be careful of my birds. I know you will take an interest in all that concerns my interest. I only hope you will first be careful of your own dear self & those sweet children. Clementine I trust will keep well then I know she will relieve you in the sewing line. As soon as Jane can be spared from nursing she & Ellen[6] (before the latter is able to cook) ought to make for those who have large families or cannot sew. But I left all to yours & Williams care & management. Do not neglect to see to those window shades & return them if they do not answer. I send the Potash for soft soap. I neglected to ask Mr Dunham to give Lady or old Jane 25 lbs of tallow from the barn—pray do so for me. The oranges are not good—they cost me 50 cts. I did not ask Dunham to take my chest of silver—perhaps it will be just as safe in the house. William has just been here he is well & says he has written to you. Amanda sends you a dress which she begs you will have made up & wear out this summer for her sake. She sends you much love. Rhinas things are all in one bundle. The cake put in the trunk is mine for you. If you choose you can send for either of my tin cases to keep your bread in—the negro shoes is for Alfred[7]—Jimper did not give me his measure. Should he be in want you can send for a pair for him.

Isa Cunningham was here this morning one of those families lost every thing they had by the fire this morning—it is a true saying—we know not what a day may bring forth—they went to bed last night surrounded by comforts—now they have not even a suit of clothes to wear. These fires are becoming serious & alarming. Do my child beg & order my servants to be ever on their guard & do you be the same.

I wonder if Hamilton Couper would not stay with you until William returns? Do Tootee ask him to do so. Should any thing happen to you in Williams absence what would I do? Kiss over & over again those sweet children for me. The medicine you will find altogether that which William sends you as well as that for Retreat. I fear you will find this letter very confused—but I have been writing it by snatches—I want to say a great deal to the servants & yet I do not know what more I can say. I implore of them to be careful of their health & conduct & add no more than they can help to my troubles. M[?] of Iron would I think be a safe tonic for all who have been so sick—beginning at 6, 7 or 8 drops in Camomile flower tea three times a day & gradually increasing one drop a day until it reaches 20. 1 half tumbler of tea is enough at a time. Once more adieu my sweet child—God bless & preserve you all

Your devoted Mother

A M King

1. Anna was staying in Savannah at the home of Thomas Bourke and his wife, Sarah, the daughter of Henri and Anne Du Bignon.

2. Middleton (number 92) was born December 2, 1837 (see appendix 2). Anna gave him to Tootee as part of her inheritance from the estate.

3. This is Ishmael 2d (number 110), born March 9, 1828 (see appendix 2).

4. "The black for dresses" I believe refers to black fabric she was sending to be made into dresses for slaves.

5. A western suburb of Savannah.

6. Ellen is number 23 on the list from William Page's will; number 32 on the 1839 list, birthday July 17, 1816; and number 13 on the 1853 list, where her birthday is recorded as January 17, 1816. See appendix 2.

7. Alfred is number 49 on the list from William Page's will and number 75 on the 1839 list, where he appears next to his twin brother, William, both born December 3, 1822. On the 1853 list he and William are numbers 102 and 103. See appendix 2.

26th June 1852 to the 29th
Allentown-Leghigh [*sic*] County
Pennsylvania

After writing a hasty letter to my dear Tootee on Friday evening Mary, Amanda, Mr Woolley, G[eorgia], F[lorence], V[irginia], F[loyd] & Tip & myself went out for a long walk—our object to visit a Furnace about 1½ miles off—Lord was too lazy to go with us. Henry & Mr Longnecker had gone to Easton.[1] We were delighted with the scenery—but the road was dusty. We however were all good walkers & in time reached the Furnace. Mr Lewis is an agent for the Company [and] has a beautiful residence opposite the Furnace. The daughters of the [a]gent had called on the girls—& their intention was to return the call. Mr & Mrs Woolley & Floyd & myself past on whilst the rest of the party past in. We could see very little to interest us, no one to explain. Neither is friend Woolley yet up to the art of shipping shillings into other peoples hands—no one seemed to care whether we understood what was going on or not. The huge engine was terrific & I was glad to get out of it. Soon Mr Lewis & Sister Mary came to invite us to the house—where we found the rest of the party very comfortably seated. Mrs Lewis is monstrous fat—& like most fat persons very good natured. They were all exceedingly polite—inviting us to take tea—this we declined but accepted their invitation to walk about the garden &c. Every thing was in most beautiful order. After a stay of some half hour we took leave & bent our way home ward. On our way home we met brother Henry & Mr Longnecker—Lord not yet recovered from his fit of laziness. Mr W[oolley] & Cousin A[manda] took tea with us—& remained until past ten.

On Sunday we went to Church—& listened to a Scotch man, very ugly & not very eloquent. Church goes in at 10—we dine at 1—then to church again at 6, leaving us breathing time of 6 hours. About 4 in the afternoon a most fearful accident occur'd. There is a beautiful spring—one which I visited with my beloved husband in 1827—& which I was at on Saturday morning (I find my dates are being confused—it was on Friday evening that I wrote to my precious Tootee & went to the Furnace). On Saturday morning Lordy went to New Haven to attend to some business of his own & to look for lodgings for us. On Saturday evening we all went out to "Prospect rock," situated about 3 miles out of Allentown. Mary, Henry, the boys, Mr Woolley & myself were in a carriage drawn by a splendid pair of black horses, driven by a white man. Cousin A[manda], G[eorgia], & V[irginia] were in a very nice light carriage driven by Mr Longnecker. Florence would not go. Well the hills here are very steep & when we were ascending a pretty high hill—we met the stage full in & out side. It came thundering down Hill & our beautiful black horses took it into their heads to buck & rear—may be I was not frightened [*sic*]. After this we went on pretty well. We had to walk (after ascending half way) up this prospect mountain, & glad was I to get out of the carriage. This Mountain is shaded by splendid trees of various kinds the earth thickly strewed with rock of all sizes (the old folks say "the devils *wife emptied her apron* full of rocks down there"). These rocks are piled up one on another beyond the tops of the highest trees. The most of our party climbed up to the very top, but I remained about 10 feet below. Floyd & Tip took off their shoes & stockings—& were never one moment still, this made me perfectly nervous. A fall off of one side would have been a fearful thing. We remained there perhaps a half hour—viewing the beautiful scenery—we could see for miles around—every spot in perfect cultivation—or here & there dotted with lovely groves of trees. The scenery is certainly most beautiful. Just as high up as carriages can come, is a little farm—Brother Henry tells me this soil is the very best for fruit of every kind—the spot was not well cultivated but the trees were loaded with apples & pears, of course yet very small. After drinking water from the well better than iced water & trying to eat some bad ginger bread—we turned our faces homeward. I walked down *to the road*, & would have walked further but from a fear of fatiguing brother Henry. We had a more pleasant ride back than going—found Flora just waking from a nap.

Well they do sit up to an abominable hour here, every one takes tea at 6 oclock & as it is not dark until near eight—all the visiting is done after tea. I had taken a long walk in the morning then this ride & walk in the afternoon made me pretty tired. Amanda & Mr Woolley again took tea with us &c.

The accident yesterday was this. There are several omnibus' here & as many forget for what the sabbath is intended it is the fashion to ride *to the spring*. One of these huge vehicles just as it was rising the Hill—being filled inside—& several on the top, the leaders got unhitched—the wheel horses were unable to drag up the load the hind wheels got off the road, the driver was drunk as was also many of the inside passengers. Over went the omnibus & it performed a complete summer set.[2] Two poor little boys were instantly killed—as incredible as it may seem the *head* of one of these poor little fellows *was driven through the top of the omnibus*—one poor boy still lives with both legs shattered & a piece of glass driven through his neck & face he was reported dead yesterday but still lives in the utmost misery. He makes the 3d boy, the 4th is brother to Sister Marys cook—a smart little fellow between the size of Floyd & Tip a pretty boy. He was dashed (as the carriage went over across the road) one leg & his collar bone broken, but he is doing very well. One of the two boys who were instantly killed was the youngest son of a widow who 3 weeks ago buried her oldest son a most promising youth. All who were inside the omnibus escaped with life—tho much cut with broken glass one little girl 1 1/2 years old was covered with blood—but not one drop of her own. Had this accident happened 50 yds or even 25 yds higher up scarcely one would have escaped with life. The omnibus not only performed this summerset—but then seem'd to bound over again—the horses apparently uninjured. We walked down last evening to look at the wreck—it was a fearful sight—quantities of blood stained the ground, & they say the inside of the carriage was covered with blood & human hair. This is a very quiet place & this awful accident seems to have struck them all with awe.

This morning I spent with dear Amanda—She has been very unwell since yesterday & Mr Woolley is very little better. I think she has been walking too much—perhaps the water may not agree with her as it is *limestone*. Mr Woolleys indisposition is from cold. Brother Henry is better—Mary & the girls are quite well as are also Floyd & Tip. Rhina & myself are about the same.

Floyd fully made up his mind to have his Dauguerrotype taken for you this morning—he regrets the want of his old straw hat & ragged clothes—thinking you would sooner recognize him in those than in his present garb. G[eorgia], F[lorence], & V[irginia] have gone out to spend an hour with cousin A[manda]. After tea I am to go over again to see Amanda & the others are to make calls. Lord promises to return here on Wednesday. I rather think he finds this place dull, for my own part I would but for *conscience* sake be willing to stay here until it is time to go home.

29th

I had just got so far when the girls came in from a walk bringing with them your dear letters to George [Georgia] & myself—I was taken with such a tremor I could scarce open the letter. I then began to glance from page to page until—"kill'd by a rattlesnake" struck me. I got so nervous I called Georgia & begged her to read the letter first—& tell me the contents. After hearing there had been no deaths—I listened to Georgia with a heart over flowing with gratitude to God for all the blessings you could tell me of. I then *insisted* on hearing all you could say to Georgia. You promised me dear Tootee to tell me all that concerns you, & yet you try to keep from me that your "cough was worse & that you were troubled again with that pain." My own beloved you can have but little idea how *much* this troubles me. I feel convinced one of your bad turns were at hand, & William would not be with you. My blessed child why are you not more careful of your precious health. What would become of me if harm befalls *you* whilst I am so far away from you & your sweet babes. Oh! my Tootee God! be merciful to us all!!

Mary & the girls had some calls to make—our dear cousin was so unwell the boys & myself went over to sit with her. I took with me both of your letters & read them aloud to Amanda. Then Mr Woolley & the boys went out to walk & I remained with Cousin A[manda]—until ten oclock. We talked over all you had written to me. I have been feeling very uneasy about that boy Edenburgh[3]—I have no doubt that sudden attack of his was all owing to his having got hold of something to eat which was not good for him. What a wretched race of beings they are. How ungratefully Rose has behaved. I suppose she ran away because Dunham wished her to go to New field! I can only hope the orderly ones will continue to do their duty & the wretched who give trouble *may be made* to do their duty. Tell those who are doing well that they shall be rewarded—& those who are refractory that I am grieved to think they would wish to add to my troubles & that time will *convince them* of their folly.

You have ere this been informed of my great disappointment relative to your Fathers visit to us. I can but hope he will be back in November—I have had no letter later than the 3d of May from him tho' 2 of later date have I received from dear Butler. What a prince of a son that boy is!—

I received a letter from Mr J H C[ouper] a day or two since of which the enclosed is a copy. I wish William to keep this & send me a list of the names & ages &c of these 115 negros. I was under the impression there were 140 negros & so informed Mr King. From what passed between Mr Corbin & myself I was under the impression the purchase could be made more advantageously to us. If dear William would just write to my husband & give him his opinion of the proposition made by Mr J H C[ouper] I would be much indebted to him. I will send Mr J H Coupers proposition to your Father in my next letter.[4]

I am very home sick dear Tootee—tho' I am really as kindly treated by dear Mary & Henry as I can possibly be. They have a most delightful house, & garden, every comfort around them & these comforts we enjoy to the very extent. I could be almost happy if you were all with me. But when I think of your distant Father & Brother—& of you beloved ones at Hamilton & my poor negros I cannot be otherwise than anxious & unhappy. God! has been merciful to us— May this mercy be continued. I hope you will get the trunks Georgia sent & the letter I wrote last week telling you what to send back to me. I will remain here until the 10th of July—then go to New Haven from thence I can write you how long to direct your letters there. Cousin Amanda is so much better as to have spent this day with us & will go to Bethlehem tomorrow. We will miss them very much & regret their departure. She is now lying on my bed talking to Florence. Georgia & Appy are entertaining Mr Woolley in the passage. This is where we sit in the forenoon & until tea—a very delightfully cool shaded spot one drawing room opens into this Hall, two beautiful drawing rooms a dining room & his office down stairs. But I will tell you all about this when we meet. I thought when I again wrote I would have had leisure & given you a quiet letter—but our dear cousin being here all day, & the children all talking so much I am confused. I often think of you & your precious children. My darling how I long to see you, you my precious Tootee & those sweet babes & my noble son William. Last Friday when the wind blew so hard here—how my heart trembled for dear William—God! grant he may long ere this reaches you be safe with you & those little darlings. What would I not give to have a peep at you all—you my beloved children—poor Mrs Gale, my good negros—my pretty birds—my garden, even the old house & dirt. I know my child you will do all in your power for me. I only hope you will not overtax your strength. *If* the negros can only be restored to health, *if* they *behave* well & *if* the seasons are favorable—I hope I may be able to meet the expenses of this to me terrible & eventful year. God! knows what is best for us. My mind is still disturbed— but *I sleep* better, this is some comfort. Kiss over & over again my precious babes. Kiss William too for me. May God! reward him for his kindness to me. My love to Mrs Gale—shake by the hand my good Pussy—Clementine, Maria, Mom Jane, Toney, Quam &c &c &c. Tell them all the kind messages your own kind heart may suggest. Cousin A[manda], Mr W[oolley], Mary, Henry, G[eorgia], F[lorence], V[irginia], F[loyd], Tip each & every one send their love kiss's &c—Rhina is terribly indignant at Rose's conduct. She sends lots of love to all her family & friends. Georgia began a letter to you but I rather think she will be too late for this evenings Mail. She has to entertain Mr Woolley. Remember me to Mr Dunham. When you go to Retreat again pray enquire particularly after the little negros. I fear in all this sickness poor Affey's children are sadly neglected. How could Rose be so ungrateful to me? It is probable she will spite me by neglecting her children.[5] I think Pussy deserves the highest praise, & she shall be rewarded if I live to return. I must now really stop my own baby. Oh! my Tootee how I do long to see you all again. It seems years since we parted. I hope to hear again from you ere I leave this. Praying the choicest blessings of God! on you I am your devoted Mother

A M King

I commenced this as a journal—I prefer the letter style. This is a poor apology for a letter or journal.

1. Mary and Henry were Henry King, T. B. King's brother, and his wife, with whom Anna and family were visiting. Mr Longnecker seems to have been a lawyer or clerk working with Henry.

2. Somersault.

3. Edinboro is number 103 on the 1839 list, his birthday May 1832; and number 87 on the 1853 list (spelled Edenborough). On the 1859 list—the inventory of Anna's estate—he is recorded with Jerry and is given no value; Jerry's value by comparison is $900. Why Edenborough was recorded as having no monetary value is unknown but it may have been because of injury, illness, or disability. "50 Negros with Their Increase" lists Edinburg as Maria's child along with Affy and Betty 2d. It is unclear whether Edenbourough and Edinburg are the same person. See appendix 2.

4. It was Anna and Thomas Butler King's hope that they could buy the property for their daughter, son-in-law, and grandchildren. By 1852 the house was in need of major repairs and the lands depleted. The "copy" from J H Couper to which Anna refers states,

Immediately on the receipt of Mr Kings letter through William, on the subject of the purchase of Hamilton I placed his offer before Mr Corbin, the Trustee of his daughter Miss Isabella H. Corbin. Before his reply to it was obtained I heard of the expected return of Mr King, and immediately after, of your intended visit to Philadelphia. Hoping to have met with Mr King in New York, I thought it better to communicate with him personally rather than by letter; but being disappointed in this, and not having any assurance of the time of Mr King's arrival, I have concluded to address you both as early as possible. Mr Corbin declined selling at $50,000 and at 6 per cent interest; but will, if he concludes to sell at all . . . take $12,000 for the lands, buildings &c at Hamilton & Couper's point. $350 per head for the negroes, being now 115 or 118 less 3 children belonging to the Hopeton gang—say for 115 $40,250—and for the Hog crawl tract of 100 acres of pine $100. Tools, carts, flats, boats horses, mules, & cattle $1650—together $54,000. The payments to be on the

1 of January 1853—	$10,000
1 " 1854—	10,000
1 " 1855—	10,000
1 " 1856—	10,000
1 " 1857—	10,000
1 " 1858—	4,000
	$54,000

With interest at 7 *percent*, payable annually on the 1st of January of each year. The first payment of $10,000 to be forfeited in the event of ultimate failure to pay the $44,000, and the debt to be cancelled by that for feiture, provided the interest is annually paid. Possession to be given the 1st of January 1853—but if the cotton crop is not then ready for market the hands are to be employed in it until it is ready, and for which no charge is to be made. The corn & pease on hand on the 1 of January to belong to Miss Corbin. If the $10,000 is paid before the 1 January 1853 interest at 7 per c' will be allowed on it. I expect to be in New York on the 8th of July and to sail for Savannah in the Alabama on the 10th. As I wish to give Mr Corbin your decision before leaving the North, I shall be glad to hear from Mr King by the 8th of July, directed to the care of Mr J. Couper Lord[?], 49 South [St or 8th?] N. York.

I observe William's name among the arrivals in New Y. yesterday, and thence infer your safe arrival at Philadelphia where you no doubt met Lord, as he called on us on Friday evening in New York. (Copy of letter from J. H. Couper to Anna Matilda Page King, June 24, 1852, WAC, SHC)

Also see Vanstory, *Land of the Golden Isles,* 155–156.

5. Affy, born October 5, 1827, is noted on the list "50 Negros with Their Increase" as Maria's daughter. On the 1839 list she is number 101. Anna wrote to Mallery, "The negros are having a funeral today for poor Affy—I wish they could be persuaded to give up the ridiculous practice—I am sure these negros from the neighboring plantations look as cheerful as tho' they were attending a *wedding* more than a funeral. . . . Rose's twins get on very well—she now has two sets of twins—I shall have to take good care of poor Affy's twins" (Anna Matilda Page King to Mallery King, April 4, 1852, TBK, SHC). I am unable identify Affy's twins. See "50 Negros with Their Increase," KWC, GHS, 15.

Allentown

3d July 1852

My own dear Tootee

I wrote to you Saturday & Tuesday last—actually time now begins to travel & if I do not mind I shall be *forgetting dates.* I feel very uneasy about you my own darling Child. What would I not give if you your sweet children & dear William were with me. It seems to me you are all dearer & more precious to me than ever you were. You were not well my darling when you last wrote—I very much fear it was the beginning of one of those attacks—& you had not dear William to take care of you. Tootee dear do not try to *deceive me.* God! bless & preserve you my precious child. I do hope ere this your dear husband is safe at home. May God! bless that dear son for his tender care of me. Tootee! he could not have been more tender had I been his own Mother, & I (poor weak woman that I am) gave him more trouble than was necessary. But I was very unhappy very nervous & confused. I dreamed two nights ago that we were just going up the Savannah river in the *State of Georgia* after having had just such a delightful passage as the one we had in coming on. I was so happy! We certainly were singularly blessed in coming on.

Two days ago Georgia received a letter from our beloved Butler up to the 31st of May. He said his Father & himself, Davy &c were quite well—that G[eorgia] & myself were the only two he had written to by that Mail. My letter has of course gone South & I fear our good friend Bourke had stopt it in Savannah to quicken my reception of it. So you my darling will not hear any thing of those beloved ones. I have not had a line from your Father since his letter of the 2nd May. But I hear through Butler that he is well or was well on the 3, 5th, 16th, & 31st May & with this I *try to be satisfied.* I very much regret your having mentioned any thing of the misconduct of the negros, it would only make them think matters were worse than they are—May induce your Father to throw up his commission—& come out at this dreadful season thereby exposing his precious life to danger, & doing away the good expected from the great sacrifice he has been making. It would be bad policy to bring him back before they are ready to come—or make them miserable if they determine it is best they should remain to the end of their term. *Hide nothing* from me but keep from them all needless trouble.

I am so much better. I begin to think it was *folly* my leaving home. I do begrudge the money it will cost me. I consulted brother Henry about the purchase of Hamilton. He *is a deep thinking* man. He thinks the *price exorbitant.* William has managed that plantation better than any other man could—or as well as any man can. He can best say whether or not the cotton crop has for the last 10 years averaged over $5000. The interest on this $54,000 annually would be $3780, pay of competent overseer $700, leaving for all other expenses but $520—if those *old negros* those invalid women—those old Mules—all of which will probably pass off in a year or two are numbered with those *115* negros the price for negros & stock are *exorbitant.* Then consider the extortion of using these negros for getting out the crop, taking away the services of the negros & working animals without the least deduction. Put the matter all together it is a bargain *I* can have nothing to do with, & which I hope your Father or Butler will have nothing to do with. If they have saved any money I would rather they would invest it in any other property. If they had the 54,000 to lay down—even then I would beg the old negros & mules may be taken out of the bargain. I had a letter from Mr J H C[ouper] dated 27th June they were then at Niagara Falls, they would next—Mr E Jackson in Middleton Connecticut—& not leave N.Y. before the 17th July—he is still under the impression that your Father is with us.

Lord left us for N[ew] H[aven] on the 26th, to return on the 1st July. I had a letter from him yesterday giving 5 good reasons why he should not return before the 7th. He had been disappointed in getting the rooms he expected to secure for us. I very much fear we shall find it more expensive than we expected. This worry about money matters will take much from the benefit the change would otherwise give me. I find that some bills contracted by your sisters have been sent home, they cannot tell me the exact amount. I should like to have them settled as soon as possible. I am thinking the best way will be just to enclose you a few lines to Messrs Andersons & Co—requesting them to forward to these people the amount due them. Had I known of this whilst I was in Philadelphia I may have settled them whilst there. But as I have so little money with me—perhaps the above plan will be best. If I could but have remained at home—how much the money I am now spending may have contributed to our comfort. I must leave the repairs of the house altogether to your good husbands better judgement—I know if his health continues good he will do everything that is necessary on as economical a plan as possible. Do you not think a *door* would be best—to shut out the little entry from view—it would not cost a great deal & would add much to the comfort of the parlour in winter. If McIntosh is not able to do the work, William will have to hire some one else, tho' where he is to be found is the question.

I begin to love my little birds again & fell quite in love with some nonpareuls I saw on board ship. If they are not expensive I would be glad if dear Isa could get me two pair.[1] Henry has expressed a great desire for a good Mocking bird. I wonder if Mrs Wilson would sell me one—*feel her pulse* on the subject. I tried by hints you recollect to get a male nonpareul & she *would not* understand me.

Be sure to send me your dresses or sizes—it will be such a gratification to employ some of our *confused* leisure moments in doing something for your loved ones. My own precious child how dear you are to me & those dear children, they are never absent from my thoughts. What would I not give to just have them now around me. God! in mercy grant we may all meet again. It seems to me if I had just such a house as this the garden & other comforts—if I had *all* my family with me I could live for years without going out side the front door.

Mary King is as kind as she or any one else can possibly be to us. Brother Henry is in bad health—he is something in the state I was in—*nervous,* [though] he is now better. His wife relieves him of every care attends to every thing but his *law* business. She does every thing without the *least fuss.* I think you & her are more alike in this respect than any two persons I ever knew. She is always cheerful never idle & *yet no fuss.* She is up the first & last to be down in the family.

Our dear Cousin was very comfortably lodged a short distance from us. But they had seen all the sights to be seen here & must go to Bethlehem. We parted with mutual regret on Wednesday last.

On Thursday there was a grand picnic given by the ladies & gents of Easton & Bethlehem. Mary was not invited—but Mr Longnecker was—he wanted Mary to go & take the girls—but she concluded it would be best *not* to do so. Yesterday Henry got a carriage which very comfortably accommodated 9 persons including the driver—we stopt to see Amanda & Mr Woolley in Bethlehem. I believe they were never more glad to see us. They were heartily sick of the place & regretted having left Allentown, its comforts & our society. We went on to Easton 12 miles further, expecting Amanda & Mr Woolley to leave by the same route on their way to N.Y. at 2 that day. There was a great excitement in Easton, the opening of the rail road from N.Y. to Easton. We saw the procession the great gathering of the people—saw rather than heard 3 bands of music, for the ringing of the bells—firing of canon drowned every other sound. After dinner Mary, Henry & the boys & Georgia went to see the sights. Flora, V[irginia] and myself rested our weary limbs to prepare for our drive back 18 miles to Allentown. We regretted not seeing the stage come in hoping to get one more glimpse of our dear cousin. We had a most *delightful* drive back. Having had rain the night before (there must have been hail some where) the thermometer must have been down to 67, the atmosphere clear & bright, horses good, carriage comfortable, company pleasant—scenery most lovely. I think I shall long remember this drive. As we approached the Hotel in Bethlehem Floyd & Tip who were on the front seat said "Why there is cousin A[manda] & Mr W[oolley]" & sure enough they were soon at the side of the carriage. It seems the stage was too full & they had to remain until 5 this morning, & they could hire no other conveyance. They really seemed sorry to part with us—I am sure I was to part with them.

Floyd & Tip have gone to spend the day with the little Lewis's. I wish I had them at some good school. Unfortunately all the schools break up the 1st of August until the 1st of October. I find my ideas are getting confused again & I will have to stop writing—my eyes are certainly not so good as they were before I left home. I am so frequently interrupted by the girls poor things they are so perfectly happy here. I have not yet been able to see any change for the worse in any of them. Georgia is the same sweet—intelligent girl—Flora some times lets her spirits fly away with her wits—she is very amusing. Appy is very much improved, a real smart girl—& an industrious little girl at that.

We are very much amused with Rhina—Marys old gardener (a dutch man) has fallen in love with Rhina & proposes marriage—Rhina makes faces & says "the *cussed* old fool—who he tinks want him."

Georgia is busy with her Fathers chair.[2] I do not know if she will be able to write to you today. Flora & Appy have gone out to do some shopping.

All unite in love to you & Wm & kisses to the sweet babes. Mary & Henry send love. Rhina begs to be remembered to all. She seems to feel no uneasiness about Annie now you have her with you. Give our love to Mrs Gale, poor old woman I hope for her own sake as well as yours she may not be sick whilst with you. Say *all* that is affectionate and kind to dear William. Remembrance to Mr Dunham. I hope he will be able to protect the peaches. I now despair of making any preserves here. Not a peach in Allentown & there may be none in N[ew] H[aven]. You are to have all you want then I must come in next. I leave *none to my neighbors*. God! grant my poor negros are now healthy. Remember me especially to those you know I think most of & that behave best.

Your devoted Mother.

A M King

P.S. Georgia says she will write a few lines—We are going to make some calls this evening & hear a Whig speech. I hate old Scott so much—I do not care anything about the Election.[3]

1. Anna had grown increasingly more interested in keeping and raising birds as pets. She bought a number of birds from neighbors on the island and in Savannah, and her children caught wild ones for her as well. She named three pairs of her birds Mr. & Mrs. J. H. Couper, William Audley and Tootee Couper, and Tom and Sarah Bourke.

2. Georgia was needlepointing a cover for her father's chair.

3. General Winfield Scott, veteran of the War of 1812 and hero of the Mexican War, was the Whig Party's candidate for president in 1852. He lost the election. Why Anna "hated" Scott or cared little about the election is unknown; her husband was, after all, a member of the Whig Party.

10th July 1852

My dear beloved Tootee

I had the happiness to receive your most welcome letter of the 29th Ult on Tuesday last the 6th. Praise be to God! you were then all well. What an awful feeling this is of *constant anxiety*—now that I am with your dear Sisters I have still many of you to *fear for*. I hope your next letter will inform me of dear Williams safe arrival at home, how lonely you must have been without him. I am distressed to hear that poor Mrs Gale has been sick—as much on your account as on hers. I[t] was kind in you my precious one, to offer the poor old woman a home in my absence. I wish I was now safe back to relieve you of the charge.

Lord returned here yesterday—as he wrote you last evening he has possibly told you that on the 14th we shall leave this hospitable roof for New Haven—I had looked for ward to our going to New Haven with more pleasure than I now do. I long for *rest* some retired nook where I could read—write—sew—sleep in quiet. But it is hard to please all my party. Lord has engaged rooms & board for two or three weeks at $10 *a head per week. Pretty severe,* & would exhaust my slender purse in no time. Oh Tootee I wish I had not left home. I do not know but that worrying about money will be as bad as that of sick & dying negros. We want *a head* among us. I have no mind of my own neither have I *experience* or *judgement*—& it requires the two latter to get along in this keen country. Lord thinks himself quite competent—& so he is to fix on nice & agreeable places. Well it is no use bothering you about such matters as these. I must at once think about raising some more money for certainly what I have will not hold out the summer. Our present plan is to go to New Haven for two weeks. We leave this Hospitable roof on Wednesday next—stop possibly one day in New York, where I hope to find Amanda & Mr Woolley. I must put poor

Floyd & Tip to School some where—here comes another bother—the summer holidays begin next month—well well I must try & do the best I can.

Your uncle Henrys health requires a change. He looks feeble & is in a nervous state. Tootee dear we have neither of us appreciated your Aunt Marys character. She is truly a devoted wife to your uncle. In fact should he now lose her—I do not know how he could exist. She is never one moment idle—*no fussing*—but seems never to forget a single duty, an admirable house keeper & manager, always cheerful but—I feel that I cannot do justice to her merits & will proceed to tell you what we have been after since Sunday last.

I try to write so that you shall hear from me every Sunday. Last Sunday we of course all went to Church morning & evening. I find it hard now to keep correct run of the days. Mary expected Lord on the 7th & invited company to tea & which is drank here at 6 oclock—Mr & Mrs & Miss Gregory, Mrs Cushing & daughter. After tea Mr Longnecker who is here every evening & some 6 or 8 others dropt in. A *blind youth* who plays delightfully on the violin—we had some delightful music & in fact a most pleasant evening party. Mary & your sisters are horror stricken at my *short dresses*—so I have been kept very busy letting down not only dresses but petticoats—this is no little annoyance to me—I can scarcely walk in these long dresses, so they tell me I must take shorter steps. Upon my word it is hard for a gray headed woman to be beginning to learn how to walk again.

Do you see the condition of this letter? Can't you guess how this happened —that fool of a Rhina was talking to the old dutch gardner. She had got him to change her some money—he brought her an *old* penny which she objected to—he said "tis vas hard times monies." She said "I dont want any of your hard times talk." Their negro & dutch lingo sounded so queer I *"bust"* out laughing & you see the consequences.[1]

On Thursday evening Mary, Georgia & myself made several calls & also visited the cemetery—where they *"stack"* away the Dutch. It was to me distressing to see the rows of new made graves. This is considered a very healthy town, but with 5000 inhabitants—I should not have wondered at the number who die & yet it is a rapidly increasing place.

Yesterday evening we rode over to the water cure establishment. Mary, Georgia, Virginia, Mr Longnecker—the boys & myself. Lord was tired. Flora was lazy. I could not if I tried ever so hard give you an idea of the beauty of the scenery. The farmers are now in the midst of their grain harvest—which seems to be a fine one this season. We past a farm belonging to one old dutch man of 500 acres—the largest & richest in this county. He has but 3 daughters to inherit this wealth, & these daughters go bare legged in summer.

The situation of the water cure establishment is beautiful—just on the slope of a beautifully wooded hill, the prospect of Bethlehem & country around is beautiful—but the house itself is very uninviting—little regard to nicety I should think. The Dr can speak but little English—he seemed delighted to hear of Miss Gould, & begged to be remembered to her. He has very few patients this season—he seemed prouder of his *white* turkeys of which he has a fine flock & of the *water* (which is indeed fine) than of any thing else. Our ride home was along the banks of the Lehigh river—dear Tootee I never see a beautiful prospect—but I wish you & William were with me to enjoy it. You have often heard me speak of the beautiful banks & river of the Lehigh. As we rode on one side (a rode [*sic*] dug from the side of a high mountain) shaded by beautiful trees—close on to the river—this running & jumping over little rocks—on the opposite side the road is shaded by trees—carriages & foot passengers—then just out side the road is the canal—the boats moving slowly up & down the way.

We found Flora & Lord as well as dear Henry ready for their supper which we all partook of with good appetites. We live well here—all of the very best, breakfast at 8, dine at 1—tea at 6. I never feel hungry & yet always enjoy my meals. I actually am getting *too fat*—it will be hard for me to let out—as well as let down my dresses. I think we all sit up to late at night—the fashion here is to sleep in the afternoons—this is what I most dislike. I have not yet indulged in this. But I insist on Georgias doing so—Flora requires no urging—Appy seems not to need it. It is very pleasant to see how pleasantly Georgia & Appy get on—Flora is still devoted to Adele Picot—time & absence will cure her of this folly. Poor Flora is weak in some points—but she has many good traits of character. Georgia's voice has been much improved & in no way spoilt—she is a lovely little being this same little Geo. I believe her to be truly pious, her conduct shows this more than her words. Gods blessing will I trust rest on my precious little girls efforts to serve Him. I am very anxious to have Floyd & Tip at school. Floyd is growing rapidly—& poor fellow he is so rough.

I find that I cannot write here as I did at home. My ideas seem confused—I hope how ever to be able to remember to tell you all when next we meet. Dearest Tootee how much I wish that happy moment was at hand. Oh! my darling you can scarcely imagine how much I feel this separation very severely. I have yours & Annas & Willies Daguerreotypes on my toilet which I look at many times a day—& always before going to bed.

Tomorrow we shall of course go to church. The next day Lord goes out shooting with Mr Longnecker. In the afternoon we are going out to Mr Lewis's to tea. Tuesday we shall pack up & leave here on Wednesday.

I must write to Amanda to day & beg her to remain at Brooklyn until the 16th so that we may meet in N.Y. I am sorry they are so restless—but they came for pleasure & sight seeing—I cannot give you their address—as I do not think they will remain in any one place more than a week. If you desire to write to her enclose the letter to me. I think the fatigue of this constant motion too much for Amanda, *he* says she was quite well when he wrote. Mrs Halls address is to the care of "Benedict, Hall & Co No 21 Park Row New York."² You must not let those sweet children forget me my Tootee. God! bless the sweet babes, how I do long to see them. I long for the time when I can return home, for after all—a *home* let it be ever so lonely or poor is the best & sweetest resting place for me. It is hard for me to be reconciled to being among strangers. I am as happy here as I could be when from home. I have just eaten dinner & am more stupid than ever. How often dear Tootee have you & I said "if we were from home we would never be at a loss for subjects to write on." Now that I am here I find it more difficult to write than when I was at home. You my darling must write me about every thing beginning with yourself—husband— children—then all that I left at home from Mr Dunham down to my birds & chicken[s]. Tell Maria she is not to forget that she is to have 25 cts for every bird she raises. There are some beautiful birds here—quite as pretty as "William Couper" they call them *May* birds—large flocks of them, they are beauties, but I cant catch any. You must tell me every thing that takes place—all the sweet talk of those darlings—tell them how much I love them & long to return to them.

You say nothing of the things Georgia sent home—those two trunks, have you received them? Have you received from Sophie Picot the bills which are yet to be paid? I will try & not for get to put in this letter a line or two to Messr Andersons—which you will beg William to enclose to Mr Anderson when *he* lets Mr Anderson know the amount due & to whom it is to be paid. I have yet to write to dear Amanda today to let her know when we are to be in N.Y. Georgia had a very affectionate letter from Mrs Jaudon a few days ago—who is so kind as to insist on our spending the balance of the summer with them, but you know this would not suit *me*. I would [however] like to see those who have been so very kind to my children. Tell dear William that I never eat or see a cherry but I think how pleased I would be to *pass him* the *dish*. I hope & trust long ere this he has safely reached home. I do think he was *very very* kind to come so far for me. Tell him that I felt his kindness deeply—gratefully. The best wish I can make for him is that should *he live* to be as *helpless as I was* when I left home, he may meet with as kind a friend as he was to me. Kiss him as well as each precious child for me. My love to Mrs Gale, & a shake of the hand to every servant I left behind. My kind regards to Mr Dunham. I hope when William gets back poor Dunham will be less low spirited. Your Aunt & Uncle send love— your brothers & sisters lots of kisses. Rhina is getting quite well—she begs to be remembered to you, the children & Mrs Gale—& sends thousands of love to her child & other relatives.

I have not felt like writing since I left home. I actually began this letter directly after breakfast & have been delving at it ever since. Be sure & write all about your self—your husband your children my negros—crop—birds—chickens &c &c every word that is favorable to either will be *like a dew drop to my parched* (I cant find a word to carry out that poetical sentence). God! forever bless you my own precious child—& may you all be protected from harm is the fervent prayer of your devoted Mother

A M King

I need not repeat that I know William will have an eye to my affairs—please beg him to jog Andersons memory about the plows, has the shingles been received—is McIntosh able to be at work—has Anderson come to do the chimneys—If those trunks ever got to you—in addition to what I asked you to send me—send the piece belonging to Appys plaid silk.

1. The only apparent problem with the letter is a crossed-out word and some irregularity in the handwriting.

2. This seems to be an interim address where Tootee was to send Anna's letters and any written to Amanda.

New Haven 17th July 1852

My own dearly beloved child

My letter of the 10th informed you of our having postponed our departure from Allentown until the 15th it so happened that on that day it rained in torrents & tho' every arrangement had been made for our leaving on Wednesday your Uncle & Aunt would not hear of our going out in the rain—this was a fortunate circumstance—had we gone we should have past through N.Y. ignorant of your Uncle Andrew & Louisa being in the U.S. I do not think that any one of our party regretted being kept another day under that hospitable roof—but we were little aware of the pleasure that was in store for us. The Mails come in between 6 & 7 oclock every evening—we were sitting in the pleasant hall up stairs—Lord & Mary playing backgammon, the girls reading & sewing & I (as usual when not writing) darning stockings—When Henry came up in his quiet way & said Mary here is a letter. He looked agitated & Mary at once thought it was from her Father & conveyed some bad news—he added "it is from Andrew" & after a moments pause concluded by saying—they are in N.Y. You may depend on it we were all at once in an uproar. From Andrews letter it was very evident he had no idea of my being at the North or the girls at Allentown. I ran off & scratched a few lines to Louisa to let her know we would be in N.Y. the next day. On the 15th the weather was beautiful—at 12 oclock we left those truly kind friends—I felt like leaving a second home for really it had been made a pleasant one to me. We left in a nice carriage calculated to carry 9 persons with the driver—our trunks had been sent off in a baggage waggon. The drive to Easton was a delightful one the rain having settled the dust. I here saw for the first time rail road cars.[1] Lord gave me a choice of seats—I preferred the last car as being most remote from the Engine.[2] I expected to be frightened to death—we moved off slowly then faster & faster after a while I felt astonishingly reconciled to the movement. I took care to look straight ahead whenever we were crossing over bridges—the motion was distressing & I very much feared a return of my headache. I had been confined to bed 24 hours from Sunday evening until Monday evening with the worse headache I had had for many a day which was owing I thought to our ride to the Water cure establishment. It was a real relief to get on board a Steam boat at Elizabethtown—we steamed it up most beautifully.[3] The scenery more beautiful than I have words to describe. We got to the City just as twilight was darkening into night—Lord got a carriage & baggage waggon. I took it into my wise head to prefer the Irving [?] house to the Astor. I can't tell why—for the price is the same—Lord could get but 2 chambers & a small parlour. We had scarce ate our supper when he ran down to the New York Hotel to see his uncle and aunt. We had washed off the dust & right sided ourselves a little when Mr J H C[ouper] & Mr Corbin called—they had scarcely been seated when in came dear Louisa, Andrew, Mr John King & Lord. The two former seemed overjoyed to see us—I am sure Mr Corbin & Mr Couper must have been amused at the number of kisses given & received. Then Louisa ran off to see Flora who was fast asleep—& Floyd & Tip who were too fast asleep to be roused up. Mr C[orbin] & Mr J H C[ouper] did not remain long. Then [?] such a babel of tongues that little room never heard before. Andrew is very fat & looks as happy as possible—dear Lou is very thin—she really needed a change of climate. I must not pretend to enter into the particulars for it would take too much time & space. I hope the time will come when we shall talk it all over. I like John King very much indeed. They remained quite late promising to be back at an early hour the next day. Tired as I was it was hard work to sleep after so much excitement—& now I will put by my letter until tomorrow.

Sunday morning 18th—

I could not sleep last night—I was thinking of your dear Father & my precious Butler & of you dear ones at Hamilton. I had scarce dropt to sleep when I was awoke by the ringing of bells & as two or three were just by the noise was distressing—we at once knew it was for fire. We could see the reflection against the nearest Church Steeple. My only uneasiness was on Malleys account. The rest soon again was asleep but I could not until after 5—but Tootee dear I must go back to N.Y. I found that the girls & myself needed each one a silk dress. We had fix'd on the colour &c, Louisa offered to come at an early hour & go out with the girls. We had scarce had our breakfast when Mr & Mrs J H C[ouper], Andrew, Louisa & John King & [Mr.] Savage came in & scarcely had they been seated when a gentleman was announced as "Mr Foster." To save my life I could not call to mind any such acquaintance. In came a tall gentleman with every appearance of *delight at having again met with me.* I dare say Mr J H C[ouper] will tell you how amused they all were knowing that I was utterly at fault. When & where we met before I cannot tell. His call was prolonged until after Mr & Mrs Couper took their leave—eventually—(first before I am done with Foster—let me add that he said he knew Butler to be Mrs Kings son from his resemblance to *me.*) Louisa & the girls got out. I had no time or thought to take any money out of my purse but handed G[eorgia] the whole $83. Away they went—& scarcely had they gone when the waiter announced a gentleman & two little girls—& in came Mr Bartow—Maggy, & Bell.[4] To my great annoyance The Revd Gent very gracefully stooped & gave me a smack—there was no help for it but submission. There is no use trying to tell you all he said. When going away he *repeated his favor* as unexpected to me as was the first. I was so confused in trying to make out who Mr Foster was all the time Mr & Mrs J H C[ouper] were in the room & as I had to entertain him especially, I had very little conversation with them and entirely neglected to send by them the guard chain for William. Louisa had brought 4 patterns of linen cambric for your children to make each of them a dress—these too I may have sent. But you can have no idea of the *confusion* we were in. Andrew & Lou all the time begging us to remain just one day longer—& I feeling that we could really not afford it. Well to return to the girls & *their* purchases I had charged them to get me also a bonnet & cap & provide themselves with shoes. Whilst they were away I retired to my room to see after Rhina who had a bad headache—the servants seeing so many go out concluded I was among them—so when Mr Anthony Barclay called they told him so & I had not the pleasure of seeing him. When our folks got back I found they had found nothing to suit them—had got me neither bonnet or cap—or themselves shoes & had spent *all the money* on *the materials* for *4 dresses.* This made me *feel wild.* The boys had got Mr Savage to take them to Benedict Hall & Co—but Mr Hall was not in Town. Andrew & Louisa dined with us—I was sorry to hurry off but it would not answer our remaining longer it was quite a scrabble to get ready to take the express train at $^1/_2$ past three. Especially when there stood Andrew at the door begging us to stay dear Lou had more sense—when she found I was determined on going—she turned too & helped us put away our things. Just imagine 8 persons—7 trunks 3 bags 1 valise put on & into one coach. Savage & Alex Campbell were at the depot to see us off—& rode with us as far as we were moved by the aid of horses. We found it excessively dusty—we went at a rapid rate. I could not help starting whenever we past another train. I may get used to this rail road traveling but from the experience I have had of it I do not like it as well as Steam boats. When we arrived here Lord ran to the Post Office— whilst our baggage was being taken out of the baggage car & found a letter from your dear Father up to the 16th June. Your Father was well but our precious Butler had been quite sick with *the Mumps,* had taken cold—& tho' he was better—was not able to write to us by that Mail—this account quite unfit me for sleep that night. I will now look for further intelligence with fear & trembling. It rained all day yesterday until the afternoon when Gov & Mrs Baldwin, Mrs & Miss Devereaux—Mrs Matthews & her son called—I like Mrs *Baldwin best*—she *is a real Mother*—we are invited all to take tea there tomorrow evening. *Lillie* is *beautiful* was splendidly dressed—I do not wonder at Lord's loving her as he did. Mrs Matthews is in deep mourning for her only daughter. This morning dear Malley came to us—he was here to see us an hour after we arrived—he is very *stout* & is so much the gentleman in his manners—he spent yesterday with us & will dine here to day. Lord, Georgia & Tip went to Church—I had just set down to continue to you this letter when Mr *Chapman* called—he told me he had just seen a man direct from San Francisco—who left there on the *1st July* that he saw your Father & *Butler* both of whom were well. I fear Mr Chap[man] must be mistaken—this is but the 18th July—On inquiry I find it was on the *1st June* and not July that the man left San Francisco.

[No signature]

1. Railroads were much less common in the South than in the North, and Anna, living on St. Simons, relied almost exclusively on steamboats to travel from the island to Savannah and beyond.

2. Engines created not only a good deal of noise but also soot from burning coal. Train rides in summer with open windows could be as dusty as carriage rides on dirt roads.

3. Elizabethtown, New Jersey.

4. By 1852, Rev. Bartow was a widower, his wife, Isabella, having died in 1841. Why Anna disliked him is unclear.

New Haven 23 July

My own precious child

I am going to begin this letter on a cru[m]pled piece of paper—but it is difficult for me to keep any thing in order with 3 such girls as Georgia, F[lorence] & V[irginia] to have a pull at every thing. On Tuesday last I had the happiness to receive your dear letters up to the 13th. I thank a Merciful God! that you were permitted to give so cheering an account of matters with you my beloved child & of my affairs at home. I have wished a thousand times that I was safe back with you & look upon myself as having *been mad* to undertake spending a summer at the North with so large a family with no head to manage & so slender a purse. I know my precious child that in advising me to come North you & my dear William believed you were doing the very best thing for me. There is no knowing how matters may have ended had I not followed your advice. Now that I can't help myself—I am here & it may be greater madness still to take the children home. I think as the negros are doing better I may have staid at home & have recovered my health. But I must not depress you my precious child. I must try not to look so constantly on the dark side. In the first place so far as my health is concerned I am certainly very much improved in flesh. When *I once* get to sleep I sleep soundly, & but for a few *ifs* I would be well. I will not go back to complaints—I must try and write more cheerfully to my *heroic* little daughter who in persuading her poor Mother to go from home forgot self & thought only of the benefit of her Mother—sisters & brothers.

You will be pained to hear that as yet we have fix'd on no definite place to retire to & try to live economically—there seems to be no end to the difficulty. Springfield is too much in the heart of Massachusetts for me to take Rhina there & be at ease.[1] She is certainly a great comfort to me & I do not *know how* I could have got along without her—still I am constantly [fearful] lest something unpleasant may occur. Andrew & Louisa are very anxious to settle down with us as soon as they have been at Saratoga a few weeks. He prefers New Port to Springfield. Lord proposes setting off tomorrow to see what can be done in the way of procuring pleasant & cheap lodgings. There are pleasant cottages to be rented—but I fear we are too late to get a *bargain*. This is the present plan. In my next I may be able to give you more certain intelligence.

We are very comfortably accommodated here but at vast expense. We have at length placed Tip & Floyd at school—but as the vacations come on in two weeks it is most probable I shall take them with us when we leave one week from today (that is if your sisters are not done up by the parties now in prospect. We have had a great deal of attention paid us, & if it were not for the expense I could enjoy my stay here. On Monday evening last we all took tea at

Gov Baldwins—your mother & her 6 children poor Mall could not go. On Tuesday night Lord went up or down to N.Y. just to see his Uncle & Aunt. We were all to take tea at Mrs Devereauxs. The day had been very warm & we had all been pretty well worn out with running after mantaumakers.[2] Mrs Matthews—her Mother, son & grand daughter had called for me to take a ride— the girls had a carriage to go to get their dresses tried on. We can fill a carriage & drive for one hour for one dollar about the cheapest thing I have met with in N[ew] H[aven]. We took our hour out & stopt at the Mantaumakers expecting to find the girls & Malley there—but they had not yet come—when they did come their hour had expired so I dismissed the coach & we walked home. Appy contrived to hurt her foot—& Flora declared she had head ache. Tip was not to be found—so G[eorgia], Mall, Floyd & myself started about 7 for Mrs Devereaux. Lord was expected but had not got back at that hour. Mrs D[evereaux] & her daughter received us with every kindness, her house & gardens are beautiful. They seemed really hurt at Flora & Appy not coming— we walked about the garden until dark—her flowers were beautiful. Some young gentlemen came in after we had taken tea & about eight in came Lord, Flora, Appy & Tip. Lord had got back—came first to our Hotel made the girls dress fished up Tip & had him brushed up. So we were really all there after all & spent a very pleasant evening. Yesterday we were after the mantaumakers again all the morning—it was so *hot* I could not think of the girls walking—it cost us $3—the ride but that was better than a Doctors bill. We were all invited to take tea at Mrs Matthews. G[eorgia] & F[lorence] had to trot off to get dresses tried. The little boys were not to be found. So I had to make Appy go with me. I *did not* know the way—she quarrel'd with me the whole way for compelling her to go with me. I bore it very patiently & by dint of asking the way at length got there. As they are in deep mourning I did not expect to meet any but the family. Mrs M[atthews], her son in law, Son—Mother & little grand daughter. I spent a pleasant evening Dr Matthews is I think a fine young man—at 9½ I left—he came home with us.[3] This has been an exceedingly hot day. I would not let the girls go out at all as they were to go to a party tonight. Georgia received a splendid bouquet of Flowers from one of Lords classmates today. Lord has been very particular who should be introduced to his sisters I think about 6 have been introduced—these have called several times. Dear Louisa sent Georgia & Florence each a party dress, to each of us expensive pocket handkerchiefs—to me two beautiful caps & to us 4 I can't now tell how many party gloves. She intends also to send me a bonnet—it was not trimmed when Lord left—& was to have come yesterday. I some how fear it is lost on the way.[4] I cannot convey to you an idea of their exceeding kindness to us all, & I do long to settle down quietly with them some where. G[eorgia] & Flora were dressed in white tarleton dresses this evening with natural flowers in their hair—they now regret having sent home so many of their things—but we will talk of them another time. This is a young ladies party—and in fact all but two to be given are. On Monday night they go to Miss Whitneys—on Tuesday night to Miss Devereaux, Wednesday night to Mrs Estes on Thursday night to Mrs Sanfords—the two latter I am invited to. I do not know that I shall go—& will not if I can avoid it—Lord of course accompanied his sisters. It is very gratifying to me to hear dear Mrs Baldwin & Mrs Devereaux speak of *Henry* as they all call Lord—he has been most fortunate in having so many kind friends. Well dear Tootee you may perceive that I am writing this letter whilst your sisters are dancing—I find it difficult to arrange my ideas so as to give you a description of all that is going on. I just put down matters as I can recollect them.

This evening the girls got their letters from their dear Father—these were dated the 17th June—I cannot but be uneasy about our beloved Butler. I *fear* as much as I desire to hear later accounts from those loved ones. If his letter to me has reached you you will of course know as much as I now do of his situation (Butler) when your Father wrote. I suppose you may have heard of Mr Picot's death. As much as I have cause to dislike the *whole* family I do most sincerely pity them.[5] The loss of a husband & Father is a severe blow. Adele must have undergone great trials—I had a letter from Mrs Picot today—she is in great distress—Adele will not return home for some time.[6] I also had a very affectionate letter from Mary King. Your Uncle Henry has been very unwell since we left Allentown—but has determined to go to Saratoga on the 28th. I hope his being with Andrew will cheer him. Mary & Louisa will out talk each other. I cannot but envy them their happiness for they have their husbands with them—I have my blessings too—for have I not my children? The Hotel we are in is facing the College green. It is ridiculous to listen to the students— they are so happy—singing, shouting—their vacation is near at hand. I expect to have the pleasure of seeing Mr & Mrs Hall—they telegraphed some one here to enquire if we were here—& how long we should remain. I also expect Mr Savage & Mr Longnecker next week. It is very strange that I can hear nothing of Mr Woolley & Amanda—I would give a great deal if they were with us. They know that we are here & I am surprised they do not write to us—I do not know where they are & can not of course write to them. I must now stop dearest child but I hope to write just as much more ere I close this scrawl. In imagination I kiss you my love & your sweet babes & I feel the friendly affectionate grip of dear Williams hand.

And now my Tootee let me turn back to your letters which I received on my arrival here. I am thankful to God! for the blessing of health yourself—husband & children enjoy, that poor Mrs Gale is better—that dear William had got home safe & that matters were as well at Retreat. I am deeply concerned to hear of the continued ill health of poor Dunham. There seems to be no alternative—he must either go away for a while or be *taken* away with or without our consent. If I was at home his going would be of less consequence. It is *possible* Toney may get on tolerably with the field work.—I must leave this as I have so many other matters under your good husbands directions. You say nothing of my cotton crop—has there been already too much rain? I fear so— I begin *seriously* to regret my coming North. I cannot see how I shall be able to stand the expense, or where I am to find the means of continuing here until October unless the Andersons will *advance* for me. I have a large family with me— and our expenses are enormous, it does hurt me so much to be paying out such sums to these landlords—for lodgings not so comfortable as my own at home & for food I do not really enjoy from thinking how much it costs. I fear I shall not be able to put Floyd & Tip to school as the long vacations begin next week. I have no plan [?] I want a *head* to the party. The only thing that comes *easy* to us is the getting rid of money. The expense is enormous—& then I cannot help it—our money is all going into the pockets of Hotel keepers & R[ail] R[oad] owners. I intended to get many things in N.Y. which we really need—but could not do it. The 4 dresses we purchased we cannot get made there seems to be the greatest difficulty to obtain any thing that we *really* want. Louisa told us as soon as she got to N.Y. she purchased 12 dresses & put them all out to be made & had not been able to get a single one finished. We have not yet found a man-taumaker here.[7] Dear me I would give worlds to be once more quietly at home. It may seem strange to you that I cannot find a cheap quiet place—*But I cannot.* Spring[field] has its objections—& I can find or meet with no one who can tell me any thing about Morristown. Oh Tootee I wish I had not come. I think I am to be worried more for want of money to get on with than I was even with my sick & dying negros. Do not send my note to Anderson just yet. I must hear first from those Picots to know to whom this amount is to be paid, certainly I shall not pay it to them. Surely this has been a trying year to me—God! Almighty grant the worst may now be over. Mr J H Couper told me that Hamilton would not come on before the Autumn—the only way I can suggest to insure our getting the trunk (the getting of which will prevent your sisters having to get others) will be to request William to desire Messrs Andersons to forward it to New Haven—care of H L P King. I *shall not* remain here until it can reach this place but Lord can get some one to take charge of it—& forward it to us. Your Uncle Andrew & Louisa made many affectionate enquiries after you & your babies. They asked me to let Geo & Flora go to Saratoga with them, but as Andrew did not say he would pay their expensis I knew that I could not even give them an outfit. If it is possible I will let them go to Niagara. I know not where Mr Woolley & Amanda are. I wrote a few lines whilst in N.Y. to them & directed my letter to Brooklyn. Whether they will receive it is doubtful. I do long to see them again. Mrs Hall you perceive was in Ohio—had she been in N.Y. I am sure she would have assisted me to make my purchases with pleasure. Mr Chapman told me he saw Tom Bourke in Savannah. I hope you may see dear Sarah this summer.

I really fear dear Tootee that you find Mrs Gale a heavy charge—Have you Clementine still with you? How far [h]as McIntosh got on with the house? If it was but finished I would return home at once. What has become of *Tootees* eggs that I left her sitting on? You only mentioned Mrs Bourkes young ones. Before you answer this please go over & see exactly how all things are. Tell me about every thing at home—first the negros—then the crop the birds—the fowls—garden &c &c. I hope you take your full share of the fruit. I see no chance of my getting any peaches here. Georgia enclosed you the chain yesterday. Should it be unfortunately lost I have still hair enough left of that which you sent Geo to make another. *If* I ever can *get any thing done.* If I get once more South I do not care ever to see the North again. Malley is writing at the same table with me. Floyd & Tip are loafing about— G[eorgia], F[lorence] & V[irginia] are taking their afternoon nap. Rhina looking out of the windows—seeing the thousands pass & repass to & from Church her health is much improved. Lord is gone to see if he can get a place to put Floyd & Tip to school. I must now close—As I have yet other letters to write. Your Sisters & Brothers send much love to yourself William & Mrs Gale. Kiss the precious children a thousand times over for me, do not let them forget me. I love them more than ever. Tell all the servants & negros how de for me. My love to Mrs Gale. Rhina begs to be affectionately remembered to each & every one.

> Your devoted Mother
> A M King

I will not try your eyes or patience by crossing this letter. Good night my own darling God! bless & protect you all

> Your devoted Mother
> AMK

I hope you have received the guard chain. It was too stupid our not giving it to Mr J H Couper but you do not know the confusion we were in.

1. Massachusetts was the home of William Lloyd Garrison, founder of the New England Anti-Slavery Society and of *The Liberator*, one of the country's leading antislavery publications. Garrison called for both the immediate emancipation of slaves and their treatment as full and equal members of society. Garrison represented a mi-

nority of the most radical abolitionists, however; slavery was neither universally condemned in the North nor was abolition embraced. Yet, Anna evidently felt Massachusetts was just too far into New England to take a slave, believing abolitionists would be at the ready to kidnap her maid.

2. A seamstress. A "manteau" was the name given to a formal gown worn during the reign of Louis XIV. See Russell, *Costume History and Style*, 497.

3. Dr. Matthews must be Mrs. Matthews's son.

4. Louisa's gifts of caps and a bonnet for Anna may have been partly to make up for her participation in the choosing of fabric for four dresses in New York that cost all of the $83 Anna had given her daughters to buy dresses, shoes, cap, and bonnet.

5. It is unclear why Anna had come to dislike the Picots.

6. As Mr. Picot was to have gone to France, he must have died while there. Adele must have accompanied him and remained in France.

7. This is confusing inasmuch as Anna had already told Tootee of all three daughters having fittings with mantaumakers in New Haven.

New Haven
30th July 1852

My own dear Tootee

Since my last letter to you, Georgia & myself have had the happiness to receive your dear letters. Thank you my precious child for your affectionate effort to comfort—& cheer your poor Mother. I appreciate your motives my own dear Tootee & if I *could* would follow your advice. I cannot be sufficiently grateful to the "Giver of all Good" that you were able to give so cheering an account of *you* the health of your beloved husband & of those darling children. I cannot but be uneasy to hear you are still troubled not only with that pain in your chest but that your cough has not yet left you. I think it may be owing to your nursing that dear little fellow & now regret my not seconding William in advising your weaning him in the Spring. I fear for you both, if you continue to nurse him you may be seriously injured—if you wean him in the midst of the sickly season he may suffer. Could you not just nurse him once & put him from you the rest of the night?

I am grieved to hear of the illness of poor Pussy—God! in mercy to me grant that her life may be prolonged. I would be badly off indeed should I lose her—poor Sukey was the only other one who could nurse. I know dear Tootee that you & dear William did not let Pussy suffer for want of any thing you could supply her with. As she was so much better when you wrote to Georgia I do hope in your next you may be able to say she has quite recovered from that attack. I also grieve to hear that poor Dunham is still suffering. Why did he not avail himself of Williams kind offer & go to his brother for a few weeks? So much rain after so long a drought—I fear will make the Island sickly—not a day passes over my head but I wish I was safe back home. I will not distress you with complaints as they are now unavailing. But if you were placed in my situation you would feel as I do.

On Tuesday morning Appy & myself were walking down to the Mantaumakers to get her dresses tried on—when we saw dear cousin Amanda & Mr Woolley in a carriage. I quite forgot where we were & called out "dear Cousin how glad I am to see you." They were looking for lodgings & had taken a full hours drive about the Town looking for some house which had been recommended to them. I advised their coming here. Poor Appy & myself as usual lost our way—eventually when tired out & foot sore we got put into the right track—finished our task & got back—we found our dear cousin & her good husband seated in our bed room right glad to receive us. She looks better but says she has lost flesh since we parted. Mr W[oolley] looks about the same—she is as home sick as I am. They left us today for Bridgeport, much to my regret. But there was nothing in this place to interest them. Cousin A[manda] is heartily sick of travelling—Mr Woolley is not tired yet. In a few days they are to leave Bridgeport for Saratoga—then Niagara—Canada & Boston—they promise to join us at New Port—but I fear will not remain there long. They persue a more prudent plan than I am able to do they go to cheap lodgings, where as I am compelled as it were to stop at expensive Hotels & have the misery of knowing that my hard earned money is all running into the pockets of these vile Yankees. Dear me how I have been cheated by a mantaumaker—who had the impudence to say "she would not have done the work for the price—had not *Mr Henry King* asked her." We will talk all this over when we meet & you can help me abuse the hussy.

Well I know that Georgia intends to write to you—but neither Georgia or myself can by letter give you an account of all the excitement they have been in since my last letter. They attended a dancing party at Mrs Estys on Monday evening. The music was finer than at Miss Whitneys—they had a great deal of attention paid them & returned quite delighted. On Tuesday evening Miss Devereaux['s] party came off more delightful than either of the others. On Wednesday evening Mrs Sandfords came off a perfect crowd—splendid rooms—supper &c but no dancing.

Yesterday the place was crowded with strangers—we were advised not to attempt the whole day—Lord was of course very busy (but I am before my story).[1] On Wednesday evening Hamilton Couper arrived he came to this house & at once called to see us. He first saw the girls & then called again to see me. I was really disappointed when I found he had left the Island without seeing you it would have been such an excellent opportunity to have sent us the trunk—& those flowers were wanted especially for Mrs Sandfords party.

Could mine & Georgias letter on the subject of what things we wanted been lost that you ask again to be informed of what we wished sent back? If the trunk has not yet been sent—I will repeat "the *bonnets*, the *cloaks*—the *unmade dresses*, the *caps, the flowers*." I can think of no better way of getting them to us than by sending them to Messrs Andersons—directed to "the New Haven Hotel—New Haven Connecticut." It is true we leave here on the 5th—But Lord will leave directions to have the trunk received & he will be coming back here before we leave New Port.

On the same day that Hamilton came Mr Savage—Mr *Longnecker*—Mrs Hall & a friend of hers came—the two latter came just to see us. Hamilton came to "class supper"—unfortunately for me the room they supped in was immediately under mine. It was not a *quiet supper* I can tell you. I never *heard* a happier set, the next morning Hamilton called to say good bye—I enquired if he had not a head ache—but he assured me *"quite the contrary."*

We got stage tickets & went one hour before the ceremonies began in order to get good seats—but all the front benches were taken—Georgia got a seat by L[illie] D[evereaux], F[lorence], V[irginia], Cousin A[manda] & myself had to put up with back seats. It was very hot, the church perfectly crowded—I never saw any house so jam'd. I had the happiness to see my son graduate & I have his Diploma in safe keeping. He certainly made the *most graceful bow* & in my eyes was handsomer than any of the others. I could have wished him among those who received honors—but I am glad he has come off as well as he has. One of the Professors told a friend of Lords—that "Mr King had fine abilities—& was a fine speaker & could have had a high appointment had he exerted himself." I am very glad it is over—& wish that Lord was ready to leave—but *he has so much to do*—that he says he cannot possibly get away before Thursday. Georgia, myself & Rhina are going over to his room this morning to help him pack up.

Poor Malley has now holiday—will go down with us to New Port. What a relief it would be to me if I could get into some quiet house at *moderate board*. At Hotels I am obliged to give out all my washing—this you may believe is no small item in our expenses. If I get back on this subject there will be no end to my letter. Tootee dear I was a fool to come North. Just think what comforts the money (now spending) would add to *our* comforts at home. If there was one of the party who had a head to contrive to save—I would be better satisfied.

They tell me I look better. I am certainly *much fatter*, more so than I like to be—& when I do get to sleep I sleep soundly—but my days are *restless* & *anxious*. I am so uneasy about my darling Butler & your beloved Father. Now that he has been sick it is a time of all others since he left me that I am most anxious to hear from them. And as they suppose that Lord & the girls have gone home—

all of our letters will be sent South. Your answer to this must be directed to New port Rhode Island. I some how think that we will remain there but a short time—the expense is too great. Positively if my house was ready I would return home at once, but in the fix it is in I could not come. All may turn out for the best—but at present I do not see how this can be. Do not fill your letters with any thing but that which concerns your dear selves & my poor Plantation. You say nothing of my good old Jane. I hope the poor old woman is enjoying her holiday & may live to cook me many more dinners—I have tasted nothing so good as her soups—her roasts & broils since I came North.

Lord invited us just now over to his rooms—mercy on me what a collection of odd ends. He certainly resembles his Father in this respect. I offered my services to help him pack—but he was not ready—& I fear will not be ready in a hurry. It is not astonishing that the young men should feel sad—this has been their home for years—& they part now—not knowing if they shall ever again meet. 17 of Hamiltons class have married since they parted 3 years ago. (If Lord lives) I wonder how many will be married before the class meets 3 years hence? I rather think Lord expects to be of the number who will be. Several of Lords friends have been to bid us a dieu & they seem really grieved. Lord too seems quite sad—Malley wishes he could go home at once & if he was not so fat I would consent—but he is too good a subject for fever. I shall settle all the bills Lord & Malley owe which will make a hole. I will have at once to write to Mr Anderson to get him to advance me more money. The $1200 I brought with me would have added much to my comforts at home, here I have not known one that money could buy. I certainly desire the sick house repaired & tell William I will indeed thank him if he will see to it for me. I know he will do it at as little cost as possible. The *making* & *trimming* of 5 dresses cost me near 3 times that sum, it was an abominable imposition—but one I was obliged to submit to as I was such a fool I made no bargain with the woman & when you see the dresses you will at once say "I am horrified."

I am glad to hear the peaches have turned out so well that you & your dear husband & children have had as many as you wished. I am glad you sent old Mrs Armstrong some—but more especially that you sent some to dear Sarah Bourke & the Cunninghams. I have received affectionate letters from Sarah, Phem [Euphemia] & Isa & one of Bourkes real friendly letters. I hope my dear Willie likes his puppy & you my bird cage. Tell Maria to take care of my pets. I shall not be able to purchase those you name—Whilst I was in Allentown I was crazy to get a pair of birds then money seemed plentiful since then all my fine desires are sinking down to necessities.

[No signature]

1. I believe Anna means they had been advised not to attempt to go out all day because of the number of people arriving in New Haven and preparations for the graduation ceremony at Yale that was to take place the following day.

2nd August

My own dear child

I force myself to write on this small sheet of paper to prevent my writing a long letter so as to injure my poor blind eyes. I had the happiness to receive that dear long letter of yours of the 27th & those dear letters from your dear Father & Butler which you forwarded to me by the same Mail. If you could have said *you were perfectly well* I would have every cause to rejoice today, for I had scarce read those dear letters when Lord received one from your dear Father dated the *30th* June which informs us of dear Butlers recovery—he had gone into the country for a change & was expected back to S[an] F[rancisco] that night. He may not have got back in time to write by that Mail—this is my principle motive for scratching you these lines. I know how rejoiced you will be to hear of his entire recovery. How blessed I am in that son surely never did son love a Mother more than that boy loves me.

Tootee dear I cannot forget my cares at home—you, your husband, & those sweet children are never absent from my thoughts. I would you could be relieved of that pain in your chest. As I know that writing increases it as much comfort as your long letters give me I must beg you not to write such long ones. I could not be easy if you did not write once a week—can't you persuade William to write for you? I am thankful that matters are going on so well at Retreat. I trust neither storm or caterpillars will shorten the cotton crop—I *had hoped for* a *better one.*—

I went this morning to have my Daguerreotype taken—Dressed in my very best. Floyd & *Tip ditto.* Lord & Flora accompanied me. I unfortunately left my specks at home & did not see what a fright I really am until I got back. After some half dozen failures the Daguerrean produced three as ugly looking pictures of an *old* woman as you would care to see. They tell me these (old hags) look as much like me as possible, but *I cant believe* that I am *really so ugly.*[1] Floyd & Tips are good—two of these I will send to California the other is for you my darling. I do not think I will sit for another unless it be one for poor Malley. I tried to get one taken for him today—but it was a failure. I shall send those intended for your Father and Butler by the next express.

I hope the trunk may reach this before we leave as we may find some of the things useful. I think Hamilton may have taken leave of his uncle William. I wish I could write you a long letter, write just as I feel—but I find myself too often forgetting the *good* I *receive* in the few misfortunes I have had to encounter. God! forgive me for my ingratitude. I have more than once said "if my house was in a condition to receive the children & myself I would return home"—trusting to the mercy of God! that they may escape fever. I am heartily tired of the life I ha[ve]—the only object of which seems to be "to spend money."

Andrew & Louisa as well as Henry & Mary seem to be as undecided in their movements as we are. Henry is in a wretchedly nervous state, and unless he soon recovers I fear will not last much longer. I do not think it has ever entered his or his wifes heads—that it was possible *any one* could think they ought to lend or give me a cent. Andrew's offers are not *sufficiently definite* to enable me to understand what he really intends doing. He is so delighted to have got back to the U.S. that he has not left N.Y. & its luxuries when I last heard from Lou. I am very anxious the girls should go to Niagara—but fear A[ndrew] & L[ouisa] will make too long a stay at Saratoga. I almost wish I had let them go with Cousin A[manda] & Mr Woolley. Those dear friends may be still at Bridge-port for what we know. Poor A[manda] really requires rest—& should have it—her health would be all the better for rest—& so would mine, but there is no evil which has not some good. If I was at rest both in mind & body I would soon be as fat as poor Mrs Abbott was, as it is I shall soon be beyond every dress I have.

I wish I could just put your dear letter before me & pick out sentence after sentence & comment on each one—But I have not time or head for any thing. That expression of poor Sukeys I feel to be exactly my case "I did once think I had some sense—but now I know that I have none." I have partly written a let-ter to your Father one to dear Butler & am now writing this to you. Malley is sitting near enough to be able to give my table a kick every now & then—of this he is unconscious—& I have my mouth too full to remind him of the an-noyance he gives me. Georgia has gone to walk with Miss Pope (one of Lords old flames & a very beautiful girl she is). Flora is writing to her Father—Appy trying to get through a book loaned them by a student—or graduate—said book to be returned today. Rhina has quite recovered her health—is never tired of talking of "de fool peoples." She is dreadfully afraid of being *kidnapped*. She has written to Clementine.[2]

I find it is almost impossible to get any thing I want. Every one seems de-termined to cheat me. I have not seen Floyd or Tip since they left me at the Da-guerrean establishment yesterday—they were very mad at being made to stand so often.[3] They are determined to undergo the trial once more for Mrs Gale. Poor Mrs Gale I am truly sorry to hear she is so often sick. Your kindness to her will have its reward my dear child. I hope whenever she is sick as to need nursing that you do not hesitate to call for Clementine. What has become of that beautiful daughter of hers. I wish Tison would offer to purchase her from me.[4]

I think I have enough other cares without fretting for the loss of Mrs Bourkes young ones or Mrs Coupers loss of eggs. I am ashamed to say the *time was* & that not many months ago when it would have fretted me sorely. But I have had too many more serious grievances since. And yet how much greater & more grievous may have been my losses. I must not look back & fear to look forward. Oh! that I could but feel "that all that is—is for the best."—

Georgia will answer your dear letter very soon. She has to write to your dear Father & Butty by this Mail. You are very wrong not to have sent me your dresses. I am not pleased with you for having *disobeyed* me. I think a dress for each of the dear children would have been better than toys or sugar candy and one or the other they must have—dear little souls, how I do long to see them. Georgia can find nothing fit to send Butler. Not one of our party are fit to shop. I get cheated as badly as they do. I am afraid I shall return home without having accomplished a single object that I had in coming here except being with my children.

Georgia has gone to spend the morning with L[illie] D[evereaux]. I am afraid Lord loves her more than ever & from all appearance she is not behind him in this respect. Mrs D[evereaux] has been exceedingly kind to all of us—also her aunt & cousin Mrs & Miss Whitney.[5] I think if Lord was less in love we should have left this ere this. He has a great deal to do—many visits to make & here we are stuck down at this Hotel "eating off our heads." I wish Andrew would go at once to Niagara—the season for going there is passing away—& then to take the girls down to New Port just to stay a few days would be folly—again they cannot go to Saratoga to remain over one night. It is terrible this uncertainty. I would rather be at home & have nothing but homany to eat—than be here worried as I am. Poor Amanda is *dying for homany*.

I am sorry that Quamina has been not only lazy but impudent. The vegetables would have been a comfort not only to Mr Dunham but to the yard negros. I will not express any regret for my roses their day for worrying me is I *trust over*. You must have had quite a pleasant party at Madam Caters. What room has Miss Annie *furnished so comfortably*. But *Mrs Cater is no greater fool* than I have been. Has any part of her house been finished? Her birds seem to be of the runaway tribe. I hope they will not get away from you on their way to Retreat. Be sure to caution Maria about the wires. Whenever there is fresh beef —they should have a little *scraped* very fine. I am glad to hear that the rooster is better. Never mind about the grape jelly—and as to the peaches—why did you not have a part of them preserved expressly for yourself. Of course my darling you must have a share. I see no prospect of my having any preserves made. I have as yet seen no fruit except some miserable squash watermelons. The peaches I see in the streets are no larger than pigeon eggs & look black—this is not yet the season for them to be had in perfection. We found the cherrys very good whilst in Allentown. I would ask William to employ some one to assist Dupey McIntosh. If he is lazy I hope he is not working by *the day*. Has Anderson finished the chimneys? Did he do the plastering? You must tell me how much of the work is done. When I purchased lumber for the Hospital I added what Dunham thought would be necessary to do the sick house over. I would be very glad to have it done & if there is not boards enough beg Wm to get them for me. I think the house really unwholesome as it stands. But dear me Tootee scarcely a house on the place that does not need repair.

Malley is just mending a pen to scratch you a letter after his fashion. I suppose "Hag" will soon be writing to you. Georgia is writing to her Father—Florence talking—Rhina grumbling. I must stop though I could write as much more. Kiss those darlings for us—tell them I love them more than ever & long to see their dear sweet faces again & hear their sweet prattle. Tell Mrs Gale she must try & get in better health or else she will never be able to stand the chatter of these girls. Give my love to dear William & thank him for all the interest he takes in my affairs. Tell all the servants howde for me—especially those who are doing their duty. Tell dear Anna that I am not half as happy in my fine silk dress—& white silk bonnet as I used to be in my calico dress & old cracker bonnet. Florence is so [?] she cannot go down to tea because the flies require food as well as we do—last night she was desperately hungry & had to go to supper at 10 oclock—a married lady—G[eorgia] & A[ppy] good naturedly went with her. I do not think any of them *will go again*.

All send love—are writing or will write soon to you. God! bless you my own darling Tootee—may we meet again in health & happiness is the constant prayer of your

devoted Mother
A M King

1. This is most likely the photograph that appears in this volume.

2. It is interesting to note that Rhina could read and write, although it is unclear where or from whom she learned. Though teaching enslaved people to read and write was illegal, it was not unusual for house servants, especially those who worked as closely with their owners as Rhina did, to be taught to do so. Earlier in the century there had been a movement among slave owners to teach their bondpeople the catechism in order to give them religious training and ultimately to assure obedience to their masters as taught through particular Bible passages. However, there is no evidence that this was done at Retreat.

3. Anna must have stopped writing this letter on the second and started again on the third as she began by saying she had gone to have her picture taken "this morning" and now says she hasn't seen Floyd and Tip "since they left me at the Daguerrean establishment yesterday."

4. I cannot identify "Tison" and do not know why Anna was so eager to sell Clementine's daughter.

5. Mrs. Whitney was the widow of Eli Whitney, inventor of the cotton gin.

New Haven
4th August 1854

My own beloved daughter

I sent off another letter to you yesterday my own precious child—but as writing to those I love is my very greatest pleasure I will commence another in reply to yours of the 30th July. I will begin *moderately* & hope to be able to continue so to the end.

We were all in good spirits preparing to pack up & leave for New Port— Lord had gone to finish his calls— Georgia to spend a sociable evening with a very lovely young lady—Mall escorted her. Flora & Appy were enjoying a quiet game of whist in one of the parlours & I was in & out having nothing particular to do—when letters were handed in. The one addressed to me was post marked Saratoga & in Mary Kings hand writing. After reading her very amusing account of affairs at Saratoga—I came to a P.S. from Louisa—informing me that "from a fear of return of Rheumatism Andrew declined going to New Port." Now you will bear in mind that it was Andrew who fix'd on this place & sent poor Lordy pell mell down there to engage a cottage which should accommodate *us all*—*he* thought it would cost at least $100 per week—Lord got one for $50, & it was to be ready for us by the 5th of this month. Andrew & Louisa were to be at Saratoga on the 24th July—Lord telegraphed his Uncle that the Cottage was secured—at what Price &c & received for answer "no such person at Saratoga." As he did not know when A[ndrew] would leave N.Y. or be in Saratoga—he rested satisfied until last Saturday when he wrote in full to his Uncle—& I wrote to Louisa—and this is the answer they send us. Andrew recommends "our going to Morristown and if we conclude to go there they will join us there after they had got done at Saratoga." John Cunningham tells Pheme that he paid $7 per week in Morristown—the chambers were not *very* comfortable. At this season of the year most of these smaller towns are full of persons from the large cities. We have no other inducement to go to Morristown but to *economise*—& please Andrew. It is ten chances to one if Lord goes down there & gets rooms—they will change their minds & prefer some other place. I am most painfully situated and cannot determine what had best be done.

I was in this state of excitement when Lord came in & I gave him the letter (as I thought from William)—he tore it open & that note marked private taken out first & read—he & Georgia went into the next room pretending it was some joke of yours only. They left the letter & as I recognized your writing—& that the letter was addressed to me—I did not feel at all frightened as you said all were well. But the whisperings in the next room made me suspect evil. You took the very best method you could to reconcile me to the loss of my crop, had it not been that that little private note was addressed to G[eorgia] or Lord—had it not been for their whispers which made me suspect even worse than the loss of crop, the shock would have been much greater. It is a great blow never the less—I endeavor to bow with humble submission to the will of an all wise Providence—Being too greatful to complain or repine when as yet the lives of my husband & children are spared. What would riches be to me if those dear ones could not enjoy it with me. G[eorgia] was so certain that the note contained *all that was painful* & that I should not hear it last night—she tore it into little bits & threw it into the slop basin. After reading over your dear letter I called for the note—I took out all the little pieces & tried to read them but after worrying myself for near an hour had to give it up. I wanted to know if the caterpillars were at Newfield or only on the Island. I will try and not suffer myself to think on this misfortune. I must only pray to a Merciful God! to keep from you loved ones sickness & death!!!

When I read Louisas P.S. I felt *determined* to take the very next Steamer home but your entreaties not to run the risk—your saying my house could not be habitable for two months compels me to hesitate taking a step which may hazard the lives of my children. Oh my Tootee your poor Mother is *very wretched*. I have shed more bitter tears since I came North for your Fathers absence from me—than I have shed in all my partings from him for many years past. I do not think either of his brothers are doing by me—as I am sure *he* would by either of their wives—had he been placed in their situation & their wives in mine. You recommend economy—I have endeavored to do so—but with so many to provide for it is requiring more than I could have dreamed of. To admit of Henry & his wife leaving home for his health we were forced to come here at the most expensive season. Poverty is a bitter pill for one to swallow who was born & raised in ease & comfort. I feel more for Lord & the girls than I do for myself. The washing is very expensive—they charge 50 cts per dozen for under clothes but make for this moderation by 25 cts for each dress, 12$^{1}/_{2}$ cts for boys pants, 6$^{1}/_{4}$ cts for each piece of muslin. Lord says we will find cheaper boarding *here* in this state than in any other State. The cheapest is more than I can afford.

This *morning* the trunk reached us safe. Thank you my darling for sending it to me—the cloaks & winter bonnets will be required as the cool weather comes on. The white dresses—[?] night caps—Floras silk dress—cracker bonnets were superfluous—as the dresses spoilt or to small—the rest not wanted. We have so much baggage & it keeps increasing—I left all that I thought we really did not require at Mrs Henry Kings. I really feel for Lord he has had & has every prospect of continuing to have so much trouble to provide lodgings for his poor Mother & sisters and brothers.

I shall have to send to Mr Anderson for the money the girls owe in Philadelphia—for Malleys Bill [is] over $200 & then that will not be enough. I have such a horror of debt. The last years crop set me free & but for this unfortunate trip of mine and the repairs of the house I could have continued free. But Tootee dear I must not murmur—you set me a bright—bright example of cheerful resignation to the Will of Divine Providence. May I be able to profit by it. Georgia says she begs you will take the old dresses you speak of. I think we had best have an auction and sell off all the old things it may enable me to give them new ones. The weather here has been so cool—thin dresses are not worn. It would have been well could the rainy season been here instead of St Simons—I never saw or was in so dusty a place.

I am glad to hear so good an account of my birds. If Mrs Caters do as well as Mr & Mrs Couper I shall be able to make canaries find me in chickens—tho I am so avaricious after birds I do not think I shall be able to part with one of them.[1]

My dearest Pet however are your own darling babes—as much as I thought I did love them when at home I find I love them far more since we parted. God! grant I may find all ready to meet me on our return. Be careful of your own & their precious health. *Never ride after dark*. You must continue to write me openly of every thing which concerns me—keep back *nothing*. It will give me *confidence* in all you may say.

It seems to me that I could be writing the whole time to your Father—Butler & yourself. I have written 12 letters to those dear ones since I left you. I hope in two weeks more to receive a reply to the last one written at home. I am so much distressed lest my coming North may make them unhappy. I have such a dread lest one or the other of them may deem it necessary to come to me. The cholera has broken out on board of two of the Steamers between Chagres [Panama] & Havana. It is reported to have made its appearance at Niagara—Buffalo & Rochester. I hope Cousin A[manda] & Mr Woolley may hear the report & refrain from going. They told me to direct to them at Niagara next week. If I could get her to stay with me—I would be more happy. My children are all young & inconsiderate—they cannot appreciate all I suffer. If the crop is gone I hope my poor negros may be spared to me—tell them all how de for me.

Your sisters & Brothers unite in much love to yourself—William & Mrs Gale
& thousands of kisses to our darling Anna, Willie, Bob & King. Tell Annie that
her Mother is quite well now & I hope will continue so. I hope she is a good
girl. You say nothing of poor Dunham—I do feel so much for him. To suffer
as he does—& have no one to take care of him & cheer him. I think he must
be better tho than when I left home—he wrote quite a long letter to Rhina for
Maria. I will write again dearest as soon as dear Lord can get a place to carry
us to. God! bless you my precious one and keep you from all harm—Your devoted Mother

A M King

I know if I could tell you we were comfortably situated you would be more happy.

    Since writing this letter Dear Lordy has succeeded in getting rooms for us
at about 4–6½ a piece so $30 per week for 8 of us & Rhina, the little boys will
come to us at the end of their term. The house is a very pleasant one—good
rooms &c. The landlady a very fine woman. I think this is the best we can do.
Better than to go to Morristown at 7—or to these little [?] country places at
4½ which they ask. It will save the expense of moving &c.

    1. I believe Anna means here that she could sell canaries to buy chickens—in a
sense a hobby could provide food for her family and friends.

New Haven
18th August 1852

My own dearly beloved Tootee

    Ten thousand thanks my precious child for your welcome letter of the 14th
which came to hand today—I *was getting* uneasy at not hearing from you & had
just begun to console myself with the hope that your letter may have been
directed to New Port was the reason why I had not got it yesterday when
Mr Kerr sent this one up to me. God! be praised for permitting you still to
write so cheerfully to me, for blessing you all with health. I will try & write you
twice a week. I know by experience what happiness there is in getting letters by
every mail from those we love. On Monday we had among us no less than 7 letters from those beloved ones in California up to the 15th July your beloved Father & Butler were quite well but sadly distressed about me.[1] Had it been possible it would have been best could they have been kept in ignorance of the
move & the cause. They really seem wretched about me. I am so very sorry to
have added to their cares & troubles.

    Doubtless Butler has written to you. What do you think that vile Davy deserves for his desertion of so kind a master as your Father has ever been to him? I am more mortified & hurt than I can express. It gives me a worse opinion of the race than I had before and makes me really desire to part with every one of them. Your Father said nothing of it to me—Butler barely says, "Davy has turned fool & scoundrel we think he has gone to Sidney." I fear the loss of his miserable body is not the only loss—I fear he did not go empty handed. This circumstance makes me regret more than ever my having brought Rhina with me. After Davys example I can never trust another black skin. I have not said a word to any one but Malley about Davy—And if you have not yet heard of his delinquency—*I would wish it kept secret* from all but William.[2] I know your dear father feels this keenly. I would much rather have heard of Davys death. When he beg'd me [s]o hard to let him go to wait on his master I little dreamed he would have deserted that kind master. Poor wretch bitterly will he repent him of the act before he dies. He is lazy, ignorant & not strong—but enough of him—I wish I could only forget that he ever existed.—

I hope before I close this that dear G[eorgia] & L[ord] will have returned from Saratoga—their time I doubt not has past pleasantly. Georgia wrote to me that Mr & Mrs H[enry] & Mr & Mrs A[ndrew] King remained at Saratoga 4 days after she got to Saratoga. Poor Louisa is in bad health & spirits—kept her room almost entirely. Your Uncle Henry had been benefited by the waters—Mary & Andrew the only well ones of the party & as each had a sick partner I do not think any of them realized the pleasure of a "trip to Saratoga." Mr & Mrs & Miss Chandler are represented by Lord & Georgia as highly respectable & most agreeable people. Georgias Uncles & Aunts thought there would not be the *shadow of an objection* to her remaining under their & Lords care. In fact G[eorgia] would have had to leave with them, had she deserted the Chandler party—& it would have been a little hard on the dear girl after Andrews having disappointed herself & sisters of their Niagara trip. It is a pity that I ever depended on any one but Lord & myself. For you see even dear Amanda has deserted me. I believe I mentioned in my last letter that *they* had been at Saratoga on their way to Niagara & Canada. I have written to beg them to come here just to rest after their journey—but I hardly flatter myself that they will—Mr Woolley does not like New Haven. He would rather be at Brooklyn so as to be able to run over to N.Y. any hour of the day. But for keeping the boys here at School I should prefer Brooklyn if I could get as pleasant lodgings there as we have here. I have employed a music master to give lessons to your Sisters whilst I stay here. They commenced today. I have the use of a piano *without paying for it.*

We are really very pleasantly situated. There are 3 ladies about my age—but none so active as I am—all very pleasant & sociable. Our table is good & quite sufficient. In fact there is no fault to be found with the house or its inmates. And then I have many very kind & attentive acquaintances. By the way we are to take tea at Old Mrs Whitneys this evening (her husband was the inventor of the Whitney cotton gins). She is now a widow—Aunt to Mrs Devereaux. She lives in handsome style—& is a very pleasant old lady.

I find myself getting so fat I am really *getting uneasy,* & am compelled to exercise to keep down my flesh. I felt a little return of nervousness when I received my last letters from California & did not hear from you as usual—but it did not last long. I had to write to Mr Anderson for some funds—for I had to pay not only all our expenses so far but Lord & Malleys last term which was not taken into consideration when I left home. In my usual blundering way I mentioned to him that the caterpillars were on the Island by which I may have been putting a stumbling block in my own way. I wish *William would write to them how the case really stands.* I have promised you & myself too that I would endeavor to have more faith in God's mercy & not suffer myself to fret & pine after riches or pecuniary losses, when I am so abundantly blessed in other respects. I am now where I am compelled to have ready money, & tho I economise in every way it will slip through my hands. I can but hope matters may not turn out as badly as I apprehend. I will try come what will not to repine at the will of God!

I am anxious to get home as soon as it will be safe for us to return—& beg you will be particular in informing me of the state of the country as regards the health of the white inhabitants. I really do not wish to remain until Nov—or accept of Mrs Henry Kings invitation to spend October with them in Allentown. Andrew & Louisa expect to remain with them until they return to Cuba & tho the house is very large—it would be too large a number to trespass on their hospitality. I expect them (ie) A[ndrew], L[ouisa], H[enry] & M[ary] here today on their way to Allentown.

I am delighted to hear of the improvements in dear little Kooneys health— God! bless the precious little lambs how I do long to see them & your dear husband and yet dearer self. Your poor Father was so much gratified by Williams kindness in coming on with me, he says "dear Tootee writes me under date of the 5th June that her good husband was to accompany you—This has been a great relief to me—I feel that you will be safe in his hands." I wish you would write me more about those sweet children. I never see children of their size but I want to kiss them. One little girl sits next pew to us every Sunday. She is larger & older than Bob—but I fancy I can see a resemblance & would be delighted if I could give her a kiss. I look at her so much the dear little thing has got in the habit of looking at me too—I dare say she wonders who I can be. My own darling Anna—does she still suck her tongue & my boy Willie—how I do long to hear him talk. Tootee dear I do love those children even as much as I do my own.

I am truly glad to hear of Mrs Gales improved health. Do say kind words to her for me. G[eorgia] & F[lorence] seem to love her better than they ever did [?]. Floyd is determined to have his likeness taken for her. If we are all permitted to meet again it will indeed be a joyful day.

I am sorry that after all your trouble you should have been disappointed of your company. Where were the Hazzards & Miss Mary Gould that they were not at Mrs Caters gathering? Do you think they were afraid to encounter yourself & William after their impertinence & *theft*. I was really very angry—that you should be deprived of the peaches—Maria was to blame in allowing the others to pry about my house. She could not have suspected Mary Gould of being a *thief* & was not to blame for the peaches. How mean some people can be. This is a poor place for fruit—the few peaches I have seen are miserable & from 1 to 2 cts a piece. I do not know what to say about my birds—get another if you can from Mrs Cater. Beg Maria to try & take care of those at Retreat. Tell Lady to try & take care of my poultry, for I hope soon to require them. Your Sisters & brothers unite me in love & kisses to your dear self—William—Mrs G[ale] & the babies—I intend to write to Anna & William very soon. My regards to Mr Dunham who I rejoice to hear is better. Tell all my negros how de for me— Rhina sends her love to her family & child. God! bless you my Tootee & keep you and yours in health & safety is the constant prayer of your devoted Mother

A M King

1. Butler wrote from San Francisco on July 15,

Oh! how could you take so little care of your precious self. My dear Mother I can stand *any thing* I believe & keep cool except any thing happening to you and even now though I have tried to collect my ideas I can scarcely write. Oh God! if I could only have been at home. But that pleasure I will not think of or speak of the regret I feel at being deprived of the proud joy Lord will have in escorting you. God grant the next mail may bring the news of your recovery—I feel that if I ever get back to you again I will never leave you as long as I can make enough to keep out of prison. I always felt it was my place to stay with and take care of you for I know I love you better than all the others do—they do their best though poor things they love all they can—so tis not their fault. (Thomas Butler King Jr. to Anna Matilda Page King, July 15, 1852, TBK, SHC)

2. Evidently, while in San Francisco Davy learned he could escape to Australia onboard a ship in port. The circumstances beyond this and what subsequently became of Davy are unknown. However, three days later Anna wrote Tootee,

I do not know what impression Davys conduct will make on Rhina—she seems utterly dumb stricken. It will not be becoming in me to censure your Fathers acts—

had he been less *liberal* with Davy he may have continued faithful—but your Father did it from a pure motive. I wish they had kept it to themselves—It makes me hate the poor wretch when most probably he is beyond human hate. I have no doubt but that he has been both robbed & murdered—for depend *on it* he would not have given up his money with out a struggle—I am mortified too & would have liked it kept a secret. I told Malley of it but no one else until this evening when Flora got hold of her Fathers letter—then I had to let Appy know it & poor Rhina seeing that something was wrong—looked so scared I was obliged to set her mind at ease by telling her. I can only hope she will be more faithful. (Anna Matilda Page King to Hannah Page King Couper, August 21, 1852, WAC, SHC)

Anna's hurt and outrage at Davy's "betrayal" reflect an attitude, prevalent among slave-holders, that their bondpeople owed them gratitude and loyalty. For more on the complicated issues of loyalty and humiliation associated with runaway slaves, see Clinton, *The Plantation Mistress*, 119–120; and Woodward and Muhlenfeld, *The Private Mary Chesnut*.

22nd August 1852

My beloved Anna,

I dare say you feel quite neglected that neither your Mother—Aunts or uncles have written to you. The fact is my precious little Anna I have not much time. I have to darn stockings just as I used to do when at Retreat. I will not tire you my pet by telling you all I have to do. I do not like to sew—& have no eye sight either.

Your Aunt Georgia went to Saratoga 13 days ago. I did expect her back before this. I hope she will come back tomorrow. I miss her very much she is always cheerful & happy. Florence is very funny & will make you laugh—Appy is a perfect old maid she is so particular about her trunk—no one dare go into it. Malley is a big fat boy—but you will love him very much he is so good & quiet.

You must stop sucking your tongue before Lordy comes home—or he will not love you. He likes young ladies to keep their mouths shut when they are silent. I think Floyd is improving his manners—he has a great appetite & does not like to dine with me on Sunday because you see we have very little dinner—but enough for those who are used to it.

You must kiss your dear Papa—Mamma—Willie—Bob & King—also Mrs Gale for me. I wish I was at Retreat that you could come often to see me. How are your mammy chickens—I hope Lady is raising me lots—so that I may not starve when I return home. I have the flowers yet which you gave me. I have seen no garden so pretty as mine since I left home. Adieu my own darling.

Your affectionate Mother,

A M King

New Haven
25th August 1852

My own dear child

I have this moment received your dear letter of the 17th—Praise be to God!
you were all alive at that time. Oh! Tootee dear when I see the daily funerals in
this place—read of the deaths elsewhere either by sickness or disasters, I dread
to hear from either the Island or California. It is when letters are due from you
& them that I feel the return of my old enemy. Your letters usually reach me
on Mondays or Tuesdays—these two last weeks it has been Wednesday before
they came & I would be too nervous to open them & have had to get one of
the girls to look over & tell me there was no bad news before I could read for
myself the wonderful blessings still vouchsafed to us. May these mercies keep
us constantly reminded of Him to whom we are indebted & strive with all our
might to be worthy of so great a blessing. Oh! my Tootee I feel that I have ever
been an ungrateful, unprofitable servant & wonder at the patience of God! that
I have been permitted so long to enjoy His blessings & not been made to feel
the nothingness of worldly riches. How sorely afflicted has Stephen Kings family been. I had heard of the death of Hannah Lord. James King wrote to Andrew King saying Hannah had died of *measles & that his mother was not expected
to live*![1] Just to think how they must suffer. How unfortunate they have been!
How much more so they may yet be! May God! have mercy upon them. I have
still the blessing of seeing these dear ones around me in perfect health. Rhina
was sick only one day & since she has heard of Davys conduct seems even more
anxious to please than she was before. She is very anxious to return home. I can
only hope this good conduct & desire may continue. I wrote you my weekly
letter & put it into the office on Sunday night.

Monday 11 oclock

Floyd, Tip & myself accompanied kind Mrs Baldwin on a visit to Meridon 17
miles from this. I had anticipated a pleasant day, and it would have been so had
we spent it alone. We had been invited to visit her brother—who is a minister—a widower with two daughters, a widow sister in law keeps house for him.
He met us at the cars & was very polite—gave me his arm & trotted me up a
hill to look into the free school, and down again to his dwelling—which by the
way is a very neat parsonage. I was introduced to the Sister in law & all was very
pleasant—until during dinner when he began to *question* me about slavery. I
was never so annoyed in all my life—as I was a guest I was obliged to keep in
my temper. I gave him rather short answers this did not stop him—but dinner
was soon over & he hurried off to get a carriage to give us a drive—to another
small town where we could visit a cutlery & ivory comb factory. This was very

pleasant & instructive, from the sawing of the Elephants tusk to the packing of the ivory comb. The cutlery was even more interesting—we were told the making of a knife went through the hands of 47 men before it was finished. After this we had a delightful drive until six oclock—then we had tea—as soon as we sat down my *inquisition* again commenced his cross questioning of me, which lasted all the time we were at table & some time afterwards—he asked what number of slaves I had—how they were fed—clothed—worked—treated—if we had them taught to read—what religious instruction was given them—then compared them with the free people of colour in this state &c & then asked me how I could endure to keep a fellow being in bondage. I do not think I ever endured a more intolerable evening & would have given the value of a *nigger* to have been able to leave his house. His sister in law was engaged in knitting stockings to be sent to some fugitive slave in Canada. I think Mrs Baldwin more than once tried to check her brother—eventually I told him the subject was a disagreeable one & which we should never agree on—I tried to act the lady tho' I thought he had entirely forgotten the courtesy due to me as a lady & a guest. I had many tart replies ready but restrained my tongue. I do not think I ever was so glad to leave a house as I was to leave Mr George Perkins!

We had a very pleasant ride back & when I got here found not only my dear Georgia & Lordy but also dear Henry & Mary King. We formed a delightful evening party. I never saw any one more improved than Henry King—he looks 10 years younger—was so cheerful, so kind. And Mary as joyous as ever. The transition to Miss Lines' comfortable parlour surrounded by my children & friends from that of Mr George Perkins'—made me feel really gay & happy. The next morning Mary & Henry left at an early hour—as his business was requiring him at home. They both urged our going to Allentown—which we shall do before we return home. At breakfast I was asked how I had spent the day at Meridon—I just told how impolitely I had been treated—Miss Lines & Mrs Dagget said I feared as much when I heard where you had gone. George Perkins is *perfectly mad* on that subject—that he was a perfect tirant over the people of his church—& is *loved* by no one.

Yesterday morning dear Mrs Baldwin wrote to invite me to take a drive with her & as she had two seats to offer asked G[eorgia] to accompany us. When I saw a gentleman get out I was certain it was the veritable George Perkins. And really was trying for some excuse why I could not go—when Mrs B[aldwin] named him to me as her brother *Samuel Perkins*. We had a delightful drive of some hours—to East Haven, Fair Haven & to the light house—it would have been particularly pleasant had we not been disappointed of an *oyster supper*. Mr Perkins living in the interior was most anxious for some roasted oysters—stopt at a house and ordered one which was faithfully promised—we then drove on further to the light house—got out & walked about & when we thought all was ready to be served up—we returned got out—hitched the horses—walked in & took our seats among some dozen grown women & men & twice that number of children of all sizes & ages. By & bye the woman came to say—she was very sorry but the tide was up—her husband away &c &c—so we had to leave— we were all hungry as hawks & looked really sheepish as we unhitched the horses—took our seats & drove off. Depend on it the horses were made to pay for it—it was now near dark & quite so when we got back. Mrs Baldwin took occasion to remark "my brother Samuel has all the fine *qualities* of my brother George without any of his *peculiarities*." I would have said *his rudeness*. We were very much pleased with Mr S[amuel] P[erkins] he was not only exceedingly polite—but very agreeable. I would be glad to see him again but as to Mr George —I would pack up this moment & be off if I thought I would ever have another squint of his ugly face. He is just such an *other* as that Wright would have been had he not stood in such fear of Butler & Lord. I even think they looked alike.[2]

Our agreeable friends the Kerrs go tomorrow. I am really sorry they are going—I do not think their places will be pleasantly filled by the Popes—Miss Pope is beautiful but she has lived so many years in Hotels. She has acquired rather free manners—is quite a Flirt—& is not respected as much as she should be to make her a desirable companion for my daughters. I have not heard again from Cousin A[manda]—& suppose they are now in New York. I expect Andrew & Louisa here some day this week. I do not suppose they will remain over a few days.

I will try & get the carpet, & think the old one had better be ripped to pieces & washed—it will not do to throw it away. I am very sorry about the birds— I advise the doves being taken out of the room unless the big cage Dunham made could be fix'd up for them. I would rather *twist* off their necks than let them kill my pretty canaries. I shall not let this grieve me—as it would have done the beginning of this *eventful year*. I have but little hope of making a crop. *But dare I murmur*? When so many other blessings surround me? God! forbid I should be so unmindful of the Mercy in sparing my husband and all of you loved ones. I have not heard one word of or from Mrs Hall since the day she spent with us on the 28th July.

Georgia says she will write to you very soon—if each one writes to you I would not give up the delight of scratching you letters every week. I am entirely selfish in this—as it constitutes one of my greatest pleasures. All send love to you, dear W[illiam], Mrs G[ale] & kisses to the dear babies—Rhina unites in remembrance to all the negros—do not forget to remember us all to Mr Dunham. God! bless you my own darling

A M King

1. Hannah Lord was Stephen King's daughter, James his son.
2. I am unable to identify Wright.

New Haven 12th September 1852

My own dear Tootee

It rains too much for us to go out to Church today—Georgia has taken the little boys into one room to read to them. Flora has locked herself up in their room to meditate or write letters. Appy & the two Jackson[s] have taken possession of my room—& as I could neither read, write, or even think in so much racket, I have taken refuge with Lord—he is getting ready to answer some letters—in the mean while puffs away at his cigar & brings to my memory the ways of your dear Father when he has letters to write & not the inclination.

I am not very fit to write letters myself—but I know I shall enjoy writing to you better than any thing else. Now comes the stormy season & I do not know how you may get through it. Tootee dear you are never absent from my mind. I can only trust to the mercy of God! that I may be spared to reach home & find all well who I left there. So many things crowd on—of little interest to relate—so little occurs which is really worth while repeating. I find it far more difficult to make out a letter here than when at home. I sent you a scrabble of a letter on Friday in time I hope to go by the Steamer yesterday—so that you may get it on Wednesday. I write this as your Sunday letter.—

I think if I could only have the energy to walk more I should not only feel better but be more happy—it seems almost impossible for all to get to bed before twelve oclock—& even then I cannot sleep—so that I do not feel able to rise early enough to walk before breakfast—after that is over there is always much to be done. I will scarcely be sorry when the Jackson[s] leave here—simply because they are too much in my room. The youngest daughter is a dear good child—a real old fashioned little girl—I love her for her devotion to her Mother. Mrs Preston is still here—I like her too. Last evening there seemed to be no end to calls on us. I had really hoped I had done with them—I will go the rounds once more & then stop.[1]

Lord was very much pleased with his visit to New York. Andrew & Louisa were exceedingly kind to him—in fact no fault can be found with them. It is not to be supposed that they could be content to settle down where we are— he has business in N.Y. & has also a taste for its comforts & pleasures—neither of which we can afford to enjoy.[2] Even here the pennies fly faster than I can afford they should. I must now stop & not look forward if I do I shall be moping again. I am trying hard to look on the bright side of things—I am trying to be more grateful for the blessings I enjoy. My beloved husband my precious children have been spared to me—how blessed how happy I ought to be, & how happy I would be but for *money*. Oh! Tootee what a poison this has been to human happiness. We all look to it with desire—forgetting that it is not all that is needed.

Mallery returns to School tomorrow. Last evening Mr Farren called to see me—he gratified me very much by saying that Floyd seemed wakening up & was studying with a will. I hope this will continue & as the regular school has now commenced I hope they will both be pushed forward sufficiently to make my teaching of them until your Father returns [*sic*]. It will be 5 years come November since we have all met at home. What may not the next 5 years bring forth? I have read the announcement of Mrs S[tephen] C Kings death in a Savannah paper. Some thing in the style of their summer excursion. Poor woman may her soul be at rest! I have heard nothing of young Henry King's coming North— I rather think it was only a negro story. But for *his* persuasion his Mother & Hannah may now have been alive.[3] We all naturally think it will go hard with S[tephen] C King. Still he may survive all this anguish & out live you or I.[4]

I hope the carpeting & Lordy's box have been received you must tell me what you think of the *stripe*. It would be too much waste if I conclude to use it for the stairs & get another for my bed room. I begin to fear the 30 yds are too little for your bed room—& regret not having sent you more. The fact is the two just took all the money I then had. I may yet be hard run for the means— at the same time I really would wish to get many things I really require—real necessaries. I always have thought persons coming North can find no difficulty in shopping. My experience makes it really a most difficult matter to get any thing. I never enter a store unless I cannot help it, & then expect to be cheated out of my very eyes. Defend me from Yankee shopkeepers they will tell you fifty lies in selling even as many pins. There are many ladies here prefer going down to N.Y. to shop but I am not up to that either. It is beginning to be time for us to prepare for home. So the boys & girls too will have to get warm clothing. I have some idea of letting G[eorgia] & F[lorence] go to New York next week they could be better suited there than here. Please beg William to write to Messrs Andersons about the box & carpeting—I wrote to them when they left this.[5] Do not neglect to let me know the colours & figure of the parlour carpet—it is too provoking it should not have held out. The money which I am giving to these Yankees I do begrudge—how much it would have added to our comforts at home. Georgia is hard at work making Uncle Andrew a smoking cap. Appy is working me one of that pair of ottomans. We left those that were finished at Allentown. I am now sorry that we did so as I could have sent them to Savannah to be made up ready for us to take home with us. I begin to dread making a move either by water or by rail road—there is not a week but some accident is taking place. Capt Lyon has now left the *Florida*—I shall go either in the *Alabama* or the *State of Georgia*. Many are returning South—I would not think of my own safety—but will be loth to risk the lives of your brothers & sisters. *You must keep* me advised of the real state of the Island depend on it I shall come as soon as *you* will let me. If I take passage by the middle of October—which is the time Andrew thinks of leaving for Havana—I will remain here until the last of this mouth—then go to Allentown for three or 4 days. I would like to pass the balance of the time in the City of N.Y. if I could do so at a boarding house—I could not stand the expense of a Hotel. Malley, F[loyd] & T[ip] will stay here until we are ready to Sail. When Lord will come up, pay their bills & bring them to us. There is no prospect of Lord & the girls seeing Niagara this year. I regret this—but it cannot be helped. There has been a great many deaths in this place from disentary. I have not heard of measles or whooping cough—& often think how happy we would have been could dear Anna have been with us. Dear little girl I think it would have done her good. I have not heard from Amanda since I last wrote to you. I am sure had it been left to her choice she would have been more with me. I can only hope her travelling has done her health good.

I am obliged to put this letter in the office this evening so as to ensure your getting it on Sunday next. I was invited to go to Church to day with Mrs Devereaux it rained too much this morning. They have just called to invite us to go this afternoon—but none of us were dressed for going out—so none went. *She* is very beautiful—*but more of this when we meet.* Georgia is to be home soon. Yesterday L[illie] sent me a beautiful bouquet of flowers. I divided it between Mrs Gordon, Miss Pope, Mrs Daggett & myself. A few days ago a young gentleman sent your Sisters more than a peck of fine peaches—what are called fine here but every peach I have tasted here require *sugaring*. The Isabella grape[s] are ripening—a very fine vine grows in the Fontine & had run over a tree in this yard. The young people here have permission to eat of these & depend on it the way they are disappearing is not slow. Floyd & Tip dine with me every Sunday. I was amused to day to see how they enjoyed their dinner. You or I would feel mean if 20 persons sat down to one small piece roast beef—1 very small ham & one dish of beef steaks, & yet there was enough left to feed those in the kitchen. If I could only learn how to make good bread I would try this Northern fashion of having but one piece of meat on the table. We seldom had more than one dish at Mary Kings—they fill up the table with vegetables & bread—& yet when you become used to it you would like it. What we have here is all very plain—but well cooked & clean. We have one *nigger* waiter a clumsy looking fellow with a squeaking voice who does all the carving on another table & helps those who first takes their seat.

Mrs Matthews was here last evening—her little grand daughter is very much in love with Tip—but I can't say he is with her. She is ever begging him to come & visit her. I really think I will make him go with me there on Wednesday evening next—I shall have to go cunningly to work to get him to go. I do not know how it is but he attracts *general notice*. The ladies pet him & the gentlemen all seem to wish him to sit on their knee. I think Floyd begins to look less like a cracker *& is* less jealous of Tip. Poor Lordy has shaved off his mustache he got tired of *blacking* it. I shall miss dear Malley tomorrow his seat is next to me, & he is so kind & attentive in helping me to red pepper. But it is best he should be at school—he says he is going to study hard so that he can go home with us. He has fix'd his heart so much I hope your Father will not object to my taking him home with me. Lordy has not done much reading this summer—he promises to do wonders when he gets home. I hope by Wednesday to hear again from those beloved ones in California. God! grant the accounts may be favorable. It is rather strange neither of them tells us any of their plans—or what they are doing. It is only *probable* that they will return in Dec. But they write to you & I doubt not say as much to you as they do to us. You say you have no news to give us—your letters are far more interesting to us when you write most of your dear husband, children & self with the little items about our poor old establishment. If I could only find a gold mine—I would bring home enough to make you all think it was best I should come North but as that is not likely—you will have to agree with me it would have been better had I never come. All I shall gain is *flesh* & that I do not want. When you see Mrs Cater again see if she will let me have a mate for poor little Tootee. I would rather any other bird had died before that dear little beauty William Couper. Why could not Mr Bourke have gone, or Mr Fraser. I did not value either of them in comparison with W[illiam] C[ouper]. I have not seen so pretty a bird as he was since I came North & I have looked at a great many canaries. Rhina is half dead to get home—she is not very well today—& never looks really pleased except when we tell her we shall soon get home. Poor thing she is lonely—I do not encourage her going out much. In fact after Davys conduct I have confidence in none of them. Your Sisters & brothers unite in much love to yourself & William & thousands of kisses to the dear little ones. I feel that this is a miserable production but I really feel incapable of writing a decent letter. You see I have got through my larger letter paper, & have to use these miserable little sheets. I ought really to write to Euphemia & Sarah Bourke but writing to any one but yourself & those dear ones in California is a perfect tax. Gods! Mercy protect you all my precious ones—kiss dear William & the children for me. Speak kindly to my negros in my name—& remember us to Mr Dunham—

Your devoted Mother
A M King

1. Anna wrote to Tootee on 10 September, "On Wednesday evening G[eorgia] & myself sallied out to return calls—the afternoon was very warm & we really hoped the ladies would all be indulging & be denied—but no such good luck all were at home so that we only made 5 calls—only four more due—& what do you think already *4 new ones* have called & many more threatened. I really am very much obliged to the good people for their politeness but would rather be let alone. I dislike calling or making new acquaintances" (Anna Matilda Page King to Hannah Page King Couper, September 10, 1852, WAC, SHC).

2. Andrew and Louisa were staying at the Metropolitan Hotel in New York City, which, Anna explained, "is said to be the finest Hotel in the world. It is 6 stories & each story is calculated to accommodate 30 families & *100* single gentlemen. It is finished & furnished from bottom to top with equal grandeur—The first day it was opened 300 persons were turned off—so quickly had it filled up. Andrew had his rooms engaged some weeks before the house was opened" (Anna Matilda Page King to Hannah Page King Couper, September 10, 1852, WAC, SHC).

3. I take this to mean that Henry persuaded his mother and sister to travel during the summer, and they became sick and died. Anna wrote on September 6, "I find it is too true that Mrs Stephen King is dead. I cannot believe that about Henry. No son could be so unnatural. Most disastrous has been that excursion" (Anna Matilda Page King to Hannah Page King Couper, September 6, 1852, WAC, SHC). The family suffered from tuberculosis, and the "excursion" was probably in search of a cure.

4. On September 5 Anna had written, "By yesterdays *Herald* I see the death of Mrs Stephen King coupled with that of Hannah Lords—as having died in July. How severely they have been visited. Oh! how much I do pity the survivors—How suddenly has that family been broken up. I really fear poor old Steve cannot survive such shocks. . . . I forget all their unkindness in pity to their misfortunes. Oh! that I could take one drop of their cup of bitter sorrow. I[t] seems perhaps strange that we do not feel more for them. We do feel—but Oh! not as such near relatives should" (Anna Matilda Page King to Hannah Page King Couper, September 5, 1852, WAC, SHC).

5. Anna means she wrote to the Andersons when that carpeting and box left New Haven for the island via Savannah.

New Haven
28th September

My dearly beloved child

Your dear letter of the 20th reached me last night—I felt like sitting down at once to answer it, & assure you that I have seldom missed writing twice every week to you, & joining with you in abusing the Steamboat Captains & Jimmy Armstrong. There is no denying it, that we are shabbily treated, & I think we who have absent friends should represent our case to the Post Master General. I can very well imagine how you felt when the boy brought back an empty mail bag. I am grateful to Old Fruin for sending your letter of the 17th (I think) it came safe & quick. How grateful I am to you for your regular letters—& how thankful to God! that you are still able to say yourself, dear husband & precious children keep well. I cannot but be distressed to hear of so much sickness among the poor negros. I do consider myself very much blessed in having so good & faithful a nurse as Pussy—has proved herself this awful year. I have often thought "what would I have done in all that sickness had she been taken from me." And how much I am indebted to you & dear William for the constant care & attention you have bestowed on my affairs. May God! bless & reward you for it.

To day it is hard for me to realize how lonely you must be for the town has been gay with martial music & thronged with Whigs—thousands of men & boys have been parading the streets—filling the beautiful green *8* splendid bands giving out the most delightful sounds. How much I wish you my dear children & even every darkey I have could be here just to help me enjoy this. At the same time there is a *Fair* held in the State house on the Green. I am to go this evening to see the beautiful fruit & flowers—I dare say I shall covet them. The weather too is delightful—clear & cool. If you could but enjoy all these I am sure you would be cheered. I fear you will find this a queer letter jumping from regrets to rejoicing. Just as one band passes & I think I can scribble on— another comes & I cant help listening. I wish to put this letter into the Office this evening, or I would wait until all this noise had ceased.

On Sunday night I mentioned that I had or would let Appy go down to hear Sontag sing.[1] They left here ¹/₂ past nine yesterday morning—& we expect them back this evening. Florence & myself have been left alone—but we manage to get on pretty well. Last evening we went to see Mrs Matthews who joined us in a long walk. We got back after six o clock & found Floyd & Tip had been to the Office & brought us 7 letters, one from you—3 from James King (to G[eorgia] F[lorence] & myself), one to Flora from a young friend, & 2 to Rhina—before bed time I got another letter—from Mrs Jackson & a Savannah news paper up to the 23d Sep. Mr Jackson writes to his wife *that she can come home whenever she likes as Savannah is perfectly* healthy, for *the better class*— the news papers say the same. I do hope you will in your next letter be able *to give me leave* to come. I really cannot stay here many weeks longer—I am really frightened at the expense I am incurring.

I had just got this far when Mrs Daggett [&] Mr & Mrs Olmstead came to invite Flora & myself to go to the Fair. We got admittance for 12¹/₂ cts each, had we been permitted to touch—or eat of what we saw we should have been well paid for going. I never saw so beautiful a display of fruit, flowers & all sorts of vegetables. The variety of grapes, peaches—variety of pears—plums—& flowers—then the variety of vegetables of every kind surpassed any thing I could have imagined. We all looked on these with greedy eyes mouths watering. I have seen as fine peaches before—but certainly never such grapes or pears. Then the flowers—Oh! I never saw such Dahlias. They were placed in various forms to exhibit their beauties to the greatest advantage—there was a bouquet of all sorts of flowers more than two feet high & splendidly arranged—then the mammoth vegetables—of all sorts. In the upper rooms were some very fine paintings—Landscapes & portraits, fine musical instruments—patch work quilts, chairs &c &c. To my great surprise a gentleman came up to me & addressed me as Mrs King. It was *Mr Hugins* he expressed great pleasure at meeting with me again. He enquired after all of his Island friends. The last he had heard from the Frasers was directly after the fire at John Demeres—he says he will call to see us. He recognized me—but did not know Florence.—

The green still presents a most animating sight. The various bands playing all sorts of soul stirring tunes. Very little work has been accomplish'd in New Haven today. I am sure the *Democrats cannot work* when such music is playing. Now do not be longing for any of that nice fruit I have been telling you about—you will get none of it—neither shall I. I like the music best. I wish—but—*but* there is *no use to be wishing*. I do hope your Sister & brothers will come to night. Our time here is drawing to a close & we have many calls to return, besides that I am most happy when they are all around me.

I left no flower seeds at home to be planted. It is too early yet to get *fresh* seed of any kind. I wish I could get some of those splendid Dahlias, nothing in the form of a flower could be more beautiful than those I saw this evening. It made me feel badly to see oranges & lemons in full bearing & know that ours are all killed at home.

I do hope poor little Emily may get well.[2] I would have supposed that Maria had seen enough of death this year to make her careful of her children. Mr Dunham wrote a letter for Maria to Rhina on the *21st* the day after your letter was written & *said she was better*. It seems rather strange that you have never mentioned how much cotton we had gathered. Oh! Tootee what short-sighted mortals we are. When poor Dunham was working all ways to get that cotton to grow—& getting the ill will of the negros—how little we thought that neither Affy, Suckey—Emoline or Mily—would not live to see it come to maturity. Well I must try & forget my misfortunes in the *remembrance of the many greater blessings I enjoy.*—

I am very glad to perceive from James Kings letter—that his Father had succeeded in getting an escort of mounted riflemen. Steves letter was dated 11th August. They expect to reach home about the 1st of November—poor James feels the death of his mother & sister most deeply—& really seems grateful for our sympathy. He dreads the effect it may leave on his poor old Father. God! knows I feel for all of them. Oh! my Tootee *our trouble is all before us.* May we be prepared to bow with submission to our fate, & be thankful for the many years of happiness we have enjoyed. *Let us enjoy our present blessings.*—

In my last I mentioned our intention to leave New Haven on the 4th—this will give me time to hear again from those loved ones in California. I think you may as well continue to direct to New Haven—Tho' if I leave for home on the 16th October you will not write after the 8th of that month. In the midst of all this writing—here comes *Lord, Georgia* & *Appy,* dear children how glad I am to see them again. They are quite well & seem really glad to get back to Miss Lines. They left Andrew & Louisa quite well. I am so sorry they have not yet been to see the Jaudons. The girls met with some new relatives in New York—they seem to make a great deal of fun among themselves about these new relations. But you will have to wait & hear from themselves all about them. Florence is so funny—by the way she had a long letter from Jinny Grant yesterday—who mentions as a great secret—the intended marriage of Miss Cater & Mr Postell. The report of Longnecker & Georgia had reached the Grants. Who could have told such a thing?[3] I must stop now dear Tootee. I have to count clothes for the wash—& my head is a little confused by the return of my children. They send thousands of love to you & William & as many kisses to the dear babies. If Mrs Gale has returned to you give her our love. If it is a relief to you her being away—I am glad she remains there. Rhina will write to her Sister shortly. I had almost forgot my love & kisses to dear William & my darling babes—kiss them all for me dear Tootee—& make the little ones give you a kiss for me. Remember me to all my servants—& do not forget my remembrance to Mr Dunham. Mrs Matthews thinks if you would do those peaches over by boiling them in syrup they may come out of their wrinkles & be fit to eat. You can try a few & see how they will do. Lord has just stept in & sends love & kisses—God bless you my own child

> Your devoted Mother
> A M King

Has Lords box come to hand?

1. On September 18 Anna wrote to Tootee, "In one of my former letters I mentioned my intention to let Georgia & Flora go to New York for a few days. . . . Flora did not wish to go but Andrew & Louisa were particularly anxious that she should accompany Georgia & Lord declared he would not go without her so she got ready— Just when all was ready some gentlemen called & there I sat on pins & for fear they would be too late at the Depot—well to make short story of it they did get out in time. I do miss them so much—only poor Appy & myself left" (Anna Matilda Page King to Hannah Page King Couper, September 18, 1852). Then, on September 25, she wrote,

> I have not heard from Georgia since Lord & Flora left her on Thursday. I do not think she has written over a dozen letters since I came on. She no doubt is much taken up with entertaining her Uncle & Aunt. Flora soon tired of the excitement. From what she tells me nothing but the purse of the *Fortunates* would induce me to

go to the Metropolitan. Andrew & Louisa have a splendid suite of apartments—they pay $9 per day for board & Lodging—this tells when weeks roll on. The extra's no doubt are great—Andrew seems never tired of making his wife the most costly presents of jewelry. These will keep—She has purchased dresses & there accompaniments that appear to me ridiculous—as the fashions will change even if she comes North next summer—but it is no business of mine. I have some idea of letting Virginia go with Lord on Monday. She is so fond of good singing—& Sontag—is not only a fine singer but a *virtuous woman.* . . . I would not indulge Virginia—but she may never hear good singing again. No one thinks of asking me to go—I suppose they all look on me as much of a fixture here as I am when at home. (Anna Matilda Page King to Hannah Page King Couper, September 25, 1852)

2. Emily, number 100 on the 1853 list, was born September 11, 1846. She is grouped with her mother, Maria, and siblings Tilla and Henry. On the 1859 list she is number 79. A/C, Selected Pages from the Record Book of Retreat Plantation, GDAH; Inventory, WAC, SHC.

3. Someone had evidently "reported" that Georgia and Mr. Longnecker were either courting or engaged.

New Haven—October 3d 1852

My dearly beloved Tootee

If I do not send this letter to the office tonight you will be disappointed on Sunday next in getting a letter from me. I must say that I do not feel much like writing—I never do by *day light.* My room has always so many talkers in it—it worries me more than you can think. On Sundays Floyd & Tip come here from Church with us—I am sorry to say we do not feel like going in the afternoons—I have to keep the boys with me until it is time for their supper &c &c.

Lord & his sisters got back yesterday in time for dinner. They seem to have enjoyed their visit very much—tho' it was really too short for much pleasure. They are delighted with John Kings wife & children—Saw also Mrs Preston that good lady seems to take matters very easy she is staying at her sons. I guess if she was paying board she would not be so content to remain North until the 30th October. What an age to look forward to—& yet the time will soon pass. I feel obliged to be governed by your advice & have thus very reluctantly decided to remain until the 30th of October. We must leave this next Friday—dear me how I dread to move. If I could just get into the Steam Ship at this place & steam away for home it would not be so bad. I miss dear William now very much. Dear me I do wish I was safe at home. We have not yet received our California letters. I hope tomorrow will bring us pleasant ones from those beloved ones. I do hope and trust we shall not find that they have postponed their return. I have never seen in the papers or heard any one say they have seen his resignation *formally announced*.[1] I am so much afraid he may be induced to hold on until next Spring—I know your dear father will do all for the best. I can only hope he may have made enough to enable him to return to us.

Dear little Tip is again well—tho he & Floyd both have bad colds. It seems a hard matter here to get rid of colds. The weather is delightfully cool & bright & if I could be induced to exercise freely I would feel better than I do—but I do hate the parade of dressing every time I put my head out of the house. This will be a busy week with us—Several visits to make—trunks to pack &c &c. I shall certainly leave New Haven with regret—*I shall never see it more.* Yesterday evening Georgia & myself took tea at Mrs Baldwins—Flora had head ache—Appy a *toe* ache. Malley, Floyd & Tip came in afterwards—we were all invited but the boys could not be got. Miss E[lizabeth] B[aldwin] is certainly a very pleasant intelligent young lady. And we spent a very pleasant evening. They have done every thing in their power to make us be on sociable terms with them. But we are every one miserable visiters.—

We all went to Church to day—Flora, Tip & Myself to St Thomas', Georgia & Floyd to Trinity & Appy to the Center Church. Georgie Devereaux communed today for the first time. I wish L[illie] was as pious as Georgie is—Mrs D[evereaux], L[illie] & G[eorgie] all have bad colds—the two young ladies are to be here tomorrow—G[eorgia] & F[lorence] sat in their pew today. Yesterday evening a man shot himself very near this—poor wretch—he had *been drinking*—he did not kill himself dead—for hours his sufferings were very great. Another poor man—was burnt so badly two nights ago that he died yesterday. I do not know what tempted me to tell you this. Because I suppose I have very little to tell about. Mr Gibson called yesterday to invite G[eorgia] & F[lorence] to go to Chapel this evening. I had to entertain him as the girls had not yet returned from Princeton. It was a hard matter for me to find talk for him & he did make a most [?] call. We got on *caterpillars* at last—on this subject I am most *eloquent*. George Gordon called the other day on Georgia & asked to see me—I do not care when G[eorgia] or F[lorence] are present how many call—they are neither of them ever at a loss for something to say. Mr Gibson has just called to take G[eorgia] & F[lorence] to Chapel &c.

I had another kind letter from Mr Hall yesterday—he has shipped the 8 yds carpeting to make out the parlour carpet. I assure you dear Tootee I ought to thank Mr & Mrs Hall for their attentions—they are more so than any one else I have met with. He offers to get comfortable board for me whenever I can make up my mind when I shall go to New York, & insists on Floyd & Tips staying with them. If it is possible I would like to remain a few days in New York before we sail. I believe Andrew & Louisa are yet in New York. I should like to be at Allentown at the same time they are as it is probably the last I shall see of them. I will try & write you again before we leave New Haven. We shall have a great deal to do—& I dare say will leave a great deal undone. I do not think there ever was a family as large as mine who accomplish as little as we do—We have no *tact*. I every night determine to do a great deal the next day—the day comes & is over & nothing done. We want you & William here. I have had a box made to put such clothing as we do not wear in & will send it on before we go. Our baggage even tho' we have but one trunk and bag a piece is very troublesome. I am going to try & make two trunks answer for our visit to Allentown. And with all this show there is nothing of value in our trunks. I presume you know that Hugh Grant, Eugenia & Fraser have come on—& the rest of them gone to Marietta. Florence got a letter yesterday from Jinny they were to leave in the Steam Ship yesterday for New York. Georgia has had several very long letters from Fanny. She intends G[eorgia] to be God Mother to her baby.

I am very nervous as the time draws near for me again to venture on the great deep. You see I can scarce spell—much less make up a tolerable letter.[2] Tootee dear as long as I live & have a husband—I will never again leave home without him. I find it so difficult to decide myself what is best to be done. I feel it is a most difficult matter for Lord—I can but hope we shall eventually all reach home in safety. I think if I can but do that it will be like taking a mountain off of me. Oh! that I could but awake tomorrow in my own bed room find Maria by my side saying "you aint guine get up today?" But there must be many nights before I can sleep again on my own bed. God! grant it may be a happier sleep than the *last one* I had there.

You must not think it unkind your sisters not writing oftener. I am sure it is not from want of love, but they see me writing so often to you—they think I tell you all they could, & they are always busy doing *nothing*. I begin to be really sorry that I cannot let them go to Philadelphia—they are all anxious to see their old school friends. One of them mentions that Adele Picot was to leave France last Wednesday for the U.S. Flora is making herself very merry about their visit to the chapel this evening. She declares she will not be a *third* again in any party—but dear me I will not pretend to repeat her nonsense—she certainly is very amusing, & is a most affectionate girl. I can only repeat—how anxious I am to be once more at rest in my own home. I do envy Amanda & Mr Woolley—they have had a far happier & pleasanter summer than I have had. Your Sisters & brothers send thousands of love & as many kisses to you—William & the babies. In this of course I unite. Flora has just run up out of breath—she says I have a "gist" to tell you—a Mrs Hall told lady Daggett that she "saw Father & Butty at a ball in San Francisco & that Father looked as young as *Lord does*." I think this rather *a stretch*. The husband of this Mrs Hall keeps one of the Hotels in San Francisco & is making a *big lump*. I must stop now.

Tell all the people how de for me. I hope poor Dunham is better [?] Mrs Gale
got [illegible]. God! bless you my Tootee

>Your devoted Mother
>A M King

I hope there is a good chance of groundnuts—I have promised to send Simeon
Baldwin a supply.

1. T. B. King wrote to Secretary of the Treasury Thomas Corwin hinting he would
like to resign his post as collector the coming August, but then decided to stay until
March 1853, when a new administration would be inaugurated. Corwin and President
Fillmore, however, considered his letter a formal letter of resignation, and a successor
to the post was named to begin his duties in November. Steel, *T. Butler King*, 90.
2. Anna had misspelled and then corrected the word *deep*.

Allentown
10th October 1852

My own Tootee

I must [not] omit writing to you to day tho' I fear I shall not be able to give
you as long a letter as usual. You will perceive that we have returned to Allentown, & had you witnessed the hospitable greeting which met us yesterday you
would not doubt but that we are really welcome. Every thing looks *so nice*—&
pleasant. But we can talk over all this when *we meet*.

Well to begin—We found it a pretty difficult matter to get ready to leave
New Haven—there were so many begging us to remain—so many things to
be collected & packed. I began on Thursday night & by hard work was all
ready to start by 10 oclock on Friday night. I met with an hundred interruptions—by callers &c but never the less we did all get ready. Poor Lordy was
trotted nearly off of his legs. Mall came to us after tea & did great service in
seeing the baggage off at ten. By the way I may as well now mention that the
box & *trunk* I mentioned were directed to be sent by the *Florida* yesterday, & I
wrote to the Messrs Andersons requesting them to forward these to you as
soon as possible—the carpet went the week before. The trunk contains only
the girls winter bonnets—& some other light articles—& if *dry* need not be
opened. The box contains all sorts of odd ends—if dry I would not give you
the trouble of opening it—it would be too much trouble—but if wet it cannot
too soon be looked into—did *Lords box ever arrive*. Mr Anderson said it had
reached Savannah safe.

We were really sorry to leave New Haven. This is the pleasantest season to
be there—Oh! it was lovely—that green cannot be forgotten. And then we

made so many pleasant acquaintances. In fact it required some little effort to leave. Lordy would have been so happy there too—but we could not return home without taking leave of our kind friends here, & the longer we staid in New Haven the harder it would be to leave—so off we came. The hack men said we had but five minutes grace—so our leave taking was a hurried one. It always requires two hacks to move us & our baggage. Two young gents accompanied the girls to the boat (I had determined to take the boat instead of the cars down). Well we did get down & found them still putting in freight— the young gents remained about a half hour & then took leave. We went into our state rooms & to bed—but the old *Traveller* never [?] from the wharf until near one oclock. I rather think it was a trick of "Mr Hackmen." I slept however until awake before seven to prepare for leaving the boat. Two more hacks were procured & away we went to the North river to take [a] boat for Elizabethtown. I told Lordy I could not go all the way to Easton without breakfast—so he stept a-round & found an eating house hard by—the Landlord of which promised us breakfast at $^1/_2$ past 7. Lord had to run off to get some money changed & did not get back until we had *tried* to eat some of as uninviting stuff as could be produced. The coffee was worse than the second drawings which I give my negros. Sausages which smelt—bah! I will not tell you what detestable stuff we had—paid $2 & came out no better off than when we went in. We did eat a little bread. Lordy was made all but sick—by having to ride 80 miles without breakfast. We had quite a comfortable ride up to Easton there we got a tolerable breakfast for $1.75—for 7 of us 25 cts less than we gave for breakfast for 6. Then we got a 4 horse omnibus—to take us on 18 miles further to Allentown—for this we gave $9^1/_2$ including toll. Our trunks 7 in number were placed on the top, tied down & covered with canvass. We 7 & 4 carpet bags were inside—it rained—but all was kept dry. Our omnibus—our 4 horses two drivers &c &c brought every old man—woman & child to the doors & windows as we rattled along. It was difficult to say which were most amused, *ourselves* or *these lookers on.* Eventually we rattled up to Brother Henrys hospitable mansion— they were all drawn to the door by the noise we made. The fine dog Nero— foremost. Our reception could not have been warmer. Every thing looked so nice, so comfortable—soon after we sat down to a most bountiful supper— broiled chickens—ham—& cakes, hot griddle cakes &c &c quite a contrast with our miserable breakfast. I got to bed early last night & had a good sleep.

I received your dear Fathers letter of the 30th August. I wish I could know exactly *how matters are with him.* His letter does not lead me *to suppose he has been successful.* The drafts he sent me—were on persons who owe him the money here. I fear there is some doubts *of their being paid.* I have decided it will be best for Lord to go to New York tomorrow to see after it. I am sorry to give him the fatigue—but it *is worth the attempt.* I am so much afraid your Father will be for leaving Butler behind—Oh! I do not know what to be hoping for—for my child while we are so much blessed with health—with life—how can we murmur at what God! sees best we should not possess. Wealth is desirable but it does not constitute all the happiness of the world. We still have a little—I will try & be content.—

Andrew & Louisa are still in N. York. I hope they may come here before we leave—my present plan is to stay here until the 22nd then go to New York to remain until the 30th when we will leave for Savannah. We have engaged passage in the *Alabama* for the 30th. Hamilton took our passage for us—we were too late in applying to get births in the after cabbin. I dread the idea of going to sea—but it is an evil *I must encounter.* Tip was so often sick I was obliged to bring him with me. I was sorry to leave Floyd but he was well *& is improving.* Two weeks will soon pass over & we will then meet in New York. I had to stop writing to go to dinner—& a *hearty one* has made me so stupid I can hardly finish this scrawl. I will write you again before the week is over. You will not receive my letters as quickly now as you did whilst I was in New Haven that was *one* of the reasons I liked to stay there.

Your sisters & brother send thousands of love—Mary & Henry are not aware of my writing to you. Give the warm love of all of us to dear William—Kiss each dear child for us—in about 4 weeks more I hope to be with you my beloved child. God! grant we may then all meet in health & happiness—Rhina begs to be remembered. How de to all of the negros.

Praying God! to bless you I am as ever

Your devoted Mother
A M King

Mr Woolley was so kind as to write me from Savannah they must be now quite settled at home.

Allentown 15th October 1852

My dearly beloved Tootee

What can be the reason that I have no letter this week from you? God! forbid you are sick or William or either of those dear children? I certainly am very unhappy the last few days. So many circumstances seem combined against me. Thank God! as far as I am aware there is neither sickness or death but painful suspense & disappointment. First we have not had a line from Lord since he left us—we have been expecting him since yesterday. Next no letter from you (tho' the girls have had letters forwarded here from New Haven) next two short letters from your beloved Father dated 15th September—he complains of a lame hand—is to leave California on the 1st or 14 Nov *but leaves our beloved* Butler there until his successor arrives. He decidedly disapproves of my taking Malley home—re commends my even leaving Floyd & Tip, Florence & Appy at school here. Then to add to all this uneasiness I must be looking over the vile *New York Herald.* The Editor is a perfect viper—he says "T Butler King removed from Office—serious charges against him." Now this has put me into a perfect fever. Brother Henry has cut out the piece & enclosed it to Mr Filmore—requesting him to stay his decision until my husband returns. Now my child you cannot wonder why I should be so unhappy. Certainly if ever a man served his country well & honestly—that man is *T Butler King,* & yet what reward has he received? May God! forgive his persecutors & slanderers—they are many & bitter. How short sighted are we poor mortals—only a few weeks ago I thought if I only had money enough to carry me comfortably home & could hear that your dear Father & Butler were well—that all were well with you—& these dear ones keep well—I would be content. Now I have money enough & to spare for that purpose. I have not heard that any of you are sick & yet I am made perfectly miserable *by not hearing from you*—Butlers remaining longer in California—This news Paper report—& Lords silence. I am really miserable. My darling child are you sick? or William? or those dear children? Oh! how unhappy I am made. This evenings mail brought dear Butlers letters to Georgia—Lord & myself. These letters give no particular information relative to any particular subject—says nothing relative to *his* remaining after your Father has left—or of your Fathers coming. I have been writing all day to those beloved ones far away. I wrote to Lord last night—& to Andrew. Henry would go at once to Washington City but for the delay of Andrew. It really seems as if A[ndrew] & Louisa are bound to thwart all of our plans. Your sisters are so anxious to spend a few days in Philadelphia. Mary kindly offers to go with them but cant budge until Andrew comes or says he has given up coming.

We have taken passage for the 30th. I will leave this for New York on the 23rd or 25th. I think most likely the former. The weather has been very stormy the *last 36 hours very* cold with high wind today. I do hope all this bad weather will be over before we start home. G[eorgia] [&] F[lorence] have gone to return a call this evening—if I was only in better spirits I could give you an account of two young ladies who were *invited to tea here* & staid until after *dinner the next day.* Adele Picot has returned to this country, consequently Florence is more anxious than ever to go to Philadelphia. I will write again in a day or two. I would have written you a longer letter—but I am out of spirits altogether. Oh! my Tootee if any misfortune has befallen you or yours? God! be merciful to us all. Oh! that I had never left you. Your Sisters & little Tip—your Uncle & Aunt all send love to William & yourself & kisses to the babies. Praying God! to bless you all—I am your devoted Mother

A M King

Allentown
17th October 1852

My beloved Afflicted Children!

I cannot address you singly as the Father & Mother of that departed babe you seem now equally dear to me! In what words Oh my children can I express the agony I have endured since the rec[eip]t dear William of your afflicting letter of the 8th & can it be possible that I shall no more on earth behold that beautiful face—hear that sweet voice—hold in mine that soft dimpled hand or fold to my fond heart that form so beloved?[1] Oh God! thy ways are inscrutable. But this we do know "that He doeth all things well." In the first moments of anguish this is hard to understand or believe. It is nevertheless *true*. He gave you that precious lamb to keep for a few short years—he endowed her with beauty & attractions above most children—he permitted your hearts to be wrapped up in this lovely flower. He now takes her to himself, to draw your hearts to Him who now shelters that sweet lamb in His bosom. My children may God! grant that the death of this beloved child may draw your hearts to *Him who died for you*. God! gave his only son to die the cruel death of the cross—that through him the sins of the world may be forgiven—can we not then trust this blessed babe to the keeping of Him who died that we may find a place in a better world[?] Oh! my children I feel that I have set you but a poor example of *Christian Fortitude*. I suffered trifles to disturb my happiness *when I may have been happy—Now that real trouble assails us I feel crushed to the earth— fearful what the morrow may bring forth.*

With all of your love for that child my William you can bear it better than my Tootee can. Her station is indoors with every thing to remind her of the chasm which *death* has made in your family. Her love was not greater than yours—but her *cares* were. Her health is not so strong—May God! give you strength to bear with Christian fortitude & resignation this terrible blow. If we could but with the eyes of faith look beyond the dark & narrow grave—we would see that loved one now in the glorious garb of an angel—singing hymns of praise. She will never again feel hunger or thirst—pain or death. It is true she has no longer a place on earth—but she occupies a better place in heaven. Let us try & be reconciled to the will of God! She can return no more to us but we *may* go to her. Let us take this chastening not only as a *mercy & blessing to that dear angel* but also to our bereaved selves. Your tears will flow, the wound of your hearts will still bleed—but if we seek help and consolation from God! we will find rest & consolation. We *must all die!* a *fearful truth?*! Our precious Isabel has past through the dark valley a little before us—her path was made smooth by the love of our Savior who said "suffer little children to come unto me & forbid them not for of such is the Kingdom of Heaven." "It is not the will of my Father that one of these little ones should perish."[2] What divine consolation. Let us take hold on these promises & seek consolation from Him who alone can give us rest. Now is the accepted time—Let lay all of our sins,—all trouble at the feet of our blessed Savior—looking to Him only for forgiveness & consolation. The blessed influences of the Holy Spirit will make the burden of our grief lighter.

This blow was so sudden. It is true I had become very unhappy at your silence—I began to fear sickness—I was not prepared *for death*. How changed in a few hours have been our feelings—but yesterday poor Appy had dressed *her* doll—& finished her dress, how proudly she folded up the dress not to be opened until we reached home. They then each one made out a little memorandum of what was to be got for each dear child. The mail came in late & good brother Henry went down to the Office he brought us your letter to Lord. I begged Georgia to open it & let me know why Tootee had not written. I soon too soon heard the sad cause. Oh! what hours have since been past! How fortunate that dear Cousin Amanda was with you at that trying moment. May God! reward her for all her kindness to us. My poor child! may God! preserve you & you my William what a task to write that letter. *I fear much for you my Tootee.* Remember my child there are yet 3 precious children left. Oh! may they be spared to you. How I long & yet dread to return to you. How different from the happy meeting we were so fondly anticipating. Oh! my Tootee, my Tootee. May God grant no further misfortune awaits us.

Your letter of the 4th I have never received. I hope I may not be too soon by taking passage on the 30th. We have had severe frost here & hope the cold weather has extended to Savannah & the Isld. I have ever regretted leaving you this summer each mile which took me from you seemed to drag back my heart to you & those beloved children. Too late, too late now for repentance. Oh! could I have foreseen this event no power would have induced me to leave you. But my children remember it is the Lord who gave & it is the Lord who has taken to himself this darling child. He knows best what was for her good. Had you possessed the wealth of the world you could not have provided for her as God! will. Had she lived she may have become unfit for her now happy home. Had she lived through this illness—she must sooner or later have died. Let us try to grieve no more—but place our firm reliance on His power & mercy who will reunite us, to part no more. Her Grand Parents—her Uncle & brother have welcomed her to a better happier home than we can offer her. Sweet sweet darling Bob! How much I shall miss you—how I grieve for your loss. But sweet innocence you are blest forever. May we meet in Heaven!!!—

Georgia amidst the confusion of last evening wrote to you my Tootee. Lordy got here about 9 oclock—He [is] truly sympathetic with you & will write to you dear William. Poor Appy! Bell was her own hearts darling.[3] Thank God! Anna is yet spared—had she gone—what would have come of Butler in that far distant country.[4] What sad news I have to give him poor fellow. In your Fathers letter of the 15th September—he informs us of the necessity there will be for Butler to remain after he leaves for the Atlantic States. This adds much to my trouble. But he is in the keeping of a Merciful God! I can but hope that my nine children & my husband & my William & 3 remaining grandchildren may all ere long meet & then may we with humble grateful hearts offer up our prayers & thanksgivings. How much Malley & Floyd will grieve—alas who that ever knew that precious child can otherwise than grieve for her loss. Bright happy now angel child—for your poor Mothers sake try to be resigned my Tootee.[5] For poor Tootees sake & for your other dear children do you my William look to God! for consolation. God! grant no further affliction awaits us ere we meet. From Mary & Henry we receive the kindest sympathy. How fortunate that we were here when this blow fell on us. I hope to hear further from you ere we leave this. God! grant you may tell me of no further misfortunes. I hope to be calmer in a day or two. I have tried to offer you consolation—I fear my agony but adds to yours. May God! bless & protect you & those 3 remaining darlings—kiss them for us—All unite in love & sympathy

Your devoted Afflicted Mother
A M King

1. William wrote to Lord of Isabel's sudden illness and death on October 8 (the day she died).

2. Her headstone in Christ Church cemetery reads: "Isabella Hamilton, second daughter of William Audley and Hannah M. Page Couper, Born August 1, 1848, Ob. October 8, 1852, Aged 4 years 2 months and 7 days. 'It is not the will of your Father which is in heaven that one of these little ones should perish'" (Cate, *Our Todays and Yesterdays*, 275).

3. Lord wrote,

This mournful intelligence met me most suddenly on my return late last night from New York where I had been since the first of the week; in my absence your letter had arrived and been opened by Mother who was anxious on account of your long silence—I hastened to her room and found her in extreme grief, which my efforts could but little alleviate. She grieves for Bel intensely, but not less for you dearest

Sister—her heart seems near to breaking, she feels so much for your sorrow. Poor Appy seems well nigh heart-broken. I believe Bel was her particular favorite, and she has been working all the Summer for the dear little Girl. Georgia, Flora, and I try to fulfil our duty of consoling Mother. Cuyler too feels very deeply. Mother reproaches herself that she did not go home when Mr Woolley did, for then she would have been with you dear Sister, and now she fears Cousin Amanda will not remain till we arrive, but I am sure she will not leave you. (Henry Lord Page King to Hannah Page King and William Audley Couper, WAC, SHC)

4. Butler had a special attachment to both his sister Tootee and his niece Anna.

5. Tootee's first letter to Anna after Isabel's death was written October 18. She began,

What shall I write you—I cannot write I can only think & feel and suffer. . . . May God in Mercy preserve us so—no words can tell our anguish I cannot write any thing of all our loss & suffering—You can know it—Poor William—God alone can help us—oh may he draw us to him in the right way—oh may he draw us for his dear sons sake—Cousin Amanda and her kind husband were obliged to leve us a few days ago—We are all alone in our sorrow— . . . Oh my mother my mother pray for us—We are better—calmer now—I entreat you not to be uneasy and unhappy for us. God will watch over us and he alo[n]e has any power in life or death. Anna, Willie & King send you kisses—our angel who is in Heaven spoke of you the last day she was with us. . . . Do not grieve more than you can help. Do not wear *mourning* for her who is now an angel rejoicing with her God—Oh her poor Mothers heart is nigh broken. May God have pity on poor us You shall know all about her if we live to meet—write it I never can—. (Hannah Page King Couper to Anna Matilda Page King, October 18, 1852, WAC, SHC)

July 4, 1853, to November 25, 1854

> If your dear Father yourself & Floyd were here last week
> I think for once in my life I would have been completely
> happy.

Anna returned to St. Simons and once again her letters to family members far away were full of news from home about the condition of the crops, the weather, and the comings and goings of her children, grandchildren, and a steady stream of visitors.

Retreat 4th July 1853

My dearly beloved Lord

We have not received a line from you since your letter from New York after your return from New Haven. I know you are too apt to procrastinate—still in these days of disaster both by land and water you must not think it exacting if I require one letter *at least every two weeks* from you. Time was when it gave me no trouble to write letters but now it is a real labour—not only bad eyes but I can never find all the requisites. I have just succeeded in finding one worn out pen—got some ink in another room—and this paper is not the best. But enough of this. I can but hope you have ere this quietly settled down to your books and are making all possible effort to make up for lost time.

We are all pretty well just now. Appy was quite unwell last week from cold but is again able to eat her allowance. Butler received a letter a week ago yesterday from Mr. Harrington advising his going on to Washington. Butler knowing the delays attending such matters telegraphed Harrington to enquire i[f] the matter was pressing. Unfortunately the wires were out of order so up to Saturday there was no reply. Consequently Butler will have to go tomorrow— he may probably find an answer on his arrival in Savannah which will decide his going on to Washington or permit him to return to wait for further orders. Whenever he does go I hope his time may allow of his seeing you and his other brothers.

We have received no further intelligence from your dear Father. I had a very kind letter from your Aunt Louisa and Butler from both his Uncle and Aunt on Wednesday last. They will not come to the States this summer. At least they have not yet determined on doing so. They were both in good health.

On Wednesday last we all spent the day at Hamilton not going at 12 and returning before dark—we started at 7 in the morning—breakfasted—lunched and dined there. The object to help Tootie sew.[1] Matty[2]—Cousin Amanda—Florence and myself did most. Georgia was taken off to write a letter to [?] "dear *Fan*" in reply to one sent down by a man in a canoe that day. Appy got interested in some book & Eliza Jackson was too *much in love* to be steady at any one thing. On the whole we had a pleasant day of it. We intended to keep up this practice until Tootees work was done but the Bishop is expected to land at Hamilton tomorrow night & this will prevent our going there this Wednesday. Tootee and family dined with us on Saturday. They are as usual. King talks as much as ever of you & he [is] interested at any time by your name being mentioned. John Audley grows finely and is really a good baby.[3] Butler did intend to start yesterday in the *Planter* but that uncertain boat passed us before day light on Sunday morning. Eliza Jackson will go on with him to Savannah poor child she is desperately in love with Butler. The piano is entirely out of order—the guitars ditto—so we have but little music. Butler will carry on the part of the piano which requires repair & I hope may get some better strings for the guitars so we shall once more have sweet sounds. By the way were you not to have sent some new music for your Sister?

The little room is now finished—portico & all—& it is quite an addition to the comfort of the old house. The desk—lounge—work table—rocking chair —foot stool all complete. Dear Georgia seems delighted—Butler pleased. [?] owes much to Mr. Woolley—he worked hard at it and got more work out of Old Peter than has been extracted in years. Now if Butler was not going away I would hope my dove cot would be made—as he is going I can't say when it will be done. We have taken up the carpets and put down matting and look more like summer in a Southern climate.[4]

We had a very pleasant rain yesterday more is wanted but this has been a blessing for which we are most thankful. Malley writes to us that the Baldwins were in affliction on account of the death of the gentleman who was engaged to be married to Miss Elizabeth. Were you acquainted with him? Mr Bourke has lost his situation in the Custom House. I would regret this more did I not think it was one which exposed him to temptation.

Mr. Cuylers youngest brother was murdered last week he was a very worthy man and has left a family. M[argaret] Cuyler is going to spend her summer at Sing Sing. I cannot find a piece of news to give you that would interest you. I wish you would write *me fully* how you are situated in Allentown. I do hope your dear Father will soon return and make some other arrangement for you.

Butler says when he gets to Washington he will Telegraph you where and when to meet him. And now my beloved son I must conclude this scratch regretting I have so little to communicate that is interesting or amusing.

All here—that is your Sisters, brothers and cousin also Matty unite in love to you—the servants beg to be remember'd.

Praying God! to bless you my beloved son I am as ever

Your most affectionate Mother

A M King

1. Catherine Clinton explains that "the plantation mistress found the production of cloth and manufacture of clothing to be her most demanding tasks. . . . Each slave required a winter and a summer set of clothing. Southern women were also in charge of supplying blankets and clothing to slave families" (*The Plantation Mistress*, 26–27). Tootee may well have been responsible for the clothing of Hamilton slaves (though they belonged to the owner of the property rather than to her husband). Additionally, she had been given a butler and nurse by Anna for whom she could have been making clothing. The women could also have been making clothes for Tootee's children, particularly underclothes.

2. Matty Lara was the King daughters' new tutor, recommended to Anna by Andrew and Louisa King, who took her into their home in Cuba after she was deserted by her husband.

3. At the time of Isabel's death, Tootee was pregnant with John Audley Couper.

4. Seasonal housekeeping tasks could include cleaning and changing curtains, cleaning and airing mattresses, and taking up carpets and scrubbing floors. In addition, kitchen utensils, especially copper pots, were carefully cleaned to avoid verdigris poisoning. Summer cleaning might include taking up carpeting and putting down matting made of hemp.

Retreat 14th July 1853

My own dear Lordy

It is seldom that I have permitted a Tuesdays Mail to depart without writing to my sons when absent from me but I find that I cannot now write at night and on Monday your dear Sister spent the day with us. I have to acknowledge two dear letters from you one by the Sunday Mail to me and yesterday I took the liberty to open and read the one to Georgia. I am thankful to find your health good and also that you do not complain *much* of the dullness of Allentown. But you are there for study and not pleasure my beloved boy and should think of little else. This is the rugged path of life begun with you. If you will persevere it will I trust become smoother as you advance. We have informed you of dear Butlers having left us for Washington. I hope by the next mail to hear of his arrival in that City. He will of course write to you where to meet him. Unless he particularly desires to visit Allentown I should think it best you should meet him in N.Y. I am grateful to be able to say we are in our usual health—as yet no fever among the white family—tho some severe ones among the negros Rhina, Christian[n], Clementines two younger children, Polly and two hog boys have been very ill all are now better except Phillip whose fate is yet doubtful.[1] It is no small comfort my dear cousin being with me not only her kind sympathy but I depend more on her judgement then [*sic*] I do on my own. We have been sadly disappointed by Williams having changed his mind as to our dear Tooties going to the Up Country. I cannot but think that Mr J. H. Couper is at the bottom of it. William seemed so willing that she should go—we were all helping her to get ready until the day that his Lordship dined at Hamilton when suddenly William came to the conclusion that she could get well at home. So we have to submit tho' I must say we are all sadly disappointed and dread the consequences to herself and those poor little ones—dear little Cooney was so delighted on Monday to hear your message to *him* he said "Mudder tell Laudy come back me want to see Audy." He still prays for you "Pray God! bless Audy make him a good boy" He has done this of his own accord. John grows finely and is certainly the best baby—he is exceedingly fair and quite fat—Appy would even give up her good appetite could she be as purely white as he is. Mr. Woolley and Cousin Amanda staid a week at Hamilton they returned to Retreat yesterday and will leave for the North a week from tomorrow. Oh! that Tootee and her children could go too.

   Yesterday your sisters left for the Grants. Little Tip went also. I have long promised to let him make Fraser Grant a visit. They will return on Monday next. Mattie would not go. So here am I—the Mother of 9 children and not one with me. It was much against their inclination my being left alone but I thought they had best all go together not having a fancy for 4 trips when two would answer. They went very early in the morning to avoid the thunder storms. For the last week we have seen fine rains falling all around us—but none came here until yesterday evening. You may imagine the state of the crops—gardens and roads but we had no *musquitos*. What a blessing you will say. The mornings from 8 to 12 were oppressively hot—but then the sea breeze would come and I have not felt a hot night. Well about the rain of yesterday one cloud [?] at the south the other at the South the other at the North may be I did not watch them these clouds had given us the go bye so often I did not believe they were coming to us at all but the one from the North came down beautifully. The one from the South did good service to Jekyl then went to sea—by and bye the North and South cloud met for consultation when

down came a streak of lightening right on to Dunhams bell post—the thunder
was terribly loud the post is torn to pieces—fortunately Dunham had taken
shelter from the rain at McIntoshes (the negros were working in that field) so
he escaped the *fright* it would have given him. I am thankful it was the post and
not a house that was struck. We shall now plant peas and hope to make provisions. I know you have no taste for crops *whilst growing*. The melons have been
fine at Hamilton—we have figs now and some peaches—none of which I ever
see without thinking of you dear boys and wishing you could partake of them.
I have been sending your share of peaches to Cooney he says "Mudder very
good." I have seen nothing of Hamilton Couper since you left or any of that
family which certainly does not *break my heart*. Postells grandmother and sister are now at Mrs. Cater. Georgia and Appy called to see the young one on
Monday last—I hope if you should meet Sarah Hazzard in N.Y. she will not
walk over you.

   We have been expecting Bishop Elliot on the Island since Tuesday the 5th
but he has neither come or has he written to say why! The uncertainty keeps
us all uneasy. Your sisters would have gone last week to the Grants but for this.
We continue to find Mattie all we can desire. She is indeed a lovely woman.
What a pitty that her husband still lives—She as well as our good cousin send
love to you Mr Woolley his regards.

   I have had no other letter from your dear Father—Oh! how anxious I am for
his return. Oh! Lordy *if* I only had the means how pleasant it would be for all
of us (dear Tootee and her little ones too) to meet him at the North. But as this
cannot be I can but hope we may all meet here on[e] of these days. I hope you
will continue to write to us frequently. Your letters are a great comfort to me—
your silence never fail[s] to make me uneasy. May God! bless you my beloved
son but how can we hope for blessings from Him we do not love and try to
serve? The servants all beg to be remembered—I know your sister would write
to you but for the pain in her fingers—your devoted and most affectionate
Mother

                         A M King

                                                              15[th July]
Your dear Sister and family were here yesterday evening they were a[s] usual in
health. Cooney said when I told him I [h]ad a letter from you "wer Audy—him
coming home"? and his dear face brightens and his head one side as he always
holds it when in earnest.

   The cause of the Bishop not coming is owing to the illness of 3 of his children. Dunham says he was in his house when the *bell* post was struck—and was
never so scared in his life—

My sick are all better except poor Phillip he will not out live the day.[2] Thank God it is not one of my own who are so low.

Your Mother
A M King

1. Phillip is number 64 on the 1853 list, his birthday June 29, 1844. See appendix 2.
2. In a letter dated July 1853 Anna wrote to Lord, "Poor little Phillip died on Saturday evening the rest of the sick are fast recovering" (Anna Matilda Page King to Henry Lord Page King, July 1853, TBK, SHC).

Nov 53
Retreat Monday night 28th

My dearly beloved husband

Could I have imagined it possible you would have been so long delayed in N.Y. the three letters directed to you in Savannah would ere this been received by you in N.Y. It does indeed seem hard you are thus kept from your home & family. I do not intend, or desire to complain. I can only try to be patient & hope for the best. You say that yourself & dear Butler are well. I try to be satisfied with this.

Yours & dear Buttys letters of the 12th & 20th have been received the first acknowledged & now await you in Savannah. I scarcely know where to direct this so as to ensure your getting it. Surely you are not still in N.Y.? I even hope you have left Washington for home & on your way whilst I with 3 candles am trying to scratch you these lines (not with the candles but by the light they give me.) I regret not sending my other letters to N.Y. You must desire to hear how we are. Thank God! I am able to say, *we* are all well. William went to Brunswick to attend court this morning our dear Tootee & her children came over to us—& as the weather is unfavorable has remained the night—my good Cousin Amanda is also here so the family tonight is pretty large. Do you know husband dear that Butty writes me it is possible you may be obliged to remain even after he can start for home? This is so unexpected. I scarce can understand it. I hope & trust it may not so turn out. I would suggest your making enquiries about the new land route—for those old Wilmington boats have become very crazy. Mr & Mrs Woolley, Mrs Bourke & Miss Dubignon came "the Massachusetts route" from Wilmington—were one day one night & until 3 the next day reaching Augusta—Amanda says she did not find it unpleasant. Do you & Butty think of this rather than trust going to sea in those old boats to Charleston—then to sea again to Savannah. I do hope the weather will become more

settled before our dear boys leave for home. I have never known a more unpleasant Autumn—perpetual high dry winds.—

We have had two dear letters from dear Lordy—& 3 from Malley—all were
well—by the last Mail we have Russells report. In every branch Malley has the
highest mark—& dear Fuddys is as fair as I could possibly expect. I was waiting your return to decide about poor little Tip. The more I think of his entering a public school the more I shrink from it—he is so backward. There is a
new select school open'd in Savannah by a Mr Fay—only 17 boys perhaps 20.
Mr Hugh Grants son is at it—Mr Grant represents it as very desirable—
Cousin Amanda offers to take Tip to stay with her. It does seem to me a more
desirable & unexceptionable plan to let Tip go—Mr Woolley will *not permit
Tip to get into improper company—his morels as well as health will be strictly attended
to.* Let him begin to struggle in this school it will prepare him to go to a larger
school & among perfect strangers. I hope my beloved you will not object or
disapprove of my having made arrangements to send Tip. I believe that my
ever constant Friend Amanda as well as Mr Woolley will watch over our child
with the care of parents & will do all in their power to urge on his improvement & take care of his health. We that is Georgia & myself have him at his
books every day—but he requires emulation & it is but little better than lost
time to him. With his rearing & temperment it would be really all but cruel to
throw him all at once into a distant school with none to take care of him. If our
dear Malley & Floyd are permitted to return home it would be Feb before they
are to go to the Up Country. If you see fit to alter this plan just let us try first
if mine may not be a good one.—

I do hope you will not be longer detained that ere another week rolls over
we may have the happiness to welcome you home—dear dear husband how
anxious we all are to see you once more at the head of your own table in your
own house with your wife at its head your children around you & your own servants to wait on you. Dear little Geo has taken to house keeping—she would
do it well had she a good cook & a well stored larder—Geo & myself each had
a letter from Sister Mary by the last Mail—She has recovered her health but
your dear good Brother was quite unwell. Some thing of the same complaint
he had when we were in Allentown. I wish to know from you or Butler what
has become of *the washing machine*—I am certain that I heard you say you had
purchased it—If so it has never reached Savannah. I wrote to the Andersons
about it—they say they have not seen or heard of it. I do hope it was not sent
on one of the several vessels which were lost between New York & the South.
I am really distressed should this be delayed.

I wish I could just have been divided one half—one half stay with you the other come home with our girls & boy—I do not like the idea of your being alone. You know how you have been sick & no wife no child with you my own dear husband. And yet if you do not get back before January who is to attend to this Hamilton affair—but surely they cannot expect you to stay there until then? Our dear children—Cousin & Mattie send thousands of love you. The servants send many "huddys"—poor things they are so anxious for your return. It is now raining smartly which I hope will bring down this everlasting NE wind—keep down the dust—& let my garden improve May God! in his infinite mercy protect & bless you my own beloved & restore you in health & happiness to your devoted & most affectionate wife

A M King

Amanda saw your brother Stephen & his family a few days ago—all were well. He has just purchased Morgin Smiths lands on the Satilla for $35,000. The plantation, not the negros.

15th Dec 1853

My own dearly beloved Husband

Butler & myself had the happiness last evening to recover your welcome letters of the 6th from New Orleans. Rejoiced to hear you had so far got safe & were able to write cheerfully and hopefully. What a fatiguing journey you must have had yet bad as it was I would rather have been with you than to be here with all the comforts of home without you. Oh! my husband yours has indeed been a hard fate—& what the end is to be God! only knows. Surely no man ever worked harder against adverse fortune than you have. I would not discourage you believing you to be more happy in trying to better your fortune by this kind of excitement than you would be at home looking back on the past. I try to be patient—& if I say nothing to these dear dependent beings around me I feel only the greater pain at being so eternally separated from you.

It is really unfortunate that the first payment could not have been raised—so that Butler could take *possession on the first January. I do* not think I could raise it in Savannah. I am glad you do not wish me to have an interest in that purchase. It will be just as much as I can do to pay my expensis of the year—with the present crop. As happy as we were at the North—I now regret having gone —The money there spent—could have been so much more profitably employed. But it is past.—

I feel very unhappy about you—you say there had been no frost in that plague stricken country? Oh my husband may God! protect you from such disease. We have had no frost here even to kill potatoe vines—And yet it has been too cold for comfort. On the 7th it rained & blew very hard & became exceedingly cold. Still no frost to kill the most tender plant. The 30 bags I sent on was sold as soon as landed at 38c which Jackson thought a very full price at the rate cotton selling—the "Dubignon" cotton bringing 35. Why hang the people say I. He must be an idiot or warped with prejudice who will say or think Dubignon or any other [?] south of Savannah equal to ours. I cannot help myself but I cannot but think there is unfair dealing in this—for the last 20 years Molyneux has been buying every bag of which cotton we send to market. And he gets our cotton for less than other purchasers pay for far inferior cottons.—

Butlers presence is a great comfort & relief to me. He has en eye & mind to correct the growing errors on the place. I beg you will without loss of time write to him what is to be done about this purchase. He will write to you himself by this mail. Our dear children from Hamilton spent yesterday with us— William has a bad cold with that exception all were well. We are in our usual health here. All trying to be as happy as circumstances will permit us to be. I hope the storm which we had here on the 7th & 8th did not reach you on your way to Galveston. Oh! the perils you will encounter! Neither you or dear Butler give me any idea of when you may be able to return from the West or when you will be able to come home! Can you give me the relief? Oh! my beloved how hard is our fate—I will try & bear it—but it does seem so hard. If there was any *certainty of* remuneration I would feel better—but all uncertainty is hard to bear. It is too me really astonishing how you can be so sanguine after all your disappointments.

On Monday Georgia, Butty & myself went to West Point—to call on the Hazzards. They have a host of as rough looking young men (friends of their eldest son) as I ever sat in the same room with. Mr & Miss Chisolm—nephew & niece of the Col are also there. Tho' brought up in the city of N.Y. and Mrs Waldo they are no great things. The Old Col & the young men were going the next day for Blackbeard—Postell & McIntosh join'd them. It took three boats to accommodate the party—Butler was invited to join them—but he had the good sense & taste to decline. The Old Col goes as Captain of the crew.

I have nothing new to tell you concerning the plantation. Our dear children all send thousands of love to you. We pray God! to protect you & permit you to return in health & safety to your home. The negros seem quite disheartened by your prolonged absence. God! bless you my dearly beloved—do not call this a complaining letter. If I loved you less I could better bear your separation from your devoted wife.

A M King

19th December 1853

My own beloved husband

I have been looking over the news papers and find that the Gale of the 8th did extend to N[ew] O[rleans]. I got the map and find the distance you had to go was 500 miles by sea. Oh! my husband I so much fear that you were exposed to its violence. May the mercy of God have protected your precious life from danger. Oh! I am so perfectly wretched about you. Oh my husband! my husband! Butler thinks I ought not to expect to hear from you for two weeks to come. If God's mercy has spared you still how much I must suffer until I do hear. I am to be pitied!!

I am grateful to be able to say we are in our usual health. The mail was not received until this morning the boat not passing until last night. We had letters from Malley and Floyd they were well on the 17th and mentioned having heard from Lord who was well on the 6th. This gale of the 8th was very severe North as well as South of us. The [?] Cutter *Hamilton*, Capt. Rudolph was lost off Charleston. All perished save one man. The *Old Jackson* (Capt Day) is undoubtedly lost between Savannah and Norfolk. Oh! my God! protect my beloved ones from a watery grave. Mall and Floyd were expecting to leave New York last Saturday and as if the fates are against my peace of mind on that night I was awakened by as severe a gust of wind as I have heard for many a day. It *did* not last long. Our dear children try to keep up my spirits by being cheerful themselves. The girls are at their lessons until dinner. The evening we all assemble in our old cheerful looking parlour some times we have music some times reading aloud and the time passes pleasantly until 10 oclock—when we separate for the night. Florence has appointed herself locker up of doors and fire outer. Virginia is my bed fellow. I never lie down on our comfortable bed— but I think how differently you may be accommodated. Butler thinks the Capt of the *Mexico* could never have suffered you my love to occupy a mattress on the floor of his dining saloon. I hope the dear boy may be right in this. If not it would be a disgrace to Steam boat captains. I have formed a very low opinion of the part of the world you have been sent to. May you be permitted to give me a more favourable one on your return and when Oh! my love am I to hope for that happy time? Remember your 4th year has begun. Worse than any "naval officer" I have ever heard of. If Gods Mercy permits you to return home this time—*you leave me not again* as long as we live.

Butler is putting the place in better order. His presence is both a relief and benefit—as well as happiness to me. What a dear good son he is to me!!! I went to Hamilton on Saturday—William is suffering from a bad cold which has been hanging on him for some weeks. The other dear ones are quite well (as says her message to me this morning). Butler will probably write you by this mail as will also Georgia. What a blessed child this Georgia is! She certainly is as perfect in character as human nature can be. If you were with us how happy we all would be.

Oh! my husband when will you return? I cannot enjoy even my flowers without you. I try by keeping constantly employed to amuse my poor tortured mind—but I can enjoy nothing—not even writing to you. As long as you remained stationary at the North I could expect to hear regularly from you and knew you were comfortably lodged—but this venturing on the great deep—this going to Texas has almost driven me beside myself. I do not forget that the Great God! has you in his holy keeping yet He may see fit to withdraw His protecting hand. I can but pray His mercy may continue and that we may all meet again in happiness. Our dear children one and all unite in fond love to you. The servants beg to be remembered. If permitted to receive this scrawl do not be anxious by my complaints. Loving you as I do I cannot feel otherwise—or refrain from expressing as near as feeble words will permit the distress I suffer. Oh! what would become of me had I not a Heavenly Father to look to for help! His mercies have long been continued to us. What dangers you have encountered—how often raised from a bed of suffering. How often gone—how often permitted to return. Oh! may the God who has so often—so mercifully blessed us permit you again to return to your loving devoted wife.

A M King

3rd April 1854

My dearly beloved Lordy

I actually am so cold I can scarce hold my pen today—nevertheless I must write to the beloved ones all of whom are in a colder climate than I am and must suffer more than I do here in my comfortable room and a good fire to warm my chilled blood. If this was the 3rd of March I would rather enjoy the temperature of the weather. But as this is "Spring time" crops up and young poultry hatched it makes all the difference possible. Mattie is all but frozen in fact the white family *look blue*. Now should there be a killing frost the cotton will be *kilt*[—]with extra labor that can be planted over. But the two orange trees will not put forth fresh blossoms—neither will the peach trees. Well there is certainly no use in fretting—or worrying you with such troubles.

We received the Wednesday mail along with the one due yesterday as we were on our way to church. One letter from Malley—the only one from my dear absent ones. Malley reported himself and Floyd in good health—One from Mrs Henry King—thanking me for the orange preserves and Elk horns. She said "a day or two since I noticed in the papers the arrival of your good husband at the Metropolitan Hotel." When we got back from Church we overhauled the papers and there sure enough in the Herald of the 2nd was his honored name heading the list of arrivals at the Metropolitan. Thank God! he has been permitted once more to reach that city. I can but hope the time is not now distant when I may welcome him once more to his own home. We have a very kind letter from Mrs Jaudon—She sent me quite a supply of flower seeds which I hope to plant tomorrow—*hoping* they will reward her kindness and my care by getting up and growing and producing flowers. My present hobbys are the flower garden—young poultry and birds. I am very sorry that up to the 26th Mrs Jaudon had not received her jar of orange preserves—Mrs Hale and Marys were sent at the same time both have theirs. It was but a small offering— yet I would be sorry any one but themselves should have the benefit of them. I am so sorry to hear of dear Adas illness. I suppose you and Julia keep up your correspondence and know more about the family than I do.

Butler got a letter from Tom Bond yesterday inviting him to stand grooms- man for him on the 20th. Unless he mends his habits—the poor girl will make a poor bargain of it—And yet I truly pity Tom Bond. I can but hope his choice of a wife is good—and if so, her influence may make a better man of him. This is a secret between Butler and myself—he teases the girls half to death by say- ing *he has a secret*. They will be disappointed when they hear what it really is. The scarlet fever is in a house very near to Mr Woolleys—I am very uneasy about Tip and if he was with me, perhaps he would be worn off [*sic*] for this ter- rible fever is raging in Brunswick. Wood and Dart each lost a child from it this last week poor Wood has another child at the point of death and to make it worse for those unfortunate parents residing in Brunswick Charles Dubignon carried the Whooping cough there with his children. There is no fever we are liable to have, that I dread more than I do this same scarlett fever. I heard just now from poor Tootie. Anna is the only well child she has to day. King and John[1] have bad colds Willie had just cut his wrist very badly—herself and William in their usual health. I stopped to see poor old Mrs Armstrong yesterday—her health continues to be much the same—I remained until evening—it was after I got back we had the gratification of hearing of your dear Father. I saw not many at Church 5 from Hazzards, 1 Gould, 2 from Postells, 4 Hamilton, 1 Armstrong, 2 Couper overseers and ourselves comprised the congregation. A poor en- couragement for Mr Brown to paddle himself so far to preach. I hope tomor- row to be able to go as far as Mrs Caters—I have not yet called there. Butler wanted to pay Postell an April fool trick on Saturday—but it was raining so much he feared it would prevent its taking effect It was to notify that a meet- ing would be held at Frederica all the gentlemen would be present—he (But- ler) would carry drinkables and Mrs Stevens provide dinner. He knew the prospect of enough to *drink* would be a bait Postell could not withstand. Oh! what a failing this is with too many young men. My own dear Lordy—in mercy to your own dear self do not indulge in this most serious failing. *Stop* now when it is quite in your power to control the growing appetite for so deadly a poison—the scrap I enclose I cut from a paper the other day—I made Butler read it—I now send it to you. Read it my son and take it as it is intended—for your own good my beloved son.

I really am sorry to send you such a scratch of a scrawl—but my hand is so cold. I dare say Butler or Georgia will be writing to you if not by this mail certainly by Friday—Tootie desired I would send you much love for herself and William and kisses from the little ones. Your sisters and Butler send much love and if you like you may include Mattie, also.

I must conclude this my dear boy—I have yet three other letters to write for tomorrows mail. The servant[s] always beg to be remembered to you—May God! bless you my dear boy. I hope the Wednesday mail may bring me a pleasant letter from you. Very tenderly you[r] affectionate Mother

A M King

1. John Audley Cooper was also called Johnnie (Johny or Johnny).

Retreat 17th April '54

My own dear Lordy

I have not received a line from you since your long & very pleasant letter dated New York a week ago yesterday. I had a very long letter from your dear Father—it was dated 2nd Inst. I fully expected & fondly hoped he would write either to Butler or myself before he left to go back to that much dreaded Texas.[1] I was doomed to be disappointed—hearing neither from him or from you. But I was not without some letters from my beloved ones—I had a short one from dear Butler written on his reaching Florida. He found his friend at Mrs Madisons also Old Mrs Dummit & was enjoying his visit very much. I heard also from Malley & Floyd—both were well, & I hope are doing well. Floyd has entered the Military Institute. On himself will depend his remaining after June or being turned out.—

Your dear Father expresses much gratification at seeing you—mentioned your having told him you "were studying hard."[2] I am sure my beloved son when you see how hard he is toiling for his children—what sacrifices he makes—what risk of life he incurs—you will not be idle—you will not throw away the advantages we are giving you. I can only *hope* your dear Father may realize his present hopes of success above all that his precious life may be spared. He says he may be with us in June—God! grant he may. Just to think Lordy if he is permitted to come to us in June he will have been absent three years & seven months. If you ever marry Lordy never do you be so long absent from your wife.

O how rejoiced we will all be when he once more enters these doors. The darkies will have to have a holiday—I hope the fields may be free of grass at the time.

The wind has been blowing a perfect Siroco since yesterday morning—Georgia—Florence & myself went to church through a perfect cloud of dust & sand, the wind from the NW. It has been very cold since last night—I can but hope there will be no frost. It seems so strange to be sitting by the fire & have *pans of blackberries* brought in.

On Saturday we promised to go to Hamilton this evening to eat ice cream & blackberries. We have given up the notion. On Saturday we spent a very pleasant day at Hamilton. When all are to go over Tootee always has to help us over. When her carriage came Mattie was busy sewing in a pair of sleeves to a new dress so she begged to remain & go with me. When we got over we met William, Tootee, Georgia, Anna & Willie very busy over a basket of beautiful green pease—shelling them for dinner. I gave a helping hand—& the work was soon over. W[illiam] & Tootee were really proud to say they would set before us 7 dishes of vegetables "to say" Summer turnips, green pease, beets, new potatoes, aspargrass, celery & Lettuce. And I doubt if [a] Philadelphia market could ever produce better of their kind. With a nice dish of broil'd chickens—a dish of boiled whiting, & a ham, we had a real nice cheerful dinner. In the evening Georgia & myself called to see old Mrs Armstrong—I am glad to say the poor old lady is better.

These sudden changes of weather has produced a number of cases of cholera morbus among our negros. 4 taken ill the first night 10 cases in all—thank God! all have got over it. The little twin boys born 10 days ago are doing well.[3]—

Your little pet King is growing more remarkable for intelligence & sweetness every day. If you were now at home you would love him more than you ever did. Oh! he is so very sweet. Johny has been suffering very much with teething.

The wind was so high yesterday, last night & today I very much fear the *Walaka* will be much behind the time. She did not pass here yesterday until long after our breakfast—& I should be very sorry to have Butler detained beyond the time he had fix'd. His plan when he left home was to continue on to Darien, attend Tom Bonds wedding on the 20th & return home on the night of the 22nd. He & Georgia agreed that she should get on board at Hamilton & go with Butler to Darien. Georgia is so good—so sweet a child! I hate ever to refuse a request of hers—& yet I wish she was less devoted to Fanny Troup.

Mrs Grant has gone on to Charleston for her daughters. Mr & Mrs Bourke are now on a visit to their friends in Savannah. They have promised to come here when they get back from Savannah. Margaret Cuyler & Mrs Churchill are to be here next month. So you may be sure I am feeding my chickens all I can—but still they will not be fit to eat in May. Lordy I have 449 young chickens—

120 young turkeys & 60 young ducks—& expect lots more to hatch. Do you not think the feeding of them will make the corn fly? How glad I will be if I can raise enough to give you *every* day a good dinner. Tootee has a number of chickens but I have distanced her in Turkeys & ducks.

The Island is even more dull than when you left us—I am sorry there is so little visiting. I want every one to see my garden in its beauty. I have now 92 difference kind[s] of roses in bloom forming I may say *thousands* of flowers—the honeysuckles—honey flowers—verbenas—phlox—nasturtion, & many others the names forgotten—form a perfect blaze of beauty. I wish you could all be at home in the month of April—May, June, July, August, September, October, Nov, Dec, Jan, Feb, March—that means the whole year [?].

The Scarlet fever is still very fatal in Brunswick. God! grant it may not come here. Now my dear Lordy it is near dark I will have to conclude. Your Sisters send much love. Cooney says he is going soon to write to you, & that I must send you a kiss. I may as well make short work of it & say *all* send love to you. Georgia will write to you when she returns from Darien. Flora & Appy when the spirit moves them. The servants beg to be remember'd. You must excuse this miserable scrawl—& all the mistakes you may find. I feel that I am becoming exceedingly careless in writing. May God! bless—guide & guard you & may you be restored to me in health & happiness.

Your affectionate Mother
A M King

1. Thomas Butler King had been traveling at breakneck speed. On March 23 Anna wrote, "By the last Sunday mail I had another letter from your dear Father making two letters in 4 days. The last dated 'on board Steamer *Shotwell Harbor* of New Orleans 11th March.' He had encountered a terrible tempest in passing the Gulf had for 2 days been awfully sea sick but then wrote himself quite well. He remained in New Orleans only a few hours had received our letters from the St Charles—was on his way to Memphis, Little Rock and Louisville then on to New York to which place you had best direct your next letter" (Anna Matilda Page King to Henry Lord Page King, March 23, 1854, TBK, SHC).

2. Lord was attending Harvard Law School.

3. Nancy is number 40 on the list from William Page's will; number 81 on the 1839 list, her birthday recorded as June 13, 1819; and number 49 on the 1853 list. See appendix 2.

Retreat 3d July '54

My dearly beloved Lordy

Another week begins & I again have the pleasure of holding a little communion with you. Georgia wanted to write to you today but I have persuaded her you would rather hear from us twice a week than get all of our letters at one time only once every week. So Tuesday mails *must* carry a letter to you from me. Friday's I give the others the pleasure. By yesterdays Mail I received a dear letter from your Father dated 23rd & one from Butler dated the 27th Ulto. How it is that letters come & go so irregularly—the P[ost] M[aster] alone can tell. My letters of the 18th to your Father & Butler both written & mailed on the same day here, were received at an interval of 4 days by them in N.Y. As I can't make these Post Masters mind their manners I may as well let the subject drop. You no doubt know even better than I do the movements of your Father & Butty. Feeling that the sooner the former leaves N.Y. the sooner I may hope to see him—I have been hoping by every Mail to hear the day named for his returning to Texas. Now that they tell me he will go this week I find myself as uneasy as ever—from a dread he may get sick on the way. The weather is so terribly hot here—what must it be in Texas. I have so great a horror of his getting Cholera or any other sickness again when from home. Oh! Lordy how hard—how nobly your poor Father struggles to retrieve his lost fortune & as far as I can understand from there letters he is no better off than when he began. Knowing his disposition so well I feel that he never will cease his efforts as long as health lasts & yet he meets with so many disappointments. I have become completely disheartened about his ever succeeding. An entire shipwreck is made of our domestic happiness—the time we are separated in life the survivor will look back on with many a bitter regret. I can't but be painfully anxious about the future. If you carried out your intentions to see them off from N.Y. I suppose you are now with them. I regret every day you are absent from your studies—but I can never regret the time you devote to your noble Father & brother.

Your father & Butty think Malley will be running some risk of being made sick by coming home when others go into camp. From the papers I learn there is a great deal of sickness in the Up Country as well Alas! as in every part of the U.S. If M[alley] & Floyd *are prudent* I cannot but think there is more safety in coming home than in camping. Malley's letter was dated the 23d why so long on the way "can't say." He will not be at liberty before the 20th of July. Alic Couper is expected tomorrow night. There are on the Island at present, The Linens, Miss Postell, Lem Clark, Young Elliott (the Bishops eldest son), 2 Cunninghams—their little nephew & niece; Jinny, Sally & Fraser Grant. The L[inens] at the Hazzards; Miss P[ostell], C[lark] & E[lliott] at Mrs Caters; the Cunninghams & children at Hamilton; the Grants here. On Tuesday Mrs Troup, 2 children & 2 servants accompanied J[inny] & S[ally]. She had been here but 24 hours when she fancied her little girl to be ill. So she asked me to send her back home. It took one carriage (2 horses one man) & 1 man, 1 cart & 4 oxen

to take her to Hamilton with children, nurses, trunks, baskets, bundles &c—
then a boat & 4 more men to place her within riding distance of her Fathers
home. Fraser & Tip had to go to take her over the [?]—this called for the use
of 2 more horses. How rejoiced I am dear Lordy it was not *your fate to have her
as my daughter in law*. She is ready to go crazy & does act like a crazy woman
th[e] moment little Minnie grunts. Has worn herself to little better than skin
& bones ab[o]ut this scrap of a little image of "Brady." If Jinny & Sally make
as anxious Mothers for the sake of all connected I hope they may never marry.[1]

On Friday evening we had another collection of petticoats here—no less
than 12 & only Tip, Fraser & Robert Couper to vary the scene. Mrs Rust—
Marg C, Robert, Mrs Cater, Emma Postell & S[arah] A[rmstrong] took tea—&
if you will believe it they kept it up until near 12 oclock. They acted Charades
which I think less troublesome & more amusing than Tableaux. Mrs R[ust], MC
& R[obert] remained until Sunday morning. On Saturday the Misses Cunningham dined here, 15 sat down to dinner—before the dessert was over William, Tootee & all the children came. The Misses C[unningham] staying to
tea—a repetition of Charades, music &c & ending off with "a bathe" about
$^{1}/_{2}$ past 11 oclock—they had also before dark a drive & ride on the beach. This
evening all that can go are invited to the Hazzards—tomorrow the Grants
& 2 of your Sisters spend the day at C[annons] P[oint]. Wednesday evening
Mrs Cater gives a tea fight—to which the folks here are invited.[2]

Postells negros have not had an allowance of food for weeks—they are going all about begging & offering to buy with poor chickens a little food. But he
has in the midst of this managed to put up a nice portico in front of his house
& is making a fence round the yard with tabby pillars. I am told it looks very
well. Old Mrs William Armstrongs son Tony with his two motherless sons, are
at Woodville. The poor old lady has been very anxious to make me a visit but
just when she was well enough to come my house filled with company & she
had to postpone her visit. The Grants will remain with us until next Friday. If
I find Butler will not be here before the 15th I think I may as well let your Sisters go home with Jinny & Sally & be done with it. Mrs Bourke wrote to Georgia that some business had prevented them from coming on Tuesday or Friday
last as they had promised. As they have put off coming so long I hope they will
not come until Butler returns home. By the way I have a piece of news to give
you I had nearly forgotten. On Wednesday last I received a letter from Andrew
dated 19th June in which he says "I am now in Havana Louisa on the Plantation—I have determined to take passage on board the *Isabel* on the 8th or
22nd July—will make you a short visit prior to our going North." I suppose
if they do come here they will wish Mattie to go North with them to which I
shall make no objection—there has been so much company here since the first

of May your sisters have had but little to do with their lessons. We all love her very much but when money is so scarce it is hard to pay so high a price for barely the pleasure of her company.

Thus far the crops look well. We had a fine rain on the night of the 28th & would be glad of just such another tonight. Fruit is turning out very so so. Not near the peaches we had last year. Melons thus far very inferior—figs just beginning to ripen—grapes got the rot. Chickens won't grow—beef wont keep over 24 hours—& no end to company. You see I began this on a small sheet of paper. I was up this morning by time it was light. Last night Appy & Sally left their windows open without the netting—the Musquitoes came in by hundreds—Appy & S[ally] actually had to get up & clear out of their room. First they walked in the garden & gathered flowers then they went on the beach all before 6 oclock. We actually were *all* seated at breakfast table by 7 oclock this morning. Georgia says she intends giving you a long letter by the Friday mail—you may expect an account of the party at West Point & Mrs Caters. All your sisters & Tip desire lots of love to you. Our dear little Cooney still looks badly from his fever. It would be a great relief to us all if he could be taken North this summer—but from all accounts you have all sorts of sickness there—please Lordy dear be *careful of your health.* Do nothing which will provoke an attack of Cholera or yellow fever or any other complaint. I have written a long letter to go by this mail to Mary King. I hope you may be able to make your Uncle a short visit this summer. Stay no time that you can avoid in the City of N.Y. I must now conclude—May God! bless & protect you my dear boy.

Your affectionate Mother

A M King

1. Eugenia (Jinny) Grant married Mallery King in 1862.
2. I believe Anna means a "fête" rather than a "fight."

Retreat 12th July '54

My dearly beloved husband

This is mail day. I can only hope I may receive favorable news from you all. On Sunday I got dear Butlers letter of the 4th wherein he says "Father Lord & myself are well. I have just finished helping Father to pack up. Mr W[oolley] & himself leave tomorrow afternoon." We also had letters from Mal & Floyd dated 3d. The latter had been suffering from a bad cold. Mrs Fraser apprehending he was getting rash fever had him consigned to her care. He had got well & returned to the Institute. Malley says nothing of his own health but as he said he was studying hard for his examinations I trust he was well. The dear ones at Hamilton were all well yesterday. The ring worms still distress Virginia. Every remedy we have tried has failed. We commenced the iodine last night.[1] Georgia & Florence, Mattie & myself are in our usual health.

I have not written to you for more than a week. In the first place I waited to write composedly. *Thank God! I can do so today. Our dear little Tip is nearly quite recovered* from an accident which on the 4th may have been fatal. He is now in the next room amusing himself again with his machinery. The dear little fellow has been showing such a turn for machinery, I have encouraged him in it, not supposing any harm could or would happen. He had got a can which held 2 gallons—attached to it parts of an old clock to carry a small saw & just when all was fix'd to his perfect satisfaction it exploded—he was leaning over the can to see the machinery in motion at the time. The steam & hot water burnt his eyes, face, arm, chest & thigh severely (I am getting too fast on in my story).[2] Again *I say he is nearly well*—feel no anxiety about his eyes—thank *God! they are safe* & we have every reason to think in a few more days will be as beautiful as ever they were. The Grants were still at Retreat. Fraser Grant is a very good boy—much of Tips gentle disposition & correct habits. They are much attached to each other & were so perfectly happy that day. Florence & the Misses G[rant] had gone to Cannon's Point. As I sat in my room I could hear all the boys said. I think I now hear their merry laugh & hasty steps as they would run into the chamber under me for some thing they wanted. They were by the garden wall. Finding the steam would force out the cork they wire'd it down fast.[3] Fraser was seated rather below the can—Tip was in the act of letting off the steam when there was a report like the firing off of a musket. I thought I heard Tip laugh. The next instant a fearful cry from Fraser. You may depend on it I re-echo'd the scream which Appy & Georgia & the servants took up. I ran one way they came into the house by another door. When I met with the crowd all was confusion—every one assuring me *Tip* had escaped injury—& as he was as active as any one else in helping poor Fraser—(whose cries were unceasing for help). I called out for ice & sweet oil & soap. Tip went & helped crack the ice & brought a piece to Fraser—then took the oil—washed it over Frasers face— Drank a half tumbler full of it himself—washed it over his face & chest—then for the first time said he was suffering dreadfully but no cry or groan did he utter. He began to gasp & said Oh! Appy I believe I am dying. I cannot get my breath & my eyes are bursting out & those beautiful eyes look'd so unnatural so glazed & red. I then feared the steam had done its work on my poor boy— got him to bed—put ice water on his eyes & made him eat ice. Poor Fraser was scalded on one side of his face, one eye, one arm & a place on his body but altho all these places on each boy blistered immediately—they never complained of any other hurt but their eyes. Our blessed Georgia showed far more presence of mind than I did—Mr Dunham immediately came to offer his services—Geo desired one messenger to go for William—another for Mr J. H. Couper, and a boat to be sent for Mr Grant, writing herself to each of these. William had just left home for the maine & was sent after whilst dear Tootee came to us. The girls were just leaving C[annon's] P[oint] when Georgias note to Mrs Couper was handed in. Mrs Couper was so shocked her countenance betrayed what we had desired should be kept from the girls. Now that our distress is over—Florence gives a ridiculous account of their rapid drive home—But enough of this. Let us forever thank a merciful God! that it was no worse.

The top of the can was found in the top of a tree. This may have been driven into our boys face—he was knocked off the wall to a considerable distance. The steam went no further than his *throat*. His right eye was most injured—was fearfully swollen. He had scarce any pulse at first—but before night it raised—he had fever for 4 days & the pain in his eyes was intense. Ice water has apparently done the good work. I will just mention a very simple *anodyne*. Dear Georgia resorted to her Homeopathic book[4] & was directed to dissolve "*casteal Soap in alcohol* & give 3 drops in a little water to be taken every five minutes["] if the patient had inhaled steam & to quiet the nerves—it acted like a charm with all the pain they were suffering they actually in a few minutes after taking the first drops went to sleep & slept better than we ever could have expected throughout the night—& during Tips confinement to bed—whenever he was becoming restless he would call for the "soap & water" & would be quickly quieted & though we sit up with him every night it is to keep the cloths on his eyes wet. The weather until last evening has been *intensely hot*. I found he was getting much debilitated by being kept in bed in a warm dark room & as by Sunday his eyes ceased paining I brought him down stairs & one eye is now quite well—by keeping the other cover'd & the blinds all closed he has the range of the house & is doing far better than we could possibly *even have hoped* for. He has proven himself his "daddys own child." I could not have thought it possible one so young could have borne such pain, *blindness* & confinement in a dark hot room with the fortitude & patience he did & then it was beautiful to see the feeling of affectionate solicitude the one felt for the other. Dear Tip seemed at first to forget his own suffering to encourage & assist Fraser, & when Fraser heard how much worse poor Tip was off than he was—he was all anxiety for Tip.

Mr J H C[ouper] was sick & could not come—his wife sent an express after the girls giving all the cures Mr J. H. C[ouper] could think of. Mrs Grant got here about 12 that night—poor woman she was dreadfully alarmed—tho' Georgia had assured her Fraser was not at all seriously hurt. Mr Grant was sick—Dr Troup[5] accompanied Mrs G[rant]. I think so little of his skill I never even asked his opinion of Tip, & noticed Mrs Grant did not consult him about

Fraser. Next morning Mr Grant & Dr Holmes came as far as Hamilton. Fraser was thought able to go home. We have since heard that he was getting fast well. I would have thought badly of Dr Holmes for not coming to offer me his services—but in the first place I did not think he knew much—and on the next— he spoke at Hamilton so handsomely of *you*. He said "a friend of mine in Charleston knowing how highly I thought of Mr King sent me a paper containing the paragraph in his favor—of course we who know the man all believe he is sound to the back bone—but these lies would chafe (rubbing his fat arm) make his friends feel sore." After this I could not think hard his not coming over to see Tip. Dr Troup was at H[amilton] & told Mr Grant & the Doctor (Holmes) th[e] boys were *very little* injured—I was going to say confound his picture—but he is not worth a thought.[6] The neighbors have all been kind in sending or coming to enquire after Tip.

I have just been made happy by your dear letters of the 6th from N.Y. & 7th from Washington. I had also letters from dear Lordy, Malley & Floyd, & Georgia one from kind Mrs Jaudon. Thank God! you were *all* able to report good health. How was it—there *could be any uncertainty about Mr Walkers going to Texas* with you? Oh! my blessed husband how I tremble for your safety. For you to be travelling so far south at this Season of the year & that too when so much Cholera & other sickness is prevailing seems to me all but madness. Had you gone in *May* I would have been less anxious. I can but trust in the Mercy of God! & try to hope all this will end well. I cannot understand all you have been trying to do—I can't understand why you have so constantly labored without some reward. I do hope my beloved husband if you fail in this effort—if Gods mercy spares your life to return home—you will be satisfied you have done all you could for your children & be content to spend the balance of your life with those who care more for your life than all the wealth the world contains.

Malley speaks hopefully of his coming home—but says he will not be accompanied by Floyd—as none in Floyds class can get leave of absence. I regret this exceedingly. Floyd has been so little with me the last 13 months & at his age more likely to be weaned from home affections & home influence. I am in hopes dear Cuylers eyes will be sufficiently recovered for him to accompany Malley on his return to the Up Country—if it is so Butler can't take him to Roswell.

13th

We are all up & about this morning—the sudden death of Clementines youngest child a boy of 5 years old has cast a gloom over the happiness of us all. This boy has been subject to fever—tho' a remarkably large child for his age. He had fever on Monday—on Tuesday until one oclock he seemed quite well— running about & quite merry. At one the fever returned—I was not aware of this until yesterday before breakfast. When Clementine told me she had been up with Herbert all night & that he was still very sick. On going to see him I found him restless—complained of pain in his head—tongue white.[7] I did all I could think of but it did no good he expired at 12 last night. I feel more for poor Clementine than for the child. She has in all my troubles shown such tender feeling for me & she is so fond a Mother. But I try to feel "Gods will be done." We have had so little sickness among the negros—when I began this letter I was in hope to be able to write cheerfully.

We had no rain—on the 28th until the 10th Inst, during this time the sun was intensely hot. I think I never felt it more parching—we had a good rain on the 10th, 11th & 12th which came in well for the planting of the last pease. I have not seen Toney lately to enquire about the cotton. The corn William thinks will be amply sufficient—but not so abundant & we first thought the ears not so large owing I suppose to the weather becoming dry just when filling.

Mr Roswell King died about 10 days ago of Rheumatisms.[8]

I hear every week from Amanda & hope ere long she will make us a visit. I presume they will go North this summer. The Isld was quite gay—for a little while. For the young peoples sake I was glad of this. Miss Isa Cunningham is staying with us for a few days—Georgia begs I will say for her she will write to you by the next Mail. They—that is G[eorgia], F[lorence], V[irginia] & Tip unite in warm—warm love to you. I hope dearest you will take every possible care to avoid sickness. Gods mercy accompany your efforts to keep well. Oh! my beloved how hard it does seem you should be exposed to so much danger. I will not annoy you by saying more of the painful anxiety I feel—it will do no good.—

Praying God! to bless, protect & guide you safe back I am your devotedly affectionate wife

A M King

Tips left eye is quite well—there is very little inflammation in the right eye— we keep it covered & he says the eye only feels a little weak.

---

1. Iodine could be toxic to ringworm (a fungus) and therefore a cure. Information from Drs. Marston and Slutsker.

2. The machine Tip built was a steam-driven toy sawmill. Steel, *T. Butler King*, 122.

3. The cork served as a safety valve. Ibid.

4. Homeopathy was one of the three most popular alternatives to mainstream medical practices in the antebellum era, which relied on harsh purgatives and bloodletting. Homeopaths believed that "a drug that induces a symptom in a healthy person will relieve it in an ill one and that drug potency increases as dosage decreases" (Keeney, "Domestic Medicine in the Old South," 283–284).

5. Dr. James McGillivray Troup of Darien, Georgia, married Camilla Brailsford,

whose family owned Broadfield, a rice plantation on the Altamaha River. Vanstory, *Land of the Golden Isles,* 124–125.

6. Anna is disparaging Dr. Troup's assessment that the boys were not seriously injured—especially as he apparently did not see them.

7. Herbert could have been suffering from malaria, viral encephalitis, or a bacterial infection. His white tongue was probably caused by dehydration. Information from Drs. Marston and Slutsker.

8. Anna refers here to Roswell King Jr., who became the overseer of the Butler plantations when his father left coastal Georgia to pursue more lucrative business ventures in the North. See Bell, *Major Butler's Legacy,* 530–532.

All well   Retreat 23d July 54

My own dearly beloved husband

I thank you ten thousand times for your affectionate letter to Virginia & myself from Mobile & for the few lines your tender considerations induced you to send me from New Orleans. It is no little comfort to hear this frequently from you on your perilous journey. May God! continue his merciful protection to you my beloved husband. We none of us deserve Gods blessings—but your object is so pure I can but hope He will bless & prosper you—but above all pray your precious life be preserved form danger. On Thursday night— our dear Malley came—he looks very well tho' not as fat as when he left us. He says Floyd was quite well when he left Marietta. Last night our dear Butler came & reports Lordy well on the 20th. Tip looks so well it is hard to convince those who did not see his injuries, that he was so badly hurt. His right eye is still a little weak & cannot yet do without his blind. Mrs Lara has been complaining—is now better & the rest of us are all in our usual health & no sickness among the negros.

Mr Woolley & Amanda are now at Hamilton—he will return to Savannah— but my dear Cousin has consented to spend the balance of the summer with us. We have at present quite a full house—fortunately there are a plenty of chickens—figs & melons—we sit down 14 to table & tomorrow our dear ones at Hamilton & Mr & Mrs W[oolley] will be here. On Thursday evening we are all invited to take tea at Mrs Caters—Theatricals are becoming the order of the day—I hope nothing will prevent my going—in my next I hope to be in good spirits & write you all about it.

Mr Bourke came for his wife & Miss Dubignon last evening—he will however leave them until next Friday—as they are anxious to attend Mrs Caters party. We are also all invited to the Hazzards tomorrow evening & in return for all their activities we will have to have a tea fight ourselves in all this week. The Cunninghams leave the Island a week from Tuesday—they are both very estimable women—give us little trouble as possible. Mrs Bourke & Kate are also very pleasant visiters. At the same time this constant company is very wearisome & expensive.

The weather continues hot & dry. I am told North of us there has been a great deal of rain. When we complain of the heat here surrounded by so many comforts I always think of you dearest—how much worse off you are. Oh my husband when I reflect on all you are undergoing I am filled with wonder & admiration as well as with fear & trembling. All I can say may God! help & prosper you.

I have begun this scrawl today—because it is not likely I shall have much leisure tomorrow.

Monday 24th

We are all in our usual health today—we have literally a house full—our dear ones from Hamilton with my dear Amanda & Mr Woolley increasing our numbers at lunch Mr Postell a Mr Clark & Dr Royal. Fruit comes in beautifully on this occasion. In addition to the pleasure of having so many friends around us we have had a splendid rain, no wind—the rain very much wanted. Dear Butler has written to you. So much company in the house I fear will prevent the girls from writing by this Mail.

Your dog Rock is in good health & the admiration of all who see him. Florence has a little black terrier marked precisely like Rock & as remarkably small as Rock is large. Rock is learning to eat Homany—no little relief I assure you.[1] I hope nothing may happen to them & when you come home dearest—he as well as all the rest of us will be here to welcome you once more to old Retreat. Dearly beloved I hope the day is not far distant when you will once more enjoy the comforts of your own home.

Dear Tootee wants to add a few lines. In all the confusion I am puzzled to make out a long letter—so I will just [let] Tootee have her say.

My own Precious Father.

Mother is writing so I have stolen a little place to just remind you, Father dear that I still am here—dear Father you fear we shall forget you. Now I think we will have to fear that you may forget us. Yes you have so much to ocupy your time & thoughts—But my own Father we never have—never can doubt your fond affection. Was it not tantalising to have you as near as Augusta—it was provocating.—

We are all here today with our dear good Mother—All but you my beloved Father dear Lord & Floyd—if—if—but what is the use of if, if's—God knows best—and you, I pray will yet be restored to your devoted family. I pray for you My Father & that is all your little daughters can do—Oh May God bless & protect you my Father. Your little boy is quite well—and I fancy is growing more like you every day—he is not as much spoiled as he was—but indeed it is very hard for me to correct him—first his name—then his sweet winning ways—he speaks of you and says when he gets to be a big man he will help you work so you can come home. Thank God we are all well now—Oh may we all continue so & you my Father May he preserve you from all danger.—

I am so miserable a pens woman, my beloved Father that I often feel ashamed to write to you—& then with little children my time is much occupied. It has been so very delightful hearing from you so often since you left New York. I have now taken more of Mother's letter than she gave so must say goodbye. Oh Father my heart yearns to have you with us—My dearest Father.

May you be blessed & prospered is the prayer of your ever devoted child

HC

25th

This day you hoped to reach Austin God grant you have been able to do so & are as well as this leaves us all at Retreat & Hamilton. We shall all—but especially your poor wife long to hear again from you my precious husband. We are obliged to send off our letters very early on Mail days—I am just dressed & feel very blind & stupid—I enclose a piece I cut from a Savannah paper of the 21st. Butler is so disgusted Mr W[alker] is named first—when all the credit & work is yours. God for ever bless you dearest.

Your devoted affectionate wife
A M King

1. Rock had been a gift to Thomas Butler King when King was serving as the collector of the Port of San Francisco. He was evidently a very large dog and Anna was happy when Rock developed a taste for hominy, which was far cheaper than meat. Anna Matilda Page King to Thomas Butler King, December 7, 1856, SHC.

Retreat 31st July '54

My own dearly beloved husband,

I am sorry I cannot begin with "all is well" our dear little King is again sick—was taken with fever on Saturday & when Tootee wrote me this morning it was not yet off. It has moderated however—we can hope he is on the mend. The rest of us both here & at Hamilton are in our usual health. Butler tells me it is too soon to expect to hear from you. Still this did not prevent my being disappointed when I found that the mail yesterday brought me no letter from you neither did we hear from Floyd—but Malley had a letter from one of the cadets just from Marietta who said he left Floyd quite well. We heard from dear Lordy on Wednesday last—he found Carlisle so insufferably hot—he was just leaving for Springfield. If I had time I could write you a very long letter & mean to make this as long as I can.

On Thursday evening I actually dressed & went to Mrs Caters there were so many of us to go it took 3 turns of the carriage & 3 extra horses to get over. 24 persons assembled. Play—"the rough Diamond"—Appy had a conspicuous part—"Margery" & really did it beautifully—the best that night after that the mock Doctor. Before it was over a storm began to rise & remembering the many turns to be made before we could all get home I became fidgity. Then came a report that Andrew & Louisa had come to Hamilton. Butty rushed off to give them welcome when I got home I met the dear boy drenched with rain water & not a little annoyed at the false report sent him. No Andrew or Louisa had come. It was past 3 before we retired that night. On Saturday morning the Bourkes left us & I was busy all day cleaning up & preparing for A[ndrew] & L[ouise]. I had to go to Hamilton in the evening to see our little darling boy. I could not remain all night as your brother we doubted not would arrive that night. Butler & Malley went over after tea to await the arrival of the Steam boat. About one they returned accompanied by dear Andrew & Louisa. And very happy we all are to have them once more at Retreat. The bustle caused by their arrival made me melancholy so like when you dearest used to come home. I do not know how long they will stay—I hope their visit will be a pleasant one to them. They really seam to be quite happy to be here. They brought us each a very pretty dress & the girls each a very pretty fan—all chinese—& dear Andrew also sent me before he came 2 more box's of fine sugar. I hope their being here will induce brother Stephen to make us another visit. They are all now but me taking their lunch, all so merry, Mr Brown & Miss Armstrong added to the number. I never permit any thing other than *sickness to interfere with my writing to you or our boys. You may take this as a gentle hint if you please.*

The weather continues very hot. On Thursday & Friday night we had fine rains—but it is no cooler in the day for it. Dear Butler intends writing to you today & is better able than I am to tell you the condition of the crop. No sickness of consequence among the negros. From what I can understand Andrew's visit to the States *is for pleasure.* When he so suddenly determined on coming I apprehended it was from the condition of Cuba. I am so glad they have come

& that too before all the fruit was over. I never see a fine peach but I wish I could present it to you my own beloved the peaches here do not require *sugaring* & Andrew really enjoys them.

I must tell you a compliment paid our dear Malley by Mr John Anderson who is of the board of visitors of the G[eorgia] M[ilitary] I[nstitute]. He wrote thus "The writer would congratulate you on the standing of your son Mallery at the Institute, & the very beautiful & perfect examination he passed." This gives us all no little gratification. I was so well pleased I ran down & read it aloud to several of the family assembled Malley being of the number he blushed like a young girl. Mallery is really a fine noble boy—he looks well too in his uniform his figure much improved—perfectly erect without being stiff. He tells me Floyd is much grown. I am in hopes being in this institute will compel him to go straight. Tips eye gets stronger—& you can now scarce perceive there [sic] having been injured. He is a dear gentle boy—I wish he had been a [end of sentence missing]. Poor little fellow in a few more days I must send him far [a]way among perfect strangers but there is no help for it.

I never feel the heat but I think how much worse it must be where you are. I have not a comfort or enjoyment but I wish you could partake with me. I have not a distress—but I think if you were here you would comfort me under it or dispel it altogether. My own beloved how cruel is this separation.

I shall ride over to see Cooney this evening & hope before I close this to give you more favorable accounts of him. He is a child of uncommon interest to all of us—so very intelligent & affectionate. Poor Tootee is in constant dread of losing him. Little John grows more interesting every day—he is a mite of a thing but very knowing & very interesting. Anna & Willie begin to grow. William is still hard at work on the wharf. Your Brother & Louisa desire much love to you. Our dear children send a thousand loves & kisses. The servants all beg to be remembered. Please husband dear take especial care of your precious health for the sake of your affectionate & devoted wife.—

A M King

August 1st

The last day of July was about the hotest days I think I have ever felt—sea breeze not in until sun down & then but light—musquetos in abundance—the first of August bids fair to be the same. I can only hope you are well dearest to enable you to bear the heat where you are. Hamilton Couper was here to dinner yesterday which made it too late for me to drive over to see our little King—I however heard from Tootee—the fever was off & he was up—but looking badly—the rest of the family are well—ours as usual but hard to be got up. Butler is now sitting next to me writing to you. May God bless & preserve you dearest

Your loving wife
Anna

Retreat 6th August '54

My own beloved husband

Thank you ten thousand times for your welcome letters of the 18th & 19th July. How mercifully you have been preserved from sickness & danger—Gods mercy has been great—may it be continued to us all. His mercy permits me to say we are all well—all here & at Hamilton—our dear little boy having recovered from his fever. On Wednesday I had the happiness to receive the welcome letters above mentioned, by this days Mail we heard from Lord & Floyd—they were both well.

Yesterday we all dined at Hamilton—on Thursday they all spent the day here, 20 sat at dinner. Young Stephen [King] & his brother (D[aniel] Lord) being of the number. They are still here & will remain until the 9th. Brother Stephen is not very well & entreats Andrew to make him a visit. Considering it his duty to comply Andrew & Louisa will return with S[tephen] & D[aniel] L[ord] & I have consented that Georgia & Florence shall accompany them. They intend being absent one week. Yours, Lords, & Floyds, presence was alone wanted to make the past week *a perfectly happy one*. The only object—Andrew & Louisa had for visiting the States was to try & obliterate the unpleasant occurrences of 1852. I do *not wonder now—that they were prejudiced against us*. I would have been the same.[1] We will not open old sores. I am rejoiced that they have come. And they both are so happy here. Louisa so affectionate so cheerful—so sweet—and Andrew in his quiet way so happy. They will not leave us before the 1st September—perhaps not then. We shall one & all do all in our power to make their stay as pleasant as possible.

Our dear boys have to leave us on the 8th how sadly we will miss them. It is my desire that dear Butler should go with Tip to Roswell. He thinks he need not be absent over one week. I hope he may not be obliged to go to Washington whilst—Andrew & Louisa are here.

The weather still continues excessively hot & we begin again to want rain. A[ndrew] & L[ouise] coming from a warmer Country do not complain of the heat as much as we do. There is no sickness of consequence among the negros —tho I have again to mention the death of one of the most faithful of servants poor afflicted Hannah I hope is now at rest. She died on Thursday night.[2] For years her sufferings have been greater than words could express—yet never a groan or complaint escaped her lips. Patiently she endured her sufferings. To her owners she was all we could desire in a servant—in fact as servant, daughter, sister, wife she had not her equal. She was in her senses to the last & willing to leave this for a better world. Poor thing let her be ever so ill—her countenance always brightened when I told her I had heard from you. Tho I know death to her was a relief—still I can't but sorrow for the departure of so good, so faithful a servant as Hannah ever was to us. Thank God! she seemed prepared to die. Thank God—she was not taken from me by sudden death.

The papers announce the death of Miss Filmore also the death of Mr Ex president Filmores brother both from Cholera. Dear dear husband how mercifully we have thus far been dealt with. With all your other trials—death has been kept from us only that precious babe in 20 years. And in removing her *we* see Gods mercy to her parents. She was their idol—they now love her through their God! & Saviour. When I look around on our goodly sons & daughters—see the health they enjoy I wonder how I can murmmur for want of *money*, that bane to human happiness. But God! is my judge—he knows I want it not for myself—but for them. I do not mean to flatter myself you will succeed—then I will be less disappointed if you do not. Your being in debt is no stain on your good name—all who know the truth—know that you gave up to be sacrificed a princely fortune, that your embarrassments were caused by the hand of God! that you have striven hard—made every sacrifice of your happiness—run every risk of your precious life to redeem this lost fortune, & if you do not succeed it is because God! sees best you should not. Oh! that you could once more be your own master—live quietly the evening of your days under your own roof, waited on by your loving wife & affectionate children—come home dearest—come home & rest from all your labours.

Malley & poor little Tip begin to look grave at the near approach of their day for leaving home. Andrew & Louisa are so sorry to part with them. Butler they seem to look on as their own son, dear Butler he has such a way of waiting on every one of the family without seeming to do it—no one is oppressed with his attentions & yet none of us seem as if we can get along without him "he is his Fathers own son—his mothers pride, his Sisters & brothers joy" so says Florence—& so we all feel towards the dear boy.

The last week I have said has been an exceedingly pleasant one. When they are all gone except Appy, Mattie & myself I will have the house right-sided—count over my stores put up chickens to fatten—So that when they get back from Satilla I shall be able [to] give them as good as the place can afford. I love to have them here & think they are equally pleased. Dinner bell has sounded—I will put this away until Tuesday—hoping I may still say all is well.

8th

We are all well this morning—dear Tootee & her dear children have just left us having passed the night here. W[illiam] staid until near 12—we had just in the family for dear Louisa's & Andrews amusement—Tableaux & Charades— they were well got up & very good.

We all feel sad at the near approach of our good Mallery & dear little Tips departure. It is possible our good *Butler* will go to Washington before he returns home—we can only hope [torn] will not find it necessary to do so—we are so reluctant to part with him. I am [torn] much hurried in getting the boys ready—all unite in warm love to you my own dear husband—praying God to bless, guide, protect us all—In great haste & confusion

Your devoted wife
A M King

1. This is unclear.
2. Anna wrote in her daybook under the heading "Deaths of negros from June 1854": "My good and faithful servant Hannah after years of suffering expired on the night of 3d August. For honesty—moral character—unselfish & perfect devotion to her owners she had not her equal—she died resigned with firm trust in her redeemer" (Selected Pages from the Record Book of Retreat Plantation, GDAH).

Retreat 10th August '54

My own dear Lordy

We have all been in so much confusion the last two weeks I am not certain when I last wrote to you. I received on Sunday your affectionate letter from Springfield—I am glad you were there—I cannot but regret your long stay in N.Y. though you acted for the best & my most serious objection was the dread of Cholera. I am glad you hesitate going to Niagara—if we can believe news paper reports—the Cholera is raging there. Dear Lordy do not rashly run into *any kind* of danger. Either your precious life—or fair name. Now I have often spoken to you & Butler on the subject of engaging the affections of a girl with no serious intention of uniting yourselves to them for life. I think it cruel & depend on it my son sooner or later you will incur the name of male flirts— which no prudent or sensible woman will or can admire. If you have no serious intentions you should avoid rather than seek the society of Emelia. To me she has been represented as being amiable—it is cruel to sport with her tender feelings—if you love her sufficient to marry her—if you think it best you should (*think well*)—do so—if not avoid rather than seek her society. It is both cruel & dishonorable to engage her affections basely for your amusement. I wished much to have written to you last week on the subject—but had not the time. I fear this is too late—even if you felt inclined to follow my advice—to have any effect.[1]

I really do enjoy this visit from Louisa & your Uncle—she is *so sweet*, so perfectly happy to be with us—*all* of her *prejudices* have been removed *ample cause had she to be prejudiced.* All I now blame her for—was not telling us at the time. It was on Brother Henrys account she was silent. Their visit to the States was on account of this coolness. They will stay with us certainly until the 1st September perhaps longer. It would delight you to see how happy they both are to be with us. Unfortunately Steve & D[aniel] Lord came down last week charged with the mission from their Father not to return without your Uncle & Aunt. Louisa would not go without two at least of your Sisters. So Geo & Appy consented to accompany them. If your dear Father, yourself & Floyd were here last week I think for once in my life I would have been completely happy. We were all well all so happy.

Last Thursday dear Tootee &c spent the day here. Again on Monday she came for the night. It was one of the most delightful nights I ever noticed— the weather had changed from intense heat to delightful cool temperature— the moon gave a bright light not a misquito felt seen or heard. For Andrew & Louisas amusement they had Tableaux on the piazza & beautiful ones they were—William, Steve, Butler, Malley—Tip, Anna, Willie, Geo, Flo, Appy, Mattie, all took part in it. The evening passed off delightfully & beautifully— every one in good spirits each one trying to forget that the next night our dear Butler, Malley & Tip would be on their way to Marietta—that on Wednesday morning Andrew, L[ouisa], G[eorgia], A[ppy], S[tephen] & D[aniel] L[ord] would leave us for Wayne [?]—the latter consideration not so distressing as the former they would be away but one week. It will be months before we can hope to see Malley & Tip again & very probably Butler would receive intelligence in Sav[annah] which would oblige him to go to Washington.

On Tuesday Tootee left us for home, by 12 oclock there came on a terrible storm of rain, hail, wind &c it lasted many hours—the boat fortunately stuck in the creek—when the rain subsided at about 4 the boys started for Hamilton. Many tears were shed dear Louisa seemed as much grieved in fact—shed more tears than I did—it is not often I can shed tears you know Lordy. It did grieve me tho' to part with my poor little Tip. Malley can better take care of himself is more used to being among strangers—my dear little Tip it is his first trial & he is so backward in his education—it is a hard trial for him. Dear Butler readily consented to go with Tip. Next day the other party left at an early hour, they had our little Anna also with them.

On the return of the boat I had the happiness to receive one I love next to my husband & children—our dear Cousin Amanda. It is a great happiness &

comfort her being with me. By the way Lordy dear let me entreat of you to be more careful in your use of *burning Fluid*. Cousin A[manda] lost a valuable servant only last week by this Fluid—she said she was filling her lamp it took fire & she was so badly burnt as to live but a day or two suffering intense agony. Our poor Hannah too is gone poor *faithful—honest—good Hannah*! Tho satisfied hers would ever be a life of suffering—still it grieved us [to] part with her. I have every reason to hope she is now at rest. The negros generally are healthy. God! grant there may be no more death among them. Your old horse Cherry died yesterday, about a month ago she actually had a colt quite a promising little thing—was in excellent order & not used at all on account of this colt— it may have been the intense heat. If the colt lives I want you to give it to Cooney. He is so delighted you wrote to him. He said to me "now you see you may know my Lordy loves me when he sent me my pistol & my letter." Dear little fellow he begins again to look better—his illness pulled him down not a little. I have yet to write to your brothers—& must bring this to a close. I have not heard from your dear Father since his letter of the 19th July. Florence—Mattie & Cousin A[manda] send much love—the dear ones at Hamilton always beg I will add their love. Tootee finds writing very painful—she often speaks of wishing to write to you—if this finds you at Springfield give our love to your good cousin John & his estimable wife. God bless you my son

Your affectionate mother

A M King

1. Stephen Berry writes about Lord's relations with women that he "was not unfeeling, but rather saw courtship as a clash of wills, stylistically similar to lobbying for a railroad contract or important bill. Travelling with his father as a representative of the Southern Pacific Railroad, Lord made the comparison quite explicit. 'The uncertainty of Legislation,' he wrote his brother, 'is so great that that of women is fool to it. With a woman you may understand 'yes' for 'no' and return to the charge, but with Legislation, if you let it floor you, you have to stay down" ("More Alluring at a Distance," 879–880).

Retreat 17th August 54

My own beloved Lordy

I dare say Butler or Geo will be writing to you today—but I can't consent as long as my sight lasts to let a whole week pass over & not give you a line from my pen. By your last letter I presume you are now at New Port. In my last I expressed my regret that you had determined to visit that place & gave you my reasons. The more I think of it the greater the anxiety I feel. I now not only regret the injustice to the young lady—but I now fear lest should her brother think you are trifling with his Sisters happiness, he may take a *Spaniard vengeance on* you. Be on your guard my beloved Lord do not let a foolish vanity jeopardize your valuable life—or tarnish your fair fame. If you desire to make her your wife—continue your attentions—if not withdraw at once your particular attentions. Money *with* a wife is never an objection[;] to make it a sole object is a sin & a shame. Dear Lordy I want to say a great deal but do not know how to proceed. Consult your own good sense—your really kind heart your sense of honor & I feel satisfied you will (if you will follow what they will dictate) do what is right. I neither advise or would desire you to be *constantly* at hard study. Still I think your prudent plan would have been to set apart 4 hours at least of every week day of this long vacation to study. I shall be better satisfied when I hear you have returned to Cambridge.

Georgia has a letter from Mary King dated 30th July at Niagara. Your Uncle has been very sick was then better—as soon as strong enough would go to Saratoga ere they returned home. I am still without further letters from your dear Father by yesterdays mail. I received a news paper directed by him to me from Austin dated 29th July. This paper mentions the arrival of Mr Walker & your dear Father in Austin. I hope soon to get a letter. I do not build up hopes in my own mind that he will be successful. I have a fear that after all he has undergone to accomplish the grand project he will meet with disappointment.

We do not expect dear Butler back before the 19th. Tuesday had been a day of considerable excitement to me. Just as I was satisfied I had lost a boy 14 years old by drowning—I saw the boat leaving your Sisters, Anna, Your Uncle & Aunt—turn the point in the face of a fearful looking thunder storm. Andrew or the 4 men rowing I knew had no skill on water but thank God! they reached the shore in safety—that all but over power'd by the intense heat. They had a pleasant visit but were not the least sorry to get back home. Dear Lordy I wish you could be here with them. Louisa & her good husband is just what they were when we met for the first time in N.Y. She is all life—all sweetness and Andrew seems perfectly happy to see her so happy. It was hard for me to get to sleep on Tuesday night—I suffered so much for the melancholy death of poor Norton. By & bye Cousin Amanda woke me to listen to some one in Butlers room. I did not feel like facing a foe that night—still felt that I ought to go down & see who was in the room. Just then I again heard foot steps—woman like. I went to the window & bawled out—"who is there" when dear Butler answered "it is me Mother." He wanted to give us a surprise in the morning—all however found it out except Andrew whose joyful surprise was very gratifying to Butler. Butler left your brothers all well.

The dear ones from Hamilton were with us yesterday for the day—the rain kept Tootee & the children until after breakfast today—William went home after ten last night. Dear Cooney is looking very much better he is very sweet & is never more so in my opinion than when talking about "my own dear Lordy" the way he always mentions you. I pray God! a joyful meeting is in reserve for you & him. Tootee is not very well—the rest of the family are well. I have had considerable sickness among the negros mostly children—all are on the mend. On Monday evening Jimper told poor Norton to drive a certain horse into the stable—had he *done* it *himself* poor Norton would not have been drowned. This boy had a defect in his eyes—& could not see 50 yds from him. The horse he was sent after was just down on the beach. Norton (from his foot marks) ran every foot of the way to Club creek—then back to our beach creek there Mr Dunham & the negros traced his steps & there they stopt—as he had never ran away or shirked his work. We knew of course he had been drowned in crossing the creek. Before dinner on Tuesday his body was lodged by the ebb tide just below this house. His loss is serious—the manner of his dying the more distressing. 4 less than when you left us. This is the misery of slave holding.—

I wish you would write to your Uncle Andrew—he seems hurt you have not done so—I hope my next letter will be filled with nothing but good news— that I may be spared the pain of re counting a death. It is painful enough to recount the death of a negro. God grant *I* may never have to tell you of the death of one of the family. Butler is much engaged with plantation affairs & entertaining his Uncle still he may intend writing to you by this Mail. One & all unite in warm love to you. Take all possible care of your precious health for the sake of your devoted & affect[ionate] Mother

AMK

(all well)   Retreat 24th August 1854
My own dearly beloved husband,

It was my very great happiness yesterday to receive your most welcome letters of the 31st July 2d & 5th of August. To hear you were in health would have been sufficient happiness—to hear you have succeeded in your mission is an unexpected pleasure—God! grant you may be spared to enjoy the fruit of so hard labour—so great a risk of life—so great a sacrifice of comfort & domestic happiness. Not having heard from you since your letter of the 24th Ulto. & that only received on the 18th Inst—I continued to direct my letters to Austin. I regret this only because you will not on your arrival in N.Y. find letters from us. And I think after all your trials & hard labor—it is hard suspence on our account should be added to your worry of mind.

I have began this letter before breakfast. All under this roof were well when we retired last night. Yesterday dear Tootee—the children—Cousin A[manda] & Mr Woolley spent the day with us. All were well except Tootee who has been complaining of fullness of the head for some days—it was better yesterday & I hope will wear off. There is no great sickness among the negros—cases of fever every day but not alarming. In my last letter I mentioned our loss by drowning of one of Roses sons a boy entering his 14th year. He went to pen up horses—attempted to cross the creek & was lost. These unexpected—unlooked for deaths are far more trying than after we have carefully nursed & done all in our power to prolong the lives of our slaves. I do not know how it is but we certainly lose more negros than any one of our neighbors—but I must not—will not repine—you my blessed husband our own beloved children are yet spared to me. Tho' God! alone knows for how long—*Brother Andrew begs me not to urge you to return to your home just now.* In the first place the yellow fever is making fearful ravages in Savannah—with cruel culpable deceit this fact has been held secret until concealment could no longer be kept. I see too (God! help me) it is in New Orleans & Mobile—places you will pass through on your way to N.Y. where the Cholera has long been & is still doing its work. Between all these fires—how are you to escape? May the Mercy of God! protect you my love. The papers also report yellow fever in Charleston. Then those loathsome—horse leaches of creditors will be pouncing upon you as soon as you put foot in Savannah. This would be bad enough in Winter when a detention would not be perilous but now a stay of only a few hours may be fatal. Dearest husband I know, you know, your own business best. I am crazy to have you home once more but I dare not let my selfishness induce you to jeopardize your invaluable life or the distress of having you leeched out of what you have so hardly won.

I do hope you are using every necessary possible precaution to avoid fever or Cholera—that even now when I am trembling for your safety you have passed safely through your journey & may [be] near if not safe in N.Y. There I hope you may no[t] be detained. Let me recommend your going to Saratoga for at least two weeks—then to some place known to be healthy. In the mean while it may be determined what will next be done—when we are to meet *&* *where*. Gods! mercy grant it may be *here & in perfect happiness.* You say dearest "you may rejoice in moderation as much as you please" &c I do rejoice that at last your labours have been crowned with success—but at the same I tremble lest at too great a cost. So well do I know your noble nature I know you would never be content to set down on the little pittance left of our once ample fortune that you would work at whatever cost to your ease of person—age to whatever risk of life & as long as health & strength would permit. If you can now realize the worth of your labors I trust you will now be content with what you may have—once more *rest*—you need it. I grieve to hear you have nuralgia in your arm. I was in hopes you had got rid of that enemy. I wish I was by to rub it out with my "mustang liniment."

I rejoice to be able to say dear Appy has got nearly rid of those *splotches*—(we called them ring worms). Our good Cousin Amanda found out that a tea made of the leaves of the "walnut tree" was good—Appy had not drank of it a week before they nearly all disappeared—this tea should be drank cold—$^1/_2$ pint a day sufficient—it is a great purifier of the blood. Butler is writing to you—he will inform you of Mr Dunhams intention to leave our employ at the end of this year &c also that he left our dear Tip safe & well in Roswell under Mr Pratts care. Butler thought it would be better for Tip to go at the time he did his eyes appeared to be quite well. We have had one letter from Tip since Butler left him. Roswell is a healthy place. Mr & Mrs Pratt [are] exceedingly kind to the boys under their care. I wish now that I had sent Tip there in January instead of Savannah. It was *my weakness*. By yesterdays mail we heard from Mally—he & Floyd were well. Mr Woolley was driven from Savannah by the yellow fever—the inhabitants are flying in every direction—2 persons died in the house next *his* the day he left. The Cunninghams write that there is a perfect panic throughout the city. The love of making money will keep their brother at his post & they cannot leave him to die maybe alone. This has been & will be a year of trial to many—*God! grant it may not be to us*. Our last letter from Lord was dated the 7th from Springfield—I hope poor dear boy he may escape fever & Cholera. Oh husband dear how much I have to make me happy & yet how much to make me anxious. God! forgive me if I am not sufficiently grateful for the first—or sin by so constantly looking forward for evil.

It is delightful to us all having dear Andrew & Louisa with us—Louisa is so sweet & Andrew so good in his quiet way. I believe them *both to be perfectly sincere*. I love them both very dearly & hope they will not leave us until they are ready to return to Cuba. I will write again on Monday & hope to be able to say as I now do—*"all is well."* Our children both here & at Hamilton our dear brother & Sister unite in warm love to you my precious husband. May our prayers be granted for your health & safety. God! bless and guide you—guard you from every evil is the constant prayer of your devoted wife.

A M King

25[th August 1854]

The family here are all well. Brother Andrew adds another love to you and says "if you can't come South before it is time for him to leave for Cuba—he will go to you" as he cannot leave the country without seeing you.

Your own

Anna

(All pretty well)   Retreat 28th August '54

My own my beloved husband

I wrote you a long letter on Friday last acknowledging your three affectionate letters of the 31st Ult 2nd & 5th Inst. This letter I hope will reach N.Y. almost as soon as you will. By yesterdays mail we had the happiness to receive
your two messages by Telegraph one from N[ew] O[rleans] the other from
Augusta. Thank God! you were so far safe—thank you dearest for the kind
consideration which prompted you to relieve our anxiety by these dispatches.
The papers announce yellow fever both in N[ew] O[rleans] & Mobile. May the
mercy of God have preserved you from infection. May it be continued to you
& keep you from Cholera in N.Y.

This seems to be a year of affliction to many. The Savannah papers gloss
over the state of things in that City. From private sources—the City has not
been so severely visited since 1827—when you may recollect you hired the pi-
lot boat to bring us round rather than run the risk of passing through the city
on our return from the North. Hamilton Couper & Postell left S[avanna]h on
Saturday they give a dreadful account of the fatality of the fever. Mrs Joe Burroughs (eldest daughter of Judge Berrien) her husband & little daughter were
at the point of death. Their eldest Son dead—his wife (the daughter of Judge
Law) considered past hope. These gentlemen say the deaths average 20 per
day. The news papers make it *comparatively* light. 280 passengers went South
in the Mail Steamer on Saturday 700 left the same day for the North by the
N.Y. & Philadelphia steamers besides hundreds that are daily going to the Up
Country by the cars. The yellow fever is also in Charleston—probably to the
same extent as in Savannah. Tho' the Charleston papers make light of it. As ardently as I long to see you my own beloved husband I hope & trust you will not
venture South through such danger. If Gods! mercy spares your precious life—
when you have finished your business in N.Y. go to some Watering place—
Saratoga may be the best. After your years of exposure to trying climates I do
think your constitution must require this step. May the blessings of God! rest
on you my precious husband—His holy spirit guide you—his mercy protect
you—& permit us all to meet again & that ere long.

I am thankful that I have no evil news to give you. Our dear Tootee is not
well—I fear there *is a cause for this.*[1] Her good husband & the dear children are
as well as the hot weather will admit.

In my last I mentioned that dear Appy had got rid of *those splotches.* I flatter
myself her general health is better—Georgia looks pretty well white washed—
but says she feels perfectly well. Florence looks very well. Louisa does not gain
flesh as fast as we could wish, but she is *cheerful* & *quite happy with* us. Andrew
is fat & hearty, very quiet. Our dear good Butler was near being made sick by

his rapid travel to Roswell & back home then Mr Dunham went away for 5 days on some business of his own—this obliged Butler to attend to the business of the Plantation which added to the stirring of the bile—& made him very unwell for several days. He now says he is quite well. Mrs Lara is in her usual health—as for myself you know I am *tough*.

My dear Cousin & her good husband are staying just now at Hamilton. I have no case of fever today. Dear Butler will give you the state of the crop.

Yesterdays Mail brought us letters from the dear boys. They were all well, our dear little Tip has written us three letters since Butler placed him at Mr Pratts School. He says "Mr & Mrs Pratt are very kind to me & I think he is a good teacher—the only faults I have to find is that the place is dull & Mr Pratt whips with a cow hide. I have not got it yet & hope never will." Mr J. H. Couper called to see brother Andrew on Saturday. He was at Marietta a few weeks ago—& gave us the gratification of hearing that dear Mallery is 3d from the head of the highest class (these three being much older & among the first at the Institute). For character & application none stand higher—he is loved & respected by the Teachers. This I know will gratify you as much as it has ourselves. Floyd is not killing himself with study—he unfortunately (I think) got into the entire good graces of Mrs Brumby (wife of the principal) this lady rules her husband as much as he rules the students. So whenever master Floyd wants an indulgence he has only to go to madame & he obtains it. Mr Couper says Floyd looked remarkably well—but he as well as all the other boys are dreadfully tan'd by the sun. The only covering to their heads in this hot sun are cloth caps with a leather front one inch wide. Tips vacation begins the first November—Malley & Floyds 20th December. If please God! Tip can return to Mr Pratt the first of January—he will have no vacation until the next Nov.

Louisa has just brought me a letter from Andrew to you—I believe it expresses no more than he really feels. He is naturally lazy about writing—*some thing like yourself dearest only when he is driven to it will he* take up his pen. He has been hurt by your never writing to him. I convinced him this morning your long silence has not been caused by want of love for him & his sweet wife—but press of constant care on your mind & the quantity of other writing to be done. I believe if ever a brother & sister in law loved a brother purely & disinterestedly it is Andrew & Louisa who loves their brother Thomas. I will keep them as long with me as I can. They add much to our cheerfulness & happiness. I am so glad all is now as it should be with us. They are convinced we love them from no *mercenary* motives. If your precious life is spared our dear boys who are away keep well—if Gods mercy spares these dear ones on this Island—if—but alas how many *ifs*. I was going to say if all keep well & we have a hope of seeing you & of all meeting again I will try & be cheerful if not happy

until all our wishes are consummated. I will try *& hope* all will yet meet again—
hope even tho' it is with trembling. Poor old Cupid always grins his joy when
I tell him I have heard from you. He says "If I can only put my eyes on Mossa
once more before I die—I will be happy."

The girls intend writing to you by this mail. I say nothing about your business dear husband—you know it is more for your own sake than for mine that
I wish you success. You are *too apt to be too liberal*—leaving the first sharing of
the loaves *and fishes* to others which ends in your getting *no share* at all. Try to
realize enough to purchase Hamilton my heart is set on this. My mortification
has been great—besides that it will be a much surer investment than any other
you can make. Be not too trusting *of those* New York men. They are too keen
for you. But enough if you have not had sufficient experience what I in my ignorance can say will avail nothing.

I have heard nothing from Lord since his letter from Springfield of the 7th
August. God grant all may be well with him. At church yesterday we saw the
most of your neighbors—on Wednesday Louisa, Andrew & myself are going
to Cannon's Point. The dear ones from Hamilton have promised to spend the
day here. I have just had a note from Tootee in which she begs her best her
warmest love to you. She is suffering from her hot ride to Church yesterday—
neither is our precious little Cooney well. We are all so anxious for that dear
childs safety. Praying this may find you in health—that the Mercy of God will
protect you from all evil & that we may again meet in happiness I am

> Your own affectionate & devoted wife
> A M King

>   29th
Last evening Andrew, Louisa, Butty and myself drove over to Hamilton Appy
& Flora on horse back. We found dear Tootee & our sweet little Cooney feeling better. All are well here. God grant dearest you may be as safe & well as we
all are this morning—write as soon as you can to your own loving wife

> Anna
> Retreat St Simons Isld

1. She was once again pregnant.

>   7th September '54
My one dearly beloved husband

Knowing how anxious you must be for our safety this trying season I shall
avail myself of every opportunity which offers to write to you. We had no mail

on Wednesday no mail boat left Savannah. The *Planter* came out & we hope will be on her return this evening. I hope to send this by her. Thank God! we are all pretty well dear Louisa getting strong again. Andrews cold better the rest of us as usual the dear ones at Hamilton *ditto.* We confidently hope the Sunday mail will bring us comforting intelligence from you my own dear husband as well as from our dear boys. I presume ere this Lord has seen you. How I do envy him the happiness. I am jealous even of the dirty Irish waitress & chambermaid. They see you, hear you speak and here we who love you so tenderly are debarred even from hearing often from you. Dearly beloved how long is this to be my cruel fate? I am fearful of saying that which may annoy you inducing you (by my complaints) to do that which you think contrary to your interest. I hold my peace when my heart urges me to implore of you to come home at any risk—not of your precious life dearest. I would rather you would remain away as long again than by returning risk you ever being made *ill*—much less you[r] invaluable life. At times I feel worn out with anxiety & desire to see you. Then I try & be patient—try to be cheerful & hopeful that the happiness of having you once more at home is yet in store for us *all.*

This is in truth a stormy day—high wind—some rain & very high tide. I am trembling for our crop. Butler says "there is no use crying" but I can't help *thinking.* I hope it will not carry away Williams nice wharf. It was quite finished on Monday last & will I hope long stand a monument of dear Williams patient endurance of hot sun, ingenuity & industry. If it stands there will be no more boarding steamboats in small boats or watching a loaded flat for days & nights waiting for Steamboats. But for the stormy weather our dear Tootee—her family & dear cousin would now have been with us. Her visits for the day is at all times cheering to us. We understand that though the fever in Savannah is on the increase there are fewer deaths—the Physicians seem to understand better than they did at first the treatment of the disease. We are in great uneasiness about poor John Fraser his Physician wrote to William that *his* was a case of bilious & not yellow fever. Poor fellow! God grant he may recover. H[annah] Page wrote to me this morning that Mr Postell had fever—this is all I have heard of any of the white inhabitants of the Island being sick at present. Gods mercy grant this may not be with us another *1852.*

Butler is writing to you & will tell you all about Plantation affairs I am so glad to shift the burden off of my shoulders on to his strong young ones. I think as little as I can possibly help when he is at home & well does he discharge these duties. Louisa is quite content to stay with us as long as they remain in the U.S. Andrew however speaks of going North the first of next month. If money was plentiful—if all could go & if you can't come to us gladly would I say we will all come but as I fear all these ifs are not to be removed that you my own pre-

cious one cannot think it prudent to venture. I must content myself to wait patiently as I can until it will be prudent for you to return home ere I can have
the happiness to see you again. This is a sad trial! God! help me to bear it!!!

The wind is so high & so jerks this house I find it hard to write. I rather think
the *Planter* will have to lie to until it subsides. But I must finish this & send it over
to Hamilton. Butler holds himself in readiness to go to you whenever you say
"come on." I shall hate to have him go—but have not the heart to keep him
from you. I doubt not you are very much occupied—I can only hope you will
be able to find time to write to me often & fully. Andrew had a letter from
Brother Henry last Sunday—he affirms that he had Cholera when out west
but was then quite well. Have you ever answered his last letter? Henry is truly
a good man—well deserving the love of all of us. We heard last week from
young Stephen King—they were all (in health) as usual. I believe your brother
has made a very good nice crop. Andrew did think of making him another visit
before leaving Georgia. I have done all I could to dissuade him from going
again—fearing it will make them sick. I have been exceedingly gratified by this
visit of theirs to us. Louisa says (and she acts as if perfectly sincere) that all she
has to love in the world after her husband are ourselves. She is truly sweet &
loveable. When they go God! knows if we shall ever meet again. I hope we will
all ever remember these pleasant days passed together with unalloyed pleasure.
If *circumstances* will allow of your coming to us my blessed husband whilst this
fever rages in Savannah you will I trust use every precaution from infection. In
the last Savannah paper I see noticed the treatment of a Dr P. H. Wildman. I
enclose it to you—yet trusting you may never be called on to use it.

The girls will be writing to you by the Tuesday mail when I hope again to have
this pleasure. Yesterday evening our dear Tootee & Cousin A[manda] com-
missioned me to send warm love to you & William his best regards—the children kisses. Cooney—says "I love Uncle Tom now & want him to come home
very bad." Butler sends his own love in his own letter. G[eorgia], F[lorence] &
V[irginia], Andrew & Louisa send thousands of love & Mattie her regards. The
servants all beg to be remembered. Praying God! to bless you dearest—keep
you from all danger & restore you to your home & to your devoted wife

                                    A M King

                                    Retreat 22nd September '54

My own beloved husband

We are in the midst of another storm. God! only knows how much it will add
to our losses—but if human life is but spared I will with his help try to be cheerful. His mercy forbid I should presume to murmur. In the last letter which I
wrote you I then mentioned the weather was rainy. We had gone over but 40

acres after the storm of the 7th & when it again set in to rain & has been rain-ing ever since off & on until yesterday noon when it set in with a will—I have never seen a greater fall of water in twenty four hours than in this last. Our yard & [?] is like a pond. We are doing all we can to let it off—rest assured dearest I will [use] every means in my power to keep fever from the family. I fear most for the dear ones at Hamilton the house is so old & decayed so very unwhole-some in wet weather. Let me not look a head for trouble—rather be thanking God we are yet in health as well as life. Not as those poor sufferers in Savan-nah. If deprived of the luxuries we may still have the necessaries of life & if pos-sessed of all the luxuries—how would they be enjoyed if all did not live to share them. When I think of how thousands are this moment suffering from loss of friends sickness & actual poverty. I look on myself with fear & trembling lest Gods wrath may be kindled against me for daring to be discontented at the loss of crop—negros & horses. If others are more blessed with fortune than I am. Surely none other is more blessed in a good affectionate husband—& devoted promising children than I am.

On Tuesday I accompanied Tootee & Amanda to call on poor Mrs Dr Fraser she gave us a melancholy account of the state of things in Savannah—Bears her own irreparable loss thus far better than could be expected poor thing she does not yet fully realize it. Dearly beloved risk not your precious life by attempt-ing to pass through that City in the condition it now stands. Should you be de-tained there—nothing but death shall prevent my going to you.

Saturday 23d

You must not think it strange my writing to you by snatches. In the first place I have long made it a rule to write to each dear absent one once every week (a duty as well as a pleasure) and it serves too to remind you of my existence. Then it is so pleasant to me—to write by piece meal like tasting a sweet morsel—not devouring the whole at once. May Gods mercy have protected you my blessed husband. As has thus far we have been protected. We have not had much wind with this storm—tho' it may yet come as the wind still sticks to NE. But rain we have had without measure. It commenced on Saturday night—over flowing again the land, then every day showers until Thursday 21st then it came on like another flood all that day & night—all yesterday—holding up last night. The yard a complete pond. I begin to hope just now that the worst is over.

Florence, Appy & Mattie are gone to spend the day with Tootee—just for a little exercise Andrew & Butty are gone to see how the poor cotton crop looks. Louisa & Georgy have put on india rubbers & gone to walk. I your loving wife take the chance to hold a little communion with you my precious husband. Oh! may God! protect you & all of us & permit us to meet again in life. We try to be cheerful—but do not at all times succeed—Again we are doubtless of having a Mail. Not only on account of the weather but on account of the brutal conduct of some people in Jacksonville. They actually fired 4 times at the *Welaka* on Tuesday last—one ball passing through the ladies cabbin. So great an outrage I hope will be punished in some way or other to prevent other recurrences of the kind. I hope "at all events" the culprits may be made to pay the damage done the boat. Butty tells me that he understood Capt King will go as far as St Marys with the Mail so we hope we shall have a mail tomorrow. And I hope dearest it will bring for me a long letter from you.

Tho' full of apprehension lest sickness will follow so much rain. Still we try to pass the time cheerfully. Our visiting even Hamilton has been nearly put a stop to—the mornings are too hot and we fear being out after dark. After the girls have got through their lessons & I have my wanderings—we settle down in my room Louisa or Georgia reading aloud whilst the others sew—In this way the time passes very pleasantly. Yesterday we got through *The household of Sir Thomas More* by his daughter Margaret More. Beautifully written it is. This little book was given me two years ago by an old friend—Mrs Joseph Burroughs—Now the eldest daughter of Judge Barrien—lately & by this fever the widow of Joe Burroughs—her oldest son one of the first victims of this dreadful fever. Poor "Veleria." She came to see me when we were in Savannah in the Autumn of '52—and did seem to sympathize with me in the sorrow I felt at the loss of my little grand child—God knows I now, truly feel for her—she has in the space of a few weeks lost her grown son—her husband and a brother in law. Oh husband dear! when I look around me and count over my early friends—how many are less blessed than I am how many widowed—and how many bereft of grown children. Truly God! has been merciful to us. We have had our trials which have caused you & I to live years separated—still we have lost but 2 in 21 years to grieve for. We feel tho separated in the body our hearts are still united in form & faithful love. I have every cause to love honor & trust in you my own beloved. And God! knows I have done nothing to make you distrust me or love me less than when near 30 years ago we were pronounced man & wife. And look on our goodly sons & daughters our son in law & our dear grand children not one thus far thank God for whom we have had cause to blush. They all have faults who is perfect dearest? No not one. But their virtues are greater than their faults. "Praise the Lord Oh my soul! and all that is within me, praise his holy name."

24th Sunday noon

As yet no Mail. We fear there will be none to day. We all feel dull & apprehensive—William intends going to Darien tomorrow. I will finish this letter

& send it by him if no boat passes between this & tomorrow morning. Neither Andrew or Louisa are very well—they speak of leaving us in the first boat for Savannah—will stop at Thunderbolt—hire a carriage to take them to meet the cars. For the last few weeks there has been a considerable disturbance. I have heretofore kept it from you but now that they speak of going—I will tell you the plain, unvarnished story.

I shall have to go back to I can't now remember what year. When Louisa took Mrs Lara under her protection. A poor friendless widow be witched orphan of 16 years old. From that time until they came here the first week in August "Mattie" stood as No 1 with Andrew & Louisa. Some years ago before Mr Savage came here you may recollect Andrew proposed that he should pay her for teaching our daughters music, french & Spanish. This we declined not having room for her. When we met in New Haven in 1852 Brother Andrew asked me what I intended doing with my daughters. I told him "try & get a good Governess & bring them home." He at once proposed his Protege Mrs Lara. Spoke of her in the very highest terms & of their love for her. I acceded. But when I lost my precious Isabel—my conscience led me to dread the introduction of a Catholic in the bosom of my family. And I told Andrew when we parted in N.Y. not to send her, until he should hear from me on my arrival at home. This he says he did not hear—probably not as he is a little deaf—& several persons being near I did not speak loud. I did not write as I said I would—I put it off until too late. She came. We were all prepared to love her on Louisa's & Andrews account. I have never seen Mrs Lara do an unladylike—imprudent act her reluctance to bodily exertion, the only real disadvantage I could discern she could possibly be to the family. This I thought induced our daughters to keep as much within doors as she did. I have ever looked on her conduct toward our sons as perfectly modest & proper. We all treated her with great kindness—first on Louisa & Andrews account & then on her own account. But I had no intention of keeping her after this year.

Soon after Andrew came we talked the matter over he said "all the money she had was in his hands—it was not sufficient for her to live on & he advised her to get some other situation & continue teaching a few years longer & she made up her mind to follow his advice.["] Then A[ndrew], Louisa & our daughter went to see brother Stephen. When Andrew proposed to Brother S[tephen] "that I should keep Mattie she to instruct Stephens little girl, & Anna—Stephen paying Mattie $500—per annum—I did not like to but as the proposition was accepted by Stephen—and considering the advantage it would be to Anna & feeling deeply for the motherless Nina. More than all, not supposing you would object—I accede[d]. Soon after, I perceived a coolness on the part of Louisa, to Mattie who bore it with respectful even cheerful indurance. Think-

ing it did not concern me I made no comment on it, even to my children.
When on the 14th our dear ones from Hamilton all dining here the whole matter exploded. Andrew & Louisas coldness & contempt for Mattie made known
to me. It was that they had taken into their heads & (there is no driving the idea
out) that Mattie was trying to catch Butler. The idea to all of us was prepos-
terous but nothing we could say could change their opinion. Neither of them
would speak to Mrs Lara and things were becoming so very disagreeable.
Henry King & John Fraser being here. Mrs Lara begged me to allow her to
keep her room—only coming down to give music lessons. This gave additional
offence—so Andrew went up into her room & there they had a real quarrel. In
all this Andrew & Louisa are much to blame. If they really believed she was trying to catch Butler—the terms on which they had lived with her for 10 years
admitted of their questioning her by themselves—if by look or manner their
suspicions were confirmed—then they may have warned Butler & myself. Instead of which they treated her with contemptuous coldness until she withdrew
from their sight—then Andrew went into her room & added insult to contempt by accusing her of trying to gain his affections. This she denied saying
positively she thought no more of B[utler] as a husband than he did of her as
making her his wife. Andrews manner was very insulting. She does possess a
violent temper—this she has never denied to us—she lost all command over
herself—& ordered him to leave her room. Now in this I can not blame her—
I would have done the same.

    After all this (after telling us that Mrs De Lara was illegitimate doubtful her
being married to Dr Lara—ungrateful to them & a schemer to get our son to
marry her) Andrew thinks or says "I have done nothing to injure her—but she
has been very ungrateful & insulting to me." I intended to have kept this from
you until we met but as Andrew will certainly mention it to you you would naturally & very properly be surprised by my being silent on the subject. I have no
reason to think their suspicions correct. I feel for the poor friendless woman—
Those she most loved & trusted on earth have turned to be her worst enemys.
I blame her for not (as soon as she saw Louisas coldness) demanding the cause.
I blame her (tho I cannot wonder at her) for the words she used to Andrew she
was provoked to it. I would have expressed the same to both Andrew & Louisa—
you have often told me my husband that 2 wrongs never made a right. I attribute A[ndew] & L[ouise's] conduct to having lived so long in retirement—
their minds have become morbid. I have no doubt we all displease them by not
taking a stand on their side—never a word has passed between Mrs L[ara] and
myself on the subject. I treat her when we meet just the same. She has said
nothing to me or I to her. I am trying to act well my part. I side with neither.
I am kind to both parties. I can but hope the worst is over. Under such cir-

cumstances I do not press your brother to remain longer. With prudence & money I think they can pass from here to N.Y. without taking infection. I cannot turn Mrs Lara out of doors—for no harm I can see she has done. Dear Butler has acted nobly throughout the affair. It has been hard work to please them & not side with them. Much could I tell—but not on paper. I wish you to be on your guard. Do not condemn poor Mrs Lara when there is no cause. I cannot turn her out of our house until the year is up.

I love both Andrew & Louisa very dearly—And really grieve such has been the termination of their visit to us. We were all as happy—as the absence of yourself and the boys would admit of. And they too seemed so happy until this crotchet entered their heads. Had they done right—all this would not have happened—as it is I fear there is no keeping it a secret—and as news of this kind always gains instead of losing there is no telling what will be made of it. Andrew is very anxious dear Butler should go on North with him. This Butty has no desire to do unless you want him. And unless you do dearest I think he had better remain quietly at home. I hope you have not been wearied out by my prolixity. I did not intend when I began this letter to touch on this annoying subject but as the boat may come on & they leave us—I think you should be prepared for what they will certainly tell you. I feel very sorry for Mrs Lara—I do not think her guilty of what they accuse her as regards Butler. What she was before she left Cuba they knew as well then, as now. They then ascribed to her every virtue—every good quality a woman could possess. I do not think her any worse for having lived 21 months with us. I will try to keep cool & correct both in my judgement—& conduct to both parties. Should there be a Mail on Tuesday you will have letters from some of the girls & from Butler. All unite in love to you my blessed husband.

God! bless & protect you—

Your own devoted wife

A M King

24th September

We are all well to day.

Retreat 4th October '54

My own dearly beloved husband,

I received Lordys letter yesterday of the [blank] by which we are all rejoiced to hear of the continued good health of yourself dear Butler & Lordy. I hope by this time you have made your visit to dear brother Henry—are about closing your business in N.Y. & will soon be ready to turn your *face once more home-*

ward. Oh husband dear God grant this long hoped for return to your home & family may be one of unalloyed happiness to us all. Gods mercy still permits us to say "all are well." Georgia & Virginia each have colds—but not severe. I spent actually 7 days with our dear ones at Hamilton—the eighth day Amanda & myself went to make a call at the Hazzards dined with Miss Gould & returned to Retreat in the evening. On Wednesday Mr Woolley kindly went to Bryans landing for our daughters & Mrs Lara they got home safe & not a little gratified by their visit to the Grants. Poor young things it is very natural they should occasionally wish a change.

By the papers received yesterday we see the absentees are invited to return to their homes in Savannah. Our good cousin Amanda will leave us next Thursday for home—we shall miss her very much. Yesterday evening Hamilton & Alex Couper were here. The former returns to Savannah tomorrow. The Couper family remove to Hopeton on Wednesday. We have not had the slightest frost on this Island—tho' several times the weather was quite cold. On the night of the 29th we had quite a heavy rain—& off & on—on all day on Monday but it cleared off warm favorable neither to health or the last gleanings of cotton our fields are as green as they should be in August—& very little has opened since dear Butler left home. The Harvest of corn took 8 days the pease at this place 9 days the gang are now at Newfield harvesting pease—the negros unusually healthy. I have heard only of one death that of Mrs Staunton tho Mrs Oatman thought to be past hope is convalescent. Mr Randolph Spalding is also recovering.

We heard yesterday from our three dear boys Mallery, Floyd, & Tip—all were well. John Fraser found it necessary he should return to Savannah on the 1st fearing it would not be safe for Tip to stay a night in Savannah before the board of health pronounced it safe to do so he left Tip to come down with John Couper who was waiting in Marietta for this said report from the Board. I hope now by next Wednesday I shall see the dear boy. In a letter I received last week from Tip he said "I received a letter from dear Father on opening it out dropped a paper I took if up & what do you think it was dear Mother? My own letter to Father—he sent it back to show me how badly the words were spelt. I felt very small I assure you—deeply mortified he had so much cause to find fault with my poor letter." When Virginia got your last letter—she opened it exaltingly but when she read it she was deeply mortified & wept it was so different from the last letter she had received from you. Did *they* not tell you of the fault of other members of your family—of mine—Georgias & Florences? But I will forbear you. Butler & Lord cannot be more sick of the subject than I am. It would be well for me could I forget that such persons as A[ndrew] & his wife ever existed. I would certainly be more happy.

Georgia wrote to Butler by the Friday mail. I hope the Mail next Wednesday will bring me pleasant intelligence from you & our beloved sons—giving me some idea of when we may hope to see you. I hope you will all be careful how you eat *oysters*—accounts in Newspapers show an increase of Cholera produced by eating oysters in N.Y. I shall not have time by this Mail to write either Butler or Lord—hope to be able to do so by the next. I have always written to you & my children just as I felt is the reason I expressed myself so fully. If I have annoyed you I am sorry. Yet you could not have been half as much so with the subject as we have been by *the promoters* of it.

Our daughters & Cousin A[manda] send much love to you Mr Woolley his regards. Say all that is affectionate & kind to our beloved sons for me & their sisters.

I hope your visit to Allentown was pleasant. I know Henry would be glad to see you—his wife is certainly very hospitable. May God! bless & preserve you my own dear husband—my most fervent prayers are for yours & our beloved childrens happiness & welfare.

> Your affectionate & devoted wife
> A M King

Private

                    17th In health all well   Retreat 16th October 54

My own beloved husband

The mail yesterday which is the first we have had since the *4th* brought no later intelligence from you than your letters to Butler & Georgia of the 22nd Ult. I opened the one to Butler barely to see if of later date than the one to me by the mail of the 4th & have read only the date. I can but hope the confusion in the P[ost] O[ffice] in Savannah is the cause of my not hearing from you yesterday. We had no less than 5 letters from dear little Tip & 2 from Mallery. They & Floyd were well on the 12th Inst.

I hope ere this reaches you our dear Butler will have arrived safe in N.Y. I very much fear the impression Andrew will try to make on you to induce you to influence our beloved Butler to accede to their plan of having him go to Cuba. Butler *promised* me he would make no such agreement *at present*—God! *grant he never may.* You have been so long separated from Andrew & are now so much occupied by other matters you will in the first place be overjoyed to see him as *he well may* be to see you. He will boast to you of his great wealth & of the advantages it would give Butler to go & live with them on a high salary &c &c from what I have gathered from Andrew & Louisa—he owes now fully to the amount of the share he holds in that estate. $40,000 of *borrowed money* he has to pay for the two shares which belonged to her brothers—he owns but his wifes share—the rest belongs to the Molineaus—besides this the immense amount he is to pay or has paid of *borrowed* money for his machinery. He or the estate may give Butler the 4000 a year as salary but at what cost to *soul & body* may not this be to our beloved son. *If* he should undertake the business he would try to discharge his duty faithfully—just imagine the exposure to that climate. But this would not be the *worst* of it. Just look at *Andrews appearance look into the cause.* For Butler to be shut up on that plantation with no other society but Andrew & his wife—he would be *utterly* ruined in both *body & mind.* Andrew has been here over two months—I do not know what his mind and habits were before he left this country. It required no great penetration to discover he was of excessively weak mind (*could not tell the same story, twice, the same*)—was *muddled* half the time, completely under the *thumb* of his wife. So much for Andrew who I can't but *pity*, though his *deviation from truth* & submitting to being a tool in the hands of his wife inspired *contempt.*

His wife is still more to be dreaded, of a jealous vindictive temper, passions as strong as those of her *color* usually are. Had she been as prudent in her conduct towards Butler! They accuse Mrs Lara of indiscreet conduct. I have already told you this *is false.* If Louisa carries on before *you*, as she did here—you will think with us! that if she was one hundredth part as modest & well behaved as Mrs Lara we should all have been better pleased—for her *kissing* and *hugging* were so disgusting—it became revolting to *visitors* as well as our selves— the wonder to me is *her* husband *permitting* it or that Butler *submitted* to it all. So great was her boldness to Butler—the very servants *sneered* at it. *What* would Butler have thought if he had seen one of his sisters fondle Andrew as she did him. What if Tootee had kissed & hugged Hamilton or John Fraser as she did Butler—they are as near to her as Butler is to Louisa.[1] What would you have thought if when I was of *her* age—I had kissed—hugged—fondled one of your brothers. Would it not have caused you *suspicion* & disgust. If she goes on before you as she did here—I need say *no more.* And poor weak mind'd muddled Andrew!!—As much as I love my Butler as much as I can *now* trust to his honor I would rather follow him to his grave than see him go to Cuba. It is not likely she will go on before *you* as she did *here* but believe me when I say She is *jealous, vindictive* & of *ungovernable passions*, neither does she *regard truth*—tho' more guarded in *this*, than her weak husband. If it please God! we ever meet I can tell you much more. What I most grieve at, is, that my beloved Butler was so *completely blinded.* In fact during the latter part of their stay here—he seem'd perfectly miserable. It was a bitter pill for us all to swallow their *triumph*, in having him go with them. They said over & over again *they would stay until you wrote for Butler*—they could not go without Butty. *He & I* invariably answered unless you wrote for him Butler would not leave me. Here they did stay, tho' conscious their conduct had rendered us all uncomfortable. Andrew assumed a very unpleasant dictatorial manner to William and when Mrs Lara appointed William to receive the money Andrew borrowed from her—he be came perfectly outraged—his wife accusing William to *me* of having acted *indelicately* in accepting the trust from Mrs Lara. And when they did go—she addressed Tootee as *Mrs Couper* & purposely avoided bidding good bye to William until after she got on board—tho he was standing on the wharf. She is as fickle in her fancies as she is violent in her dislikes—it will take but little to make her hate Butler as much as she now *loves* him. I think Butler was perfectly right in his endeavours to treat as *your Brother* his uncle Andrew whilst under your roof. I tried to do the same. I shut my ears & eyes as much as was possible to every think [*sic*] against Andrew & Louisa. But *memory* was still alive. Could I have supposed all which was to follow the first knowledge I received of the cause of her hate to Mrs Lara my course would have been different. My object was peace. It was new to me, quarrels, under our peaceful roof.

My idea is—she will not let Andrew return to Cuba as long as Butty remains in N.Y. *I entreat* of you to *advise our dear Son* to return to me as soon as you can *spare his services.* God! grant you may soon return to us yourself. If we have but little of this worlds goods, thank God! we are pure in *birth* & *principles* and *have* been happy within ourselves. I *will not* believe that their influence will ever render us otherwise. Their boasted wealth has never increased my respect for either of them but I did believe they were both true friends of our family. I believe poor Andrew really loves Butler but he will only *love him or any* one *of the other children* as long as his wife *will tell him to do so.* In 1852 both Andrew & Louisa treated both Lord & Georgia very unkindly. As regards Georgia, Andrew was less unkind than his wife was. I again say—we have parted with them may we never again meet. With my consent a child of mine shall never be under their roof or their *influence.* I do not think I was ever more unhappy than I now am my whole thoughts are taken up about you & Butler. I dread lest you should allow your noble mind to be warped by their misrepresentations.

I know nothing about the plantation affairs further than regards the sick— only two cases of fever have occurred since Butty left & they are light. We have had no rain since the 30th the water between this & N[ew] F[ield] is fast drying up & looks badly. During the day the sun is very hot, mornings & evenings very cool & pleasant, heavy dews at night. Our dear Tootee & the children are here for a morning visit all are well. I know of no sickness among our neighbors if we could have occasional showers I think the Island would continue healthy. God! grant it may, that sickness or death may not be added to our other troubles. I can but hope the Wednesday mail may bring us pleasant intelligence from you beloved ones. That you my beloved will be able to tell me when I may hope for the happiness of seeing you. Oh my husband what labor both of mind & body you have undergone what risk of life have you not run, since you last saw your old home. It is hard to bear when all this has been for nothing. But Gods! will be done. If you can be content to live on the little we have—to be satisfied with our lonely life—it will be our endeavor to cheer you in your solitude to dispel all your regrets by our affectionate loving attentions. Let us but continue our love & *confidence* in each other. Let us live on in harmony if we are even to die in poverty. Come home dearest husband. We will do our best to make you happy.—

Mallery has probably written you of the decline in the G[eorgia] M[ilitary] I[nstitute] poor boy he is much chagrin'd & disappointed—I hope we may be able to find the means to send him as well as Floyd elsewhere to conclude the education of the one & carry that of the other. Malley thinks the present term will be brought to an end the 15th of November. Tips vacation begins the 1st of November. John Fraser has offered to take charge of him & bring him down to Savannah as soon as there has been a frost in that City & send him home to me. John will leave for Marietta the end of this week.

I have written a long letter to Lord giving him the best advice I can—poor Lord! it is hard to convince him he will have to depend on his own exertions for a living. In justice to the younger boys it is full time he should begin to do for himself.

I have no doubt Georgia who never neglects a duty will write to you by this mail. Florence tells me she has written. I will write to my own beloved Butler having already written to Lord, Malley, Floyd & Tip. It grieves me to write the unpleasant *truths* I have lately been filling my letters to you. But I felt it to be my duty. I know you have great influence with our beloved son. Help me to save him—if he goes to Cuba he will be lost to himself & to us & in the end be poorer in purse than he leaves us. Just keep your eyes open & if she goes on in N.Y. as she did here you will think as we do. He would not admit the truth when with us. It may irritate him as it did when told of it here should you tell him the contents of this letter. Keep the contents to yourself—unless you have the cause we have had to doubt her purity.

All send love to you & my beloved boy. Praying God! to bless—to protect & to guide you safe—both safe home I am as ever your devoted wife

A M King

17th

I fear you will think I was over excited when I wrote this letter. I acknowledge I am never very calm when I think over what has occurred. It is to save our beloved Butler from ruin I have I have [*sic*] tried to open your eyes to the *true* state of the case.

1. Anna refers here to Tootee's nephews by marriage, Hamilton Couper and John Fraser.

Hamilton
25 & 26th October 1854

My own dearly beloved husband

I dispatched a letter to you & Butty only yesterday, if received you will not be surprised this is dated from Hamilton instead of Retreat. This days Mail has been received & brought me your affectionate letter of the 16th also one from our dear Tip of the 20th. Thank God! you were able to say yourself & our dear sons were well & that dear little Tip assures me of his own good health. Our daughters & Mrs Lara left Anna & myself at Retreat yesterday before breakfast. William saw them safe over the rough water. Tootee was sick & as I had not come over with the girls he could not go all the way with them he got into his sail boat & went along until he saw that they would go safe. My good cousin went to visit the Bourkes in the *Planter*. I am so comfortable here with our beloved daughter & dear William & my darling little grandchildren I do not think I shall return home before Monday. Cousin A[manda] will then be back & I can go home without the dread of being too lonely.

On *your account dearest* husband I am glad to hear of your prospects brightening. I try to think as little of it as possible only praying you may be given strength to bear all the disappointments you may meet after having worked so hard—undergone so many perils & at so great a sacrifice of our domestic happiness. Tootee is up today & I hope will have no more pain yet a while. William has gone to Oatlands—I heard from home just now all was well there.

I have read your letter with attention & *no little pain*. It is as I feared it would be. You have taken part with the strong against the weak. The only part of Mrs Laras conduct to Andrew King or his wife which I told you I disapproved of was her letting her temper get the better of her when he went into her private chamber to *insult* her. Had any man dared to insult *me* as *he did her* I would have turned him neck & heels out. Still I was, *sorry for her sake* that she lost [her] temper. I again say their conduct to her was cruel, base, & cowardly. It was all their doing Mrs Lara ever was an inmate of our house. All they tell you of Mrs Lara *if true* was known to them when *they sent* her into my family. When they came here, *& without* consulting *me* or *Tootee & William* made arrangements with Stephen that *I should keep Mrs Lara & take charge of Stephens daughter*, & let Anna share the instruction of Mrs Lara. From the first knowledge we had of Mrs Laras being in existence, to the time they quarrelled with her they had both of them (Andrew & his wife) represented Mrs Lara to us, to be all that was *perfect* in every sense of the word. If Andrew King believed or had any reason to even doubt her *not being* the *lawful wife of De Lara* how could they have invited such a woman with *her paramour to be inmates of their house—how dare* he recommend *& send to me to be an inmate of our house a companion of our* daughters—an illegitimate, abandoned woman, artful &c. As regards her loss of fortune—they did not to the last deny her having lost her all by that Bank, neither need they for I have seen not long since a letter from Davidson one of the Executors of Broadfoot on this subject. As to her age—In '52 Louisa told us in New Haven her "dear Mattie" was just 22. No my beloved husband you have allowed that poor weak brother of yours & his malignant, vindictive & I fear impure wife to turn you against a lone woman who I firmly believe is innocent of all they charge her with (*that she can help*). Mrs Andrew King threatened "to turn her out of doors—to crush her, destroy her—she should not have a roof to cover her—a cent to buy her bread."[1] This was said by her before Mrs Lara ordered him [Andrew] out of her bed room. If he was an honorable man he would have *himself offered* to pay her the money he *had of hers*, not when she asked him to do so—refuse to do so before the year was up & putting off that year from January to April. What is more they cannot with truth say she lived on them on their charity. The $5\frac{1}{2}$ years she was under their roof she gave Mrs Andrew King regular lessons on the piano & Guitar & did as much of their sewing as would of itself have paid her board. Neither did Louisa deny this after the quarrel, for when Andrew called her "an object of charity" Louisa said ["]no Andrew she earned her living when with us." I did not intend again to write to you on this disagreeable subject but your letter compels me to it.

Andrew King & his wife left here triumphant—they left with a determination to poison your mind against this friendless lone woman they left determining to keep her out of her money as long as they could. Oh my husband do not let your noble mind be swayed by such as they are. Andrew it is true is your brother but she could *never have* been your Sister. Deeply do I regret their visit to us. They found us as happy a family as could be, when the beloved head & 4 sons were absent. We did all in our power to make them as happy as we were. I tried to keep peace—I treated them with kindness. They have done, they are doing, & will try to make us as unhappy as they can. Oh! let them not succeed in this too. I shall now request Mrs Lara (I have from the first to this day, *studiously avoided saying anything to Mrs Lara about their conduct to her). I will now ask her to tell me all that* from her *first unfortunate* acquaintance with Mr & Mrs Andrew King to the time of their coming to Retreat this summer. *I will have it all written down she will take an oath to it* before a magistrate & I will read it to you when you & dear Butler get home. In the 22 months Mrs Lara has been with us *I have never had cause to doubt her varacity.* All I ask of you my beloved husband is to let your own noble pure heart govern you. Put a stop at once to *their gossip*—I had for peace, to do this. Butler had to do the same. They are gone from the peaceful home they found me in. I sincerely *hope I may never see either of them again.*

As soon as Mrs Lara returns I will request her to seek another situation. I shall owe her about $450—this sum I will ask the Andersons to advance for me. Mrs A L K[ing] represented her acquirements in Music, French & Spanish to me as perfect as was her lady like deportment. I cannot conscientiously say that I have ever seen any thing in Mrs Lara to disapprove of. I can but hope *she will* find a *better protector than she has yet found in this cold world* & may do well. I liked her first from *the character given of her by her now bitter calumniators. I learned to like her better for her* correct amiable deportment. That our Florence & Virginia have improved so little under her tuition I blame them & myself more than Mrs Lara. They neither of them will ever play in company I have not compelled them to do this. Their French even Mrs Andrew King cannot find fault with—their Spanish I hope they will never *need in Cuba.*

Since I have felt myself compelled to mention this disagreeable subject to you I have been robbed of half my pleasure in writing to you or Butler. I speak of it as little as possible to our daughters. I have a constant dread less they may injure my beloved Butler. God! grant they may not succeed in this! Oh my husband return to us bring home my Butler. Let us be again a happy family. Money may add to happiness but it does not constitute happiness, unless *united with love, respect, confidence.* We had but little money but love, confidence in each other was perfect when those people came to Retreat. I am just about as miserable a wife & Mother as *they* could wish to make me. Do not let them rob us of our *Butler.* Would you have Butler like Andrew? No, no, come home! come home! Oh! that you were both now here. *I will not retract a single word I have written on this disagreeable subject.* All I have said in writing I would have preferred saying in person. I would you had been at home this summer then none of this may have happened—at all events you would *have seen & judged for yourself* of the propriety of Mrs Laras conduct & the *impropriety of theirs.*

God! grant you & dear Butler may be here by the middle of next month. By letters received from Savannah today, we have heard of the death of Parson Prestons oldest son & that Lovat Fraser is far gone in consumption. Oh! how much real misery is in this world, God! has mercifully blessed us with life & health. Why should we allow the false hood & malignity to interrupt our happiness. If Lord is still with you ask him how Andrew & his *wife* treated him about the New Port cottage commissioning Lord to go & hire a cottage then denying having ever done so. How unkindly *she* treated both Lord & Georgia *with cold contempt,* if they dared do *so to two of our children* how much more they will dare insult & belie a friendless woman. If I had not burned the letters I received from Louisa—from the time they first knew Mrs Lara to their coming here (I did so unfortunately this very last spring when putting my papers in order) you could read for your own satisfaction, the terms used in favor of Mrs Lara their loving her as they would a child of their own their desiring to adopt her as their daughter, the pleasure & comfort Mrs Lara was to them.

Mrs Lara['s] *amiability* & *accomplishments*—her *independent spirit refusing* to be *indebted to them for board & lodging after Louisa* would take *no more lessons* from *her—their great distress her going to the De Chapels.* If you had time to listen to *all* they will tell you & would *pay attention to what they say* you will find as many contradictions as stories. Andrew *runs so far wide his wife the whole time drawing him within possibilities.* You thank God! that your *wife & daughters are amiable charitable* &c &c always *telling the truth* &c &c. Have a *sensitive repugnance* to *injustice* of any *kind* &c. *Thank God! every word true! We have each a love of truth,* We *are each by nature,* education, & *birth pure* & lovers of charity & common justice. I told Andrew & his wife that in no one instance had I ever seen an *imprudent* act or heard an imprudent word *or seen an imprudent look* from Mrs Lara. Thus far *I say to you* the same. All I heard of Mrs Lara before she came here was through Andrew & his wife, no woman could have been more highly spoken of than she was by them. All I have seen of Mrs Lara after a residence in my family of 22 months no woman could have *conducted herself with more modesty & general* decorum than she has. Her age is of no importance tho Louisa wrote to me that her marriage with De Lara was before her "dear Mattie" was 15 & that she had grown taller after coming to live with them. Mrs & Mr De Lara were both Catholics—were married by a Priest—Andrew *saw the certificate of their marriage* & De Lara published their marriage *on his coming to Charleston.* Mrs Lara is claimed as Cousin by the Simmons in Charleston. I am sorry my beloved husband that so revolting a subject should take up so much of a letter between me & a beloved husband who I have not seen for near a twelvemonth.[2] But I can't bear that your generous noble mind should be perverted. If you & I live or who ever lives to see it, Andrew & his *wife will yet have cause to repent their cruel conduct* to Mrs Lara. Let him pay her money. The more he now says against her the more he will have to unsay.—

I am glad for one thing—they have shown *their true character* he a weak, muddle minded untrue man. She a *violent, vindictive, calumniating jealous* woman loving one moment hating the next & leading him to do & say what she pleases. Let *them but leave my husband* & *children* as *they found them* & I ask no greater favor from them. I fear they will prolong their stay in the U.S. All I ask of you is *to suspend* your judgement until we meet which God! grant may be soon, & to give *no encouragement to our beloved Butlers going to Cuba*—or to their *fulsome gossip*. And tell *Butler to be as little in public with her* as possible unless you & Andrew are present. I have said my say & I hope have done no more than my duty in saying what I have.

William has gone to Hogcrawl after Cattle today. Our beloved Tootee sends you & her brothers a thousand loves—the children send their kisses. Yesterday when Cooney saw I was writing he asked to whom & when I told him said tell Uncle Tom "I think it is time he came home." I think so too. Just to think the 9th of next month will be 4 years. I may not write on Monday unless the letters on Sunday calls for an answer. I cannot write to my beloved Butler or Lord today—Give my fond love to both. May God! bless you belov'd and quickly restore you to your home your children and your devoted wife.

A M King

We are all in our usual health this morning. Our mails are again in a state of confusion. We had one on Wednesday have *another today* & then will have to wait until next Wednesday for the next. I can scarcely expect to hear from you again today. My dear Cousin got back last night & gives a melancholy account of the health of St Marys. John Floyd oldest son of Geo Floyd—Hamilton (his cousin) are among the victims to yellow fever. At *Fancy Bluff* 2 deaths from yellow fever 2 others dying—3 recovering. Death in every direction—God has mercifully spared us. Let us try & live more worthy of Gods mercy. I understand a number of deaths have lately occurred along the S[outhern] R[ail] R[oad] on the St Marys river—of yellow fever. Mr Woolley saw Dr Curtis at St Marys who told him up to Tuesday last there had been 35 deaths from yellow fever in that little town 82 cases on hand. Mr W[oolley] did not land—& slept but a few minutes at the wharf. I will write to my beloved Butler & Lordy by the Mail which will leave the Island on the 29th. All send love to you my husband & to our good Son & dear Lordy if he is with you.

May God! preserve you in health.

Your own wife
A M King

1. Louisa's outcry that she would "crush" Mattie was no idle or empty threat. Without reputation and Andrew King's patronage (or Thomas Butler King's), she had few, if any, options in life. Without her husband's support, Anna could do little to help Mrs De Lara. For more on women's position in the antebellum South, see Wyatt-Brown, *Honor and Violence in the Old South*, 37.

2. Unclear.

Hamilton 28th October 1854

My own dearly beloved Lord

I have not written to you for more than a week & then I addressed it to Cambridge. By your dear Father & Buttys letter of the 16th we find you were still in N.Y. tho your returning to Cambridge was spoken of to be "in a few days." As by experience, yours, & your fathers, few days, usually run on to [a] few weeks or months, I will direct this to your fathers care N.Y. In my letter to your Father of the 23d I begged him to send you home for your health. My own dear Lordy why do you continue to abuse the good constitution God gave you. Why Oh! why will you waste your strength, your time, in dissipation trifles & folly? Turn from this my beloved son. Lordy dear! it has always been painful to me to find fault with my children more so, when they have been long absent from me. Still I feel it to be my duty & I will advise you as long as I am alive & able to see or hear or speak.—

I trust a long life is before you—it will be a useful one to yourself—or one of misery to yourself & family it is perfectly within your power to be an industrious sober man of business—this character will be certain to secure you the respect & confidence of all classes. Oh! Lordy I can't say any more to you. You are not wanting in good sense. You know the duty you owe to yourself your indulgent parents—your sisters & brothers. Above all to the God who formed you who has given you all the blessing you have so long enjoyed—who now sustains you & who will be your friend if you will but put your trust in him & turn from all your follys. I am indeed troubled by your waste of time & money yet more so my beloved son to hear of a return of your back complaint. My son! what will be the end of all this? Think of this my darling son, think of the misery to your self the misery to your parents your loving sisters & brothers. Your Father & mother have set you good examples—& given you every opportunity to make you all we could desire you to be. But enough! If still in N.Y. you will see why my letter is dated Hamilton. I do not expect to return home before Monday or see your dear sisters before Wednesday next.

As far as I know we are all well. This Island has been unusually healthy this summer & autumn. How dreadful has been the ravages of yellow fever in Savannah Darien & St Marys. Even Fancy bluff has not escaped it was brought to F Bluff by the Capt of Scarletts vessel—he died 6 persons look infected from him—two are dead—2 were dying when last heard from the others slowly recovering—35 persons died in St Marys many others took infection returned to their homes & died. John Floyd died on Tuesday last. His cousin Hamilton died of yellow fever at his grand mothers. Rosalie has been at the point of death but is recovering. In Savannah they are still dying tho' slowly. There are so many returning unless we have frost it is feared many will die. George A. Read who married Miss Younge is dead. Lovat Fraser had fever in Charleston has got to Savannah apparently in [the] last stage of consumption his poor Mother & Aunts went on yesterday to take care of him. Last accounts from Randolph Spalding, Mr Bourke & Mr Toman had been sent for R.S. being exceedingly ill. On Thursday last there were 82 cases of fever in St Marys.

We have been wonderfully blessed with health. When I look back on the past summer & think how perfectly miserable we were made by the conduct of Andrew King & his wife—It will take time even if our blessings remain to recover from the poison that couple let out in my house. I some times fear we shall never be the same again. I am sick of the subject. They found us a cheerful [family] confiding (in each other) happy to have them share our happiness. Andrew commenced with undue liberties—he went to Stephen King & offered "that I should keep Mrs Lara here another year or for years take charge of Nina & her maid that William should send Anna to share with Nina Mrs Laras instructions—that William should on his part find a first rate saddle horse a new saddle & bridle for Mrs Lara & to find feed not only for that horse but also for one Stephen would send down for Nina["] & this he told us after he came back with an air of "you can't object to any arrangement I have made." I was fool enough (in consideration of the advantage it may be to Anna) to consent. Directly after the green eyed monster began its work on Louisa. But Lordy dear I can't go over the whole story of poor Mrs Laras wrongs.

I feared it would be so yet grieve none the less to see how completely Andrew & his wife have poisoned your dear Fathers mind against Mrs Lara. I wonder at Butler allowing it. What has become of your fathers discrimination? If Mrs Lara was all that Andrew King and his wife makes her out to be. If, an illegitimate impostor [?] if deep, artful, the mistress of Delara all this if true they knew before they saw that she was trying to catch Butler. It is saying very little for their own purity—their taking into their house a deep designing woman & her paramour Delara of their keeping under their roof 5¹/₂ years this woman all that time Louisa filling her letters to me with the perfections of this woman— her great distress when she wrote to me "that the independent spirit of her dear Mattie made her quit them to teach the De Chapel's when she would no longer take lessons from Mattie.["] Of Mattie refusing to get her a situation in my family—even then offering to pay Mrs Lara if I would take her. Then in '52 his in a manner forcing her on me after which Louisa wrote to me & when they came both of them thanking William & Tootee (she with tears in her eyes) for their kindness to her dear Mattie. I repeat, if Mrs Lara was all they tell your Father she was & is. How dare they to have sent such a woman to me. No Lordy! it is all a lie. A base lie. No other eye but the green eyed Monster in Mrs Andrew Kings eye could see any love Mrs L[ara] had for Butler.

Andrew King is a very weak minded man lead [sic] by the nose by his artful vindictive jealous hard hearted wife—a disgrace to us her being his wife. Whilst they were under your Fathers roof Butler & myself made it our duty to treat him as your Fathers brother. Now they are gone and we earnestly pray we may never see their faces again. And if they will but let Butler alone I hope never to hear of them after they return to Cuba. If you have had the reading of my letters to your dear blinded Father I need not repeat the fears I expressed to your father for Butler. It was a bad day your dear Father made her an inmate of our house. God! grant it may not be a worse one [than] when she entered (I insist it shall be) the last time my peaceful home. Your Fathers loss of fortune—all his absences have not caused me the misery I endured after the out break they kicked up here—the loss of Fortune the separation from my husband I felt as a misfortune—their conduct has brought awakening to disgrace which I fear has not yet ended.

Lordy you & Georgia tasted in 1852 a little of their changeableness—their venom. If with your Father tell him to reflect on all they may say—all they have said their conduct as well as their words. And judge for himself. I am sorry to perceive that my beloved Butler seems to be as blinded as your Father. When Mrs Lara returns I will for the first time speak to her of Andrew & Louisas conduct to her. I will request her to write down all Mrs Andrew King & her husband has said to our family. We have heard but their story—let us have hers & see what has been told her of us as well as what we have been told of her. I certainly shall believe her word as quickly as I shall theirs. Poor Andrew cannot tell the same story twice alike. He pique [?] themselves on their wealth and yet Andrew will not at once pay Mrs Lara the money he has of hers—he will not do this, when he is trying all in his power to blast her character & drive her from our roof & protection. A poor weak muddled minded man. A violent vindictive black hearted woman. I pity whilst I despise him—of her I have a perfect horror. With all the faults they now attribute to Mrs Lara with the stain on her birth the stain on her character they sent her here as a companion to my daughters an inmate of my family. With all they now tell of—they had had her 5½ years in their house—it is 10 years since they first met. All this time Louisas letters were filled with praises of their dear Mattie.

Oh! it is a black bad business. They or she wrote to Mrs Lara—the first object of their coming to the States was to effect a perfect reconciliation with our family. They came we did all in our power to render their visit pleasant to themselves as it was certainly to us the first 3 weeks. Had they gone a way then all may have been well. It was best however they remained to tear the vail from the eyes of your sisters, William & myself. Butler saw but darkly through their characters & I fear still sees but darkly. Now your dear Father tells me to send Mrs Lara away. Where is she to go if she gets no situation how long will the $450 I owe her support her. Oh! Lordy view this conduct on their part as you will it leaves a black cowardly stain on Andrew King's character—he is but the tool of his wife.

If you are still in N.Y. you can show this to your dear Father & to dear Butler. Lordy! sooner than see Butler go to live with those people in Cuba soon would I follow him to his grave—as much as I do all but idolize that son. I feel it would (if he lived) end in ruin body & soul to him. It must have been that Gods mercy kept me calm the last part of those peoples stay—a more miserable house hold (with no fault of this family[)] could not have existed. Each member of my family from me to Appy were watched by the inquisitorial eye of that jealous vindictive woman. If she saw Butler talking to me or to one of his sisters—if two sisters talking together [unreadable] not loud enough for her to hear she was in a fever. If not all smiles to her [blank] away she would go to "sweety" then the poor demented husband would go poking after Butty. "Wify" was crying & Butler called on to find out who had made "wify" & go & coax her back to smiles. I made up my mind to treat them as the brother & his wife of your dear Father. I went through it all—& kept peace. But when I saw their triumphant looks when it was so Butler was to go with them I really lost patience. They could not conceal their triumph over the poor Mother & Sisters. They felt they could do, [illegible words inserted above] their fiendish plan would succeed—they would poison your dear Fathers mind against poor Mrs Lara & induce him to take part with them against her if they could (against all of us—& make him desire me to send her off. She the _____ dared show her hatred to my own H[annah] P[age] & to her husband when about to depart. She said "I will crush her ruin her. She shall not have a roof to cover her head— a crust of bread to eat." When Mrs Andrew King said this of Mrs Lara it was clench fist—glaring eyes. And if Andrew King is not made to pay Mrs Lara— such may indeed be poor Matties fate. If you could but know all those people did—you will not think I paint [the] matter in too glowing colors—all is true. I will not repent or take back a single word I have written to your father, to Butler or yourself against either Andrew or his wife—but can add much more.

Your dear Sister is in better health. I have been here since Tuesday but will return home tomorrow the weather is to day quite warm. John Fraser will bring down Tip as soon as it will be safe for John to return to Savannah. In a letter from John to Tootee by yesterdays Mail—he spoke of Malley & Floyd as being quite well. Sandy Waynes Sister Julia & young Hartridge made a run-away match last week. So the world goes. I must write to dear Butler as Georgia is not here to answer his letter—Your Sister William & Cousin Amanda send love to you. Cooney loves to hear of you and sends many kisses. If you do not return with your father in order to recover your health I implore you to be careful of yourself. Avoid taking cold. I am really tired of writing—see what a scratch I have sent you—God! bless & guide you my own beloved Lordy. Whenever you do marry take care there is no stain on your wifes birth & that she is not jealous vindictive or unthoughtful.

Your own Mother
A M King

I wrote a long letter to your dear Father & sent it yesterday. I shant read this over.

Retreat 8th November

My own dearly beloved husband

I have just had the happiness to receive yours & dear Butlers letters of the 30th Ulto & one from dear Floyd of the 3d in which he mentions Malley, Tip & himself as being in good health. I am truly thankful a merciful God! permits you all to report favorably of health. I have been suffering from great uneasiness on your account & that of dear Butler & Lord lest you have eaten of oysters as others had done & suffered. We have been having oysters since the first week in September or there abouts. I made it a rule to eat a full share of them myself—not that I cared so much for them but that if unwholesome I should suffer with the rest. None of us have experienced the slightest inconvenience. I will however send for no more just now.

Our dear ones from Hamilton are here today. Appy & G[eorgia] still have colds with this exception we are all in our usual health—neither is there a case of fever among the darkies today. Truly God! is good to us my blessed husband. Throughout this trying year—To what danger have you not been exposed? What have you not undergone & yet you were spared you my most loved earthly treasure—next to you my husband our beloved daughters, sons, grand children are spared—surely God! has been merciful to us. Oh! that we could serve Him better. I grieve dearest that in the midst of your other trials & annoyances our letters on a certain subject should have added to your annoyance.

Had Andrew & his wife left here direct for Cuba I should have said nothing about them to you, until we met. Had they not boasted of what they intended to make you believe against a friendless woman—& even misrepresenting your own daughters conduct in the affair to you I would be more forgiving to them for the discomfort they gave me the last part of their visit here.

I have just received a letter from Mrs Dechapelles with whom Mrs DeLara resided as governess for three years—Mrs Lara has constantly corresponded with Miss DeChapelles since her coming to us & very naturally informed her young friend her reasons for not visiting Cuba this winter. When Mrs L[ara] wrote to Miss DeChapelles, she was not aware of the extent of the calumny heaped on her by her former friends & most enthusiastic admirers. I will just copy a part of Mrs DeChapelles letter to me. "My daughter Selina has just received a letter from her friend Mrs Lara in which she apprizes her of the unkind treatment she met with lately from Mr & Mrs Andrew King—I feel indeed distressed at this occurrence on account of Mrs Lara, to whom I feel attached as a kind and estimable friend. And I am sure she feels unhappy at such strange and incomprehensible conduct from those she had regarded for so many years as warm friends & protectors. As she mentions that in their anger Mr & Mrs King's insinuations of her past conduct in this country, might have left an unfavorable impression on you & your family, who have but a short acquaintance with her, she begged me to address to you a few lines to do justice to her character. During her three years residence and intimacy in my family I can testify that she proved herself every thing that I could desire as a teacher, companion & friend to my daughters—and a correct & perfect lady in her conduct. It was a painful separation, which we all felt keenly when she left us. I cannot express to you our regret at the knowledge that she will not visit Cuba this winter as we had anticipated she would have divided her time between us & her friends at the [home of] Louisa. I beg you dear Madam to write me a few lines in answer to this and let me know if your opinion of our friend does not coincide entirely with mine during your acquaintance with our friend at Retreat as a proof for me to refute any calumny that may be brought against her during her stay in your family."

I am sorry my husband to bring up this disagreeable subject again. Before we were aware of the impression those slanderers had made on your mind—Hannah Page had invited Mrs Lara to stay with her until she could procure another situation—she would earn her board by instructing Anna & Willie but since we find the slanderers did succeed in poisoning your mind—we fear such an arrangement will not be pleasant to you. Your children would not throw the slightest shadow on your comfort & happiness either at home or when you are abroad if this arrangement is at all disagreeable to you say no & Mrs Lara will accept Mr & Mrs Woolleys invitation to take up her abode with them until she can obtain a situation as governess in some family.

As regards Virginia—her health will not allow of her spending another winter at the North. You recollect what a hardy little child she used to be—ever since her going to Picots she has become subject to violent colds & cough which almost invariably settle on her lungs giving severe pain in her chest. I should like her to have further instruction—but cannot consent to having another Governess in the family. Georgia & Florence are really now too old to attend to regular lessons. G[eorgia] & Virginia are well read—Neither Florence or Virginia will ever conquer their [?] as regards playing before even the family or singing—What they all most require is society. It is not likely we shall ever be able to afford it—but a few months spent in Savannah during the winter—or at the North in Summer in some city where they could see some thing of refined society is all they require. Tootee has just come in & begs I will give you her tender love & say so far as your kindness to her children is concerned she thanks you heartily knowing how long I have served Tutors & governesses she would not, even advantage to her children, desire it. If William lives with strict economy they hope in a year or two to be able to afford a teacher of their own. Neither Anna or Willie, are robust children it will be best, they should not be kept close at lessons yet.

Dearly beloved do not think me unkind—do not think I willingly would for a moment disturb your peace of mind by so often dwelling on unpleasant subjects. If you are permitted to return home I will show you the characters given us by Mr & Mrs Andrew King in Cuba—very pretty ones they are. But no more of this in this or any other letter. I must not, will not disturb you or dear Butler any more as long as we are separated. Yesterday Cousin Amanda Mr Woolley & myself dined at Hamilton. Margaret Couper & her governess dined & took tea here. Tomorrow Mr & Mrs Woolley leave us for Savannah. I shall miss my dear cousin sadly. We have as yet had no frost tho' frequently it has seemed quite cold enough for frost. I am sorry you could not find time to visit your brother Henry. I think him a good man though his wife is certainly not a sincere woman or truthful. Oh! how beautiful is truth.

I have been clearing out the weeds from our flower garden—trying to make it look to please you dearest. I wrote to you on the 4th—Georgia also wrote to you. Florence & Appy will write to you by this mail. I hope dearest we may soon be able to tell our thoughts to each other in words not the everlasting scratching on paper. We send two letters to dear Butler which came in this days mail from California—I will also write to the dear boy myself. I will also add a line or two to let you know how we all are on the 11th—the later the intelligence from those we love the more agreeable. If you are able to return home in all this month or the first of December had not Butler better wait & return with you? Gods mercy protect & restore you both to your home.

Friday 11th

Yesterday we all went over to Hamilton to see my dear good Cousin A[manda] & her kind husband depart for their home in Savannah. It is with deep regret we part with our cousin—she has ever proved herself to be our grateful true friend in sickness—in time of prosperity—in time of adversity in joy & in sorrow—always & has ever been the same to me & to you too dear husband.—

We some how confidently expected dear Tip last night—sent back the carriage to await him at Hamilton. At quarter of 11 [t]he *St Johns* past—I first sat down stairs listening for the carriage—then went out & stood at the gate—by & bye the carriage came but no dear child was within it. I can but hope Mallery is going strictly by my orders not to send Tip until there had been a frost in Savannah—I will write to day & tell him to come. I must now conclude. Georgia will write to you by the next Mail—we both of us wrote to you by the last Sunday Mail. All unite in love to you & dear Butler & Lordy if with you— God! forever bless you my husband.

Retreat 25th November 1854

My own dearly beloved Lordy

Your affectionate letter of the 12th was most joyfully received on the 22nd. Truly gratified are we to hear you were then *better* (if not entirely recovered) from your back ailment. These attacks give me great uneasiness about you my beloved Lordy. What will become of you should this weakness of your spine become a confirmed disease what will be the consequence? I fear a miserable cripple the balance of your life. Oh my son why can you be so reckless of your own health. You were so long absent from your studies I think you had better have come home. There are no inducements here (unless a man is determined on it) to indulge in any kind of dissipation. Putting aside the happiness of your parents sisters & brothers—if you value your own good my son take more care of your *health*. Could you now see poor Lovat Fraser—you would see what the consequences are to a "fast liver." Had he been a prudent man in his youth— he would not be now lingering out the last of a misspent life despised by more than by those who pity him. This may be unpalatable truth—but truth nevertheless. Reflect seriously on what has been *your life*—forsake every evil habit my beloved boy—do so at once—& take a fond mothers word for it—you will not only enjoy better health—but will be far more happy—more respected by all whose good opinion is worth having. I wrote to you that all the letters sent

home from Cambridge had been returned to you—except 4 from myself—
they were of old date & contained too much of the *late war* "or attack of *King—
DeLara—Cuba Phobia*" as your dear father calls it to be pleasant reading to you.
Say what you will think what you will Andrew King & his wife acted most dis-
gracefully from beginning to end. I will say no more about them.

    This is Saturday this cannot go before Tuesday. On Monday (my usual day
for writing) dear Tootee & the children will be here. William [h]as to go to
Court. Whenever Cooney is here he thinks it my duty to attend to all his little
wants. I will have other letters to write & will add to this. We were at Hamilton last evening William was so much better he had determined to go to Darien
today—he did go & Geo & Florence are spending the day with your sister.
Horace Gould has actually sent 4 of his children to spend the day at Hamilton—they want to see sugar made—poor little dears, neither the Mother or
father to make them behave a nice time Tootee will have—fortunately the day
will not be long. Florence wrote to you by yesterdays mail—I am happy to be
able to say we have heard since then better tidings of poor Tom Bond. It was
brought by one of the Hazzard negros—the Col & his sons returned last evening from their hunt on Blackbeard. Tom was found alive—quite speechless
from cold exposure hunger & thirst—but still alive. When or where we did not
hear. I hope William gets back we shall hear better still of poor Tom Bond—
the two negros who were with him are certainly lost. Oh! what poor Tom must
have suffered. If he lives I trust he will be a better man & never forget the mercy
God! has shown him on this occasion. Emma Postell, his wife & Mrs Cater
were to have gone to Savannah in yesterdays boat sent their baggage to Hamilton but were too late themselves. I am told James Postell is still in very bad
health. I have not seen him since July.

    It has been raining very heavily. I hope dear William is not out in it he has
been very unwell from a bad cold & that irruption on his legs. I have not heard
of the Bourkes or *from* them since they left here in October. Frank Scarlett has
gone North for his nieces—I rather think the Miss's Parland will create quite
a sensation among the beaux this winter. Had their grand aunt Mrs Staunton
lived—I understand their intention was to have spent the winter in Savannah.

    I hope tomorrows mail will bring pleasant intelligence from your dear Fa-
ther & brothers—his last letter was dated 13th at Metropolitan dear Butlers
the 15th Washington City. I have another bitter disappointment your father
was obliged to return to N.Y. I am sick at heart it see[m]s as tho' we are never
to meet again in our own happy home. Dear Butler says "I am on my way
home" but gives no time when we may hope to see him. We heard from Malley & Floyd last Sunday they were well. In less than one month from this we
hope to see the dear boys. And I hope & trust in January you will be with us. I

will now put aside my paper to resume it on Monday—till then God bless you
my boy.—

Sunday 26th

We have just received the Mail & with it letters from your beloved Father dear
Butler yourself & Floyd. Thank God! you were all in life on the 20th—18th—
14th & 10th. Oh! Lordy dear I wish Andrew King & his wife had never come
to Retreat—their seems no end to the trouble it has made. Here we are all
alive—blessed with health enough of worldy goods to keep starvation from
our doors—whilst thousands of others are grieving for lost friends & relatives
we are made unhappy. You cannot be more sick of the subject than I am. I am
more grieved than words can express that your beloved Father cannot be made
to view the matter in the right light. That his love for one who (unfortunately) is
his brother he has by that brother been influenced (though he will not confess
it) against his wife & daughters. He seems actually to hate Mrs Lara—blaming
his wife & daughters for taking her part instead of that of those weathercocks
& as vindictive as they are changeable. I would not have touched on this subject again but your Father seems to be *offended* with my beloved Tootee for having invited Mrs Lara to stay with her until she could recover her money from
Andrew King or find another situation. Tootee did this *before* she understood
your fathers dislike to Mrs Lara. I will request Mrs Lara to accept Cousin
Amandas kind invitation & depart for Savannah this week. I hope this arrangement will not be found fault with. I shall have to request Messr Andersons to
advance for me what is due her.

I fear poor Williams health will be none the better for the drenching rain he
was in yesterday. It poured down for several hours & he exposed to it all. G[eor-
gia], F[lorence] & Tip got home & brought (if William got the right story) a
most shocking story of poor Tom Bond. His boat swamped on Saturday night
on *Wednesday* Randolph Spalding & another gentleman met with what they supposed to be his dead body lying about half a mile from the horses had crawl'd
2 miles *when,* no one knows—they supposed him dead—but after a little per-
ceived the face to since from the *flies*[. H]e had been *subsisting on the grass*
around him—head bare—feet black—after getting him to the house—he recovered sufficiently to turn about his head—the only word he utter'd was *water*. This is what was told William in Darien. Dr Holmes [h]ad been sent for—
he returned to Darien before William left—saying Tom was dead! Merciful
God! how he must have suffered! His poor wife was with him. Eugenia Grant
wrote to Florence that on Saturday noon her mother & self were in Darien &
saw poor Tom he was looking remarkably well, was in high spirits & spoke of going the *next day* to join the other hunters on Sapelo. Mr Grant begged him not

to use the Sabbath for such a purpose he went home & it seems his wife urged him to go on Saturday night rather than on Sunday. I will not harrow your feelings by dwelling longer on the heart sickening subject I can but hope in all his agony poor Tom tried to make peace with his God! & died forgiven.—

Mrs Morris died before Dr Troup reached Virginia. We see no mention made in this days paper of Emma Postell—therefore hope the report we got by the *St Johns* was not true. No doubt some of the girls will write to you by this mail. All send love—I fear you will not be much cheered by this letter—though to hear we are all in our usual health must be gratifying to you. Be careful of your precious health for the sake of your devoted Mother

A M King

Portrait of Anna Matilda Page
King (Courtesy of the Coastal
Georgia Historical Society)

Portrait of Thomas Butler
King (Courtesy of the Coastal
Georgia Historical Society)

Portrait of Major William Page (Courtesy of the Coastal Georgia Historical Society)

Portrait of Anna Matilda Page King (Courtesy of Harry Aiken)

Portrait of Thomas Butler King Jr. (Courtesy of the Coastal Georgia Historical Society)

Portrait of Henry Lord Page King (Courtesy of the Coastal Georgia Historical Society)

Portrait of Virginia, Georgia, and Florence King (Courtesy of Edwin R. MacKethan III)

The house at the Retreat Plantation (Courtesy of the Coastal Georgia Historical Society)

LEFT TO RIGHT: Jacob Dart, M. J. Coulson, Captain Charles Spalding Wylly, John Floyd King, and Neptune Small (Courtesy of the Coastal Georgia Historical Society)

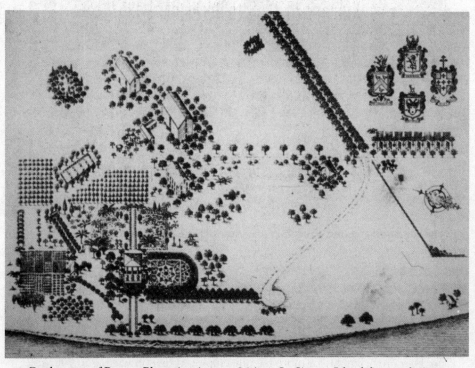

Garden map of Retreat Plantation (1755–1863) on St. Simons Island, known during
the eighteenth century as Orange Grove

January 20, 1855, to December 1, 1857

Bless the man who first learned to write. What a comfort
it has been to me.

*Although Thomas King finally returned to Retreat after an absence of nearly four
years, he did not come home to stay. Business soon called him away, and Anna once
more remained behind to manage the plantation and household. Mallery, Floyd, and
Cuyler were sent to schools in Georgia and New York while Georgia, Florence, and
Virginia remained at home. Lord studied for the bar exam and Butler alternated between working for his mother as plantation manager and as his father's business partner and assistant.*

Savannah 20th Jan 55

My own dearly beloved husband

Our daughters have gone to the Theater. I am alone this evening I cannot be more profitably or more happily employed than in writing to you. You
must make every allowance for the irregularity of my writing blotted words &
crooked lines—I cannot see to do better. It is near two weeks since we parted
do you not think I may reasonably have expected the scrape of your pen by this
time? I am perfectly aware how busy you must be—if you could not write[,]
Butler or Lord may have written to me after seeing you—and given me some
idea—when you would be able to return. I looked for Lord & Van [Rensselaer]
today but understand that no Steamship will be here before Tuesday. Mr Anderson tells me he has received by the express a trunk & box belonging to Lord.
These he must have shipped before (or the day) you reached N.Y. the 13th. If
you only got there on the 13th you did not proceed as rapidly as you expected.
Your dispatch says "all are well"—with this I try to be satisfied. I do not know
whether I shall leave here this day week or Tuesday week. I am very anxious to
return home—our dear boys must be so very lonely certainly not later than
Tuesday—but for the boys & the scarcity of money I would like well enough
to indulge our daughters with another week.

I wanted your council sadly today. Postell brought on 13 of his wifes negros to be sold. They were mortgaged to his new Factor for $5000. *Smarts* wife who you recollect came to us begging us to buy her & her 6 children the oldest 13 the others all boys. They were valued, that is, the woman & 6 children for $3100—60 days credit. But the Andersons have been advancing for me ever since August—I have not the money. I am sorry as the woman is prime & the children very promising.

I heard today from Tootee all were then well at Hamilton & Retreat. I hope to see her here on Monday. I feel certain the little change will do both her health & spirits good. She mentioned your having engaged oxen from Piles. I thought we had enough for the present—money with me is exceedingly tight. I assume you and I [?] will be still lighter before the year is out unless fortune for once smiles on your hard efforts. God knows you have worked with both head & body hard enough to have made a dozen fortunes. I both wonder at and admire your perseverance—had it been me I should have given up years ago—May God! yet bless your efforts my beloved husband.

Major Grant & son arrived this morning himself & son—son in law & three daughters—three nephews our daughters & several young gentlemen formed a party to go to the Theater this evening. Mr Dummit called to see us this evening—he is on his way home from the Legislature of Florida. Tell Butler that Mr D[ummit] looks thin—but says he is well. I thought I had paid all my calls—but find new ones are made daily. I shall try & return them all before I go. It is now 10 oclock. I will add a few lines some time tomorrow as this letter cannot go before Monday morning. I believe I mentioned in my last having heard from our dear Tip. He had reached Roswell safe & was well on the 16th.

Sunday evening

We went to hear Bishop Elliott this morning—who gave us a very excellent sermon. A little drizzle this morning which only served to render the walking more disagreeable. Since then high wind making matters still worse. Our dear girls are all well & enjoying their stay here every day more & more. The Misses Grant start for Charleston this evening they go the Island route—Sarah Hazzard her grand Mother & brother went to Charleston yesterday. There is a number of cases of Cholera on the river plantations which they attribute to eating unsound rice. In a number of cases it proved fatal.

Our daughters send a thousand loves to you & dear Butler—Lord can scarcely be still with you. God! grant dearest these hurried lines may find you & our dear son or sons in health. I know I need not hurry your return that you will come as soon as you possibly can. I will go home & try to get the house in order for you. What happiness could you be here to return with us. I try not to think it probable such happiness is in store for us. Praying God! to bless, guide, protect, & prosper you. Ever until death your affectionately

devoted wife

Anna M King

Retreat 17th Feb 1855

My dearly beloved husband

I can but hope the Mail tomorrow may bring us letters favorable to your return home. Yesterday Lord got a letter from dear Butler of the 6th you were still in N.Y. & not one word relative to your leaving that place or when we may hope to see you both here. Your *three* weeks are lengthening sadly my beloved! I know from no *fault* of yours but certainly your misfortune. Oh my husband I sadly fear no benefit is ever to result from all this labor—all this waste of time & money. Give it up dearest come home & take better care, than I can, of the little that we have. It will require the strictest economy as well as good management to keep this little property in possession. I may be wrong in writing this to you—but it is just as *I feel*. You or Butler tell me nothing—whether all is a failure or whether any *substantial* proof of success has been yours I know not. I have but my *fears* to dwell on.

William has gone on bravely with the field work. With all his efforts the manure for corn will fall short—but it must be endured—I cannot afford to *buy* manure. I think he said he will finish grassing on Monday. I am anxious he get the balance of the cotton into the market—but it will be so poor—the better plan is to try for a better crop the present year & hope and hope for better luck & better times.—

Georgia & Virginia are up & about faces yet a little swollen. Florence imprudently exposed herself last Tuesday took fever & was for three days very sick. To day she is able to set up in her room but feels weak & has no appetite. She was very bilious I gave her a blue pill since then she has been getting better. I had a bad pain in my side—took a blue pill & am also better. Tootees children all have whooping cough—King suffers more than either of the others. Tootee herself has a terrible cough which is both trying and dangerous in her condition—I went over to see her yesterday & will try to do so again this afternoon. Lord, M[allery] & F[loyd] are well. Mrs Van Rensselaer still suffers from headaches—She certainly is a very amiable woman & bears cheerfully the solitude of this place. I can only hope the change will be beneficial to her health. Corty has gotten bravely over the chicken pox. Malley thinks he will be obliged very soon to go back to Marietta. I can but hope you & dear Butler may come before he leaves. It is full time that Floyd should also leave—But with sickness

& company in the house it is slow work getting on with sewing. Lord ought also *soon* to go if he can find a place. He has been exercising very freely & finds it no injury to his back. I heard from dear Tip yesterday he was quite well & seems satisfied. We have not had much sickness among the negros *principally* young children from colds. I will not close this until the mail comes tomorrow hoping to get such pleasant letters from you & Butler.

Sunday morning

The Mail has not yet come. I must however send this in time. There is a letter here for dear Butler from San Francisco—I am doubtful whether to send it or not—If the mail today brings no letter telling us you are on your way home I will send it on Tuesday. There is no Tuesday boat from Savannah the *Planter* on Wednesday. *St Johns* on Thursday & *Welaka* on Saturday. Tootee is still quite sick—Florence is very much better the rest are as usual.

Our love to dear Butler accept a thousand loves from your children & your devoted & affectionate wife

A M King

Retreat 26th March 1855

My own dearly beloved husband

I wrote to you yesterday but as the letter was sent by the *St Johns* it is possible it may be lost on the way. We shall have no Friday mail. The *Seminole* has met with some accident down South. No Wednesday Mail—all this is trying especially as it is more than a week since I have had the happiness to hear from you. My own beloved I know it is not from forgetfulness of your poor wife that you do not write to me twice every week. And yet it would be conferring on me a very great favor as well as happiness to hear oftener from you. I fear you have not only a great deal to occupy your time & thoughts but much also to annoy you. I am much distressed myself just now. In my letter yesterday I mentioned that our dear Butler had gone on a visit of a few days to Savannah—a certain lady being there. I went with him to Hamilton. Mr J. H. C[ouper] was on board the boat got out on to the wharf & told Wm and Butler that he had just received a letter from Mr Corbin—ordering him to sell to old Barret the Hamilton property on this Island. So ends my much cherished hopes—I am not only bitterly disappointed but sorely distressed. I do not think William will like to continue on the place as Old Barrets overseer—when he will leave—where he will go is not yet determined on. I need not dwell on this painful subject.

I can only hope you will soon be at home—may you return to us in health. I cannot sufficiently thank God! you are able to bear up against adverse fortune. If we were young my husband—if our children had learned to be content on hard fair & homespun clothes the want of means would not be so severe a misfortune. But we are both going down hill & they have been living too much on hope & expectation. If you were but here to comfort me perhaps I would feel better.

Our dear Tootee is in very feeble health. I can but hope she may be able to stand the trial which must now be very near. The two elder children are now with me—their cough is much better—dear little Cooney & John yet cough violently—but they bear it bravely.[1] Floyd is now quite well enough to go to school.[2] I will send him as soon as I can raise the money. I can but hope he will now feel the necessity there is for him to learn how to get his own bread. I think it of no use our dear Lord waiting your return. Oh! that he would make up his mind to hard work at once. I grieve to write so despairingly.—

Another trouble which may be made worse if not attended to soon. Young McIntosh is fast becoming a confirmed drunkard. William and Butler & Lord were informed by good authority that McIntosh gets negros men & women at his house, drinks & carousing—terrible proceedings (as described by a respectable white man who witnessed it). It is doing us a great injury—as doubtless some of our negros go there—then it is ruining the young man himself to hold the lighthouse longer. He is a good carpenter—if compelled to work at his trade for a living he may stop drinking—his salary as Light House keeper supports him without working. William says "it will not do to go to work openly—for a number on the main perhaps worse than even McIntosh would be trying to get the place." James Armstrong has given up drink—has become a member of the Church. He is very poor & would be glad of the birth—William is also under the impression that *you* could have McIntosh turned out and James W Armstrong appointed—you are the best judge of this. It certainly never will do for him to corrupt the negros in this way. I hope & trust my own beloved husband you will soon be at home. What is the use of your remaining?

Florence is spending the day with poor Tootee. Appy, Floyd & Anna & Willie send much love. Our dear Butler will I hope be home by Thursday night. I feel that he is capable & willing to attend to the place in your absence. I would he was at some work for himself. Butler is now 25 years old—full time he was at some settled business. May God! bless him he is a good son to me. And may God bless and preserve you my precious husband. My heart bleeds for your trials and disappointments. Your devoted & affectionate wife

　　　　　　　　　　A M King

1. The pregnant Tootee had been suffering from whooping cough since mid-February. Anna's letter to her husband of March 18 reported that "for the last ten days

poor Tootee has been able to leave her room—but she still suffers from her cough & is very feeble. Our best hope is that she will not be confined until some time in April. . . . King at times coughs alarmingly—poor little fellow he turns perfectly purple in the face & seems just about to expire—this is at night. During the day his cough is less violent. John actually grows fat on it—& yet he too coughs very violently. . . . The cough is now among our little negros—& among those at Hamilton" (Anna Matilda Page King to Thomas Butler King, March 18, 1855, TBK, SHC).

2. Floyd had been exposed to the mumps by his sisters and had "painful and numerous boils all over his body" (Anna Matilda Page King to Thomas Butler King, March 18, 1855, TBK, SHC).

St Simons Isld 21 May 1855

My own dearly beloved husband

Yesterday Butler Lord & myself each had the happiness to receive your affectionate letters of the 12th & 13th. These assure us of your being then in good bodily health—which ought in itself be happiness to us. And so it is— only we grieve to find your enemies still prevail and you say nothing of the object you had in returning to N.Y. You certainly bear up most nobly under your many great trials. God! be praised for this dear husband—it is He who gives you strength so to do. I wish I had some of your fortitude, your hopefulness. In this I am distressingly deficient but let me not dwell on this most painful subject. It seems to me most cruel to express to you any of my feelings—still I do it. Pardon me my beloved husband—I must however tell you what I have been obliged to do.

We have been living beyond our means which unfortunately most planters (who have nothing but crops to depend on) do. The loss of half the crop last year & Dunhams management of that gathered after the storm has entangled me to the amount of very near $4000. Our sons must have schooling—and as long as company will stay I have been compelled to keep up the table. Mr G. W. Anderson proposed that I should get Mr J. H. Couper to give his note as my Trustee—for the amount payable the first Dec next. The sum is due to J. W. Anderson—but he very kindly offers to let me use it in paying these other debts & for our boys schooling clothing &c. Then he would be my only creditor & it amounts to the same thing in the end.

Butler intends writing to you by this mail tho we both hope & pray you may at this moment be on your way home. The gin you speak of is *not the one* so highly spoken of in this part of the world. He will give you the name. Frank Scarlett showed Butler his & says he obtained 5 cts on the pound from its use & that he gets 300 Lbs a day from it—the cost I think is $150. I think the name they go by is McCarthy gins.[1]

Butler went this morning to see Mr J. H. C[ouper] who very kindly & at once gave his notes as my trustee. If these notes are accepted Butler will start the first of next week with Floyd to Cass County. This school was recommended to me by Mr John W Anderson, but I do not like to send Floyd there alone. I think it best that Butler should go with him—see the place he is at—and tell Mr Goulding on what we desire Floyd should attend to.[2] It is true dear Floyd has lost much time—but his stay at home has improved him in other important respects. He *now promises he will try to improve.* He now seems to *feel the necessity* of his so doing. He now *feels* he will have to depend on his own exertions to get on in this cold world. It will be June before I can get money even to pay Lords passage to Savannah—he has been talking to me on the subject. I think he had better go on see Mr Ward, enter his name as you advise—be advised what books to get—obtain them & return here to study & read.[3] I hope before long we shall be free of company when he will have nothing to interrupt his studies. He has had repeated attacks of ulcerated sore throat. He wants energy and a determination to face the foe. I hope when he realizes the *necessity* he will go ahead. A situation for Mallery must if possible be obtained as soon as he is capable of filling one on some R[ail] R[oad]—he thinks the end of this year.

On Saturday we had some rain—it commenced with some thing like a Tornado—fortunately it did not last long. The corn was knocked down some but it is getting up again. William says the cotton was not a bit hurt—he says the cotton & corn are both promising. Had he not taken hold when you were obliged to leave we would have been in a sad plight. God prosper him in his new business—he is a noble fellow blessed is our Tootee in having such a husband. Oh husband how beautiful it is to see the effects of a change of heart in that man, surely it was good he was afflicted. Oh! that my trials were equally blessed.—

Butler was accompanied home by Daniel Lord, he is as tall as Butler but very thin & delicate—poor Stephen! his visit to Cuba was an injury more than a benefit. Butler says it is melancholy to see so large a frame going away to skin & bones, his strength of body all gone. His Father & brothers urge his going West—but he will not consent to leave home again. Your brother Stephen Butler says looks remarkably well, his little girl also has a cough. They have wealth but surely we have more to make us happy and grateful.

The *Israelites* left the Island last Thursday night.[4] Barret will have the place for $50,000 he says he will give no more. Corbins last letter said $55,000. I rather think he is pushed for the money—it will end in his taking 50. If they were genteel Christians it would be not so bad but vulgar upstarts as they are, the idea of having them as neighbors is revolting in the extreme. Tootee says she can bear with the old man for two reasons he *spoke well of you* & *petted her children*. Georgia is spending the day at Hamilton—you have not answered her last letter—what a blessing she is to me. All here and at Hamilton send you thousands of love—God bless you my precious my beloved husband. May his mercy guard, guide & restore you to your affectionate wife

A M King

1. A Macarthy gin is a single-action gin with one oscillating blade to remove the fiber from the seed. It consists of a large leather roller approximately 40 inches long and 5 inches in diameter. According to Frederick Wilkinson, it should produce thirty pounds of cotton per hour. For more on how the gin works, see Wilkinson, *The Story of the Cotton Plant*, 77–78.
2. Francis R. Goulding's preparatory school in Kingston, Georgia.
3. Lord had returned home to prepare to take the bar exam in Savannah.
4. The Barretts, who were then in the process of purchasing Hamilton, were Jewish.

Retreat 10th September 1855

My own dearly beloved Lord

Your Father received your welcome letter by yesterdays Mail—yours the only one from 5 beloved sons absent from us. Thank God you were able to write cheerfully. Your father is much occupied today—& your sisters have to entertain Joe Bond—it is probable neither Father or Sisters will find time to write— but the Mail must not go without a few lines from your home my Lordy. Tho I verily believe you would rather any other of the family should write than your poor dispirited Mother.

Well to begin, your Father, G[eorgia], F[lorence] & V[irginia] as well as myself are in our usual health. The storm which threatened on Friday & Saturday past off with not much damage to the cotton. The wind has gone more to the South & we flatter ourselves will clear off these clouds & enable us to gather cotton. Your dear Sister on Monday last got William to try and extract the tooth which has given her so much pain. He failed in the attempt—since then she has suffered *very much* from pain, not only the tooth but that entire side of her face & head, which she bears with her usual fortitude. William deemed it expedient he should visit the Fair at Atlanta, but left your Sister very reluctantly—she would not consent to come here during his absence. She is so soon to leave Hamilton she thinks it necessary she should stay there to take all possible care of her things. I have been there every day since William left & last evening Florence went to stay some days with her. As your Sisters have returned home one or the other will be with her until William returns which will be on Saturday night. I will not pretend to say any thing of the merry time G[eorgia], F[lorence] & V[irginia] had at the Grants let this suffice—they were perfectly delighted the whole time they were there—& each one declares she envys not the enjoyment you may have at Saratoga, the six days of pleasure they had could not have been exceeded by any enjoyment among strangers. Georgia hopes to give you a discription of it. So I will just say no more on the subject.

During there absence your dear Father & myself were at home all alone. I must admit at times we did feel lonely—still not unhappy. I found occupation in looking over old papers for him, & on the plantation he has more to do than time or hands can accomplish. He is now off in the field. Time alone can determine what the cotton crop will be. That terrible drought did so much injury nothing but a late autumn will safe [*sic*] us. As yet we have but 7 bags gathered—at this time last year we had 27.

Your dear Father came in just in time for lunch & in attending to his wants I have pretty near forgotten all I had to say. I cant say how the Election goes on—thousand of lies are being manufactured against him. I would he had kept quiet & let the country elect their Long. It makes me sick at heart.

I am sorry my son you should neglect your reading for any cause—I would *seriously advise* you *to return home early in October & devote your whole mind to prepare for your examination in November. Think how many little minds will rejoice at your failure—how many affectionate hearts will be [?] by so great a misfortune.* When your father hears again from the main he may be able to give you an idea how close will be the Election—it would seem hard he should lose it by *one* or *two* votes when if his sons were here he would gain it. I wish now that Butler had gone with you—then he would have had enough of the North before the first of October. I am glad yet sorry but I will not say for what. I can say with perfect sincerity I am glad you have seen your Uncle Henry & Aunt Mary. Your letter to Butler I will forward by the Mail tomorrow. If Georgia writes to you today she will tell you she has had a letter from S[arah] B[utler] since you left Philadelphia.[1]

What an awful accident on the R[ail] R[oad]. I am so thankful dear Lordy you were not on that road when the accident occurred. More than one Mother may now be mourning the loss of a son. Your Sisters were to have returned home by the Steamer on Friday—but the weather was so rainy they could not get to Brunswick—your father had to send the boat for them on Saturday. Joe Bond had politely escorted them down & expected to return yesterday with Dr Troup but as that gentleman has not yet made his appearance Joe will probably take the Steamer tomorrow night for Brunswick. Capt[ain] Duree & his daughter are at Mr Postells they have a house full there 7 besides the family. Your Sisters will call to see Miss Duree this evening. Your dear Father sends his love & says he will answer your letter as soon as he can get time—I am glad you write to him so often. Continue to do so my son, he needs all the love & attention his wife & children can show him. Your Sisters send much love. Cooney says he "thinks it is time you should come home" and so do we all. I wrote to Mary King not long since my love to her & her good husband. I pray God you may be kept from all harm & soon restored to

Your affectionate Mother
Anna M King

1. Sarah Butler was the daughter of Fannie Kemble Butler and Pierce (Mease) Butler. Pierce Butler's mother, Sarah Butler Mease (for whom his daughter was named), was the oldest of eight children born to Major Pierce Butler and Mary Middleton Butler. With the condition that Pierce and John Mease change their name to Butler, Sarah's youngest sons inherited the family fortune. Pierce Butler is best known for his marriage to the English actress Frances Anne Kemble, which ended in divorce in 1849. The journal she kept during a visit to her husband's plantations in the South contributed to the demise of their marriage. Their daughters Sarah and Frances were close friends of the King children. For more a more in-depth account of Butler family history and the Kemble-Butler marriage, see Bell, *Major Butler's Legacy*; Clinton, *Fanny Kemble's Civil Wars*; and Kemble's *Journal of a Residence on a Georgia Plantation 1838–1839*.

16th September 1855

My own dear Lordy

Your affectionate letter of the 30th August is the last we have receiv'd from you. Your dear Father has not yet answered that letter. He is out so much during the day & so tired when he comes in he has little inclination to take pen in hand. I am now sorry I said any thing to you about Johnny being sick—but when I wrote there was every reason to fear his attack would be serious. Thank God! his fever lasted only 24 hours & he is now as well & merry as ever.

William got back last night but we have neither seen or heard from him since he came, but will I hope before I close this. Your Father went to Brunswick yesterday & your Sisters & myself dined at Hamilton. The weather was very hot but as there was no gent in the way in thin wrappers we past a comfortable day.—

Your Father did not return home until this morning—he brought the melancholy *tidings of poor Steves death*. We all felt he would not long be with us but did not expect the end so soon. It grieves us much—the more so that your Sisters had not paid their promised visit to him—if the weather continues as favorable as it now is they will go this week to see their Uncle. Surely he is afflicted. And poor dear Steve!! I verily believe he loved us all sincerely—& deeply do we lament his departure (Gods mercy grant) to a better world. Mr Scarlett told your Father of the event—& he was too much shocked to ask at what time. Your Father did not see Mr Bourke who unfortunately was _____.[1] Poor Bourke why cant he give up this terrible practice. Let his case be an example for you to shun my son. See what misery his weakness brings on his Mother & wife. We did not hear from your younger brothers today—but from a note I have just had from Tootee she says "William saw Mallery who was well & who reported Floyd & Tip also well."

Monday

We saw the dear ones at Hamilton all were pretty well last evening. Tomorrow G[eorgia] & Florence intend starting for Satilla. If by going they can impart the least consolation to poor Brother Stephen so far—so well. I very much fear they will do no good & may be made sick by the jaunt. I hope my son you may gain a good stock of health by this trip of yours. I still think you ought to be here by the first Monday in October. Your Father will probably write to you & dear Butler by this Mail. The weather is now as hot as in July & August & very dry. I think Georgia has written to both you & dear Butler.

May God bless you my son all send love to you & Butler. By the way Lordy it is full time we should be thinking of furnishing your bed room in Savannah. I am told for $30 a bed stead wardrobe set of drawers—wash stand & 3 chairs can be had of what they call "cottage furniture." If you can get it I will pay for it on delivery in Savannah.[2] Perhaps your Aunt Mary can advise you where to get it.

I hope the next Mail will give us a letter from you. Trusting this may find you in good health & spirits

I am as ever your devoted Mother
A M King

1. Tom Bourke was evidently still battling a drinking (or drug) problem.
2. Once Lord had passed the bar, the plan was for him to begin practicing law in Savannah.

Retreat 23d Dec 1855

My own dearly beloved husband

This days Mail brought me your welcome letter of the 5th written in N[ew] O[rleans] P[ost] Marked [the] 6th. It has been a long time on the way. When the Mail bag was opened and the glad cry "a letter from dear Father" all rushed to hear the contents—all are grateful for the good news that you had not then experienced any ill effect from your exposure, but the truth must out—*all disappointed* not to receive later accounts from you. I hope (& trust I shall not be disappointed) the next mail will bring a pleasant & *later* intelligence from you.

Your beloved self alone is wanted to render a reunion of our family complete.
Florence informed you by the Friday Mail of the arrival at home of dear Floyd
& Cuyler. The carriage had just left to await them at Hamilton, when some
one rapped at Tootees out side door, when she opened it in marched the two
boys, they had landed at the creek. They are in fine health & much grown. Floyd
I think fully as tall as Malley & very stout. Cuyler is taller than I am—it worries me to find his *voice changed*. It is a pity, he is very quiet, quite a love of a
boy. Last night or rather this morning William & Lord came to pass Christmas with us. We sat at table 9 children—4 grand children & a son in law, not
one ugly or evil dispond [*sic*] among them. Last night little Willie expressed
himself in his way—"I have been looking at Mothers sons all look so well and
seem so happy in one instant they may all be dead without a moments warning
& may be none of them are prepared to die" and with that he burst into tears
as tho his little heart would break. It was a strange speech for a little fellow like
him to make. Johny & the baby[1] got soon over their ailment then dear little
King was attacked with a kind of Cholera but thank God! he too is again bright.
Hannah Page & several of the negros have had similar attacks it must be owing to the damp variable weather—we have had cold sufficient to materially injure the crop but nothing else looks as tho there had been frost.

Butler will write about plantation affairs. I gave him your letter to read. I
shall ship what cotton is ready tomorrow. I am told there is no demand for
S[ea] I[sland] but as I owe Mr Anderson so large a debt conclude it best I should
place the cotton in his hands. I can but hope he will not sacrifice it. I am truly
gratified to find that dear Floyd *now* really desires to study, he says he feels
the importance of an education. I can but hope he will yet do well. Dear boy
he seems very happy among us. William intends taking his family to Savannah
on the 4th. I shall miss them very much but he says his life is so dreary in Savannah he cannot bear to be without his wife & children—dear Tootee will
not be as comfortable there as with us, but of course yields to the wishes of her
husband.

                                                                        24th

Tomorrow will be Christmas day & again dear husband you are far away from
home & family. It is painful beyond expression to us I am sure it is so to you.
Our nine children are together once more. Oh! that the father was here also.
God! grant you may be as well this moment as we all are. Georgia, Mallery &
Tip have gone to help dress the Church for Christmas. It seems a head over
heels day with all of us. The weather warm—foggy & drizzly. All busy & very
little being done. I got up with a determination to be very industrious but it
was late before breakfast was got over with—then poor Ruthey had one of her

attacks which always unnerves me. With one thing and another I have done very little. I need not however annoy you with my annoyances.

I find the Friday boat is still South some breakage I presume—so Florences letter is still at Frederica. Tootee & myself rode over to Hamilton on Tuesday last, every thing looked sad & dreary there. I am told Mr J. H. C[ouper] wishes to dispose of Cannon's Point. I hope he may. The lands on the Island are being monopolized by so few the society of the Island gets lower & lower. I have not yet talked with Butler *on the subject—does he understand where you wish the head rights placed?*

Butler has just returned from shipping 44 bags prime cotton if it would only bring 50 cts I would be at ease. The cause of the delay of the *Seminole* is that she got on fire and was burned to the waters edge—the occurrence took place at Jacksonville no lives lost. Floyd & Tip have lost all their best shirts & under clothing, pocket handkerchiefs & all their soiled clothing were in a bag. Tip says before dark he put all their baggage together—it was very dark when they got to the creek—the baggage put at the head of the boat immediately after leaving the Steamer. Tip asked the mate if he was sure he had put in all the baggage. The mate asked how many pieces—Tip told him 5—the mate then said the bag is left but I will land it on Friday at Frederica. But I rather guess they will never see the bag again. Daniel Lord & his little Sister came down in to-nights boat. They left Brother Stephen well—also James & family & Henry. You see we have a house full. Oh that you were among us. Good night my beloved husband. Gods choicest blessings be yours. All unite in love to you. The servants beg to be remembered to you.

> Ever & forever your devoted wife
> A M King

> 25th

Christmas day—I do not say "merry Christmas" to you my beloved. I know such will not be the case—but I hope you are well & in good spirits. God! forever bless you

> Your wife
> Anna M K

Memory dearest Father takes me back to last Christmas when you my beloved Father were with us—we miss you Father dear—but let us all pray to a merciful God—that it may be our happiness all to meet again in health love & happiness

> Your ever devoted child
> H[annah] C[ouper]

We are all so sorry dearest Father that you are not here to day & hope you are not having a dull day in Texas.

Your own affectionate daughter
Virginia

Darling Father surely if you were here this merry Christmas day our earthly happiness would be complete. May God! in his infinite mercy and goodness grant that you are well and that this may be the last Christmas day you will spend *from* your devoted family.

Your very affectionate daughter
Florence

God bless you! dearest Father this beautiful Christmas day. All your children are here with Mother—but the Head is wanting. So our happiness is incomplete! may you be successful in all your [?] [?] and in health [missing last page].

1. Helen Rosalie Couper, also called Tusie, Toozie, Toosie, and Tuzie.

10th January 56

My own precious child

How are you all this bitter cold day? Dearest child how sadly I miss you & your precious children. I know that your good husbands happiness is first to be consulted still that does not lessen the pain your departure gives me. So lonely I feel. Just imagine no one at home but Cuyler & me. Dear boy he tries by his affectionate devotion to cheer me. He is attentive in carrying out the orders Butler left him to have executed—but the house is still—nothing but the whistling of the horrible wind & the singing of the canaries & the coughing of Anne to break the stillness. I keep busy to keep away care.

Oh! Tootee dear you do not know what I suffered the day you left me. It seemed to me I was perfectly bewildered after you were all gone. I went into your room & saw the dear babys pillow—its old cloak & your silver cup. Did you not intend to carry these? I picked up every thing you left & locked them in your wardrobe. And then Clementine cut me to the heart by saying "And Miss Hannah thought hard of your not letting her have a little girl to follow Johny." Now Tootee I "think hard" of you for not telling me this. You know there was no other than Bell & when I insisted she should follow Johny after Lindy went you seemed not to care for her services. You possess too much false delicacy. You know my daughter that my old servants are all failing from one cause or another. It is full time I should try to raise others (if they live) to take their place. I do not give Bell to you because in the first place I have so often heard you say "you would never have a little negro girl brought up among your children" then again Georgia was anxious to have a tractible girl to learn to sew & wait on her & asked me for Bell & I gave her for that purpose. I am sure Georgia would have cheerfully let you have her during your present stay in Savannah & if you had only had the frankness to tell me you wanted her she should have gone with you. Whether your Sisters go on the 15th or not Tip will (God! willing) leave me that day & I will send Bell with him. Remember she has never had whooping cough & you will please keep her very close. I have promised to let Clementine go as maid to your Sisters. It will be economy my doing so to take care of their things. I would not have cared for Christian[n]s remaining at home had Maria not have been laid up. She does nothing for me—but help her mother put the house to rights in the morning & puts the chambers to right—but for her child as soon as Maria is well enough I could send her to you.[1] I have no nurse to give her but the one she has & I am sure you do not want Julia about you. Now be frank if your want C. after Maria gets well say so—if you want Bell keep her 'til you come. Nothing is gained by false delicacy. I do feel for you this cold weather you & your babies—God! grant the exertions you made in preparing to leave may not make you sick. Oh! Tootee it would be terrible for me to hear you are ill—God forbid!!

I have your sausages ready 33 strings—$^1/_4$ barrel lard 2 of your jars (are quite full the other was full when the lard was hot). I will keep until further orders the "jowls & chines" will be put into a barrel with the pickle. They would not keep if sent dry. I have the corn now grinding to fill a barrel of grist. If I can sift it I will but from present appearances fear I shall have not one to do it. I want to kill some of my own hogs tomorrow. I would have done so today but hoped last night Butler would be here to superintend it for me. I will send you a cheese tomorrow—a line by the *Welaka* will give you a better idea of what is sent. I wish William would charge me with the freight of what goes tomorrow & whenever I do send any thing to the house. I am so sorry Cousin A[manda] is not in S[avanna]h the first trouble to you will be so great & then dear Tootee you are so regardless of your precious health when you imagine you must do a thing. I am so worried—so anxious about dear Butler, Floyd & my three precious girls if I was only sure they did not attempt to start today I would feel easier—it is so bitter cold & the wind so high—they would all perish with cold— so much for pleasure seeking.—

This cold is filling the hospital with sick negros—I can see that they have bad colds. I fear it will be worse instead of better. Kiss each dear child for me. Tell them Mother already longs to see them & hear their dear voices. Every thing belonging to them & to you is sacred to me. I dreamed two nights ago— that I was in some town & had Cooney with me. In crossing a wet place I fell down & the little monkey ran laughing away—I went after him as fast as I could but lost sight of him (you may imagine the trouble I was in) at length I concluded the best way for me [was] to return to the Hotel where we were all stopping & inform his father—when I got into the house—the sweetest sounds that ever met my ears was the cries of dear Cooney—he had got back in some way & you were tuning [?] him for the trick he playd me. So much for my dream. Had I not dream'd he was found—I should not have told you my dream and would have been very uneasy about Cooney. God bless his dear little heart & may God! bless & preserve you all my children and restore you all in as good health to me as when we parted. It is very cold. How much I wish all I love were this night—safe under this old roof. I am sure you would all be more comfortable & I am sure I would be more happy—the wind still blows. Surely dear Butler did not attempt to come home today—I know poor fellow he would do for the best. If he was any where else than at Mr Grants I would be satisfied he would be prudent. God! help me how many causes I have for anxiety. My poor Malley! I fear he had a bad time of it going North. I have heard nothing further from your dear father. Dear Tootee do you not think I have much to make me anxious & miserable? I shall look anxiously for a letter from you dearest. I hope Wm has been able to select the negro blankets & the shoe measures were not lost on the way. Tip sends much love to you all. My love to Wm & my beloved Lord also to John if he did not come to the Fancy ball which I heartily wish had never been thought of. Kiss each dear child & tell them to kiss you for

Your affectionate Mother

Anna King

I will try & write a few lines by the boat tomorrow I will do my best to get the things sent—but poor Sam is no longer there to watch for me.[2]

Friday morning

After writing to you last night I sat by the fire thinking where you all were. Of dear Butler his brother and sisters perhaps the most—when I heard some one enter the house I hailed fast enough you may imagine & dear Butler answered. It is only me Ma. The wind & intense cold was too much for the girls but he would not remain knowing my anxious nature. He you may be sure had a cold time of it. Left at 4 yesterday afternoon—put up a big sail & busted it down—Postell came with him—expecting his carriage to meet him at Hazzards. Butler went up to the House with Postell of course no carriage there Hazzards horses out—So Butler rushed back on his Turkey legs to the boat—landed at Hamilton and on "them thar" same legs came home in double quick time. The boat was to meet Floyd and the girls at Bryans landing today but the weather is not only bitter cold but boisterous & rainy. B[utler] says the party went off beautifully—kept it up until 7 A.M. I will try my best to put the things on board the *Welaka*—but you know what my negros are & this weather will keep back the *Welaka* nothing will spoil. I send a letter for you which came on Wednesday. Give my dear Lordy a kiss for me the same to your own dear children.

Your own Mother

A M King

1. Maria's daughter Augusta was born December 25, 1855. See appendix 2.

2. There is no record of Sam's death in the "Deaths of negros from June 1854." See Selected Pages from the Record Book of Retreat Plantation, GDAH.

Retreat 17th January 56

My own beloved Lord

I wish you would read this letter of yours over again. You may not have *intended* to wound my feelings—I have long made it a practice to place the last letter of each beloved absent one next my heart—I cant wear this one the old letter must remain there until I receive another worthy of you my son. My very heart sickens at the name of money that root of so much misery in this world— I wish to understand *distinctly* how much you expect me to allow you. It is useless my going *over* the old ground again. You are as well aware as I am that I am deeply in debt. I could not in January last pay what was due for '54. The short crop in '55 & low prices at this time when the bills for '55 are fast coming in makes me really *miserable*. You my son should *learn* to economise you should spare your Mother every *unnecessary* expense. You say I expect you to live on $240 a year in Savannah when I allow Malley 6 or 800. Do you remember *how much* each year since you went to College you received? & how many years it has been since you first left home? You are not now *going to school neither have you high board to pay*. You three older sons have each one spent yearly far more than my circumstance would warrant—Floyd & Tip the last year seemed much inclined to follow suit. Not one trying to see how *little* but how *much* could be wasted. Dear Butler latterly has been earning his. You have had dear Lordy every advantage that our means could possibly afford. I have strong hopes you will ere long prove all has not been in vain. Malley must now be assisted on his way by one more years expenses. I was not aware it would cost 6 or 800. Neither did I *promise* so large an amount. Think of two years short crops & low prices—*think* of the out lay necessary for your younger brothers & that your three sisters must have some consideration & then tell me how I can support all? I expect at the end of the year to pay your share of the house.[1] I must know what you will absolutely require. And now my son I will stop the subject.—

Your Sisters Florence & Virginia are much indisposed from violent colds. Georgia seems to be getting one—Floyd also—Butler took cold on his way from the Grants that terrible windy day. Miller Grant carrying measles to Elizafield has confused all the previous plans for your sisters and their going to town. Even if that did not—Flo & Appy are now too unwell for any time to be appointed. Appy may be getting measles for what we know—I have not seen her so unwell for a long time. Florence's throat is very sore as well as suffering from a bad cough. I cant see to write any more. I had also a letter from your dear Father—he said he was well on the 26th. I wrote to Tootee what poor Mal said of his terrible passage on North. Florence has written to you. And given all the news she could pick up. And now my beloved son I must say good night—May God bless you. I hope your next letter may be such as should be prized by your affectionate

Mother
Anna M King

1. His portion of his rent in Savannah.

10th Feb 1856

My dearly beloved Child

I am very sorry the weather was so unfavorable on Thursday & Friday—if it rained in Savannah as it did here—the streets would be in no condition for you to walk out even on Saturday. I had hoped in your next letter you would have been able to give me your opinion of my poor Appys personal appearance—she has never before had so much fever my poor little one! how I do long to see her. God! grant she may have no more put backs & may soon again be well. She cannot be taken too much care of—she is so apt to take cold & every one goes straight to her chest. Florence wrote to me on the 8th and assures me her Sister is gaining strength. I am truly grateful to all who have been kind to my poor little girl. I know Clementine to be very kind hearted. I owe her much for her constant attention to Appy. I am sorry Appy & herself have had so sad a visit of it. That yourself & family Geo, F[lorence] & Lord can yet say "we are about" is a great comfort to me. Oh Tootee what a wearing & tearing of the heart is this suspense as regards the life & safety of my husband & children.

Another Mail & again no further intelligence from your poor Father. The papers say Austin is more than usually sickly. This long silence makes me fear he is ill & not able to write. I can only pray I may be mistaken. I can only hope God! will be merciful to us & spare the life of the best of husbands & fathers.

As much as I want to hear from you all I now dread Mail days—fearing some bad symptom in Appy—some evil to the others. I am distressed for your precious children—would it not be safer to bring them here? No mumps here & I do not think their chance of getting measles would be as great as in Savannah. I do not urge it as I would wish—These diseases all go lighter with children than adults—still I dread hearing they are all down & I poor me not with you. I heard from Malley he was well on the 1st—but not from Tip. He promised to write to me every week. God! grant he may not be sick. It is a pity I was not prepared to receive your work by the Planter. I expected a parcel from you & sent over to Hail the *Welaka*—on her return it was dark when she past Hamilton & did not stop. Prince[1] told Alfred the *Planter* had left a box which he saw on the wharf in the rain & had put it away for who ever it belonged to. This was on Friday night & we heard of it on Saturday—Butler called at Hamilton on his way from New field & found it was for me as the top was made up of two boards & the box broken in the bargain, of course everything was wet, but make yourself easy my love nothing of yours injured—I dried them in my room. The bread (thanks to you) I put into the oven. The mutton sent me by you or the girls I put to roast as it was smelling a little sourish & we had it today for dinner—rather underdone but Butler says it will be nice broiled tomorrow & we will have it for breakfast. Flora sent a dozen oranges—So the box contained quite a treat—bread, mutton, oranges, thanks to all to whom we are indebted. I am truly sorry I did not get the work on Friday or until late on Saturday. The pants I will set Rhina & Maria at on Monday—if I can induce them to exert themselves they may be done in time to go in the *St Johns*. It will be well to enquire for them—the rest of the work I will get done as soon as possible. Christiann is very much better but it will be well not to make her sew too soon you know one of the miserable effects of Measles is the weakening of the eyes. As yet her child shows no symptom of getting it but I think it will have it.

If Mr Morris's charges are not beyond my means I will send Floyd the last of March. I should like to make him more shirts—I want you to see if you can get me 10 tucked bosoms at DeWitt & Morgans—the wove tucks are most durable. If they have none on hand perhaps they would send to N.Y. for them. They asked me $1.25 a piece for them last year that is high. Those they sent me were coarse for that price. I shall not want them before the girls are coming home—by that time I will mention other things I want you to select for me.

Monday morn

Many annoyance[s] this morning they began last night—when William hears of it he will say "I have all along said those fluid lamps are dangerous things" but in this case, as in every other that I have ever heard of all blame rested on the one handling it. I was very nervous & would not go to bed. Floyd was asleep as also Tulla[2] & Annie. I found the two lamps in my room had neither of them an extinguisher was too lazy to go down for them myself—did not like to make either of the girls get up as they have bad colds. I hated the idea of losing one or two cents worth of Fluid—So I thought to empty one in to the other & use my thimble to keep the Gas—most foolishly I stood by your Fathers beauro—on which were many letters not yet opened placed under your fathers cushion. My tucking comb which dear Geo made over to me the new box Homeopathic medicine & too many other little things (you know I always keep my dressing table very much littered). I could not see without a light to empty one lamp into the other—so I took very wisely a paper box put the first top with wick very safely into it—leaving it burning but propt up then took out the other & more foolishly still placed it by the lighted one. Both had long wicks both blazed up all among letters read & unread—had I been content to have brushed only these on to the oil cloth it would have saved me much fright & trouble—but I swept everything off lamps & all—All was in a blaze & may be I did not scream "fire"—up jumped Floyd dragging in all his blankets & cumfort he put on his worsted stockings & had on drawers as he came in the little girls had got up—they threw a bucket of water over the fire—which the blankets would have extinguished more pleasantly for me. When all was extinguished I had the trouble of mopping up the water. I at last concluded to send them all back to bed—Tulla began to wheze like a broken winded horse gave her Jackson syrup. Then my dear Floyd began to sneeze I gave him Jackson syrup & another blanket & this morning as yet neither seem the worse for last nights frolic.

At twelve I thought I would try to sleep. Then I heard a knocking at the flat & found Flanders[3] was trying with all the men to get off the flat. I would have given much to the person who would advise him to go back to his bed & let the flat stay until next spring tide. I felt satisfied she would not get off. So I watched & watched—saw she had moved but still the lights were being moved about—at two all had gone out. I then went to bed. At day light this morning Peggy came blowing into the room "Abagale"[4] wrapped in a blanket—She had fever last night & Peggy was afraid of the measles in the Hospital—I gave her some aconite & sent her into Floras room. Scarce had she gone when Pussy came to tell me little Ruthy had a baby last night[5] & to make matters worse she had attended her in the same clothes she has been wearing I believe ever since Christiann sickened—It is strange how perfectly careless negros are. And poor Pussy can now be but little depended on. Our dear Butler has increased his cold in some way & feels badly this morning—I am glad he did not go out last night—had he done so I would have felt worse than I now do about it. Our work is exceedingly backward & that worries him very much—the weather has been so terribly cold & so much rain—the negros all with bad colds & many laying up—& he wants experience & advice—& it worries him poor boy. After all I have told you are you surprised I should be nervous this morning? All this you will say "after all is not so much["]? Very true & thankful I am it is no worse. Had I brushed the lamps to me just in my loose night dress I probably would not have been in a condition to write to you this morning. Could I have heard from your beloved Father & Tip yesterday—was my poor Appy restored to health & to me & all of the rest of you at home—I would feel very different from what I now do. Give each precious grandchild each sister, Lordy & cousin A[manda] a fine kiss for me. My love to dear William and to John Fraser. I will add a line tomorrow. Take care of your own precious health for your husband and childrens sake & for that of your affectionate Mother.

A M King

1. The name Prince does not appear on any of the lists; however, a Prince Hamilton is listed in Anna's record book. On August 10, 1856, she wrote: "Prince Hamilton for 13 fowls—1 62½" (Selected Pages from the Record Book of Retreat Plantation, GDAH).

2. This is, I believe, Tilla.

3. In February 1856 Anna noted in her record book a payment to Charles M. Flanders for $100. There is no further information about what the payment was for or about Charles Flanders's identity. See Selected Pages from the Record Book of Retreat Plantation, GDAH.

4. Abagail was Peggy's daughter, born July 22, 1855. See appendix 2.

5. Ruthy's baby, June, appears on the 1859 list and is noted as three years old. See appendix 2.

28th February 1856

My dearly beloved Tootee

I thank God! your dear Sister & Lordy got here quite safe at about 1 oclock—dear Lordy will tell you that our good Butler was at Hamilton awaiting their arrival—poor fellow his usual luck. His cold was very bad & made worse by their night watching & rides through the wet pine barren. We some how could not separate until near three—so the next morning it was near twelve before they had all breakfasted. Poor Floyd went late to bed & was so sound asleep he could not be aroused by a kiss from either his sisters or Lord. Our dear Virginia as well as G[eorgia] & F[lorence] seem delighted to have got home—not half so much as I am. I had become very lonely. I rejoice to add—as yet we cannot perceive any ill effects to dear Appy from her change of residence. My poor little girl how very sick she has been. Well for me I was not aware of it at the

time. I do not know what would have become of me. I wish my own dear
Tootee you & the precious children could have accompanied them. I do so
long to see you all & dear William too. I do not blame you for prefering remaining with him though I do think the children even—if they had measles
here would be more comfortable than their having it in Savannah. As yet the
disease has been favorable with our little negros. I wish your dear children were
here—that I may assist you nurse them through it—It is a disease that generally goes easier with children than grown persons. 20 have had or have it. I will
be glad when the last are over it—I had to turn Rhina out of her room. Which
she kept in very nice order, in appearance a contrast from others. The Hospital has never been so filled since it was built. Thank God! as yet no deaths.

Lord will tell you of who has been here since he came. Capt Ossenger the
only pleasant one. Mr Bourke has taken such a deadly hatred to Lieut Longfellow he did not speak to him. Some days ago Postell invited Capt Ozenger to
dine with him & yesterday was the day named. Postell told Butler he had invited the Capt & if his (Postells) carriage was not there that Butler would give
him a conveyance (just like him is it not). The Capt landed & seeing no conveyance ready—did not come to the house but footed it there—when yet there
M[r] Postell he was informed had gone to Brunswick—so he footed it back &
Butler sent & invited him in—but we had nearly done dinner—he however
found enough to satisfy hunger & spent the evening.

The first Clementine has done was your collars &c. If you think it worth the
freight—send them all back when soiled & it shall be done again & again &
with pleasure—Christianns eyes are yet too weak to do nice work. I will put
her at your work the end of this week. The shirts for William I presume you
will wish done first. All shall be done as soon as I can. I thank you my darling
for the fish—I beg dear Tootee that you will send no more. The bread was very
acceptable the more so as I am out of wheat flour. It came in beautifully last
night—when those people were here. It is getting dark now & I must conclude
until tomorrow.

29th

All pretty much as they were yesterday. Appy took a drive yesterday & Floyd
went shooting this morning & actually returned having killed 11 doves & one
hawk. The doves—a turkey—a barrel of oysters (got yesterday) a barrel of potatoes & 10 chickens will go with Lordy. I sent Neptune last evening in my
little wagon to old Charles for your fowls—he got back this morning & I went
with Slate & pencil to take an account of them & was very much disappointed
to find but 10 & one of them with sore eyes. I will give that one to my little sick
negros & send you one of mine in its place. I would gladly send you more than

Charles' chickens could I get them for love or money—but none are to be had. Spring time is coming.

I am very sorry you sent back little Bell. I am certain you must miss her services small as they were. I am sorry you sent her back—As regards the rest of that family my dear Tootee I am sorry to perceive that you consider the matter in the light you do. It is very unfortunate as it has resulted that I was ever so weak as to make that promise. I did not at the time consider that the little I have should be held together. I gave you Middleton from the time he was a child—but did not think it necessary I should give you a deed of him—I will do so now if you prefer it. I would prefer consulting with your Father before giving up all right to Christiann her child & future children. I now tell you in good earnest. That I considered her as yours & Nora[1] as Annas—her future children as yours[.] Clementine must remain with me as long as your Father & I live—Bell I want for Georgia. Depend on it my Tootee I will ever do all that I can to assist you. At this time I am exceedingly pressed and unless I am assisted will be in as bad a way as Postell or any other poor unfortunate person. The expenses of my family & plantation are enormous. You recollect I made Georgia a promise of giving her Rhina—Florence Maria—& Appy Ellen. They have nothing to show for them—neither will they have. They must [be] content if I can give them each a maid Georgia has long since relinquished R[hina] & Annie—Flora claims only Tilla—& Appy claims no one of Ellens family. Christiann is yours as soon as you say so. As long as she stays here she is virtually yours—for she is put aside to sew for you alone. Whilst you were with me I required only that she should wait at table on Sundays. I do not wish to give you the papers for C[hristiann] until I speak to your father. Especially as I gave you Middleton without his knowing any thing about it. The only thing you can object to in this may be the short delay. As there is no doubt he will approve still the compliment is due him—and now Tootee let this subject be dropt— you are to understand distinctly that M[iddleton] is yours & C[hristiann] & her child as soon as you "say send her to me." I do not think you weighed every word you used. You are too good to affectionate a child to cause me the slightest pang intentionally. Fearing her eyes are yet too weak to do nice work I have not yet given her yours—I will get them done as soon as I possibly can. Mr Bourke will go today & I hope soon to get regularly to work again. I again repeat my offer to have your dresses, muslin, or any other washing done for you which Ellen can not do. If your children have measles I will send you Clementine—unless she is laid up at the time—which frequently happens when I most require her services. The only important work I have for her to do is Floyds shirts but that must not be considered if you need her services to help nurse those precious children.

I have this day sent in my indebtedness to Mr Anderson as he offered to try & get a loan for me. I earnestly hope he will be able to do so that I may pay dear William for his aid last year. I have named the amount due to William on that account. He can see Mr Anderson and if he has raised the money for me claim the [$]500 due him. I did hope that in January dear Butler would have got the money due in California it has not yet come & may be months yet coming. My whole crop sold for $5200 which by no means covered what I owed Anderson. Money money Great Father how much trouble it does cause.

I found more thread than I could possibly require for all the work to be done before you come so I send back a part. Remember I owe you needles & I dare say thread—I wish you would let me know when you require grist. I would send a barrel to day—but have none ground & Butler is so busy cracking cotton seed I did not ask him as you said you would let me know when you were out. I send all the eggs I can now spare. The hens do not lay well—but set admirably. So that I have to keep them supplied—I send you by Lord [$]20 which I beg you will first pay what I owe for the corn &c I begged you to get in my last letter. Keep the balance to get what I may require you to select.

I earnestly hope my beloved child you will not delay your return until May. I do so long to see you all. God! grant all may return to me. This letter you will find very crazy but my mind is much disturbed—My love to dear William kisses to my precious pets—love to our good cousin & to John—Your Sisters—B[utler] & F[loyd] send a thousand loves—Your devoted Mother
A M King

1. I am unable to identify Nora.

March 31—1856
My own beloved child
Although it is but two days since we parted it seems an age since I bid you, your precious children & our dear cousin adieu. John doubtless told you that that Steamer did not leave the wharf until past 11 oclock. Could I but have known this, I would have had one more hour to stay with you, & would not have missed telling Clementine good bye. Whenever I have made up my mind *to start* I have a mortal terror of being left & always become confused. The hope of seeing my beloved husband as soon as the *St Johns* should meet the Northern Steamer made me nervous. Too soon I was convinced the *St Johns* would not connect & then the hope became strong that *he* had come on the last Tuesday boat. Margaret D & myself were glad of each others company until we both tired of talking, so we each sought our state room. I had a book & did

not again come out until dinner. A very pleasant day it was—we never stuck once. I took leave of Margaret at ten o clock she went to bed & I returned to my book—by the time we got to Frederica my lamp was nearly burnt out & eyes very blind. So I took down my little bird—*threw my bottle over* board & prepared for landing—it was past 11 when we got to Hamilton—where we found our good Butler ready to receive us. His first question was "is Father with you"? The next "how are the children?" Until the first questions I had hoped your beloved Father would appear from behind Butler to welcome home his runaway wife. We got here safe—Floyd had gone to bed—your sisters ready to welcome us home & they kept me talking until past two oclock. I got up at my usual hour—they slept it out you may be sure the next morning it was near 12 before all had breakfasted. Thank God! I found dear Butlers cold better. Florence, V[irginia] & F[loyd] saying "quite well" & dear Geo relieved by having had 2 more risings in her ear. She is still obliged to be very careful of her eye—but no more pain. My little negros all better than when I left for Savannah.

I was foolish enough to sit up until after ten last night & had just got into a sound sleep when I was awoke by Rhina's coming into my room with a candle. My first impression was that little *Nat*[1] was worse (as he had shown a bad symptom last evening) the next instant I saw my blessed husband! I could scarce believe my eyes. Thank God! once more he has been permitted to return home. He soon told me he had seen you & the dear children. What a pity he did not reach Savannah three hours sooner. What a wonderful man he is dear Tootee he got to Darien at dark was some two hours in finding a boat—reached Frederica against wind & tide at past eleven—Mrs Stevens fortunately had a horse to lend—but the poor brute had the *itch* & had been smeared all over with Sulphur & Lard—she had a *blanket put over* him before the sadle—to protect your father from the greese—your father was obliged to trust to the horse to keep the road it was so dark—& he actually was here in his own bed room before twelve hours since he had ate the lunch at Riceborough he looked as fresh and as cheerful as though he had just come from a pleasant drive. Whilst Rhina was getting him some supper he went from room to room rousing up his dear children God! be praised for his great mercy to me. How oft has He permitted this blessed husband after all his perils by sea & land to return safe to his home & how well he looks. Oh if he was but free from his persecutors those who seek to have the pound of flesh next his noble heart—how happy I would feel now. Thank God! he was able to tell me our precious Johny & Tusie were no worse than when I left them. Yourself and those dear little ones are ever in my thoughts. And then dear William & our good cousin will have their share too & Mr Woolley & John neither are forgotten.

I found that it was just as I supposed it was why no letter came on the last

Wednesdays Mail. Neither Geo or Appy could write & Florence *intended* to do so—The officers spent one of their unconscionably long evenings here which prevented her writing on Tuesday evening & she of course *was late* the next morning & lost the mail. She wrote to you by the Friday mail & *thinks* she will do so by this—but I have my doubts. Tell dear William I am sorry he forgot to get me the *rice seed.* I did not like to worry him by *repeating my request on that subject*—for I knew he was very busy & I know now that he must have forgotten the promise made me. Please beg him to send it as soon as *he possibly can.* So that I may not have to buy rice next year. I cannot send the grist this Tuesday but will do so next Tuesday. When I hope to be able to send Willies shirts also. I hope Clementine has been to Dr Sullivan & that he may be able to do something that will cure that lump. I am the more uneasy from his differing in opinion with those other Physicians. She is loved by all of us & to me an invaluable servant. Tell her that her Mother & children are in their usual health & send her much love & tell her I was worried after I left that she did not come to bid me good bye.

I found letters here from dear Tip—poor boy he has been again suffering from risings in his head & deafness & bad colds—had he not suffered a great deal he would not have mentioned it. How is the one that was threatening you my darling? And our dear Cousins tooth—I hope it has ceased acking her. Tell my darlings—Anna, Willie—Cooney & John even little Toosie I miss them— kiss them all for me. Your Sisters have been making the most of the few flowers now in bloom—& their arrangement is beautiful—I wish you had them. They went to the Church on Saturday—Rhina did all she could in the time allotted her one of the three roses is dead—but the other two are vigorous—neither is the geranium dead. The Phlox is getting up all over the lot & they planted other small annuals. And now dearest I must stop with this & write to Mall & Tip. Tell dear cousin I have not time to write to her by this Mail but I hope to do so ere long. I hope the next Mail will being cheering intelligence of each & every one of those precious children—remember *you can't be too careful.*—

                                                                   April 1st
I suppose you are aware of your poor Fathers intention to return to Texas. Oh what a cruel fate is ours. He intended to take this days boat back to Savannah— but after counting over & over the time he has—thinks he may remain with us until Friday—I beg that William or John will be prepared to receive him *at the boat* you know the dangers which surround him. It will do neither you or I any good to dwell on this painful subject—How fortunate he was in getting from Darien on Sunday night—he could not have weathered the storm of wind & rain we have had all yesterday last night & today. It is again as cold as winter—

fortunately no cotton up—*ice* was here on Friday last—All send much love to you, William & cousin & regards to John & kisses to the babies—With affectionate devotion

Your Mother

AMK

1. I believe this is one of Nancy's twins, Nathaniel.

May 1st 1856

My dearly beloved child

I am indeed grateful to a merciful Providence you are once more able to say you "are all well." God! grant this blessing may be continued to you, and in less than two weeks we may have the happiness of seeing you safe back to the old place. I long for the sound of those dear childrens voices. Florence actually tosses up her arms as tho' little Toozie rested on them in reality. I long to have you back & trust our meeting will be one of unalloyed happiness. Please Tootee dear do not over fatigue yourself in packing up as when you went from us. It is really unfortunate that your only house servant should be lame & Ellen again sick. I can't imagine how you manage to get along at all. I hope our precious Butler will be back on Saturday night—he was far from well the day he left us. Did you notice his cough & how thin & badly he looks? Oh! Tootee dear I am very unhappy about Butler. Another Mail & yet no tidings from your Father. He may have written—And yet I am in painful uncertainty—Oh! Tootee this constant separation is hard to bear!

The Steamer came on provokingly early on Tuesday. Butler had scarce time to pack—I had been trying from Saturday to arrange my business—& yet at the 11th hour not time to arrange the flowers which I had myself gathered be[fore] breakfast that morning. And fear it was all love & labor lost—that all withered before they reached you. This terrible drought is telling seriously on every thing, but as it is just what we can't help—we must bear with patience. I wish we could invest our little all in some other business not dependent on Seasons. In my hurry in making out my ruinous memorandums the other day I entirely forgot—*a lock for my safe & one for the small door leading into the garden*—also vinegar & tea—5 lbs tea (such as William likes) 3 gallons *table* vinegar. I cant go the book case dearest this year. I have so much else that are really more necessary.

I am very glad you got me the *white horse shoe*. Miss Mary Gould says Mrs Cater has a beautiful plant of that description from which she will [give] a cutting

to *no* one. I must be content with the Plants you have got for me. Unless I can
have better protection for plants in winter it is folly to get tender ones they so
frequently die before ever blooming *once.* Before you come my most beautiful
roses will be over & they have been so very beautiful—I never had your Mountain rose in such perfection. The roses are not only numerous but perfect. I cut
them down last winter.

On Tuesday Capt Ottinger came & brought me one Banana Plant & some
Cuba oranges. Butler had not been gone an hour before he came—my first
thought was I wish these oranges had come in time for me to send half to my
little darlings but it is as well they did not—for of the whole number not more
than 6 or 8 had any juice in them—but all beautiful to look at. He staid until
12 oclock—little Longfellow (as ugly & insipid as ever) was here also. I will tell
you more of that evening when we meet. Have I raised your curiosity? Capt O[t-
tinger] went to sea next morning & says when he comes again he hopes to bring
us some melons from Florida. He certainly is very pleasant & amiable in manners & conversation. The best of him is he really appears *to be a good Christian.*

Yesterday evening your sisters G[eorgia] & F[lorence] went with Rosalie to
take tea at the Hazzards. I did not like their long ride in so dark a night—but
they got back safe. I was reading in the little room & Appy practicing on the
piano when a rap at the door aprized us of other visitors. She ran off to change
her dress—I smoothed my hair put on a cap & received Capt Frenchard &
Mr Mazaros—& would you believe it they sat until half past eleven. I was determined to finish my book & like a silly old woman after they did go I sat up
until 3 oclock & up at my usual hour 6 this morning consequently I feel very
cross & stupid. I have no doubt these officers will now for some time be here
every evening. If they would only not stay so late I would like it very well on
the young peoples account. For propriety sake I feel obliged to sit them out.

I fear Butler will forget the paint box & fine drawing paper I asked him to
get for Geo. She has been trying to paint flowers & has succeeded so well I
would like to encourage her. Rosalie says she gave $5 for her small box of paints.
William I believe is a good judge of such things—& if you have time & the
money get them for her. I do not think I will give them any thing more in the
dress line this summer—one of our great faults is having too much at one time.
So much waste. I am trying to take up carpets & brush up the old house for
warm weather. Hard work with half sick servants they get on slowly. I hope
Butler did not lose the memorandum I gave him for matting & I forgot the
door mats to be purchased by him at the same time.

I fear I shall not be able to write to our dear cousin by this mail. The fact is
I feel it my duty to keep up a constant correspondence with my beloved children & my noble husband when ever my letters can reach him. I do not write

now as when my eyes were younger. It is a labor to get through a letter & when I write to you I think it is like writing also to Lord & Cousin A[manda]. Your writing me two long letters every week seems to bring you almost in the same house. In my minds eye I see you my precious & can almost imagine I hear your loved voice. Bless the man who first learned to write. What a comfort it has been to me.

Your Sisters are very busy preparing for the Brunswick ball. I hope it may not be a failure. Your sisters will go over to Mrs Bourke probably on Tuesday afternoon, if the wind does not blow too hard. The[y] will return Thursday, & you I hope will be here on Saturday night following—you must be careful to appoint the time that we may have carriage & cart to meet you there. All send much love—My love to dear William & to John. I have written to dear Lordy— also to our good Cousin—When will she make me a visit? How pleasant if she would come with you dearest—Kiss my darling children for your

Devoted Mother

A M King

If the jars of plants could be placed in an open box or basket they would come safer. I cant find the tape you sent for Willies shirts. I will have them done up to be ready for him when you come. Clementine is still very little able to do work of any kind she looks miserably thin.

Retreat 29th May 1856

My dearly beloved husband

I received a letter yesterday from Lordy who informed us of your safe arrival in Savannah on Sunday last & of your having left him in health. This is Thursday possibly you are now safe in New York—at least I hope such is the fact. Dearly beloved! God grant the day is not distant when you may be permitted to rest & enjoy the fruits of your labors. It is very pleasant to feel whilst writing to a beloved one that there is every probability of the letter being received. Depend on it as long as you remain in N.Y. you may expect a letter from me twice every week. William left us on Tuesday—I knew well how to feel for poor Tootee having by [?] experience felt how great is the pain of parting with a husband. Like a wise little woman she is occupying her time in teaching Anna & Willie.

On Tuesday Mr & Mrs J H Couper & their daughter Margaret came—the two former remain until tomorrow. Writing of that gentleman reminds me of his singular & most unbrotherly conduct to poor William. I believe I told you that Mr J H Couper had made so capital a bargain for himself in the Sale of

Hamilton & the negros—he had *given* the woman Becky & her daughter to Tootee. Both William & Tootee consider'd his conduct as very generous & were very grateful. But to their surprise & mortification Mr J H Couper *now tells* William *he must* pay $700 for the *negros*. William expected when he offered to make the purchase to pay this amount but when his brother *gave* the negros to Tootee he relied on their being a gift—& the amount he had intended for their purchase was otherwise employed.

God grant you may be successful & be able to help our dear Tootee the next year. Her husband is a noble fellow & will work himself to death to support in comfort his wife & children. When she first married you know I gave her Middleton—but nothing to show him to be hers. The girl Christiann I have always promised should be hers. This woman is unfit for any other than house work. For reasons I would rather not name in a letter I do not wish her to be longer in my house.[1] My wish is to give her & her brother to Tootee by a deed & when the time comes that our little property is to be divided let it be understood that this man & woman will count as *two* of her share. I intended to have talked to you about this when you were here—but put it off for a more fitting opportunity until too late. If no war, & William can keep afloat for one or two years more—as far as human eyes can see he will do well. Now is the pinch. I can but hope this crop may be a good one & that we may be able to help them.

We had a little rain last night & it is so close & warm this morning I can but hope we shall have more. We are all pretty well. Lord says you promised to Telegraph from New York on your reaching that city. I hope you will devote your first leisure moment to writing to me. I may be able to add to this before mail hour tomorrow. Our daughters & Butler unite in warm love to you. The children send much love & many kisses. Cooney says he "does not think Uncle Tom will forget his promise about the [?] horse." I think we should never forget promises made to a child. They lose confidence in our word.

And now dearly beloved I must conclude. May God protect you from harm—be your guide in all *things* & restore you in health & happiness to your

Devotedly affectionate wife

Anna M King

30th

Butler had the officers to dine here yesterday the dinner went off very well— & in the evening the young people had a little dance breaking up at a very reasonable hour. All are yet sleeping except myself. God bless you my blessed husband. Your most affectionate wife

AMK

1. The reason for this is unclear.

Retreat 2d June '56

My dearly beloved husband

By the Mail yesterday I received a letter from dear Lordy beginning with "I have received a telegraph from dear Father dated at the Metropolitan Hotel day before yesterday saying that he had arrived safe and well." Thank you my husband for your kind thoughtfulness in sending that message. More do I thank the merciful God! who guarded you from danger on the way. Oh how mercifully He has dealt with us. Lordy was well—he said Stephen King was still in Savannah—neither himself or Nina had been very well but nothing of much consequence. I heard also from dear Malley & Cuyler—As you have probably ere this seen the former I need not give you the purport of his letter relative to poor Floyd. If Mallery is correct in his opinion of Mr Maurice & his school I think it wise in him to remove his brother & very proper in Floyds disliking to remain in that school. I had promised Cuyler he should come home in his summer vacation provided he had studied well. He writes the vacation is but for one week & he thought he had best not come & I think so too. So I shall not see the dear little fellows until next December if it please God! to spare our lives. I can but hope that both he & Floyd have awakened to the necessity of their applying their minds more to study.

I flatter myself that dear Butler coughs less. He was out from dark until day light on Friday night & Saturday morning patroling—& I do not perceive that he coughs more. The Misses Wylly's negros became rebellious—& instead of J H Coupers taking the matter into his own hands—he preferred calling on Butler. Who had all his trouble for nothing the faulty negros were not to be found. Tootee & her dear children are well the baby is improving rapidly. Geo & Florence are pretty well—but dear Virginia is becoming very dyspeptic. As soon as she finishes eating her dinner she is obliged to leave the table from pain in her chest & also has frequent attacks of palpitation of the heart. She says in '54 she had these same symptoms & found after I got some claret wine & she drank some every day at dinner that she got over it. I shall send for some today & hope she will again be relieved of so distressing a complaint. I am in my usual health. We are again suffering for want of rain—but Butler & Toney say the cotton is looking well & I can see that the corn is beautiful. No sick negros to day. This is all that will most interest you my husband. Margaret Couper stayd here until Saturday morning. On Friday afternoon Mr & Mrs Bourke & Miss Catherine Dubignon came. Every evening the Officers are here so you see there is no chance for moping. I would really like a few weeks of perfect freedom from company—to rest & collect the means to feed. Mr & Mrs & Miss D[ubignon] go tomorrow and the Officers speak of going on Wednesday & right glad I shall be. I hope dearly beloved you will find your orders for land traveling has been fulfilled. Remember my husband you have devoted wife & nine affectionate children to live for. Without you what would be life to us? To me life would be worse than a blank. It is true Gods! mercy has preserved you through countless dangers. Still to a certain extent man is a free agent & we should not tempt Providence by going knowingly into danger.

Tootee received a letter from William which he handed to Jimper on Saturday night at Hamilton—as the weather was fine we hope he got safe to Pelatka & is now roughing it in Florida. As you are not skeptical on the subject of table tipping I will tell you some of our late experience. I have not time or space to write ⅓ of what has been communicated if they can foretell the future—time will prove the truth. Yesterday I asked for my sainted Mother. She said "she was perfectly happy with Christ—for 12 years after she died she occupied the 7th sphere but now she is in Heaven with Christ & those who died in childhood" (our William—dear little Bell & the infant Tootee lost). My beloved Father was happy too—but not yet so high as she was—but would be (The girls asked her which of them she loved best) "she said she loved them all." That Florence was the prettiest because she resembled my Father. I asked her if she could & would place her hand on my forehead—she said "not now." We asked when & begged she would last night at 11—she tipped "yes." So at 11 Tootee, G[eorgia], F[lorence], V[irginia] & myself sat down. She required the room to be dark. Evidently there was an effort made. I did wish it but must acknowledge I was a little frightened. She then spelt out "not to night." We asked when she then spelt out "when you my children are more developed." How long before we are? "In 4½ months" when we shall have physical manifestations. She said "she loved you—that you were at heart a good Christian—had done your duty nobly as a man a husband & a father." I asked her about her death—after tipping her age—how long sick—who was her Physician & when she died—how many years & months & the month & day of the month—she then spelt out "A voice came unto me saying [unreadable]" after answering several other questions—said my Father wished to communicate with me. The table then turned over into my lap—then into Tootees, then into those of G[eorgia], F[lorence] & V[irginia] for good night. My beloved Father tipped for me. His message was "you woo trouble to constantly my child, read, hope, trust." Then the baby awoke & Tootee had to leave—& it being late—he promised me he would come back another time and finish his communication. Now if we are really communing with the spirits of departed ones. They all tell us God! approves of our so doing & I mean to try again. Our darling Willie spelt out "My Mother love your God." It certainly is very wonderful! There is no doubt of the truthfulness of the past if they are as correct in predicting the future you may go on with your present work with confidence of success. I have not time [to] mention the other extraordinary communications—some very pleasant.

As we have so much company I very much doubt either of our daughters having time to write to you by this Mail. They all unite with Butler in fond love to you. Mr Bour[k]e expresses much regret his absence from B[runswick] when you went there. I hope dearest the next Mail will bring us a letter from you. May God! bless & protect you my blessed husband—is the constant prayer of your affectionate & devoted wife

Anna M King

Be sure you give me your opinion of the war question.

We are all as usual   8th June 1856
No 5—

My dearly beloved husband

It is now 15 days since you left us—full time I should think for me to have received a letter from you. By this days Mail Lord informed us he had received another Telegraphic message from you. That you had been to Cincinati (I hardly know how to spell this word). The letter was to Georgia. I have not read it—as she went to Church soon after receiving it & before I could ask her for it. The other girls tell me "you said you were well." The weather is becoming so warm I feel that you are every day more exposed to sickness. May Gods mercy protect you beloved husband. When I contrast the comforts I am enjoying at home, with the risks & fatigue you are encountering, I can't enjoy mine, & tremble for the consequences to you. May God! protect you from sickness & every other harm! Did you find the conveyance you ordered ready for your use? You of course are the best judge which will be your safest route. I know you do not care for fatigue—but I think fatigue of body can be borne better in cold than hot weather. I said the weather here was getting warm—it is hot & again very dry. It will do no good to complain so I will just stop. Our dear Butler seems to feel the effects of the heat very much—I really hope he will be able to go North by the first of August at furthest.

We have heard nothing either from William or the man he recommended to you (young Hamilton).[1] I would not like to be left alone & yet rather that, than that the dear boy should be made ill. On Saturday morning the officers made a move for St Marys—but the wind was adverse & they put down anchor until tomorrow. We shall not be long quiet for Mr Savage & probably the Grants will be here some time next week. One comfort I shall have, my good cousin promised to be with us next week. Her presence always does me real good as well as gives me pleasure. I not unfrequently think dear husband that "if I could get to some place where I would see only my own family (of course including son in law as well as his children) & dear cousin Amanda I would be really & truly happy.["] But I rather think I would be alone in my happiness— I am more certain of you than of the others. The girls would be wanting beaux & the boys Belles—So I must try & be content with life as it is. Will you be annoyed if I continue my communications with the Spirit world.

I received yesterday noon so impressive a message it has opened my eyes to the fatal fault I am guilty of. Butler was late down to his breakfast. I am not conscious that I looked particularly cross—but when I asked after his health—he said "not very well." Soon after Tootee & I got the table—in less than three minutes it began to move—the Spirit was Dummits & said he wished to communicate with me & that Tootee should call the Alphabet. This was the message Tootee asked if Butler had taken fresh cold answer "no" if he was sick— "no." Then followed "Your mothers irritability distresses him—your Mother always gets in a passion with her innocent children for nothing. She should govern her temper and you would all respect her wishes more than when she goes off in a passion, she should pray to receive strength to control her temper for if she does not she will become more irritable every day, and make a wretched family and became more unhappy every day and provoke he[r] God! past Mercy to her and draw down his punishment on her, and at last your Mother will go on to such a pass. She will go Mad, and make you all most unhappy." As sure as I am now writing—such words were spelt out to us it occupied three hours or very near it.

In the evening we again got the table. I had been so much struck with the message I had received—I endeavored to control my temper—& had succeeded beyond my hopes. Dummit made me his medium & among other strange things— spelt out as to you "At the Metropolitan Hotel talking to Gen (then corrected himself & spelt on) Governor Diamond.["] We asked at what hour Gov D had reached New York—answer "at 4 oclock this afternoon." This message was received at early candle light last evening—you can tell if the last was correct. On Saturday evening 7th June.

                                                                                                  9th
The spirit "tells me you do not particularly like my giving you his communications.["] I will give you the one of last evening as a remarkable one (between 7 & eight—I think it was he said) "He is in the Metropolitan Hotel talking with Gov Diamond about the Pacific Rail road plan." We asked if you had been about from New York—"yes"—Where? "To Cincinati." What for? ["]He went to nominate a candidate for the Presidency." Was there one nominated? "No the convention disolved without any nomination—and will meet again on the 20th June." When was Mr King in Cincinati? "On the 5th June.["] How long?

"2½ days." We then asked if Mr Walker would be nominated the answer was No. The spirits say they "can't tell the future.["] God! for wise purposes forbid they should. "They can tell the past & present & can think as we mortals do— & judge as we do, what is to come. Dummit regrets your having joined the Democrats thinks the American party at present more honest in their intentions." Admit these communications are all nonsense. He has shown me a true picture of myself & with Gods help I hope to profit by it.

I was not a little tired yesterday. When they returned from Church Neptune of course left the carriage standing before the Carriage house door until he had taken care of the horses. An ox cart was required for some purpose that stupid Jack[2] (careless as well as stupid) drove one of those ponderous wheels against the wheels of the carriage destroying one wheel entirely—bent the axle & injured the other. I[t] will take 50 or 60 dollars to repair the carriage. Most fortunately it was the one we got from William Couper. Had it been the beautiful new carriage I could not have controlled myself at all. Butler will send it on tomorrow & try & get it mended. Our dear Butler is not well today the heat is very oppressive which I think is one cause & then his bowels are out of order. All the rest of us are as usual. The Officers took leave last night which they really seemed to do with much regret. They have certainly conducted themselves in a most gentlemanly way & were very pleasant company only they would stay too late every night—Mr Brown is now here. If anything occurs worth communicating I will inform you. I must now close. All unite in warm love. I do not suppose you have had time to think either of Cooneys horse or my cans for preserving. God bless you my own beloved may He guide you in all things— guard you from harm & permit us to meet again in health & happiness—Your affectionate wife

A M King

10th
All went to bed early & I doubt not will feel all the better for it this morning— I am the only one up & dressed except the babies.

---

1. Young Hamilton is identified as Dave Hamilton in Anna's record book. He was hired, but the only payments to him recorded in 1856 were for $50 on October 7 and $75 on December 20. Anna wrote to T. B. King in September, "from all I can gather Mr Hamilton is strictly following Butlers orders. But the negros are trying him. He writes to Butler once a fortnight & will give his account of matters. Butlers crop has been the admiration of many, & the envy of some. Butler by following your directions—did all that man & the land could do for it" (Anna Matilda Page King to Thomas Butler King, September 4, 1856, WAC, SHC). Again in October she wrote to her husband of his progress, "Mr Hamilton seems very willing to do his duty but he

wants experience. And you know *negros will take every advantage* of an inexperienced manager. William Coupers health is so *wretched* he cant ride on horse back or walk far—& cannot consequently know exactly the state of the cotton or corn—which requires the first attention. In consequence of the drought the cotton boles are small & scrimped—William says he thinks there was boles enough to give a bag to the acre could they have filled out.—Our misfortune is having no one with sufficient judgement to know when to gather cotton. I think if dear Butler intends leaving you he ought to come to me" (Anna Matilda Page King to Thomas Butler King, October 27, 1856, WAC, SHC).

2. Jack, listed in 1839 as number 48, also appears on the 1853 and 1859 lists; his birthday is noted only as 1831. See appendix 2.

14th July 1856

My dearly beloved husband

Since my last on the 10th we have been jogging on in the usual way all pretty much in our usual health except the poor baby alas has again been very unwell. She is naturally so very delicate it takes but little sickness to reduce her in flesh & strength. I mentioned that the Grants were here they came with out a gentleman—And Lord thought it would be but an act of common politeness to escort them back on Friday—he did so & Butler met him at Brunswick the two returning home that evening—John Fraser came on Saturday night and will remain with us a few days. Yesterday we heard from Malley & Floyd—both were well. Tootee had letters from William up to the 2nd Inst—He was at Aligator & in good health. On Sunday we had a fine rain. Butler was perfectly willing we should now have dry weather as he is stripping fodder but at 10 today it again showered just enough to wet negros & fodder. William says there has been a great deal of rain in Florida. Georgia intends writing to you today & will I know give you an interesting letter. I am in one of my stupid fits & can think of nothing really worth writing & yet dearest when I think of you, so far away from us in this deadly climate neither wife, children or friend to care for you I cannot let a mail leave the Island without giving you intelligence from home. Dearest husband you promised me you would take every care of your precious life—Do you indeed try to do so? I cannot be otherwise than most anxious for your safety. May Gods mercy restore you to us in health and happiness—Oh how mercifully He has dealt with us—when so many have been taken we are yet on earth yet in the enjoyment of so many blessings!!!!—

Our daughters are yet looking forward to their visit to the Springs in Virginia—but I hope they possess too much good sense to *repine* if *circumstances* prevent their going. Mr J H Couper takes his daughter Margaret to Athens on the 29th—she will remain there & in Marietta until October. The Grants will remain at home this summer. We keep up the practice of riding every evening & regret when the tides do not suit for the beach which is now the case. The other evening Tootee & myself went with the children on the beach & saw three turtle tracks but had no means of getting the eggs. Lord & Georgia are singing so delightfully down stairs it distracts my thoughts—They do certainly sing most delightfully & it is a most beautiful accomplishment. By the way the Grants learnt from Bob Troup fresh from Philadelphia the doings of Mr Butler & his daughters. The daughters very naturally & properly desired to visit their Mother on her return to this country. This the Father positively forbid. And after much trouble Sarah (being of age) determined she would go & did go. Mr Butler forbiding Fanny & Sarah from corresponding. Whilst Sarah & her Mother were in N.Y. they sa[w] Mr Butler in an omnibus riding by—the Mother immediately Telegraphed *Fanny to* come to her. Some how Mr Butler got wind of her having done so & hastened back home & found Fanny just ready to set out & put a stop to it. His conduct is very much condemned by society in Philadelphia. He threatens to disinherit Sarah & both his daughters if they will notice their Mother. I am *thankful it is Mr & Mrs Butler & daughters and not Mr & Mrs T Butler King & daughters who are in this plight.* I am really sorry for Sarah Butler. I wish she was well married & then she could show respect to both parents. What can be more dreadful than a divided family!!!

I hope it will now not be long before I hear from you from Austin. I try to be *patient.* I wish I could blot the last summer from my memory. I was *nervous* & did not appreciate the blessing of having you with me. Pardon me dearest husband for having wounded your noble heart—I fear I have often done so but *never intentionally.* I feel that I am of a miserable discontented nature. May God! give me grace to see, & strength to overcome all my faults. I must now bring this to a close with giving the love of all to you and praying God! to bless you with his love his guidance—& protection from every evil and restore you in health & happiness to your home, your children & devoted wife.

Anna M King

No. 13   21 July 1856

My dearly beloved husband

Yesterdays mail brought me your dear letter of the 8th from Galveston.[1] I had hoped you were in Austin ere then—& should most certainly have been greatly distressed had I known at the time of your long detention in that deadly City. I do not pretend to say that I am now easy. *Nine* days is the test. Dear, dear husband how can you so expose your precious life to danger? God has been merciful but may you not too often tempt him? God! grant you may now be well recovered from the great fatigues you have undergone—& may be protected from *every* danger.[2]

What must be the heat of that region when we have felt it so much here. I think I have never felt the *sun* hotter. At the same time I have not a single night suffered from heat. As I have said before I cannot enjoy the comforts I possess for thinking of all the discomforts, risks, & hardships you are undergoing. Since I have thinned out the shrubbery & trim'd up the trees around the house it seems 10 degrees cooler & we have had very few musquitos.—So far none who are not compel'd to go into the sun has had any right to complain of the climate of Retreat.

Our beloved children & grandchildren are all well today—the little baby stronger but poor Tootee is in great distress of mind. Yesterday brought letters from William of the 9th & 11th. He had been quite ill at a place call'd "Alligator" and tho better was still confined to his room—As soon as he can travel he proposed going to the White Springs where my good cousin Amanda & her husband are staying. And as soon after as he can bear the journey will come to us. He has been very much exposed to the heat & rains of the country. The day before he was taken with fever [he] was out in a terrible storm of rain & wind—got thoroughly drenched with rain & had to ride after this 30 miles in his wet clothes before reaching his lodgings. I can but hope he will be spared to his wife & children. *I know too well what our beloved Tootie is suffering to wonder at her being so distressed.* Should you be ill in Texas! But I will try to put my trust in Gods mercy to keep you from every danger. William writes that the whole Country is covered with water—it rains every day without making it a bit cooler & that much sickness is apprehended.

On Thursday last Lord & John Fraser went to Cannon's Point. John was taken sick on the way & when they got back here had to go to bed. [He had] a very high fever for two days—but I am glad to say he is now up & taking Quinine. He intended returning to S[avanna]h tomorrow but must remain until able to attend to business. I am glad if he had to be sick it was here he should suffer—as we could have him carefully attended to. He really is a very fine young man. Dr Royal had been here attending to our childrens teeth. He went to Postells on Thursday & he too was taken with fever. His was caused by going fishing. John [Fraser] came to the Island chock full of bile is relieved of that & I hope will soon be quite well.

On Saturday we had a beautiful rain [and] at Church yesterday Mrs Hazzard told me the rain at their house was accompanied by hail & a perfect storm of wind which did great injury to their corn and cotton. I am thankful we had the rain without either hail or wind. Our fields (from the road) looked remarkably well. Very different from the cotton last year at this time—but there is no calculating what it will turn out. I *envied* no one their cotton or corn as I road along—but did *wish we had as good pease* as Horace Gould has growing on poor land. Our melons are remarkably fine—but the peaches very small & not many at that.

I have never seen on this island a prettier breakfast table than ours was this morning. Peaches—3 varieties of figs—musk Melon & blue berries—with ham, chicken, two kinds of bread—homany, clabber & fresh butter it was a feast fit for Kings. And I wished you were here dearest you, our boys & dear William.

Mr. James [Hamilton] Couper enquired very kindly after you yesterday. He starts next week with his daughter Margaret for Athens. Our daughters begin to despair of going to Virginia. I am sorry the plan was ever talked of.[3]

I had a letter from Floyd yesterday he was well. One of the girls heard from Mall—on Wednesday I heard from Tip. Thank God! both were able to say "quite well." I heard also from Henry King & Georgia from Uncle Stephen. Mary King had again been very ill & brother Henry troubled with chills & fever. [As] Stephen Kings health [is] improved they are now probably at Bedford Springs.

I have not heard Butler and Lord say at what time they propose leaving us. I am so reluctant to be left without either husband or son but think Butler requires a change.—God! grant he may not again get Cholera. Oh! this separation from husband & children is a sad trial! May God! protect you all! Our daughters wrote to you by the Tuesday mail. All unite in warm love to you praying fervently to Almighty God! for his choicest blessings on you my beloved husband. I am your affectionate wife

A M King

P.S. It is said "in ladies P.S. is generally the most important part of her letter." In this instance it certainly is an important one of mine. Please tell me how long you expect to remain in the inhospitable town of Texas that said Austin. Do you then immediately return to N.Y.? Take my advice dearest—go to Sharon or Saratoga—you will require great care of your health if permitted to return even without having had fever. Oh! in mercy to us be careful.[4]

Your own
Anna M K

1. Between 1853 and 1858 Thomas Butler King traveled between New York, New Orleans, and various cities in Texas as a member of the executive committee of the Southern Pacific Railroad Company. In an attempt to build a transcontinental railroad and make a fortune, King promoted, through complicated financial schemes, three successive corporations, each built on the failures of the one before. Though King and

the Southern Pacific Railroad failed, his idea of a transcontinental railroad along the thirty-second parallel laid the foundation, in both vision and technique, for his successors. See Steel, *T. Butler King*, 114–115.

2. Anna King, who constantly worried about the health of her husband and children, especially those away from home, not only followed through newspapers and information from visitors to the island the course of epidemic diseases like yellow fever and cholera, but often enclosed prescriptions for avoiding exposure as well as remedies if infected. Moreover, her husband had during his many years of traveling been gravely ill while far from his wife and family.

3. On a visit home in June, Thomas Butler King promised his daughters a trip to one of the Virginia springs but was unable to keep his promise. To make up for the disappointment King sent a pair of ponies to be used in their drives along the beach. Steel, *T. Butler King*, 124.

4. Sharon Springs and Saratoga Springs, New York, were mineral springs frequented for their healing and recuperative powers.

9th October 1856

My dearly beloved Lordy

I had yesterday the happiness to receive your affectionate and very pleasant letter of the 29th—I have much cause to be thankful your dear Father was well—you and dear Butler not only well but enjoying yourselves. Your dear Father is never so well satisfied as when he has a difficult work to accomplish— He certainly is an extraordinary man. God! bless him & I hope will reward him eventually with success his labors hard & honestly—ever more for others than for himself [*sic*]. It is *strange* that Florences letters have never reach'd you. *I do not know how often—but I do know* she has written several times. Georgia more frequently. Appys eyes are so weak & become so painful if she writes even a few lines that she has not written to yourself & I think but once to her Father since his return to N.Y. Rest assured dear Lordy you possess a large & your full share in the hearts of your Parents Sisters & brothers. We all seem willing to make every allowance for your want of punctuality—As you have experienced the difficulty weak eyes occasion you can appreciate what Georgia & Appy have now to contend with. Georgia will read & write & paint a little every day— poor Appy dare not read at all. And now we have a third—poor Tip he must have suffered dreadfully when first afflicted with sore eyes—poor boy he is unfortunate—he is one of the sweetest little fellows so gentle & yet you can see his dear Fathers spirit breaking out when an occasion presents itself. He has not grown as tall as I thought he would. I did not hear from either Malley or Floyd by the last Mail—you say they are well—which ought to satisfy me. I am glad to hear you are taking more lessons in singing—I do not think you needed *further improvement*. I really wish your dear Father would induce Malley to take lessons—To my taste he has a very fine voice which only needs a little cultivation. I fear Butler is too stiff necked for me to ask him to take lessons. Our precious little Geo is now warbling away most sweetly—I wish she too could take further instruction.—

Your sisters have a lonely time—poor girls I am really sorry they have so few enjoyments. If G[eorgia] & Appy could only use their eyes their life would not be so dreary. I hope you will be able to tell us a great many pleasant things when you come—your dear Father says "you & Butler were the leading beaux (at Saratoga) with the first people of the land & they are much courted & highly appreciated here." You write a very delightful account of the way your time is being spent—What a contrast to our hum drum life.—

When we went to see our dear cousin off we expected to see Mrs Troup & the Grants on board the *Welaka*—they were to have taken boat at Brunswick that day—but they were not on board—We have not heard since of their movements. Mr J H Couper goes tomorrow to the Up Country. We feel very dull & still since dear Tootee & her little ones left us for Cannon's Point. Your pet is again gaining flesh & I hope will have no more put backs. I will give her your kiss when she returns. Geo has written to you. Florence & Appy unite in fond love to yourself, Father & brother. It is well John Fraser fix'd on Saturday for leaving had he put it off until Wednesday he would have had another rough passage. Showers pass on all sides but none comes to this thirsty spot. Your horse is well—I saw her kicking at Sally yesterday. My love to your Father & brothers. I have written to the former & Butler—God bless you now & ever my son—

> Ever & ever your affectionate Mother
> A M King

"Chip" sends lots of love—[1]

1. I am unable to identify Chip.

3d November 56

My dearly beloved Lordy

You certainly deserve our thanks for no less than three letters from you by yesterdays Mail—you are so honest in confessing your faults we cannot otherwise than pardon your sins of omission—do you think we can those of commission? Florence says "you are a nasty boy!"—but I must not let her know that I repeat what she said—it will only make matters worse. I feel no inclination to kick you even in imagination. *I feel hurt* when you will not take the trouble to write to me—your knowing this *shall be your punishment.* I am glad to find you are assisting your dear Father be sure to cross you[r] t's & dot your I's, & *never divide your* words as I have just done—& make stops where he does—then you will please him. You know I have had some little experience in the matter.—

I did not write to either Butler or yourself last week—judging from the reports which reached us that dear Butler would be on his way to Cuba & you on your way home before my letter would get to New York. I hope you will return with redoubled energy to your business with a good stock of health & energy to carry you on. The plantation really requires dear Butlers presence or I would have no objections to his going for a short time to Cuba—I am grieved that my wants should fetter his movements *May God!* bless the dear boy!!![1] I[t] will be "a worlds wonder" if your dear Father really does get his reward for all he has undergone. It is wonderful his indomitable energy & perseverance. May God bless him too the dearly beloved husband & Father.—

Your dear little pet is just now "looking up" again—a wee bit more flesh on her bones. She can say many words & never refuses to give a kiss for Lordy. She walks alone but not with a very steady step. The dogs invariably follow in her wake—Johnny has christianed them "*Bungy—Dandy* & *Stepson.*" You cant grieve Toozie more than by threatening to whip "Daney" as she calls Dandy. Cooney has no appetite & still looks thin—the influenza doubtless causes this—For Appy says all she eats tastes the same or is without taste. We have now corn pies, which you know she "adores." She eats heartily but with a discontented countenance. I am glad you are enjoying so much recreation. I hope it will not unfit you for business.

I have written to your dear Father & Butler of the health of the family. Willingly would I exchange bodily health with poor William it is really melancholy his now wretched state of health. Your dear Sister bears up wonderfully. Georgia is succeeding astonish[ing]ly with her painting she says it does not injure her eyes—The Influenza had made Appys eyes worse. It is distressing to see how eagerly she listens to any one who will read aloud for her. I am now again the reader of the family. Tootees & Florences throat prevent their using their better eye sight—It [is] true my want of sight has destroyed my reading but I manage to stumble along tolerably well tho the pronunciation of French or Spanish words does bother me & amuse my more accomplished daughters—I am at present reading the *Conquest of Granada* for want of a more modern book of interest.—

I must now conclude having yet to write to dear Malley & Floyd—All unite in fond love—Praying Gods! choicest blessings on you my son

Your devoted Mother

A M King

1. This is an interesting and unexplained turn in Anna's attitude toward Andrew and Louisa King.

Monday morning
15 Dec 56

My own beloved child

Thank God! thank our merciful Father who has permitted you once more to write hopefully of your precious ones. Oh! Tootee dear what agony of mind have I suffered since Wednesday morning last. The only semblance of relief I had was to hide away from every human eye & pour out my soul at the throne of Mercy—praying more for you my Tootee than for the loved sufferers. Had the *Clinch* come along even on Saturday evening I would have gone to you but she only passed this morning. When my heart has been relieved to a great extent by your dear letter & what our good Butler has told us. It is true relapses are more than possible but we have hope both Father & child will now recover. On Saturday night I could not sleep until quite late. I got doctor books & read of inflammation of bowels & bladder & went to bed with the firm impression our poor baby was by that time no more. I slept & dreamed "that Butler had come & said dear William was a little better but the baby had left you before he reached S[avanna]h—that Dr Sulivan was also there & he (Butler) rather rejoiced as he did not think Dr S—— understood Williams case." I awoke feeling the bitterness of my grief for the little angel was past. I could not have felt worse had these words been actually told me. On enquiry no boat had past. Mallery had been from 10 at night waiting for dear Butler at Hamilton. As soon as we had breakfast Floyd & Tip went over it was past eleven when Floyd returned to say the Steamer was in sight. The wind was terrible with scuds of rain. I went to the top of the Hospital to watch, & at ½ past 1 the carriage was in sight. Tip rode forward as soon as I could get a Glimpse of the dear boys face I could see joy & not sorrow. Great God! how I thank thee!!!

It was perhaps better that we were not alone in all this agonizing anxiety & suspense. James & his wife were here—& Capt Ottenger & his Lieutenant were here every day but one since Monday. We were obliged to exert ourselves. The three former participated in our uneasiness. Who is there that can otherwise than kindly be interested in the fate of William Couper? & the good Capt loves William. He came on shore yesterday to hear what Butler should say. Oh how gratefully his report was received by one & all. On Saturday night Flora followed me into my room at bed time & said "Mother I felt yesterday morning that our prayers have been granted—that Brother William & Toozie are better. I was praying for them Mother dear & as I got up from my knees a load seemed taken off my heart & ever since I have been hopeful"—Thank God Thank God!

Butler says he must go back by the next boat if my fears get the better of me I may go with him. At present I am calm, & hopeful, & see so many inconveniences in the way of my leaving home. I have given up the idea. Butler has returned more in love with you than ever—dear dear boy he is worthy of all our love. He r[a]n a narrow chance of getting his death by cold on board that steamboat there were 20 passengers he had no place to sleep & ate nothing from the time he left S[avannah] until he got here at 2 yesterday. He got a place fix'd on deck to sleep & was awoke by the rain—which wet him through & he kept on those clothes until he got home. I had letters yesterday from your dear Father & dear Lordy—both were well and sent much love to you & William—Lordy little dreams how near death his little pet has been. We are all very much gratified by this visit from James & Louisa King. I believe James to be really & truly a good Christian—his wife improves every hour on further acquaintance. And the little baby is without any exception of my own babies or of yours the most perfectly sweet child I have ever known. Not so pretty as sweet & good. A smile for every one—a holding out of arms—then putting the little bald head on our shoulder. She is not so large—but strong & healthy. I never took her in my arms or looked at her without contrasting her fine health with that [of] our darling—wishing she could only have been as healthy. With an infant health is every thing. If well they will be quiet & good. Capt Ottinger intends leaving us today I have s[c]ratched off these lines in great haste—As it may be until Thursday before the *Welaka* gets back to S[avannah] James Louisa & Floyd started for Brunswick before it was quite day light this morning—The two former wish to take the cars for Wayne County—Floyds being obliged to leave school is unfortunate—I think he begins to feel the necessity of prudence tho' I do not think his movement this morning proves it. All here unit[e] in warm love to you. William—Cousin A[manda] Mr Woolley & a kiss to each dear child—Devotedly and affectionately

Your Mother

A M King

25th Dec 1856

My dearly beloved Cousin

Were I gifted with the tongue of an angel I could not in words convey to you the deep gratitude I feel to you & dear Mr Woolley for all your kindness to my poor Tootee & her loved ones. What a time you & they have had of it my Cousin.

What can be the matter with poor William? It seems to me he is far worse since he went to Savannah—What do you think of his case my Cousin? Do you think he will ever again be a well man? *Answer me candidly.* And the poor poor little baby—Most to be pitied of all is my poor Tootee. Her life is *wrapped up in his.* What mental agony she has endured! my poor poor child!! In all this trial how blessed she was in being with you my cousin, with you & your excellent husband. We can never be sufficiently grateful to you. Tho God knows we do thank you with all our hearts & pray God! to reward you in his own blessed way! & He will so, my Cousin. Malley & I were talking last night—he was so ill & I so blindly ignorant of his case & how providential it was that Mr Woolley & yourself were here—saw his danger & did (with the help or permission of God!) relieved him. I have had very many other instances of your kindnesses dear Cousin. May God! bless you for them.

It is Christmas & but that the negros are idle I could scarce believe it was Christmas. I thank God! tho' so many are absent I have 6 of my beloved ones around me all quite well except Tip who has sore throat. I think he would have been better had not Floyd kicked the covering off him last night—he was very tired & slept soundly until awakened by the cold & pain in his throat. He will return to School next week if this sore throat does not end in Scarlet fever. What a terrible cold spell of weather we have had. How I wish you were all with me. I have good fires if nothing else that is good. With all my efforts my greenhouse could not be done. So all my beautiful plants are dead—the orange trees look very sick & my two beds of beautiful pease are boilt up. I *say* I will have no more plants—& will not again waste seed by planting pease in October. I certainly adhere to the last determination if not to the first. Do not think I have forgotten the Persian vine for Mrs Davis. You know the vines were put down in box's & the day before Tootee was to leave I cut them from the parent vine intending to send by her the day she went—they had withered, & on examination found *not* to have taken root. Neither your orange preserves—I have been so pressed on all sides with work I could not spare Lady to do any for either you or I but I will now soon have them ready. Tell Tootee be sure to enquire for a box by the *Clinch* it will contain only a fruit cake—she will have to get it iced over as Clementine made quite a botch of it.

26th

I have no Island news to give you—I believe all are well. You sent me 14lbs Sugar according to my weighing—I find I am getting late & must conclude dear Cousin with love to Mr Woolley in which all here unite take all you are willing to receive from my children & from your Cousin

A M King

9th Feb 1857

My dearly beloved Child

I have again to thank you for a long interesting letter received yesterday—I cannot imagine how you can find the time to write such long letters. I prize them very much my darling—I cannot be so *selfish* as to beg you to continue to do so. I know it hurts you to write much *at a time* & yet it is [a] very great happiness to me to hear twice a week from you. Please Tootee dear take more care of yourself. I am hurt you should think I was not *comfortable* when with you. As far as accommodation & fare went I could not have desired better. I was only disquieted when I saw how worn out you were & that I could be of no assistance to you. I do want again to visit you my darling—but I really cannot now say if I can do so. Your dear Father & our noble Malley propose taking the *Everglade*—you will be sorry to find the latter too is leaving us for Texas. It is possible you may not see them—so I will just tell you their plan. When your Father was so unwell—we thought it would never do for him to go again alone—He did not make up his mind to take Malley until Saturday night— Poor Booney wants to go—but was not quite ready. He will probably return with your Father in April. God! grant they may both get back safe & well.—

Your Father is anxious your sisters should have some recreation—Appy will go to Charleston with the Grants—Butler would take her on but he is not in the first place—well enough to go roughing it—& in the next he cannot now spare the time. The specks wont do at all. I have to hold my book almost touching my nose—I will return them by Appy with the best directions I can give. The butter is pronounced good—a little too salt but that fault will help keep it from growing rancid. The *brooms* are not yet forthcoming—Tell Beach I shall certainly not pay for them until received. I cant write business today.

I began to write about your sisters movements. At present G[eorgia] & F[lorence] think of taking a run down or up to Washington under Lords care. Your Father will furnish letters to some of his lady acquaintances. I dare say they will spend a couple of weeks there pleasantly—on their return they will make you a visit. I hope you may have the room to offer them on their way to Washington. How long do the Frasers stay with you. I dare say Mr Woolley will laugh & say "I hope they will have better luck then I had when I went to see the Inauguration." God grant they may. De Witt & Morgans bundle came by the *Everglade*—I carefully examined the dress waist but saw no signs of a 2 dollar bill—The lamps were there but one of *them broken*. Do you not think me lucky? I *will think* about the china at $75—it is a big sum—if I could get Spaldings price 45c for my fine cotton I would get it—Anderson sold the 31 bags at 35—it was the *common crop*. You can very well see I am much confused in mind—I will add to this tomorrow when I hope to be less so. If this weather only holds on I shall give sore throats to those impudent hogs tomorrow. I hope in time to send you & cousin some spare ribs. I hope the oysters were not too long on the way. Jimper had to sit up all Friday night for the Old *Welaka*— & I fear your dear Father & Mall will have no better luck tonight. This weather must be much against the *Everglade*. She past here ¹/₂ past 7 on Saturday evening—the *St Marys* two hours after. The *E[verglade]* blew of her whistle at 7 at Hamilton. It was a beautiful moonlight night—your dear Father & myself walked to the creek to see her pass—met Floyd on the way who insisted on it that she was coming very slowly. All I know about it—she past went across & was in Turtle river in the time we took to walk ³/₄ of the distance from the creek & we walked not very slow. So we thought *she travelled well*. I do hope she will do well.

The box's from the North contained 3 beautiful ladies saddles for your sisters—a *failure of a likeness of your* dear Father—1 saddle for your Father. The beauros I have not yet opened—too much else to do—the stands are very pretty & seem strong. Dinner is near ready & I must stop. So strange that I have written nearly 3 pages & not one word about your husband & childrens health. Thank God the former & dear little Toozie are still improving—the dear baby must be still very weak or she would try to use those poor little feet of hers— have patience my child—if she can only be kept from another illness she will ere long walk again—I fear poor Lordy will have a bad passage from Cuba— he is to leave tomorrow—God! grant he may have a safe passage home.

Tuesday 10th

We all sat up until near two last night but no *Everglade*—I am sorry your dear Father will only have to travel the more unceasingly—I am in so great a state of excitement I scarce know what I am writing. I have to beg William the favor to make money arrangements for Virginia with Mrs Grant—I will write separately to him—I send back the Spects—I have not the time to try & follow Williams Directions—If they would send me several pairs to suit my age 59 possibly I may get suited if not why I must do without & blunder on with the ones I have—I intend sending you 6 spare ribs 4 for you & 2 for Cousin also 2 neck chines— one for you & 1 for her. The sausages & cheeses will go next week. I have killed my hogs—how I shall succeed in saving bacon cant say. It seemed my last chance this season. Floyd is trying for birds if he succeeds they shall go. Appy (if the Grants go today) will probably stay with them at the Pulaski you are so crowded—The other girls will go a week from today if Lord comes in time.

And now baby I must say adieu—I cant think what else to say. Love to W[il-liam], Cousin A[manda] & kisses to the children. With fervent prayer all may be well with you—your devoted Mother

A M King

The beef was not fat—the soup not so good as that I first sent you—do not *touch it if not perfectly* sound. Please Tootee dear ask Middleton if Mallery gave him a parcel (those 2 vest patterns to take to Robinson & Camp to make vest patterns for Tip) if so get John Fraser to do me the favor to call on those men & ask what has become of them. If you really think I had better get the set of china at $75.00 tell them to pack them *carefully* & I will pay for them as soon as the next cotton is shipped. Floyd has killed no birds. I am so sorry.

5th March '57

My own dear Cousin

I have already written two letters to dear Tootee this week & will my own dear cousin give you one of my beautiful scratches which I request you will give her to read as I will want her to answer some of the enquiries. In the first place did she receive her basket with Appys new cloak from the Pulaski the morning she left? What became of the Doctors prescription for Nancy? A Phial of medicine put up by A. A. Solomons was landed at Frederica but not letter of advice? Did she by the *St Marys* receive a small box a champaigne basket & a barrel? I believe these are all the important questions to be asked. Before I go off of the track as I usually do I will just say Nancy seems better of that alarming symptom but [not] very well—& has several times complained of *chills* tho no fever follows—I think a *wet bandage helped* her. Toney is crawling out—but Ellen sticks to the chimney corner. Thank God! I have nothing worse in the way of sickness to complain of.—

I write such volumes to dear Tootee it is difficult for me twice a week to find news. I am trying hard to prepare for vegitable gardening & to get all things snug before my dear G[eorgia] & F[lorence] & Lord get back. In consequence of the prevalence of Scarlet fever on 4 of the plantations we are kept in a state of excitement—I can scarcely hope to escape it. The measles is at Postells but I do not fear that as I do the other scourge. It is true the Hazzards & Gould[s] say their negros get bravely over it—but I don't trust their sayings. The only or greatest fear I have is that it may be here when my poor Tootee is ready to come.

We have had quite an exciting adventure with a great big old hog which Alic Boyd purchased from Dubignons negro. It got out of the pen—& as the corn is now being planted it could not be suffered to have the run of the field. Two nights ago he was met in the road—a fine racoon dog belonging to William put on him—he killed the dog with one of his enormous tusk[s]—poor William *shed tears* for his trusty dog. Yesterday Floyd & Cuyler fully armed with pistols & double barrel guns—with Jimper to assist were out from 10 oclock in the morning until dark—they took Rock & all the tarriors. They traced the beast from where he had killed Williams dog—In & out until they reached Ebo landing on the *Wrights old place*[1]—The best tarrier we have received I fear a mortal wound—Rock got a bad cut on his leg. I think the boys fired 16 times into him before he gave up the ghost. He was very fat & the most of the shot took effect in his sides. They were tired & hungry enough when they got home. If he had not been killed we would have been constantly fearing he would be in the corn field. Dear Cousin do not laugh at me for writing the history of a wild hog.

Butler got a letter yesterday from dear Georgia written the day after they reached Washington City—Georgia & Lord attended a large party on the first night—Florence would not go. I hope now that the inauguration is over they will be thinking of home. I hope they will remain at least one week in Savannah on their way home. You cant think me a weak woman for being kept constantly uneasy about my beloved husband & children—God! had been very merciful to me dear Cousin heretofore permitting them all to come back. Again & again have I been blessed in this way but this will not last forever!

I am so sorry your eyes (like my own) are so fast failing you—I love to receive letters from you my beloved Cousin. You write much to my taste. How my dear Tootee manages to be so punctual in her correspondence with me I can't imagine. She is a dear good child. I all but envy the Misses Fraser their long visit with Tootee—My poor child! I wish her *purse* was as well *filled* with *gold* as her heart is with generosity. I hope this week will end the visit of two of those young ladies. I ought not perhaps to say this but it is safe with you my cousin.

I do hope & trust my beloved ones are under cover this very disagreeable day. How Cold! & now it rains. As we are very much behindhand in work I wish the rain which we also want very much would always *be at night*. This is the third time we have had thunder since January.

Tootee asks if she shall get me the set of china. I will take it at once—but I cannot have them for *common* use—too many breakages in this house.—

I want in addition

2 dozen white dinner plates
1 dozen do—breakfast—do
2 dozen ¹/₂ pint tumbles
4 large size basins with pitchers for chambers
The extra pieces—say *fruit* & *nut* dishes—4 each.

She can add—get also—4 oblong glass dishes for preserves—I enclose the mans memorandum of the set for $75. Beg Tootee to return it to me & charge the man to pack so that there will be no breakage—As in one box it would be exceedingly heavy—they had better use two boxes. Please Cousin look out for a pair of nice Fluid lamps for my Parlor mantlepiece. I must stop now or I will be going to greater expenses & the crop not yet in the ground—it rains beautifully—I wish it had kept off until tonight. Our love to dear Mr W[oolley]. Kiss my children for me (that is Tootee & the babies) love to William.

Your affectionate Cousin

A M King

1. Ebo Landing was a landing site for smuggled Africans, Georgia having prohibited their further importation in 1798. The spot is named for a group of Ebo Africans who chose to drown themselves rather than live as slaves. See Cate, *Coastal Georgia*, 67; and Wheeler, *Eugenia Price's South*, 26, for more on this.

26th March 1857

My dearly beloved husband

Yesterdays Mail brought us a letter from dear Malley of the 7th Inst but from you we have received nothing later than your Telegraph for papers. Whenever you are silent my beloved I fear you are sick! God grant my fears at this time are groundless!! On Tuesday night we had a most delightful surprise by the arrival of dear Lordy. They reached Savannah on Monday, Georgia & Florence remained with their sister until Saturday. Floyd had so severe a return of his malady I thought it advisable to send him on in the Tuesday boat—that Dr Sulivan could better judge his case & prescribe for him. He probably will return with his sisters the day after tomorrow. Lord says, as well as does Georgia in her letter to me that herself, Florence are quite well & perfectly delighted with their visit to the Butlers. We cannot be sufficiently thankful to the kind providence which so ordered it, that you could not carry through the plan you had form'd to occupy with your daughters & Lord the rooms you engaged at the National Hotel in Washington. Had you done so God alone knows what consequences would have been. You may have seen by the news papers the misterious poisoning with arsenic from President Buchanan to the lowest boarder in that house—the cistern being cleaned out of dead rats did not stop it. When Lord & his Sisters got there (as I understand it) the cause had been supposed to have been discovered—& the cistern cleansed—Lord could get rooms no where else & could not have got in there had not the panic driven many away from the house. He took every precaution not to drink water supplied by the house not withstanding which dear Florence was poisoned—tho' thank a merciful God! but slightly—Lord fell indisposed but it did not show itself until he reached Philadelphia when for 4 days he was quite ill. Again we have great cause to be thankful it was no worse—Butler thinks Lord still feels some of the effects—Lord himself it will wear off. I enclose you a piece taken from the last Savannah papers from which we may infer some murderous hand has been at work. Doubtless Mr Buchanan was their object. Eleven persons had died of this poison when Lord left Philadelphia—probably many others will die—The Hotel has been shut up. If the suspicions incorrect God! grant the pupetrators of so diabolical a crime may be discovered. Here after I would advise all who value life to avoid putting up at the same house with a new President.

Our dear Butler Appy, Cuyler & myself are in our usual health. All with our dear Hannah Page are as usual—William & the baby still very delicate. The Scarlet fever is at Postells. Tho' it is said to be of so mild a form I trust it may not get among our negros. We are again suffering from drought—tho the corn is all up beautifully In spite of Mr J H Coupers prediction "it would rot in the ground."

Mallery must have had a dreary time after you left him at Marshall—I wish (unless you left him work to do) he could have gone back to N[ew] O[rleans] with you—his teeth ought not to be neglected. I hope you may consider it expedient his returning home with you for the summer—& then start prepared for a long stay in that savage country. I hope & trust you will be able to return here in April—& not find it necessary to go North instead of coming home. You have so often done so my beloved you must not wonder at my feeling *suspicious*. Oh how much we do want to see you my noble, beloved self sacrificing husband!!

We hope the last few days had brought us spring—but to day it is quite cold again & *dry*.

[Last page missing]

27th April 1857

My own beloved child

You certainly do all in your power to relive my anxious fears—Thank you my own good child for your letters of Friday & Saturday. The last was handed me on my way to the Steamboat at Darien. I got a candle as soon as I was settled on board & read with a grateful heart intelligence less distressing than the one previously received & yesterday I got your other dear letter by the mail. Oh! how much I am with you in thought—& so sorry I was to leave you. But I could do nothing to help you my darling & poor Tip wanted his Mothers care & cheering. Georgia & I concluded she had better remain with Tip until Sunday evening—she would then return home with the Grants & come home to-day. Tip was able to leave his bed—but it was too soon to bring him out. I hope the weather will admit of dear Butlers going for him in a row boat on Wednes-

day—which we think will be safer than landing from a Steamer in the night. I
left Rhina to cook for & take care of him. She is a real trump that same Rhina.
She is used to traveling you know—& is not to be put out of her way by trifles.
She cooks up his little messes so nicely & attends to all his comforts. I was sorry
to leave the dear boy—but he was so well—I wanted to get home & thought I
had trespassed long enough on the hospitality of the Gouldings—I would not
have thought of these however did I for a moment think that dear Tip needed
me. For three *days* I read aloud to him *by candle light*. His room was too dark to
see *even how dirty it was*. This *is strictly between ourselves*. For they (the Gouldings) were really very kind to all of us.

   Well to proceed—If dear Lordy thought best he should remain longer in
Savannah I am glad he did so. But I so fully expected him I was made to feel for
a short time very uncomfortable at the idea of going home *alone*. Mr Grant
took charge of the baggage as soon as it went down came on shore to meet me
& said he had at Lords request placed me under the captains care—but just
then Mr Nightengale came up & very politely offered to take my baggage &
bird under his own care & certainly no one could have discharged a self imposed duty more completely or more pleasantly. The *St Marys* had got her
wheel injured at mud river I believe & had to have some repairs made then the
landing of freight & taking in wood kept us at the wharf full two hours. I was
sorry I had left dear Tip in such a hurry—the boat came in before dark & did
not leave until 8. I found Sarah & Miles Hazzard & a cousin (Miss Habersham)
on board. I got Mr Nightengale to take a memorandum from your letter of
what William had put on board & then gave him a list of my baggage. He came
back & laughingly said "there are *three* box's with plants—not one has a name
on it—I have chosen the best looking for you"—& as it turns out (by your list
contained in the letter by mail) he really gave me my own. When the Hazzards
were landing I really felt sorry for them (I have myself such a horror of getting
into a small boat) thinks I to myself I am better off having a good wharf to get
on to. When we got to Hamilton judge my dismay when Mr Nightengale told
me he was sorry to say I too must get into the small boat. At first I said, indeed
I can do no such thing—But the tide was over the wharf & the Capt said he
dared not endanger the boat. I know that I made myself very ridiculous but I
could not help expressing my fears. I heard some people laughing at me—but
I did not care—fortunately it was not rough & we did not have very far to go—
at one time I thought I would leave the box of plants—& thought seriously of
taking from my bosom *the Will* & entrusting it to Mr Nightengale. He had
every thing put into the boat—got in himself & some how I followed & in the
end got safe to land where I found Neptune with several of our other negro
men. Dear Butler was so certain of Lords being with Geo & myself he did not

go over. I got here safe—found all asleep—but a light burning—was in my room before Appy awoke—I then went to Florences room & had to knock some time before I could awake her. I would not have disturbed her, but that I wanted the keys. Fully awake the two kept me talking until after two oclock. I had that evening walked out to Mrs Kells & back—then the excitement kept me awake until near morning—I however got up at my usual hour & had my nice breakfast *alone*. Dear Butler was so worried that I should have landed without his being there to receive me. He was tired that night poor fellow and was so certain Lord was with me. Before I forget to mention it, Butler will be on in the Friday boat on this way to New York called there by business for his Father. As his object is to go in the Saturday Steamship—he may not be able to go up to your house. I had a letter from your dear Father yesterday written on board a Steamboat on his way to Marshall. He assures me his health is good—& that on the 12th he had heard from dear Mally who was then well— but Tootee dear he says he does not expect to be able to return to us before June. I very much fear he will next say July & so on. I do so dread his remaining late in that climate.

From what I can understand poor Smart died for want of proper attention— first on Floras part & then on Pussys. He is now gone & it cant be helped! Nancy has had another fl—g[1] Pussy gave her Dr Sulivans medicine & she is better. Poor Ruthy has again been sick & Clementine nearly lost her baby by its falling out of bed. Poor Tina![2] she says she never was so scared in her life. The poor little thing never cried but went off into a deep sleep—the blow was on the side of the head & swelled up to great size—she seems however quite well now. Tilla is not well neither is Bell. Ellen is out still grunting—nice prospect when a house full of company is expected. Tell dear Floyd the Brunswick ball was a complete failure. I know dear Tootee you will give your good advice & so will dear William & my good cousin to—to my poor dear Floyd—I do hope he will learn to take better care of his health. It is sad to see him suffer so long—Oh entreat him to see the Doctor as often as he can & follow *strictly* his directions. His poor Father seems in great trouble about Butlers cough & Lord & Floyds indisposition.

As you may not see dear Butler I will just tell you the worry he was in last Tuesday. Cotton, barrels, basket, were all awaiting the *St Marys*—when she came the Capt refused to come to the wharf. Butler got the barrels & basket put on board. Did you get the barrel of grist as well as oysters? Did Middleton & Christiann get a bag of grist? When Clementine came & begg'd Appy to give her a card for a bag of grist to be put into a box or barrel & barely wrote "for Middleton & Christiann" on the paper & this was all the direction the bag had. As it was taken on board *the St Marys* along with your barrels & basket I hope it got safe. John Hazzard being on board may have told who it was for. Butler had the ham in his buggy—got so out of humor with the Capt about the cotton he forgot all about.

They assure me that a Champaigne basket with the *ham & [?]* & Cold hens in a box went on board the *St Johns* on Friday. On *Tuesday*—a trunk containing a ball dress for Georgia was sent in the *St Marys* to the care of Couper & Fraser. I hope it is safe. I also hope if Lord comes on Tuesday he will bring Georgias Trunks—(one at Mrs Steenbergers) her guitar & my Plants—For mercy sake I hope *Appys skirt* (or material for a skirt) will come by Lord. It is almost too late now for the season. I ought to have remembered it when leaving you.

The plants I am very much pleased with—I find my white moss rose—is no moss rose at all but a very pretty pink rose. If you go again to Parsons garden get me 2 moss roses the deep red & a white. Do not forget that splendid large *yellow rose* you spoke of. Let him put into pots 12 such roses as you may select to be sent me in the Autumn. Should they be moved now they will certainly die. My garden is perfectly beautiful—I have never seen any thing to equal the cloth of Gold—Oh I wish you & Dear Floyd & the children were here to help me say "Oh how beautiful." The cold has not injured us, but that terrible wind on Tuesday night killed some of the corn dead. & Oh! my peaches—I am so sorry they were shipped off by hundreds—very few remain—What a terrible spring this has been. Cold, dry, blowing it is well for us our cotton is on the level.

The carriages have been sent to Frederica for Geo the Grants & Miss Rhet. I am getting the best dinner I can—yet think it very probable they will not come the morning was threatening & the wind has been high. I am told Mr J H Couper will *see no one*—still I intend going to Cannon's Point as soon as I possibly can. Florence insists on it she left her ring at a large jewelry shop near De-Witt & Morgans—if she goes for your dear little ones—& I do wish dear Tootee you would lose no time in sending them to me for I so dread their having Scarlet fever (Please let none of them at any time go near the poor baby) & if William cant get it she may—She says the man took down her name. I must now stop & see how down stairs looks. Please give this to Floyd to read—it may gratify him—I do not like to send to husband or child a short letter & when I get writing to you I cant stop—it is now three oclock & Oh mercy on me I have to dress & I do so hate it. I wish I could have rested just this one week—but no rest for the wicked. Kiss my Floyd—the dear children & our cousin for me. My love to dear William & regards to John & Mr Woolley—I am so sorry to hear that dear Cousin is not so well. Do not let her give up the notion of granting me the happiness of having her here this coming summer. I will add tomorrow.

Have you yet sent your dresses to Mrs Thomson? If not & you could get a very *thin* dress for me—put it with yours & tell her to make it for me. When ever you can find time or you are able to leave the dear baby see if you can get me 2 pieces of paper hanging—I want to cover my fire boards for summer. Dont forget Moss & wool.

Tilla looks very badly. She is just like her Mother—such a fool. You cant get a sensible answer from her—her face is swelled in the morning—her tongue is *perfectly clear*. She says going *up steps makes her dizzy*. On coming up to me just now her pulse were made very rapid & her hands quite cold. *She says she had not taken cold*. I know the Dr is to see the dear baby every day—will you ask him what I had best do for Tilla. She says she has no pain—only this dizziness in ascending steps. I think the sooner you send your children the better. Let Florence know when to come for them. Quamina—Clementine & Pussy send heaps of huddy to Becky, Ellen, Middleton & Christiann all of those named are well as also is Nora. Until Capt Freeborn again takes charge of the *St Marys* I will prefer (until the *Everglade* gets going) everything I ask for to come by *the St Johns*. I do not like McNelty & his clerk looks no older than Tip. I am so sorry old Freeborn is sick.

18th

We waited until dark for our expected guests. 2 carriages a waggon & Jimper, Neptune, Sam, Frederic at Frederica to meet them there—then Butler started in his new Buggy with Man Henry & remained until Sun down—no boat. Well we dined by candle light. This morning the same was to be done over when we got a note from Georgia saying they would not be down before tomorrow. From the appearance of the weather I look for another disappointment—not only of them but of getting dear Tip home. Geo left him doing very well on Sunday evening—I find Tilla has been *unwell* ever since Tip hurt his finger & has kept the thing a secret. I am giving her Philatoken—Please ask the Dr if I can venture to give her tincture of iron—as a tonic. God bless you & yours my darling child. Kiss my poor Floyd for me—He must not read this half sheet.

Your Mother

AMK

1. Unclear.
2. I am unable to identify Tina.

Retreat 11th May 1857

My own dearly beloved child

On Saturday night Lordy & Mr Maszaros went to Hamilton to watch for the Steamer. Next morning I enquired if they had returned & was answered in the negative. I was getting to be real miserable—not knowing that Capt Freeborn was in command—I feared they had gone out side that boisterous day.[1] Direct[ly] I heard the boat passing this place & rejoiced at her safety. I really hoped dear Florence had remained with you until dear Butler came—consequently was disappointed when I saw her get out of the carriage & still more so when *only* dear Cooney followed. All along my Tootee I have felt that I could not urge you to send your dear children to me. I wished you & your good husband to do just as you thought it was best. I felt that you could not doubt but that I would be glad to have them with us. I love them all as my own children & watch over them with the same anxiety & interest that I did my own beloved ones in their childhood. I was so sorry too for Cooney, he was homesick yesterday. It was touching to see his efforts to conceal from us that he was in tears most of yesterday. Not a sound was heard but frequent applications to his eyes of a pocket handkerchief last evening. Flora took him up stairs to brush his hair—seeing how often the hankerchief was in demand she remarked "dear Cooney you must have a cold." "No Poya I dont think it is a cold but I cant help the water coming in to my eyes." I am sorry to say his bowels were much out of order yesterday & last night he had some fever. *He seems perfectly well today—no fever no disturbance no tears.* I would not have mentioned the two first but that *I shall hide nothing from you.* Where I say he seems perfectly well now & more cheerful—you may depend on it such is the act. He says he does want to see you all very much & begs if you cant come very soon that you will send Anna, Willie or Johnny to keep him company. His dear voice always falters when he names the dear little sufferer. Oh! Tootee dear how my heart bleeds for you—that expression in your last letter about her is never absent from my mind!! Is it your anxious fears my child or does the good D[octor] say so? Oh! my God! give strength to my poor child to bear with resignation thy will!

I am still more miserable about dear William surely he will follow D[octor] Sulivans advice & leave Savannah in a very few weeks. I begged Mr J H Couper to use his influence with dear William & persuade him to follow Dr Sulivans advice. If he is taken what will become of you & his little children? The very apprehension is dreadful—beg him for your sakes to try & retain a life so loved so valuable. Oh Tootee try all in your power to persuade him to go by the Doctors advice. Do not Oh! in mercy do not let him remain in Savannah another month. Beg the Dr, Cousin Amanda & Mr Woolley to urge him to do the only thing that man can do to preserve his precious life—delay may be fatal. With Gods! blessing he will return a well man & will soon make up the expense. I would to God! I could assist him. But alas I cannot!

Last evening dear Cooney told me that which makes me very uneasy. I took him to walk on the beach to amuse him. We had a great deal to say to each other—I asked him when you sent Christiann to take him & Johnnie to walk where she took them—to the Park? "No often [she] takes Johnnie & me into the lanes where my Ma does not want us to go & into negro houses—& some times she tells us to walk on & she will overtake us but we wont go for you know we may get lost so we go into these houses with her." I was fearful when I was with you & saw her so dressed up such was her habit. I desire you will not hide this from William—& my advice is that he gives her a good flogging to begin with. I am not at all surprised to hear she is becoming *too fond of the street*. If you hope to keep her in her senses—*be strict* with her. But if you indulge her—she will be *ruined*. Tell her for me that as sure as she now lives *I will punish her* if she does not do her duty as a servant. *Keep her down* & she may be valuable—give her indulge[nce]s *& she is lost*. You are too indulgent to your servants—if they do their duty you are too apt to praise them too much & Christiann cant bear praising. Even her Mother has to be kept in her place. All have to be kept there. I think it due to your children that the huzzy is kept from carrying your inno-cent children into her dens of iniquity—& where they may catch disease. God! help you my Tootee surely you have enough to craze you. I shall keep Cooney strictly from [Missing last page].

[In the margin of the first page] 12th He is quite well this morning & is good & bidable as [a] child can be. Appy is better. Lord & C[uyler] had a most fatiguing day yesterday caught but a few dozen small whiting 2 other boats on the ground—not a single drum caught— saw no deer—which I regret more than the fish. I bribed a man to go out last night for prawn. He brought very few. It is so warm I have tried to pickle them. Hope they may be good. Send to the *St Marys* for that which I will give the Capt or memorandum of—I do not yet know what I may be able to send. God bless you my darling

A M King

1. Pat Morris of the Coastal Georgia Historical Society speculates that "going out-side" may have meant traveling out into St. Simons Sound rather than staying "inside" on the Frederica River.

Retreat 9th October 1857

My dearly beloved children

I could only write to your dear Father and Floyd yesterday. The Mail has been sent but I feel like having a little communion with you my darling chil-dren. I am making this a *joint letter*—On Monday I may answer my dear But-lers two last letters. This is a gloomy day the wind blew very hard all night &

rain began early this morning. If I was dear Cousin Amanda & Mr Woolley was my husband I would be wretched about him. He has certainly important business to take him to Brunswick—but was not well enough to venture out such a day as this is. He left us in the *Flirt* at Sunrise. Our dear Cousin bears this as she does all other trials *very quietly*. Oh! that I possessed her *faith*! That all will be ordered for the best. Dear Tootee is nervous—she so dreads Williams return at this trying season of the year & in the old *Alabama* too. Willie was not very bright yesterday seems quite well today—the other children—your dear brothers & I humble self, as usual. No new cases of fever among the negros today—Little Nora was very *ill* yesterday—this is the 15th day since she was first taken sick. Her fever is less this morning than it has been the last three days. We hope both her & Emily are better. Bell doing as well as we could expect—& the rest all better. So much good I little deserve—God! grant me a more grateful heart! Neither my husband, sons, or daughters say one word of a *time appointed* for returning home. I do not want you to come before it will be perfectly safe. Yet I should like to hear some *time named*. God! grant whenever you do come, a meeting of unalloyed happiness, may be permitted us.

In my letter to your dear Father I mentioned having received a few lines from dear Floyd. I wrote to him yesterday & referred him to dear Floras promised letter for intelligence of & from you all. Dear Floyd! we miss him very much—but hope it is for his own good that he has gone away from us. Mall & Tip went to the Regatta & ball at Brunswick on the 1st. A failure it was. The 10 dollars it cost Mall & Tip had better been spent on *chickens*. I rather promoted their going for they are very lonesome now. Mr Grant, Miss Johnson & the little girls were at the regatta—reported "all well at home." Mrs Bourke—the Misses Dubignon & Fanny Hazelhurst were at the ball. On Tuesday last Malley again went to Brunswick (a business visit that time). He joined hands with Jim Postell & Mat Tunno—they returned just in time for dinner so those two beauties dined here. We had expected Hamilton Couper & had added *another chicken* so there was enough. HC did not come. Alic wrote to Mall that his brother was too unwell to take his departure for Savannah that day. The news Malley gave us was distressing as regards dear Sarah Bourke. She has had another of those distressing attacks and tho' better her friends must feel great anxiety on her account. Jennie King her child &c got to Brunswick in the Saturday boat—there she had to remain her baby having the mumps. Mrs Col Wright returned to her parents also on Saturday night. The Col sent her home alone—whilst he is gone some where else on business. How *queerly* men are now acting? Why could not Henry King have come as far as Savannah with his wife & child? Why could not Col Wright have taken his wife to her parents & then gone about his business? But it is no business of ours.

I had a long letter from Mary King on Sunday who fully expects a visit from you girls—I hope you will be able to go to Allentown for *two* or *three* days. Not longer for I am sure she must by this time be heartily tired of entertaining her husbands relations. Stephen King, Nina & servant still there. You ask me dear Geo to have green corn fix'd for winter use—all was over when your letter came & the mischief is in the tomatoes. I have scarce enough to put occasionally in soup. I have again failed in tomatto crop. You dear Florence beg that Toozie may be kept in remembrance of you. No fear of her forgetting you my darling it was very amusing to see her last evening with a bit of paper & pencil she would scratch a few marks—then show it to Tootee saying—"See Mama I writ a letter to Pouee—I tell her time to come home & I tell her bring Toozee a red hat with red plumes and red frock and red shoes." I send Florence her note—She is doing very well now—talks a great deal & often astonishes us by the queer things she says. As to Johnny he is "a perfect brick" so full of life it is at times hard to manage him but so good humored it is equally hard to get vex'd with him. When he gets in a rolic[k]ing humor both cousin Amanda & myself fear for our teeth. It would not take much of a jolt to knock them out. Cooney is looking better. We have had to get fires in the house & comforts on our beds it has been so cold here. Mrs Henry King speaks pretty confidently of coming out this winter. We are getting very hard run *for feed*. So eat all the good things you now have a chance at. I will stop writing now & finish this another time.

10th

It rained and stormed all yesterday. In the afternoon the *Welaka* was seen passing here with the *Flirt* towing behind her so the carriage was sent to Hamilton with Mr Woolleys trunk—We were very sorry that he determined to proceed to Savannah—I never saw him looking worse than he now does. All his amiable best traits of character has been showing forth this visit. His trip yesterday to Brunswick through weather bad enough to make a weak man sick was all for no profit. Old Scarlett had got hold of the men who wished to purchase Lands End which circumstance put an end to the sale. The *Carolina* also passed yesterday—we have a ship at anchor in the sound. Did I tell you of dear Floyds saving Postells negro & raft? He is a noble fellow that dear boy! but often too head over heels. I do not know how much Postell may appreciate the favor done him by Floyd—but poor Jacob expresses great gratitude—de claring "but for Mass Floyd he never would have been on dry land again." It occurred the night before Floyd left. When he was going Jacob said "good bye my dear Massa—As long as I lib I will bless you for saving my life." All the sick except Emily seem on the mend this morning. I am so glad poor Bell did not leave us. Under providence we are indebted to our good Cousin & her kind husband for her recovery. This long sickness among the negros has put back every thing like sewing. For the last three weeks I have had to give up Clementine altogether. And nearly that length of time Christiann has done little for Tootee. Altogether it is a most worrysome time. God grant my dear children may keep well. In a pecuniary view of our case—it would have been more prudent had you all remained at home. If you all gain health I must not regret the expense.

12th

Yesterday I received your sweet letter my Georgia—also one from my beloved husband. A thousand thanks to both. Ten hundred thousand thanks to Almighty God! your being able to report all doing well. I do feel very anxious about dear Virginia—when any thing like pleasure is in view—she is too apt to forget every thing else. My children Geo & Florence watch over that child—leave it not to her prudence to guard against taking cold if she will not be governed by your judgement & advice refer at once to your dear Father. You must not remain much longer North. A bad cold would be fatal to my poor Appy!!

As unpleasant as this bad weather is—I hope the wind will keep where it is until the *Alabama* gets in—for William seemed determined to leave in her on the 10th. I wish he had remained if only one week more in New York. I am much relieved of anxiety on your account by the account you dear Georgia give of your life in the New York Hotel. I hope so good a beginning will end pleasantly. I can't but be worried about my precious Appy—And my noble Butlers case now. I fear it will be his *ruin*. Mrs S may find a richer Son in law but it will be a hard matter for her to find his equal in every other desirable quality. A second Mrs Deveroux I take Mrs S to be—I can but hope L—is purer more noble than Lily is or was. I would write to my beloved Butler today but I have really no time. I have to write for negro clothing shoes & blankets—My sick negros are all better today. Your Sister brothers & the children and our dear Cousin send much love to you one & all. I have written to your dear Father this morning. Tilla is well all to a bad cold—so is Anne.

19th October 1857

My own dearly beloved husband

I wrote you a hurried scrawl by the Friday Mail—which I hope has not been delayed as it would relieve you of anxiety on our account. Thank God I am still able to say the family are "as usual" & that I have had no new cases of fever among the negros since the 15th a longer cessation than has occurred since the month of July. I have but one patient now & that one our dear Tootees servant & nurse Becky. I hope she will soon be better for her sickness gives her mistress the entire care of poor Rosalie which is most tiresome work.

Yesterday's Mail gave us letters from dear Lordy, Georgia, Virginia, & William. I am glad it was not sickness that detained poor William but our joy for this mercy was sadly dampened by the intelligence given of you my beloved. William says on the 12th "Mr Kings cold is better" God grant it was! But Oh! husband all hope of seeing you before you go to that *Hated* Texas is crushed. I will force back all complaints. I *know* you are doing for the best but I cant help saying ours is indeed a *hard fate*!!! I felt so convinced you would be able to come home as soon as it would be safe for you to do so. I remained where I thought it was my duty to stay. Could I have believed you could not come—I must have gone to see that loved face heard that dear voice—& left these precious ones to their fate. God! is good & Oh how merciful he has been to us my husband! I will try & hope that mercy will be continued—that yet we may meet in life— health & happiness. Dear Lordy says he is to accompany you—I am glad you are not to be alone in that vile country. I hope dear noble Malley has a chance of good employment—*he is chafing under his loss of time* & looks anxiously for your promised letter. He has been very devoted to me & our little business here. Our crop they say is the best on the Isld—I pity those who have a worse prospect of a cotton crop. But there is comfort in feeling all that man could do has been done to ensure a good one. I heard also from our dear Floyd he was well—& is not only satisfied with his school but expresses a determination to do his best to improve. He acknowledges great kindness from Mr J H C[ou-per] & that gentleman declares Floyd was so attentive to *his* comforts & the charge of the baggage that he is under great obligations to Floyd. So they seem to be mutually pleased & grateful.

Our daughters G[eorgia] & V[irginia] express some intention to return in the Steamer on the 17th. From all I can hear Savannah is perfectly healthy. I think there must have been a slight frost there on the night of the 16th. It was quite cold here but in going to church yesterday I could see no evidence of their having been one. Brunswick has been & is still very sickly—several deaths—the vile Burnett who assisted in the murder of poor Wood among the number—so Brunswick has been relieved of one of the bad men. Scranton has lost several negros. Mr Woolley told me that draining was very imperfectly done this summer which is doubtless the cause of this fever & then they have no less than 7 quack doctors to help on disease. I received a box two weeks ago directed to dear Butler from New York. Thinking it may be another pumpkin I had it opened & found a handsome ice Urn of Silver or plated ware & nice tub—water bucket—&c for chamber—are they yours, or dear Butlers, or whose? I am taking care of them. I am busy today preparing the house for winter—How sad I feel that you my beloved will not just now enjoy its comforts & see how nice & *clean* it looks!! But I have said I will try not to complain!!!

Have you any idea how long you will be detained in Texas? How sorry I am that I did not send by dear Butler—or to you in N.Y. your thick dressing gown—& your fur coat. If Malley is to join you—shall I send them by him? And please dear husband give me clear directions where to direct my letters to you & dear Lordy. I do not write to him by this mail—because I am doubtful of his being still in N.Y. & have really not the time to write more than to you & to dear Floyd. I do not intend to write to our daughters if they do not leave on the 17th they certainly will before this can reach New York. Our children send thousands of love to you my beloved—& to our beloved Lordy. May God! of his infinite love & mercy guide each & every one of you in all your ways— guard from every evil & restore you all in health & happiness to your homes to your devoted wife

Anna M King

20th

Nothing new this morning. Mall has written to you. God bless you my husband.

St Simons Isld
7th November 1857

My dearly beloved Lord

I am afraid you think I have neglected you my darling—I would have acknowledged your affectionate letter of the 25th Ult. last week but in the first place I was doubtful if my letter would ever reach you. If I directed to New York you would certainly have left there before it could reach its destination, and Texas has no Post Office at all. Your Sisters three left here for the Grants yesterday before the Mail came—your letters to Geo & Flora I took the liberty to open. Up to the 1st you & your dear Father were still in that pic pocket City New York, and as uncertain as ever when you were to leave.

What beautiful courage what indomitable perseverance my beloved husband possesses. Either his wife or Sons would years ago have given up striving against adverse fate & sank into nothingness. If ever man deserved success it is the same noble husband of mine. I try to school myself into the belief that if he meets not his reward in this world of trial & disappointment he will in that better world to which we are all hastening.

I wrote to your dear Father yesterday & directed my letter to St Charles Hotel New Orleans. For once in my life I hope I have *nicked it*. By the same mail Florence wrote to you. If it were not that I think your dear Father should always have one of his sons with him I would have rejoiced to see you with dear Butler & the girls. You cannot desire to see your home more than we desire to have you with us dear Lordy. But home in these hard times will not be rest without employment. I wrote to your dear Father yesterday relative to dear Mallery—who *feels deeply his present life*—he feels that he ought to be pursuing his profession that time & employment *lost now*, is to him a *serious drawback*. I do hope & trust your dear Father may be able to obtain for him suitable employment. Even should dear Butler be able to go to work for himself—let him not put *my ease* in competition with dear Malleys welfare or advancement. I have never desired a Son of mine to be a planter. Slave driving is trying both to the temper & morals of a young man. Our dear Butler inherits from his dear Father the talent for managing negros and taste for agriculture—if he had a plantation of his own, it would do for him to continue the employment. But already too much of his life has been wasted here. I think in justice to our sons they ought to be working for themselves. Please dear Lordy urge your dear Father to use his best endeavors to obtain a situation on a R[ail] R[oad] for our noble Malley. It will grieve me to part with him—but I am ready at any moment to sacrifice my own happiness for the welfare of husband—sons or daughters.

You will hear that dear William Couper is now seeking employment as overseer. He found that neither his health or purse would allow of his living the coming year in Savannah. All this will be better explained by Butler than by me. Your sister bears this coming down as a good wife should. The more depressed poor William is, the more cheerful she appears in order to cheer him. Your little pet Rosalie is gaining strength—& is not only Lordys pet but the pet of the house. She is both intelligent & amusing. She is delighted with the bonnet you sent her. As the girls would say "it *was so sweet of Lordy*." When Tootee found she would not reside this winter in Savannah she said in the hearing of Rosalie "I will sell the bonnet Lord sent Toozie." The poor little [child] cried out "no you shant sell my pretty hat—Lordy gave it to me."

As yet we have had no frost—for the last two days the heat is equal to summer weather. I very much fear we shall have more fevers. Christianns little child is now desperately ill. I have a still more serious fear that you & your dear Father are going too soon to New Orleans. May God! protect you both. I expect your Sisters home this afternoon. Geo will doubtless answer your affectionate note. William has a cold the rest of us are as usual. And now dear Lordy I will conclude until tomorrow when I hope to tell you of the safe return & good health of your sisters.

All here unite in fond love to you & your dear Father. God! bless & keep you from evil—   Your devoted Mother

A M King

8th

Family as usual—Sisters got back safe last evening—Tootee goes with William to Savannah tonight to pack up her things. Christianns child is dead.[1]

1. Six days later Anna explained,

Christianns little Nora was taken with fever on Friday Morning & died at 5 oclock on Monday morning. From her symptoms I think it was congestive fever. Well I did all I could for the poor little thing—& I pity her grandmother who has been devoted to her ever since she was born. Monday was a day of real confusion to us all. I was warned at two oclock A.M. that Nora was worse so I got up & went to the Hospital where I remained until the poor little thing expired. On that day your Sister had to get ready to accompany William to Savannah. . . . Tootee had a great deal to do, of course I gave her every assistance in my power but we could not expect work from either Clementine or Christiann—but all was done that she required. (Anna Matilda Page King to John Floyd King, November 13, 1857, TBK, SHC)

1st December 1857

> This day 33 years ago I was
> married to my beloved husband!

My dearly beloved Lordy

Your affectionate letter of the 22nd was received this morning—Thank God! you were then able to say your precious Father & self were well. I am thankful for the *misery* spared me—When I read of the loss of the *Opelousas* I never imagined your father and self could possibly have been in her. It was indeed a most providential detention. I am no believer in *accidental* escapes dear Lordy. Surely the Good God! so ordered it that you should not be exposed to that danger. Poor Genl Hamilton!!

You say you will now remain until after the 7th this is the 1st—this letter will not leave the Isld until the 3d—I hope it may find you in N[ew] O[rleans] even if you leave that place five minutes after receiving it. It seems strange so few of our letters had been received up to the 22nd. Butler, Geo, Florence, Mall & myself have written many letters—certainly as many as three every week & directed them to the St Charles beginning the last week in October. The letters by todays mail to Butler & myself are the first we have had from you since you left N.Y. Those of the 14th & 22d all I have had from your dear Father since he got to N[ew] O[rleans] I do not complain knowing as I do how incessantly he is not only occupied but (dear Soul) perpelex'd & annoyed. Surely he possesses no ordinary energy & perseverance else he would long since have given up in despair. We are all pretty much "down in the mouth" as we say here. Our noble Butler tells me nothing of his troubles but it is very evident he is suffering much anxiety—He certainly does love hard. I dread the consequences to him should this engagement be broken off. Then poor Malley *feels* that he ought to be at work. *Tip* feels that he ought to be at School. I can't command the means if I knew where to send him.

William left us yesterday for Savannah—he has applied for the management of the Butler Estate. I fear in that he will not be successful. If he can do no better he will oversee Hamilton at $600. Your dear Sister tries to be cheerful but succeeds only when William is present. She, King & Johnny have been very unwell from influenza. So has B[utler], M[allery], G[eorgia], F[lorence], & Cuyler but thank God all are now better. Florence & I went to Church on Sunday only 14 persons present including Mr Brown & a *nigger*. Miss M Wylly—Miss Gould, Miss Harris—Mrs Miles, Mrs Hazzard & all the little Goulds are down with influenza. Yesterday the Cater folks all went to Savannah to attend Miss Emma Postells wedding. She is to marry a Mr Hopkins—an Englishman clerk I think to Mr Green. People say a very good catch for her. Mr Fox is absolutely engaged to Eugenia Grant. He met them in Savannah returned home with them and there he still remains. Your Sisters & brothers were to have gone to Elizafield on Saturday but the weather prevented. They go tomorrow if the weather is favorable. I am trying to persuade Old Smart[1] to go too—he wants cheering. There is to be a grand regatta of three days on the second day, a grand ball in Brunswick about the 15th January. R Spalding chief manager.

I think the next time you & your dear Father occupy different Hotels & are to start in the same train I would advise your going over to *his* Hotel & starting together. He wrote to me all about how it happened. I did hope to see you here in December—you now speak of January. I trust not later. Let me entreat of you dear Lordy—never to feel *confident* when on board any of those Louisiana or Texas Steamers. Never undress sleep light & have your senses about you—more over keep close to your dear Father that you *may help* each other. May God! protect you from such a fate as poor Genl Hamiltons!!!

I hope when your Sisters return from the Grants they may be able to write news & other pleasant matters. My mind is so taken up with cares & anxieties my letters are not very enlivening. I heard from dear Floyd on Saturday—he forgot to date his letter. I am so thankful he escaped that fatal fever. Oh how merciful God! has been to us!!! All here unite in fond love to you & your beloved Father. I will write to him tomorrow.

God bless you dear Lordy & restore you in health & happiness to your devoted Mother.

A M King

1. I am unable to identify Old Smart.

January 6, 1858, to August 10, 1859

When I think of all the trouble that is before me I pray God! to let me be the first to depart. His will not mine be done!!!

This year and a half proved difficult for Anna and her family as Retreat's depleted lands, low cotton prices, and unfavorable weather plunged the plantation further and further into debt. T. B. King remained away from home and no closer to realizing a profit from his labors. Anna struggled to provide an education for the two youngest boys while she continued to support Lord and looked for the means to provide diversions for Georgia, Florence, and Virginia. Butler traveled between Retreat and his father's latest railroad meeting and became, more than ever, the emotional center of his mother's life.

6th January 1858

My own dear Floyd

Your affectionate letter of the 29th Ult was received yesterday. And a very sensible letter it was dear Floyd.[1] I am indeed thankful to perceive you are now sensible of the necessity of close application to your studies and appreciate the efforts your parents have used for your obtaining a good education. Much valuable time has been lost dear Floyd, but even now much useful knowledge may be acquired if you will persevere in the wise resolve you say you have made to make study your whole business & to avoid mixing in society & evil company.

I saw the letter written to Mr J H Couper by the gentleman he engaged to give you & Bob[2] private instruction. I am sorry he has left you but hope his place has been supplied by one equally efficient & attentive to you. He spoke well of your application—said *you had worked hard* regretted your having given up the study of French—this is to be regretted as you would find that language not only a useful but an elegant accomplishment. But if you found the time could not be spared from other more necessary studies it was perhaps well you gave it up at least for *the present*. This gentlemans letter was sent to me by Mr J H Couper. I enclosed it to your dear Father last week. I think in the end dear Floyd you will find the relinquishment of society—avoiding dinner parties, balls, & *parties* whilst you are at school—will be amply made up to you by the improvement of your mind. Such pleasures are very aluring to youth it requires a strong mind to resist. The first effort at resistance is the hardest to conquer the next less so & so on until in the end *duty to yourself* will be a pleasure & you will come off a conqueror. Dear Floyd I have a great deal of good advice in my head and heart—but I find it difficult to put it down on paper. All that I will now add—is that I am grateful & proud to find you are now doing well and pray God you will continue to do so. I shall make every effort to get the means to send dear Cuyler to the Bloomfield academy. Mr Grant applied for admission for Fraser & Cuyler at Mr Serls in Charleston—his answer was that he took no boy over 14 years old. In fact from the first I felt it would be too expensive for us. But dear Cuyler wanted to go with Fraser.

Butler had a letter yesterday from your dear Father dated New Orleans 26th Dec. He & Lord were then well. Still detained in that City, he has met with much annoyance—but is still hopeful of success. Dear Floyd if he does not succeed I do not know what will become of us. We made a very poor crop last year & the little we did make will be sacrificed as there is no demand for S[ea] I[sland] cotton.

William returned from Savannah yesterday morning his health is now quite good. He will take charge of Hamilton—the salary is a mere pittance but as long as it is *no worse* we must not complain. Little John has been quite sick for a week—his throat shows some symptoms of Mumps—very much swollen & fever every night but he can eat acids with impunity—which shows it cant be mumps. Anna you know is at Hopeton[3]—William—King & Rosalie with all the rest of the family are as usual. Rosalie has improved wonderfully a perfect little chatter box—possesses a most imaginative mind, employs her whole time in cooking unseen dishes, gathering unseen fruits—&c &c. She is quite plump. Georgia is at present at Mrs Troups. Malley took her there on Monday morning—*he* dined at the Grants, all were well except Mrs Troup who has been quite sick & was on Monday still confined to her bed. Geo will not return home before Saturday.

I suppose you have heard through the Coupers or your Sisters of the doings in Brunswick—how on the night of the 24th Dec Jacob Moore was shot dead by a Mr Styles. I looked for a Brunswick paper to send you as it would give you some account of it but find it has been torn up. *We* are none of us Sorry that Jacob Moore is out of Glynn County. Styles did [it] in self defence. As soon as the Houston clique found that there was no chance of their being re elected as Mayor & Council of Brunswick—they opened the jail door & let Charly Moore "slip." As there was no certainty that Charley Moore would be hung for the Murder of poor Wood it is better he should have been let out than to have had him acquited. He will now have to keep out of Glynn County.

You ask after dogs & horses. Well I believe all are well except poor old Rock. After giving him arsenic he improved very much in health his cough left him & he regained much of his former spirits. For the last week we remarked that his cough returned. Yesterday he again vomited blood & this morning was found dead! Poor old Rock!! Florence has had him buried near her summer house— Butty put him into the compost heap—but she had him dug up & planted just there. Pluto is a poor devil—& would have been shot long ago had you been here to give the word. *Brass* as Butler calls the puppy I got from William—does not gain in our estimation—the two terriers are the only dogs we have worth their feed. Your horse is kept in good order—Malley rides her. Poor Henry has been laid up all winter with Rheumatism poor little fellow he has suffered very much nothing that I can do seems to benefit him long.

We are busy now putting the gardens in order. Since the 21st November the weather has been very mild no time yet safe for killing hogs—living every day more scarce. The Hawks every day lessen the number of fowls—& none to be purchased. Malley as yet not certain when he will leave home. He sticks to Butler & poor Tip to the Engine—the working of which gives much trouble—the pump is so defective. Our lands are so worn out Butler is preparing to plant at Oatlands this year. When the people are at work there Butler & Mall ride up & back every day between breakfast and dinner—sometimes on horse back sometimes in the buggy.

All here unite in warm love to you dear Floyd—if I had the time I would write a longer letter. Before I close I must add a request that you will try & be more careful in your spelling. You are again getting careless. Also that I am sorry your letters have not been answered by either your dear Father or dear Lordy they are I know much occupied & it takes 10 days some times longer for their letters to reach us. To the St Charles Hotel New Orleans, they desire we shall continue to direct our letters—when they do go to Texas—they could not yet tell us—& whilst in Texas I presume they will remain long in no place. May God! bless you my own dear Floyd & give you strength to pursue always that which is right in His eyes as well as in that of your affectionate Mother.

A M King

P.S. Did either of your Sisters ever tell you how strangely Malley recovered the signet ring your Father gave him? You know he was under the impression it had been stolen from him when you & him as cadets camped in Augusta. It will be news to know who has had it so long—it was discovered on the finger of a negro man belonging to Miss Wylly. All Butler and William could get out of him was that he "picked it up on the road." Dear Malley is glad enough to get it back again—it was somewhat injured by negro possession.

1. Floyd was now attending the University of Virginia.
2. Robert Couper.
3. Anna was living at Hopeton to study with a tutor hired by J. H. Couper for his children.

10th January 1858

My dearly beloved Lordy

I had yesterday the happiness to receive your dear Fathers letter of the 31st Ult. He said nothing of the health either of himself or of you—neither did he say one word relative to your leaving New Orleans or returning home. In fact about nothing else but his uneasiness about our dear Butlers unhappiness. Dear Butler! he is exceedingly annoyed that I have ever mentioned his unhappiness. Perhaps I was wrong as his dear Father has not been able to carry out the plan of establishing him in business & it only makes your dear Father unhappy too. I gave dear Butler your Fathers letter to read. He made no remark when he returned me the letter, as he kissed me when he did so—shows that he felt & appreciated his dear Fathers kind feeling for him. Dear Butler—he keeps his troubles locked up in his own noble heart. He has never told me why he is so troubled—enough that I see he is unhappy but I cant help him poor fellow.—

1858 has opened gloomily for us all. There is your dear Father & you working in the dark—he has not seen his home for nearly a year & God only knows when we shall ever meet again. Dear Butler having all his fond hopes blasted by the caprice of an ambitious Mother who apparently cares little for her daughters happiness—then dear Malley chafing that he has no employment. Poor William and your dear Sister going to begin the world anew & I utterly unable to find the means either to keep Floyd at school or give poor Tip a chance of further education. Put this dark side on one side & on the other place this picture (as far as I know). My beloved husband—you my darling & dear Floyd are well & working hard. My beloved Butler is doing the best he can to prepare for another crop. Malley—Georgia—Florence, Virginia—Cuyler— Dear Tootee her husband & children are all alive & all so loving. Oh! God! give me a grateful heart for all this blessing! We are not the only family who feel the want of money. It is true the suffering of others do not alleviate our wants. I do not know why I write you all this—so I will just think of my blessings whilst I continue this scrawl. I wrote to your dear father last week & I presume dear Butler will answer his kind letters by this Mail. Malley is gone for dear Georgia who has been at Mrs Troups since Monday last. Florence, Tootee—William & Willie & Cooney are at Church. Johnnys throat is better.

William finds the old Hamilton house so uninhabitable until that is repaired—they will live in the Point House. The distance from the old settlement is a serious objection to their remaining in it longer than until the old house is put in order. Dear Tootee has been hard at work the past week unpacking & preparing to move. We shall miss her sadly—how beautifully her character unfolds under trials. She tries to cheer her husband & he tries to look poverty bravely in the face. They have just returned from Church—where they saw Miss Hazzards guests the Misses Dillon, Davis & another Miss (name not remembered), Mr Lounds & a Mr Jones. These people came from Savannah with Miss Hazzard who has been on a visit to "Cousin James Potter." Your Sisters & brothers are invited to a tea fight—tomorrow evening at West Point. They will probably go—if only for the change.

I am sorry to say the last accounts of Mr Bourke he was very ill on Jekyl. Postell had Dr Hazelhurst to see a sick negro. So they had to send here for the Doctor for Mr Bourke—we have heard nothing since. Mrs Bourke was with her husband. Charly Moore & Hornsby were let out of jail as soon as Styles was Elected Mayor. Old Jewel has left Brunswick—so what with shooting running away & going away the town of Brunswick has been rid of some of its obnoxious weeds. The nearer the time for the long talked of Ball & regatta—the fainter the prospect of your dear sisters going to the ball. Florence & Appy are very anxious to go. Butler & Malley entirely *indifferent.*

Your sister says she hopes ere long to be able to answer your last affectionate letter. All here unite in warm love to you & your beloved Father. Please Lordy dear answer this as soon as you possibly can, & if in your power tell me when I may hope to see your dear Father & self. Oh! that it may be soon. Just to think how little I have seen of your dear Father since 1849. The older we get the longer we live the greater our separation. This is *sad*! I do not complain—but I feel it deeply!

You must excuse this scrawl. My warm warm love to my beloved husband. Praying for your health & safety & that you will soon return—I am

Devotedly your affectionate Mother
A M King

11th

Our dear Georgia returned safe & well with her brothers Mall & Tip last evening. Mall remained at the landing whilst Tip *footed* it up—fortunately for all parties he met Georgia accompanied by Miss Grant & others of the family on their way to the landing (for once dear Georgia was ready to come home). Mrs Troup better—the rest quite well. Geo brings intelligence of Henry Dubignon to this effect. As hard as times are they have horse racing at Savannah. At dinner after the race (all pretty jolly I presume) Mr Dubignon threw a bottle at the head of a Mr Lamar (Uncle to Charley Lamar). Charley said "if you do that again I will shoot you"—Dubignon repeated the insult when Lamar shot him—the ball entering his cheek & lodging in the head—when the informant left S[avannah] the ball had not been extracted. I am most sorry for dear Sarah Bourke. When I hear of such things how I tremble for my husband & sons. Love to your dear Father for me & for all to yourself also dear Lordy. God bless you now & ever.

Your devoted Mother
A M King

17th Feb 1858

My dearly beloved Lordy

Thank you heartily for your affectionate letter of the 22d. I received one from your dear Father dated two days later by yesterdays Mail and which I have just answered. If I mistake not the Texas Legislature adjourns early in February. I therefore hope you will be in N[ew] O[rleans] as soon as this will reach that City. And that in your next you & your dear Father will be able to say when we may hope for the happiness of seeing you at home. In this I trust I may not be disappointed.

Dear Lordy do not for one moment suppose that I *now* ever blame your noble Father for his long absences. When he worked entirely for the public I did blame him. Now I feel that his exertions for his family are as great as they are self sacrificing that he suffers even more than I do. For whilst he is undergoing every hardship—I am in a comfortable home—whilst he is combatting with designing dishonest men with only one dear child to make him feel he has one to love near him—I am surrounded by a large [?] of loving and beloved sons & daughters & grand children. No I do not or cannot feel that it is his fault that we are so much separated—but you must admit it is to me a great grief. We are too old now dear Lordy to live independent of each other. It is so long now since he has been leaving me for months & years—I fear I am getting used to it. Something after the fashion of getting used to hanging. Your dear Fathers last letter was less hopeful—I can but hope all may yet be well.

Butler & Malley are decidedly of the opinion it will be necessary for the maintenance of the family that we make a settlement in Texas. I am willing to agree to whatever your dear Father thinks will be for the best. Dear Butler is doing the best he can with our old lands—Dear Butty!! he is very unhappy. This is the day that Lettie Gamble is to be married to Mr Holyday ("Mr Recreation" as Florence calls him). He invited Butler to be groomsman—unfortunately he directed his letter to Darien—so it was delayed & not received until too late. I want dear Butler to see L.S. & then he may be able to decide if there is any *hope* of their ultimate union. His being tied down at home—is much against his recovering from the depression caused by this unexpected & bitter disappointment. Oh! that I could see him again the cheerful son he used to be. God grant your dear Father may be able to get a good situation for dear Malley he does seem at times so gloomy feeling the time which is wasting. I can but hope there will be no necessity for dear Floyd to leave The University—he seems to be doing well there. A return of his complaint is scarcely as serious as that of the reappearance of the Tiphoid fever among the students there. We miss dear Tip very much—he is a dear boy well worthy the love we all have for him. Your dear Sisters G[eorgia], F[lorence], & V[irginia] I have never seen in better health and spirits. They take a great deal of exercise—go to bed early get up early—walk—eat well—& are so cheerful. We have been exerting ourselves so long to cheer dear old Smart that it has become quite a *habit* you see to be cheerful.

They have become very much interested in the flower garden—which bids fair to look well this spring. The[y] feel it is hopeless to expect a new house—so they are trying to make changes. Whether for better or worse you will judge in the old one. Even the poor pillows are being enlarged—filling pillow cases &c &c dear children! As it costs nothing but sewing I let them do as they please. You will be delighted with the improvement in dear little Rosalie—she possesses a wonderfully fertile imagination. The other day Tootee was talking at some length—she said "hush ma when you talk so much you tell stories—when me talk much I tell stories"!! At times she really is pretty. Dear dear Tootee!! she finds herself poorer now than when she first married.

The Grants are expected here tomorrow. It is strange how generally disliked Mr *Fox* is! Henry Dubignon is fast recovering it is hoped he will regain the sight of his eye. Mrs B[ourke] [is] still in Savannah. Bourke has Harringtons house & is getting it repaired.

All here unite in warm love to you & your dear Father. God bless you both dearly beloved. Write soon & tell me you will soon return to your affectionate Mother

A M King

2d March 1858

My dearly beloved Lordy

This days Mail has brought us no letters from our loved absentees—I do not complain dear Floyd & Tips last letters are not yet 2 weeks old—I know that neither of them love their pens. And it is scarce time (7 days) to get one from you or your dear Father—His most welcome "message" dated 23 Ulto relieved me from great anxiety you had got safe to N[ew] O[rleans]. Oh! how good— how merciful has God! been to me.

I hope dear Lordy the next Mail may bring some one of us, an answer to the many letters you found awaiting you at the St Charles. And that you may rejoice our hearts by saying *you will very soon be at home.* It is now over a year since I last saw my beloved husband I try not to complain—knowing all he suffers knowing how nobly he sacrifices every other feeling but that of desiring to benefit his family. Surely he is a noble man!!

It is so cold dear Lordy I can scarce write—both fingers & ideas are frozen. I like cold weather when no fear of plants or fruit or what is of more importance *crops* being injured—It has been so mild since the destructive frost on the 21 & 22 November. I began to hope old fashioned seasons were returning. The few bearing orange trees are in bloom & black berrys. Now if this wind holds in the same quarter it has been freezing from since the deluge of rain we had yesterday I fear all will be lost—but as we cant help ourselves we may as well stop fretting.

I saw your sister and family on Saturday—King & Johnny are recovering from their attacks of sore throat & sore mouth. Your little pet Toozie improves gradually in strength & good looks. She can actually now lie down & get up *without assistance*—a feat (only for the first time in her little life) only accomplished last week—& how proudly the little creature will go through with it— calling for us to look & see her "dit" up until perfectly exhausted. I mentioned to your Father that Miss Gamble *was not* married on the 17th Feb. What a slippery family—She gives the blame to the old Col this time. I wish our dear Butler could take back his warm noble affections from L.S. & bestow them on my young friend Jinnie Grant—Who I verily believe would take him at a word in spite of her engagement to that despised Fox.

I dare say Geo & Flo will write to you by this Mail—It is so cold I am obliged to sit near the fire which heats my glasses more than my hands & renders writing really painful to me. Butty & Mallery are shooting at the little robbins they have killed a great many or have wasted much shot & powder. The birds are very fat said to be good eating. They killed 40 the other day also 6 snipe & 2 ducks. Dear Malley is *crazy* to be at work—will it be possible for your dear

Father to get him a situation—All unite in love to you & your dear Father—
God bless

31st March 1858

My dearly beloved Lordy

Thank you a thousand times for your welcome letter of the 18th which was
received yesterday. It is no small relief to hear you had got safe and well to
Shreve Port—God grant you as safe a passage back & over all those dreaded
waters. A trip across the Atlantic (it seems to me) is less hazardous, than the
travel of 100 miles on those rivers. Dear Lordy God! protect you & your dear
Father from every evil. I could not sleep last night—was afflicted with visions
such as those which tormented me in 1852. I was not asleep dear Lordy when
startled by seeing you holding your right hand with your left & that right hand
filled with blood from a terrible wound—how received I dont know. Then I had
other visions—then the rats over head—the mice in the room kept me awake
pretty much all night. It has been raining all day—we all feel gloomy—but if
we in the comfortable old home feel so, what may be your feelings if in just
weather you & dear Father are shut up in uncomfortable lodgings? I think we
should not complain when we think—how much worse off you may be. I have
just concluded a long letter to your noble Father—telling him all were well
yesterday at Hamilton all well here this morning. This blessing should comfort
us even if deprived of many others which we long for. None so great as the desire to see your dear Father & self. You say not one word of when we may hope
for the happiness. Have you really no idea when you hope to be with us? Florence is writing to you today—I hope she may be able to give you a more cheerful letter than I fear mine will be. Let me try to forget my discomforts of last
night & think what to tell you of *home*.

Well the corn fields & gardens are looking spring like. Dear Butler & Malley drive almost daily to Oatlands or New field—your Sisters to Hamilton &
the last few days have twice extended their drive to make calls higher up the Island. This gives them an opportunity to air their nice dresses & gain an idea or
two of how our few neighbors are getting on. All pretty much of a sameness—
Miss Mary Gould speaks for making a visit to the Up Country by way of a
change. For the same purpose Mrs Cater has gone to Savannah. Your Sisters
G[eorgia] & V[irginia] have concluded to make Stephen King their long promised visit on Monday next—if Butler gets through planting so as to spare the
hands. Mrs Tunno & daughters expected at the Hazzards this evening. On Saturday last William, Butler, Malley & little Willie went fishing—Tootee & the

chicks came to us. Just as we had finished a pretty good dinner the fishing party returned—William had caught one drum—but as it had no roe we did not prize it. Butty secured a mess of whiting & dear Malleys luck was *crabs*.

On Sunday we saw the most of our neighbors at Church & heard from Mr Brown that Fannie Troup was not so well as she had been. Anna wrote to her Mother that Rebecca Fraser was then at Hopeton & would visit us before going to Florida. On Monday Malley went Alligator hunting—killed two—but could not get them—Flora (the nurse) begs for young alligators for the little darkeys. She assures Butler & Malley "that Alligator meat will make de children grow faster dan any other food." As I would be very glad to have some dozens of these little homany eaters grow big enough to work—I beg your brothers to provide the means.—

Our poor Tootee has very few of the comforts now that she had when living on "the Hamilton Estate" $600 a year to provide 7 persons with every want except homany requires close living. Thank God as yet they have no Doctors bill to provide for. Dear little Rosalie still requires the most particular care—she must be clothed & fed "just so" to keep her from relapsing into bad health. She is a dear little creature—but much spoilt. The three little boys are well. Anna is improving very fast—We hope Mr J H Couper will soon move to the Isld. Anna has been with her parents—but 24 hours since the first week in December. I believe this day disolves the partnership of Couper & Fraser. The whys & wherefores I cannot understand—It is hard always to believe "that all is for the best." You will know all about it when you come home.—

Mr Corbin did not visit the Island when in Georgia. I have mentioned to your dear Father our last intelligence from Floyd & Tip. Middletons thumb is still in a bad state but he suffers less pain—it is very hard on poor Tootee to be deprived of the services of both Middleton & Christiann at the same time— the latter has an infant now three weeks old. Neptune & Ila were married on Sunday evening last the poor bride had to foot it to Oatlands the next morning & he has not seen her since. I dare say Flora will give you a description of the marriage ceremony as performed by Hercules.[1] Poor Butty said & with deep feeling too "Only to think Mother even Neptune can marry the woman he loves when I can't"—Oh I do wish he had never loved L.S.—how much she has made him suffer dear, dear Butler! All unite in warm love to you & your dear Father—All long to see you at home—

God! forever bless you my darling with his love—guidance & protection & restore you in health & happiness to

Your devoted Mother

A M King

Is there no prospect of your dear Father obtaining a situation for poor Mally? Please urge it all you can.

1st April—all well here & at Hamilton.

1. Hercules is number 180 on the "Register of Negros Belonging to Thomas Butler King," number 50 on "A List of 50 Negros with Their Increase," number 113 on the "A/C of Negros in April 1853," and number 42 on the "Inventory of the Estate of Mrs. Anna Matilda King."

16th June 1858

My own dearly beloved husband

Your affectionate letter of the 7th reached me yesterday. When you were permitted to write "my health is restored["]—Dare I murmur that *all* my prayers have not been granted? Oh! husband dear! when are you to return to us—What other man but you—would have the heart to persevere in a work which seems doomed to utter failure. Oh! how you have toiled—overcoming difficulties just to see greater ones rise up—I do not understand it at all. All I do understand is that you are spending life and strength for nothing—If you love us—do not remain longer in New Orleans—Oh run no further risk of your precious life. I dread next to hear you have gone to Texas or must return to New York. How is it all the labor & risk is thrown on to your shoulders—Is there another man in the company who has worked as hard or been as long separated from his wife?

Night before last we heard the whistle of a steamer at Hamilton—as in your letter of the 2d you hoped not to be detained later than the 8th I could not help hoping the boat stopt to land you—but alas—no husband & Father came! Thank God! you were able to say so favorably of your health. I fear you have so much to occupy your mind you can scarce realize the state of your bodily health. I had a letter from dear Tip by yesterdays Mail. He & Floyd were well—our poor dear Cuyler writes in very low spirits—Fraser Grant returned home on the death of his Sister—and probably will not return to Bloomfield—as He & Tip are like brothers our dear boy feels the loss of so true friend—We are much gratified by perceiving a very great improvement in the writing & spelling of dear Tip—both Floyd & himself seem to be using every effort to improve.

It troubles me much you have not been able to obtain a situation for dear Malley—Depend on it my beloved husband—that idleness is destructive to youth. Poor Malley does so long to be striving to earn his bread—Do my husband use your own influence & try to obtain that of others to get him a situation. We all stand waiting for you to do something for your sons—time goes on—other young men are working for themselves—our dear Butler has been sacrificed to the good of his poor Mother—Lordy is doing nothing Malley nothing—Oh it does make me so wretched—The old plantation every year yealding less & less. This year promises no better than the last. The high winds in April injured us more than any one else on the Isld. We have had more wind & less rain than any one else—you know the effect on our light dry land. I know not why I write you all this—God! knows I do not want to add to your troubles. This dry NE wind drives me almost mad.—

The health of the family is about the same as when I last wrote. Our dear H[annah] Page would have us all to spend yesterday with her. I could have enjoyed the visit—had you been able to write to us, when you would be with us. God! grant dearest husband the time may not be distant when you may return to us. I know it must be warm where you are—You must much need your summer clothing—and here they all are in your drawers at home. That you may so regulate your movements as not to be detained in Savannah, I will just say one boat leaves on Monday—one on Wednesday & one on Friday—each one starting from 9 to 10 oclock A.M.

The Grants have all gone to the Up Country. But dear Husband I need not detail to you the movements of our acquaintances—I do feel so wretched about you I cant write cheerful letters—And yet I have so much to be grateful for—What a blessing to be able to tell you we are all in our usual health—What happiness to hear from you & our youngest sons that you are well—God! forgive me for my repining *after.*—

Georgia & Florence wrote to you by yesterdays Mail—All unite in love to you dear husband—Hoping & praying for your speedy return ever & forever

Most affectionately, Your devoted wife

A M King

30th June 1858

My dearly beloved Floyd

I did not have time to write to you by the Monday Mail—I intended to devote a part of yesterday to you—but our dear Tootee came for the day, directly after breakfast, and again I could not find time. I wrote to dear Tip on Monday morning informing him of the hope we were entertaining of seeing your dear Father this week—as yet he has not come. His last letter was dated 15th June in which he said "I hope to leave New Orleans on the 19th will have to stop a day or two in Mobile & then proceed home as fast as Steam can carry me." If he left New Orleans on the 19th surely he will be here this week! You know that vile Yenga (I don't know how to spell the name) has had the P[acific]

R[ail] R[oad] Sold. A pretty termination to all our grand expectations—How it will end God! only knows—Your Father says "it is the legal opinion of both Judges & lawyers *the sale* is utterly *void.*["] The case has yet however to be tried. The terrible drought is telling distressingly on our crop for the last week the sun has been intensely hot. As I am allowed to keep in the house as I please—I would say I have not suffered from the heat—the nights are delightful no insects & cool sea breezes. But those who have to brave the out door employments tell a different story. God only knows what will be our fate if we make no crop this year. Your dear Father says "In April last how willingly would I have changed places with any of these planters on the Mississippi—the floods came & now these late beautiful—valuable plantations are nothing but ruin—up wards of fifty *Millions* of dollars have been lost by the over flowing of the river."

Your Sister is about the same—the rest of us are as usual. Your dear brothers got home safe after a pleasant visit of 15 days to James & Henry. D[aniel] Lords eyes are better—but he went to Savannah on Friday to consult Physicians as to what may make an entire cure. Our dear Cousin is better—she has suffered a great deal—William says he heard at C[annon's] P[oint] that Maggie was enjoying herself in Marietta. Your Sisters heard from Sallie Grant on Saturday last they were in Marietta all well except poor Mrs Grant who was worse since leaving home—very weak & nervous. Fox had joined the family—They seem to be dependent on him for advice as to where they should spend the Summer.

On Monday next Mr Bourke—William, & your brothers are going on the reef for a fish frolic—expect to be absent three days—they have hired a sail boat. I will feel better satisfied when they get safe back again. You would have enjoyed the fight they had with a big alligator on Sunday last. It had taken one of my hogs & it took Malley—John & Jimper with all the strength they could put out to haul him out of his hole. The next day they killed 4 & brought home the fifth alive about $2\frac{1}{2}$ feet long. I feel much disposed to cook the fifth for my ducks—these make 23 which your brothers have killed since Spring. They are now very numerous on the Isld. The one killed on Sunday was $9\frac{1}{2}$ feet long—enormous body and head—a very old Alligator.—

I see by the papers the fruit crop in the Up Country is very heavy. How is it we have no peaches at all? We now are getting fine melons—but the drought keeps back figs—Every thing is burning up—Well well complaining will do no good. Your horse and dog as well as Henry are well. I find it is time to close this hasty scrawl. All here unite in warm loving love to you—Praying God to bless you dear Floyd

> I am ever & Ever
> Your devoted Mother
> A M King

14th August 1858

My dearly beloved husband

Lord got by this days Mail a letter from dear Butler dated the 8th Inst. His report of your health Thank God! was still favorable. How did it happen, there was no letter from you to me? Butler said you would go to Saratoga the next day, so I suppose you were busy packing up. I verily believe I am older than you are (tho' you never would acknowledge it). It is true you are not in as good health as I am at present—but when did I ever neglect writing to you. When you do not write I know some thing is *wrong*. Do you remember when Appy was but *one day old* I sat up in bed & added a P.S. to the letter written before she was born? I believe if I was now ill in bed & there was no one else to write to you I would try & do it. So dear Husband if you are not too sick to write I hope you will write to me at least *once* every week. Even when your letters are not cheering the getting of one always quiets my mind.

I hope from what Butler said—you & he are now at Saratoga—where I trust you will receive much benefit from the waters. I hope dear Butler will also be benefited. I had letters today from Floyd & Tip—both were quite well up to [end of sentence missing]. They are boarding at $18 per month in a very pleasant village. It is amusing in what a patronizing way Floyd writes of Cuyler, he means it well & I hope Cuyler is wise enough to be governed by Floyds advice. They both say they will devote a part of every day to their studies. Robert Couper is fast recovering from his late illness. He & one other young man from Florida—one of Tips schoolmates are spending their vacation at this village.

I had a letter also today from dear little Nina King. Her selfish Father still keeps her in the mountains of Virginia—on the 3d Inst they were at the Healing Springs in Virginia. She poor child could not stand the white Sulphur. She says "the waters of the Healing springs are good [for] all kind of irruptions, & scofula[1]—spinal, Bronchitus and weak lungs—all of which pleasant things I have. I have some hope, I may get well, but some times I feel just like I should die—I am so sick & weak—the Dr says my left lung is affected. I cough all the time." She says her Father had been sick—but was then better.

I heard from dear Tootee this morning—all there pretty well—little Johnnie seems to be recovering from his attack. I hope to see them before I close this. Our two sons & three daughters at home are quite well. There has been so many hands sick dear Malleys work is in a jumble. He is as steady as a well trained ox—never seems flurried—but goes on making the best he can out of little. The wind is again NE & I fear will give more fevers. *Fewer* cases today than since the sickness began. I am thankful to be able to say our good servant Clementine is very much better. She was very ill for several days—more so, than I ever before saw her. She is a good servant.

Old Mrs Canon is very sick—I have been to see her several times. Mr & Mrs Bourke intended returning to Brunswick last night—but the Misses Wylly dined here on Thursday & prevailed on them to spend today with them—they will return here tomorrow & leave on Monday night. Maggie Couper came on Thursday & left us last evening. We are hoping for rain—that which fell on Wednesday was very acceptable but not enough. I have written to Andrews wife by this mail—He has been so kind a brother & Uncle I could not resist thanking her & him for all you & our dear children have received from them. Andrew has proven himself to be the *only* brother you have May God reward him by continuing his prosperity.

I send you three letters received by this Mail—Butler requested we should continue to direct to the New York Hotel. I will add to this tomorrow. Until then adieu dear husband!—

15th

I have nothing of importance to add to this letter—I saw dear Tootee yesterday evening little Johnnie is doing well—the rest as usual. We had yesterday some appearance of rain—which is much wanted but today it looks as dry as ever. I will write to dear Butler by the Wednesday Mail. Mr & Mrs Bourke request their kind regards to you & Butler. Our dear children send a thousand loves to you both. Devotedly your affectionate wife

A M King

---

1. Scrofula is tuberculosis of the lymphatic glands, especially of the neck; it is characterized by the enlargement and degeneration of the glands.

24th August 1858

My dearly beloved Floyd

I did not write to you by yesterdays Mail—but as I did to dear Tip—you got intelligence from home even if second handed. None of your sisters are present for me to enquire who wrote to you. I know Georgia sent you a piece of music. The Mail for today, has not yet come. I hope it may bring letters, from each dear absent one. Your Sister & family were to have spent this day with us—but it rains. Georgia & Appy were to have gone to Cannon's Point this morning on a visit of a couple days—but the same rain keeps them at home.

Last night Lordy had a very long letter from Mr Bourke written yesterday. Mrs Bourke was recovering from her distressing attack. I do not know who is most to be pitied—Sarah or Mr B[ourke]. I believe he would give every dollar he has to restore her to perfect health. It is indeed an affliction these attacks of hers.

Mr Bourke informs us—that a most brutal outrage has been committed in Brunswick by a Dr Moffet—assisted by a man named Fraser. Dr Moffet owned a little negro boy some 12 or 14 years old. With or without cause the boy ran away from his Master—he either returned voluntarily or was brought back to his master. The Dr was going to flog him—the poor boy tried to run off—when the brute seized him—took him down on the wharf—where he & this man Fraser *flogged him until* morning. Before 12 at noon the poor little boy expired—was quickly put under ground & the master left for Savannah. Now if this Dr Moffet gets clear—I think the abolishonists may well talk of cruelty to slaves!

I still have a great deal of sickness among the negros—thank God! none dangerously ill—but still so many sick is very trying. Poor Malley does the best he can—but with so much sickness it is hard to get along with the work. The mail has just brought me a letter from your beloved Father dated 17th Inst—He & dear Butler still at Saratoga the former hopes he is gaining health—the latter enjoying himself. John C Fraser *is also at Saratoga.* Georgia had a sweet letter from our dear Tip dated 18th. Thank God you were both well. Georgia also had a letter from poor Mr Maszaros—poor fellow! to add to all his other misfortunes he has been *sick* for several weeks. Poor fellow!! We heard nothing by this mail from Mr Woolley & fear our dear cousin may be worse—or that he is sick himself.

The negros are still very sickly—as yet thank God! none have died or been *alarmingly* ill. I find on looking back that I have twice written about the sickness of negros. God! help me I am so bothered about them they are ever in my thoughts. A note from dear Tootee just now informs us the health of her family is the same as was yesterday when your Sisters were there—no one actually sick—tho' neither Johnnie or Rosalie are quite well. I have nothing more to add dear Floyd but a fervent prayer that God! will in mercy keep you & dear Tip from every evil.

All unite in love to you both.

Your devoted Mother
A M King

St Simons Isld
Wednesday 6th October 58

My dearly beloved husband

Your letter of the 23d Ult was received on Saturday the 2d Inst—that of the 30th came yesterday. In the former you did not even mention dear Butlers name. This gave me much uneasiness—I felt convinced something was *wrong.* It struck me as strange you should mention your brother and his wife and say not [a] word of our dear boy. Our dear ones here tried to persuade me all was right. And I was so taken up with poor Annie it did not occupy my thoughts as it otherwise would have done. Thank God! you were able to *assure* me that our beloved son was again able to be up. God grant he may have no further relapse.

As unhappy as I am this morning—I feel my sorrow can be much greater than that caused by the death of a favorite servant. God! has spared my husband and children thus far & I am thankful!! Our dear children and grand children are yet in their usual health. The health of the negros seemed improving—fewer cases than since the fever began and I began to hope the worst was over. On Tuesday last (the 28th) Annie and Henry—the only 2 of the house and yard servant[s] who had kept well were taken sick. I treated them as I had done the others. Annies fever never intermitted, Henrys did. I treated her as I had *successfully* treated others of the same type. On Sunday she became so delirious I was induced to get the advice of Dr Postell, who chanced to be at Mr Postells on a visit to his wife and child who had been very sick. He came and assured us he could see no danger to be apprehended if we would carry out his prescriptions. That her liver was not exactly in a congestive state but much engorged or some such term—this from sympathy acted on the brain. I had a blister on the back of her neck & on her legs. Whilst in that state of Delirium nothing could be gotten down her throat. With Blisters mustard Plasters & cupping her temples she came to her senses. Being much alarmed about her my good cousin and I sat up with her on Sunday night—carried out to the letter Dr Postells prescription—& we hoped for a favorable result. During the night—her fever subsided—but not off. It then increased—yet as her medicine acted—we yet hoped. On Monday night we left her as we thought doing as well as we could expect—in the morning found she had past a restless night—fever high, skin dry & her mind flighty tho she answered our questions sensibly. Thinking the liver in fault—we put a blister over it (her bowels were never distressed) at 8 yesterday morning she began to sleep. At first we rejoiced & thought she would awake improved—let her sleep two hours—when it was time to begin giving her calomel & opium to act on her liver. But all we could do could not rouse her. I literally covered her with blisters and mustard plasters—had her feet in hot mustard baths. Nothing could break this terrible stupor. Ice had been kept on her head from Sunday & William got ½ pint of blood from her temples. I believe my cousin did every thing that could be done for her. She died at 9 last night—a loss to me not to be replaced—I had raised that child from a little girl and loved her much. Poor Rhina is broken hearted for Annie was the only child she ever had. I deeply regret having left her on Monday night. I was tired—but feared if I sat up—Cousin A[manda] would & it may make her sick. I put Pussy to watch with Rhina telling her if she saw any thing wrong to call me but she did not do it. Pardon me if I have worried you by this minute account of the death of my favorite little servant. I do feel very sad. But when I think God! has yet spared my beloved Husband and children—I feel this is but a light affliction. Oh! when I think of all the trouble that is before me I pray God! to let me be the first to depart. His will not mine be done!!!

We have had no rain since the 25th and for some days past—the sun has been very hot the water left in the ponds and ditches in a bad state. Our dear Malley went to Satilla on Monday. He is looking out for Hicory—William joined hands with him & sent the flat to Henry Kings Plantation [1]—Mall wanted to see after this & to visit D[aniel] Lord. Our dear Tootee, William and the children were here yesterday—thank God they were all well. Say all that is loving and kind to my darling Butler—I cant write to him by this mail—but One of his sisters has done so. I got up with the sun this morning that I may not let another week pass without writing to you. I have lost but one week since you left us—what has become of our letters the Post Masters only can tell. No letter bearing date of 22nd & 15th has been received from you. Tell dear Butler I shall not believe he is recovering until he writes to me himself—& that his man Henry is doing well. Our daughters G[eorgia] & F[lorence] wrote to you on Monday. All unite in love to you & dear Butler. Praying God! you may soon be quite well that you and our dear Son may be restored to us in health and happiness—I am ever & forever

Your devoted wife

A M King

My love to Andrew & his wife.

---

1. Anna meant to say Stephen King's plantation.

12th October 1858

My dearly beloved Floyd

We were very thankful for your long letter of the 28th Ulto received on the 9th. As you are perfectly conscious of the fault of want of punctuality I need not again remind you of the pain your silence causes us. I wrote to you by the mail of the 6th—telling you of the death of poor Annie. My grief for her is great—She was the brightest—most healthy of our young servants—was 14 years 7 months old strong & healthy. How strange that she should go—when more than one hundred, as sick as she appeared to be for the first 5 days, should go & all the others recovered [*sic*]. I had two little boys whose fevers lasted without intermission 15 days—and with deadly symptoms & yet they got well.

I do grieve so for my favorite young servant. I cant replace her—& miss her so much!!! Poor Rhina is calm—but looks entirely broken hearted!—

I still have many sick but none *ill* that *I can judge*. I believe the white folks who have been sick on the Island are doing well. In my last I mentioned that Mallery was on a visit to D[aniel] Lord. On Friday afternoon Lord went to meet M[allery] in Brunswick—found D[aniel] Lord with him—on another visit to us. Mr Woolley also came down with them. He only remained until Sunday—On Saturday Maggie, Alic, Mrs Dr Fraser & Miss Graves dined here—it was most irksome to me to have company but it could not be helped. On Sunday Mr Woolley returned to Brunswick & our dear Cousin went to Tootee—I miss her very much—but Tootee wants her even more than I do. Poor Tootee suffers much from palpitations of the heart. I spent the most of the day yesterday with her & may go again this afternoon. From the 24th Sep until last night there had been no rain—I hope the rain which fell in torrents all last night will improve the atmosphere and put a stop to this fever among our negros—I have had a sad anxious time of it. I am sad & weary! But God! be praised my husband and *children* are yet spared me. I am afraid to grieve for Annie fearing a worse misfortune may befall me.

On Saturday I had a letter from dear Butler who assured me his health was rapidly improving & that your dear Father continued to improve—Dr Gray assures your Father that had his disease been longer neglected mortification would have taken place & *of course death*! Great God! what a blow that would have been to us! Now Dr Gray says a perfect cure will shortly be effected! Thank God! thank God!!!!! The Grants (we are told) are now in Marietta—and will be down as soon as there is frost—I presume Mrs Grants health improved. The Troups & Dents went North last Wednesday—the latter leaving little Lillie Brown for Florence to take care of—I can only hope the child may keep well. She does not give much trouble—very bidable—Her *tender parents* will not be back before November. This world is made up of strange people!!

You are now I hope safe back to your studies and I hope have received the letters I directed to you there & will answer them without fail. All here unite in love to you—

Praying God! to bless you with His love protection and Guidance

I am your devoted Mother

A M King

13th

I saw dear Tootee yesterday evening—she was suffering less than she did on Sunday & Monday the rest well—Geo remained the night & Florence will spend the day with her sister. Your brothers go to C[annon's] P[oint] for the day. No negro so sick as to make me uneasy today that is that I know of—the gang is at Oatlands—weather very uncertain & unfavorable for cotton gathering. God bless you dear Floyd.

Sunday 17th October 1858

My dearly beloved husband

Thank you a thousand times for your affectionate letters of the 7th & 11th Inst both received by yesterdays Mail. Dear husband I cant realize the *mortal danger you have been in*—I cant be sufficiently grateful to God! for blessing the means now employed for ridding you of so dangerous a complaint—truly God! has been merciful to me ungrateful woman that I am! How many blessings still surround me—and yet I am grieving—grieving for the death of a favorite servant girl—forgetful that we must all die—that not only must I die—but I may have the misery of seeing those I love better than life—whose lives are dearer to me than my own soul—taken, & I left to mourn their loss. God! be merciful to me—ungrateful sinner that I am!!!

Our dear ones yet keep free of fever. I went to Hamilton on Friday evening to remain until Saturday evening with our dear Tootee & good Cousin Amanda. I witnessed one of those distressing attacks of palpitation of the heart, which dear Tootee has been suffering daily from for some time past. Dear Tootee thinks the frequency & violence of these attacks are owing to *her situation*. She does not expect to be confined before late in Nov—She eats so little—(some days not a mouth ful). She scarcely ever takes food—(let it be ever so little) but it brings on one of these attacks. When she throws it all up. She is very weak & thin. Yet God! bless (the daughters of her own heroic Father) she bears her suffering with not—only patience, but cheerfulness! May God! in mercy spare the life of this precious one!! Oh that I could transfer to her my iron constitution.

You say nothing certain of dear Butlers movements. If he determined to be here at the next court—he is now on his way—I try not to be anxious for his safety the *weather here is stormy*. If so where he is—God protect him from harm!! I had a kind letter from Mr & Mrs Bourke yesterday they assure me you are looking quite like yourself again also that dear Butler had recover'd his health. We are glad to hear Sarah is improving in health. Should you see them—thank them for their kind letters to me. We did not hear from either Floyd or Cuyler the past week. It was quite cold enough for fires & blankets from Thursday night until last night—for several days past no cases of fever among the negros—I can but hope the worst for this season has passed. From the news paper we learn the health of Savannah is improving—I have already stated to you & Butler there are but two steamers which leave S[avannah] during the week on Monday & Friday morning. I can but hope my beloved boy is not on the ocean this stormy day!

Dearest husband how nobly you have borne your misfortunes—how patiently your bodily affliction—how wonderfully you keep up your spirits! God bless you my precious one. Our dear children do all in their power to cheer me. God! bless them!! D[aniel] Lord left us on Friday night—& it is quite probable James & his wife will be here tomorrow night. All here unite in love to you & dear Butler if still with you—Our love to Andrew & his wife—May God! bless them for all their kindness to you & your children.

> Devotedly your affectionate wife
> Anna M King

18th

Lord drove me over to Hamilton last evening. I found our dear child on the sopha trying by *keeping perfectly quiet* to ward off an attack of palpitation—she had eaten a little dinner. Little Toozie had suffered from toothache all Saturday night—which we think gave her the fever she had—poor baby what a martyr she has been to the ills flesh is subject to. The rest were well. Our dear ones here are free of fever & cheerful. Weather still very unsettled—two sharp showers this morning—wind NE the wind was very high all night—There is no use in fretting.

When do you think you will be able to return home? Be careful not to leave one hour before your Physician says you can *do so with perfect safety.* Try now *for a perfect cure. How dreadful may be the consequences if it is not!!!* H[annah] P[age] begged me to give you & dear Butler much warm love for her. Dear dear Tootee! I hope tomorrow may bring me another of your dear letters. I enclose a note for dear Butler if he is not with you—I doubt not Louisa will do me the favor to select the article for me. God forever bless you my own beloved husband & restore you soon in health and happiness to your devoted wife.

> Anna M King

21st Dec 1858

My dearly beloved husband

I acknowledged one welcome letter of the 11th by the mail which should leave this place last evening. By this days mail I have your dear letter of the 15th in which you desire Lord should start for N[ew] O[rleans] as quickly as possible. We expected him to return from Savannah last night. Had he done so there would have been no delay on his part. We hope nothing will prevent him from being out tomorrow night. Should the boat going North be delayed he will go in her—if not must wait for the Friday night boat. The fog & high winds have made all the boats uncertain—I only write this to prepare you for a delay which I can't help. Neither would he, could he have supposed you would require his services in any way.

I am very thankful to be able to say dear invalids go on improving in health. Our dear Tootee still requires great care to ward off a relapse. She suffered for 9 months before her child was born & has been so fearful ill since then.[1] How thankful and rejoiced we are to hear so favorable an account of your own precious health. Surely God! has been most merciful to us! I feel satisfied, were it in your power you would stop to see our dear boys. Your not being able to do so will be a great disappointment to them but all disappointments are endurable as long as death does not cause it.

After dear Tootee was pronounced out of danger. We so fully expected you would be at home & had then no idea either Butler or Mallery or Lord would be absent. I lent a willing ear to our dear girls request that we should try and have a cheerful Christmas—Father & brothers all being away their present prospects are not very promising. Another disappointment to be endured! I hope and trust nothing will prevent your being with us on New Years day. I of course can have no idea what your plans may be for dear Lordy. Oh it does seem a cruel fate which has attended all your efforts. Could you but have succeeded we could have gone *some where* where we could have had all of our dear children settled around us. These partings are so painful and the older I get the more frequent they become. Dear Lordy has been so affectionate considerate & lovely since his return home.

We have heard nothing from dear Butler and Mallery since they left us on the 13th—neither do we know when they will be back. You can scarcely regret more than we do your not getting tidings from home for so long a time. Neither could you direct us or we imagine where letters would find you. God! grant this constant exposure and fatigue may not be injurious to your health. If Lord can take it—shall send you your fur coat. Why will you travel night and day? Dearly beloved—you forget the possibility of taxing that iron constitution of yours too far. In mercy to us be more careful of yourself.

Please dear husband do not be imposed on by the company—you have done most of the hard work to run the most risks & made the greatest sacrifices and may have no reward after all. Our dear daughters send thousand of love— Georgia says "Oh if I were but a man to be with dear Father." Her whole heart was set on going to N[ew] O[rleans] with you this winter. God forever bless you my darling husband—Your devoted wife.

A M King

1. On November 6 Anna wrote to T. B. King, "On the afternoon of the 4th I received a hasty summons from William to go to our dear Tootee at ¹/₄ of 9 she gave birth to a son. About a half hour later suddenly appeared the most alarming symptoms for two hours her precious life hung on a thread. Thank God! her valuable life has been spared to us" (Anna Matilda Page King to Thomas Butler King, November 6, 1858, WAC, SHC). The baby was named Thomas Butler Couper.

16th January 1859

My dearly beloved Floyd

The only letter received from you since Dec 1858 was one directed to Lordy received after he had left us for N[ew] O[rleans] as I mentioned in my last to you. Georgia by the return Mail forwarded it to him—he left there before it reached him. So we are without intelligence from you for several weeks. I have [?] a letter dear Tip in reply [?] yesterday from him. It is true it is no later than [?] but it was a great relief to hear at all from him. He mentions having spent the Christmas Holydays with you, but not one word of the health of either of you. How careless you boys are!!

I will now proceed to tell you about our noble selves. On the 4th Georgia and Florence went to Satilla—on the 5th Butler and I started for Savannah he, being in treaty with a man for a tract of land in Lounds County—thought it possible my presence would be necessary to consumate the bargain. When we got to Savannah—I got hold of a news paper—giving an account of a terrible R[ail] R[oad] disaster—14 persons killed—no names mentioned & on the Road dear Lordy had to travel to reach N[ew] O[rleans]. You can imagine my anxiety—Fortunately relieved by soon after seeing a dispatch from Lord to John Fraser—dated beyond & after the disaster between Macon & Columbus. Thank God!! Also another dispatch from your dear Father telling Butler to remain in Savannah until the 17th when he (your Father) [hopes] to be in S[avannah]h. As he dear Soul never can tell what disappointments are in store for him & I had left Appy and Malley alone & she not very free of cold, I determined to return home on the day I had promised—Butler concluded his purchase but the papers were not finished—So I returned alone. When I got to Hamilton I found Florence had left Georgia to remain a week longer at Satilla. She poor child little dreaming of the near prospect we had of seeing your dear Father at home. Stephen King promised "if Geo would remain another week—Nina should come down with her.["] On Wednesday night Butler returned from Savannah—where he had left your Father & Lord—they to come on Friday night. On Friday morning dear Malley started to reach the cars by eight oclock for Satilla to bring down Georgia 2 days sooner. On Saturday morning at about 4 A.M. your dear Father & dear Lordy did get here. The latter quite well—the former very unwell from a severe cold contracted two weeks ago his cough is very bad—I can but hope the worst is over. He speaks of being obliged to go to Washington in a short time but not for long. When he does I hope he will be able to see you and dear Tip. About 12 today dear Malley brought dear Georgia safe home—As the weather had changed again cold Nina did not come. All at Hamilton are well except Rosalie who has been suffering from a bad cold. William, Tootee & the three little boys were here yesterday. I spent 5 days very pleasantly with our dear good cousin—Mr Woolley was very kind & did all in his power to oblige me & make my stay pleasant. I have now given you a hasty sketch of all that has taken place since my letter to you of the 3d.—

When in S[avanna]h the Weather became colder than it had previously been during this winter—ice remained unmelted in the streets throughout the day—it moderated on Wednesday until yesterday—the heavy rain on Friday night brought us another cold change—much to my relief as during the first cold [?] my best hogs had been slaughtered. I find the hot or green house a perfect protection to my plants. One bunch of bananas has ripened perfectly [?] [?] flavor.

As it is near dinner time I must conclude. All here unite in warm love to you praying God! to bless you my beloved boy with his choicest care—I am devotedly your affectionate

Mother
A M King

21st Jan 1859

My own beloved Sons

Try beloved sons to prepare your minds for a most unexpected & awful calamity. It seems strange that I his fond Mother lives to tell you I have no longer on earth a beloved son *Butler*—that you my boys have no longer a beloved & loving brother Butler. Great God! that I live to tell you this—We are all crushed by the sudden death of your & my precious Butler. You know my darlings he has from childhood had an affliction of the heart. He often said it would end in death. Since last March he has been more than usually free from these attacks. On Tuesday last—18th he had one—kept his bed until 3 but so anxious was he to be with his dear Father he left his room—dined with his us & afterwards walked with your Father & Sisters. On Wednesday we all went over to bid dear Tootee & William adieu as they were to start for Savannah that night. Your three brothers and dear Father went on horseback—our precious Butler & your dear Father extended their ride to Vas'field [?]—If our precious one felt badly he never told us—after tea he had an attack of hiccough's—this was relieved by a little Soda—but had them again until he went to sleep

(so Lordy & Malley say) Yesterday morning he was up & dressed all to his cra-
vat before either Lord or Malley were—he had gone out without this—&
when he came in—he went to his glass—put it on & whilst brushing his hair
he felt a twitching of the lids of his left eye & that his *face was looking swollen* &
the left cheek contracted—he turned to Lord—& in attempting to point out
this stra[n]ge symtom—found he could not articulate distinctly—he immediately came into the breakfast room—where your dear Father & Sisters little
boys & myself were breakfasting—stood behind your Fathers chair & said—
"Father I do not know what is the matter with me look at my face["]—We both
thought it was an attack such as Lord had years ago—your Father & I jumped
up—calling for the galavanic battery & tubs of hot water. Your Father took his
dear arm & when the[y] got to his room door felt the hand to be stiffening—
He said my son your hand seems spasmoned—he replied "Yes Father the
spasm is extending all over me—*I think this 'will be the end.'*" As quickly as possible his feet were put into a hot bath—clothes stripped off—and while a bath
was being got to put him in—he was rubbed with pain killer—his t[h]roat &
chest seem to swell out & he complained of *nausea*—begged Malley to put his
finger down his throat—& called for an emetic (saying his stomach seemed full
of bile.)—as soon as it was possible a boat was sent for Dr Curtis & a man on
horseback for DW the precious one until one oclock continued perfectly calm—
giving directions to us to do for him—he was put into a warm bath & when taken
out—wrapped in blankets & placed in bed. He said he felt like sleep, he begged
that wet towels should be kept on his head—& for quiet—soon he complained
of palpitation & asked for aconite which Georgia gave him. (I have left out
the first most startling symtom. Before giving the mustard emetic & Hep [ink
stain ?] which he himself asked for (his hands being paralized he could not do
it himself) [he asked] Malley to put his finger down his throat—a little *blood*
came the first throw—then it came up in *volumes* [double underlined]—Great
God!! what a *sight*—we hoped that in retching he had ruptured a blood vessel—
but it was from his noble heart—the blood came. He was apparantly more
easy—as he seemed drowsy—every thing was hushed & for the first time since
going into the room with him at 9 in the morning—your dear Father went
to see if the boat was coming. In less than 5 minutes those left with him—
screamed for your dear Father our precious one was *in strong convulsions*—from
that time his mind left him. Your Father in spite of his struggles suceeded in
taking blood from his left arm—these awful convulsions—continued until a
minute or so before his noble soul left his body—his last breaths were as quiet
as an infants—his soul departed without a struggle leaving his beautiful countenance calm as when sweetly sleeping. He had been gone about 15 minutes
when Mr Bourke and Dr Curtis came. After looking at his precious body &

hearing of his constitutional aff[l]iction of the heart—the way it had come on—
the Dr assured us all had been done that man could do—had we done nothing he would have died in 15 minutes—our efforts prolonged his precious life
6 hours, that the disease had come to a crisis & that no human aid could have
saved his valuable life.[1] He got up yesterday morning feeling as well as usual—
6 hours after his soul was with his God & Savior. Oh we are crushed by this
terrible blow—as unexpected as it is terrible. Since his return from the North
our precious Butler has been entirely his former self. So loving—so considerate so cheerful!! He was to have left us on the 24th for Lounds County to see
after the land he had just purchased—Malley on the same day intended to leave
for Mississippi to join Mr C Hardee [?] in surveying the swamps in that sec-
tion. Your dear Father was to leave in the *Everglade* this night on his way to
Washington City. On Wednesday night your dear Father past a better night
than he had done in 3 weeks. We got up so happy—every thing seemed favorable present & future. Oh what a change did those fearful 6 hours make. Now
all is grief & our only consolation is that it is the hand of God—that has in-
flicted the blow. We must not murmur—and Dr Curtis is of the opinion our
precious darling Butler must soon have left us from that affliction of his heart.
Had he lived to leave on Monday—he may have died on the road with no one
but a servant with him. He probably never would have come back to us—our
noble son! the best of sons and brothers—Oh God! it is terrible I cant realize
so dreadful [a] loss.—

Your Father says if life is spared him he must leave us for Washington some
day the coming week. I know if our precious Butler was alive & either of the
others taken—he would have advised your being sent for. Your Father thinks
you had better wait until he meets you in Charlottesville. He will go there to
see you and give you the means of coming home. He fears you may miss each
other on the way—should you start off on the receipt of this melancholy letter.
God! give you both the strength to bear up under this awful affliction. Your
poor Sister went with Wm to Savannah on Thursday morning—they could
scarcely have reached Frederica when our darling Butler was death struck.
What a blow to her poor child—She so fondly loved our darling Butty.—

Your dear Father says he has not the heart to write to either of you. I direct
this letter to you my Floyd—go at once to my poor Tip break the crushing news
to him gently—then my darlings be you together in Charlottesville until your
poor Father meets you. All who are now here send fond love to you—Praying
God! to comfort you under this bitter trial

> I am in affliction as in happiness
> Your devoted Mother
> A M King

1. It is likely that Butler had some congenital heart defect or a cardiac injury from an illness at an early age such as rheumatic fever. The acute event that killed him may have been an embolic stroke (a blood clot "thrown" from the damaged or poorly functioning part of his heart—possibly a valve), which would account for the paralysis of his face and extremities. It is difficult to explain his gastric bleeding, but it may have been the result of gastritis or an ulcer and caused by the extreme stress of his terminal illness. He may have died from internal bleeding, or perhaps the convulsions signified additional strokes leading to his death. Information from Dr. Larry Slutsker.

18th March 1859

My dearly beloved son Floyd

With what different feelings do I now attempt to address you my son. But a few months back what pleasure to write to my absent husband and children. Now alas I have no pleasure in any thing. I know and feel this to be wrong and sinful—Oh how many blessings are still left me. For how many years did our merciful God! stay his hand whilst millions of others were suffering grief want and death. How joyous we were—how bountiful fed how often spared—Oh God forgive me that I cannot feel "thy will not mine be done." I try to be still—the dealings of my Heavenly Father now seems dark to me but a day of disclosures is at hand—when every dealing will be vindicated then all darkness will disappear. Eternity will unfold how all, all was needed, that nothing else, nothing less, could have done! If not now, at least then, the deliberate verdict or a calm retrospect of life will be this "The word of the Lord is right and all His works are done in truth."

Our dear Georgia wrote to you on Monday last. Our precious Florence, Appy & Cuyler got safe home on Tuesday morning 4 oclock. I have not heard from either your dear Father or dear Lordy since they left us. I can but hope they are safe from harm. I try to be willing to resign all I have left to the keeping of my God! and Saviour—Oh why can't I as willingly resign my darling son Butler to a merciful Saviour. Why will ever a doubt enter my mind that he the most beloved son and brother is in perfect bliss. I try to forget that terrible day I try to for get that that noble beauteous face and form is mouldering in the cold grave. I try to lift my Eyes—my heart my thoughts to his now gracious home in that house of many mansions in the home of a merciful Saviour—who suffered and died and rose again for such as my beloved was on earth—so pure in heart—so kind so just—so noble—Oh! my son—Floyd think how he did his duty—to his parents—sisters, brothers servants—neighbors—of his honesty —truth & almost perfect character—& try my darling to be to us what he was in life—looking to God! the Father, God the Son and God the holy ghost for help to guide you through life & when called to a better world—there to meet and be welcomed by our Saviour and there to be united to the brother you love so well & that other dear brother so long an angel in Heaven. You ask me my darling to give you advice—my darling what better advice can a fond Mother give than to implore of you to read your bible and there in learn your duty to your God—your Saviour and to your neighbor—Do this my son and you will be much happier in this world and what is far better be sure of a welcome in that heavenly mansion where there will be no more trouble—sickness—or death. Encourage the trust in an over ruling providence it gladene'd my poor heart to *perceive you cherished.* In your walk through life be honest and upright—quiet and peaceable—ready to do good to all—forgive as you hope to be forgiven. Oh that we one and all could take our blessed Saviour as our example in all things—Try my son to take him for yours.

Dear Georgia spoke of writing again to you but I begged her to defer it—as I know she has many letters which require answering. You will be distressed to hear of another misfortune the Grants have met with—Probably Robert Couper may have had earlier intelligence from Hopeton—All we know is that their comfortable home at Elizafield was burnt to the ground on Tuesday last at mid day—the roof took fire from a spark from the chimney—Mr Brown may be here tomorrow & I hope will be able to tell us more was saved than our present information warrants our hoping. Most truly do I feel for the Grants.

You will be sorry too to hear that at present we have no certainty of our dear Cuylers get[ing] in with Major Downey—Sarah Bourke wrote that he would take him—then Fraser Grant wrote that he could not—then Mr Bourke wrote "that Major D[owney]—would provided Cuyler could be in the same class with Fraser["]—This last letter was received two days ago since then the weather has been such dear Malley could not go over to learn more definitely how it will be. On Monday God! willing—he and Cuyler will go over to Brunswick— I can but hope all will be well arranged. Dear Floyd [I] have not said one word about how much we miss you my darling—God! grant you had a safe pleasant journey—& will write to us as often as you can find time. Trust my beloved you may be permitted to return home in July & may find our number the same as you left us. For your dear sake I will see that your horses are taken care of— Dear G[eorgia] & F[lorence] have gone to that sacred spot. The wind is very high & the weather very cold but it does not fret me as it would have done last year at this season. I must try and see all my trials as coming from a merciful God! blessed when He gives, blessed when He takes. All we have are His. All unite in fond love to you—your poor sister has a bad cold—& still very lame— Johnnie had croup on Saturday night. Toozie too was threatened with it. All hope and pray for your well being my darling Floyd both here & hereafter— Let us all pray for the comfort which our Saviour has promised to all who be-

lieve in him—will love and obey him. Then my darling death will have no ter-
rors—the grave no victory.

> Your devoted Mother
> A M King

22d March 1859

My dearly beloved son Lordy

Yours & your dear father['s] letters of the 10th from Holmorville & yours of
the 16th from Waresboro were received on the 20th & 21st. Truly thankful
to God! we are to hear you had so far been kept from sickness or disaster. I have
never before felt it a task to write to my loved absent ones. I am so forcibly reminded that there is *one* loved one absent with whom, I can never again hold
communication or hope to see return to his earthly home. When a Mail is received (even mourning his absence every moment of my waking hours) there
is a feeling of disapointment that there is no hope of ever again in life hearing
from him when your dear sisters return from the hallowed spot which covers
his so late beatious form—a feeling of disappointment comes over me that
they bear me no message from Him—You say truly my son that it is my duty
to submit to the will of God! For submission to the will of Him who cannot
err—I pray unceasingly—But none but my God! can know the agony I suffer
how much I *feel* the loss of such a son as my Butler was to me. It was his own
peculiar gift a gift given him by his God! the love he bore his poor Mother—
the way he showed it was so lovely—How painfully empty seems now our so
late happy home. Not a room but brings his dear loving face which ever expressed love & respect for His mother to my mind—not a chair but he has occupied—Every tree & flower is associated with his loved memory. Would that
I could ever look up to that happy home where I must believe. He is now so
happy. Do not do me the injustice to think I am not grateful for the good husband and many loving & beloved children yet left me and for the rich consolation this gives me. I do not love you all the less for grieving that his loved
place among you is vacant. My constant prayer is that as one after another goes
from our circle to return no more on earth we whose days are prolonged, be
knit more and more closely together. May we be faithful to our God! to ourselves & to each other "And do thou most merciful Saviour form amongst us
those ties which death cannot destroy.["] May we each one receive strength to
return to the duties of life with increased diligence & purer aims—So that
when we are called to follow our departed friends—we may be found in the way
of righteousness and with a hope within that shall triumph over the grave, and
lead us into that world where all tears are wiped from all eyes, and we shall be

joined to the glorious assembly of the just made perfect, and look back upon the trials of this life as the instrument [of] a good and merciful God! to bring us to Him through Christ Jesus our Saviour.

The weather here has been very unfavorable. We think & feel how many discomforts you and your dear Father must be exposed to God! protect you my beloved husband & son from every evil. It does seem most trying that your dear Father has to be thus mixing with men who can have no sympathy with the subject which must most occupy his mind—& you too dear Lordy how often you must suffer. May the glorified spirit of your beloved brother be permitted to guard you from every evil! Oh! may that same spirit guide me in my duties & heal the wound which God! can heal!

Dear Georgia will write to your dear Father today & dear Malley speaks of writing to you. I hope you may receive these letters my dear Lordy—you must be anxious to hear from or of us. Malley & Cuyler went to Brunswick yesterday. Major Downie has consented to take dear Cuyler and our kind friends Mr & Mrs Bourke insisted he should stay with them. Malley accepted on the condition he should be considered as a boarder. So dear Cuyler will be very comfortable. Your sister was here last evening she still looks very badly. I believe more from mental than bodily. I believe more from mental than bodily ailment. What a brother what a *friend* she has lost!!

All the dear ones here unite in the warmest love to your dear Father and self. May God! of his infinite mercy keep you both safe—& restore you to your devoted Mother

A M King

Retreat 2d April

My dearly beloved husband

This the third day since you and dear Lordy left us. Oh how sad is this separation. More so now than it ever was before. How good our Heavenly Father has been to us what seas & miles have been between you and your home—how often has your precious life been in peril in storm & in sickness! our Heavenly Father has preserved you & restored you again & again to your home & loving family. How many years of happiness have I wasted in gloommy anticipation of misfortunes which have not yet over taken me. What spirit of continual fretting and moping over fancied ill that temptation to exaggerate the real or supposed dangers which surrounded my beloved absentees—tho disadvantages of our condition, magnifying the trifling inconveniences of our everyday life into enormous evils. Old as I am I am trying to amend this serious fault, and try and be thankful, for the many blessings still given me by a merciful God!

D[aniel] Lord & Nina tell us that you got safe to Brunswick. I presume you & dear Lordy left for Waynes County on Friday. We had Jimper at Hamilton all last night to receive the buggy & horses—but the *Everglade* did not bring them. So we conclude you have made some other arrangement for their return. William and our precious Tootee were here last evening—She looked ill poor child. The rest of us, are, as you left us.

Dearest husband how painful it must be for you and dear Lordy to mix with men who if they know your sorrow feel no sympathy for you. We at home have no such trial. We can sit every evening in his room—we can talk of him & mingle our tears without interruption. Oh my husband how ardently fervently do I pray that God! will in mercy fill all our hearts with His holy spirit—to strengthen us in all good resolutions—guide us in all our ways. May we first earnestly seek to please our God! Trusting all we have into his wise & merciful keeping—all we have are His gifts—And Oh for how many years did our Merciful Father spare us from real sorrow. Now that our God! has seen best to recall the precious boon (in the person of our most beloved son) loaned us for this many years. Let us not murmur—but rejoice in the many blessings still left us. Looking to Jesus! for help in this our deep sorrow—Looking to Him to guide us in the strait and narrow path which will lead us to his mercys seat. Sometimes I feel comforted—then again all is dark dark. God! be merciful to me a sinner! Tomorrow will be communion—Oh! may I be able to partake of that bread & wine as one worthy to receive the mercy & forgiveness of our Lord & Saviour—by feeling all I have are His—To him I can alone look for forgiveness & salvation.

I am conscious I write almost wildly thought upon thought rushes through my mind. In looking up all of His letters I opened one addressed to me when you & him were on your way from California to Washington City. In alluding to you How beautifully he expressed his gratitude to God! for Having given him such a Father! Oh how he loved us on earth—how he still will love us all in his new and far more happy home—if we will strive to do the will of God! in this world Our Saviour will prepare a place for us all "in that house not made with hands eternal in the Heavens." Oh my husband let us pray without ceasing that death will only be only a reunion with our departed treasures!!!

I trust soon to hear from you and dear Lordy. All here unite in fond love to you both. Praying God! to protect you soul & body from every danger I am your poor sorrowing but ever devoted wife

A M King

4th
Your most welcome letter was handed me by Rhina yesterday—I am glad I permitted her to visit her Father—had she not gone I would not have heard

from you & dear Lord so soon. I feel more willing now, more content—to leave all I have in the hands of a merciful God! I look back with horror on so often mistrusting His kind Providence. How often have we parted—how often have our beloved sons left us—all were permitted to return. I now feel a trust that all now absent will be permitted to return. I pray you & our dear sons will be guided in the right way. Oh that every word we speak our every act—may be guided by Gods! holy spirit. Write to me of him the dearest and the best of sons. those absent in the body tho our mortal eyes will never more in this world see that precious one. Yet I feel his spirit is sometimes with me. Do not shrink from naming our beloved—How his glorified spirit must rejoice when we try to please God! Oh! that we indeed may be a God! loving—God! serving family that as each one falls asleep in Jesus it will be to awake to the glad welcome of those gone before (us—redeemed by the blood of our Saviour)—there to be united forever & forever!!

Dear Georgia has written to our dear Lordy—dear Mallery to you—by this Mail. If permitted I will write to Lord by the Wednesday Mail. Our dear children unite in fond love to you & our son. God! bless & restore you to your devoted wife

A M King

St Simons 4th April

My own beloved son Lord

I thank you much for your affectionate letter of the 1st the receipt of which I begged your dear Father to thank you for in the letter I concluded to him this morning and sent by this days Mail to the care of Genl Knight. Georgia also wrote to you by this Mail & Malley to his father. I did not know there was a letter for you by the Saturdays Mail it will go with this on Wednesday.

I do not think I ever perused a letter from you my darling with more heart felt gratification than this now open before me! That gratification arises from the view you take of the mercies we have so long received from our God! feeling inspired by the removal of our choicest blessing. The Lord gave, the Lord has taken blessed be the name of the Lord!!

We heard from Mr Browne yesterday a most excellent sermon. Showing with some, affliction hardens the heart—with other[s] it worketh righteousness. Such I trust will be the effect on the hearts of his parents—sisters—brothers. For how many years did our God! pour down blessings on us. For so long we all seemed to forget this world was *not* our abiding place. We received and enjoyed His blessings—too often forgetful of the Giver. I look back on the years of happiness past & feel how ungrateful I have been what would I not give could I but live them over again—but would I make a better use of those years?

I fear not. You say "I need not allude to your duties as Mother to the rest of the family, for as no one ever discharged them better, so no one understands them better." Alas my son! when I think of the example I have set to my beloved children of fretfulness about trifles—discontent about that which God! in his wisdom withheld from us over anxiety lest danger should befall my absent husband & children—that want of patience & trust. Above all the example of a true Christian Mother. Oh! how my heart is torn and rent. Oh that I could but dreamed my Butler was so soon to leave me. That I could but have heard him express a firm belief in His saviour. His acts showed he was forgiving, as he hoped to be forgiven—his last few weeks on earth seem'd to show he was at peace with all—if at peace with all around him—can I be presumptuous in believing he was making his peace with Him who searched that noble heart? How often did he set his Mother the beautiful example of Charity—justice "doing unto others as I would have them do unto me." What I blame myself much for is my not setting you all the example of a true Christian mother making religion an inviting pleasing subject for you all to follow. I was not a true Christian my son—else it would have been my example to you all. The past cannot be recalled it may not be too late to implore of my remaining children to *seek diligently after the true treasures* laid up in Heaven. Search the Scriptures for in them you will find eternal life. It is not all who say Lord Lord [and] shall find forgiveness but they who doeth the will of the Father.

During much of his life how well he did did [*sic*] do the will of the Father his beautiful discharge of his duty as a son a brother friend—neighbor—master. Surely God! is rewarding him now? If our then bleeding saviour forgave the thief on the cross. If He forgave his unfaithful disciples—blotting out their sin as soon committed—Surely our beloved was forgiven & is now in perfect happiness—Surely he is with his God! and Saviour. I will try to discharge my duties better than I have ever done before looking [to] Christ for strength & guidance. Praying for Christs sake the Holy spirit will dwell in each dear heart—fitting us for that better world where I hope we will be united to our loved ones. Let us each try to obtain grace to do our duty to our God! to each other & to our selves—to our neighbors—friends—servants and fellow beings—then my darling when our time comes—when the Father call us He will find us ready. Let us not put off the hour—"but watch."

We regard *your wish* each time has one of the most beautiful flowers been placed in your name & we will continue to do so until please God! you return to do that duty yourself.

I trust my darling you are trying to guard against any word or act which will jar the feelings of your kind Father. Our darling Butler was perfect in his conduct—& manner as a son. I know my dear Lordy it was his nature to be so. I know too it is your manner but you will endeavor my son to correct your every fault do not depend on your own strength that you will find but weakness. Look to God! through Christ—for help! under every trial—think how our Saviour bore all that man could do to him. Oh that we could all look only to Him. As precious as have ever been the souls of my husband and children to me they are doubly so now. By the sudden removal of our most beloved Butler—I believe our God! has some faithful end in view—by the removal of that prized, most cherished earthly prop. God! would imbold more of His tenderness by taking to His Heavenly Mansion. He is drawing our hearts close to Himself.

5th

Feeling it a duty we [owe] our friends the Grants dear Georgia is most anxious to spend a day with them. The few days your dear Father & self were with you she could not spare from you—then Nina & D[aniel] Lord came & dear Malley thought it would not be well to leave him even for a day. D[aniel] L[ord] proposed leaving last night but he did not go. Poor Malley has the doctoring of another fine mule. What a terrible disease it must be. Thank God! it is confined to the brutes. Tho' we must feel their suffering & loss, it is not like the suffering and loss of human beings.

I presume Georgia informed you of Mr Postells speedy recovery. An attack of Pleurisy I believe. I hope the sudden changes we have had from summer heat—to almost winter cold has not given colds to your dear Father and self neither to Nep[tune] or John—and that you will find the roads more passable than through your first route. I love to think you are doing all in your power to assist and comfort your dear Father. Just think dear Lordy if our precious Butler is permitted to see us—how rejoiced he is, at every effort we make to please God! in the faithful discharge of *all* our duties to Him—to each other—ourselves and all around us. How it must grieve his glorified spirit when we do wrong in thought word or deed. How much nearer I feel to Christ—since I believed my darling was in His Kingdom how much more I prize the Gift of Gods! only son—since I believe through Him my beloved has been saved—And that we all will be saved if we will but do our duty in this life. Let us try to assist each other in the love & duty we owe our God! and Saviour. What fault you see in your poor old Mother—tell it to me my darling & I will with Gods! help try to mend it. I saw our dear Tootee at Church on Sunday. I hope to see her ere I close this. I wish you could have given us more definite directions where to address to you—but I suppose you could scarce tell yourselves.

A letter to your dear father from Marshall—I will give it to Malley to read & determine if necessary to send with this. Georgia has just returned from Hamilton all as usual there.

I had a very dear letter from our dear Floyd today—How well he expresses himself—Floyd (if he lives) will be a noble man. His greatest fault now is being too impulsive—All your sisters & dear Mall unite Praying God! to bless you my darling son I am ever & forever your fond Mother

A M King

6th

Malley is so fearful the letter from Dr Fouls may be lost or never received by your dear Father—he advised its not being sent. He thought he would make a copy of it to send—but on opening it saw "private." His delicacy forbade his reading the letter.

The weather is very cold this morning—we feel for you dear ones—How much better off we at home are—God! grant neither your dear Father or self or either of the servants with you may suffer from this journey God! protect you from every evil—

Your devoted Mother
A M King

dear Tootee was here last evening—she is about the same.

9th April

My dearly beloved husband

Your dear letter to me & our dear Lordys to our precious Georgia were received on *Thursday*. Thank God! you were able to assure us of your safety & good health. God! continue in His mercy—to guard you from evil during this our most trying and painful separation. Oh my husband none but—He who searcheth the heart can know what you have undergone. Believing that you have ever acted conscientiously I cannot—will not blame your present course. I have ever believed your aim has been pure—My only dread is—you may not have time to devote to more vitally important thoughts. I believe you have ever looked to God! to bless the efforts you were making—if so you could never strive for that, of which He disapproves! May He bless you my beloved & restore you to us in health.

We have addressed letters to you & dear Lordy to Mill town & Troupville— This I will direct to Thomasville. I know it will be a relief to you to hear from home. I am thankful to say—we are no worse in health than when you left us. Dear Malley has still that cough—of which he makes light. The lightwood tea certainly did him no benefit. He is now trying another remedy. Our dear H[annah] Page spent yesterday with us. She thinks or says her health is improving. God! grant it may be!

Our dear Cuyler came to us last night—he seems quite well. He says he hopes to be benefitted by Major Downies instruction & that Mr & Mrs Bourke are all kindness to him. We heard from dear Floyd I think I wrote you on Tuesday last.

We had a very heavy rain on Monday last—none since then—but very cold & today a high cold wind. Dear Malley finds it difficult to conquer the grass but he is doing his best. The mule is slowly mending.

I received by this days Mail *the much covetted likeness* not so strikingly like our best beloved, as the one *he* gave you but I am thankful it is in my possession. Oh my husband at times I feel my grief too heavy to bear—then the good God! strengthens me & I feel willing to try & do my duty to you & to our other dear children. In every instance given us in the Holy gospel—of those raised from death by our Saviour—*He gave back to the Mother her son* to the Sisters the brother—to the parents the young maiden. Is not this a proof that God! will give back to us our Son in that better world. And Oh how joyous will be the welcome we will receive from our beloved sons—& how joyfully was he welcomed into the joys of his Saviour by that Saviour—his brother grand parents & many friends.

On Sunday last whilst dear Tootee was kneeling by the sacred grave some one touched her & on looking up there stood poor old Mrs Davis the tears were coursing down her cheeks. She said "Oh he is safe safe in heaven. He was a good friend to me. Oh you do not know how kind he has been to me." Oh our blessed son! no one but His God! & the recipients of his charity—his kindness knew how oft he carried out "as much as ye did it unto the least of these, ye did unto me." And *he* is now reaping his reward!

Oh that his dear brothers will follow the beautiful example he set them as a son—brother—friend—master—his loving kindness to all. As long as we remain in this earth—it is our duty to fill worthily the station wherein God! has placed us. I try to hope all will work together for our good. Oh how precious to me the souls of my husband my children—Let us each strive to be worthy the love of Him who died for us. Then death will have lost its terror. It will prepare us to throw of[f] life as [an] old and useless garment, and look, on, and welcome death as a redeeming friend.

It is quite possible none of our dear ones will write to you by this Mail— D[aniel] Lord & Nina are still here & occupy much of their time. I will if possible write to dear Lordy—never the less give him a fond Mothers love. All our dear children unite in love to you & Lordy.

Devotedly your affectionate wife
A M King

12th April 1859

My dearly beloved Floyd

When I look back to this day *one* short year ago—how changed are the feelings of our two families—the Grants & our own! On this day twelve months past—our dear Georgia, Virginia & Mallery returned from Satilla—they had heard their loved friend was much better! & how thankful I was to get them safe home again. Before the close of that day Oh the agony the Grants were suffering & we here so happy and all unconscious of their grief. Little did we then think in nine months and eight days more he our best would be sleeping the same sleep! Oh! my God! have mercy!!!

It seems hard that our precious Georgia has yet been prevented from going to Mrs Grant. Their kind hearts will not blame what others may think neglect. Dear G[eorgia] bears the disappointment well—knowing how much dear Mallery has to contend with in the management of our little property. He the precious noble son—bears his crosses without one murmur—his whole aim seems to be to do his duty & safe me trouble. Our dear Cuyler came to us on Friday night—his health seems good—he brought letters from the Grants. A very kind one from Mr Grant to me. He writes so affectionately of my children. He who we mourn—He says "was like one of my own." He calls you "our noble Floyd" —Your letter to him was sent by one of his sweet daughters for our perusal— a letter which did justice and credit to your head and warm heart my Floyd! Cultivate all those tender liberal feelings my darling—it will render your life on earth more happy and your path to that better life less choked with thorns and brambles (envy and malice) the seeds of which are sown by the evil one in our hearts.

Mr Grant & dear Jinnie I presume went to Savannah last night. *She* wrote most entreatingly that our precious Georgia would accompany them. In the first place D[aniel] L[ord] & *Nina* are still here—then I really had not the money to defray her expenses. As dear Cuyler did not bring his books—& would lose Mondays recitation if he did not get back on Sunday night—dear Malley took him back late on Sunday evening—Mr Bourke was absent dear Sarah was in her usual health. When our dear Cuyler comes again (which he proposes to do the coming Saturday) he will bring his books & need not return before Monday morning.

I have not heard from either your dear Father or dear Lordy since their letters of the 6th. They were then well & getting on as well as they could possibly expect. It is my pleasure to mention to them every letter we receive from you my dear son. As they will be on the move until please God! they are restored to us—I can't advise you where a letter from you will probably find them. Our Mail has not yet come—I hope to acknowledge a letter from you before I close this—If not I will try not to be uneasy. Dear dear Floyd how many precious days & hours of happiness have I lost by cultivating my mistrust of Gods! goodness and mercy. Now that His hand has been laid on me I feel His past mercies—I look in vain to hear some loving voice say "Mother, see your fears were groundless" and from whom did I more frequently hear those words—than from him—whose voice will never again sound on my mortal ear. My own precious most tender—most loving son Butler! I long for the time when that loving voice will welcome me in his Heavenly home. Oh my Floyd let us all strive to enter in at that straight gate. Oh! the joy to hear the words of our blessed Redeemer welcome thou to the joy of the Lord! How wonderful it is my Floyd that in all my long life I being so peculiarly blessed did not appreciate the mercies I received. Oh what blessings still are mine! My cup is still full to the brim with blessings infinite, double for all my sins have I received—I adore Him for the past and for the future I cheerfully trust Him. I had but a loan—no more, and if the Great Proprietor sees meet the loan He lent me to recall becomes it me to murmur? Rather let me own His undeserved kindness that my noble husband so many loved sons and daughters are still spared me. So many preserved from day to day. The monuments of Gods! for bearing love! We were all too well contented with the happiness of this world—In taking first the best—the one we all leaned on. Oh how much I am at a loss for his support & advice. Oh what a son—Brother, friend, Master!!!

Thank God! on the 2d Inst you were well your sweet letter to dear Georgia is now before me. I am most grateful no harm befel that precious "copy." Fearful that some harm may befall the original likeness your dear Father took the "copy" for me with him. The one claimed from Mrs Baird has been received—we do not think it as good as the one He gave his Father. Oh! how fervently have I prayed God! to let Him visit me in my dreams—His beautiful hair—his last letter to me—his likeness—are under my pillow every night—the pillows his loved head rested on supports that of his sorrowing Mother but tho never absent one instant from my mind whilst awake I cannot dream of him. Oh how I pray that his glorified spirit may be with us. He is a strong link—between Heaven and earth. Oh may that link never be broken or made weaker!! But may it draw us closer and closer to that Merciful redeemer who will love us if we will but give our hearts to Him. I have never seen our flower garden more beautiful than it now is. The only pass time which seems to give pleasure to your Sisters is to gather these beautiful flowers for his sacred grave. Last Spring at this time how he admired these beauties—Where he is—flowers never die. Your rose bushes are looking very healthy—your cuttings apparently doing well. Each letter you get from home must bring our sorrow fresh to your mind—It is harder for you to realize our loss than we who witnessed his end.

Yet we too find it difficult to realize. Oh my Floyd I wish that you and dear Cuyler could have been at home those *few last perfectly* happy days. When his beautiful spirit show[er]ed love on all around him.

I have just heard from our dear Tootee—I have not seen her since Friday last—when she spent the day with us. She *says* her health is improving. Your dear Father has all the horses which can draw except Old John & Tallulah. We are very tender of Old John—and seldom use him—but for visiting his masters grave. I have been at Hamilton but once since our affliction. Your dear Sister comes to us whenever William can find the time to drive her over. Your horse has nearly recover'd—Malley will not use him for fear of another relapse. Dear, dear, Mallery what with sorrow, striving to make a support for us—and sick horses he has had & still has much to bear him down. But he goes on doing the best he can—And is I trust looking to God! for his reward. Oh how warm & tender his love for that best & noblest of brothers!!

I believe your cousins will leave tomorrow night—dear Nina seems so happy here it will seem unkind to regret their long stay—but to me the presence of any but my own family is very irksome to me. I desire no other society but that of the Grants. How close sorrow draws to each other mutually suffering friends. What beautiful resignation Mr Grant expresses. God! grant me the same. My whole mind is so absorbed by this great anguish I can think or write of but little else my darling—you feel the same in communicating with us—you can understand how it is. I must not neglect to say our dear Mallery *says* his cough is better—the rest of us are as usual. I have as yet heard nothing of dear Cuylers things that you promised to send him. July is not far distant—I pray God! you may be spared to return & that you will find all you left at home. Your Sisters and dear Mallery unite in warm love to you my darling—Praying God! to protect you from every evil. To guide you in all good ways—I am your devoted Mother

A M King

13th
Our dear Tootee was here last evening. Our family & hers in our usual health. Ever & forever your fond mother

A M King

7th May
My dearly beloved Floyd

The Mail has just come and brought dear Mallery your affectionate letter of the 28th. Thank God you were able to say you were then well. And I am also thankful to add the good & Merciful God! permits me to say in point of bodily health, we are as usual. Dear Georgia wrote to you by the Wednesday Mail informing you of the unexpected happiness we experienced on Monday night—by the return of your dear Father & dear Lordy. On what day they contemplate making a third start I can't inform you. When I said "in our usual health" I had forgotten that our dear Lordy had been suffering from a return of pain in his back. He says it now only feels weak—keeps very quiet & I hope & pray he will soon get over it.

In your reply to this—I beg you will name the sum you will require to pay up your bills and return to us—and at what time. But a letter received to day from John C Fraser saying "As some change was being made in his business he requested we would not draw on him again immediately.["] So *be sure not only to give me time but say exactly what will be required.*

Each day but brings the stronger conviction of the sad bereavement we have sustained—time does not assuage my grief for the departure of my most beloved son. Oh my Floyd what would become of me if I did not believe that our beloved is among the Redeemed! Yesterday in the agony of my distress—doubts of his salvation began to intrude—then came the sweet consoling thought "like a voice in my ear—a still small voice" saying "how often when you have been distressed for his safety—have I restored him to you. Cant you trust him now with me?" Oh the comfort that gave me. Could it be that an Angel put those thoughts in my mind? Oh that I could at all time "only believe."

Oh how I do pity your dear Father—how much more he has to contend with, than I have with a heart crushed by the loss of such a son has he to contend against the machinations of those who would wish by injuring him to defeat his election. God! will order all for the best.

On Thursday dear Cuyler returned to us. D[aniel] Lord also came. The latter tells us that Henrys wife has presented him with another daughter—now three weeks old & named Jane. Henry has been sick—also James King—but both recovered.

I had a very sweet letter from dear Jinnie Grant yesterday—all were well. Mrs Grant was prevented coming to see us by the high wind—which has been blowing now 9 days. It has again been so cold as to make fires necessary for comfort.

I saw dear Tootee two days ago—she thinks her own health improving. Johnnie still looks badly—the rest—as usual.

Your request was complied with—the most beautiful of your roses with violets were placed in your name. Oh how sacred have all the flowers become—for no other purpose are they gathered—it now seems my sole object in cultivating them. Yesterday Tip went to old Mrs Demeres & from the Magnolia tree which her daughters gave to our Butler—he brought several most beautiful flowers—In the afternoon dear Georgia accompanied Tip to the spot and paced them over him—their beauty like his own soon perishes—but thanks be to God! through Christ—the beauty which made him so dear to us will never perish—but is now growing brighter & brighter to all eternity!

Your dear dear Father bids me say—that he has not written to you—which he regrets—all owing to his present state—the little time he can spare from actual labor both of body and mind is given to rest. He will I hope soon be able to write to you. He is now writing a report—which he hopes will do away the falsehoods now circulated against him—truth is on his side—If the good God! knows all is true in his noble heart—it matters not what man thinks or says. All here unite in warm love to you—I pray without ceasing that God! will make each dear son and daughter his by adoption as they all are by creation that when we leave this world of trial we will be united to the loved ones gone before us to dwell forever with God the Father God! the Son & God! the holy Spirit! I call on the father—the dear Sons the precious daughters to unite with me in this prayer. If accepted through the Son—come death how welcome will be the summons. "Arise let us go hence."

Your affectionate—devoted Mother
A M King

9th

Our dear Tootee & family are spending this day with us. Your dear Brother Cuyler detained by weather—your dear Father & Lord will probably go to Savannah this evening. Cuyler will also or proposes taking the S[team] Boat for Brunswick.

Oh my Floyd how earnestly I pray to God! you will not be lead away by the world. Let not this affliction be sent in vain. It is true we could not have met with a heavier affliction—your dear Father & I looked to your precious Butler to be the one to supply our loss to his Sisters and brothers. But there are yet 10 more to be taken—Let us all try to be ready when we are summon'd. When I look back on the years gone by & feel how poorly I have discharged my duties as one to whom so many children have been given to raise for Christ—I do not think I can say one word out of season now—How earnestly do I pray that all my darling son ever did wrong may be visited on me his poor heart broken Mother. Not on him Oh my Saviour but on me be the punishment.

No one can find grace unless they seek it through Christ. No one can receive the good gift unless they ask it. Unto none can the door to Heaven be opened unless they knock—Oh let us all seek—ask and knock—on earth our blessed Jesus never once turned from the vilest sinner—neither will he refuse forgiveness now to any who go to him with faith in his promise to forgive—if we truly repent and pray for grace to sin no more. Praying for you all the time—I am your devoted Mother

A M King

[On black-bordered paper] 18th May

I began this on the wrong side of the paper. Be sure and inform me what money will be required and when.

My dearly beloved Floyd

Yesterdays Mail brought Mallery an affectionate letter from you. We cannot be sufficiently grateful to the giver of all our blessings—that you are able to say you were quite well. I could not write to you by the Monday Mail but your dear Sister Georgia did so. To hear from your home my darling must give pleasure even when now our letters bear the badge of mourning for one who no longer gladdens our hearts by his presence. But praise be to God! many blessings are still left us on earth. And through Christ who died for us—has risen, & has prepared room in his kingdom for all who will love and obey him in this life. We have hope that the best of sons and brothers is now with his Saviour and that though he can no more return to us—we shall go to him. Oh my Floyd— had we all been seeking for a place in the better world instead of valuing our temporal [one] looking so much for happiness in this world how much less would have been the terrible shock occasioned by the sudden removal of our beloved. Now we feel this is not our abiding place. Thank God! this grief has not so far as man can judge hardened any of our hearts. We all feel that God! has chastened us for a good purpose. May that purpose be accomplished without further chastisement. May we one and all come at once to the feet of Jesus.

On Sunday last your Sisters Florence & Virginia were confirmed. I verily believe had my three sons gone up also I must have shouted aloud my joy. Thanks be to God! the work of grace has commenced in the heart of my beloved Lordy. He was powerfully affected by the Bishops most touching convincing sermon that day. If the good God! will but have patience a little longer I hope and trust all, all will take up the cross & follow the Lord Jesus. We were so struck with the sermon I begged the Bishop to let us take a copy of it & dear Georgia is now making that copy. You I trust will read it my darling and feel the folly of putting off the day for seeking your souls salvation.

The Bishop came to us on Saturday. Sunday returned here from church— dined at Postells on Monday, returning here that evening—went to Cannon's Point yesterday—will dine at Hamilton today & leave tonight. His visit at this time was mostly to comfort us. Oh what comforting prayers what consolation he has given us all. I must not neglect this opportunity to say how grateful we all are for the sympathy we have received from Mr Brown. How much I lament my own prejudice against him—still more my ever having encouraged the prejudices of my children—the fault is more mine than theirs. God! forgive us one and all. He was with your Sisters when they went on Saturday evening to change the flowers on that sacred grave—& said "I would feel that I had neglected a sacred duty if I did not visit this sacred spot whenever I came to the Island." He feels for and with us. No one is without faults. Let him or her who is without fault cast the first stone. Had true charity dwelt in our hearts we would never have searched for faults in him. My child is more mine than thine God! forgive me, as I trust He will forgive [the] dear child who has followed the evil example set by your Mother.

On Friday night your dear Father and Lordy came home & dear Cuyler accompanied them. Your dear Father seems more sad every day—he never mentions the name of our departed. Would he speak of him as I do I think he would suffer less. He is very thin looking so care worn.

Virginias shoulder is no better—it is probable she will go on to consult Dr Sulivan to night. I saw your dear Sister on Monday evening and heard from her today all there are as usual.

Your dear Father, Sisters and brothers unite in fond love to you. Leaving you in the hands of a Merciful God! I am

>Your devoted Mother
>A M King

25th June

My own dear precious Georgia

It being quite probable I may be able to send this by the *Everglade* this evening and knowing how glad you will be to hear from me I will try and write to you this morning it being quite possible I may not be able to write by the Monday Mails. Dear Florence wrote to you on Wednesday sending you what you had left here for Mr. Maszaros. She of course mentioned the safe arrival of our dear Floyd! He did not get over until I was asleep when he came to my door I thought he was your dear Father poor fellow he came up very quietly. Thank God! he was permitted to return again to the home and family he so dearly loves. He gave us your letters my precious Georgia. How strange it seems that you my darling are gone from us.[1] God! grant it may be only for the Summer & Autumn. You beg me not to miss you my precious child could that be possible? Yes my own precious child I do miss you more than words can express.

As our family circle lessens we seem to draw closer to each other. Even dear Malley now sits at supper with us & last evening he and dear Floyd & myself sat on the Front steps discoursing serious subjects and altho his sacred name was not mentioned his beloved image filled my thoughts and I believe was present with theirs also. But when is he absent from our thoughts? I love to believe his glorified spirit is often with us Oh my Georgia what would become of me, if I had no hope of ever seeing him again? The nearer we can walk with God! the surer will be that meeting—I feel it to be so. And my darling pray for your poor Mother that her faith shall never again fail. "Lord I believe help Thou mine unbelief."

Malley opened Andrews letter to your dear Father—he did not seem quite certain of coming to [the] U.S. this summer. I yet hope he may & that you will be able to accomplish our cherished wish. Oh how blessed we are in having so correct a likeness—but they want that lovely loving smile. Oh my Georgia may I believe that those beautiful eyes are now looking down on his poor sorrowing Mother? If so he will know [how] much I love him, how much I grieve for his loss to us how much I long to be united to him again. My own beautiful my good son Butler. This day makes 22 weeks since that noble form has rested in the grave 22 weeks and three days since that redeemed spirit has been with his Saviour but 22 weeks and 4 days ago I begrudged every day that passed feeling if I lived trials must come. Our good God! saw how content I was with the blessings of this world. He took my best treasure to draw my best affections to a better world. Even tho' so many weeks have past since that terrible day now as I write I cant realize the sad certainty that he will return no more on earth to his mother. But praised be to God! God our Saviour God! The Holy Ghost we can & I trust will go to him. I no longer begrudge time—every day brings us nearer to that Saviour who will restore!

Try my precious to carry through all the plans we two drew together First praying to God! that in so doing we shall do no sin. I pray tomorrows sun will not go down ere you shall be safely landed in N. York. I think of you & pray Gods! choicest blessings on you my precious pearl. I feel that you are in the hand of a merciful God! praying for grace to feel His will may be to restore you to us in life and with improved health. We heard nothing from or of your dear Father or Lordy by the Tuesday mail can it be that I am so absorbed by the certain sorrow that I no longer anticipate evil to come? or can I be so blessed as to be able to leave all coming events to a wise and merciful God!!?—

On Monday night our dear Florence gave all the letters to Tilla—they were forgotten. Tip took them to Brunswick—I regret most the letters to Capt Ottenger and John Fraser. We had a very heavy rain on Wednesday very gratefully received. The rain prevented your dear sisters from going to that sacred spot. Before sun rise dear Florence went on Thursday morning—we thought it too damp for dear Appy who has been *suffering*. I know you will rejoice to hear we are all love & forbearance to each other. God! give us *grace* to live each day as if we knew it would be our last. Flora & Appy have gone to Hamilton to see poor Tootee—Appy rode over last evening. Flora, Floyd & Lily walked up the road whilst dear Malley & I visited the pig pen and cast [?] house. We then all assembled in his room. On Wednesday dear little Willie was quite sick—he was free of fever yesterday when heard from by M[alley] & F[lora] in the morning and again when dear Appy rode over in the evening—I fear I shall not see dear Tootee before Sunday. I have been greatly disappointed by our precious Florences feeling not fit to partake of the Holy Communion the coming Sabbath. It is now my precious child that you are missed most seriously. I cant use the sweet convincing arguments you can. I have experienced the dread of unworthiness she speaks of—but it is only by going to Jesus trusting to His merits His willing ness to receive all who will believe in Him who so freely offers His salvation—"Believe only believe." I have not talked with dear Appy. Oh! That I could but see each dear Son each dear daughter go boldly to the Throne of Grace take hold on those gracious promises—& never let go until welcomed to the joy of their Lord and Saviour.

Your dear Sisters have returned leaving all in their usual health except dear Willie who has a return of fever—I would not tell you this dearest Geo but I promised to hide nothing from you. We can but hope the dear boy will recover from this sickness—For his dear Parents sake I trust God! will restore him to health. Dear Tootee has sent me to read a very affectionate letter she received from Mrs Cunningham also a little book "Christian consolation on the death of relatives and friends," by the Revd Hugh White A.M.—Late curate of St Marys Parrish, Dublin—For sale at the Depository 683 Broadway. This offering to Tootee was anonymous. She thinks it comes from Mary Tunno Interlined with pencil marks applying all the comforting words to our precious most beloved son & brother. Oh how much kindness we have received. God! will reward them all such kindness.—

It again rains—I fear it will again disappoint your sisters of the dear Grants visit. We hope to see dear Cuyler & he thought the Frasers & his dear sisters would come with him. See what a long letter I am writing to you my Georgia. I am grateful to your uncle & cousins for their kindness's to you. It would seem stranger if any could be unkind to my "little pearl." I hope you may meet with nothing to jar your feelings my love. I know I can trust to your *propriety* of conduct. It must be a very contrary spirit which could not live happily with you my darling—but do not forget the "sleeping & riding."—

Your little maid has not forgotten your orders—she came of her own accord today & is at this very moment picking my hair. I admit it is a luxury but one

I would not indulge in had you not so earnestly desired it. She has finished Toozies blue dress and is now making the one you gave Lily. If all children gave as little trouble as Lily does I would like a half dozen such in the house. I presume Florence mentioned the queer note she received from Mrs J.K. She made no mention whatever of me &c&c. I really do not know what to do. I do not like the idea of those little boys being left all summer with servants and yet some how I shrink from undertaking so heavy a charge. If the parents are content to leave them where the[y] are I had best let them stay.

Can you tell me where I can find the bombazine I got for your brothers hats? Tilla says when you fixd Lordys hat you left it up stairs that she brought it up to your room & put it on the bed—Bell has been looking all over your things but cannot find it—& poor Floyd is in want of a piece for his hat. Of course if you have taken it with you I cant expect it to be sent back but it would save me the trouble of hunting further for it.

I am sorry to hear from Mrs C[unningham]s letter that our dear Cousin was still very—unwell did you get the loan you desired? I hope it will not be long before she will be with us [*sic*].

I hope tomorrows mail will bring letters from your dear Father & Lordy. Think dear Georgia of the six sons God! gave me, the two most beautiful and beloved we believe are with their Saviour God! Two of the now eldest & the youngest are absent and two are with us. Oh God! grant that we shall all so walk in life that when lifes journey is finished we shall all be accepted by our Saviour Christ welcomed to His Fathers Kingdom and made one family undivided our circle united to be separated no more forever & forever!!!—

How sweet it is to commune with the absent whom we love—I could spend the whole day in writing to you my Georgia—I hear the voices of your dear sisters and brothers I know they are safe & near & yet him who we cannot see or hear may be nearer still—by his fond sorrowing mothers side—feeling sorrow only because those he loves are in sorrow, yet rejoicing if that sorrow will lead to their everlasting happiness & reunion with Him in his Saviours home.

The bell rings for dinner and I must stop—Praying God! to bless you my darling child keep you from every evil your sisters and brothers unite in fond love to you. Bell is the only servant near—she says "tell un huddy." I wish we could name some hour that we could pray at the same time for each other & those so dear to us. My love to Nina & her Father—James & his wife—if you tell Maria howde for your affectionate mother

A M King

P.S. The bombazine was found in Appys drawer just brought to me—

---

1. Georgia was traveling with the Stephen King family.

Friday 8th July

My dearly beloved Georgia

I am sitting in your own room writing at your table thinking of the many miles which now separate us. How much changed I must be my Georgia—I feel now none of that torturing anxiousness which oft times made me miserable, when I had so much to make me happy. I do not deny that I miss your sweet presence very very much—But the hope that the change will benefit your health that a merciful God will permit you return in some measure reconciles me to your being so far & for so long a time from us. Our darling Florence has, and is, & and will I know, continue to do, all in her power to fill your place. She devotes herself to me and dear Appy & the boys are all so kind to their poor mother. Florence got up early this morning to write to you, in answer to your welcome letter by yesterdays mail. She forgot the hats. They I hope will go on Monday.

Possibly Flo informed you of the change in our Mails [they] go North *Monday* and *Friday*. [We] Receive on Thursday and Saturday. I will make no comment on this change. It commenced raining this morning at past 7—& has gone on thickening every hour since, and so cold a fire would not be objected to— very unwholesome weather. The change took place during the rain on Monday night the hardest of which your dear Father, Lordy & Malley were exposed to from this to Hamilton. It was so dark they got into the bridge Providentially no one was hurt or was the carriage or horses injured. As the Steamer did not pass until 9 oclock—& we heard from Lordy after they reached Savannah—I hope like dear Malley the[y] escaped all injurious consequences. They hoped to be along in this night's boat—but will now stop [no] longer than to take in Neptune & the horses proceed—to Brunswick & take the cars tomorrow for Waresboro. They hope to be back home one week from tomorrow.

I suppose that Florence told you that dear Cuyler accompanied the Grants home yesterday—he had to pay Major Downey who has given 2 months vacation. For this I am truly sorry. Poor boy he has not had one pleasant Friday to return home. This rain looks like continuing & so cold. Did not Florence tell you of the fright we had on Saturday night last? supposing some poor negro had been drowned between this and the light house. The mercy of God! kept Joe, Charles & Edenboro from being drowned. They were on their way to Brunswick the boat swamped—they held on to her until she drifted ashore near the tide gauge. But let me not be filling my paper with such as this. I thank God! their lives were spared for there owns sakes as well as for ours.

We were very sorry to part with those dear girls your Sister had intended returning with them but little Rosalie showed symptoms of having one of her bad turns and as the weather has turned out today she is best at home. Next Tuesday it is probable she will go. I am anxious she should go the little change will do her good. Poor Tootee she has a wearysome life & well does she discharge her duties. Dear Tootee with 4 of her children were with us on Wednesday William could not come & Willie remained with his Father.

Saturday 9th

I have just finished the perusal of your sweet letter of the 3d—it met me just preparing to retire to my room to continue this letter to you which I began yesterday. You will be as grateful as I am that I am able to say we all are in our usual health. Last night dear Malley set off through all the rain for Hamilton. In the first place he had to see 4 horses & the buggy put on board the Steam boat for Brunswick—hoped to have a few minutes talk with your dear Father and dear Lordy whilst this was being done—& to meet and bring home dear Cuyler. When the Steamer stopped at the wharf the Capt said he had no room for the horses so the boat left barely giving your dear Father & Lordy time to say they were well & to desire the horses &c sent over in a flat today. D[aniel] Lord landed with Cuyler. He did not bring little Willie with him—his excuse was that it was raining. I will urge his bringing him the next time tho I do not think the dear boy will be as happy with us as he is at home. And such is the scarcity I really cannot urge the three to come. Were it otherwise I would be too glad to repay some of the kindness you are receiving from their grandfather. Thank him for me my sweet child! I know my dear child that you repay his kindness by your devotion to his only daughter. I am distressed to hear the Doctors opinion of dear Ninas case. Distressed almost as much for you as for her. Your own Father is of the opinion that occupying the same sleeping apartment is as dangerous as to sleep in the same bed. Dearest Georgia I know how delicately you are situated—I am as reluctant as you can be to hurt the feelings of either Brother Stephen or Nina. But remember my child how dear you are to us. The duty you owe us. Enquire the candid opinion of Dr Green—And if he thinks you run the slightest risk either tell it yourself to Brother S[tephen] or beg him to do so! Will you my precious child obey me in this? I can but hope your plan may be the best. I am too much of the old school to like it altogether. I hope it may not end in your not going at all to any mineral spring. After writing to you my last letter I received a beautiful letter from Mr Savage. I will try and answer it, in the meanwhile give him my grateful acknowledgments for the kind sympathy he expressed for cherishing so just an appreciation for our precious one. Oh my Georgia I must reserve that subject for a separate page. Too sacred to be mixed up with less serious matters.

In my letter of the 25th I certainly must have added the joy which was mine by your precious sisters joining Tootee & me at the Holy table. Look over that letter again. My constant prayer to God! is for the souls of my precious children. Oh my Georgia it seems to me could I believe they would be saved I would be willing to lay you all by our Butlers side then lay me down too & die. I pray His precious memory may never be otherwise than it now is. His place filled so nobly must remain vacant. Oh my Georgia I miss him more & more my beautiful my noble son Butler! All last week my mind was filled with this image of him standing in all his beauty looking from up to his Saviour to down to his poor sorrowing mother. This idea was so comforting to me. I see him now my Georgia & Oh how bright & beautiful is that face. Your sisters are busy preparing their flowers. Your offering & dear Lordys are never forgotten. The flower season is nearly over & yet even then seems some to be found. It seemed to gratify the Grants to assist in these offerings of love to his sacred memory. Oh my Georgia!!! I am so sorry Andrew has not arrived I fear he will not visit the states this summer. I am so anxious our plans should be carried out. Do not have one taken from the one you have. If I could but have dreamed of how soon he would leave us, I would have begged one the last time we were together in Savannah. At times I feel as if I cant live any longer without him then the Good angel whispers be still. "What I do now you know [unreadable] you shall know here after."

You ask who sleeps with me. When your dear Father is away Flora has slept with me every night but one (when Jinnie was here). She is perfectly devoted in her affectionate attentions. Reads to me every night—& tries her best to fill your place. Appy is also very affectionate—Your brothers all love. Thank God! I have yet so many blessings. Our precious Tootees greatest happiness seems to be when she can spend a day with us—how short those days seem to both of us. She promises to come this evening. Our dear Cousin Amanda promises to be out in two weeks—her health still very weak Mr Woolley quite well. Your letter to your dear Father I will keep for him hoping to hand it to him one week from today. The one you left for dear Lordy I found yesterday in his drawer & read it. Dear Geo it does credit to your head and heart—Continue to write to him such sweet holy advice & God! will bless you my child & may send the blessing also on your brothers. My greatest comfort is to rise early—dress & go down in *his* room and there I hold communion with our God and Saviour—there dwell on the memory of our beloved! There offer my prayers for the living— there pray for a happy reunion with the dead. Oh my Georgia. I some times feel that my prayers are heard & then I can go forth to my duties cheered.—

These damp mornings I have left the gathering of peaches to Maria still I place them in the basket & am gratified to see your sisters and brothers enjoy them. We have an abundance of melons [&] figs but not many peaches. Miss Mary Gould has sent peaches to us three times much finer than those we have of our own. I am doing tomattos but difficulties for cans. We have yet to prove if bottles will answer.

Florence wrote to you by the Friday Mail (I made a mistake—we still have two chances weekly for sending letters—Mondays & Fridays). Sending you I think three letters which came for you—these were directed to Sharon Springs care of S.C.K. Malley speaks of writing to you poor dear boy he has so much to fatigue & worry him but outwardly he bears all patiently & I trust grace is given him to bear with patience all his trials. I will add a line if permitted on Monday.

10th

Flora had one of her headaches yesterday—& tho better I thought she best stay at home. D[aniel] Lord did not wish to go. The weather is again hot & looked showry [unreadable] for the buggy. So dear Malley concluded but 4 could go— Virginia, Floyd, Tip & myself with little Lily set out when about half way it came on to rain wetting Floyd & Tip so completely we had to turn back. But Thank God! our day has not been wasted I gathered my sons & daughters in your room & there we read one of Peabodys excellent sermons "Communion of the dead with the living." In my heart I prayed the spirit of our beloved was permitted to be with us. I trust my prayer was granted.

I am writing a volume to you my darling I do not fear tiring you my precious I know I am very [unreadable]. If I could only find words to express what I feel. I want to write on no other subject but the one ever uppermost in my mind. Of him alas I can tell you nothing new. But I can tell you that at times our God! and his God! sends me comforting thoughts. I no longer dwell on the dread of his present life. I see him now in the beautiful attire [unreadable] drawing me to his Saviour My precious Son!!!—

Your dear sister, W[illiam] & Rosalie were here last evening—dear Tootee! she seemed so disappointed that Anna could not be with her this week—it rained all Friday. I had a sweet letter from your dear Father by Jimper who went with the horses. He wrote to Malley. They were well yesterday—your Father says "You are a blessed good wife to cheer me on in what I hope and believe to be best, and what can a man do more than to act according to the best of his judgement? I may fail, but if I do I shall have consolation of the approval of my conscience. Dear Lord & I start early tomorrow for Waynesville expect to reach Waresboro on Monday & hope to be back on Thursday or Friday next." You see by this that he is less sanguine of success. But in this as in all else I am trying to feel Thy will Oh God! not mine be done.

Mr Savage informed me that he too was a mourner mourning for a sister. A fond mothers heart feels, hers to be a heavier affliction. Yet I pray God! to comfort him. Oh my Georgia How fervently do I pray that we (Father, Mother, Sisters, brothers) may keep our hearts at peace with God! in whose presence we may at any moment find ourselves with that Redeemer at whose judgement bar the great account of life may be so speedily demanded. May our every day be spent as we would wish it had been were it to be our last. Oh that this could be our rule of life. Then come death & how welcome opening the door into that house not made with hands Eternal in the heavens. 25 Sabbaths since he left us (we trust) for that happy home. What ages to us—!!! D[aniel] L[ord] tells us that Fanny Rilys Father died about 2 weeks ago. God! comfort the widow & fatherless!!!—

But for the rain—dear Sarah Bourke would have come with Tip on Friday night. Mr. Bourke is in Savannah.

11th

[O]ur dear ones at Retreat & Hamilton are as usual. All unite in fond love to you all send love to Nina & regards to Brother S[tephen].

I conclude in haste But with prayers for your health & welfare

Your devoted Mother

A M King

I fear the Triplex [unreadable] pills which we get from A A Solomons & Co are not such as your Father—try & get me 6 boxes & bring home with you.

> Liver Triplex pills
> Hegeman Clark & C.
> Rushton Clark & C. No 165. 273. 511.756
> Broadway New York City

Saturday 16th July

My own precious child

I was sadly disappointed that my promised Saturday letter was not received today. It seemed particularly wanted to soothe my poor distracted mind. Yours to Virginia (which you mentioned in your letter to dear Malley) came today. We must now wait until the 21st before we can hope to hear again from you.

Dear dear Georgia I know no one loves our departed treasure more fondly than you do—& yet my darling circumstanced as you are, how often may you be led to do things which jar on our feelings. It seems to me the head dress you speak of & undersleeves are not suitable to deep mourning. Consult your feelings, my precious Georgia not fashion or the example of others. Was the piano put into your room by request? If so how inconsiderate of your feelings!!—

We have had much to distress us all this week. Flora wrote to you of dear Johnnies illness & how sick Willie has been the latter tho very thin seems fast getting over his attack but it seems hard for our precious Johnnie to pass the crisis. During the day he seems better but for every night he is very ill. Every day but this Florence & I have taken turns to be with dear Tootee during the day. You know William always thinks he needs no assistance when his children are sick at nights, especially Johnnie. When I left him last night it was after dark—& he seemed so free of fever so cheerful I had hope the worse was over but this morning Dr Curtis was here (to see a sick negro) and says Johnnie was again worse last night—Tootee wrote to me by the return of the carriage which took the Dr over that he was still restless with fever and could not sleep. This is the 6th day since he was taken ill. God! only knows how it is to terminate. Oh my child I will not doubt the wisdom of an all wise & merciful God! If it be His will to take our precious lamb to Himself I can only pray strength and resignation will be given his parents to their loss. Dr Curtis is still with him. If he would be candid I would have more reliance on his word when he says there is no danger to be apprehended.

Florence wrote by yesterdays mail informing you that your dear Father was not Nominated. All we can say "it was not the Lords! will he should be." Dear Malley got home last night leaving your dear Father & Lordy still in Brunswick—Mr Styles trial was in progress and they deemed it their duty to stay by his side. They hope to be with us this evening. And I trust they will be. So falls to the ground many of the of the plans we formed. Under present circumstances I see no prospect of _____—but let us keep his memory closer in our hearts & minds.

I am more than disappointed I am grieved that Andrew has not come to the States—I fear he will not this summer. This seems my only chance to get the copy I so much want. It is when sickness and death comes poverty is most felt. I am so nervous and miserable today I ought not to write to you and yet my Georgia I cant resist doing so.

I had a letter today from Capt Ottenger—I en close it to you—you will find in it as much disappointment as I did. Oh Georgia the slightest doubt of our precious Butlers happiness drives me almost frantic. I will not let myself do so much injustice to the Saviour who died for him to the good and merciful God! who created him! No one can write as I feel—Oh how hard to feel with those who mourn!—

I can but hope my Georgia you will have left N.Y. City ere this reaches that place. I earnestly entreat of you never to sleep in the same bed with [Nina]. I wish you could have separate rooms. If still in N.Y. be sure and inquire of D[r] Green if it can possibly injure you to sleep in the same room with dear Nina. Remember my child the grief it would cause us should your health be injured by it. I will take this letter to Hamilton and if your dear Father & Lordy land there from the *Everglade* will have it put on board that it may reach you two days

sooner than the regular mail. I will also keep it open that I may add how Johnnie is. Your dear sisters are preparing for their sad visit—Your offering is never
forgotten. All unite in love to you—Praying God! to bless you with his love I
am your fond

Mother A M King

Retreat—Tuesday
19th July

My dearly beloved Georgia

I am now almost sorry that we informed you how ill dear little Johnnie has
been knowing how uneasy you would be on his account. I will at once say We
have now every hope he is convalescing. It is now eight days since he was taken
sick. I have not seen him since Sunday evening he was then better—it was so
hot yesterday noon I did not go over when I heard he [was] better. I have just
now heard from Tootee who says our dear little boy is so much better today William has gone to Brunswick. The best proof we can have that the precious little
boy is indeed better. His case throughout has been uncommon & very obstinate. I will not venture to say how much medicine Dr Curtis gave him and until last night—without the slightest effect as his liver & bowels are returning to
a proper state. I have hope all is well. Willie is nearly well tho' thin and weak.
The rest are as usual.

As dear Florence wrote to you yesterday she doubtless informed you that your
dear Father & your four brothers went to Brunswick. Mr Styles has throughout shown so much feeling and so much interest in all that concerns our family your dear Father & brothers feel it is their duty to stand by him in his trial
by man.[1] The good God! will we trust prove him innocent even in the judgement of man. Before I close this I hope to be able to tell you of his acquittal. If
permitted to see what is passing on earth how gratified must be the spirit of our
beloved Butler to see that his Father and brothers view Mr. Stiles case in the
light he did that they are acting as he would have acted had he been spared.
Tomorrow will make it Six long months since he left us. Oh my Georgia if he
is indeed with his Saviour! And can we doubt that he is not?—How selfish is
our sorrow—We know not from [what] evil he has been saved! Yet Oh my God!
how much I love that noble son how much I miss his counsel his support his
assistance. You know the perfect faith we had in his judgement. I believe my
other sons love me tenderly but they have never been called on to think for
their poor Mother. And somehow I shrink from telling your poor Father of my
debts. This last failure I trust may not prostrate his noble mind. God! grant
that he and your brothers will view it as another of the means God! in his wis-

dom and mercy is using to wean them from the riches of this world and leading them to strive for that which no man can rob them of.

Your dear Father and Lordy came home on Saturday night—all Sunday they seemed too tired to talk much and you know I am not given to ask questions. I gave him the letter received from you in his absence. He was sitting in your little room. In passing I saw he was in tears. I did not ask him to let me read the letter. Afterwards I saw that he gave it to dear Lordy to read. I would my Georgia I could write as touchingly as you can. Oh my child cease not address[ing] yourself to the hearts and consiences of your surviving brothers. You may help much to lead them on the way to God! I am so anxious for their souls salvation. Oh my Georgia that I could but have set my children a brighter Christian exa[m]ple. Now that I am bowed down with grief they may look on my efforts to serve my God! as too gloomy—I used to crave this worlds treasure for my children but never with the craving I now feel for the riches of Gods holy spirit for them. Oh my child pray with your Mother that all all will be drawn to their God! and Saviour whilst on earth then after death we will be united to our Saviour & through him to our blessed Butler there to meet our other loved ones to part no more. Oh my child I still look back on the years of unvalued happiness which are past never to return and forward to the trials which may be still in store for me—Praying forgiveness for the past & for the future strength to bear all that God! may see fit to bring upon me. I try to look not on the prosperous & happy but to look rather on the blessings still around me. Yet a loving husband and eight loving children! Dearest Geo it is great happiness to write to you—I believe you understand me better than any one else does and yet my letters are all confusion of words. But He who searches the heart knows how hard I am trying to go into the path which will lead me to my Saviours home!!

Your dear Sisters were at the Church last evening your brothers still in Brunswick with your Father. I was alone. And yet my Georgia I never feel alone—I can now go more frequently into his room there commune with my God! there pray for the living—there pray for a reunion with him who though dead to us is alive forever more! Oh my son Butler!!!

The sun is so intensely hot the flowers perish as quickly as did his beautiful form. Thank God! through Christ Jesus that more beautiful soul is alive forever more.—

Malley & Cuyler returned home after ten last night—they went to Mr. Grants—Your Father and Lord will remain until the trial is over.

We hope to be able to go to Hamilton this afternoon. It is now some days since we have had rain until the sea breeze sets in the day is intensely hot. I think Sunday was the warmest day we have had for 2 years. Not a breath of air all day that was cooling—I am glad your dear Father and Lordy were [not] at home.

The fruit is far better than it was last year. It is gratifying to see how your dear Father and brothers enjoy it. I am trying to preserve all I can tho sugar is high. And I am every day reminded of the necessity to economise. I am so grieved there appears no prospect of our obtaining the portrait. I now wish I had even braved the annoyance of your dear Father and given you the one we so value. We will feel the want of money now more painfully than we ever did before. What an opportunity you would have had remaining so long in New York to have overlooked the taking of that much wanted likeness, & the copies for your poor brothers. I cannot trust it by mail. I will try and wait. I think dear Georgia if there be no prospect of Andrews coming to the States, all I can now do with the $50 will be to get 5 lockets one side for hair the other for his likeness when we can get it taken. If a 6th locket could be got with the 50 do one for each brother father & mother. If you have left N.Y. before you get this you may pass through on your return from the Springs. By that time you will be able to judge the movements of Andrew. Your dear Father is much distressed that you occupy the same room with Nina. I hope you have consulted Dr. Green.

And oh my Georgia I know how you love him. Yet such is your yielding nature I fear you may be led to do many things which you will look back on with regret. I know you are constantly surrounded by strangers who know not, or care not if they knew—the grief in your heart. If you I find I could speak to you much better than I can write [sic]. I do not think you ought to have gone to the Jaudons. If you do not "use your grief as a club to knock down others with" a certain retirement and seriousness is needed to remind others that there is a cause and will save you many a pang. Please darling do not be hurt at what I say. I mean not to wound your bleeding heart. But let us feel as deeply as we can it will not prevent others from judging from appearances. To visit or wear fancy mourning is not in accordance with my feelings. To please Nina you are not called on to do violence to your feelings. I warned you of this my precious child when I consented to your acceptance of your uncles invitation. But enough my child all I pray is that you will be governed by your own feelings.—

21st

Yesterday was the 6 months since we had no more beloved Butler! Oh what a day to me his poor sorrowing Mother. I got up early & went into the room from which his spirit left us. In that room in which his six hours of suffering was witnessed and I hope felt more by us, than by him. I must not go back to that horrible day—Oh my son my blessed Butler. After I had got through the house duties I retired to my room—my precious & most sensitive daughter Florence soothed me by reading to me two of Peabody's sermons "Sources of Consolation" & "Consoling views on death." How much I am indebted to dear Mrs Hall for that volume. Oh my Georgia. Would that I had more faith—that faith which hopeth all things believeth all things. Yesterday was a dreary day to me. I feel no better today. God! be merciful to me!!!

I have just received the precious letter which ought to have come on Saturday only 2 days later than the one to Mallery 7 days longer on the way. I am glad it came at last. Oh Georgia dear how the praise you give me shames me when I reflect how unworthy I am. God! knows that I am trying for a new life but there is so much to correct so many old ways to forsake. I pray for strength to be always on my guard to bridle my tongue to stop the hasty conclusion. May that grace yet be mine. Oh for that charity "which beareth all things forgiveth all things." I am sorry for a letter just received by Florence from Mrs. James King I would not tell it to you my Georgia but to beg you to be on your guard with her. Poor thing she may not mean to jar our feelings she knew but little of the treasure we have lost. She may never have experienced the agony we are suffering. "This is what she writes"—["]Papa has placed Cornelia under Dr Green so will doubtless remain in N.Y. longer than they at first intended. We really know nothing of their movements or intentions than was conveyed in a hasty note a week or more ago. They must be very much engrossed in some way, grave or gay, or ere we must have heard from them."

The thoughtless words uttered relative to those children have given us uneasiness. Mrs King is fully under the impression her children are [to be] with us. The more this season advances the less we feel it will be safe to have even one of them here. D[aniel] Lord advises their all remaining at home. They are accustomed to that climate—it would be certain sickness to run out here as they do at home. Willie would not be happy with us. We would be glad to do any of brother Stephens family a service—we fear it would not be a kindness to bring them here. In every family but our own there has been more or less fever. Last night Rebecca Fraser passed south. I hope it may not be health she is seeking. We hope our good cousin will be out tomorrow night.

The boat was sent last evening for your Father & brothers—but they have not yet come. The weather still continues intensely hot & dry. I do hope and trust you have ere this left N.Y. You say nothing in your letter of your own health. It was on account of your health dear Georgia that I consented to part with you. Do not that, my darling, which will be detrimental to it. Each mail brings disappointment—nothing further from Andrew. If the vases are expensive dear Geo you will have to get less expensive lockets. I long to place his beautiful curls where there will be less injury but do not get the lockets until you have reason to think Andrew will not come. I wish you could have sent the vases at the time the railing came. I cant think if you return by land how you will bring them with you. I will ask Malley about the watch & let you know before I close this. No risk of losing it must be ran. I wish you had taken dear Floyds advice and offer. His watch he never wears.

Now that they have moved out to that house we see too little of them. Oh how unlike the social happy evenings of former days. Before the death angel took from us our best beloved. I had a kind note from Sarah Bourke on Monday last she said nothing further of her own health but that it was their intention to leave for the warm springs the last of this month.

Dr Curtis was to have returned on Monday last but nothing has been hear[d] from or of him since dear little Johnnie had a slight return of fever yesterday but he seems to be getting well slowly. We still have Lily Brown with us, certainly the best little child I ever saw. We are willing to keep her as long as her parents will spare her to us. She is so bidable and so perfectly amiable.

In all this heat your dear Father & Lord have come. Mr. Styles was honorably aquited last night I am glad your dear Father & Lordy stuck to him throughout. It is what our blessed Butler would have done had he been spared. The trial ended very quietly.

I have been writing this letter so long & cant read it over I would not be surprised if I have made many repetitions—& that you will have to go over it more than once to understand it. I want to write to Mr. Savage in answer to the beautiful letter he wrote me. But some how I put it off. I am sorry dear Floyd did not return with your Father we hope to see him tomorrow night that is if he has any money to pay his way down. I will add to this tomorrow.

22d July

I did not finish this letter yesterday intending to add to it today—I was hurried this morning and only sealed without finishing the direction. I wanted to consult Lord whether I should write Metropolitan or Mason & to my mortification just now Mr. Gould sent it back. I am so sorry as it may be Monday before it can go. If the J H C[ouper]s take boat at H[amilton] tonight it will go. I will have yet to wait and see Malley about the watch. We got Tillas medicine safe & thank you much as yet no improvement in her.

It grieves me to tell you that our precious Johnnie still has fever every day. I hope nothing but a good rain will prevent my going over to see him this evening. It is strange but I love that beautiful boy. I am not as much trouble[d] as you would expect—is it the greater trouble which dwells in my mind or that I am more satisfied that He in whose hands the dearly loved child is knows best what is good for him?

At home we are as well as this hot dry weather will allow the heat is terrible and so dry. Your Father wanted to write to you today but said he really lacked the energy. All unite in warm love to you. Love also to dear Nina & remembrance to Maria. May God bless you my precious child.

Your Mother

A M King

1. He was on trial for the murder of Jacob Moore. See Anna's letter of January 6, 1858.

28th July 1859

My own precious child Georgia

Florence wrote to you by the Mondays Mail. Since then we have by this days Mail been blessed with your long letters to your sisters up to the 20th and yours to me of the 17th. As we had continued to direct to the Metropolitan after hearing of your detention in N.Y. I fear you will again be without intelligence from home for some days. This will I know cause you some uneasiness. I am thankful to be permitted to say that all who you love at Retreat are as usual. Dear little Johnnie has had no fever for some days and tho suffering from a great many boils on his face and a discharge from his ear his most serious symtoms are disappearing. Willie has a slight return of fever—but only for one day. I have not seen dear Tootee since Sunday evening. I shall hear from her before I conclude this scrawl. On Tuesday Mr. & Mrs Bourke came down as your Father sent up for them they got here soon after breakfast and as they were to go to Savannah tomorrow night they left us last night in the Steamer. In the morning the tide did not suit and for several days past we have had thunderstorms accompanied by severe wind. The one yesterday at 4 was very severe & it is now so dark by the approach of another I can scarcely see how to write. I had to stop writing a short time—the rain did fall in torrents—but seems now over—and has cooled the atmosphere very much—I hope to be able to drive over to see our dear Cousin Amanda as well as our other dear ones at H[amilton]. I heard just now from dear Tootee who reports favorably of the dear children. Lordy & Malley promised Tootee to dine with her today but the rain came up before they were ready to start. So instead of clam soup with her—they will partake of scro [?] which is next best. You ask me my precious what your dear Father intends next to do? I am as ignorant on that subject as you can be. He says nothing to me—is perfectly quiet. Oh what a changed family is ours. Gods! mercy grant all this sorrow may yet be turned into joy. We are like a parcel of shipwrecked mariners—suddenly from a prosperous voyage cast on to a desert isle. Cant even yet realize all we have lost by the removal of our best son and brother. You ask me if I still feel him at my side. Yes my Georgia I feel him there now but oftener he seems to be looking down on me from high when my prayers are most fervent that beautiful face looks radient with joy. When that stoney feeling comes over me, When the evil one whispers me to murmur— then I think that beautiful face looks sad! Oh my Georgia time cannot reconcile us to our loss!

Friday morning

Thank God! I had more comfort in prayer this morning than I had yesterday at any time. I felt more in the immediate presence of my God! and Saviour and I felt that the eyes of my beloved Son was also looking on me. Oh my Father in Heaven! My Saviour Jesus Christ have mercy!! We all seem to be in a state of apathy. The heat of the day drives your brothers to the house they now sleep in. Our evenings are sad and nearly silent—little Lily is the only one happy! and she seems to divert your brothers and even your dear Father. I believe dear Florence and Virginia are both preparing a letter to you by this mail. After dinner the rain apparently over your dear Father[,] Flora and I set out for Hamilton leaving Appy & Floyd to follow on horse back. Soon after we got to H[amilton] another storm of wind and rain came on. I felt fearful on their account finding the rain not likely to be altogether over we left about dark and drove all the way home in rain and were rejoiced to find dear Appy for once in many days had been prudent—she and dear Floyd safe and dry within doors. Our dear Cousin looks thin and feeble—the same goodness stamped on her face. Mr. Wooley will not be out until some time in August. I hope you are now safe and pleasantly situated at Sharon Springs. I will find no fault with the mode of your getting there. As Mr. Maszaros goes with you I hope you will get there pleasantly. It was very kind in brother Stephen to insist on your having another dress as I believe the offer was made in sincerity and I know he can afford it. I hope you did avail yourself of it. You are not very careful of your things my child and having to be dressed every day requires many changes. How was it that any but yourselves got admittance into your room—*If a letter* could be so easily abstracted other things may go of more value. I hope that circumstance will teach you, Nina, and Maria a lesson. I have heard nothing of Andrew King. I mentioned to your poor Father our plan about that sacred likeness—he said "I wish you had given *her mine.*" Now you know dear that liberty I did not feel I could take. Now I wish I had dared for I fear it will be long ere another so good a chance will offer. If these heavy rains continue I fear our crop will again fall short if so my darling.—

I answered Mr Savages letter by the mail of the 22d. I dispatched by the same day a very long letter to you, and requested Mr. S[avage] if you had left for Sharon that he would have the kindness to order it forwarded to you. I presume however you left at the Metropolitan such directions. In that letter I told that dear Mal particularly requested the watch should not be sent by express. Not to send it unless some trustworthy person should be coming to Savannah. And Georgia dear please keep in mind, the more than intrinsic value of that watch. Do not let it be lost or injured. On Florences & Appys account I would be glad for Mr. M[aszaros] to come but I fear he will not be repaid for the trouble of coming. He cannot feel as we feel and your dear Father does not seem inclined for company. But if he does come your brothers and sisters will do the best they can to make his time pass agreeably. I am writing in haste and in the confusion of clean-up—contriving for dinner &c. All here & at H[amilton] unite in fond love to you—Our love to Stephen & Nina & how de to Maria. From a fond Mothers heart go thanks to them for all their kindness to you my precious child.

Praying God! to bless, guide, guard and comfort you I am your sorrowing but devoted mother

A M King

If Col Hardees invitation was extended to Nina I cannot see anything which would prevent your accepting Miss Anna's invitation to visit her. She is the only one with whom you could converse freely about our beloved. She loves & cherishes his memory Oh my Son! My Son!—

30th July 1859

My dearly beloved child

Your letter of the 22d has just been read, first by me, then by your dear Sisters, F[lorence] & V[irginia] my darling we feel so grieved to have added to your grief. He who searcheth the heart knows such was not our design it was barely to guard you from that which would have added fresh wounds to your already lacerated heart. Oh my child if we have done this very thing forgive us!!

By this days Mail your dear Father got a letter from your Uncle Andrew dated N.Y. You evidently knew nothing of his arrival. If not—if you left N.Y. in ignorance of his being so near you—at once write and ask if he has with him that precious likeness. Tell him your object—and I believe he will do all he can to assist you in carrying out our wishes. And now my darling let me go on to tell you that we are all at Retreat in our usual health. Tho' very much depressed. Not only have we this deep and abiding sorrow ever uppermost in our minds but we have other causes to perplex & distress us. Your dear Father not being nominated leads to other disappointments—which in our embarrassed state in pecuniary matters—gives anxiety, & adds to the depression. After suffering from drought since a week this day (with the exception of one day) we have had a deluge of rain daily. In the hands of a merciful God! let us leave the future only praying all these trials may work together for the salvation of our immortal souls. It was only last night that dear Florence remarked "I am glad that dear Georgia is not here to share with us these anxieties." In our family we feel with and for each other. If a man is going up hill he may find many to lend a helping hand. If *down hill* many more are ready *to push him lower*. Your dear Father being defeated in the nomination—will deprive him of the power to do for his sons. Dear Lordy feels his situation keenly mortifying. He told me last evening "If the company would but pay him what it owes him he would try and get in with Mr. Savage." He also said he "felt it was impossible for me to help him." I think it was in 1857 that Andrew offered to assist dear Lordy—your dear Father then thought it best Lord should act with him in the P[acific] R[ail] R[oad] business. You know how that ended. I can but hope matters may take a better turn—as it is I know not how I shall be able to carry on the education of your younger brothers. When these troubles thicken around me I think of that noble son on whose judgement I could depend. But all this sorrow all these crosses and disappointments do not come by *chance*. Oh that we could view it in the right light—that all all are ordered by a wise Providence. Let us do the best we can placing our trust in a merciful God!! and believe "He doeth all things well."

Oh my Georgia to write to you of our beloved is the only subject that I love. It seems at such times his beloved spirit is with me—Oh how he loved (& I believe still loves) us both so tenderly—I frequently close my eyes that I may see that face beaming with love up to His Saviour then down on his poor sorrowing Mother! When this poor heart is stoney that loved face looks sad—When the "Comforter" is near then all radient with joy.

31st

I am truly gratified by Miss Annas kind visit to you. I wish you could accept her kind invitation I know of all who you may visit when away from us no one will feel with you as she does. After the rain yesterday afternoon Flora—Appy and Floyd went to the church—your Father and I to Hamilton. Theirs was a sacred duty to the dead—ours what we deemed a duty to the living. They brought back "no messages of love"— Oh how silent all voices are when they come back to me—a kiss—& our thoughts are on that silent spot. Oh Georgia dear if I could but only dream of him. I believe God! in his wisdom thus tries my faith.

We found Johnnie still suffering from boils & running from one ear—but running about & cheerful—the rest as usual. Our dear Cousin will probably come to us this afternoon or tomorrow. She looks very thin & pale. Hamilton Couper went on to Savannah yesterday morning. He looks (I am told) very badly and is gone to consult Dr. Sullivan. You say we must direct to you at Sharon until the middle of August—knowing how anxious you will be about home try and find out brother Stephens plans—how long he will remain there and where he will go next. Andrews letter was dated 24th. I fear you did not know of his arrival. He gave no plan for the summer. F[lorence], V[irginia] & I all sent you long letters by the Friday Mail. I do not know why it is your poor Father has never written to you. He repeatedly speaks of doing so, as do also your brothers. Tomorrow will be the anniversary of the birth of dear little Isabel—had she lived 11 years would have been her age. One month and 17 days more will be the anniversary of our beloved Butlers birth day. Oh my God! my God!—

I have never yet been able to record the 20th January 1859. Oh my Georgia would that I had not lived to see that day.

Your dear Father seems so lonely. In his other trials how he leaned on our Buttie—how he misses support his loving attentions [*sic*]. He reads your letters to us dear Geo. I did not mean him *to read* this last but he got hold of it and was troubled your feelings had been so wounded.

Mr. Savage wrote to Wm that the railing would soon be shipped—Since then we have heard nothing more. Oh that I was able to order the monument at once. Lord and Malley have gone to the church. Last Sunday his Father, Mother, four brothers and two sisters & his dear little Anna stood around his sacred grave. I believe his spirit was there too. If permitted to know our hearts how thankful he must be that God! gave him the heart he possessed on earth to so faithfully discharge his duty as son and brother that he is so much beloved and lamented.

1st August

[T]he rain continued so late last evening your sisters did not go over to Hamilton—I hope they will do so this morning, so that our dear Cousin may come to us. I do not wish to take her from poor Tootee but as she said *she would come* I will try and go the oftener to your poor sister. Florence intends to send your bracelet—what a pity you did not send for it whilst in N.Y. All here unite in fond love to you Oh my Georgia may a merciful God restore you in health to your sorrowing but forever

Affectionate Mother
A M King

Give our love to Brother Stephen and dear Nina and remember us to Maria. Florence will tell you that Bell is well and is behaving well. They all wish you were at home—I believe they love you sincerely—and well they may!—

10th August 1859

My own precious beloved Georgia

I hope you may have attributed your not hearing from us to the uncertainty of the mails. Such however was not the reason why no letter for you left this house on Monday last. Dear Florence had sat up late on Sunday night to write you a long letter. On Monday morning your dear Father could not spare the piece of paper she had written you she would enclose—so rather than not send it—she concluded to wait. I had got 3 pages written but such had been my gloom I could not infect you with the same. So my letter too remains in the house. I hope it is more the state of the weather which affects us all than even the deep sorrow which time does not lighten. Since the 24th July we have had but 4 dry days not gentle refreshing showers but each day & often each day and night a perfect deluge. The injury to the crop adds to our depression. What can we do my Georgia but pray for faith to feel "All is for the best."

How grateful we all feel to brother Stephen for taking you from home this summer. If all my dear children & your dear Father could have spent this summer from home—! but we *know* not that it would have been best. All all is ordered by a wise Providence.

Florence wrote to you that dear Malley & Tip went to the Grants on Friday. It was arranged that your dear Father should return Mr. Grants visit on Monday when your brothers would return. On Sunday Mr. Brown concluded to take passage with your Father spending the night here for that purpose. On Monday morning your Father did not feel well. Nothing serious but not well enough to encounter the heat. On that night too we expected dear Lordy home. Johnnie had a return of fever on Sunday and his ear still discharged. William concluded he would at once take him on to Dr Sulivan[.] So you see there was some getting ready &c. On Monday evening I went over with dear Cousin who proposed remaining with Tootee until yesterday morning when we would send for them to remain here during Williams absence.

I waited for your brothers so long a heavy rain over took us on our way home, wetting dear Malley (who drove) to the skin. Tip & I got off with less. At one the Steamer landed the two Lords & took off William and dear little Johnnie. Your brother Lord was not very well yesterday but says he is quite well today—your dear Father & Lordy have gone to call on Mr Snead at Col Hazzards. This gentleman has done his duty in vindicating your persecuted Father. It is due to him this attention.—

Yesterday morning the carriage came back empty from Hamilton—little Rosalie was threatened with croup. Tootee could not venture to bring her out in bad weather. I fear the weather will deprive us of the gratification of having them here—William may or may not return tonight. We were sadly disap-

pointed by not hearing from you on Saturday last—it is true we had two letters on Thursday but these were not to your sisters or me just loving letters to
your Father & Floyd—told us you were well & that was all.

Now that peace is proclaimed—Appy looks alone to your letters for matters
of interest. Our precious Florence is so constant so beautiful in her devotion
to us all, especially to your poor Father & I, we have not suffered for want of
your tender services. We all miss you sadly—we long to see you, but we feel
that it was good you should leave us to regain health both of body and mind.
We have nothing to divert our thoughts from the solemn fact that the chasm
in our family circle can never again be filled—and we know not how soon it
may be made wider. The future was never so dark as now. All we can do is to
pray for submission. To drink of the cup offered us by our Heavenly Father—
who better knows "the need be." Oh Georgia this has thus far been a year of
trial to us all. The greatest came like a clap of thunder from a cloudless sky.
Since that terrible day many blessings have been continued yet all we now feel is
so uncertain. For so many years I *believed* yes I dared believe—all the blessings
a good God had given me would be left with me as long as I lived. I shut my
understanding against all warning—I never saw. I would not see the danger I
was in of losing my choicest blessing the severing blow came when least expected when least prepared. Oh my Georgia!!—

11th

This [is] 29 weeks since that terrible day. Last night as Florence and I walked
the piazza we talked over the happy Wednesday evening 29 weeks back—
When you and dear Lordy sang *his* favorite song. The pride he showed for the
pleasure you two gave us. The piano ceased its sounds from that night—the
next day the voice of weeping was heard! Oh my Son my Son would I could
have died for thee!

I have received your letter my precious child & dear Florence also your
sweet letter of the 2d Inst Post Marked 4th. Surely we are much blessed. How
many are stript of all they had called their own, and left alone in the world.
Praise be to God! never had woman a better husband never a Mother more
tenderly affectionate children. Yes my Georgia tho' my hearts idol has left me
to return no more, each day takes us nearer to the new home Christ has given
him—and through Christ Jesus we can hope a place in that new home is being
prepared for each one of us. I long for that better world my Georgia. The trials and disappointments of this world adds much to the joy of knowing there
[is] another and a better. May the God! who created us the Saviour who died
for us—draw our hearts to that better world. Give us grace whilst we remain
here to act in all things in accordance with his divine commandments. And

when we have done our appointed task here may be all all to meet to part no more. I cant believe that my God! gave me that noble son of His own f[r]ee will—& has taken him away forever and ever from me. Yes my Georgia though the parting has withered our hearts thanks be to God! not one heart has been hardened by the affliction. On Tuesday evening I was leaning out of the window—dear Lordy came an[d] leaned out by me & said "this night 29 weeks ago Malley & I returned from our Long Isld hunt." I said dear Lordy I am glad you have kept count of the days that have past—he said "Mother do you suppose *it* is ever out of my mind." Our dear cousin told me that *their minister* (a Mr Adams) had been a classmate of our beloved Butler. That he felt deeply our beloveds departure speaking of him as "a noble fellow." This from a Methodist minister shows he had the praise of one who looked deeper for true worth than an ordinary school companion would. It rained last Saturday evening on Sunday morning by the time it was light dear Florence was culling fresh flowers— & went to the church—She did not go to church. Our dear Cousin had her seat. To you dear children there seems to be comfort in visiting that sacred spot. I too often think of that beautiful form mouldering beneath those flowers and not of that still more beautiful spirit far above me. My thoughts are more comforting when in that room where last those beautiful eyes rested on me when last that loved voice named his "Mother."—

Your dear Father was present when I received your letter he requested me to read it aloud to him, but as soon as I came to *him* he got up and left the room. He never names the son he most loved. Our deep sorrow for that loved one makes our other trials lighter—I need not say we have much else to depress us. I have said nothing to you of the base conduct of Mr. W H Styles. I have not told you that he is the author of "Philippi" that when your Father traced it to him—he demanded a retraction or to meet him with pistols—that he would do neither the one or the other—but continues his base slander. I knew nothing of this until Mr. Styles had refused the challenge. Florence will send you papers which will better enlighten you than I can. As Mr Styles refuses to fight— We have only lament—your dear Father has been forced to take the steps he has done. He never by word or deed had injured Mr Styles—black must be his heart to make the attack he has on your Father. As I believe your dear Fathers life will not be jeopardized—I try not to speak or think of Mr. Styles. I have long prayed that the hearts of his enemies may be changed. I still pray that this man may repent of the cruel unjustifiable attack he has made on your Father. Florence will send you Mr Bourkes letter by it you will see the estimation with which Mr S[tyles] is held by all honorable men. I would not have made that quotation from Mrs Ja[me]s Kings letter but to put you on your guard. She is almost a stranger to me. And I know how unsuspicious you are my Georgia.

D[aniel] Lord left us last night—I do not know how long Mr Snead is to stay. Company of strangers is very irksome. It has rained heavily since 7 this morning—I heard last night from Tootee, William and Johnnie will I hope be out tomorrow night—up to yesterday morning Johnny had had no return of fever—it is so dark I must stop until tomorrow.

The *railing* has been paid for but we do not know if yet received in Savannah. Dear Florence may tell you that on Saturday last Tip accompanied Fraser to visit dear Fannies grave. They spent one night at Mr Wyllys—I do earnestly hope Doctor Troup will consent to the removal of her sacred remains. I will hope too that those so loved by me (but from weak superstitions so much neglected) will also be removed to consecrated ground.

I would not know Mrs Tucker if I met her but I will remember her kindness to me in *1829*. It was she who procured for me the nurse, who took care of our beloved Buttie at his birth. Was she one of the enquiries after him?

12th

Another day has dawned. And thank God! we are all up. Your dear Father has a cold but is better than he was yesterday. Cuyler went to stay with Tootee night before last. Malley went for him after the rain last evening—they brought the latest accounts from Hamilton. Rosalie was better—but Anna had fever—with some symtoms of rash. Nothing at all alarming but very wearying to poor Tootee. 3 out of six have now had this rash fever. Mr Bourke came out in the last boat—he said Johnnie was doing well—they will be out tonight I hope. Sarah had had one of her attacks at the Indian Springs.

In writing in this disjointed way I omit much which I want to say repeating what I have already said. I am grieved to hear dear Nina has taken cold—poor child!! Give much love to Nina & Stephen. A grateful Mothers heart acknow [word unfinished] their kindness to you my precious child.

Florence and I will probably go over to see the dear ones at Hamilton. I hope my precious you will not be over anxious about us. Remember the very hairs of our head are numbered that we and all we call ours are in the keeping of a merciful God! Let us cherish that faith which will make us believe that all our trials are sent for wise purposes. I am much hurried—& must close tho I would be glad to fill this sheet.

I hope you have ere this written to Andrew—I am glad you visited that wonderful cave. Your Father, brothers & sisters send much love the—servants are well and beg to be remembered. God bless you my child!

Your devoted Mother
A M King

Epilogue

Anna's world was crumbling around her. By 1858 the estate was in debt to her Savannah factors for approximately $10,000 and Thomas Butler King appeared no closer to returning to Retreat and joining forces with his wife to either make improvements in the existing homestead or move their planting operations elsewhere. He had, with Butler, attempted to buy additional land on the island and in Ware County, but raising capital or finding credit was all but impossible. More important, however, with Butler's death Anna's emotional strength faltered and could not be restored. Though she turned to religion and her family for solace, nothing could ease her anguish. She died on August 22, 1859, seven months after Butler's death. Those closest to her believed she died of a broken heart. Life at Retreat was never again the same.

With the coming of war in 1861, the King family was further separated and bereaved. Thomas Butler King was elected to the state legislature and participated in Georgia's decision to secede from the union. Though initially against secession, he stood with his state and the Confederacy in their bid for independence. Early in the war, Gen. Robert E. Lee asked the inhabitants of the Sea Islands to move inland because he was unable to defend them or their property from the formidable Union navy. While Thomas Butler King journeyed to France and England on behalf of the state of Georgia to solicit aid for the Confederacy, his daughters, grandchildren, and bondpeople moved to Ware County. All the King sons joined the army, leaving William Couper to support and protect the women. Georgia met and married a young officer, William Duncan Smith, who died of pneumonia before the war's end. Mallery, on leave from his duties in 1862, came home to a newly constructed cottage, The Refuge, and married his childhood sweetheart, Eugenia Grant. In that same year Lord was killed at the Battle of Fredericksburg. Neptune, who traveled with him, ventured out onto the battlefield to retrieve Lord's body and returned it to his family in Georgia. Thomas Butler King died on May 10, 1864, surrounded by his daughters, grandchildren, and son-in-law.

The years following the war brought many changes to the lives of the remaining Kings. In 1866, Florence married Gen. Henry Rootes Jackson. Georgia remarried on June 9, 1870, to John Joseph Wilder; and one month later Virginia married John Nisbet. All three sisters lived in Savannah and remained physically as well as emotionally close. Cuyler remained a bachelor into his late forties, but in 1899 married Henrietta Nisbet (no relation to Virginia's husband). Floyd, who never married, followed his father into politics, representing his adopted state of Louisiana as a U.S. congressman for four terms. Hannah and her family eventually made their home in Macon, Georgia.[1]

Though certainly they were aware of the growing number of self-liberated and emancipated bondpeople moving throughout the South, relatively few of the Kings' enslaved workers left the family before the end of the war.[2] Rhina continued to work for the family into the turn of the century. After Lord's body was laid to rest, Neptune accompanied the youngest King son, Cuyler, to war. When the King family returned to St. Simons after the war, Neptune was given a piece of land as a reward for his service to Lord. On it he built a house for his wife, Ila, and their children.[3] After emancipation Neptune took the last name Small and became a well-known figure on the island and beyond. His grave in the slave cemetery at Retreat bears a bronze plaque with the words: "Neptune belonged to Mr. and Mrs. Thomas Butler King of Retreat Plantation. When their son Capt. H. L. P. King enlisted in the Confederate Army Neptune accompanied him to war as his body-servant. Capt. King was killed at the battle of Fredericksburg, Virginia on December 13, 1862. When night fell Neptune went out on the battlefield, found the body of his master and brought it home to rest in the family burying ground at Christ Church, Frederica, St. Simons Island."

A copy of a newspaper article that appears in *Old Mill Days: St. Simons Mills, Georgia, 1874–1908* records "Neptune's Story," an interview with Neptune Small by J. E. Dart. I reprint it below.

Well, genl'mens, Ise b'longs to de King fambly since my longest 'membrance. I use to sorter had to look after Mas' Butler, Mas' Mallory, Mas' Lord, Mas' Floyd, an' de balance. Well, one day on St. Simon's Mas' Butler he tooken sick, and 'fore a doctor could come he was dead. Well, missus she grebe and grebe and follow him; I tink de same year de Janneray afore de war. Well, it most brake up de family, cos dey was all lovin' peoples. Well, when we heard "Fo't Sumpta" surrender, all my young masters say we must go; dey don't take adwantage of 15 colored peoples to keep out de war. Well, I went wid mas' Lord, cos when he was a boy he wus mostly wid me. At fust it wus nothin', but w'en we ento to "Furginny" de truble commence. You kno' I use ter cook fur him and kinder take care of him, cos I wus leetle de oldest. Well, any of you genl'men wot ben in de march from de vally to the place call "Fredericksburg," mus' kno' wot a time it wer' wen about 25 miles off we could hear de canon an' see de town aburnin', dat is de lite on de sky. De army marches on tell we cum to whar Mas' Lord say was "Mary Hite." Jus' under de hill I make a fire to cook supper. W'en supper was reddy I go to call Mas' Lord. He be talkin' to some big officers, an' I wate tell he git thro', and I say: "Supper reddy, young master." He cum an' eat he supper, but don't talk lik mos' de times; w'en he thro' he look in de fire a long time. I ben busy washin' de dishes w'en all a sudden he say: "Neptune, a big fite to-morrow mornin'; good mens will eat deir las' supper to-nite." It makes me feel kinder lon'some to hyar Mas' Lord talk so, cos he always ben so happy-hearted. Well, de nex' day I see de canon gwine by, an' de solders marching by, an' de gen'rals ridin' by, an' I know'd trouble wus comin.' Jus' afore 12 o'clock I hyar de canon commence te shoot, den I hyar de muskets begin, den I see de wounded mens goin' ba'k, and den—but gentl'mens, "war broke loose on dat day"; all day it gwine on, and I keep sayin', Mas' Lord can't cum, cos de big gen'rals is keepin' him to carry orders. Nite cum, but no Mas' Lord. I stir up de fire to keep he supper warm, but no Mas' Lord. I still hyar de canon an' de muskets, an' I say to myself, "dey ain't thru yet." Well, after it git good dark I lef' de supper by de fire to go look fur Mas' Lord. I met a' officer on a hoss. I ask him if he see Mas' Lord. He say not since 2 o'clock. I makes no answer, but my heart cum up in my thro't, an' I know'd den he mus' be hurt. I gone towards de Confed'rate line, wher' dey ben fiten all day, an' I ask de oficer could I go out an' fine my young master. I don't know he [unreadable]. Who is yer young master, [unreadable] Mas' Lord King. De oficer say, "I hope you'll fine him out dere, but look out fur de Yankee pickets." I crawl down de hill; ded mens was ev'ry wher', but none look like Mas' Lord. At las' it wus very dark. Den I cum to a' oficer layin' on he face. Som'body had pull off he rite boot and lef' de lef', cos it wus so blody. I hyar som'body say, "wat' yer doin' dar?" I say, "lookin' fur me young master." He say, "who?" I say, "Mas' Lord King." He say, "dat is him." I say to myself, "no, dat ain't my young master," and I gone furder down de line. Wen' I git nearly a quarter mile; I say to myself, "I kno' how I can tel if dat is Mas' Lord." I see my old missus run her han' thro' his hair wen he bin a boy, and she used to say, "My boy, you have such beauterfil hair," and I used to feel it myself, cos it wus so nice an' curly. I crawl back, an' I put my han' in he hair, but de blod was clot, and de hair didn't feel lik Mas' Lord's; but I turn he head over w'ere de blod was not so t'ick. I turn he face up so he could look in old Neptune's face, an' I say, "my young master—Mas' Lord, dis is old Neptune; supper is ready; I ben waiting fur you—is you hurt bad?" But he never answer his old nigger—he, he, he Genl'mens, wate on old Neptune a little w'ile—I can't talk now. Genl'mens—he, he; Lord have mercy—he was ded! I take him up in my arm. De shells bust an' de bullets rattle, but I ain't 'fraid dem. Mas' Lord, my young master, dey can't hurt him; and Old Neptune don't care. De nex' day sum offercers put him in a pine box to go to Richmon'. I say well, when I git to Richmon' dats something else. When I git dere I got de best coffin dey had, an' we cum to Savannah and burry him dere. Since den he brothers and sisters bring him to St. Simon's at de old Frederica church and burry him w'ere de people am restin'. Sometime old Neptune. He hair is w'ite an' rumatiz is got him, but in de spring time I goes an' see dat no cows eat de flowers of'n his grave, an' keep de grass from growin' too clos' Well, genl'mens, I could tell about the Atlanta campane, but I can't tell too much now. Som'how old Neptune's eyes ain't strong like dey used to be, an', an', water cum in dem so easy w'en I talk 'bout old St. Simon's an my young masters in de good ole days afore de war cum, dat tooken so many good boys away. Good day, genl'mens—good day; Neptune will tell you som mo' some time.

Among the many reasons "Neptune's Story" is so compelling is the time in which it was written. Catherine Clinton writes in *Tara Revisited* of the postwar restoration of the South's image both by and among southerners and in the country at large. In part, rehabilitation of the Old South as manifested in the popular image of the "faithful servant" is one of its most powerful, troublesome, and persistent legacies. The article in which "Neptune's Story" appears begins, "The story of Neptune Small is so full of tender pathos, so replete with the history of those memorable days, now fast passing away, and bears so directly upon the bravery, the chivalry, the devotion to the just cause of a family whose record, whether in the halls of Congress or upon the field of battle, in civic or military stations, stands forth peerless and without a model or shadow in the annals of Glynn County or any other, that it is told for the entertainment of Times readers."[4] One wonders how much the telling—and the recording—of this interview reflects this refashioning of the plantation past and the ongoing power of whites late in the century to elicit what they wanted or needed to hear from formerly enslaved people.

It was Neptune Small who beckoned me to enter the world of Retreat, and it is with him that I end. There is much we cannot know about the lives and thoughts of the Kings and the people they enslaved, but the journey through Anna King's letters is a start to understanding a critical chapter in our collective past.

Notes

1. Marye, *Story of the Page-King Family,* 97–98.

2. Even more interesting is the fact that Retreat was used by Union forces, and later by the federal government, as a settlement for former bondpeople and as headquarters for the Freedman's Bureau. A list of King enslaved people compiled in 1859 names 142 people. In 1864, someone in the family took inventory again and listed 106 people resident with the family in Ware County. Only two, Joe and Jimmy, were recorded as having "gone to the Yankees." Selected Pages from the Record Book of Retreat Plantation, GDAH.

3. A portion of Neptune Small's property was sold to the city of St. Simons and turned into a park that bears his name. Neptune Park sits at the end of Mallery Street and along St. Simons Sound.

4. Graham, *Old Mill Days.*

Appendix 1

The Page-King Family of Retreat

Children of William Page (1764–1827)
and Hannah Matilda Timmons (1759–1826)

Thomas William Page (1782–1790)
Martha Page (1783–1783)
Ann Page (1784–1784)
Eleanor Page (1786–1786)
Louisa Page (1788–1788)
Phillip Page (1791–1792)
Hannah Elizabeth Page (1794–1801)
William Page (1795–1803)
Anna Matilda Page (1798–1859) m. Thomas Butler King (1797–1864)
Harriet Elizabeth Page (1802–1804)

Three Generations of Descendants of Thomas Butler King (1797–1864)
and Anna Matilda Page (1798–1859)

Hannah Matilda Page King (1825–1896) m. William Audley Couper (1817–1888)
  Anna Rebecca Couper (1846–1928) m. Charles MacLean Marshall (1846–1911)
    William Audley Couper Marshall (1872–1930)
    Helen MacLean Marshall (1873–1964)
    Percy MacLean Marshall (1883–1950) m. Julia Ketchem Weed (1887–1976)
  William Page Couper (1847–?) m. Ida Blackman
  Isabella Hamilton Couper (1848–1852)
  a son (1850–1850)
  Butler King Couper (1851–1913) m. 1st Meta Habersham
  m. 2nd Josephine Sibley (1867–1957)
    Butler King Couper (1906–1993)
    Constance Maxwell Couper (1897–1985) m. 1st Boling Reynolds
    m. 2nd George House
    m. 3rd John W. Haney

John Audley Couper (1853–1905) m. Martha Cecil Stubinger (1867–1901)

   William Audley Couper m. Augusta Beall

   Selina Fraser Couper m. Clement Murphy

   George Mortimer Couper m. Margaret Chisolm

   Margaret Maxwell Couper (?–1970) m. Charles Oswald Sanger (1893–1957)

   Hannah Page Couper

   Helen Josephine Couper

Helen Rosalie Couper (1855–1896) m. Eckhart Von Walther

   Lisa Von Walther (1896–1896)

Thomas Butler Couper (1858–1909) m. Sarah Nesbit

William Page King (1826–1833)

Thomas Butler King (1829–1859)

Henry Lord Page King (1831–1862)

Georgia Page King (1833–1914) m. 1st William Duncan Smith (1826–1862)

m. 2nd Joseph John Wilder (1844–1900)

   Anne Page Wilder (1873–1956) m. Jefferson Randolph Anderson (1861–1950)

     Page Randolph Anderson (1899–) m. Henry Norris Platt (1888–1956)

     Jefferson Randolph Anderson (1902–1903)

     Joseph Wilder Randolph Anderson (1905–1967) m. Edith O'Driscoll Hunter (1909–)

Florence Barclay King (1834–1912) m. Henry Rootes Jackson (1820–1898)

Mallery Page King (1836–1899) m. Maria Eugenia Grant (1836–1909)

   Mary Anna Page King (1867–1946) m. Calvin Donnell Parker (1865–1929)

   Frances Buford King (1869–1956) m. Franklin Dunwoody Aiken (1861–1942)

     Mallery Page King Aiken (1895–1960) m. Dorothy Stair

     Franklin Dunwoody Aiken (1896–1985) m. 1st Margaret Philips Trawick (1899–1945)

     m. 2nd Venie Corley (1910–1989)

     Buford King Aiken (1897–1982) m. John Harold Horlick (1888–1960)

     Isaac Means Aiken (1899–1991) m. Alice McDonald Harrison (1900–1993)

     Florence Lord Aiken (1902–1974) m. Frank Duncan MacPherson Strachan (1901–1966)

     Hugh Fraser Aiken (1906–1951) m. Roberta Claire McGinnis (1909–1988)

     Fannie Bryan Aiken (1907–1984) m. 1st Thomas Edward Keegan

     m. 2nd David Mozo

     m. 3rd James Clark

   Florence Page King (1871–1955) m. Henry Baker Maxey

     Maria Eugenia Maxey (1897–) m. 1st Sherman Watkins

     m. 2nd Barrington King

     Anne Page Maxey (1899–1976) m. 1st Douglas Nightingale (1888–1951)

     m. 2nd Dean Dunwoody Atkinson (1899–1991)

     Florence King Maxey (1902–1992) m. Joseph Gipson Riley (1891–1969)

   Thomas Butler King (1875–1877)

Virginia Lord King (1837–1901) m. John Nisbet (1841–1917)

   John Lord Nisbet (1872–1938) m. Margaret Idella Holoway

   Marianne Nisbet (1874–1947)

   Florence King Nisbet (1877–1963) m. Phillip Thorton Marye (1872–1935)

      Philip Thornton Marye (1901–1901)

      John Nisbet Marye (1904–1962) m. 1st Sarah Hurt

      m. 2nd Frances Rozelle Shawver (1916–)

   Virginia Lord Nisbet (1879–1963) m. Richard Willis Heard (1871–1959)

      Virginia Lord Heard (1905–1997) m. Edwin Robeson MacKethan (1907–1989)

         Edwin Robeson MacKethan (1939–) m. Elsie Frances Hopeton (1940–)

      Richard Willis Heard (1906–1992) m. Alice Riddle Read (1913–1996)

      George Alexander Heard (1917–) m. Laura Jean Keller (1924–)

   Nannie Page Nisbet (1880–1927) m. George Shorter Alexander (1874–1928)

John Floyd King (1839–1915)

Richard Cuyler King (1840–1913) m. Henrietta Dawson Nisbet (1863–1944)

   Henry Lord Page King (1895–1952) m. Sarah Evans (1895–1989)

      Henry Lord Page King (1920–1976) m. Eileen Taylor (1926–)

      May Lindsay King (1922–) m. Warren Duncan

   Mary Nisbet King (1900–1970) m. Ranald Trevor Adams (1893–1959)

      Ranald Trevor Adams (1925–) m. Jeanette Chichester (1925–)

      Richard King Adams (1926–1936)

Information courtesy of Edwin R. MacKethan III.

Appendix 2

The Bondpeople of Retreat

Register of Negroes Belonging to Thomas Butler King, November *1839*

Number	Names		When Born	Age
1	Old Sarah			86
2	Dorcus			56
3	Edward	Carpenter	Mar. 13, 1802	37
4	Byna		Feb. 6, 1804	35
5	Ishmael	Driver	Aug. 14, 1809	30
6	Richard		1810	29
7	Ansel		July 5, 1813	26
8	Ben		Apr. 3, 1819	20
9	Thomas		Jan. 2, 1822	17
10	Ishmael 2d ⎫	Byna's children	Mar. 9, 1828	11
11	Clementine 2d ⎭		Aug. 12, 1831	8
12	John		Mar. 18, 1782	57
13	Phillis		May 28, 1784	55
14	Frank	Byna's child	June 11, 1838	1
15	Sarah 2d	Isaac's wife	Dec. 18, 1811	28
16	Polly 2d		Sept. 4, 1831	8
17	Dorinda		June 1, 1835	4
18	Vickery a *girl*		Nov. 7, 1838	1
19	Peter		Nov. 3, 1791	48
20	Old Betty			87
21	Cupid	Driver	July 21, 1777	62
22	Lizzy	his wife		49
23	Cupid Junr.		Dec. 1814	25
24	Abraham		July 31, 1817	22
25	Neller 2d		Dec. 4, 1819	20
26	Mark		July 29, 1824	15
27	Lady		Nov. 11, 1786	53
28	Toney	Driver	May 22, 1808	31
29	Jane	his wife		

(continued)

Number	Names		When Born	Age
30	Bella		Feb. 1839	
31	Hannah		Dec. 7, 1812	27
32	Ellen		July 17, 1816	23
33	Allick Boyd			
34	Jannet		Oct. 16, 1838	1
35	John		Feb. 22d, 1825	14
36	Quamina		Jan. 22, 1794	45
37	Jean		Mar. 1779	60
38	Neptune	Carpenter	Aug. 4, 1796	43
39	Sukey	his wife		39
40	Abner		Oct. 1, 1820	19
41	Lydia		Apr. 15, 1823	16
42	Sanders		Sept. 4, 1827	12
43	Neptune Jr		Sept. 15, 1831	8
44	Emiline		Aug. 3, 1833	6
45	Linda		Apr. 29,1838	1
46	March	Driver	Aug. 14, 1806	33
47	Peggy	his wife		
48	Jack	his child		8
49	Delia	"	Mar. 26, 1836	3
50	Jimmy		Apr. 28, 1838	1
51	Ruthy		May 12, 1808	31
52	George	her son	Apr. 4, 1821	18
53	James	"	Oct. 16, 1823	16
54	Amy	her daughter	Sept. 28, 1825	14
55	Anthony		Oct. 30, 1827	12
56	Sam		Dec. 1, 1829	10
57	Betty		Dec. 1837	2
58	Stephen Dick			59
59	Phoebe	his wife	1781	56
60	Lucy		Sept. 14, 1807	32
61	Hagar		Sept. 14, 1829	10
62	Linda		June 1834	5
63	Prince		July 9, 1810	29
64	Phillis	his wife		
65	Jean 2d		Nov. 1, 1812	27
66		her child		
67	Marcia 2d		Jan. 24, 1816	23
68	Phoebe 2d		July 13, 1820	19
69	Big Peter	Carpenter	Dec. 1783	56
70	Polly	his wife	Aug. 20, 1801	38

Number	Names		When Born	Age
71	Dianna		Aug. 25, 1819	20
72	Myrtilla		May 1786	53
73	Maria		Dec. 1, 1817	22
74	William ⎫	twins	Dec. 3, 1822	17
75	Alfred ⎭		Dec. 3, 1822	17
76	Rhina		May 21, 1825	14
77	Peter		Oct. 5, 1827	12
78	Sarah		Feb. 11, 1833	6
79	Alick		Oct. 6, 1791	48
80	Mary Ann			30
81	Nancy		June 13, 1819	20
82	Richard Robert		Oct. 1836	3
83	Joshua		July 9 1838	1
84	Ned		Aug. 12, 1821	18
85	Allick Jr.		June 24, 1826	13
86	Sukey Jr.		Apr. 14, 1830	9
87	Ruthy		May 24, 1828	11
88	Lucinda		Mar. 5, 1832	7
89	Marcia		1788	51
90	Jerry		Oct. 23, 1808	31
91	Smart		Mar. 30, 1812	27
92	Rose		Jan. 2, 1814	25
93	Norton		1804	35
94	Charles 2d		1833	6
95	William		July 1836	3
96	Caezer		Aug. 16, 1838	1
97	Flora		Apr. 26, 1818	21
98	Laura		Sept. 16, 1820	19
99	Sarah		Mar. 31, 1824	15
100	Joseph		Nov. 4, 1825	14
101	Affey		Oct. 5, 1827	12
102	Betty		Oct. 3, 1829	10
103	Edinboro		May 1832	7
104	Pussy		Feb. 20, 1794	45
105	Clementine		Aug. 20, 1813	26
106	Middleton		Dec. 2, 1837	2
107	Christiana		Apr. 17, 1839	
108	Charles		Oct. 6, 1818	21
109	James		Jan. 25, 1829	10
110	Illa		Dec. 30, 1834	5

(continued)

Number	Names		When Born	Age
111	Julian	Ruthy's child omitted	Jan. 27, 1834	5
112	Old Minty			65
113	Patty			51
114	Scipio			39
115	Hannibal		June 12, 17[?]	[?]
116	Charlotte		1797	42
117	Minty 2d		July 9, 1820	19
118	Hannibal		Feb. 12, 1823	16
119	Sam 2d		June 24, 1826	13
120	Caroliana		Oct. 1831	8
121	Patty 2d		May 1834	5
122	Nelly		May 1837	2
123	Dick Armstrong			41
124	Betty		Nov. 6, 1804	35
125	Dick Junr		Oct. 23, 1824	15
126	Cilla		Aug. 2, 1827	12
127	Baptiest or Battis		Nov. 1, 1831	8
128	Carolina		1798	41
129	Lucy Armstrong		1812	27
130	Peggy		Nov. 15, 1830	9
131	Suram			53
132	Judy		Dec. 22, 1793	46
133	Renty		Apr. 10, 1821	18
134	Suram Jr		Nov. 2, 1828	11
135	Will		Nov. 26, 1799	40
136	Anthony		May 6, 1829	10
137	William		Aug. 1837	2
138	Sylvia		1800	39
139	Cook Sam			57
140	George		July 9, 1818	21
142 [sic]	Battis—or Baptiest		1807	32
143	Myrtilla 2d		Aug. 28, 1812	27
144	Lucy 2d		May 25, 1830	9
145	Robbin		Dec. 1 1832	7
146	Harriot		Aug. 1836	3
147	a girl ⎫	Twins		
148	⎭			
149	Adam		June 27, 1815	24
150	Cathrina		July 19, 1818	21
151		her child	June 1839	

Number	Names	When Born	Age
152	Darcus 2d	May 4, 1824	15
153	Amarritta	Mar. 19, 1821	18
154	Hercules 2d	Sept. 13, 1828	11
155	Old Caezer		65
156	Jeffry	Aug. 27, 1812	27
157	Minty	Aug. 31, 1815	24
158	Hannah	Feb. 8, 1835	4
159	Caezer Jr.	Oct. 8, 1820	19
160	Molly	July 19, 1823	16
161	Neller	1777	52
162	Phillis	Oct. 26, 1820	19
163	Israel	June 6, 1828	11
164	Beck	Oct. 1830	9
165	Margaret	Sept. 1833	6
166	Maguire Betty	1800	39
167	Lizzy	July 18, 1821	18
168	Harry 2d	Jan. 10, 1824	15
169	Summersett	May 1, 1828	11
170	Old Harry		67
171	Fuller Mary		57
172	Hannah	Feb. 23, 1820	19
173	Billy	Aug. 22, 1838	1
174	Pender	Jan. 10, 1823	16
175	Billy	1791	48
176	Cinda	1817	22
177	Eve	Sept. 18, 1832	7
178	Dick Ward		55
179	Elcy		54
180	Hercules	1797	42
181	Louiza	1814	25
182	Paul	Jan. 23, 1839	
183	Jack	1796	43
184	Old Sue		58
185	Davy-Piles	1805	34
186	Rhoda	1806	33
187	Morris	Dec. 1833	6
188	Sally	Nov. 1836	3
189	Dido		52
190	Debrah	1806	33
191	Dido Jr.	1825	14

(continued)

Number	Names		When Born	Age
192	Peter Armstrong		1801	38
193	Hannah		Aug. 6, 1828	11
194	Robert		May 1834	5
195	Mary		1837	2
196	Miley	Sukey's child omitted	1836	3
197	Jonney		1800	39
198	Charlotte Ward			46
199	Tom		1800	39
200	Jacob		1806	33
201	Duncan		1806	33
202	Tom	Carpenter		61
203	Abby		1816	23
204	Simon		June 1834	5
205		her child	1837	2
206	Old Cloe			57
207	Cloe Jr		1819	20
208	Rose 2d		1821	18
209	Maria		1814	25
210	Caroline		July 1837	2
211	Henry	Bricklayer	1803	36
212	Sancho			45
213	Isaac	Blacksmith		42
214	Lymus	Mason		41
215	Charleston Alick			45
216	Armstrong Caezer			61
217	Sally			51
218	Henry		1815	24
219	Peggy	Caezer's daughter	1824	15
220	Jack		1826	13
221	Caeser Jr.		1829	10
222	Scipio			59
223	Peggy			[?]
224	Davy	Body servt	1813	26
225	Congo Dick			50
226	Hester		1809	30
227	Darcus	her child	Nov. 1830	9
228	Tom Colquit		1805	34
229	Patience—Boyd			50
230	Charlotte	her daughter		32
231	Dick		about	8
232	Patience 2d		about	6

Number	Names		When Born	Age
233	Sary		1819	20
234	Peter 3d		1817	22
235	Joe	Carpenter—supposed to be		30
236	Flavia			60
237	Davy		1824	15
238	George	Carpenter	1808	31
239	Jane	his wife	1814	25
240	Sarah Jane		1831	8
241	Hannah		Feb. 1835	4
242	Hagar		Apr. 1837	2
243			Oct. 1839	
244	Robert	Carpenter	1814	25
245	Celena	Matthews	1819	28
246	Ishmail		1802	37
247	Martha		1811	28
248	Caroline	her child	1829	10
249	Dolly		1824	15
250	Maria		1829	10
251	Milly		1826	13
252	Cumsey		1829	10
253	Peter Jr.		1833	6
254	Brister			60
255	Maryann			56
256	Tom	Carpenter		55
257	Cilla			52
258	Peter			45
259	Phoebe			40
260	Richard			47
261	Maryann			50
262	Byna			60
263	Kate			50
264	Mary	Matthews	June 1836	3
265	Larkin			28
266	Phoebe	his wife		21
267	Lewis	once Driver		50
268	Maria	his wife		45
269	Brister			50
270	Molly	his wife		50
271	Cherry			25

(continued)

Number	Names		When Born	Age
272	Dicy	supposed to be		21
273	Little Prince	supposed to be		12
274	Edward 2d		1835	4
275	Tonsel			47
276	Charlotte			35
277	Sampson		Mar. 1836	3
278	June		1814	25
279	Jim		1821	18
280	Pompy	supposed to be		53
281	Susanna			
282	Clarinda			
283	Flora			
284	Catoe			
285	Rhina			
286	Abraham			
287	Dick			25
288	Martha		Aug. 10, 1838	1
289	Tella ⎫	omitted in the		31
290	Boston ⎭	proper place Blacksmith		29
291	Old Toney			68
292	Little Toney			33
293	Sam			50
294	Dean			25
295	Luke 2d			20
296	Fortune			58
297	Stepney			49
298	George			38
299	Henry			43
300	Bob Paisley [?]			48
301	Bob Habersham			38
302	Peter			33
303	Hamilton			33
304	Robbin			20
305	Edmund			20
306	Luke	supposed		38
307	Almarine			28
308	Old Bess			68
309	Daphney			38
310	Flora			36
311	Little Rachael			33

Number	Names		When Born	Age
312	Sue			30
313	Affey			28
314	Big Rachael			47
315	Minty			19
316	Charlotte			23
317	Nanny			19
318	Caty			17
319	Elery			42
320	Litty			33
321	Big Rose			33
322	Celia			15
323	Rose			33
324	Sylvia			28
325	William			16
326	Joe			15
327	Charles			14
328	George			15
329	Ned			10
330	Will			10
331	July			12
332	Davy			10
333	Stephen			7
334	Richard	or last night		3
335	Harry			4
336	Joe Stiles			7
337	Elizabeth			14
338	Peggy			9
339	Beck			1
340	Patience			
341	Sarah			
342	Clarissa			
343	Tenah			
343 [*sic*]	Washington		Mar. 1836	3
344	William Gary		Dec. 1836	3
345	Francis		Apr. 1837	2
346	Moses		June 1837	2
347	Adam	(Affeys)	May 28, 1838	1
348	Comfort		Jan. 28, 1838	
349	James	Rachaels child	Aug. 1839	
350	Nanny [marked out]	of Bess	1839	

(continued)

Number	Names		When Born	Age
351	Bella	of Sylvia	Oct. 1839	
352	Solomon [?]		1839	
	Patience	Alicks daughter omitted		

CENSUS TAKEN FOR THE UNITED STATES, AUGUST 1840

First class	under 10 years	93
Second class	10 to 24	107
Third class	24 to 36	63
Fourth class	36 to 55	66
Fifth class	55 to 100	26
	Total	355

A/C of Negros in April 1853

				When Born	Age
1	Cupid [marked out]	born	dead	July 21, 1777	76
2	Boney or Cupid Jun			Dec. 2, 1814	38
3	Abraham [marked out]		to the Yankees 1863	July 31, 1817	35
4	Neller			Dec. 14, 1819	32
5	Mack [marked out]		to the Yankees 1863	July 29, 1824	20 [sic]
6	Lady			Nov. 11, 1786	66
7	Toney			May 22, 1808	44
8	Jane	purchased		1820	33
9	Bella		born	Mar. 12, 1839	14
10	Jane Jun			Sept. 10, 1848	4
11	Hannah [marked out]		born	Dec. 7, 1812	40
12	Alic Boyd	purchased	born	1812	40
13	Ellen [marked out]		born	Jan. 17, 1816	37
14	Jannet [marked out]		born	Oct. 16, 1838	14
15	Hannah Jun		born	Dec. 20, 1842	10
16	Charlotte			Aug. 30, 1845	7
17	Julia			July 16, 1848	4

18	Abel			Dec. 24, 1851	1
19	John			Feb. 22, 1825	28
20	Quamina			Jan. 22, 1794	59
21	March			Aug. 14, 1806	46
22	Peggy	purchased	born	1813	39
23	Jack	"	"	1831	22
24	Delia		born	Mar. 26, 1836	17
25	Jimmy		"	Apr. 28, 1838	15
26	Pleasant			Mar. 1840	13
27	Hannah Matilda			Mar. 1842	11
28	Cilla			Feb. 28, 1845	8
29	Maria Jun			May 11, 1847	5
30	Nelly			Sept. 6, 1850	2
31	Ruthy 12 [marked out]	dead	born	[?] 12, 1808	44
32	George			Apr. 4, 1821	32
33	James or Jimmy			Oct. 16, 1823	29
34	Amy			Sept. 28, 1826	27
35	Ella		born	May 11, 1845	7
36	Sam			Dec. 1, 1829	23
37	Julia Ann			Jan. 27, 1834	19
38	Balam			Nov. 7, 1852	
39	Betty			Dec. 1837	15
40	Abner			Oct. 1, 1820	32
41	Liddy			Apr. 15, 1823	30
42	Frederic			Feb. 3, 1843	10
43	Adelet			Sept. 26, 1847	5
44	Sanders			Sept. 4, 1827	25
45	Neptune			Sept. 15, 1831	21
46	Linda			Mar. 1836	17
47	Mary Ann [marked out]	purchased	born	1802	51
48	Richard		Born	Aug. 19, 1811	42
49	Nancy			June 13, 1819	33
50	Robert			Oct. 10, 1836	16
51	Richard Jun			Oct. 15, 1840	12
52	Mary			Oct. 17, 1842	10
53	Elizabeth			Jan. 12, 1844	[?]
54	Ansel			Sept. 23, 1845	7
55	Gabriel			Feb. 27, 1848	5
56	Victoria			Sept. 14, 1849	3
57	Ned			Aug. 12, 1821	31
58	Alic Jun			June 24, 1826	26

(continued)

59	Patience		July 15, 1823	29
60	Ruthy Jun		May 24, 1828	24
61	Sukey Jun		Apr. 14, 1830	22
62	Betty or Lucinda		Mar. 15, 1838	20
63	Clara Fisher		Dec. 25, 1842	10
64	Phillip [marked out]	obt 1853	June 27, 1844	8
65	Cornilia or Camilla		August 1848	4
66	Modina		Dec. 10, 1850	2
67	Jerry		Oct. 23, 1808	44
68	Smart	obt	Mar. 30, 1812	31
69	Rose		Jan. 2, 1814	39
70	Charles Jun		Mar. 1834	19
71	William Jun		July 1836	16
72	Caesar		Aug. 16, 1838	14
73	Norton [marked out]	drowned 14th August 54	Jan. 1841	12
74	Sye ⎫ twins		Aug. 8, 1846	6
75	Rose Jun ⎭		Aug. 8, 1846	6
76	Mary Wylly		June 5, 1850	2
77	Joseph		Mar. 17, 1852	1
78	Flora		Apr. 26, 1818	35
79	Lizzie		June 16, 1846	6
80	Henrietta		Aug. 7, 1849	3
81	Anthony		Oct. 2, 1851	2
82	Laura		Sept. 10, 1820	32
83	Sarah		Mar. 31, 1824	29
84	Joseph		Nov. 4, 1825	27
85	Betty		Oct. 3, 1829	23
86	Louisa		Jan. 12, 1851	2
87	Edinborough		May 1832	20
88	Tobey		Jan. 18, 1847	6
89	Pussy		Feb. 20, 1794	59
90	Clementine		Aug. 20, 1813	39
91	Charles		May 1818	35
92	Middleton		Dec. 1, 1837	15
93	Christian		Apr. 17, 1839	14
94	Isabella		Apr. 12, 1846	7
95	Herbert [marked out]		July 7, 1849	3
96	James or Jimper		Jan. 25, 1829	24
97	Ila		Dec. 30, 1834	18

98	Maria		Dec. 1, 1817	35
99	Tilla or Myrtilda		Dec. 6, 1840	12
100	Emily		Sept. 11, 1844	8
101	Henry		Feb. 11, 1846	7
102	William ⎤	twins	Dec. 3, 1822	30
103	Alfred ⎦		Dec. 3, 1822	30
104	Rhina 37		May 21, 1816	26
105	Annie [marked out]	died 5th Oct 1858	Feb. 9, 1844	9
106	Peter Jun		Oct. 25, 1827	25
107	Sarah Jun obt [marked out]	May 1853	Feb. 11, 1833	20
108	Peter Sen		Dec. 1783	69
109	Polly		Aug. 20, 1801	51
110	Ihmael		Mar. 9, 1828	25
111	Clementine 2nd		Aug. 12, 1831	22
112	Frank		June 10, 1838	14
113	Hercules		Sept. 1797	55
114	John ⎤	twins	May 1, 1849	3
115	William ⎦		May 1, 1849	3
116	Adam		May 30, 1851	[?]
	8 dead			
	108			

October 1857

	Sukeys daughter Mily died April 23	1853
1853	Sarahs son Albert born 18th Mar.	1853
1854	Floras son Hercules born 21st Feby	1854
	Ruthys son Dawson born 28 Feb	1854
	Nancys Twins ⎱ Nathaniel 8th April	1854
	⎰ Harper "	1854
	Toneys Jane's son Toney born 24th April	1854
	Ameys daughter Jean born 4th May	1854
	Bettys son Almarine 21st August	1854 [marked out]
	Lucindas son Alic 17th September	1854
	Lauras daughter Mary 9th October	1854 [marked out]
	Ellens daughter Patience 5 November	1854
	Christians daughter Elenora 13 May	1855 [marked out]
	Sues daughter Emoline 8 July	1855 [marked out]
	Peggys daughter Abegale 22 July	1855

(continued)

	Bettys daughter Marcia 7th October	1855
	Marias daughter Augusta 25 December	1855
	Julia anns daughter Mina 27th Dec	1855
1856	Ruthy Juns son June born 10th Feb	1856
	Floras son Ferdinand 28 April	1856
	Ameys son Prince 6th August	1856 [marked out]
	Sarahs Daughter Margaret 28th August	1856 [marked out]
	Do son Ned 28th August	1856
	Clementine Juns daughter Binah 31 August	1856
	Clementines daughter Justina 11th Nov	1856
	Little or Ruthys Betty's daughter Nancy 15th March	1857
	Sue's daughter Cornelia born 11th July	1857
	Betty's son Quamina born 23d July	1857
	Jane's daughter Sally 27 Septem	1857
	Laura's son Singleton 15th Dec	1857
	Chistiann's daughter Therese 6th March	1858
	Ruthy's son Julias Caeser born 18th Sep	1858
	Nancy's son Thomas born 19 Dec	1858
	Sue's daughter Alice born 19 Dec	1858
	John's Betty's son John 4th April	1859
	Amy son Alonzo August	1859
	Pleasant's Dorinda	1859
	Sarah's daughter Hetty September	1859
	Maria's Herbert October 18th	1859
	Ila's Elenora ″ 25th	1859
	Tilla's Anne ″ ″	1859
	Juliann's Robert Enoch Nov	1859
	Ruthy's Charity	1860
	Flora's Nella	1860
	Jeannett's Corrine	1860
	Ruthy's Elizabeth	1863
	Lind's Jim	1862
	Matilla's Kate	1862
	Julia's Darcus	
	Betty's son Lee	1863

DEATHS OF NEGROS FROM JUNE 1854

Maryann died June 23, 1854

Herbert died suddenly July 13, 1854

My good & faithful servant Hannah
after years of suffering expired on the
night of 3d August 1854
> For honesty—moral character—
> usefulness & perfect devotion to
> her owners she she [*sic*] had not
> her equal—she died resigned
> with firm trust in her redeemer—
> 1854

Norton was drowned on Monday
14th August 1854

Peggy's boy child aged 12 hours
18th August 1854

Maria's infant daughter
7th September obt 11th 1854

Almarene July—1855

Mary [?] February 1856

Dealia's first child of lockjaw
7th Oct 1856

Nancy's still born son Nov 24th 1856

Old Cupid honest & true to his earthly
owners departed this life, 4 A.M.
29th Jan—1857

Ellens son—4 days old March 1857

Liddy's daughter—8 days old
March 1857

Smart—died on Monday
20th April 1857

Christiann's daughter Elenora died
of 3 days
ill—congestive fever
9th November 1857

Dealia's child still born 8th March 1858

Little Emoline died 8th July suddenly
1858

Little Prince died—11th Sep.—1858

Peggy infant dead born August—1858

Julia ann infant—lock jaw 1858

Amey's twins 28th September premature
1858

My valued servant Annie died of fever
Oct 5th *1858*

Delia's child—[?] suddenly 1859

Linda's "   "

Liddy   "   premature

Mily—died of fever Oct. 1859

Quamina—most honest & true—
a faithful servant & good man after
a short illness of 24 hours departed
this life [?] March 1860

Inventory of the Estate of Mrs. Anna Matilda King

No.	Negroes	Ages	Valuation
1	Abram	43	$800
2	Alick Boyd ⎫	47	800
3	Ellen ⎭	43	500
4	Jennett	21	1000
5	Hannah	17	400
6	Charlotte	14	900
7	Julia	11	600
8	Abel	8	500
9	Patience	4	300
10	Alick ⎫	33	1000
11	Delia ⎭	23	1000

(continued)

No.	Negroes	Ages	Valuation
12	Charles Jr. ⎫	25	1000
13	Lucinda ⎬	26	1000
14	Alick	5	300
15	Alfred ⎫	37	1000
16	Liddy ⎬	36	600
17	Frederick	16	700
18	Adalette	12	500
19	Abner	39	900
20	Sanders	32	1000
21	Ruthy's Betty	22	1000
22	Nancy	2	200
23	Boney ⎫	45	800
24	Sarah ⎬	35	900
25	Toby	13	600
26	Albert	6	400
27	Ned	3	200
28	Margaret	3	200
29	Hetty	0.4	100
30	Clementine	46	700
31	Middleton	22	1000
32	Christianna and ⎫	20	1000
33	Child Theresa ⎬	1	200
34	Isabel	13	800
35	Justine	3	200
36	Ishmael	31	1000
37	Frank	21	800
38	Clementine Jr. ⎫	28	800
39	Binah ⎬	3	200
40	Jerry	40	900
41	Edinborough—no value	27	000
42	Hercules	62	200
43	Laura ⎫	40	700
44	Singleton ⎬	2	200
45	Jimmy	36	900
46	Sam	30	1000
47	Jimper ⎫	30	1000
48	Linda ⎬	23	1000

No.	Negroes	Ages	Valuation
49	Joe ⎫	34	1000
50	Ruthy ⎭	31	900
51	Dawson	5	250
52	June	3	200
53	Julian	1	200
54	Lady no value	73	000
55	Quamina	65	100
56	John ⎫	34	1000
57	Betty ⎭	30	1000
58	Louisa	8	600
59	Marcia	4	250
60	Quamina	2	200
61	John	0.8	100
62	Mack ⎫	35	1000
63	Amy ⎭	34	1000
64	Ella	14	900
65	Jane	5	350
66	Lonzo	0.5	100
67	March ⎫	53	700
68	Peggy ⎭	46	500
69	Jack	28	1000
70	Jimmy	21	1000
71	Matilda	17	1000
72	Cilla	14	900
73	Maria	12	800
74	Nelly	9	450
75	Abagail	4	250
76	Maria	42	850
77	Tilla and ⎫	19	1000
78	child Anne ⎭	0.3	100
79	Emily	15	900
80	Henry	13	600
81	Augusta	4	250
82	Herbert	0.3	100
83	Big Peter ⎫ no value	76	000
84	Polly ⎭	58	150
85	Nella ⎫	38	800
86	Flora ⎭	41	700

(continued)

No.	Negroes	Ages	Valuation
87	Lizzy	13	900
88	Henrietta	10	550
89	Anthony	8	450
90	Hercules	5	300
91	Ferdinand	3	250
92	Ned	38	1000
93	Patience	36	200
94	Clara	17	1000
95	Rhina	33	1000
96	Peter	32	1000
97	Pussy	65	200
98	Charles	41	700
99	Neptune ⎫	28	1000
100	Ila ⎬	25	1000
101	Leonora	0.3	100
102	George ⎫	38	1000
103	Sukey ⎭	29	1000
104	Camilla	11	600
105	Modina	9	500
106	Cornelia	2	200
107	Alice	1	100
108	Robert ⎫	23	1000
109	Julianna ⎭	25	1000
110	Balaam	7	400
111	Mina	4	250
112	Enick	0.4	100
113	Richard ⎫	49	500
114	Nancy ⎭	40	500
115	Richard Jr.	19	1000
116	Mary	17	1000
117	Elizabeth	15	1000
118	Ansel	14	700
119	Gabriel	11	500
120	Victoria	10	500
121	Nathaniel	5	350
122	Harper	5	350
123	Thomas	2	200

No.	Negroes	Ages	Valuation
124	Rose	45	600
125	William	23	1000
126	Caeser	21	1000
127	Siah	13	600
128	Rosa	13	600
129	Mary	9	400
130	Joseph	7	350
131	Toney ⎫	51	1000
132	Jane ⎭	39	800
133	Bella	20	1000
134	Jane	10	500
135	Toney Jr	5	350
136	Sally	2	200
137	William ⎫	37	1000
138	Pleasant ⎭	19	1000
139	Dorinda	0.6	100
140	William	10	500
141	John	10	500
142	Adam	8	400

A List of Fifty Negros with Their Increase Bequeathed by Will to A. M. King

(KING-WILDER COLLECTION, GEORGIA HISTORICAL SOCIETY, SAVANNAH)

†1	Jimmy	17	Pussy
2	Jane	18	Clementina
3	March	19	Charles
4	Ruthy Jun	20	Lady
5	George	21	Toney
6	James	22	Hannah
7	Amey	23	Ellen
8	Marcia	24	John
9	Jerry	25	Cupid
†10	William	26	Lizzy
11	Smart	27	Cupid Jun
12	Rosi	28	Abraham
13	Flora	29	Nellar
14	Laura	30	March
15	Sarah		
16	Joseph		

(continued)

31	Quamina		63	Marcia 2d}	Fionas
32	Peter Jun		64	James⎤	
33	Polly		65	Ila ⎦	Pussy
34	Neptune		66	Middleton⎤	
35	Sukey		67	Christiann ⎬	Clementina
36	Abner		68	Louisa ann⎦	
37	Liddy				
			69	Jannet}	Ellens
38	Alic				
39	Maryann		70	Indianna}	Pollys
40	Nancy		71	Sanders⎤	
41	Ned		72	Emoline	
42	Patience		73	Neptune⎹	Neptunes
43	Alic Jun		74	Mily	& Sukeys
†44	Myrtillas		75	Linda	
†45	Henry		76	Walter⎦	
46	Maria				
47	William		77	Ruthy 2d⎤	Alic &
48	Alfred		78	Sukey 2d⎬	Mary ann
			79	Betty 3 ⎦	
49	Binah				
50	Hercules		80	Robert ⎤	Nancys
			81	Richard⎦	
	Increase		82	Myrtilda}	Marias
51	Anthony⎤				
52	Sam		83	Ishmael⎤	
53	Julia ann⎬	Ruthys	84	Clementine⎬	Binahs
54	Betty ⎦		85	Frank ⎦	
55	Affy⎤		86	Rhina⎤	
56	Betty 2d⎬	Marias	87	Peter ⎬	Myrtillas
57	Edenburg⎦		88	Sarah⎦	
58	Charles⎤				
59	William				
61 [*sic*]	Cesar⎬	Rose's			
62	Norton 2d⎦				

Of the original 50—4 have died marked by a cross leaving at this day *Eighty three*

Bibliography

Primary Sources

Georgia Department of Archives and History. Selected Pages from the Record Book of Retreat Plantation.

Georgia Historical Society Manuscripts Collection. Savannah, Georgia. King-Wilder Collection.

Otto, Rhea Cumming, comp. *1850 Census of Georgia (Glynn County)*. Atlanta: Georgia Department of Archives and History, 1973.

Southern Historical Collection. The University of North Carolina, Chapel Hill. Thomas Butler King Collection; William Audley Couper Collection.

Warren, Mary Bondurant, and Sarah Fleming White. *Marriages and Deaths, 1829–1830, Abstracted from Extant Georgia Newspapers*.

Interviews

Lackritz, Eve, M.D. Medical Epidemiologist, Centers for Disease Control and Prevention, Atlanta, Georgia. Interviewed by editor December 6, 1995.

Marston, Barbara, M.D. Assistant Professor of Medicine, Division of Infectious Diseases, Emory University School of Medicine, Atlanta, Georgia. Interviewed by editor December 14, 1995.

Slutsker, Larry, M.D. Medical Epidemiologist, National Center for Infectious Disease, Centers for Disease Control and Prevention, Atlanta, Georgia. Interviewed by editor December 14, 1995.

Secondary Sources

Alexander, Adele Logan. *Ambiguous Lives: Free Women of Color in Rural Georgia, 1789–1879*. Fayetteville: University of Arkansas Press, 1991.

Bagwell, James E. *Rice Gold: James Hamilton Couper and Plantation Life on the Georgia Coast*. Macon, Ga.: Mercer University Press, 2000.

Bailey, Cornelia Walker. With Christena Bledsoe. *God, Dr. Buzzard, and the Bolito Man: A Saltwater Geechee Talks about Life on Sapelo Island*. New York: Doubleday, 2000.

Bell, Malcolm, Jr. *Major Butler's Legacy: Five Generations of a Slaveholding Family*. Athens: University of Georgia Press, 1987.

Bennet, Jennifer. *Lillies of the Hearth: The Historical Relationship between Women and Plants*. Camden East, Ontario: Camden House Publishers, 1990.

Berry, Stephen. "More Alluring at a Distance: Absentee Patriarchy and the Thomas Butler King Family." *Georgia Historical Quarterly* 81, no. 4 (winter 1997): 863–896.

Biographical Directory of the American Congress, 1774–1961. Washington, D.C.: U.S. Government Printing Office, 1961.

Blassingame, John W. *The Slave Community: Plantation Life in the Antebellum South*. Revised and enlarged edition. Oxford: Oxford University Press, 1979.

Bleser, Carol, ed. *In Joy and Sorrow: Women, Family, and Marriage in the Victorian South, 1830–1988*. Oxford: Oxford University Press, 1991.

Boydston, Jeanne, Mary Kelly, and Ann Margoles. *The Limits of Sisterhood: The Beecher Sisters on Women's Rights and Woman's Sphere*. Chapel Hill: University of North Carolina Press, 1988.

Brady, Patricia, ed. *George Washington's Beautiful Nelly: The Letters of Eleanor Parke Custis Lewis to Elizabeth Bordley Gibson, 1794–1851*. Columbia: University of South Carolina Press, 1991.

Buczacki, Stefan. *Creating a Victorian Flower Garden: Original Flower Paintings by Alice Drummond-Hay*. New York: Weidenfeld and Nicolson, 1988.

Burr, Virginia Ingraham, ed. Introduction by Nell Irvin Painter. *The Secret Eye: The Journal of Ella Gertrude Clanton Thomas, 1848–1889*. Chapel Hill: University of North Carolina Press, 1990.

Cashin, Joan. "Decidedly Opposed to the Union: Women's Culture, Marriage and Politics in Antebellum South Carolina." *Georgia Historical Quarterly* 78 (winter 1994): 735–759.

———. "The Structure of Antebellum Planter Families: 'The Ties that Bound Us Was Strong.'" *Journal of Southern History* 56 (February 1990): 55–70.

Cate, Margaret Davis. *Early Days of Coastal Georgia*. Photographs by Orrin Sage Whightman. Fourth edition. St. Simons Island, Ga.: Fort Frederica Association, 1966.

———. *Our Todays and Yesterdays*. Revised edition. Brunswick, Ga.: Glover Bros., 1930.

Censer, Jane Turner. *North Carolina Planters and Their Children, 1800–1860*. Baton Rouge: Louisiana State University Press, 1984.

Chambers-Schiller, Lee Virginia. *Liberty, a Better Husband. Single Women in America: The Generation of 1780–1840*. New Haven: Yale University Press, 1984.

Clinton, Catherine. "Equally Their Due: The Education of the Planter Daugther [sic] in the Early Republic." *Journal of the Early Republic* 2 (April 1982): 39–60.

———. *Fanny Kemble's Civil Wars*. New York: Simon and Schuster, 2000.

———. *The Plantation Mistress: Woman's World in the Old South*. New York: Pantheon Books, 1982.

———. *Tara Revisited: Women, War, and the Plantation Legend*. Foreword by Henry Louis Gates Jr. New York: Abbeville Publishing Group, 1995.

Coats, Alice M. *Garden Shrubs and Their Histories*. With notes by Dr. John Creech. New York: Simon and Schuster, 1992.

Coleman, Kenneth. *A History of Georgia*. Second edition. Athens: University of Georgia Press, 1991.

Cooney, Loraine M., and H. Rainwater, comps. and eds. *Garden History of Georgia*. Atlanta: Peachtree Garden Club, 1933.

Coulling, Mary P. *The Lee Girls*. Winston-Salem, N.C.: John F. Blair, 1987.

Davis, Angela Y. "Reflections on the Black Woman's Role in the Community of Slaves." *Black Scholar* 3 (December 1971): 3–15.

East, Charles, ed. *The Civil War Diary of Sarah Morgan.* Athens: University of Georgia Press, 1991.

Elliott, Brent. *Victorian Gardens.* Portland, Ore.: Timberwood Press, 1986.

Farnham, Christie Anne. *The Education of the Southern Belle: Higher Education and Student Socialization in the Antebellum South.* New York: New York University Press, 1994.

Faust, Drew Gilpin. *Mothers of Invention: Women of the Slaveholding South in the American Civil War.* New York: Vintage Books, 1996.

———. *A Sacred Circle: The Dilemma of the Intellectual of the Old South, 1840–1860.* Baltimore: Johns Hopkins University Press, 1977.

Ferguson, T. Reed. *The John Couper Family at Cannon's Point.* Macon, Ga.: Mercer University Press, 1994.

Fox-Genovese, Elizabeth. *Within the Plantation Household: Black and White Women in the Old South.* Chapel Hill: University of North Carolina Press, 1988.

Franklin, John Hope, and Loren Schweninger. *Runaway Slaves: Rebels on the Plantation.* Oxford: Oxford University Press, 1999.

Fraser, Walter J., Jr., R. Frank Saunders Jr., and Jon L. Wakelyn. *The Web of Southern Social Relations: Women, Family and Education.* Athens: University of Georgia Press, 1985.

Friedman, Jean E. *The Enclosed Garden: Women and Community in the Evangelical South, 1830–1900.* Chapel Hill: University of North Carolina Press, 1985.

Garraty, John A., and Robert A. McCaughey. *The American Nation: A History of the United States to 1877.* Volume 1. Sixth edition. New York: Harper and Row, 1987.

Gere, Charlotte. *Nineteenth-Century Decoration: The Art of the Interior.* New York: Harry N. Abrams, 1989.

Gomez, Michael A. *Exchanging Our Country Marks: The Transformation of African Identities in the Colonial and Antebellum South.* Chapel Hill: University of North Carolina Press, 1998.

Goodwine, Marquetta L. *Frum Wi Soul Tuh de Soil Cotton, Rice and Indigo. Gulla/Geechee: Africa's Seeds in the Winds of the Diaspora.* Volume 3. St. Helena Island, S.C.: published by the author, 1999.

Gordon, Ann D. "The Philadelphia Young Ladies Academy." In *Women of America: A History,* ed. Carol Berkin and Mary Beth Norton, 143–154. Boston: Houghton Mifflin, 1979.

Gould, Virginia Meacham, ed. *Chained to the Rock of Adversity: To Be Free, Black, and Female in the Old South.* Athens: University of Georgia Press, 1998.

Gray-White, Deborah. *Ar'n't I a Woman? Female Slaves in the Plantation South.* Revised edition. New York: W. W. Norton, 1999.

Green, R. Edwin. *St. Simons Island: A Summary of Its History.* Westmoreland, N.Y.: Arner, 1962.

Hellerstein, Erna Olafson, Leslie Parker Hume, and Karen M. Offen, eds. Estelle B. Freedman, Barbara Charlesworth Gelpi, and Marilyn Yalom, assoc. eds. *Victorian Women: A Documentary Account of Women's Lives in Nineteenth Century England, France, and the United States.* Stanford: Stanford University Press, 1989.

Hine, Darlene C., and Kate Wittenstein. "Female Slave Resistance: The Economics of Sex." In *Black Woman Cross-Culturally*, edited by Filomina Chioma Steady, 289–299. Cambridge: Harvard University Press, 1981.

Holmes, James, M.D. Compiled, edited, and with an introduction by Delma Eugene Presly. *"Dr. Bullie's" Notes: Reminiscences of Early Georgia and of Philadelphia and New Haven in the 1800s*. Atlanta: Cherokee Publishing Company, 1976.

House, Albert V., Jr. "The Management of a Rice Plantation in Georgia, 1834–1861, as Revealed in the Journal of Hugh Fraser Grant." *Agricultural History* 13 (October 1939): 208–217.

Huie, Mildred Nix, and Bessie Lewis. *King's Retreat Plantation, St. Simons Island, Georgia Today and Yesterday*. St. Simons Island, Ga.: published by the authors, 1980.

——. *Patriarchal Plantations of St. Simons Island, Georgia*. Brunswick, Ga.: published by the authors, 1974.

Hull, Barbara. *St. Simons, Enchanted Island: A History of the Most Historic of Georgia's Fabled Golden Isles*. Atlanta: Cherokee Publishing Company, 1980.

Jones-Jackson, Patricia. *When Roots Die: Endangered Traditions on the Sea Islands*. Foreword by Charles Joyner. Athens: University of Georgia Press, 1987.

Kagle, Steven E., and Francesca Sawaya. "An Examination of Eight Personal Narratives by Women in the Antebellum South." Essay Review. *Mississippi Quarterly* 50 (1997): 143–154.

Keeney, Elizabeth Barnaby. "Domestic Medicine in the Old South." In *Sickness and Health in America: Readings in the History of Medicine and Public Health*, edited by Judith W. Leavitt and Ronald L. Numbers. Second edition. Madison: University of Wisconsin Press, 1985.

Kemble, Frances Anne. *Journal of a Residence on a Georgia Plantation in 1838–1839 by Frances Anne Kemble*. Edited by John A. Scott. Athens: University of Georgia Press, 1984.

Kilbridge, Daniel. "Philadelphia and the Southern Elite: Class, Kinship, and Culture in Antebellum America." Ph.D. diss., University of Florida, 1997.

King, Spencer B., Jr. *Darien: The Death of a Southern Town*. Illustrated by Irene Dodd. Macon, Ga.: Mercer University Press, 1981.

King, Wilma. *Stolen Childhood: Slave Youth in Nineteenth-Century America*. Bloomington and Indianapolis: Indiana University Press, 1995.

Lander, Ernest M., and Charles McGee, eds. *A Rebel Came Home: The Diary and Letters of Floride Clemson, 1863–1866*. Columbia: University of South Carolina Press, 1989.

Lane, Mills. *Architecture of the Old South. Georgia*. With special photographs by Van Jones Martin and drawings by Gene Carpenter. Savannah: Beehive Press, 1986.

——, ed. *Neither More nor Less Than Men: Slavery in Georgia, a Documentary History*. Savannah: Beehive Press, 1993.

Leavitt, Judith Walzer, and Ronald L. Numbers, eds. *Sickness and Health in America: Readings in the History of Medicine and Public Health*. Second edition. Madison: University of Wisconsin Press, 1985.

Lebsock, Suzanne. *The Free Women of Petersburg: Status and Culture in a Southern Town, 1784–1860*. New York: W. W. Norton, 1984.

Leigh, Francis Butler. *Ten Years on a Georgia Plantation since the War, 1866–1876*. Introduction by Charles E. Wynes. Savannah: Beehive Press, 1973.

Leslie, Kent Anderson. "A Myth of the Southern Lady: Antebellum Proslavery Rhetoric and the Proper Place of Woman." *Sociological Spectrum* 6 (1986): 31–49.

Lovell, Caroline Couper. *The Golden Isles of Georgia.* Boston: Little, Brown, 1933.

McMillen, Sally G. *Motherhood in the Old South: Pregnancy, Childbirth, and Infant Rearing.* Baton Rouge: Louisiana State University Press, 1990.

———. "Mothers' Sacred Duty: Breast-Feeding Patterns among Middle and Upper-Class Women in the Antebellum South." *Journal of Southern History* 51, no. 3 (1985): 333–356.

Marye, Florence. *The Story of the Page-King Family of Retreat Plantation, St. Simons Island and of the Golden Isles of Georgia.* Edited by Edwin R. MacKethan III. Darien, Ga.: published by the author, 2000.

Miller, Byron S. *Sail, Steam and Splendour: A Picture History of Life aboard the Transatlantic Lines.* Foreword by Frank O. Braynard. New York: Times Books, 1977.

Moore, John Hammond, ed. *The Diary of Keziah Goodwyn Hopkins Brevard, 1860–1861.* Columbia: University of South Carolina Press, 1993.

Museum of the Confederacy. *Women in Mourning.* A catalog of the Museum of the Confederacy's corollary exhibition held November 14, 1984, through January 6, 1986, Richmond, Va. Essay by Patricia R. Loughridge and Edward D. C. Campbell Jr.

Nissenbaum, Stephen. "Wassailing across the Color Line: Christmas in the Antebellum South." In *The Battle for Christmas: A Cultural History of America's Most Cherished Holiday.* New York: Vintage Books, 1996.

Numbers, Ronald L. "The Fall and Rise of the American Medical Profession." In *Sickness and Health in America: Readings in the History of Medicine and Public Health,* edited by Judith W. Leavitt and Ronald L. Numbers. Second edition. Madison: University of Wisconsin Press, 1985.

Palmer, Colin A. *Passageways: An Interpretive History of Black America.* Volume 1: *1619–1863.* New York: Harcourt Brace College Publishers, 1998.

Parrish, Lydia. *Slave Songs of the Georgia Sea Islands.* Foreword by Art Rosenbaum. Introduction by Olin Downes. Music transcribed by Creighton Churchill and Robert MacGimsey. Athens: Brown Thrasher Books, University of Georgia Press, 1992.

Patterson, K. David. "Disease Environments of the Antebellum South." In *Sickness and Health in America: Readings in the History of Medicine and Public Health,* edited by Judith W. Leavitt and Ronald L. Numbers. Second edition. Madison: University of Wisconsin Press, 1985.

Pope, Christie Farnham. "Preparation for Pedestals: North Carolina and Antebellum Female Seminaries." Ph.D. diss., University of Chicago, 1977.

Pryor, Elizabeth Brown. "An Anomalous Person: The Northern Tutor in Plantation Society, 1773–1860." *Journal of Southern History* 47, no. 3 (1981): 363–392.

Ramey, Daina L. "'A Place of Our Own': Labor, Family and Community among Female Slaves in Piedmont and Tidewater Georgia, 1820–1860." Ph.D. diss., University of California at Los Angeles, 1998.

Robertson, Mary D., ed. *Lucy Breckinridge of Grove Hill: The Journal of a Virginia Girl, 1862–1864.* Columbia: University of South Carolina Press, 1994.

Rosenberg, Charles. "The Therapeutic Revolution: Medicine, Meaning, and Social Change in 19th Century America." In *Sickness and Health in America: Readings in the History of Medicine and Public Health,* edited by Judith W. Leavitt and Ronald L. Numbers. Second edition. Madison: University of Wisconsin Press, 1985.

Rothman, Ellen K. *Hands and Hearts: A History of Courtship in America.* New York: Basic Books, 1984.

Rothman, Sheila M. *Living in the Shadow of Death: Tuberculosis and the Social Experience of Illness in American History.* New York: Basic Books, 1994.

Russell, Douglas A. *Costume History and Style.* Englewood Cliffs, N.J.: Prentice-Hall, 1983.

Savitt, Todd L. "Black Health on the Plantation: Masters, Slaves, and Physicians." In *Sickness and Health in America: Readings in the History of Medicine and Public Health,* edited by Judith W. Leavitt and Ronald L. Numbers. Second edition. Madison: University of Wisconsin Press, 1985.

Scott, Anne Firor. *Making the Invisible Woman Visible.* Urbana: University of Illinois Press, 1984.

———. *The Southern Lady: From Pedestal to Politics, 1830–1930.* Chicago: University of Chicago Press, 1970.

Seidel, Kathryn L. "The Southern Belle as an Antebellum Ideal." *Southern Quarterly* 15 (July 1977): 387–401.

Smith, Julia Floyd. *Slavery and Rice Culture in Low Country Georgia, 1750–1860.* Knoxville: University of Tennessee Press, 1985.

St. Simons Island Public Library. *Old Mill Days: St. Simons Mills, Georgia, 1874–1908.* 1970.

Starr, Paul. *The Social Transformation of American Medicine: The Rise of a Sovereign Profession and the Making of a Vast Industry.* New York: Basic Books, 1982.

Steel, Edward M., Jr. *T. Butler King of Georgia.* Athens: University of Georgia Press, 1964.

Stowe, Steven. *Intimacy and Power in the Old South: Ritual in the Lives of the Planters.* Baltimore: Johns Hopkins University Press, 1987.

Sullivan, Buddy. *Memories of McIntosh: A Brief History of McIntosh County, Darien, and Sapelo.* Darien, Ga.: Darien News, 1990.

Tise, Larry. *Proslavery: A History of the Defense of Slavery in America, 1701–1840.* Athens: University of Georgia Press, 1987.

Vanstory, Burnette. *Georgia's Land of the Golden Isles.* Athens: University of Georgia Press, 1981.

Vlach, John Michael. *The Afro-American Tradition in Decorative Arts.* Athens: Brown Thrasher Books, University of Georgia Press, 1990.

———. *Back of the Big House: The Architecture of Plantation Slavery.* Chapel Hill: University of North Carolina Press, 1993.

Wheeler, Mary Bray. *Eugenia Price's South: A Guide to the People and Places of Her Beloved Region.* Atlanta: Longstreet Press, 1993.

Wilkinson, Frederick. *The Story of the Cotton Plant.* New York: D. Appleton Company, 1903.

Wood, Betty. *Women's Work, Men's Work: The Informal Slave Economies of Lowcountry Georgia.* Athens: University of Georgia Press, 1995.

Woodward, C. Vann, and Elisabeth Muhlenfeld. *The Private Mary Chesnut: The Unpublished Civil War Diaries.* Oxford: Oxford University Press, 1984.

Works Projects Administration. Georgia Writer's Project. Introduction by Charles Joyner. *Drums and Shadows: Survival Studies among the Georgia Coastal Negroes.* Athens: Brown Thrasher Books, University of Georgia Press, 1986.

Worth, John E. *The Struggle for the Georgia Coast: An Eighteenth-Century Spanish Retrospective on Guale and Mocama.* Introduction by David Hurst Thomas. Anthropological Papers of the American Museum of Natural History. New York: American Museum of Natural History, 1995.

Wright, Richard Nowell. "Planters and Scholars: The Common Bonds of Higher Education in Antebellum Georgia." Master's thesis, University of Georgia, 1996.

Wyatt-Brown, Bertram. *Honor and Violence in the Old South.* Oxford: Oxford University Press, 1986.

———. "The Mask of Obedience: Male Slave Psychology in the Old South." *American Historical Review* 93, no. 5 (1988): 1228–1252.

Index